A Hands-On Introduction to Forensic Science

Cracking the Case

A Hands-On Introduction to Forensic Science

Cracking the Case

Mark M. Okuda
Evergreen Valley College
San Jose, California, USA

Frank H. Stephenson, PhD
Thermo Fisher Scientific
Carlsbad, California, USA

CRC Press is an imprint of the
Taylor & Francis Group, an **informa** business

CRC Press
Taylor & Francis Group
6000 Broken Sound Parkway NW, Suite 300
Boca Raton, FL 33487-2742

Printed and bound in India by Replika Press Pvt. Ltd.

Printed on acid-free paper
Version Date: 20140711

International Standard Book Number-13: 978-1-4822-3490-9 (Hardback)

Visit the Taylor & Francis Web site at
http://www.taylorandfrancis.com

and the CRC Press Web site at
http://www.crcpress.com

Contents

Preface

The aim of this book is to present a novel way of teaching forensic science and, more importantly, a different way of presenting any science discipline whether it be chemistry, physics, or biology.

Most science textbooks today are formatted and presented in a compartmentalized manner; students are likely to encounter a chapter entitled "Cell Structure and Function" in a biology textbook, or "States of Matter" in a chemistry textbook, or "Newton's First Law of Motion-Inertia" in a physics textbook, or "Blood Spatter" in a forensic textbook. These compartmentalized units present an extensive list of vocabulary words as well as scientific principles and concepts to be mastered. The student takes notes, conducts lab experiments and, at the conclusion of the unit, is evaluated by some form of written assessment. This cycle repeats itself with the next chapter until the course is completed at the end of the academic year. This format often lacks the connections learned in prior chapters to the current chapter under study. Science, on the other hand, is about making connections.

The disconnect that commonly exists between science textbooks, science courses and the way real science operates will be addressed in this manuscript. Science works with a problem or an observation which requires an integrated approach involving many different disciplines of science coming together and the connections that these disciplines can provide to help solve a problem or explain an observation.

This book attempts to capture the student's interest by means of a unique format. It begins with a story about two characters who go about solving a missing persons case. It reads like a murder mystery novel, with each succeeding chapter revealing new characters, new information, and new physical evidence to be processed. Following the storyline, the reader is introduced to the appropriate science necessary to process the physical evidence. The final component of each chapter consists of a series of lab activities that train the student in processing, analyzing, and documenting the physical evidence revealed in the narrative.

The final chapter takes all of the evidence and presents it in a mock trial setting where information is presented in a court of law and the jury decides the fate of the suspect.

We hope that by reading this book you will gain a better appreciation of how science operates in the real world and the important role it plays in our lives. Having gone through this experience, some of the readers may even entertain the idea of pursuing a career in forensic science or the legal system. Enjoy the journey upon which you are about to embark.

Authors

Mark M. Okuda received his BA in biology with a minor in chemistry from the University of the Pacific. He went on to receive his MA in natural science from San Jose State University. Mark taught for 33 years at Silver Creek High School and currently serves as an adjunct faculty member at Evergreen Valley College teaching human heredity and forensic biology. During his tenure as a high school science teacher, Mark was the recipient of the Santa Clara County Teacher of the Year, Synopsys Outstanding Science Teacher Award, East Side Union High School District Innovative Teacher Award (Forensic Science), and National Biotechnology Education Conference Teacher Award and held a patent for a biotechnology kit marketed by Bio-Rad entitled "Secrets of the Rain Forest."

Frank H. Stephenson received his PhD in molecular biology from UC Berkeley and performed postgraduate work at UC San Francisco Medical School. He spent several years with Berlex Biosciences as a senior research scientist prior to joining the Technical Training Department at Life Technologies, where he teaches forensics, DNA sequencing, and real-time PCR. Frank has taught molecular biology with the UC Berkeley Extension program and, for ten years, served as a part-time faculty member with Foothill College, where he conducted evening classes in PCR. Dr. Stephenson has published several books in the biotech field, including *DNA: How the Biotech Revolution Is Changing the Way We Fight Disease* and *Calculations for Molecular Biology and Biotechnology: A Guide to Mathematics in the Laboratory*. This textbook evolved from summer workshops in forensic and DNA analysis given at Life Technologies to high school teachers and students in collaboration with his coauthor, Mark Okuda.

1
Crime Scene

Police Headquarters, Monday 9:12 AM

"Jenkins!"

His head pulled upright like that of an African gazelle at a watering hole when startled by the sound of a twig snapping accidentally under the paw of a stealthy predator. *A sneeze?* he thought. Maybe. Alert, he strained to filter out the background din. Nothing. He went back to his reading.

"Jenkins!"

There it was again but closer this time.

"Where's Jenkins?"

He recognized that growl, and by its Doppler shift, it was coming up fast behind him. He jerked his heals off the wastebasket and yanked the steaming coffee mug from his lips, splashing a dose on the pages of his latest issue of *True Detective*, which he quickly flung shut and slipped under a stolen vehicle report. Lieutenant Robert Jenkins, swiftly wiping several fugitive doughnut crumbs from his chin, reeled his head around to see the department head, Captain Stan White, strutting down the path between the rows of desks littered with a full dozen detective staff who were either tapping away on computer keyboards, talking prattle, or flipping through stacks of papers as they squeezed their telephones between ear and shoulder. They parted like cars on a two-lane yielding the right of way to a black and white, sirens blaring, as the captain barreled through them. They closed ranks behind him in his wake. Captain White cultivated a no-nonsense, tough guy image and wore it tight to his skin like body armor. He downshifted as he approached Jenkins' desk and, as if he were a traffic cop flagging a commuter through an intersection, waved a manila folder in a southbound direction. "In my office, now!" he grumbled. Jenkins pried himself from his chair and merged a pace behind him.

Every time Jenkins stepped into the captain's office, he felt as if he was trespassing the bounds of a mausoleum. It wasn't decorated in a way that invites company or makes a soul feel cozy. Thin parallel layers of light sifting through the cracks of thick wooden blinds hanging like ribs against the windowpane etched a grate of glare and shadow across the opposite wall tiled in bronze plaques, framed certificates, and a collection of photographs picturing the captain shaking hands with a generation of mayors. A human skull stared vacant from the top of a filing cabinet, and the cadaver of a desiccated weeping fig collected dust in the back corner, a present, at one time, from his department to celebrate 20 years of service in law enforcement. Captain White dropped into a frayed armchair. As he lurched himself forward against a cluttered and scarred mahogany desk, his chair scratched along the linoleum like a lid sliding closed on a stone sarcophagus. He twisted the knob on the side of a banker's lamp that then spilled light over a pile of forensic journals and glowed as green as kryptonite through the cover glass.

"What's up, Captain?" Jenkins asked as he closed the door behind him, flicked the light switch on, and took up a standing position by the gallery wall.

The captain shot a brief but annoyed glance at the overhead light. "We've got, what we thought, is an unclaimed vehicle in impound, a white Subaru station wagon," the captain replied, placing the fingers of his right hand lightly on the manila folder and skimming it back and forth across a small clearing on the top of his desk. "We were just about to sell it off on auction when Gonzales over in Motor Pool noticed a large stain on the cargo liner."

"Blood?" Jenkins inquired, starting to feel a little like a dog being teased with a Frisbee.

"We don't know yet."

"How long has the car been back there?"

"That's a problem," the captain replied. "It's been over six months. According to an inventory log, it was towed from Seaport Boulevard on January twenty-third."

"And no one followed up? No one checked the registration?"

"Apparently, it fell through the cracks."

"Any record of who may have had access to the vehicle since then?" Jenkins pressed.

"No."

"And the towing company? Any record of who towed the vehicle?"

"Fell through the cracks," the captain responded.

"Fell through the cracks?" Jenkins asked incredulously.

"Do you remember Sergeant Hayes?"

"Of course, he got transferred downtown to credit card fraud."

"It was his case. When he left, it fell through the cracks."

"But cases get reassigned," Jenkins noted. "Yeah, it's the responsibility of the department…er, ah, never mind Captain."

Captain White glared up at Jenkins. "Anyway," the captain continued, "I just had Henderson check it out. The vehicle's registered to an Erica Holmes in the city."

"Can she come get it? I hate to think of the accrued storage fee she'll have to pay but at least she'll have her car back and maybe we can get an explanation for the blood stain."

"Again, now, we don't know it's blood, and, unfortunately, she can't come claim it," the captain replied.

"Why not?" Jenkins asked, cocking his head slightly like the old RCA beagle.

"We got a hit on a cross-reference. She's a missing person."

"This just keeps getting better," Jenkins said, starting to salivate like one of Pavlov's dogs. "How long has she been missing?"

"A report was filed on January twenty-fourth."

"The day after her car was towed?"

"It seems so," the captain responded. "Now, for the part you're not going to like."

"You're giving the case to someone else?" Jenkins asked, deflated.

"No, I'm giving you the case, but you're going to be working with a partner." The captain seemed to brace himself for what he knew was coming.

Jenkins stood there for a moment and let his brain sift the particulates like a coffee filter. "A partner?" Jenkins asked skeptically. "Is this a disciplinary action? Captain, I can handle a missing persons."

"Bob," the captain responded, his voice taking on an edge, "I'm tired of relying on the backlogged county lab. We've acquired the equipment and we've hired someone to do DNA for us. She's a graduate from Berkeley—a molecular biologist—and I want her to work with you on this one."

"She's fresh out of school?"

"Yep."

"Oh, for Pete's sake, Captain. Don't saddle me with some wet-behind-the-ears rookie—some CSI wanna be! You can't expect me to...."

"You'll be fine," the captain interrupted.

And there they were. Those three words: "You'll be fine." This was hardly the first time he'd heard them, and he knew they weren't meant to reassure. But, rather, they were a demarcation—a line he didn't dare cross. They were the signal that the discussion was over and that any further attempt to influence an outcome would be a waste of both their times.

"Here's the missing persons report," the captain said, handing Jenkins the manila folder. "Your partner's name is Helen Chang. She'll be meeting you at the Subaru in the back lot." With that, the captain turned his attention to a stack of reports piled on the left side of his desk. "And Jenkins!" the captain said without looking up.

"Hmm?"

"The light!"

"Right, Captain," Jenkins sighed, flipping the light switch off and stepping out of the office. He did not catch the captain's glance again as he left the room, closing the door behind him.

Back at his desk, Jenkins lifted the metal case containing his crime scene evaluation equipment onto his desk and flicked the latches open. He verified its contents against his checklist:

- ☐ Barrier tape
- ☐ Screw drivers (Phillips and FH)
- ☐ Graph paper, sketch paper
- ☐ Clipboard
- ☐ Pencils and pens
- ☐ Flashlight
- ☐ Steel tape measure
- ☐ Compass
- ☐ Magnifying glass
- ☐ Ultraviolet light
- ☐ Eye dropper
- ☐ Sterile saline solution
- ☐ Evidence envelopes
- ☐ Evidence bags
- ☐ Sealable plastic bags
- ☐ Test tubes
- ☐ Cotton swabs
- ☐ Spatula
- ☐ Cotton
- ☐ Latex gloves

- ☐ Digital camera, memory cards
- ☐ Batteries
- ☐ Forceps
- ☐ Brush
- ☐ Photo log sheets
- ☐ Collection vials
- ☐ Methylumbelliferyl phosphate
- ☐ Video camera and tape
- ☐ Fingerprint kit
- ☐ Hemastix
- ☐ Chalk
- ☐ Tongue depressor
- ☐ Sharpie
- ☐ Ruler
- ☐ Camera lenses
- ☐ Lint pickup roller
- ☐ Numbered marker tents
- ☐ Tripod
- ☐ Clear packaging tape
- ☐ Distilled water

Satisfied that all his equipment was in place, he headed through the gauntlet of detectives that cluttered his passage to the back of the building.

"Hey, Bob!" a rough voice called from his right. It was Detective Sanders. "Heard you have a new partner. Just be yourself there buddy! If she bails on you, I win five bucks."

"Was I the last person to know about this?" Jenkins sighed to himself shaking his head slowly as he left the floor into the hallway.

Lieutenant Bob Jenkins had been a detective for close to a quarter of a century, and he'd seen it all, from the missing toddler he'd tracked down to the digestive system of a neighbor's boa constrictor to the serial killer, the whack job from The Mission, who dispatched his victims with a syringe full of Drain-O. (The Press had dubbed that psycho "The Pipe Cleaner.") The assaults, the kidnappings, the black mailings, the murders. ... Jenkins had come up against each one on that unsavory list. And every time he closed a file, every time he cracked a case, he gave credit to, what he believed, his best crime-solving tool ... his gut. He could feel a crime scene. Its color. Its texture. Its layout. Its smell. Everything told a story, and it was his gut that took it all in. It was his gut that nagged him to look in places others on the force wouldn't dream of. It was a feeling in his gut that had always led him to the bad guy. His gut spoke only to him. Jenkins worked alone.

But now, here he was, the guy they mockingly called a gumshoe and a maverick, getting partnered up. His gut began to churn. A partner! he thought. And a graduate from Berkeley! At least the tie-dye T-shirts have gone out of style. But she'll probably have a tattoo on the small of her back and her ears will be plugged into an iPod—someone consumed by the latest gizmos and gadgets. How am I going to make a criminalist out of someone like that? Solving crimes is about interrogating witnesses, chasing down leads, and crawling around the dirt inside the criminal mind. It's about getting all that grunge hurled at you and trying not to let too much of it stick to your heart in a permanent way. She'd better at least be damn good with DNA.

Jenkins paced down the corridor towards the back impound lot carrying his case in one hand and the manila folder in the other. He flipped the folder open with a downward snap of his wrist and read the missing persons report. There, in the upper right-hand corner, was a picture of Erica Holmes. *Young, pretty,* Jenkins thought. *Probably a boyfriend or an ex-boyfriend, jilted, turned stalker.* Jenkins' mind almost always went first to murder.

Missing Persons Report Form MPR 1182

Date: January 24, 2014

Case Number: CA087953

Name: Erica Holmes

Date of Birth: January 7, 1988

Address: 2834 Cherry Hill Rd
San Francisco, CA
94122

Description of Missing Person

Caucasian female, 5′4″, 120 lbs, blue eyes, blond hair, last seen wearing blue coveralls and black Converse tennis shoes.

Distinguishing Marks

None

Reported by: Dwayne Holmes (father)

Information on Case

Erica Holmes is an auto mechanic at The Nuts and Bolts of It Auto Service & Repair shop at 317 Geary, San Francisco. By her father's statement, her boyfriend, Sam O'Neill, had picked Erica up at her home at 8:30 A.M. on January 23, 2007 and dropped her off at work at the service station. O'Neill's vehicle was in for repair at this location and Erica had allowed him the use of her vehicle, a 2001 white Subaru Legacy station wagon, until his vehicle was operational. At the time of this report, Erica has been missing for 34 hours.

Investigating Officer: Winthrop Hayes

Jenkins toggled the sheet with a finger. The second page in the folder was a vehicle registration form.

AUTO — REGISTRATION VALID FROM 10/02/2013 TO 10/02/2014 — TYPE 11 — LICENSE NUMBER 4GRSR2

VEHICLE IDENTIFICATION NUMBER: 3FASP15J6R16185A8

MAKE: SUBARU

BODY TYPE MODEL: SW

CYLS.:

DATE FIRST SOLD: 00/00/2001

CLASS: CR

Yr. Model: 2001

DATE ISSUED: 09/30/2013

TYPE VEH.: 12S — MP: G — AX: — WC: — UNLADEN/G/CGW:

TOTAL FEES PAID: $96

4010

REGISTERED OWNER

HOLMES ERICA P
2834 CHERRY HILL RD
SAN FRANCISCO CA 94434-3010

CA

L0030
R0058

LIENHOLDER

C

14102004039199

STATE OF CALIFORNIA
DEPARTMENT OF MOTOR VEHICLES
VALIDATED REGISTRATION CARD
READ REVERSE SIDE - IMPORTANT INSTRUCTIONS

X 1604350

Jenkins pushed through the double glass doors that emptied to the stairway above the expansive back impound lot. From the top of the landing and across the pit of derelict automobiles, he could see the white Subaru station wagon parked against the chain link fence on the far side of the blacktop. He could make out the figure of a woman in blue jeans and a pale T-shirt meandering towards the vehicle. Jenkins realized that he was now in a race. He skidded down the steps and zig-zagged his way through the maze of cars. Trying to suppress an overwhelming urge to pant, he arrived at the Subaru. But he was too late.

The Subaru's hatchback door gaped open, and the bottom half of a woman, bent at the waist, leaned out from the cargo bay. Her light blue T-shirt hiked up to her waist and exposed a circular design tattoo at the base of her spine. A cell phone was holstered to her jeans by her left back pocket. A small tackle box sat on the pavement a few yards from the Subaru's back bumper. Jenkins cleared his throat, loudly, deliberately, announcing his arrival. The woman, visibly startled, quickly came upright and faced him. Jenkins scanned her as if he were in an MRI machine. Wire rimmed glasses magnified her dark eyes—exotic. Warm. Her hair, nearly black, had a slightly reddish tint to it and was pinched back, through a crooked part, into a ponytail. She had a soft, pleasing, and reassuring face. Although each ear was pierced, she was not wearing earrings. She wore almost no makeup to speak of but her lashes were so dark that they may have been cosmetically enhanced, Jenkins couldn't quite be sure. A silver necklace spelled the name "Helen." She wore neither a diamond engagement ring nor wedding band and neither did she have a tan line on her ring finger to indicate she had ever worn either. But she could have been too young for that anyway. She brushed a stray lock of hair behind her left ear and Jenkins caught a glimpse of a pale and narrow two-inch scar running down the inside of her left forearm. Jenkins scanned her for the iPod he knew had to be part of her accoutrement. A thin, rectangular shape distorted her left front jeans pocket and two white wires ending in black earphone pads dangled from the opening. That must be it, he thought. His gut, it occurred to him, was uncanny.

"Bob? Good morning. It's nice to meet you," she said politely while quickly stretching out her right hand. "I'm Helen Chang." A spark danced across her eyes when she spoke.

"I can see that," Jenkins replied, pointing to her necklace. "And call me Lieutenant Jenkins." She was pleasant. Affable. Jenkins wasn't in the mood for either. He took her hand, grudgingly, and shook it twice, though lightly. Her hand was slender and feminine, feline almost, but sturdy and durable nonetheless. Jenkins, still winded, took in a few breaths. "Have you ever heard of Edmond Locard, Miss Chang?" Jenkins asked on the exhale.

"I don't think so," she replied.

"In 1912, a young woman was murdered in Lyons, France," Jenkins began while setting down his case on the hood of the adjacent vehicle. He popped open its lid and removed a roll of yellow barrier tape. He tied one end to the chain link fence, then proceeded to drape the yellow plastic ribbon in a large rectangle around the Subaru, using a rearview mirror and antennae of adjacent vehicles as posts, leading the other end back to the chain link fence at the front of the vehicle. The words CRIME SCENE DO NOT ENTER, reiterated on wide yellow ribbon around the automobile, now twisted gently in a subtle morning wind. "Her boyfriend, Emile Gourbin, a bank clerk, was suspected of the murder and was taken into custody," Jenkins continued. "He had an airtight alibi, however. Or so he thought. He had spent the night of her murder, he claimed, with friends of his out in the country. The forensic scientist, Edmond Locard, was called onto the case. He went to the morgue and examined the body of the victim. She had marks, bruising, around her neck. She'd been strangled, Locard concluded. He went back to Gourbin's prison cell and collected scrapings from underneath the suspect's fingernails. When he looked at that material under a microscope, he found skin cells covered with a cosmetic powder. Analysis showed that that powder was made from a unique collection of compounds. Locard then had the police recover the victim's cosmetics from her home. Her face powder, it turned out, made by a local druggist, had all the same components as the cosmetic clinging to the skin cells scraped from underneath Gourbin's fingernails. When confronted with this discovery, Emile Gourbin confessed and was convicted of her murder."

"Do you think that has something to do with this vehicle?" Helen asked.

"More so now than before since you opened the hatchback," Jenkins replied. "The point is that every time you touch something, you leave a little of yourself behind and you take a little of what you touched away with you. That's Locard's exchange principle. Every contact leaves a trace, in both directions. You opened the latch of the hatchback door. Your fingerprints, your skin oils and sweat, and all the host of chemicals they contain are now on that latch, and you will now have the skin oils of the other people who have touched that latch and fragments of their fingerprints on your hand along with any chemical residue from the latch itself. You were leaning into the hatchback area. A hair of yours may have fallen into the vehicle or fiber from your clothing, or by static electricity, fibers from the vehicle may now be attached to you. Any time there's contact, there's an exchange of material. In forensics, we're only limited by our ability to detect that exchange."

"I think I get it," Helen exclaimed. "You have coffee this morning, let's say, for example. You leave your fingerprints on the mug and your saliva on the rim. You may take away a drop of coffee on your nice white shirt."

"Exactly!" Jenkins said while quickly flicking an extended finger at her in the air like the strike of a cobra and being quite pleased with himself for making the point. But then her words found their mark, and he quickly glanced down at the front of his shirt, and there, by the second button, was a coffee stain the size of a quarter. *Must have been from when the captain snuck up on me this morning*, he thought.

"Lieutenant Jenkins," Helen said, redirecting his attention, "Captain White asked me to see if I could recover DNA from the stain on the cargo bay liner. I was only going to swab it for a small sample."

"Yes, but let's hold off on that a moment," said Jenkins. "Won't the very act of swabbing the stain change its appearance? And might fibers from the swab slough off onto the stain?"

"Well, yeah, okay, I suppose so. But, again, I was told by the Captain to get a sample."

"What kind of person drives a 2001 Subaru Legacy station wagon, Miss Chang?"

"Excuse me?"

"Would it be a wealthy person?"

"I would think not. More likely, someone who is concerned about making ends meet. Maybe a student or a teacher or a waiter. I don't know. Why?"

"Young or old?"

"Young, I would guess. Or someone who still acts young."

"Anything else?"

"Lieutenant Jenkins, is there a point to this?"

"You don't see one?"

"No, Sir. And do you always answer a question with a question?"

"Shouldn't I?"

"I think I should go talk to Captain White. Maybe you should work with someone else on this case."

"Suit yourself, Miss Chang. But I'd hate to see Detective Sanders win five bucks."

"What?"

"We're getting a feeling for the owner of this vehicle, Miss Chang. That's all. Now, can you say anything else about the person who owns this car?"

Helen stood there a moment. She leaned her head back to the sky. Her hair cascaded down behind her like a waterfall. She took a long, protracted breath and straightened her glasses. "Okay," she finally said, "it gets decent gas mileage. Again, that points to someone who's frugal and perhaps someone concerned about the environment."

"Ecologically minded. An environmentalist. Good Miss Chang."

"It's a Japanese make so the owner's not into the 'buy American' credo. And, it's sporty—an outdoor kind of car," Helen continued. "The owner is probably athletic and likes outdoor activities, maybe biking, skiing, surfing, or snowboarding."

"Or, they want to give the appearance of being athletic and outdoorsy," Jenkins added. "A modest man's midlife crisis vehicle." He started to pace slow circle around the automobile, looking for anything out of place. Helen followed.

"I suppose," Helen said. "Or, since it's a wagon, the owner could be a parent."

"True," said Jenkins. "But the child would have to be at least six years old or over sixty pounds."

"How could you possibly…," Helen started.

"State law, Miss Chang," Jenkins interrupted. "No child seat."

"Oh, yeah, that's right."

"And what kind of car do you drive, Miss Chang?" Jenkins asked as he leaned over a moment to examine a small dent on the right side of the front bumper. He looked up to find Helen staring at the gun in his shoulder holster.

"Oh, perfect!" Helen said aghast, "you carry a firearm?"

"I'm a sworn officer, Miss Chang," Jenkins replied. "Now, about your car?" Helen stood there staring at the area on Jenkins' left chest where his revolver rested in its holster. Her lungs surged in and out at a beat above normal respiration. "Miss Chang," he repeated, "your car?"

"A Prius," she finally replied. She gathered herself together into a firmer bundle. "A graduation present from my Dad."

"Makes sense," said Jenkins. "A young professional. Upwardly mobile. Your father knows you."

"And you, Lieutenant Jenkins?" Helen asked.

"A 1980 Oldsmobile Cutlass Calais."

"Wow, who would have imagined," Helen said, trying not to give up a grin.

"Yeah, well, it's a classic," Jenkins said shooting her a quick, disapproving glance. He resumed his stroll around the vehicle. "If I were to tell you, Miss Chang," Jenkins continued, "that the owner of this vehicle is a woman, what would you say would be the characteristics of her boyfriend?"

"Why do you assume she has a boyfriend? Maybe she's single. Or maybe she has a girlfriend."

"Now who's answering a question with a question? But your point is well taken. For the sake of argument, however, let's say she has a boyfriend."

"I think people are attracted to those who share similar values."

"I agree with you," Jenkins said. "We've secured the area. Let's get busy. First, I need to photograph the vehicle, and, Miss Chang, if you wouldn't mind writing up the log," he asked, handing her a log sheet. "Please note the date, the time, location, case number … it's CA087953," he said, glancing at the manila folder, "and who's here. That's Jenkins, J, E, N, K, I, N, S."

"Wait a minute," Helen protested. "You've cordoned off the area and we don't even know if this is really a crime scene or not."

"We're going to treat it as if it is," Jenkins replied. "The owner of this vehicle is a missing person, and until we're convinced otherwise, this is a crime scene."

"Shall I close the hatchback door?" Helen asked hopefully.

"No, leave it up," Jenkins replied.

"Do I have to write in the log that I opened it?"

"Yes, you do, Miss Chang. Now, nothing personal but if you wouldn't mind moving out of the frame…."

Crime Scene Investigation

A *crime scene* encompasses the largest area that might contain physical clues to the circumstances and participants of an unlawful act. If a person has been hacking into bank records, the crime scene might be as small as their computer. When terrorists destroyed New York's World Trade Center in September of 2001, the crime scene included several city blocks. In the Erica Holmes missing person case, the crime scene is the recovered Subaru station wagon.

The first few minutes of a crime scene's processing can be the most critical moments of an entire investigation. At no other period will the investigators be closer to the moment the crime was committed. Investigators will never have the area more pristine or more unfettered from contamination. In those first few minutes, fingerprints, shoe prints, tire prints, trace evidence, and the state of the victim are all at their most informative. And yet, at no other time are mistakes more likely made that can potentially jeopardize successful prosecution of the crime's perpetrator.

Because Locard's exchange principle haunts every crime scene, human contact with any physical or biological evidence can result in its contamination or loss. One of the first acts of a first responder, therefore, must be to restrict access to all those not directly involved in the investigation. Cordoning off the area with yellow crime scene tape is the method most frequently used to limit trespassing by the unaware or by curious members of the press or public. To minimize contamination, the taped-off perimeter should allow access to the scene at only one spot, and all those entering and departing the scene should be carefully documented. The secured area should be large enough to contain the most obvious elements of the criminal act—the victim, blood stains, a discarded murder weapon, any disturbed furniture, etc.—but must also allow for careful examination of all possible paths by which the perpetrator may have gained access to the victim and then exited the area.

Documenting the Crime Scene

Once the area is secure, investigators can then perform an initial *walk-through* in which they try to glean an understanding of the nature and scope of the crime and determine what evidence should be collected and from where. Prior to removing any evidence, however, it should be photographed or videotaped to document its state and its position within its surroundings. Much of the crime scene can also be recorded by 3D laser scanning to give investigators an even more refined image of the crime scene and its overall layout (Figure 1.1). Photos of smaller items should be taken with and without a reference (such as a ruler or a coin) to give a measure

Figure 1.1 The Leica Geosystems 3D laser scanner is integrated with a high-resolution panoramic camera giving a detailed image of the crime scene's 3D layout. It is shown here in front of the Texas School Book Depository in Dealey Plaza, Dallas, Texas, scene of the John F. Kennedy assassination. (Photo courtesy of Leica Geosystems, Houston, TX.)

of scale. Although photographs provide the most accurate documentation of the physical elements of a crime scene, sketches are also made to show the relationships and distances between those elements. Are doors open or closed? Are glasses on the dining room table? Does anything seem out of place? Sometimes, even the most trivial detail can be important. These sketches don't necessarily require that the investigator be a talented artist, but they do demand enough accuracy to show the crime scene layout and the relative locations of any evidence. Careful notes taken at the crime scene can effectively supplement photo, videotape, and sketch documentation.

Information gathered from the crime scene will help the investigator file an official report. Most police departments use report forms specific to the crime. For example, a kidnapping, a homicide, and an incident of domestic violence may each have their own associated report form. The homicide report prepared for the assassination of President John F. Kennedy in 1962 is shown in Figure 1.2.

Collecting Evidence

Evidence is anything that can be used to probe the events and identify the participants of a crime. Investigators gather two types of evidence during an investigation, direct and circumstantial. *Direct evidence* refers to information gathered from statements made by a surviving victim, by suspects, and by eyewitnesses. This type of evidence, however, is notoriously unreliable. Perceptions of an event, as they pass from the eyes to the brain to the vocal chords, can be filtered and distorted in a number of ways. The accuracy of a person's account is subject to filtration by the witness' own visual acuity and is susceptible to distortion as it's refracted through the powerful lens of their bias, prejudice, and past experience. An eyewitness account is also vulnerable to flaws in continuity through the witness' own capacity, or lack thereof, for accurately remembering information and the order in which the events of the crime occurred.

Circumstantial evidence usually refers to items such as blood, fingerprints, hair, fibers, and DNA. This type of evidence is more amenable to scientific examination than is direct evidence. And, since various controls can be run with any type of scientific test designed to identify its source, circumstantial evidence tends to be more reliable. Nevertheless, circumstantial evidence still requires that a court make a judgment as to its relevance. For example, if DNA analysis shows that a suspect's blood was found at the scene of a murder, a jury still must weigh the arguments made that such evidence necessarily places the suspect at the scene during the time the crime was committed.

But what types of evidence should be collected, and how much of any one type? If a murder, assault, or burglary is being investigated, any type of evidence that can place a suspect at the scene should be collected. This is usually obvious; fingerprints, a murder weapon, bloodstains, and shoeprints can all be critical to solving a crime. Not so obvious, however, might be those items not readily visible, such things as dirt, pollen, hair, and fibers. These items of trace evidence might prove that the perpetrator came from a certain outside geographical region having a unique flora and geology. Collecting absolutely everything from a crime scene, from a couch down to the dust, however, would create a documentation and storage nightmare and might actually hinder speedy and successful prosecution of the case. Experience becomes the best teacher as to what items will have the most relevance for the investigation of each type of crime.

FORM OF HB-40

HOMICIDE REPORT

POLICE DEPARTMENT CITY OF DALLAS

Last Name of Person Killed, First Name, Middle Name: KENNEDY, John F (PRESIDENT OF U. S.)
Race, Sex, Age: w m 47
Residence of Person Killed: Washington, D. C. (White House)
Offense Serial No.: F-85950
Reported By / Title or Relationship / Race, Sex, Age / Address of Person Reporting / Phone of Person Reporting

Offense as Reported (Crime): MURDER
After Investigation Changed to

Place of Occurrence — Street and Number or Intersection: Elm St. (approx. 150' W of Houston)
Division: H&R)
Platoon: 2
Beat: 101
Officers Making Report, I.D. No., Name, I.D. No.: CN Dhority 476 HH Blessing 698

Day of Week: Fri
Date of Occurrence: 11/22/63
Time of Day: 12:30PM
Date Reported: 11/23/63
Time Reported: 5:10PM
Report Received By: Mayo
Received—Time—Typed: 5:10PM

DESCRIPTION OF DEAD PERSON

Age / Height / Weight / Eyes / Hair / Beard / Complexion / Identifying Marks, Scars, Etc. / Clothing

Coroner Notified: Joe B. Brown
Name of Coroner Attending—Time of Arrival A.M. P.M.
Name of Prosecutor Attending—Time of Arrival A.M. P.M.

Pronounced Dead by Physician: Dr. Kemp Clark, 1PM, Parkland Hospital
Address
Person With Whom Deceased Lived or Associated

DETAILS OF OFFENSE (Give Circumstances of Occurrence of Offense and Its Investigation) Use Both Sides of This Sheet.

The expired was riding in motorcade with wife and Governor John Connally, and his wife. Witnesse heard gun shot and saw the expired slump forward. More shots were heard and the expired fell int his wife's lap. Governor Connally was also shot at this time. Car in which they were riding was escorted to Parkland Hospital by Dallas Police Officers.

Witness Taken Into Custody, Address: All witnesses affidavits are in Homicide Office.
Witness Taken Into Custody, Address

Known, Suspected or Possible Motives

DESCRIPTION OF SUSPECTS OR PERSONS WANTED

Name if Known / Alias / Address / Sex / Color / Age / Height / Weight / Eyes / Hair / Complexion
Beard / Nativity / Occupation / Dress and Other Marks / Cause for Suspicion

Name if Known / Alias / Address / Sex / Color / Age / Height / Weight / Eyes / Hair / Complexion
Beard / Nativity / Occupation / Dress and Other Marks / Cause for Suspicion

Name if Known / Alias / Address / Sex / Color / Age / Height / Weight / Eyes / Hair / Complexion
Beard / Nativity / Occupation / Dress and Other Marks / Cause for Suspicion

Persons Arrested—Name—Address: Lee Harvey Oswald
Race, Sex, Age: w m 25
Arresting Officers, I.D. No.: Lt. E. L. Cunningham 464, MN McDonald 1178
Charge: MURDER

Officers Assigned to Investigate (Include I.D. No.): Dhority - Blessing - Brown
This Offense Declared: Unfounded ☐ Pending ☐ Cleared by Arrest ☐
Date
Commanding Officer
Case File: Yes ☐ No ☒
Disposition Code
By
Date
REMARKS:

INVESTIGATION BUREAU

Figure 1.2 The Homicide Report prepared by the Dallas Police Department on the assassination of President John F. Kennedy on November 22, 1963.

Packaging Evidence

Evidence can make or break a case. To the attentive investigator, it is the *silent witness* that reveals the events of an illegal act. Without it, the prosecution has little hope of tying the alleged criminal to the crime. As such, it must be handled in a way that protects it from loss, damage, or contamination.

Different types of evidence should be packaged in ways that ensure their longevity and that packaging should be clearly marked denoting it as evidence. Dry items such as small swatches of cloth, scraps of paper, or wood splinters can be folded in paper and placed in a sealable plastic bag. Nonbiological liquids such as water, bleach, gasoline, or paint should be stored in an airtight, plastic container.

Since any type of biological evidence is a potential food source for bacteria and mold, it's best that such material is stored in a way that will prevent the retention or accumulation of moisture that would encourage microbial growth and destruction of the sample. Bloodied or semen-stained cloth, for example, should be allowed to dry. Once desiccated, it can be packaged in a sealed bag and, as such, should be stored safely for years.

Each evidence bag must bear a description of the item it contains, the name of the person who found it, the case number, the date, the location where the item was found, and the name of any witnesses who observed its discovery. Evidence should be stored in a secured room that prevents its tempering with.

Chain of Custody

As evidence items are gathered, careful notes must be kept documenting where, when, and by whom it is collected. Evidence is bagged or boxed and sealed in such a way that its removal from the container is immediately obvious (Figure 1.3). It is readily apparent, for example, when tape securing an evidence bag has been torn or ripped. Such precautions can help thwart any accusations by a defense attorney of *evidence tampering*. And each time an evidence bag is passed from one person to the next, from the time it is collected until it finds its way into the court room for the trial (and even thereafter), the person accepting the item dates and signs their name on the bag. This record is called *chain of custody,* and you can bet that a defense attorney will meticulously examine that record. If they find any irregularity, you can further expect that they will either move to have that evidence rendered inadmissible or use the investigators' lapse in protocol as a way to raise questions in the minds of a jury that that evidence was tampered with, in perhaps a sinister and calculated way, ultimately prejudicial to their client (an approach that was taken full advantage of by attorney Johnnie Cochran during the O.J. Simpson murder trial of 1995). An example of a chain of custody form is shown in Figure 1.4.

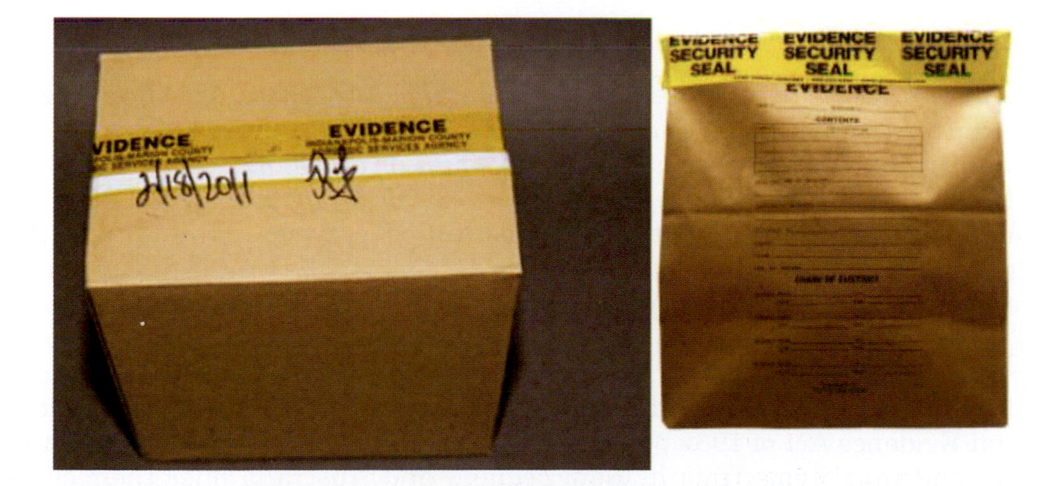

Figure 1.3 Tape is used to seal boxes or bags carrying evidence. Notice that the tape on the box on the left is initialed and dated. Notice that the initials actually overlap onto the cardboard next to the tape. Any attempt to remove the tape and to put that same tape back on again could most likely be detected as tampering. Any time the tape on the container is broken, the person breaking the tape must document it. When the lawyer, investigator, or criminalist has finished their business with the evidence, the evidence must be replaced and the bag resealed with fresh tape. (Photos courtesy of the Indianapolis-Marion County Forensic Services Agency, Indianapolis, IN.)

Chain of Custody

The item(s) described below were obtained as evidence by the undersigned during a criminal investigation conducted by the San Mateo County Police Department.

Case Number: ____________________

Description of item(s) obtained:

Obtained from: ____
(Title, name, location, contact information)

______________________ ______________________ ____________
Printed Name of Investigator Signature of Investigator Date Obtained

Temporary disposition of item(s): (where stored; show releases below)

Released by: ________________ Released to: ________________ ________
Printed name/signature Printed name/signature Date
Purpose/Reason: ____

Released by: ________________ Released to: ________________ ________
Printed name/signature Printed name/signature Date
Purpose/Reason: ____

Released by: ________________ Released to: ________________ ________
Printed name/signature Printed name/signature Date
Purpose/Reason: ____

Released by: ________________ Released to: ________________ ________
Printed name/signature Printed name/signature Date
Purpose/Reason: ____

Final disposition of item(s):

Figure 1.4 A chain of custody form is used to document who has examined or taken possession of an evidence item and when that occurred.

Legalities of Evidence Collection

The right of the people to be secure in their persons, houses, papers, and effects, against unreasonable searches and seizures, shall not be violated, and no Warrants shall issue, but upon probable cause, supported by Oath or affirmation, and particularly describing the place to be searched, and the persons or things to be seized.

The Fourth Amendment of the US Constitution prevents citizens from being strong armed by law enforcement. It provides residents of the United States a degree of sovereignty over their own property. All countries in the Free World recognize the rights of the individual against *unreasonable* search and seizer of their property by their government. In Canada, those rights are protected by Section Eight of the Canadian Charter of Rights and Freedoms. In Britain, Section 8 of the Police and Criminal Evidence Act of 1984 puts limits on the power of the police to search your property and take items from it. New Zealand and Australia offer their citizens similar protections.

However, some crime scenes (or the location of evidence involved in a crime) may be within a suspect's personal property, for example, within their vehicle or residence. The US Constitution's Fourth Amendment requires that a law enforcement officer obtain a judge's permission before the right is given to search either of these properties. That permission, called a *search warrant*, is issued by a judge and will be granted only if the officer shows *probable cause*—a compelling reason to believe that the vehicle or residence contains evidence critical to a criminal investigation.

Even with the safeguards of the Fourth Amendment, searches may be conducted under special circumstances such as when there is a life and death emergency, if evidence is in imminent danger of being lost or destroyed, and when granted permission by the property owner. In addition, when a suspect has been lawfully arrested, their property can be searched for evidence without the issue of a warrant.

In the Crime Lab

Activity 1.1 Silent Witness: Interpreting Physical Evidence

There are three ways that crimes are solved, (a) by confession, (b) by testimony from eyewitnesses, and (c) by examination of physical evidence. A potential problem with a confession, however, is that the confessor, for any number of reasons, may admit to a crime they didn't commit. Likewise, eyewitness testimony can be equally unreliable in that no two people will witness or describe the events of a crime in exactly the same way. The most important and reliable tool for solving a crime, therefore, is through careful analysis of the physical evidence. The physical evidence, the so-called silent witness, can corroborate or contradict either a confession or the testimony of an eyewitness.

In this activity, you will derive information about the participants of a crime by examining physical evidence recovered from a hypothetical crime scene.

Materials:

Laboratory notebook
Brown bags containing physical evidence collected from a crime scene

Protocol:

1. Your instructor will provide each lab group with (1) a bag containing crime scene evidence, (2) the circumstances under which the evidence was collected, and (3) a list of questions relevant to that evidence. Answer the questions based on information you might be able to deduce from each item of physical evidence.
2. Reproduce the following data table in your laboratory notebook and fill in the appropriate information. Once completed, you will be asked by your instructor to report your findings to the class.

Item Description	Question(s) the Item May Be Able to Address	Interpretation

Activity 1.2 Sketching a Crime Scene

Photography, whether film or digital, is an invaluable tool for documenting the objects and the spatial arrangements of those objects at a crime scene. With such technical devices readily available, it might seem archaic and antiquated to make a free-hand sketch of a crime scene. A drawing, however, gives investigators valuable information about the layout of a crime scene. How many feet between the bedroom doorway and the homicide victim? How far away from the window was broken glass discovered? What is the distance from the front door to the body? How many inches long is the muddy boot print in the walkway? This type of information is easy to make note of on a sketch. In this activity, you will create a rough *bird's eye* (or aerial perspective) sketch of a crime scene.

Materials:

Laboratory notebook
Tape measure

Protocol:

The class will be divided into two groups. Each group will be assigned a crime scene prepared by your instructor. The students in each group will document their assigned crime scene by drawing an overhead sketch of its components and layout in their laboratory notebook. Along with your sketch, include all supporting pieces of information (time of day, general location, weather conditions, other investigators present at the scene, etc.).

Note: In this exercise, no digital and/or video cameras are allowed at the crime scene.

Activity 1.3 Reconstructing a Crime Scene

When a case goes to trial, the court uses the notes, photographs, and sketches collected during the investigation to reconstruct, as best as possible, the physical layout of the crime scene. Arguments as to a suspect's guilt or innocence can hinge on the accuracy of those accounts.

In this activity, you will help to reconstruct a crime scene based on notes and sketches taken by other students.

Materials:

Other student's lab notebook containing description of crime scene
Tape measure

Protocol:

1. You will be divided into the same groups as those created for Activity 1.2. Exchange notebooks with a student in the opposite group. Using the information provided in the student's notebook, reconstruct the crime scene they had examined. Place all the objects of the crime scene in their relative positions as documented.
2. When your group has finished, the instructor will take a digital image of your reconstructed crime scene.
3. For comparison, your instructor will display digital images of (1) the actual crime scene setup by your instructor on day one and (2) the crime scene you re-created based on your classmate's notes from their laboratory notebooks.

Analysis: In your laboratory notebook, record your responses to the following questions:

1. What parts of your reconstruction were reproduced accurately when compared to the real crime scene?

2. What parts of your reconstruction were reproduced incorrectly when compared to the real crime scene?
3. If you had to repeat the previous activity (Activity 1.2), what would you do to improve the accuracy of your documentation?

Activity 1.4 Documenting the Position of Objects at a Crime Scene

When investigators document a crime scene, whether it's by digital photography or by sketch, they may often make note of the relative positions of the items within the scene by their relation to the points of a compass or by the place they occupy within an imaginary geometric grid. Accurate measurements of where items are located will help a court re-create a crime scene, if it is necessary, at a date later than when the original investigation was conducted. Reference points used to take measurements and to position evidence items within a crime scene, therefore, should not be items that can be easily moved.

Investigators may use either imaginary triangles or rectangles to record the position of an evidence item. Constructing a rectangle containing an evidence item within its bounds requires the lengths of two adjoining sides and fixtures at a right angle to each other (90°) from which to reference (Figure 1.5). By placing an evidence item at the corner of a rectangle and knowing the lengths of the two sides that meet at that corner, an investigator can precisely re-create its location.

Accurately determining an object's position within a triangle requires the length of one side and the two angles formed by lines leading from either end of that imaginary line to the object. For example, if we know that the distance between two reference markers is 10 ft and the angle of a line drawn from the evidence item to one reference marker is 34° and the angle of a line drawn from the evidence item to the other reference marker is 80°, we can draw lines having the proper angle from each end of the measured line until those two lines intersect. The distance from each marker to the evidence item can then be determined (Figure 1.6).

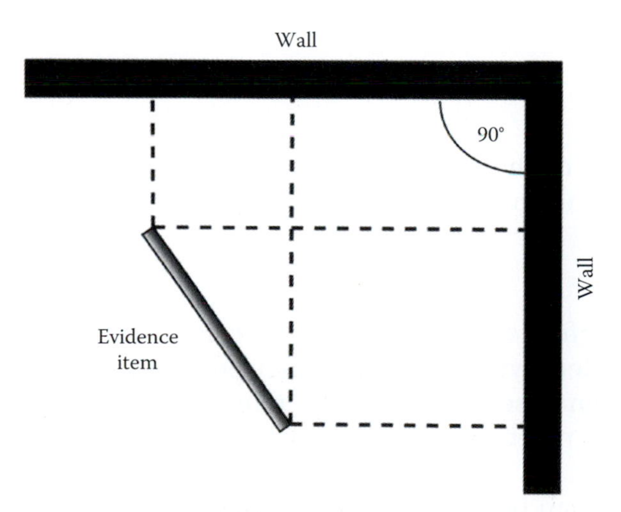

Figure 1.5 Using rectangles to map the location and orientation of an item within a crime scene requires a nearby reference marker having sides at a right angle to each other (here shown as two walls). By knowing the distances of at least two points on the evidence item from each wall, the evidence item can be precisely placed at its original position if the crime scene needs to be reconstructed.

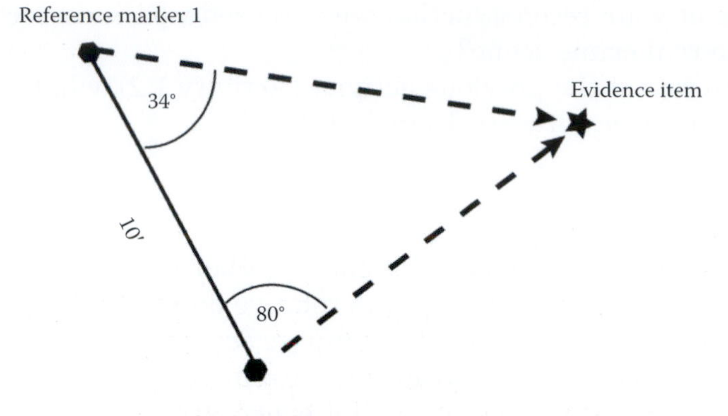

Figure 1.6 A straight line between two reference markers (designated 1 and 2) measures 10′ in length. The angle formed by that imaginary line and a line leading from Reference Marker 1 to the evidence item is 34°. A line leading from Reference Marker 2 to the evidence item creates an 80° angle. To re-create a crime scene, an investigator or officer of the court can draw the 34° angle line from Reference Marker 1 and the 80° angle line from Reference Marker 2 until they intersect. The investigator will then place the evidence item at that intersect point.

Noting the location of an evidence item in relation to the points of a compass requires that the investigator must also know a little bit about geometry. A compass heading is based on a 360° circle (Figure 1.7). North is designated as 0°. Moving clockwise around the compass, due east is 90°, due south is 180°, and due west is 270°. All directions in between are designated by their corresponding angle from magnetic north.

In this activity, you will document the location of an evidence item within a crime scene using a digital image, compass orientation, and/or coordinate position within a geometric grid.

Materials:

Laboratory notebook
Ruler
Protractor

Protocol

Describe the position of the evidence item within each digital image by using its relation to the positions on a compass or by using its location within an imaginary geometric grid.

Analysis

In Figure 1.8, the surfing wet suit booty (center) is the item of evidence. It was discovered beneath the deck window of a burglarized apartment. Assume that the deck railing and the garden hose wall are at 90° to each other.

In your laboratory notebook, record your responses to the following questions:

1. What method(s) can be used to describe the position of the surfing booty on the porch deck shown in Figure 1.8?
2. What items should not be used as reference points and why?
3. Draw a re-creation of this image in your laboratory notebook. Using a ruler, draw the appropriate lines to identify the position of the evidence item (the surfing booty).

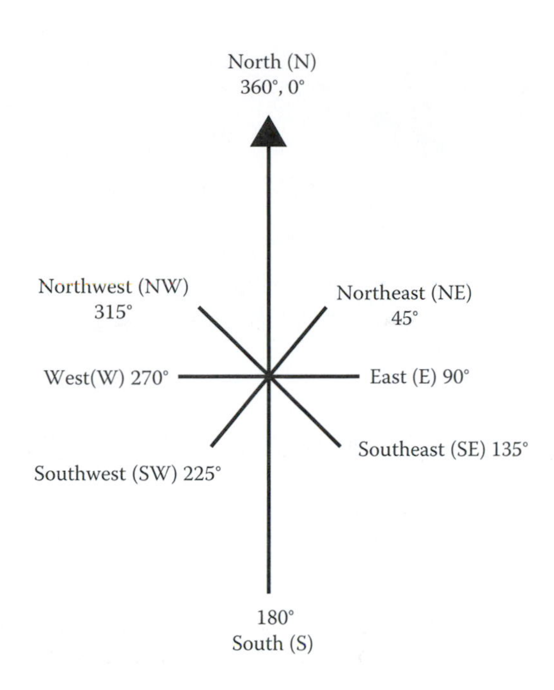

Figure 1.7 The headings of a compass are related to the degrees of a circle. If the object is facing due north (N), the compass heading will read and point to 0°. If the object is facing due east (E), the compass heading will read and point to 90°. If the object is facing due south (S), the compass heading will read and point to 180°. If the object is facing due west (W), the compass heading will read and point to 270°. If the object is facing north east (NE), south east (SE), south west (SW), or north west (NW), the compass heading is reading 45°, 135°, 225°, and 315°, respectively. If the object is pointing between 0° and 45°, the orientation is north, north east (N, NE). If the object is pointing between 45° and 90°, the orientation is east, north east (E, NE). The same nomenclature applies to the other compass quadrants. Note that the compass headings are magnetic north, not true north.

Figure 1.8 Digital image of a surfing booty on a porch deck. 1 represents an example of a possible measurement that can be taken (from the edge of the deck to the heel of the surfing booty). 2 is another possible point of measurement (from the wall of the house to the back rim of the surfing booty). B is a potted plant and C is a sponge. N represents north.

Figure 1.9 Aerial photograph of a surfing booty adjacent to an outdoor brick barbecue. Line 1 is a measurement from the brick wall to the booty's heel. Line 2 is a measurement from the corner of the brick wall to the toe of the booty. Line 3 is a measurement from the brick wall to one of the corners of the brick (marked as "C"). Line 4 is a measurement from the brick wall to one of the other corners of the brick (C).

4. The surfing booty measures 25 cm heel to toe. How far is the heel of the surfing booty from the garden hose wall?
5. Using the compass heading given in the figure, describe the orientation of the evidence item (e.g., what direction is the toe pointing?).
6. What fixed objects in Figure 1.8 can be used as references to re-create the crime scene?

Figure 1.9 shows a surfing booty (the evidence item) in the barbeque area of a burglarized home. Use this image to answer questions 7 through 13.

7. During the original processing of the crime scene, a brick marked "C" was placed into evidence. It is now 3 months later and the court is asking the investigators to re-create the crime scene. The brick has a width of 9.5 cm. What is the true distance of line "3"?
8. What is the true distance of line "4"?
9. What is the compass orientation of the brick marked "C"? (State your answer with respect to the front edge of the brick proximal to the booty.)
10. What is the true distance of line "1"?
11. What is the true distance of line "2"?
12. What orientation is the rubber booty in relation to the points on a compass? (State your answer relative to the direction of the toe and ankle.)

Figure 1.10 A photograph taken from an aerial perspective of a knife on the fourth stair leading up the front porch of a residence in which an assault has occurred.

13. What fixed objects in Figure 1.9 can be used to re-create the crime scene in a drawing or reconstruction?
14. Which coordinate technique (rectangular and/or triangular) would you use to determine the position of the knife shown in Figure 1.10?
15. Which fixed points would you use to establish the coordinates of the knife?
16. Which two points on the knife shown in Figure 1.10 would you use to measure distances from the fixed points you identified in Question 15?
17. Re-create Figure 1.10 as a drawing in your laboratory notebook and, using a ruler, draw the actual lines you would measure at the crime scene.
18. What is the compass heading of the knife in Figure 1.10 with respect to the direction the tip of the knife is pointing?

Activity 1.5 Sketching a Crime Scene Revisited

For this exercise, your instructor will create two crime scenes and assign a group of students to document each scene. This activity will give you practice documenting a crime scene and will give you an opportunity to apply your skills at creating coordinate systems for accurately positioning evidence items within a crime scene sketch.

Materials:

Laboratory notebook
Measuring tape
Compass
Crime scene tape
Protractor
Map of school campus (which includes compass heading)
Measuring wheel (optional)

Protocol

1. Make an overhead sketch of the crime scene assigned to you by your instructor.

2. Note the orientation of the evidence items within the crime scene in relation to the points of a compass. With a laboratory partner, take the necessary measurements needed to locate the evidence item(s) using a rectangular and/or triangulation coordinate system.
3. Share and compare your measurements with the other members of your group.

Note: No digital and/or video images will be taken at the crime scene.

Activity 1.6 Crime Scene Reconstruction Revisited

In this activity, you will use a directional compass and coordinate measurements to reconstruct a crime scene from notes taken by other students.

Materials:

Laboratory notebook
Measuring tape
Compass
Crime scene tape
Protractor
Map of school campus (should include compass heading)
Measuring wheel (optional)

Protocol

1. In Activity 1.5, your instructor divided the class into two groups—each group documenting a different crime scene. With your laboratory partner, exchange your notebooks with a pair of students in another other group and, using the information they have provided, re-create the crime scene they documented.
2. When you have finalized the reconstruction of the crime scene, have the instructor take a digital image.
3. Compare your re-created crime scene with the digital image taken by your instructor.

Erica Holmes Missing Persons Case

Figures 1.11 and 1.12 are photographs of Erica Holmes' vehicle in impound and the large stain on the rear cargo bay liner.

Questions

1.1 What was done to protect the crime scene?
1.2 What improvements could have been made in the manner in which Lieutenant Jenkins and Criminalist Chang secured and evaluated the crime scene?
1.3 How might a defense attorney use any procedural lapses made by these investigators to protect a suspect charged with involvement in a homicide case?

Figure 1.11 Erica Holmes' Subaru station wagon in the impound lot.

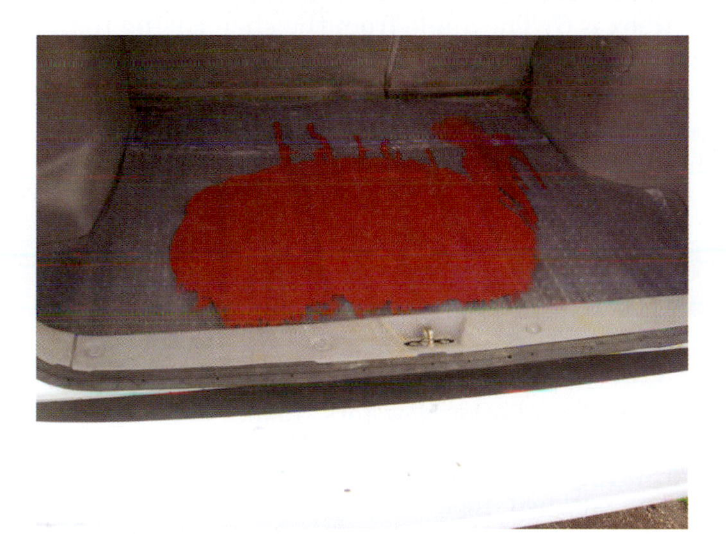

Figure 1.12 The large bloodstain on the cargo bay liner of Erica Holmes' vehicle.

Review Questions

1.1 What is Locard's exchange principle?

1.2 What defines the size of a crime scene?

1.3 What is the purpose of a crime scene walk-through?

1.4 Give four examples of circumstantial evidence.

1.5 Why is it a good idea to allow blood or other bodily fluids to dry when taken into evidence from a crime scene?

1.6 Why is it important to maintain a *chain of custody* document for the evidence items collected from a crime scene?

1.7 What is a warrant?

1.8 What is profiling?
1.9 When documenting a crime scene, why is a *bird's eye* sketch preferable to one taken from ground or eye level?
1.10 What is the rectangular coordinates method of describing an object's location?
1.11 When positioning objects within a crime scene, why is it important that the measurements be taken from fixed objects?
1.12 When implementing rectangular or triangular coordinates to describe the position of an evidence item, why is it important that two different reference points be chosen?
1.13 During an initial investigation of a crime scene, what other notation(s) (beside position measurements) should be recorded before removing an item from its original location?
1.14 What other tool would aid the crime scene investigator in addressing the issue posed in Question 1.13?
1.15 What is the triangulation coordinates method?
1.16 When would triangulation coordinates be preferred over rectangular coordinates in describing the position of an evidence item?
1.17 A shell casing has been found in the street at the scene of a murder. A signpost and a mailbox are nearby. The distance from the signpost to the front, right leg of the mailbox is 6′. The angle from the shell casing to the front, right leg of the mailbox to the signpost is 55°. The angle from the shell casing to the signpost to the front, right leg of the mailbox is 30°. (a) What is the distance from the shell casing to the front, right leg of the mailbox? (b) What is the distance from the shell casing to the signpost?

Further Reading

Evaluating the Crime Scene

Crime Scene by L. Ragle, Avon Books, New York, 1995.

The Criminal Investigation Process and the Role of Forensic Evidence: A Review of Empirical Findings by F. Horvath and R. Meesig in *Journal of Forensic Sciences*, Vol. 41, No. 6, pages 963–969, 1996.

Crime-Scene Investigation (Chapter Two) by J. Nickell and J.F. Fischer in *Crime Scene: Methods of Forensic Detection* (The University Press of Kentucky, Lexington, KT), pages 23–53, 1999.

What Educational Background Do Crime Laboratory Directors Require from Applicants? By K.G. Furton, Y.-L. Hsu, and M.D. Cole in *Journal of Forensic Sciences*, Vol. 44, No. 1, pages 128–132, 1999.

The Scene of the Crime (Chapter One) by N.E. Genge in *The Forensic Casebook: The Science of Crime Scene Investigation* (Ballantine Books, New York), pages 1–19, 2002.

At the Crime Scene by R. Platt in *Crime Scene: The Ultimate Guide to Forensic Science* (DK Publishing, Inc., New York), pages 11–23, 2003.

Crime Scene Investigation (Chapter 8) by M.T. Miller in *Forensic Science: An Introduction to Scientific and Investigative Techniques* (S.H. James and J.J. Nordby, Eds., CRC Press, Boca Raton, FL), pages 115–135, 2003.

The Crime Scene (Chapter One) by J.T. Dominick, S.A. Koehler, S. Ladham, R. Meyers, T. Uhrich, C.H. Wecht, and M. Welner in *Crime Scene Investigation* (Reader's Digest, Pleasanton, New York), pages 16–35, 2004.

Working the Scene: Evidence Collection and Protection (Chapter 3) by D.P. Lyle in *Forensics for Dummies* (Wiley Publishing, Inc., Hoboken, NJ), pages 29–48, 2004.

Profiling

Stalking on Campus: The Prevalence and Strategies for Coping with Stalking by W.J. Fremouw, D. Westrup, and J. Pennypacker in *Journal of Forensic Sciences*, Vol. 42, No. 4, pages 666–669, 1997.

An Investigation of the Psychological Characteristics of Stalkers: Empathy, Problem-Solving, Attachment and Borderline Personality Features by S.F. Lewis, W.J. Fremouw, K. Del Ben, and C. Farr in *Journal of Forensic Sciences*, Vol. 46, No. 1, pages 80–84, 2001.

Communicated Threats and Violence Toward Public and Private Targets: Discerning Differences among Those Who Stalk and Attack by J.R. Meloy in *Journal of Forensic Sciences*, Vol. 45, No. 5, pages 1211–1213, 2001.

The Contract Murderer: Patterns, Characteristics, and Dynamics by L.B. Schlesinger in *Journal of Forensic Sciences*, Vol. 46, No. 5, pages 1119–1123, 2001.

Stalking: Developing an Empirical Typology to Classify Stalkers by K. Del Ben and W. Fremouw in *Journal of Forensic Sciences*, Vol. 47, No. 1, pages 152–158, 2002.

Criminal Personality Profiling by M.R. Napier and K.P. Baker Miller in *Forensic Science: An Introduction to Scientific and Investigative Techniques* (S.H. James and J.J. Nordby, Eds., CRC Press, Boca Raton, FL), pages 531–550, 2003.

A Day in the Life of a Criminal Profiler by D.A. Wideman in *Crime Scene Investigation* by J.T. Dominick, S.A. Koehler, S. Ladham, R. Meyers, T. Uhrich, C.H. Wecht, and M. Welner (Reader's Digest, Pleasanton, New York), pages 16–35, 2004.

A Case of Stalking in the Workplace and Subsequent Sexual Homicide by K.A. Morrison in *Journal of Forensic Sciences*, Vol. 52, No. 3, pages 726–730.

2
Lifting Prints

Vehicle Impound Lot, Monday 10:30 AM

Make the best of it. That's what her father always told her. Make the best of it. She would remind herself of that free wisdom whenever she found herself obligated to a situation that was unpleasant or otherwise not to her liking. Waves of doubt cresting with regret, however, surged over her as she stared at an anonymous white station wagon with a large dried-up pool of blood in the back stuck in a forgotten corner of a police impound lot. Was taking this job the worst mistake she had ever made? What had she gotten herself into? This car had a secret, probably a dark and sinister one. It represented human beings at their worst, most desperate, and most depraved. Forgiveness and trust as discarded and decayed as the dried bloodstain. There was nothing joyous here. Someone's life could have ended in that car. She struggled not to allow herself to detach from the reality she was now feeling so close to drowning in. Make the best of it. A degree in molecular biology, two years of postgraduate study, and work as a technician in a genetic analysis lab didn't prepare her for the psychology that she was now realizing had to be a necessary part of what she was taking on. And to make things as bad as possible, for her first day on the job, she's stuck with a pompous, arrogant, anal-retentive, gun-toting gasbag. *Make the best of it* now seemed little more than platitude.

"Don't you think, Miss Chang?"

"Huh?" Helen responded, bringing herself back to the moment.

"We should start collecting evidence, don't you think?" Jenkins asked dryly.

"Yeah. Okay"

"Of all the evidence we could collect from this vehicle, Miss Chang, which do you think is the most fragile—which one is in the most danger of being compromised?"

Helen didn't hesitate. "The blood, of course," she said, "because it would have the DNA."

"Well, if it is blood, it's been there for several months," said Jenkins. "It'll last a little while longer. In fact, you very eloquently demonstrated when you opened the hatchback door that it would be the fingerprints we'd need to worry about the most. And, by the way, we do have yours on file, don't we? We kind of need them now."

"They took them when I was hired," Helen replied. "But come on, do you think that after all the time, this car's been out here you could still get prints off it?"

"It's possible," Jenkins said. "Prints have been taken from ancient tombs. We might get something. Did you bring gloves?"

"I have some in my tackle box, "Helen said. She pulled two latex gloves from a bag and deftly slipped them on. Jenkins snapped a pair from a dispensing box in his case. He tucked the fingers of his left hand into the shape of an iguana's head and snapped one of the gloves around them. He stretched, pried, and pulled the glove over each finger until his hand was completely covered.

"You okay?" Helen asked, riveted by the spectacle.

"Just fine," Jenkins said with a final snap of the last latex finger into place. "You know, putting on these gloves reminds me of a case in Wagga Wagga, Australia, back in the 1930s."

"Wagga Wagga?" Helen asked incredulously. "There's no such place."

"No, it's quite true. You'll like this story," Jenkins said.

"I'll like it? I'll reserve judgment on that."

"It was on a Christmas day and fisherman discovered a body snagged in the branches of a submerged tree limb in a river near Wagga Wagga. The body had been in the water for weeks and was badly decomposed—hard to ID. Bugs had chewed up much of the flesh and it was peeling off the bone from decay. One hand was cut off and the other was mangled almost beyond recognition. It must have had a pretty foul stench to it and…"

"Are you trying to gross me out?" Helen interrupted thinking she might have tasted the first hint of bile.

"Now why would I want to do that, Miss Chang?" Jenkins asked as he began to wrestle with the second latex glove.

"Ohhh, let me see. Because you hope I'll quit. Because you don't want me working on this case with you?"

"So, anyway," Jenkins continued, struggling to get all his fingers into their appropriate positions, "despite the poor condition of the corpse, the coroner could tell that the victim had taken several hard blows to the back of his skull. Detectives searched along the banks of the river for clues that might help them ID either the victim or a suspect. Stuck on a bush, out in the water, they found something that looked like a shriveled-up leather glove. But that wasn't what it was."

"Oh, here we go," Helen sighed.

"It was the skin of a right hand, hollowed out by maggots."

"I think I see where this is going."

"To recover fingerprints, one of the detectives slipped his own hand into the glove of human skin, inked the tips, and rolled the digits onto a fingerprint card. It worked surprisingly well. They were able to ID the guy."

"Who was he? Did they catch who killed him?" Helen asked.

"He was a drifter and yes, yes, they did find his killer," Jenkins replied. "An acquaintance of his did him in—with an axe. There was something of a hiccup during the trial though. The prosecution's main witness was shot before he could testify—murdered by his own wife. She was trying to save the accused from the gallows. She had been having an affair with the murderer."

"Are you sure this is a true story and not something you dreamed up while watching reruns of Jerry Springer?"

"It's quite true," Jenkins said as he bent over for a closer look at the handle on the driver's door. Helen crouched beside him. "I don't see anything," she said.

Jenkins brought himself upright with a groan—an involuntary sound effect he'd acquired around his fortieth birthday and, from then on, always seemed to accompany his rising from a stooped position.

"You okay?" Helen asked.

"I'm fine," Jenkins replied, irritated. "And you can stop asking me that."

Jenkins drew a deep and deliberate breath. "There are three types of fingerprint impressions," Jenkins began. "Prints made on surfaces that can hold the shape of the print—you know, on surfaces such as tar, clay, or a soft wax. They're called plastic prints. Then there are visible prints. Ones made by fingers coated with some transferable, colored liquid—grease, motor oil, paint, ink, blood. They may need no more processing than a good photograph. Then there are the latent prints. The ones you can't see, but they're there. They have to be developed in some way to make them visible. This door handle could have latent prints."

"Oh yeah," Helen said, "We're dusting for prints."

"That's one way to do it, yes. And that's how we're going to do it here. We'll need to dust and photo-document a number of places," Jenkins said removing his equipment from his case. "We may only have one crack at this so we'd better do a thorough job. We'll start on the outside of the vehicle."

"May I do one?" Helen asked.

"No," Jenkins said quickly. "That is, it's somewhat of an art. Let me take the first ones," Jenkins said placing the handle of the fingerprinting brush between his two palms and, rubbing his hands together back and forth, twirling the brush between them for several seconds. Helen watched inquisitively. "I'm removing any excess powder and fluffing up the brush," he offered. "We'll need 'before' and 'after' photos of each print location. We'll begin with the door handles. Miss Chang, if you wouldn't mind..."

With the digital camera, Helen took a close up shot of the driver's door handle.

Jenkins poured a small amount of dusting powder into the jar's lid and dipped just the tip of the brush into the powder. "You have to make sure," Jenkins said, "that you don't take up too much powder into the brush. Too much can ruin a print." In a gentle, circular motion, he then lightly brushed across the handle of the driver's door. "You need to be careful here, too. You brush too much or too hard and that can also destroy a print. Stop when the print has become visible. Another photo please, Miss Chang."

Click.

Jenkins then peeled a flat of lifting tape from its backing and rolled the tape over the area on the door handle he'd just dusted. He rubbed the tape to give it a firm contact and then, grasping one end, peeled it from the door handle. Curling the tape outward in a loop and moving from one end of the tape to the other, he reaffixed the tape carrying the lifted print onto a white index card. On its reverse side, he jotted down the date, case number, print location, and his name.

Jenkins and Helen moved methodically around the vehicle taking prints from door handles, windows, and from the various parts of the vehicle's body that Jenkins thought might carry latent prints. It was when moving around to the front of the vehicle, their last location, that the question Jenkins dreaded, but knew was coming, came.

"Can I try one now? Helen asked.

"Do you think you got the procedure?" Jenkins asked.

"Absolutely," Helen replied.

Jenkins handed her the jar of dusting powder, but, as she moved to take it, the jar slipped from her hand. Jenkins grabbed for it as it fell but he succeeded only in batting the jar upward. The fine black powder burst over him like an exploding water balloon. The jar hit the pavement and rolled almost a yard before it lost its momentum and stopped, teetering on its side.

"Oh, dear," Helen said. "I am so sorry, Lieutenant Jenkins. Honestly."

"Locard's Exchange Principle, again, I suppose," said Jenkins, spitting black dust from his mouth like a baseball player who'd just slid into home plate, face first.

Helen's jaw had dropped.

Pinching and pulling out his shirt at the stomach, "Look," Jenkins said glancing down, "I don't think you can see the coffee stain anymore."

"Oh my goodness," Helen gasped. And then it happened. Involuntarily and without warning or conscious choice, a giggle began to percolate out of her. *No, not now*! Helen thought. *Not now*! She tried to suppress it but that only made it worse. In seconds, she was convulsing in laughter, horrified and elated at the same time. "I'm sorry, Lieutenant," she said through the bursts. "But you should see yourself. You look like the drummer for Kiss?

"I need to clean up," Jenkins said. "I'll be back in a moment and don't touch anything. Is that clear?"

"Crystal," Helen replied. "I'll be right here making the best of it."

"What?"

"Nothing."

As Jenkins walked back to the building, he tried to brush the powder off but that only ground the dust in deeper. It smeared his chin, neck, and down the front of his shirt. He shuffled back into headquarters, hunching over as if he was soaking wet. He pressed his back against the swinging door of the men's washroom and rolled in. A face stared back at him from a mirror above the washbasin. It was Captain White. A crooked grin torqued his face.

"Jenkins! What on earth? Is Gene Simmons looking for a new drummer?"

"Captain," Jenkins started, "this isn't working out. You know partners don't work out well for me. Can we please put an end to this before I'm seriously injured or there's a loss of life—like mine?"

"Have we been collecting prints?"

"Captain, please," Jenkins pleaded.

"I'm counting on you, Jenkins, to help bring Miss Chang up to speed. Your experience with Detective Juarez cannot forever prevent you from working with a partner."

"Detective Juarez really did try to kill me!"

"That was five years ago, Juarez is in the big house, and you've got to move on."

"But Captain, she's just a kid for crying out loud. And you should see…"

"You'll be fine."

There it was again.

Recovering Fingerprints

The crux to solving almost every crime, whether it is burglary, forgery, assault, automobile theft, or homicide, hinges on placing the suspect at its scene. No other forensic technique is used more often to associate a person with an article of evidence than fingerprinting.

Your fingerprints and the patterns of grooves and ridges that swirl on the gripping sides of your fingertips, as well as those on your palms, toes, and the soles of your feet, are formed in the womb, and their patterns stay with you, unchanged, for your entire life. Although they serve a common purpose—to provide friction for gripping and walking—each person's prints is unique. Even genetically indistinguishable, identical twins differ by their fingerprints.

Dr. Henry Faulds, a Scottish physician, having observed fingerprints on ancient samples of pottery, proposed in an 1880 letter to the British journal, *Nature*, that fingerprints could be used as a means to positively identify individual people. None other than the extraordinary English scientist, explorer, and mathematician Sir Francis Galton took up a comprehensive study of fingerprint patterns and published his work in 1892. He identified the three major patterns—loops, arches, and whorls. That same year, Sir Edward Henry, an India, police officer, and Juan Vucetich, an inspector with the police department in La Plata, Argentina, applied fingerprint identification to the prosecution of criminal acts, and from that point on, forensic science changed forever. The first person convicted of murder based on fingerprint evidence occurred in 1910. Because fingerprinting has become so familiar, juries readily accept them as evidence in a court of law without need for lengthy or elaborate explanations from expert witness as to their worth in placing a suspect at a crime scene.

Impressions left by fingerprints fall into three types: visible, plastic (also called patent, impression, indentation, or molded), and latent (invisible to the naked eye). *Visible prints* are formed from fingers soiled with soot, dirt, ink, paint, grease, motor oil, blood, or some other liquid or powder, making them readily apparent. *Plastic prints* form by finger contact with a moldable substance such as clay, calking, putty, wet paint, or soap. *Latent fingerprints* are formed by sweat and oils of the skin and are the type most frequently pursued by the forensic detective.

Dusting for Prints

So common is the practice of *dusting for prints* that almost everyone has heard the term, seen it done on television crime shows, or been personally involved in its use during an actual criminal investigation. Dusting involves the use of a soft brush to

Figure 2.1 A Criminalist dusts for fingerprints.

lightly coat a surface carrying a fingerprint with a powder made from finely ground carbon, charcoal, titanium, or aluminum (Figure 2.1). The powder sticks to the lines of sweat and oil left by a fingertip ridges. The exposed fingerprint can then be lifted by adhesive tape and placed on a paper card or a sheet of acetate as a permanent record. More recently, iron filings applied with a magnetic wand has been introduced as another method for dusting prints.

Although black powder is the most frequently used material for dusting, powders of other colors can be used to enhance a fingerprint's contrast against backgrounds of different shades.

Porous surfaces such as paper or cardboard can absorb a fingerprint's sweat and oil and therefore may not readily yield a fingerprint pattern when dusted with standard dusting powder (though magnetic powder can often still provide a discernible result). For these surfaces, chemical reagents such as 1,8-diazafluoren-9-one (DFO) will make prints glow under laser, ultraviolet (UV), or blue-green light. Another chemical called silver nitrate reacts with the salt in human sweat to make silver chloride and a reddish-brown print under UV light. Yet another chemical agent, ninhydrin (triketohydrindene hydrate), makes prints turn purple blue under standard white light.

Fuming

Yet another method for bringing up latent prints is by a process known as chemical *fuming*. Forensic scientists have used iodine for this purpose for almost 100 years. In this technique, the object carrying latent prints is normally suspended in a closed chamber in which warmed iodine crystals sublime directly into vapor, filling the air within the chamber. The iodine fumes, reacting with the sweat and oil from the fingerprint's ridges, form brownish prints. As the prints developed by iodine fuming fade rapidly, a photograph must be taken quickly as a permanent record.

A second fuming method, and a very intriguing one at that, was discovered by accident during the late 1970s when a hair and fiber expert with the National Police

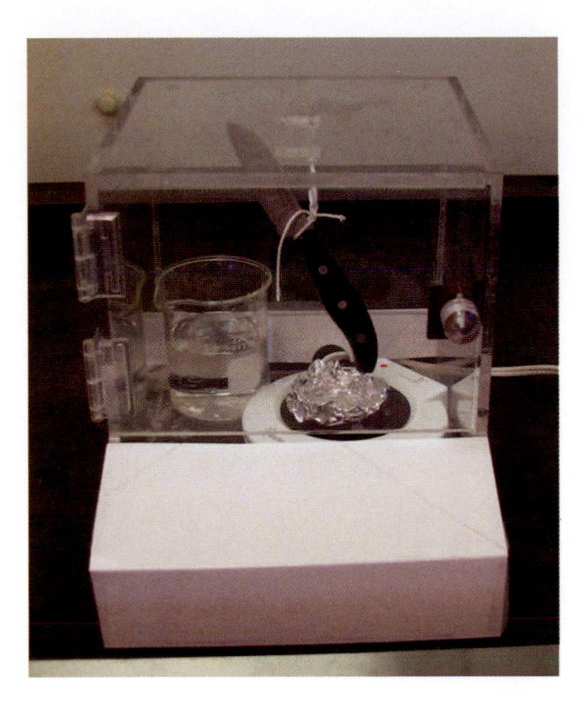

Figure 2.2 Super Glue fuming to develop fingerprints. Fuming should be conducted in an airtight enclosure placed within a fume hood. The glue is poured onto folded aluminum foil heated by a mug warmer. Heated water is placed in the fuming chamber to aid in the development. In this picture, a knife is suspended in the fuming chamber above the mug warmer.

Agency of Japan kept finding his fingerprints turning up as white, chalky patterns on the microscope slides he was using to mount hairs with Super Glue (known to a chemist as cyanoacrylate). A friend of his, a fingerprint specialist with the laboratory, refined the technique as a general-purpose method for developing prints.

Since Super Glue vapors are toxic, fuming is performed in an enclosure held within a fume hood (Figure 2.2). From several drops to a couple milliliters of Super Glue are dispensed within a small aluminum container held on a warming plate (such as that used to heat a cup of coffee). A beaker of warm water is placed within the enclosure to provide humidity. As the Super Glue is heated, vapors are released that bind to trace amino acids, proteins, and fatty acids on the fingerprint. After about an hour, the print is usually developed enough that a photograph can be taken (Figure 2.3). Alternatively, a fluorescent dye can be applied to enhance the contrast and the fingerprint can then be photographed under laser or UV light.

Photography

Photography of prints developed by dusting or fuming can be done with a standard digital camera and standard lighting. But latent prints may also become visible with no chemical enhancement by shining a laser light or light of different wavelengths on the surface carrying the print. For example, a print made from fingers contaminated with motor oil will glow under UV light. Latent prints, particularly on glass or plastic, can often become visible simply by changing the angle of the light source. UV light can help bring out the pattern of prints developed by fuming with Super Glue. An argon ion laser can bring out prints refractory to other visualization methods.

Figure 2.3 A fingerprint developed by Super Glue fuming.

In the Crime Lab

Activity 2.1 Making a Fingerprint Reference Set with an Ink Pad

A reference set of fingerprints is routinely taken from those people employed by state or national government and of those arrested or under suspicion of committing a crime. In this activity, you will gain proficiency in making a set of fingerprints. Your fingers can be designated as shown in Figure 2.4.

Materials:
- Ink pad
- Practice sheet for right- and left-hand fingerprint impressions
- Fingerprint ID card
- Scotch tape
- Scissors

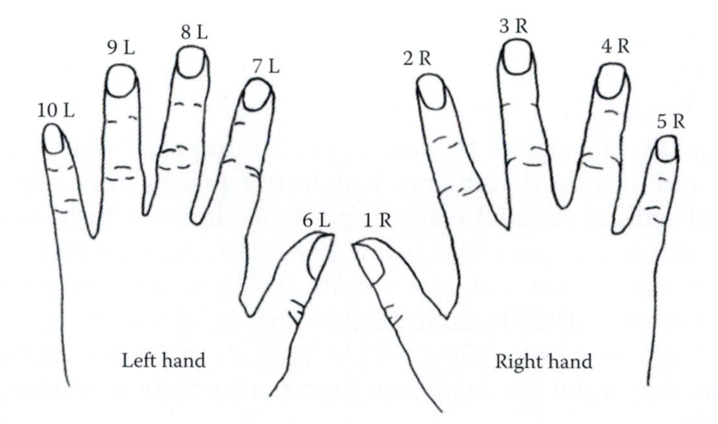

Figure 2.4 Numbering system for the fingers of the left and right hands.

Protocol: Make a set of practice and reference fingerprints using the following steps:

1. Press the lateral edge of your fingertip onto an ink pad. Using a rolling type motion, rotate your fingertip in a clockwise or counterclockwise manner against the ink pad. Make sure that ink completely covers your fingertip ridges.

2. Check the tip of your finger to ensure an even spread of ink on the ridge surfaces (but not within the furrows between the ridges). If too much ink is present, dab some of it off on a clean paper towel.

3. Move the paper towards the edge of your desk so that when you go to roll your inked finger position your lower arm parallel to the floor. When doing your thumbs, roll away from your body, all other digits roll towards the body. Applying even, light, and continuous pressure, gently roll your inked finger onto the appropriate position on the left-or right-hand practice sheet (provided by your instructor). The impression left on the paper should appear like a square. Make five impressions for each finger. It is not necessary to re-ink your finger between print transfers. Once you have rolled your fingertip onto the practice sheet, do not roll it back over the initial transfer. This will cause smudging and result in an unreadable print.

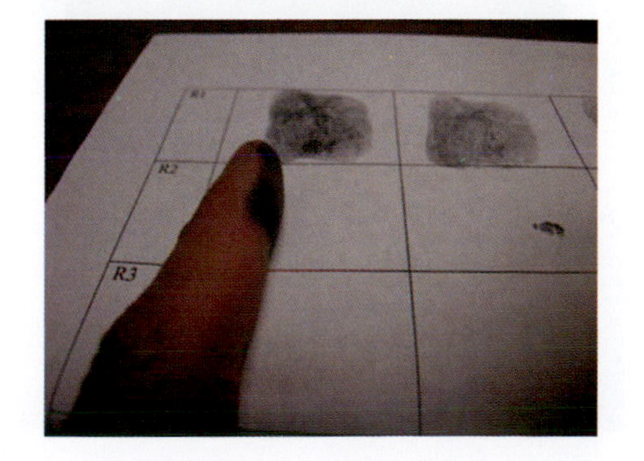

4. Once you have completed all 10 digits, have your instructor circle the best print of each digit. Using scissors, cut the print from the practice sheet and mount it on to the fingerprint ID form with tape. Turn your set of fingerprints into the instructor. These will be analyzed in Chapter 14.

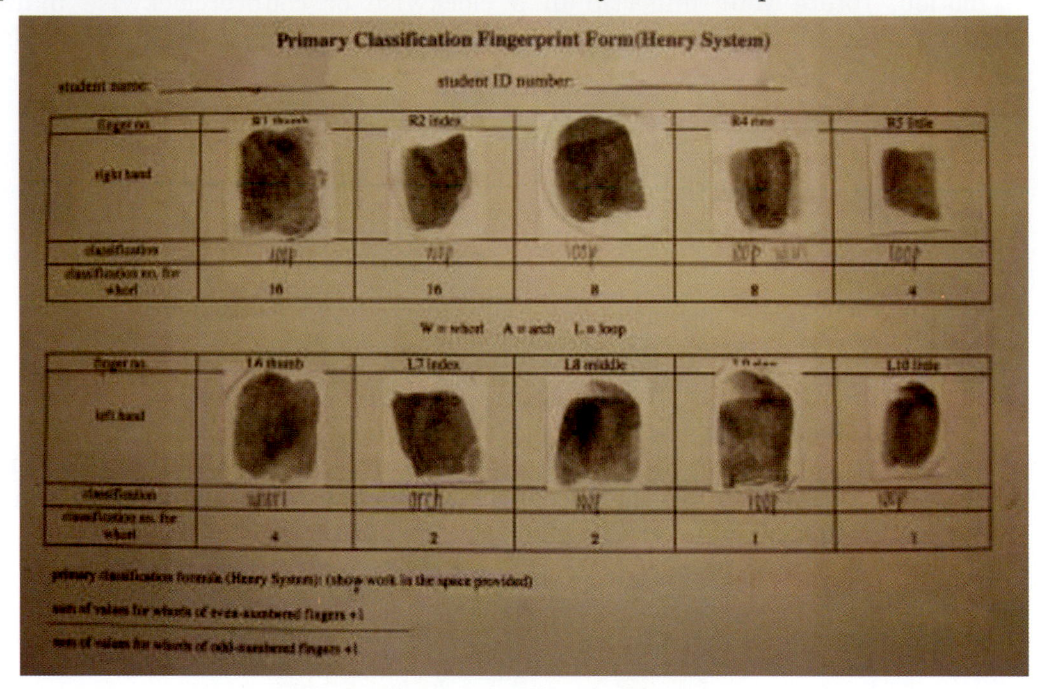

Primary Classification Fingerprint Form(Henry System)

student name: ____________ student ID number: ____________

finger no.	R1 thumb	R2 index		R4 ring	R5 little
right hand					
classification	loop	[illegible]	loop	loop	loop
classification no. for whorl	16	16	8	8	4

W = whorl A = arch L = loop

finger no.	L6 thumb	L7 index	L8 middle	[illegible]	L10 little
left hand					
classification	whorl	arch	[illegible]	loop	[illegible]
classification no. for whorl	4	2	2	1	1

primary classification formula (Henry System): (show work in the space provided)

sum of values for whorls of even-numbered fingers +1

sum of values for whorls of odd-numbered fingers +1

Activity 2.2 Making a Fingerprint Reference Set Using Fingerprint Ink

In this activity, you will make fingerprint impressions using fingerprint ink. As you did in Activity 2.1, you will first practice on practice sheets and then make a reference set on a fingerprint ID card.

Materials:

Fingerprint ink
Ink roller
Petri dish
Practice sheets for right- and left-hand fingerprint impressions
Fingerprint ID card

Protocol: Make practice and reference sets of fingerprints by following these steps:

1. Apply a small drop of fingerprint ink onto the outer surface of a Petri dish or other nonabsorbing smooth object.

2. Using an ink roller, spread the drop to create a thin film of ink.

3. Lightly press the edge of your fingertip against the ink and roll your fingertip on the inked surface. If your fingertip is not completely covered with ink, it may be necessary to roll your finger across the ink one more time.

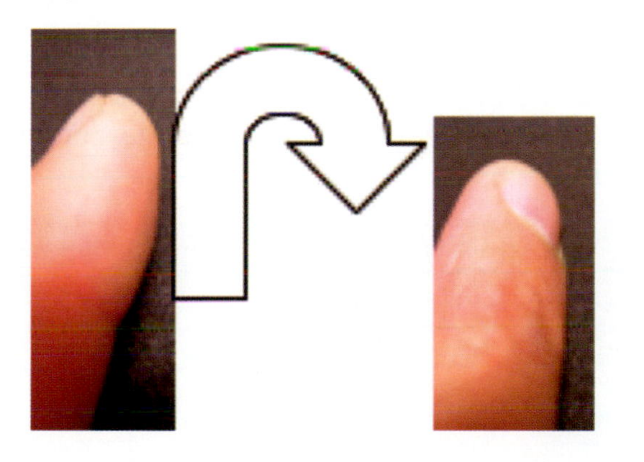

4. Check the tip of your finger to make sure the fingerprint ridges are evenly covered with ink. The furrows between the ridges should not be heavily inked.

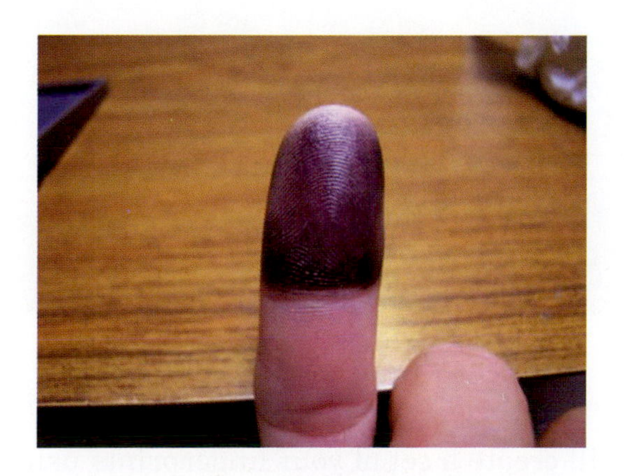

5. Move the paper towards the edge of your desk so that when you go to roll your inked finger position your lower arm parallel to the floor. When doing your thumbs, roll away from your body, all other digits roll towards the body. Transfer the print into the appropriate square of the fingerprint practice sheet by rolling your fingertip with even, light, and constant pressure once against the paper. Make a total of five transfers for each digit. Do not re-ink your finger between each transfer attempt.

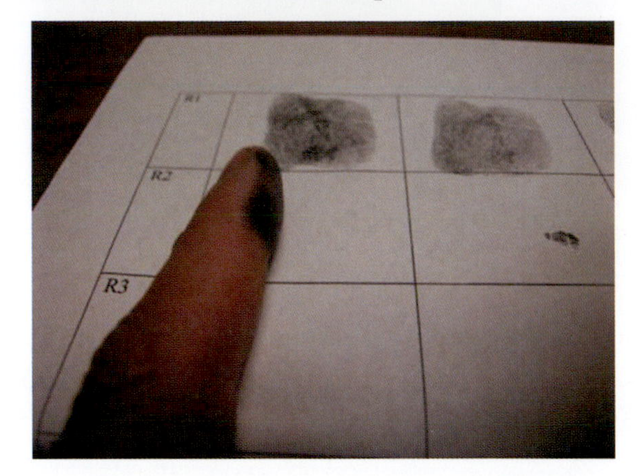

6. Once you have completed all 10 digits, have the instructor circle the best fingerprint from each digit. Cut out and tape that print onto the fingerprint ID card. Turn your set of fingerprints into the instructor. These will be analyzed in Chapter 14.

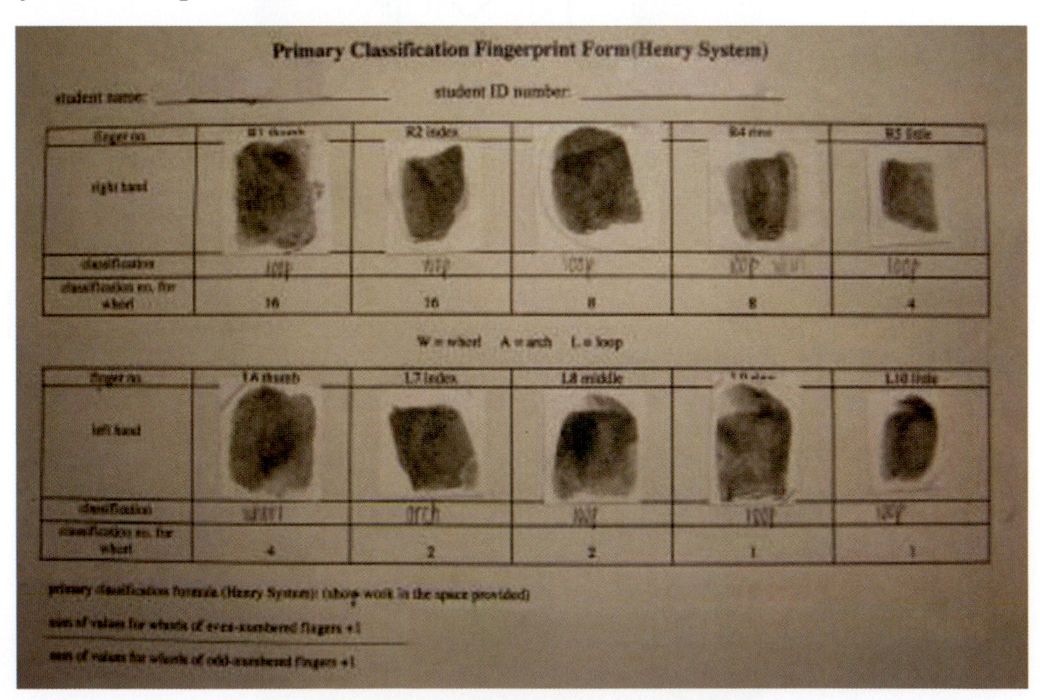

Primary Classification Fingerprint Form (Henry System)

student name: ______________ student ID number: ______________

finger no.	R1 thumb	R2 index	[illegible]	R4 ring	R5 little
right hand					
classification	loop	[illegible]	[illegible]	loop	loop
classification no. for whorl	16	16	8	8	4

W = whorl A = arch L = loop

finger no.	L6 thumb	L7 index	L8 middle	[illegible]	L10 little
left hand					
classification	whorl	arch	loop	loop	loop
classification no. for whorl	4	2	2	1	1

primary classification formula (Henry System): (show work in the space provided)

sum of values for whorls of even-numbered fingers +1

sum of values for whorls of odd-numbered fingers +1

Activity 2.3 Making a Fingerprint Reference Set from Pencil Graphite

In this activity, you will create a set of your fingerprints using the graphite from a No. 2 pencil.

Materials:
No. 2 pencil
Scotch tape
Scissors
Fingerprint ID card

Protocol: Take fingerprints from all 10 of your fingertips using the following steps:

1. Create a dark swatch on a piece of scratch paper using a No. 2 pencil.

2. Rub your right thumb (1R) into the swatch.

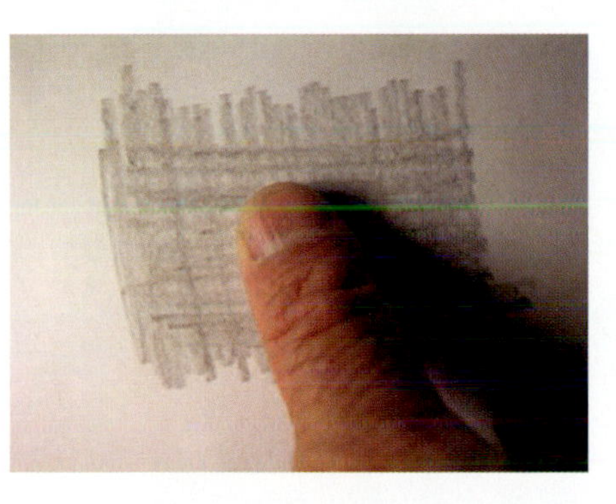

3. Lay a piece of scotch tape, sticky side down, onto the fingertip and then gently pull it off.

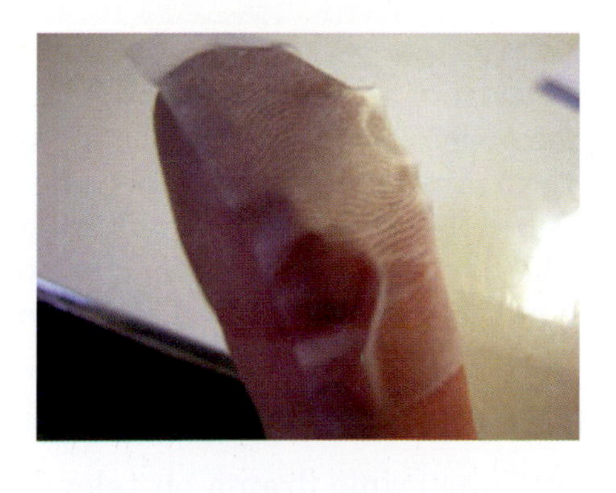

4. Place the tape sticky side up on a flat surface. Lay a clean piece of tape, sticky side down, over the transferred fingerprint so that it is sandwiched between the two pieces of tape—sticky side taped to sticky side.

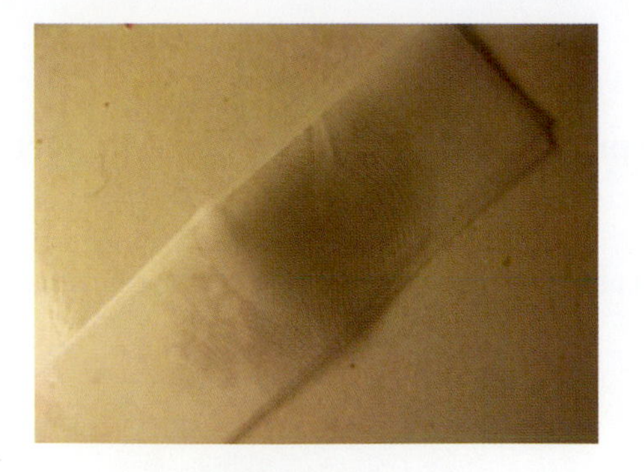

5. Using a pair of scissors, trim off any excess tape and place the print into the appropriate square of the fingerprint ID card such that the first tape carrying the original transfer is facing upwards. Turn your set of fingerprints into the instructor. These will be analyzed in Chapter 14.

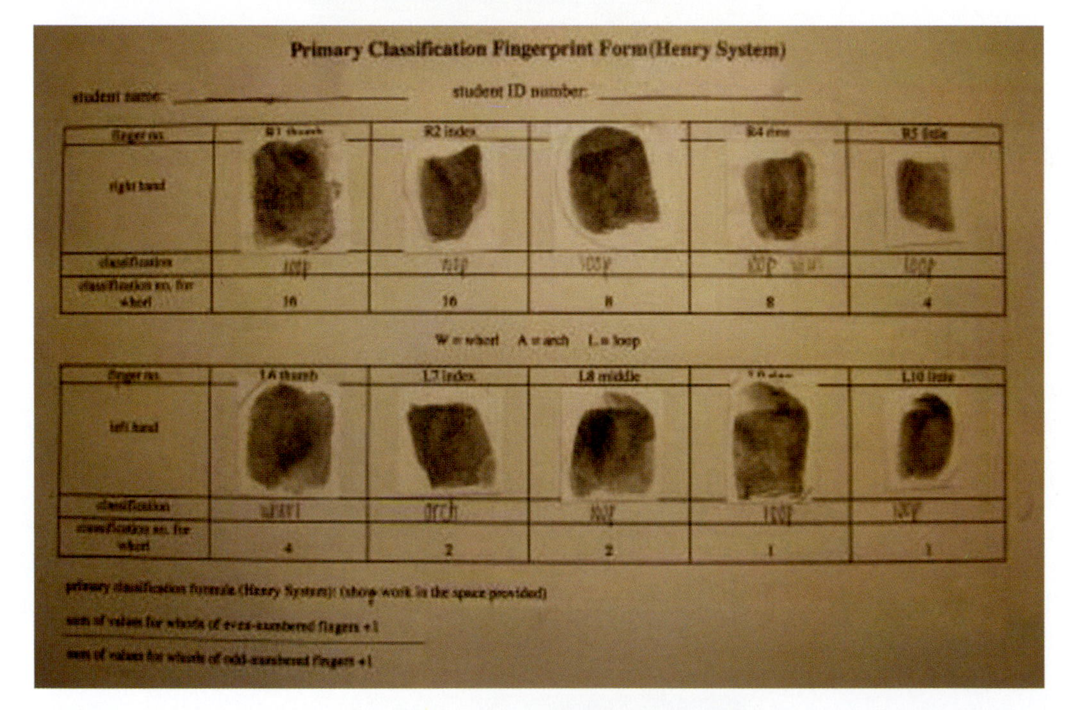

Primary Classification Fingerprint Form (Henry System)

student name: ________ student ID number: ________

finger no.	R1 thumb	R2 index	[illegible]	R4 ring	R5 little
right hand					
classification	loop	loop	loop	loop	loop
classification no. for whorl	16	16	8	8	4

W = whorl A = arch L = loop

finger no.	L6 thumb	L7 index	L8 middle	[illegible]	L10 little
left hand					
classification	whorl	arch	loop	loop	loop
classification no. for whorl	4	2	2	1	1

primary classification formula (Henry System): (show work in the space provided)

sum of values for whorls of even-numbered fingers +1

sum of values for whorls of odd-numbered fingers +1

Fingerprints made either from an ink blotter or from fingerprinting ink are actually a mirror image of your print pattern. Using the graphite technique, if you were to make the transfer and then place the sticky side face down, the image produced would be in a reverse orientation. By sticking a second piece of tape against the first, your fingerprint's orientation becomes a mirror image in the same manner as prints made from ink.

Activity 2.4 Lifting a Latent Fingerprint with Dusting Powder

Anyone who has seen almost any crime drama on television will be familiar with the technique of lifting fingerprints by the use of dusting powder. In this activity, you will have an opportunity to practice this technique.

Materials:
Fingerprint brush
Fingerprint powder
Glass slide
Lifting tape or packaging tape
Dust mask

Protocol: Working in small groups, lift a print from one of your fingers using the following procedure:

1. Obtain fingerprint powder, a brush, a glass slide, and lifting tape from your instructor.

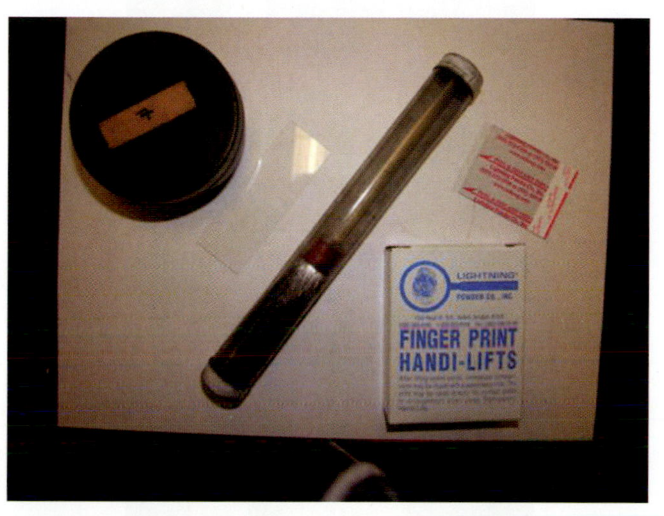

2. Cover the fingertip you're going to print with skin oil by rubbing it against your nose or forehead. Roll the oiled finger from one edge to the other onto a glass slide. (*Note*: Do not attempt to reverse or reroll as doing so will create a double image.)

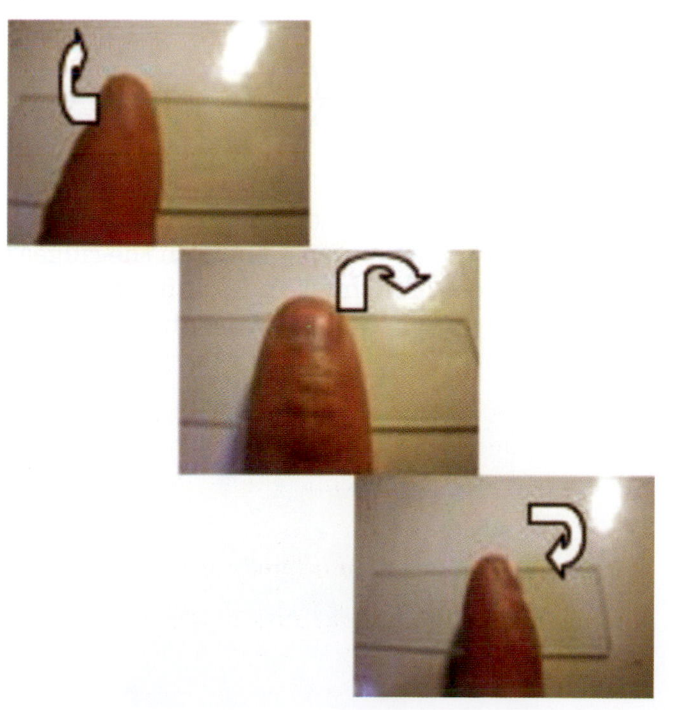

Place the glass slide on top of a sheet of scratch paper to collect and recover excess dusting powder for recycling.

3. Place a dust mask over your face. Dip the fingerprinting brush into the fingerprint powder and tap off any excess back into the container. Using a circular motion, gently bring the tip of the fingerprint brush hairs into contact with the latent print you created on the glass slide. Carefully, swirl the brush over the fingerprint until the print pattern becomes visible. Return any excess fingerprint powder back to the jar.

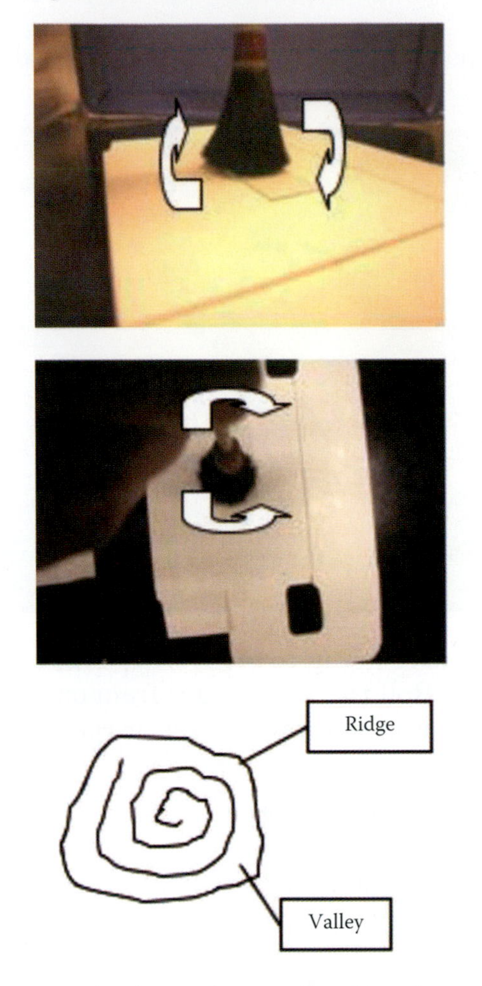

Depending on the amount of powder on the brush, you may need to repeat this process. The goal is to create contrast between the ridges and the valleys.

4. Lay the sticky side of a piece of lifting or packaging tape face down onto the dusted fingerprint. Slowly, peel the tape from the glass slide and stick the tape carrying the lifted print into your laboratory notebook.

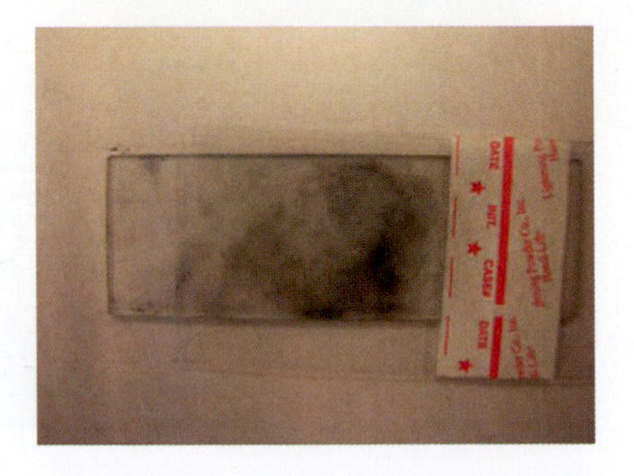

Activity 2.5 Developing Fingerprints Using Super Glue Fumes

In a closed chamber, fumes given off by heated Super Glue stick to the skin oils of a latent fingerprint and turn the ridge marks a chalky white. Since properly fumed fingerprints are chalky white in color, Super Glue fuming works well for fingerprints deposited on smooth, dark surfaces. In this activity, you will process a fingerprint deposited on a glass slide.

Materials:

Super Glue
Aquarium tank with lid
Coffee cup warmer
Beaker of water
Four-square-inch sheet of aluminum foil
Fingerprint brush
Fingerprint powder
Glass slide and/or empty beverage can
Latex gloves
Safety glasses
Lab coat
Microwave oven or hot plate
Chemical fume hood

Protocol: Develop latent fingerprints with Super Glue fumes by the following protocol:

Caution: *Fumes given off by Super Glue are toxic!* Perform this activity in a fume hood or a very well-ventilated area, and take special precautions not to breathe the fumes generated by the heated Super Glue. Handle all materials with protective gloves and wear safety glasses. If you have any questions about your safety during any step of the protocol, ask your instructor for advice.

1. In an empty aquarium stationed within a chemical fume hood, place a mug warmer and a beaker of water that has been heated to near boiling. Mold a small square of aluminum foil into a shallow cup and place it on the mug warmer. Turn the mug warmer on to preheat the aluminum foil.

2. Prepare a latent fingerprint by rubbing a fingertip against the skin of your nose and then pressing the oiled finger on a clean glass slide. Label the slide with your name and suspend it with tape from the aquarium lid. If you are developing prints on a recently discarded beverage can, place it in the aquarium by suspending it from the lid with tape. Squeeze the contents of a small tube of Super Glue into the aluminum foil cup on the mug warmer. Secure the lid over the aquarium. Watch the items for the appearance of white, chalky ridgelines defining the fingerprint. This could take anywhere from 15 to 40 min. When the prints are sufficiently developed, unplug the mug warmer and let it cool to room temperature before opening the aquarium lid and removing your glass slide. When opening the lid, allow the Super Glue Vapors to completely evacuate the tank before obtaining your samples.

3. Dust and lift the print as described in Activity 2.4. Tape the lifted print into your laboratory notebook.

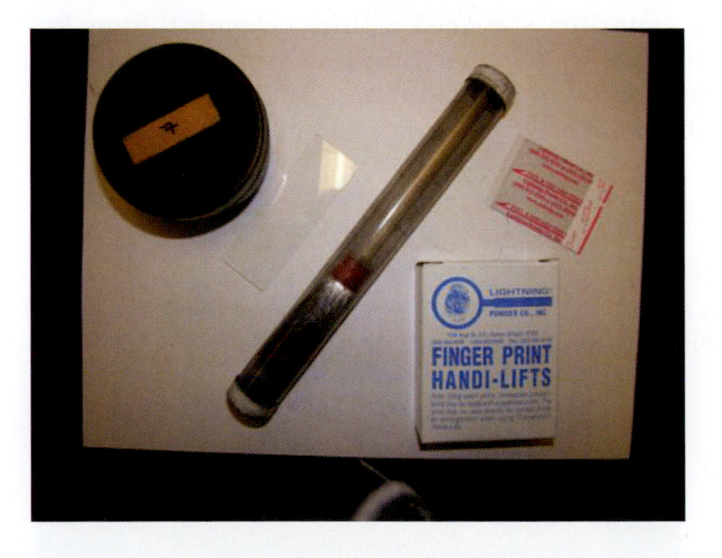

Activity 2.6 Visualizing Prints Using Biological Stains

In this activity, you will develop a latent fingerprint with dyes that are used to stain biological molecules.

Materials:

Laboratory notebook
Crystal violet and/or methylene blue
Weigh boats or similar small plastic containers
Masking tape, duct tape, and/or scotch tape
Forceps
Gloves and lab glasses

Protocol: Latent fingerprints can be developed with dyes using the following steps:

1. The dyes used in this exercise can cause permanent stains on clothing. Therefore, wear a lab coat, protective gloves, and safety glasses. Place two weigh boats on an absorbent background. Dispense a few drops of either crystal violet or methylene blue into a plastic weigh boat. In the second weigh boat, dispense enough tap water to barely line the bottom. This second weigh boat will be used for destaining your print.

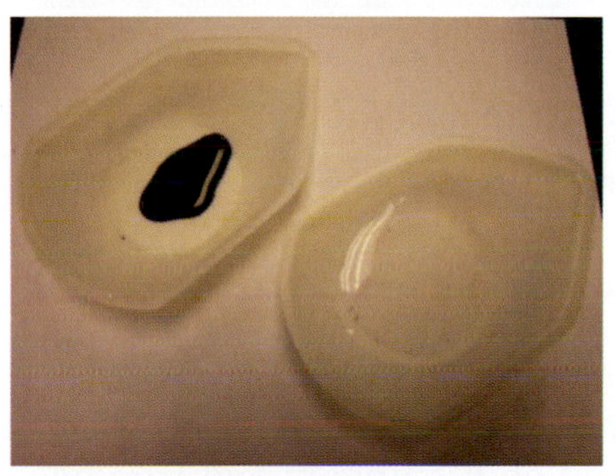

2. Press the sticky side of a piece of tape against the fingerprint area of a fingertip. With a pair of forceps, peel the tape from your finger.

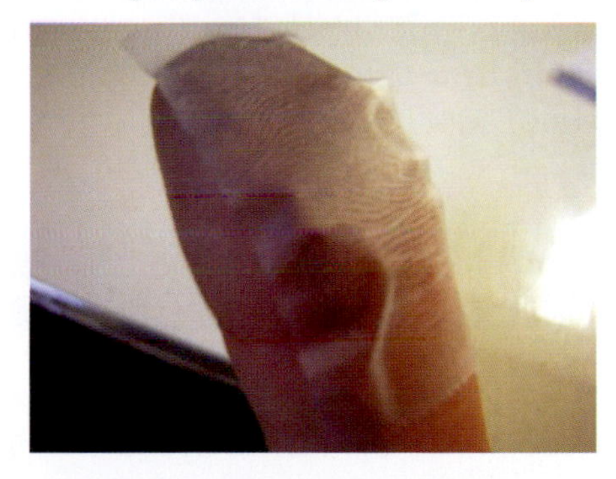

3. With a second pair of forceps, take hold of the other end of the tape, and immerse it, sticky side down, into the staining solution (see arrows). Using a back and forth motion, pass the tape through the staining solution.

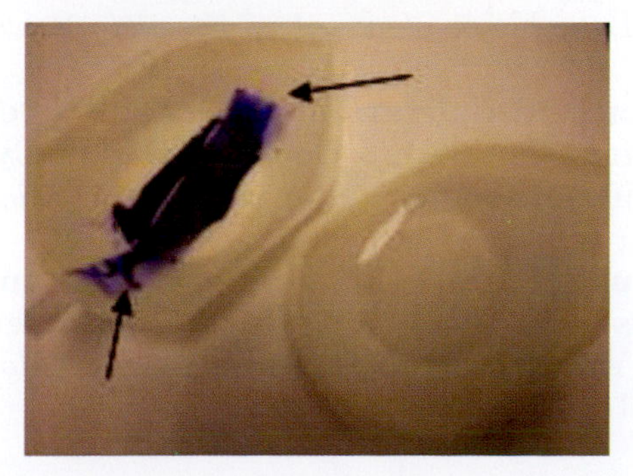

4. Transfer the tape into the weigh boat containing water, and rinse off any excess staining solution not adhering to the fingerprint. Remove the destained tape from the water, allow it to dry thoroughly, and tape the print, sticky side up, into your laboratory notebook.

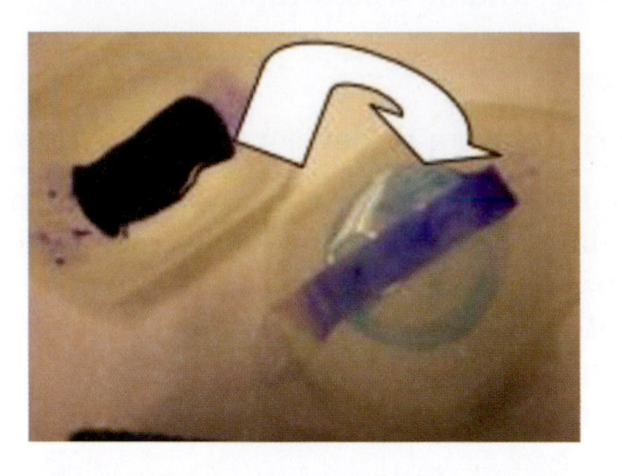

Review Questions

2.1 What is a latent fingerprint?

2.2 What biological functions do the ridges that make a fingerprint serve?

2.3 Do identical twins have identical fingerprints?

2.4 What type of fingerprint (visible, plastic, or latent) might be made by an auto mechanic who has oil on his fingers and who has closed the engine hood of your white Toyota?

2.5 Give an example of how a plastic type fingerprint could be formed.

2.6 Why does fingerprinting powder stick to a fingerprint?

2.7 What precautions should be taken developing fingerprints with the fumes from heated Super Glue?

Further Reading

Rapid Method of Super Glue® Fuming Application for the Development of Latent Fingerprints by F.G. Kendall and B.W. Rehn in *Journal of Forensic Sciences*, Vol. 28, pages 777–780, 1983.

Development of Latent Fingerprints on Paper Using Magnetic Flakes by B. Wilshire and N. Hurley in *Journal of Forensic Sciences*, Vol. 40, No. 5, pages 838–842, 1995.

Fluorescence Spectroscopy as an Aid to Imaging Latent Fingermarks in the Ultraviolet by S.K. Bramble in *Journal of Forensic Sciences*, Vol. 41, No. 6, pages 1038–1041, 1996.

A New Method to Enhance Visualization of Latent Fingermarks by Sublimating Dyes, and Its Practical Use with a Combination of Cyanoacrylate Fuming by S. Morimoto, A. Kaminogo, and T. Hirano in *Forensic Science International*, Vol. 97, pages 101–108, 1998.

Latent Fingerprint Visualization by 1,2-Indanedione and Related Compounds: Preliminary Results by J. Almog, E. Springer, S. Wiesner, A. Frank, O. Khodzhaev, R. Lidor, E. Bahar, H. Varkony, S. Dayan, and S. Rozen in *Journal of Forensic Sciences*, Vol. 44, No. 1, pages 114–118, 1999.

Obtaining Fingerprints from Mummified Fingers: A Method for Tissue Rehydration Adapted from the Archeological Literature by C.W. Schmidt, S.P. Nawrocki, M.A. Williamson, and D.C. Marlin in *Journal of Forensic Sciences*, Vol. 45, No. 4, pages 874–875, 2000.

Processes Involved in the Development of Latent Fingerprints Using the Cyanoacrylate Fuming Method by L.A. Lewis, R.W. Smithwick, G.L. Devault, B. Bolinger, and S.A. Lewis in *Journal of Forensic Sciences*, Vol. 46, No. 2, pages 241–246, 2001.

Fingerprinting the Deceased: Traditional and New Techniques by T. Kahana, A. Grande, D.M. Tancredi, J. Penalver, and J. Hiss in *Journal of Forensic Sciences*, Vol. 46, No. 4, pages 908–912, 2001.

Chemical Development of Latent Fingerprints: 1,2-Indanedione Has Come of Age by S. Wiesner, E. Springer, Y. Sasson, and J. Almog in *Journal of Forensic Sciences*, Vol. 45, No. 5, pages 1082–1084, 2001.

Latent Fingerprint Detection Using a Scanning Kelvin Microprobe by G. Williams, H.N. McMurray, and D.A. Worsley in *Journal of Forensic Sciences*, Vol. 46, No. 5, pages 1085–1092, 2001.

Luminescent Visualization of Latent Fingerprints by Direct Reaction with Lanthanide Shift Reagent by J.P. Caldwell, W. Henderson, and N.D. Kim in *Journal of Forensic Sciences*, Vol. 46, No. 6, pages 1332–1341, 2001.

Advanced Solvent-Free Application of Ninhydrin for Detection of Latent Fingerprints on Thermal Paper and Other Surfaces by L. Schwarz and I. Frerichs in *Journal of Forensic Sciences*, Vol. 47, No. 6, pages 1274–1277, 2002.

Forensic Applications of Chemical Imaging: Latent Fingerprint Detection Using Visible Absorption and Luminescence by D.L. Exline, C. Wallace, C. Roux, C. Lennard, M.P. Nelson, and P.J. Treado in *Journal of Forensic Sciences*, Vol. 48, No. 5, pages 1047–1053, 2003.

Enhancing Contrast of Fingerprints on Plastic Tape by C.A. Steele and M.S. Ball in *Journal of Forensic Sciences*, Vol. 48, No. 6, pages 1314–1317, 2003.

Genipin—A Novel Fingerprint Reagent with Colorimetric and Fluorogenic Activity by J. Almog, Y. Cohen, M. Azoury, and T.-R. Hahn in *Journal of Forensic Sciences*, Vol. 49, No. 2, pages 255–257, 2004.

Fingerprints' Third Dimension: The Depth and Shape of Fingerprints Penetration into Paper—Cross Section Examination by Fluorescence Microscopy by J. Almog, M. Azoury, Y. Elmaliah, L. Berenstein, and A. Zaban in *Journal of Forensic Sciences*, Vol. 49, No. 5, pages 981–985, 2004.

The Detection and Enhancement of Latent Fingerprints Using Infrared Chemical Imaging by M. Tahtouh, J.R. Kalman, C. Roux, C. Lennard, and B.J. Reedy in *Journal of Forensic Sciences*, Vol. 50, No. 1, pages 64–72, 2005.

Genipin, a Novel Fingerprint Reagent with Colorimetric and Fluorogenic Activity, Part II: Optimization, Scope and Limitations by G. Levinton-Shamuilov, Y. Cohen, M. Azoury, A. Chaikovsky, and J. Almog in *Journal of Forensic Sciences*, Vol. 50, No. 6, pages 1367–1371, 2005.

Beware of the Possibility of Fingerprinting Techniques Transferring DNA by R.A.H. van Oorschot, S. Treadwell, J. Beaurepaire, N.L. Holding, and R.J. Mitchell in *Journal of Forensic Sciences*, Vol. 50, No. 6, pages 1417–1422, 2005.

A Mechanistic Model for the Superglue Fuming of Latent Fingerprints by P. Czekanski, M. Fasola, and J. Allison in *Journal of Forensic Sciences*, Vol. 51, No. 6, pages 1323–1328, 2006.

Fingerprint Reagents with Dual Action: Color and Fluorescence by J. Almog, G. Levinton-Shamuilov, Y. Cohen, and M. Azoury in *Journal of Forensic Sciences*, Vol. 52, No. 2, pages 330–334, 2007.

Understanding the Chemistry of the Development of Latent Fingerprints by Superglue Fuming by S.P. Wargacki, L.A. Lewis, and M.D. Dadmun in *Journal of Forensic Sciences*, Vol. 52, No. 5, pages 1057–1062, 2007.

Forensic Applications of Infrared Imaging for the Detection and Recording of Latent Evidence by A.C.-Y. Lin, H.M. Hsieh, L.-C. Tsai, A. Linacre, and J.C-I. Lee in *Journal of Forensic Sciences*, Vol. 52, No. 5, pages 1148–1150, 2007.

Latent Fingermark Visualisation Using a Scanning Kelvin Probe by G. Williams and N. McMurray in *Forensic Science International*, Vol. 167, No. 2–3, pages 102–109, 2007.

A New Method of Reproduction of Fingerprints from Corpses in a Bad State of Preservation Using Latex by D. Porta, M. Maldarella, M. Grandi, and C. Cattaneo in *Journal of Forensic Sciences*, Vol. 52, No. 6, pages 1319–1321, 2007.

Optimisation and Evaluation of 1,2-Indanedione for Use as a Fingermark Reagent and Its Application to Real Samples by C. Wallace-Kunkel, C. Lennard, M. Stoilovic, and C. Roux in *Forensic Science International*, Vol. 168, No. 1, pages 14–26, 2007.

A Novel Approach for Fingerprinting Mummified Hands by Roy Fields and D. Kimberley Molina in *Journal of Forensic Sciences*, Vol. 53, No. 4, pages 952–955, 2008.

The Recovery of Latent Fingermarks and DNA Using a Silicone-Based Casting Material by Rita Shalhoub, Ignacio Quinones, Carole Ames, Bryan Multaney, Stuart Curtis, Haj Seeboruth, Stephen Moore, and Barbara Daniel in *Forensic Science International*, Vol. 178, No. 2–3, pages 199–203, 2008.

3

Trace

Vehicle Impound Lot, Monday 11:30 AM

Jenkins squeezed the last button through its hole and tucked his shirttail in. He always carried two spare shirts in his car. Just in case. He discovered long ago that working at a crime scene could leave its traces on you—dirt, oil, chemical dyes, blood, nail polish, luminol, vomit, paint, grass stain, dust, semen, smoke, urine, shoe polish, feces, lipstick, saliva, hair dye—it was a long list. Now he'd have to add massive amounts of fingerprint powder to it.

As he scrubbed the face reflecting in the washroom mirror, he debated accidents. Was the fingerprint powder an accident? It had to have been, he thought. No one, especially someone so new to the office, could be so brazen. He'd have to give her the benefit of the doubt. She was his new partner. He had his orders. It's what the captain wanted and Jenkins always did what the captain wanted. The assignment was only temporary anyway. Helen Chang was a lab rat, not a field agent. She couldn't handle a gun if her life depended on it. She'd be back in the laboratory and he'd be back to being the departmental pariah again soon enough.

She'd be gone either way—either he'd force it or the others would get to her in their own good time. They'd warn her that he'd ratted on his own partner before. Never mind that Juarez was the lackey of a drug kingpin. Never mind that Juarez turned a blind eye to the meth and coke deals going down with kids barely in their teens. Never mind Juarez was on the take. Never mind that Juarez had pumped a couple shots at him. It was all about *the code*. Stick by your partner. Look out for each other. Nothing's more important. Honesty and integrity, apparently, are expendable and forfeit and, along that road to Juarez's extradition, Jenkins had become an outcast. Sometimes he wished the warm lead of those two bullets from Juarez's 45 had found their target.

Jenkins toweled off one last time and made his way back to the Subaru as he tried to reassure himself, yet again, that it wasn't personal. He wasn't evil. No, that would be the captain for putting him in this intolerable and untenable situation. Miss Chang was probably a decent enough individual. He just hated having to work with her. But she couldn't possibly hold out much longer, he thought. Perhaps, even now, she might be at a tipping point. He'd try the gory, true crime story ploy one or two more times to see if that would shake her off and send her running for the exit.

"I think we're good on the prints. Let's move to the inside of the car now," said Jenkins on his return to the vehicle.

"Uh, Lieutenant Jenkins," Helen sputtered hesitantly while curling her upper lip and pointing to her front teeth, "you uh…."

"What?"

"You still have a little bit of dusting power between your teeth."

"What places on the inside of a vehicle do you normally touch, Miss Chang?" Jenkins said while mining the dust from his upper dental work with a fingernail.

"I think you got it."

"Miss Chang?"

Helen paused in thought for a moment. "The steering wheel, emergency brake, the shifting knob, the radio controls, the window controls, the door handles, turn signal, the glove compartment, and windshield wipers," she replied.

"How tall are you, Miss Chang?"

"I'm five foot two."

"You're five, one."

"Five, two."

"Everyone lies about their height, Miss Chang. They always add at least an inch. So you're actually five foot one now, aren't you?"

"Have you ever had a partner before?"

"Yes, I have," Jenkins replied.

"How did that work out for you?"

"We had issues."

"Is he still with this office?"

"No."

"Is he still even in law enforcement?"

"In a way."

"What do you mean?"

"He's making license plates. Miss Chang, if we could get back to the task at hand. The owner of this vehicle is five foot four. What would you need to do if you were to drive this car?"

"Learn how to drive a stick."

"Besides that."

"Since I'm shorter than five, four, I'd probably have to adjust the seat forward. You're saying we should dust the seat lever?"

"Yeah, but not only that. If we measure the distance of the seat to the gas pedal, we can get an idea of the height of the last person to drive this vehicle. But you've still overlooked one other place that we should dust. If you moved the driver's seat, what else would you have to move?"

"You got me."

"The rear view mirror, Miss Chang."

Jenkins slipped a gloved finger under the driver's door handle, lifted the lever, and slowly swung the door open. "We're going to be crawling around in here so we'd better look for trace before we dust."

"Trace?"

"Hair, fibers, small stuff. If it comes to it, we don't want to have to explain to a court room what our own hair is doing at a crime scene."

Jenkins cut a strip of wide transparent packing tape, looped it back on itself, and rolled it along the driver's seat. He cut the loop and stuck the tape to a sheet of white paper. "We should also roll the floor and swab the pedals," Jenkins said. "Miss Chang, my knee's acting up a bit today. Would you mind taking care of that and, as long as you're down there, measure the distance from the seat track to the heel wear spot by the gas pedal." Jenkins exchanged packaging tape, a swab with a collection vial, and a tape measure for the camera.

Squatting, Helen inserted herself between the steering wheel and seat. "Am I looking for anything in particular? Wait. There's a piece of metal down here in the seat track," she said as she worked it from its lodging place. "Maybe it's a bolt but I don't think so." She passed the object to Jenkins, underhand behind her back.

"You're quite right, Miss Chang. It's not a bolt." Jenkins carefully pinched the object between his thumb and forefinger and rotated his hand for a 360° view. "This is a large caliber bullet. Let's tag it and bag it. Do you see any bullet holes down there?"

"No, but it's dark and I'm not in the most comfortable position."

Jenkins placed the bullet in a clear plastic sealable bag, marked it for its contents, and placed the bag between two layers of cotton within a plastic box. "Did you take a lift from the floorboard and gas pedal yet and did you get a measurement on the seat track to heel distance?" he asked.

"I didn't think I needed to be a contortionist to do forensics," Helen replied dropping one knee to the pavement. "I'm sure there's all kinds of hair, dust, and dirt down here. How would we ever sort any of this out?"

"A case can hinge on the smallest fiber or hair, Miss Chang. In this one case..."

"Is this another one of your stories? Where does this one take place—Zimbabwe?"

"No, in Canada and Madawaska, Maine."

"Madawhatska?"

"Madawaska and the point is that it was just a single hair that caught a killer. One evening in the spring of 1958, sixteen-year-old Gaetane Bouchard failed to come home from a shopping trip in Edmundston, New Brunswick. Her father, quite worried, needless to say, phoned several of her friends to see if they'd seen her. The name John Vollman kept coming up. Apparently, she'd met Mr. Vollman several months earlier at a local dance".

"In Madawaska?"

"No, Madawaska was where Mr. Vollman lived and, since the dance, the two had been seeing each other."

"Long distance relationships almost never work out."

"Duly noted, Miss Chang, but Madawaska is just across the Canada, US border. Close enough that Mr. Bouchard, that very evening, drove to Mr. Vollman's place of work, a newspaper printing plant, as I recall, to confront him. Though Mr. Vollman admitted to dating Gaetane on occasion, he claimed he hadn't seen her since he'd become engaged to marry another woman."

"Oh, a love triangle. One time at Berkeley, I was insane about this guy on the volleyball team..."

"Miss Chang, if you don't mind. Mr. Bouchard returned home to find his daughter still missing. He called the police. But, on the advice of friends, he drove out to an abandoned gravel pit known to be a popular spot where couples would park and neck."

"Neck? Do you mean make out? There's this great spot up on Strawberry Canyon that overlooks the entire Bay Area."

"It was there, at the gravel pit, around midnight, that Mr. Bouchard found the body of his daughter, stabbed repeatedly and left to die. Close by, the police found a pool of blood and tire tracks. One of the investigating officers found small flakes of green paint within those tracks—fragments of paint no bigger than a grain of sand that had probably been chipped off by gravel as the murderer's car sped away. Interviews with witnesses placed Gaetane at midafternoon talking to someone in a light green Pontiac with Maine plates. A little later, other friends saw her inside a green Pontiac and yet another witness saw what could have been that very same car parked at the gravel pit at dusk. The police traced the car to John Vollman. The paint chips matched his vehicle, a green Pontiac."

"That's incriminating."

"Indeed. But what sold it was what was found at Gaetane's autopsy—clutched in her hand was a single hair just over two inches long. It matched Vollman's. He was convicted of her murder."

"Seventeen and a half."

"What Miss Chang?"

"The distance along the floor from the heel mark by the gas pedal to the front of the driver's seat is seventeen and a half inches."

"What about the height of the front of the seat from the floor?" Jenkins asked.

"Eleven and a half inches," Helen replied.

"Got it," Jenkins said as he jotted down the numbers. "If you could get a swab of the gas pedal and a couple lifts with the tape, we can try to find the entry point of this bullet."

They circled around to the back of the vehicle and studied the cargo bay with its large rust-colored stain spread across its liner. Jenkins looked for any obvious tear or perforation of the siding and back seat upholstery.

"Nothing," Jenkins said. But then, leaning forward into the hatchback, something caught his eye. "Miss Chang, roll some tape, if you would, please."

Helen tore off a slice of packaging tape and handed it to the lieutenant who then, leaning into the cargo bay, pressed it onto the liner within the area of the large stain.

"What have you got?" Helen asked.

"Hairs, it looks like," Jenkins replied studying the surface of the tape. He stuck the tape to a glass slide and placed it into an envelope onto which he had jotted down a brief description.

Jenkins leaned back into the hatchback to study a small, discolored area having a braided appearance next to the larger stain. "Miss Jenkins," he said with slight puff as he straightened, "would you mind cutting off another piece of tape, please?"

"What is it?" Helen asked as she cut a three-inch fragment of the clear packaging tape and handed it to Jenkins.

"How long were you in the hatchback area before I got here?" Jenkins asked.

"A few seconds."

"That's all?"

"Yeah," she replied. "Why? Is there some kind of five-second rule?"

"Five-second rule?"

"Yeah, you know... if you drop a candy bar or something on the floor, if it sits there for less than five seconds, it's okay to pick it up and eat."

One side of Jenkins' upper lip pulled into an arch as if it had just been snagged by a fishhook.

"What?" Helen asked innocently.

Jenkins, making no response, leaned back into the cargo bay, pressed the tape against the patterned stain, and examined the particles that clung to it. "Interesting," he remarked.

"Still have doubts that this is a crime scene?" Helen asked.

"You think it is?"

"I think it walks like a duck," Helen replied.

"Yeah, it does, doesn't it?"

"We should get a picture of the seat track where I found the bullet, don't you think?" Helen asked.

"Do you mean put the bullet back for the picture?" asked Jenkins suspiciously.

"No," Helen replied. "That wouldn't be honest."

And for a passing moment, the shadows that mark the corners of Jenkins' mouth saw a little more light.

Trace Evidence

The word *trace* refers to the last detectable remnant of something left behind. In forensics, trace usually refers to objects barely visible to the naked eye—hair, synthetic fibers, chips of paint, grains of dirt, or specks of pollen. Items of trace evidence are so small they must be recovered with tweezers, by sticking them to tape, or by collecting them on a filter in a vacuum cleaner and then examined under a microscope.

Trace evidence is all about Locard's exchange principle—you sit down and fibers transfer from your clothing to the chair and vice versa. A hair falls from your head and settles on the back of the chair. You stand up and take with you fibers from the chair's upholstery along with strands of fur from the cat that fell asleep in that same chair a week ago. A criminalist evaluates trace evidence by its association. Does it match other recovered evidence? Trace evidence can place a suspect at the crime scene or it can place them in association with the victim. Sometimes, trace evidence is all an investigator has to go on.

The Microscope

What makes the examination of trace evidence possible is the microscope. There are three primary types of microscopes used in forensic studies—transmission electron, scanning electron, and optical microscopes. Each has its own technology, magnification properties, and uses.

The transmission electron microscope (TEM) uses electromagnets to focus and transmit electrons through the object being examined. Denser materials will stop the electrons in their path, producing an image of the object based on its areas of different densities. Since electrons have a very small wavelength, TEMs can resolve images to a much finer level than a standard optical microscope. The better TEMs can magnify images by up to 50 million times their actual size. Viruses not seen by a standard optical microscope, for example, can be visualized with an electron microscope. The smallest structures within a cell can be imaged using TEM (Figure 3.1). These instruments can help forensic pathologists determine the cause of death when a disease agent is involved.

The scanning electron microscope (SEM) sweeps a finely focused beam of high-energy electrons back and forth across the surface of a specimen. The instrument collects the electrons scattered (reflected back) by the object and x-rays and electrons dislodged from the object by the moving beam. An image is produced by the amount of electrons detected at any one point—the more electrons, the *brighter* the image. SEMs can magnify objects up to 250,000 times their actual size (Figure 3.2). SEMs are used to visualize samples of pollen, soil, fabric, fibers, and gunshot residue.

TEM and SEM are expensive pieces of equipment and are usually maintained only in larger, more well-financed facilities. All forensic laboratories, however, no matter how modest, will at least be equipped with an optical microscope (Figure 3.3).

The optical microscope, also called a light microscope, is a device that transmits light through a specimen mounted on a stage. In a compound optical microscope, a series of lenses focuses the light passing through the specimen to produce

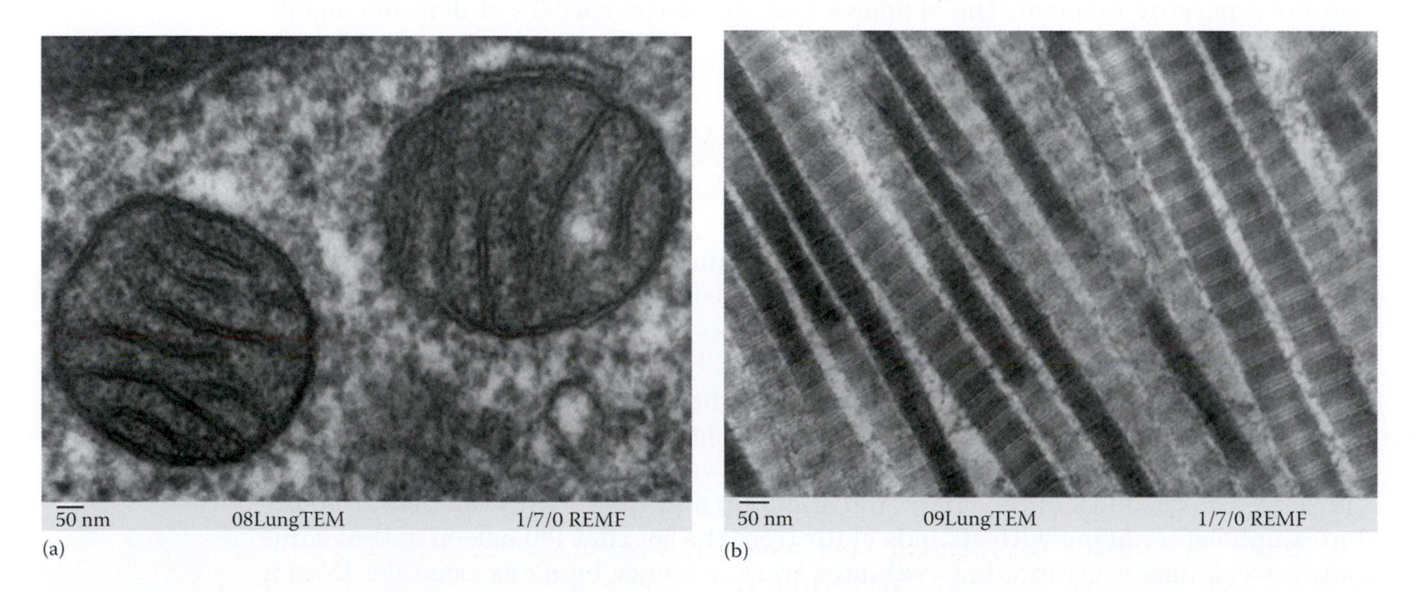

Figure 3.1 TEM images of lung tissue showing (a) mitochondria and (b) connective tissue comprised of collagen type I fibers. (Images from the Dartmouth Electron Microscope Facility, Dartmouth College, Hanover, NH.)

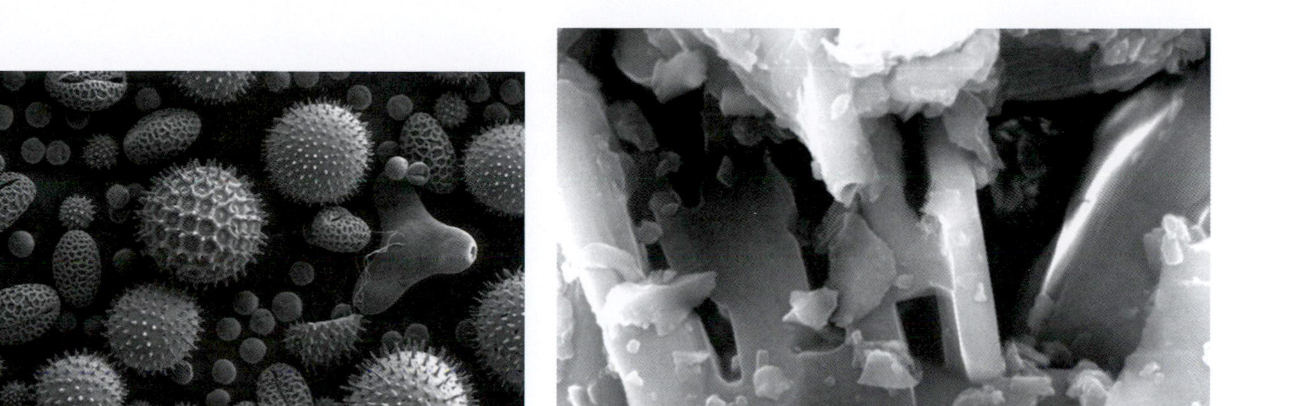

Figure 3.2 SEM images of (a) pollen from sunflower, morning glory, hollyhock, lily, primrose, and caster bean and (b) volcanic ash from the 1980 eruption of Mount St. Helen in Washington state. (Images from the Dartmouth Electron Microscope Facility, Dartmouth College, Hanover, NH.)

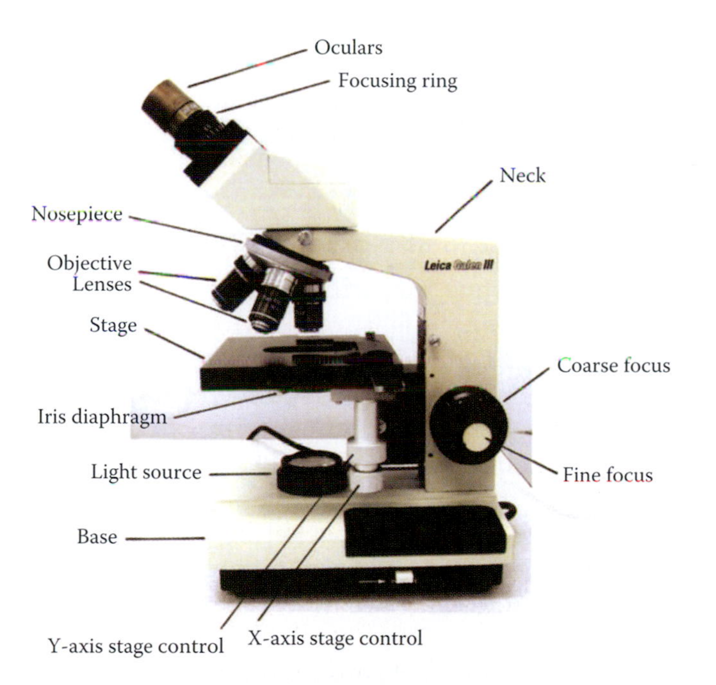

Figure 3.3 The parts of an optical microscope include a series of lenses and a light source.

a magnified image either on the ocular eyepiece or on a mounted camera. The more light transmitted through the specimen, the lighter the image. An area of the specimen that is particularly thick will transmit less light and appear darker. Biological specimens (cells and tissues) can be stained with a variety of dyes to highlight certain features of the material. Ocular microscopes can magnify

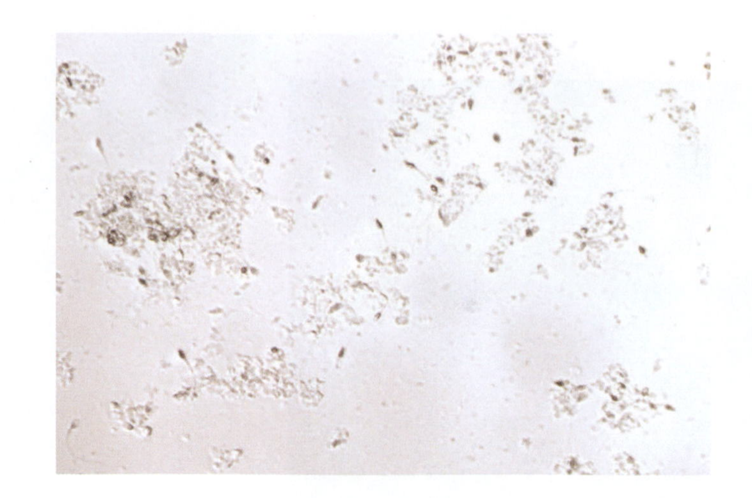

Figure 3.4 Sperm cells collected from the victim of a sexual assault can be viewed with an ocular microscope. Microscopic examination of semen evidence can give an investigator an idea of how much DNA they can expect to recover for subsequent typing. The sperm cells shown here were magnified using a 40× objective lens. Each sperm cell contains 3.5 pg (3.5×10^{-12} g) of DNA. DNA typing can be performed with as few as 10 sperm cells. Intact sperm cells have a long threadlike tail. In this photograph, there are a number of sperm heads that have lost their fragile tails.

objects 1500 times their actual size and are used to examine hairs, fibers, tissue, and semen recovered from sexual assault cases (Figure 3.4 shows sperm within a semen sample).

Hair

You shed over 100 hairs each day. If you walk into a room, spend a few minutes there, chances are, when you leave, you will have left a hair or two behind.

All hairs have their own unique features. Hairs differ between individuals by width, cross-sectional shape, and color and by the way they curl or twist. Hairs on your own body differ from each other as well. A hair from your head is different from one from an eyebrow, which is different than one from your leg. Head hairs are usually round. Those from an armpit are more oval shaped while those from a mustache are more triangular.

Hairs are anchored to your skin at a pocket of cells known as the *follicle*. The hair shaft, growing from the follicle, has three parts, the outer surface called the *cuticle*, a core called the *medulla*, and the area that surrounds the medulla known as the *cortex*.

The cuticle, the hair's outer layer of cells, can look like the skin of a snake when viewed under an electron microscope—having all the appearance of layer upon layer of overlapping scales cascading away from the follicle. Human hairs have flattened scales with rough, irregular edges (Figure 3.5). Those from a cat are cone shaped. Those from a dog wrap almost completely around the shaft and look like stacked waffle cones.

Below the outer cuticle is the hair's cortex. It contains the *melanin* pigments that give a hair its color and, in humans, makes up the largest portion of the shaft. The shape, distribution, and density of the pigment particles within the cortex help the examiner identify the hair's source.

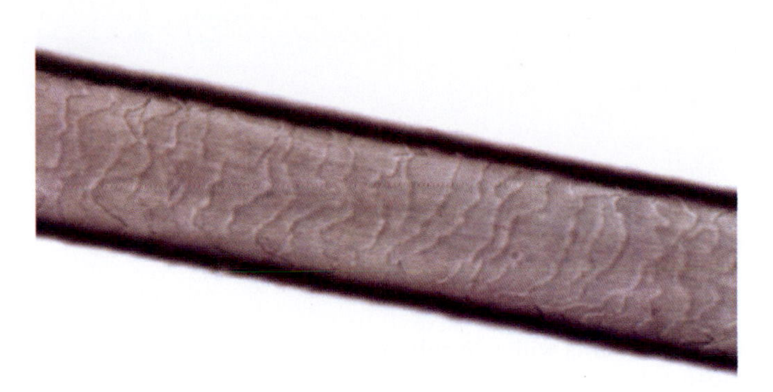

Figure 3.5 The scales along the cuticle of a human hair are irregular and jagged in shape. Image taken at 40× magnification.

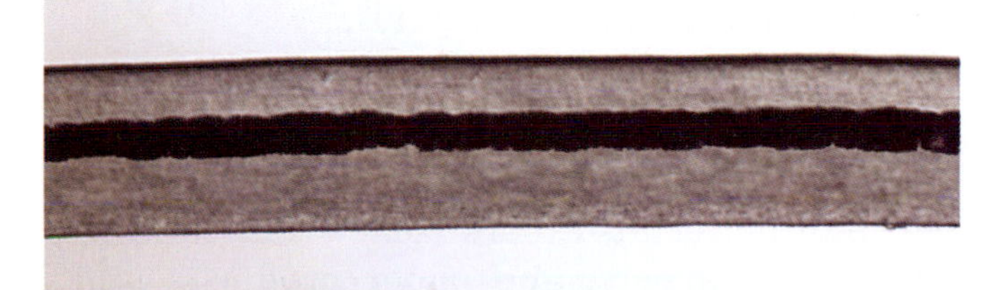

Figure 3.6 A human pubic hair has a broad medulla compared with most other hairs from the human body. Image is 400× magnification.

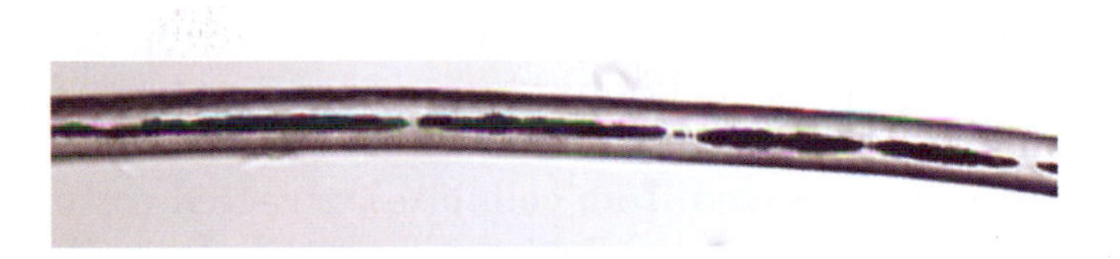

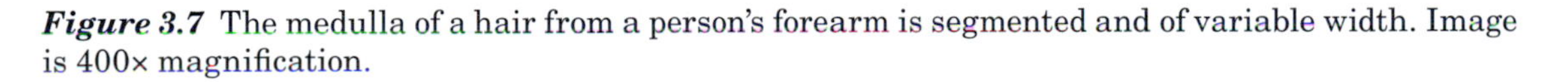

Figure 3.7 The medulla of a hair from a person's forearm is segmented and of variable width. Image is 400× magnification.

The medulla is the central core of cells within the hair shaft. It can be continuous or fragmented into regular sections, and its width can vary between hairs taken from different areas from the same individual (Figures 3.6 and 3.7). In very fine hair or in naturally blond hair, the medulla may be completely absent. Examiners use a ratio called the *medullary index* to help them determine if a hair is from a human or nonhuman. If the ratio of the width of the medulla to the width of the shaft is 0.5 or greater (the medulla makes up over half the width of the shaft), then the hair is probably nonhuman (see Figure 3.8 for a photograph of the medulla of the domestic cat). Most human hairs have a narrow medulla with a calculated medullary index of roughly 0.3 or less.

When a hair is brought into the crime lab as evidence, the criminalist will compare the evidence sample with samples taken from a suspect and the victim so that its source can be identified. Even if a hair found at a crime scene seems to match that from a suspect, that match alone is not discriminating enough for a court to say that a certain hair definitely, positively belongs to the suspect. However, if the hair was pulled from the skin, it will probably have follicle cells

Figure 3.8 An animal's medulla is wider in relation to the hair's diameter than that from a human and, in the case of a house cat, is segmented into stacks of oblong packets. Pictured here is a hair from a domestic cat. Image is 400× magnification.

attached to it from which DNA analysis can be performed to obtain a match evoking greater confidence. Even shed hairs lacking follicle cells can still be DNA typed using their mitochondria (see Chapter 11).

Fibers

A *fiber* is any threadlike material. Fibers come from clothing, bedding, towels, furniture upholstery, rugs, carpets, and paper products, and it's hard to keep them off you. Fibers differ by shape, twist, thickness, color, chemical composition, and density. They are categorized into three groups, natural, manufactured, and synthetic.

Natural fibers are derived from materials produced by plants or animals. Cotton, hemp, and flax are the most common types of plant fibers encountered by a criminalist since these are woven into clothing, ropes, and bedding (Figure 3.9). Wool, cashmere, and mohair are derived from animal fur.

Manufactured fibers are derived from cellulose-extracted cotton and wood pulp. The fabric rayon, for example, is manufactured from cellulose. Many baby diapers, cigarette filters, and feminine hygiene products contain rayon.

Synthetic fibers are manufactured by laboratory chemists who string together long chains of single molecules into a goo-like substance known as *polymer*.

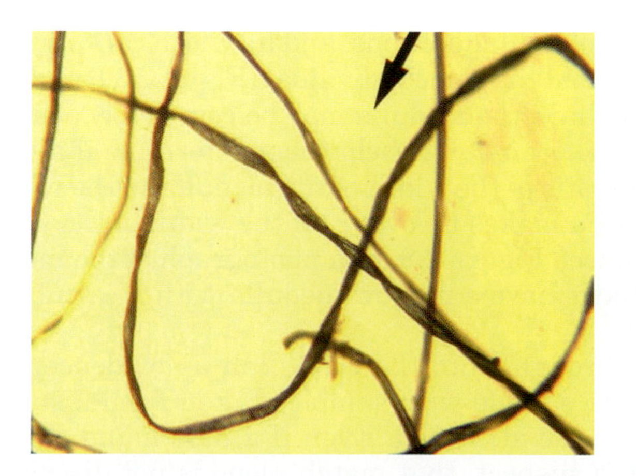

Figure 3.9 Fibers of cotton are twisted and have an irregular width. Image is 100× magnification.

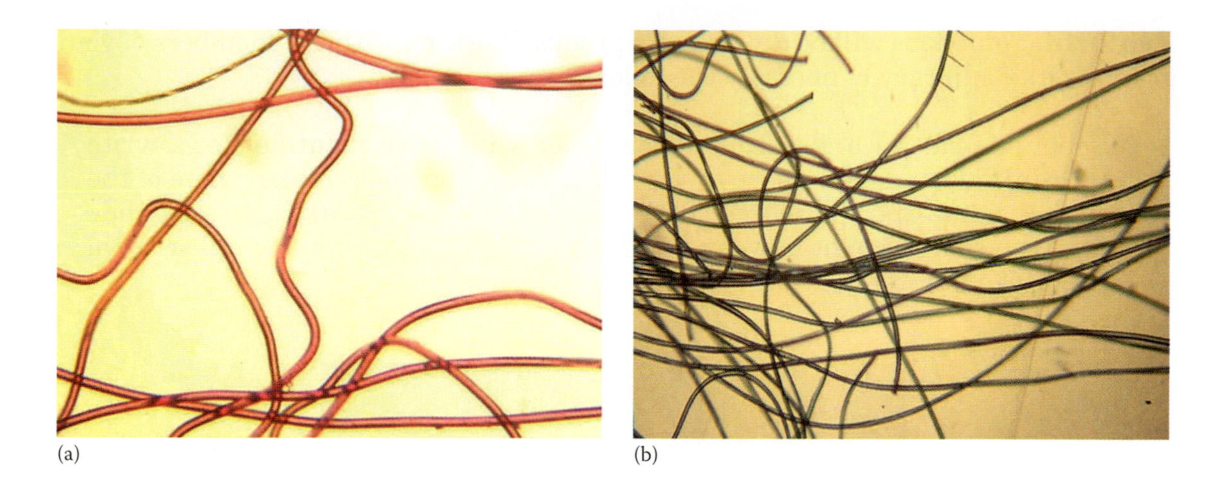
(a) (b)

Figure 3.10 Nylon (a) 100Å~ magnification and polyester (b) 40Å~ magnification show smooth surfaces and constant diameters characteristic of synthetic fibers.

The polymer is turned into a fiber by forcing it through tiny holes whereby it solidifies upon meeting air. Consequently, synthetic fibers bear the geometric shape of the opening through which they were extruded. Nylon, polyester, and spandex are all synthetic fibers. Nylon, first developed in 1939 and derived from petroleum, is used to make seat belts, sleeping bags, windbreakers, and carpets (Figure 3.10). Polyester, developed in 1953, can be found in rope, filler for sleeping bags, and the trousers worn by pro golfers. Spandex, invented in 1959, is found in swimsuits and exercise clothing.

Many synthetic fibers give a fabric an undesirable sheen. To reduce their shine, manufacturers add to their synthetic fabric a material such as finely ground titanium dioxide that acts as a *delusterant*. Since different fibers are manufactured with different delusterants dispersed within the fiber at different densities, their pattern and composition can aid in their identification.

In the Crime Lab

Activity 3.1 Identifying Fibers from Known Sources

Within an assigned group, you will prepare microscope slides of fibers taken from known sources. Fibers can be collected from upholstery, carpet, clothing, pets, and people and can be of wool, cotton, nylon, polyester, fiberglass, hair, fur, or any other type of strand-like material.

Materials:

Glass microscope slides
Cover slips
Clear fingernail polish or glycerin
Forceps
Sharpie marking pen
Compound microscope

Protocol: Your class will be divided into groups. Working with the members of your group, make a library of fibers by the following protocol.

1. Label one side of a glass microscope slide with some identifier (e.g., write your initials and a number). In your laboratory notebook, make a note of the sample name and the source of the fiber you will be mounting on that slide (e.g., the source might be your cat). Have the fiber ready on a small scrap of paper nearby.

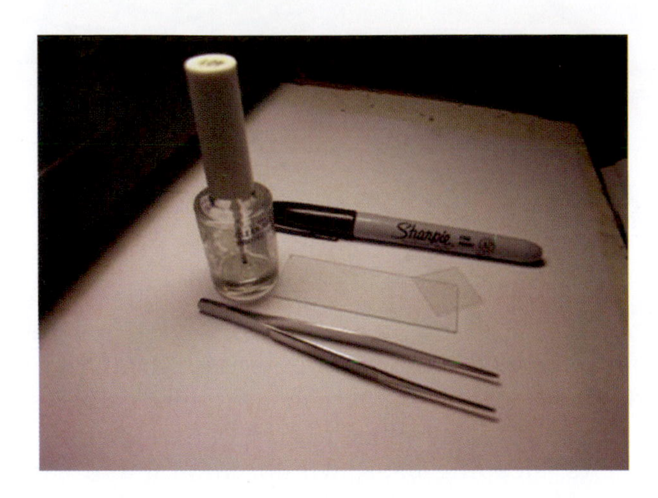

Note: To save on the use of slides, you can place as many as three different samples of the same fiber type on to the same slide.

2. Using the brush applicator that comes with the fingernail polish, place a few drops of the liquid in the center of the glass slide.

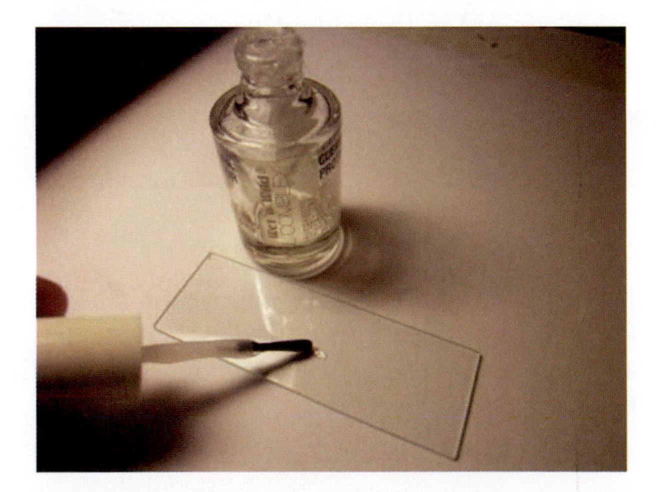

3. Using a pair of forceps, place the fiber into the fingernail polish.

4. Carefully place a cover slip over the fiber. You may need to gently press your finger on top of the cover slip to spread the fingernail polish beneath the cover slip. Avoid introducing bubbles. Allow the liquid to completely dry before proceeding onto the next step.

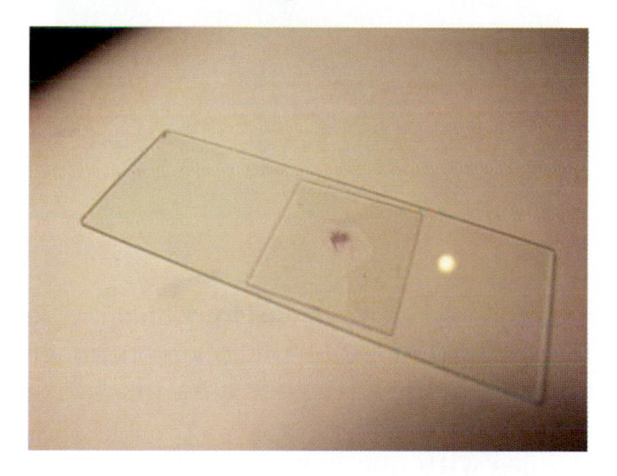

5. Place your permanent slide on a microscope stage and view the specimen under the lowest power. Make adjustments to the light level as necessary.

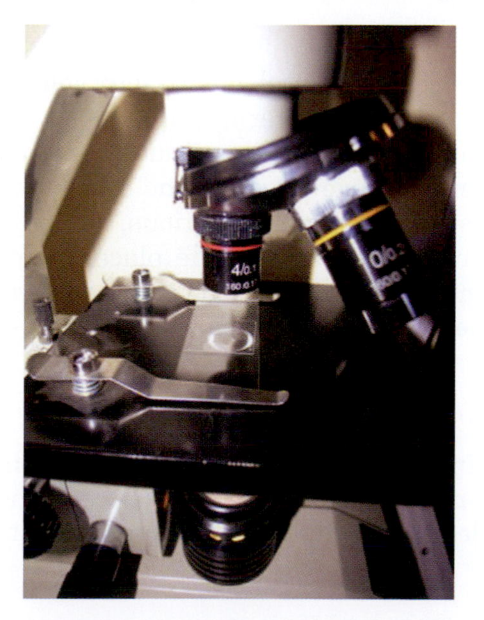

6. Carefully swing the objective to the next level of magnification. Using the fine adjustment knob, make adjustments to sharpen the image as needed. Make appropriate changes to the light level as necessary to bring in a clear image with good contrast.

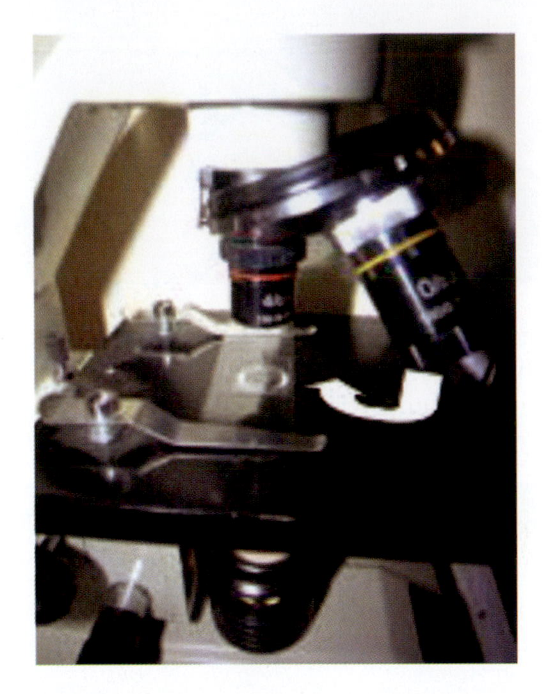

In your laboratory notebook, write down your observations for each sample. Include a drawing of the item. Note the serial number of the microscope, magnification, and light setting. Repeat this process for your other trace evidence samples.

7. Exchange your samples with another group. Do not tell them the source of the samples you prepared. Likewise, you will be given samples from another group of students in your class. As a group, make your best determination as to the samples source.

In your laboratory notebook, create a table with four columns for the sample's identifier, your observations, your best determination as to the possible source of the fiber, and the fiber's actual source (the actual identification of the fiber will not be revealed to you until after you have filled out the first three columns).

After you have completed making observations, return the slides to their source and store the slides returned to you in a safe place. Meet with the students with whom you exchanged samples and reveal to them the source of the fibers. With this information, complete the table described earlier.

Activity 3.2 Locard Exchange Principle

The Locard exchange principle states that every time two different objects come into contact with each other, material is exchanged between them. Pick up your pet cat or walk through a puddle of mud, and it might appear that the exchange is terribly lopsided. But if you were able to look close enough, you'd find that the cat now had some of your skin cells, hairs, or clothing fibers clinging to its fur. Likewise, not only did you leave footprints behind in the mud, those footprints would carry bits of fiber from your shoes or molecules of synthetic rubber from their soles. It is by making use of the Locard exchange principle that cases are solved. In this activity, you will see this principle in action. You will determine what types of foreign material have adhered to your clothing and whether or not these materials can be traced to their origin.

Materials:

Clear packaging tape
Compound microscope
Glass slides
Scissors
Sharpie marking pen

Protocol:

In your laboratory notebook, re-create Activity 3.2 Data Table. Allow enough room to enter your observations. In the appropriate column, describe the type of clothing covering your upper body, your lower body, and the type of shoes you are wearing.

Activity 3.2 Data Table

Area of Clothing	Description of Your Clothing/ Shoes and Predominant Color(s)	Description of Foreign Object(s) Revealed during Microscopic Examination
Upper body		
Lower body		
Bottom of shoe		

Follow the steps outlined in the following to recover material from your clothing.

1. Make a loop of packaging tape (sticky side facing outward) that will allow you to insert two or three fingers snuggly into the loop. Press the loop of tape (sticky side facing outward) onto your upper garment of clothing several times.

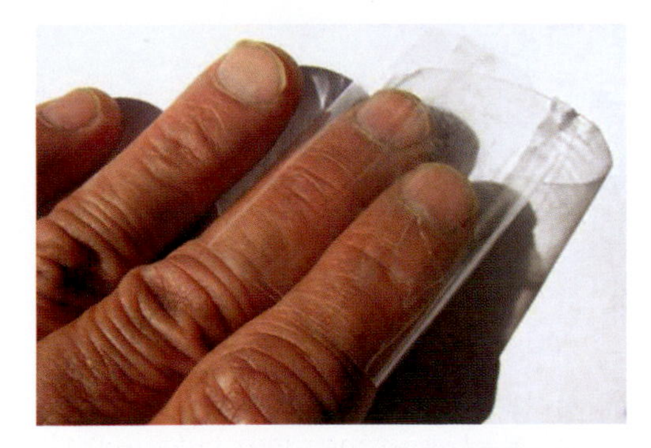

2. With the loop of tape still on your fingers, press the sticky side onto the surface of a clean glass slide. Using a sharpie pen, label the slide to identify the article of clothing from which the fiber sample originated.

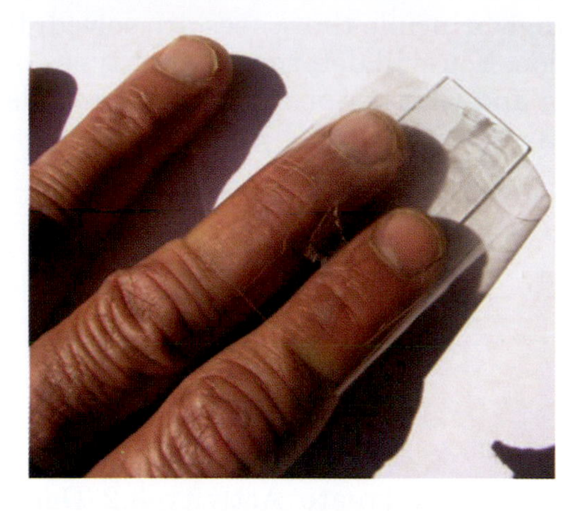

3. Remove your fingers from the loop and trim any excess tape not adhering to the slide with a pair of scissors.

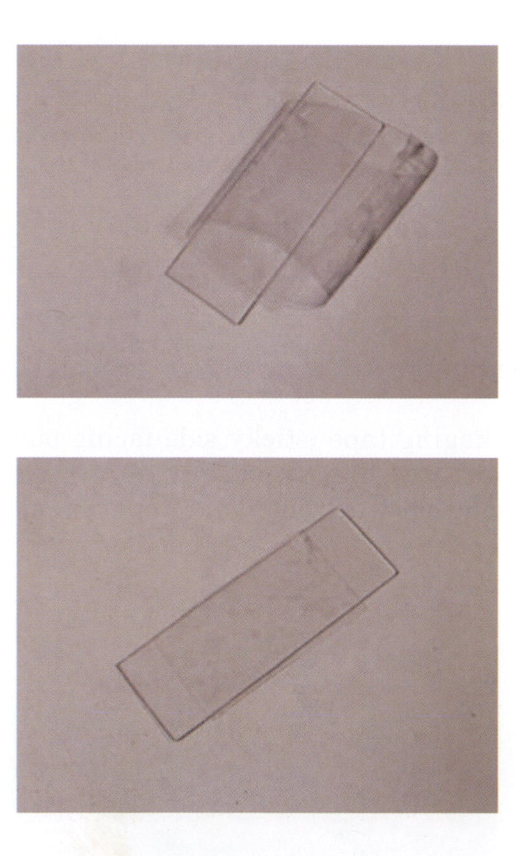

Repeat steps 1 through 3 for samples from garments below the waist and from the bottom of your shoes.

4. Place one of your prepared slides on the stage of a microscope and view the specimen under the lowest power. Make appropriate adjustments to the light level as needed for optimal viewing of the specimen.

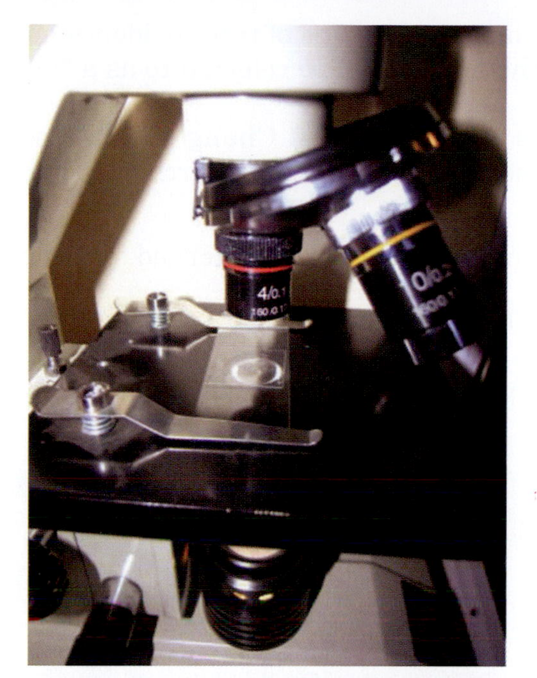

5. Carefully swing the objective to the next level of magnification. Use the fine adjustment dial to sharpen the image. Change the light level as necessary.

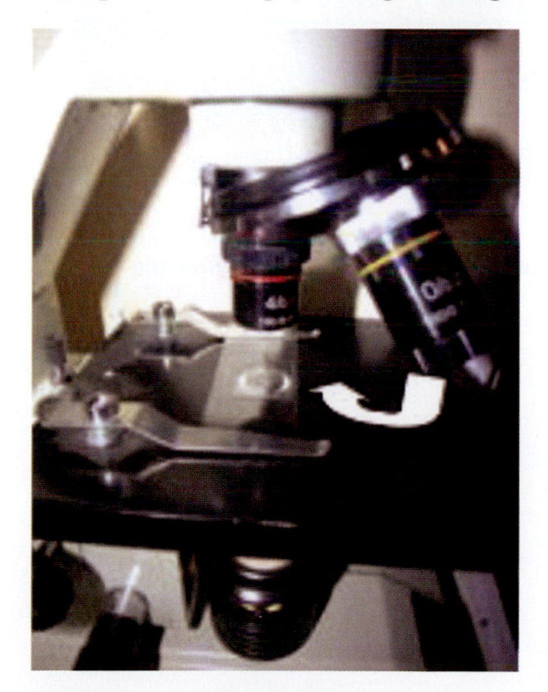

If the microscope has multiple lenses, rotate to the highest level of magnification. If resolution quality at this point is compromised, return to the previous level of magnification to make your observations.

Examine all three slides and record your observations in the Activity 3.2 Data Table in your laboratory notebook.

Erica Holmes Missing Persons Case

Preliminary note: Any filamentous type of trace evidence not positively identified as either a hair or a synthetic fiber will be referred to as a "fiber" during the course of this investigation.

Lieutenant Jenkins and Criminalist Chang collected several items of evidence that can be classified as fibers during their search of the abandoned vehicle. These included the following:

Evidence Item 14: Fiber from the braid-patterned stain on the hatchback liner.

Evidence Item 14, a small collection of fibers, was recovered from the patterned stain on the cargo bay liner. (A small swab of material taken from the pattern stain for DNA analysis is designated as *Evidence Item 5*.)

Close up of the pattern stain from which *Evidence Item 14* was recovered.

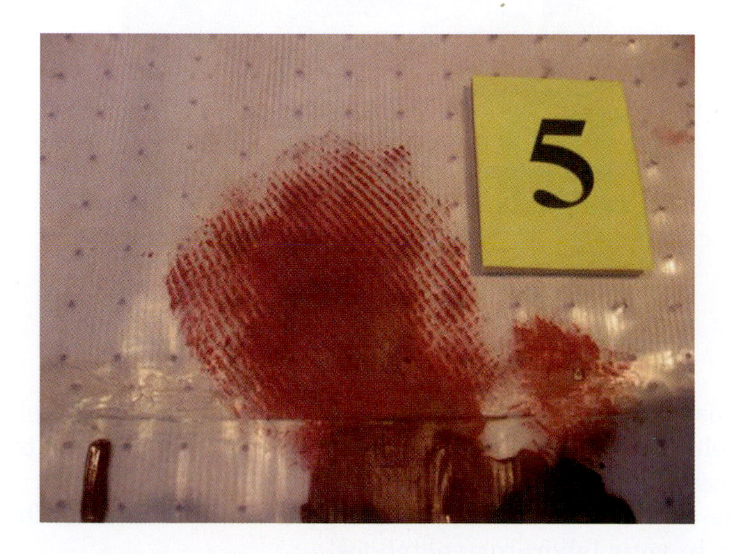

Evidence Item 14 fibers are shown in this microscopic image (above) to reveal their color and general morphology. Image is 100× magnification.

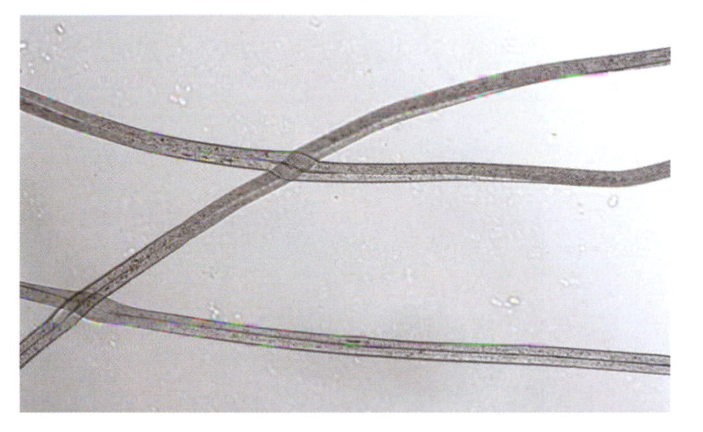

The photograph earlier shows the microscopic examination of *Evidence Item 14* under white light at a magnification of 100×.

Evidence Item 15: Fiber from the large stain on the hatchback liner.

Evidence Item 15 was recovered from the large stain on the cargo bay liner. In this photograph, it is seen as a strand within the large stain to the left of the evidence tent.

Zoom of *Evidence Item 15*.

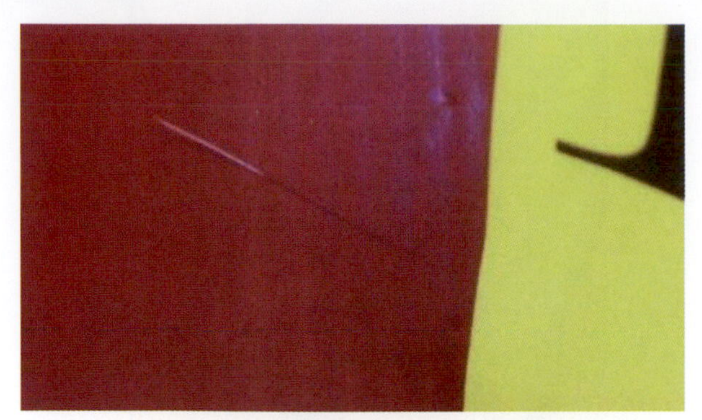

Microscopic examination of *Evidence Item 15*. Image is 400× magnification.

Evidence Item 16: Fiber from a stain adjacent to the braid pattern stain on the cargo bay vinyl liner.

Evidence Item 16 is a fiber within a smudged area close to the pattern stain identified as Item 5.

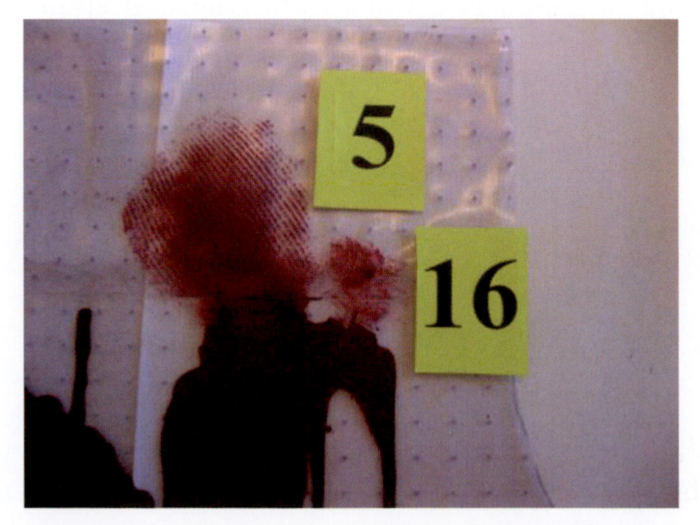

Enlarged image of *Evidence Item 16*.

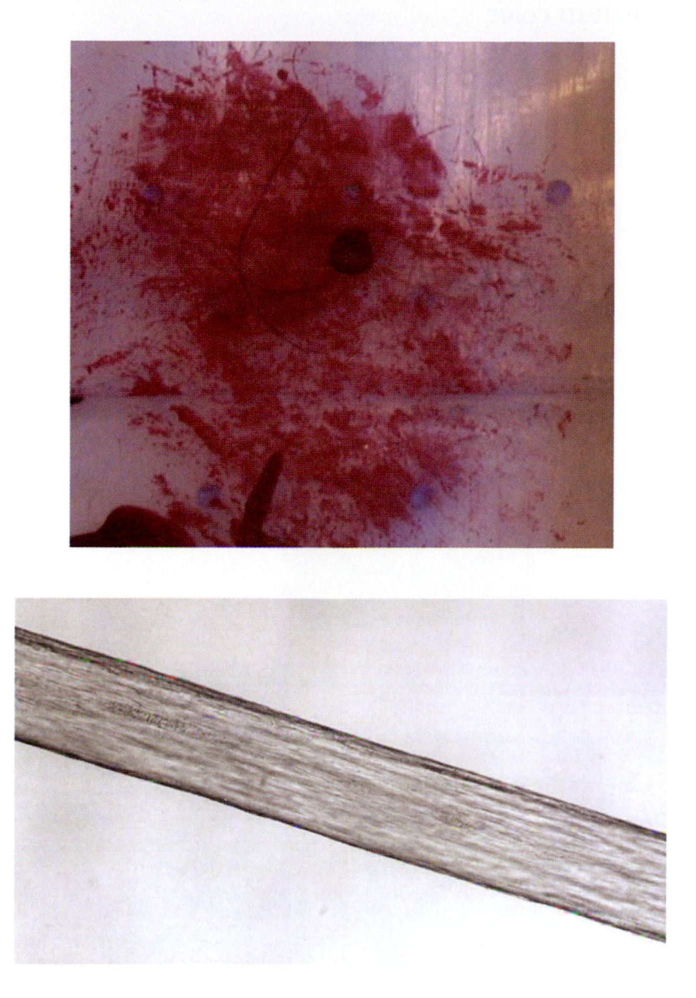

Microscopic examination of *Evidence Item 16*. The fiber was rinsed with water and ethanol to remove the red stain that coated it. When cleaned, the fiber is light (blond) in color. In this image, the microscope is focused onto the center of the fiber in an attempt to distinguish a medulla. Image is 400× magnification.

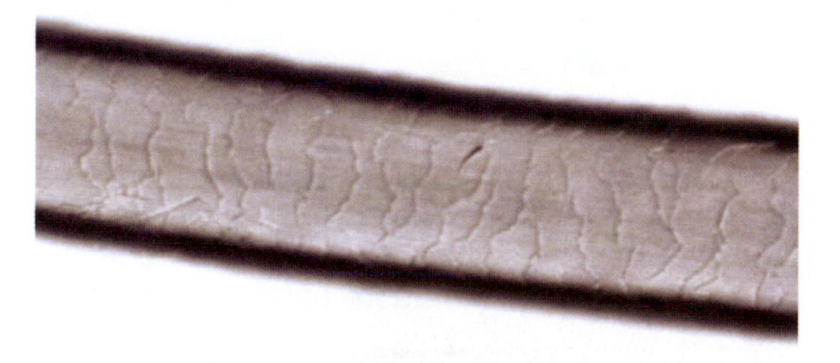

In this image of *Evidence Item 16* (at 400× magnification), the microscope is focused under white light to show the fiber's surface features.

Evidence Item 17: A fiber taken from the bullet found within Erica Holmes' vehicle. The fiber is olive green in color.

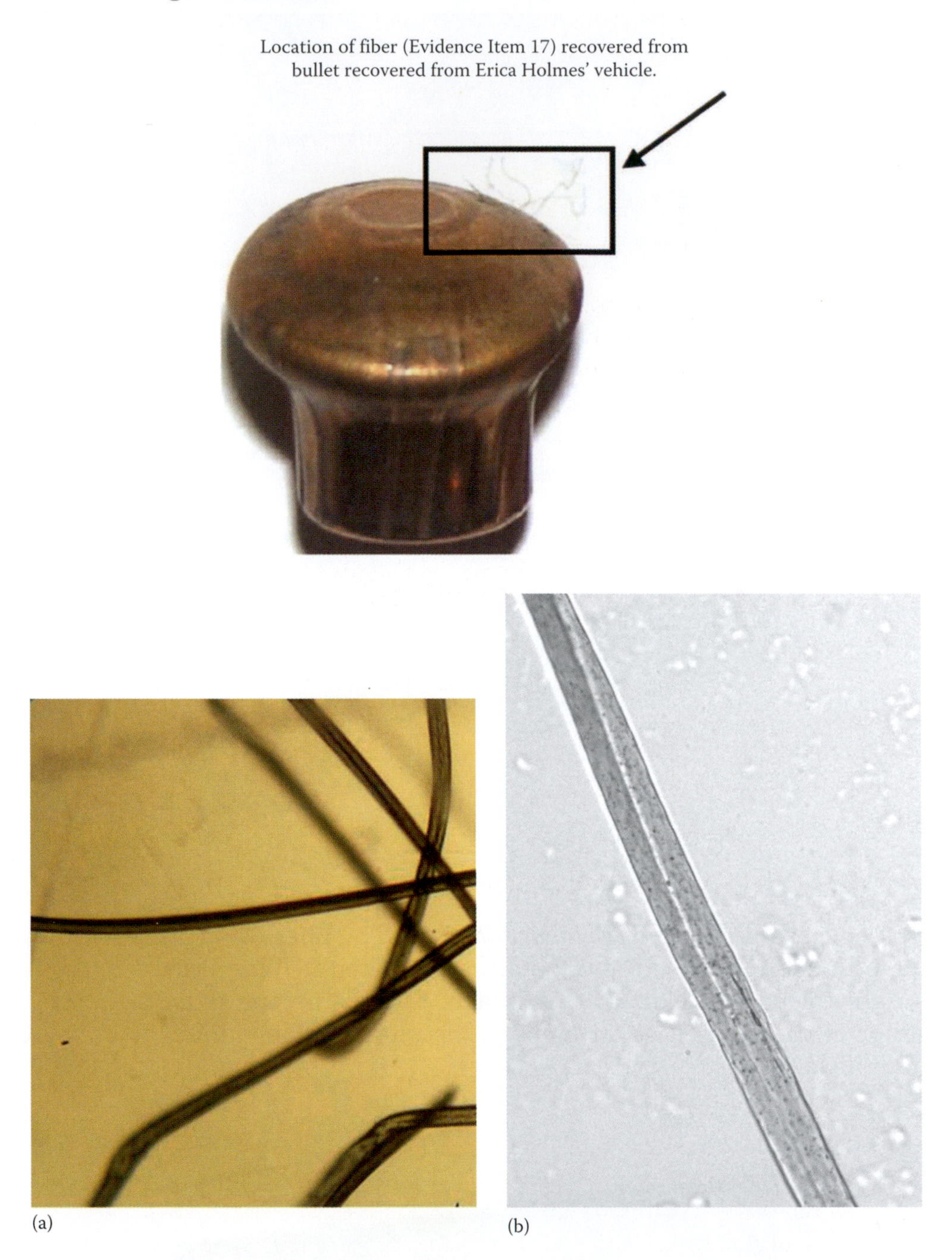

The images earlier (Image a at 100× magnification, Image b at 400× magnification) are microscopic examinations of *Evidence Item 17* to show the fiber's greenish color (Image a) and under white light to better show the fiber's morphology (Image b).

Here, you will identify the types of fibers collected from the vehicle (the bullet will be examined at a later time). You will complete an evidence report for each item. Remember, when filling out an evidence report, any inaccuracy, any omission, or any unsubstantiated conclusion could be seized upon by a defense attorney in an attempt to persuade a jury that the investigation was either carried out in an inept or inadequate manner or that the prosecution is making a deliberate attempt to lead the jury toward deciding a guilty verdict for their client. Be accurate. Be complete. Be honest. Do the best to your ability. You can use the fibers analyzed in Activities 3.1 and 3.2 as reference libraries to aid you in the identification of these evidence items.

In your evidence report write-up, you should use such terminology as, for example, "the fiber is consistent in appearance with cotton" or "the appearance of the fiber is not consistent with that coming from a natural source." If you think you have an absolute, irrefutable identification, then say so. If you cannot make any conclusion, then say that your results are inconclusive. Leave no room for doubt as to which area of the vehicle the evidence was recovered from. Remember, on the witness stand, you will have to defend what you record in the evidence report! You might also have to justify why some observation or conclusion was not included in your report.

Record your observations, drawings, supporting information, etc., in your laboratory notebook.

The Last Person to Drive Erica Holmes' Vehicle

Helen Chang, while looking for evidence along the floor by the driver's seat of the Subaru station wagon, took measurements of the seat's height and its distance from the heel mark in the carpeting below the gas pedal. You will explore whether or not those measurements can be used to estimate the height of the last person to drive that vehicle as this might provide a clue as to the circumstances of her disappearance.

For this exercise, you will take measurements of length. When dealing with almost any type of measurement, you will need to consider two of its most important aspects, accuracy and precision. *Accuracy* refers to how close a measurement is to the truth—to its real, actual value. *Precision* refers to how reproducible a measurement is when taken with a specific piece of equipment or instrument. For example, let's look at a precision sky diving team flying over the Western United States. Each member of the team jumps from the plane in turn, all aiming for a red bull's eye target on the ground. Each lands one on top of the other in a field in Arizona. Their skydiving, therefore, is very precise. However, the target that they should have landed on is in Nevada. Their accuracy, therefore, leaves much to be desired.

We will use two methods to estimate the height of the Subaru's last driver. In the first method, we will plot the area of a rectangle formed when the height of the driver's seat is multiplied by the distance from the heel mark by the accelerator pedal to the front edge of the seat. In the second method, we will use these same measurements along with the Pythagorean theorem to calculate leg length and overall height.

Estimating the Height of the Last Person to Drive Erica Holmes' Vehicle: The Area of a Rectangle

This protocol will require that you take measurements from a number of different vehicles and/or have a number of different people sit in the driver's seat of the same vehicle with each of them adjusting the seat to a distance from the accelerator that they find the most comfortable. Record the height of each driver (in inches) along with the measurements described in the following protocol.

Materials:

Tape measure or ruler
Different makes and models of vehicles
A collection of students of different heights
Computers with Microsoft Office (Excel)

Protocol: Use the following protocol to estimate the height of the last driver:

1. With a tape measure or ruler, measure the height of the driver's seat from the floor to the seat's center edge. Record this result in your laboratory notebook.

2. Locate the heel mark worn into the carpeting or mat cover by the vehicle's accelerator pedal, and measure the distance along the flooring from the front edge of the driver's seat to the heel mark. Record this distance.

Take multiple measurements using different vehicles and/or different drivers. Obtain at least 15 sample measurements.

3. For the measurements of each driver, calculate the area of a rectangle that would be created by multiplying the height of the driver's seat by the distance from the seat to the accelerator pedal's heel mark. This value will be in square inches.

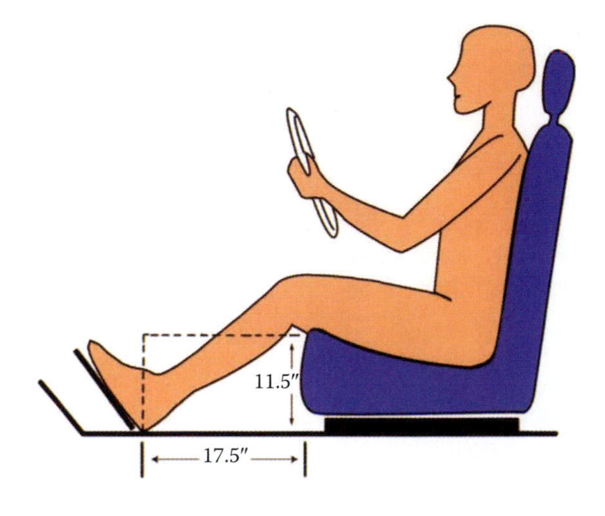

You will now use a mathematical technique called *linear regression* to estimate the height of the vehicle's last driver. Using the Microsoft program Excel, you plot all your data on a chart where the x axis represents height and the y axis represents the area of the rectangle you calculated from the seat's height and its distance from the gas pedal heel mark for each of your test subjects. The Excel program will then draw a *line of best fit* (a *regression line*) through the data points and report an R^2 (R squared) and an equation for the best-fit line given in the standard form of $y = mx + b$. The R^2 value will give you an idea of how well the data points line up along the regression line. For the regression line, y is equal to the area of the rectangle for each driver, m is the slope of the line, x is the height of the driver for each corresponding area measurement, and b is the point where the regression line crosses the y axis. You will use this equation to calculate the height of the last driver of the Subaru station wagon under examination in the police impound lot. Excel will provide the values for "m" and "b" in the equation; you will provide y and solve for x.

1. On a computer, open the Microsoft Excel program. Click to open an Excel workbook.

2. In the spreadsheet that opens, type in "height (x)" in column A, row 1, and "area in square inches (y)" in column B, row 1.

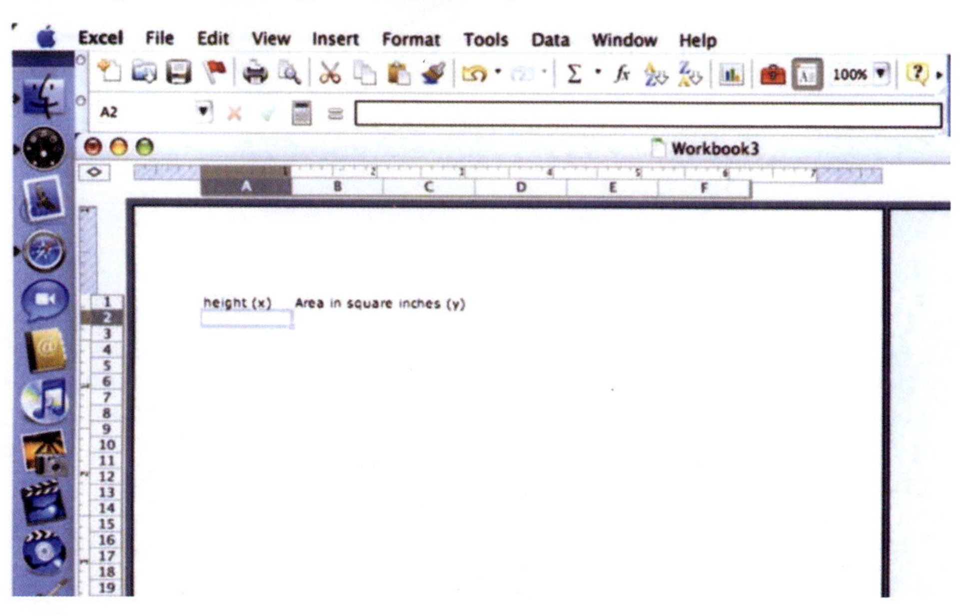

3. Enter the values you obtained for your measurements from your shortest driver to your tallest driver. You may also, at this point, give a title to your document if the software version allows it.

Linear Regression Analysis of Driver's Height

height (x)	Area in square inches (y)
58	120
60	115
61	142
61	130
61	135
62	121
63	135
64	150
64	160
65	155
65.5	162
66	170
66	155
66.5	168
67	170
67	172
69	170
71	182
73	185
75	200

4. Without selecting the header titles, highlight the values you entered for height and area.

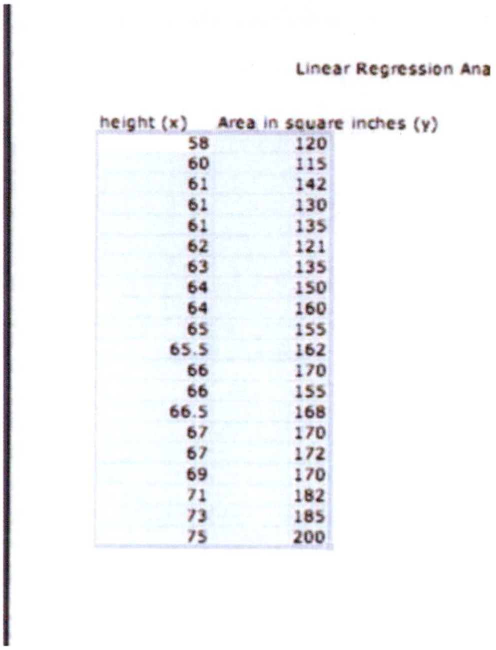

Linear Regression Ana

height (x)	Area in square inches (y)
58	120
60	115
61	142
61	130
61	135
62	121
63	135
64	150
64	160
65	155
65.5	162
66	170
66	155
66.5	168
67	170
67	172
69	170
71	182
73	185
75	200

5. Click the Chart Wizard icon button in the top tool bar (it looks like a bar graph) to open the Chart Wizard/Chart Type window. Select the "XY (Scatter)" chart type. Click "Finish." (Newer versions of Excel will allow you to label the x and y axes at this point.)

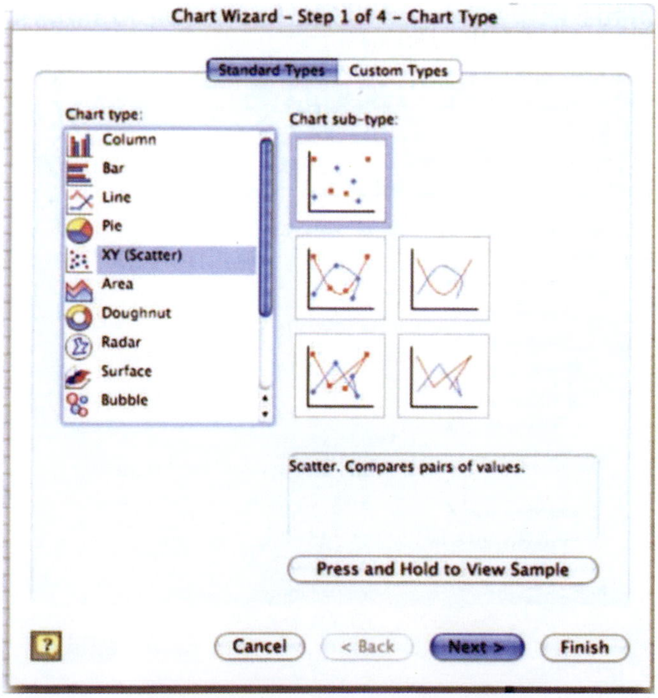

Chart Wizard - Step 1 of 4 - Chart Type
Standard Types
Custom Types
Chart type:
Column
Bar
Line
Pie
XY (Scatter)
Area
Doughnut
Radar
Surface
Bubble
Chart sub-type:
Scatter. Compares pairs of values.
Press and Hold to View Sample
?
Cancel
< Back
Next >
Finish

6. A chart will appear on the workspace. You may not like its appearance, but this can be changed as described later.

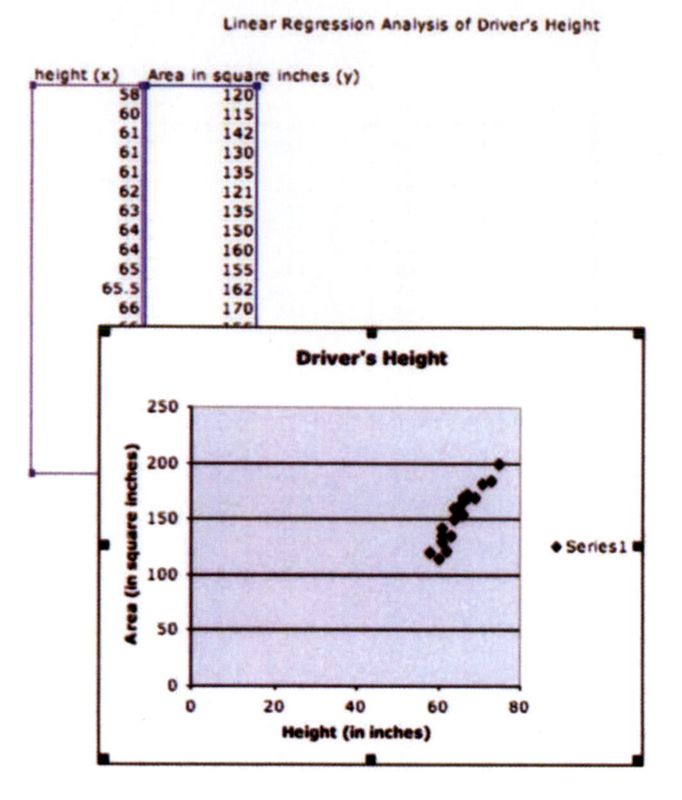

7. To change the range of values on the x axis, click the mouse on any number on that axis. This will allow you to change the minimum and maximum x values displayed.

Format Axis

Colors and Lines | Scale | Font | Number | Alignment

Value (X) axis scale
Auto
Minimum: 56
Maximum: 80
Major unit: 2
Minor unit: 0.4
Value (Y) axis
Crosses at: 56
Display units: None ✓ Show display units label on chart
Logarithmic scale
Values in reverse order
Value (Y) axis crosses at maximum value
Cancel OK

8. To change the range of values along the y axis, click the mouse on any number along its axis. This will allow you to change the minimum and maximum y values displayed.

Format Axis

Colors and Lines | Scale | Font | Number | Alignment

Value (Y) axis scale
Auto
Minimum: 100
Maximum: 220
Major unit: 10
Minor unit: 2
Value (X) axis
Crosses at: 100
Display units: None
Show display units label on chart
Logarithmic scale
Values in reverse order
Value (X) axis crosses at maximum value
Cancel
OK

9. By altering the values along the axes, you can spread the data points over a broader range to produce a more easily readable chart.

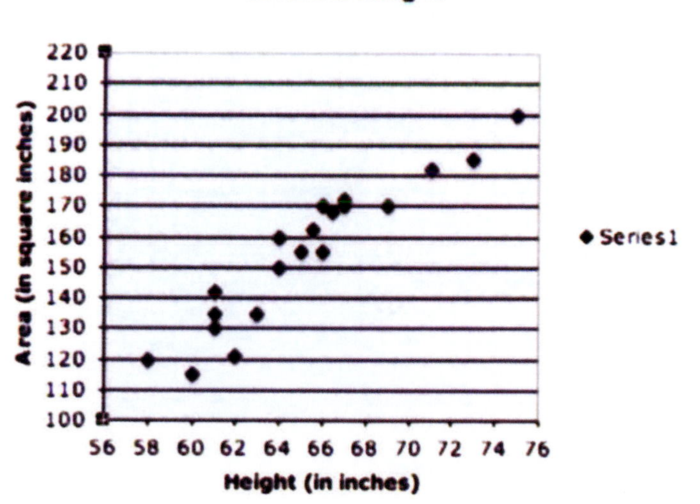

10. Pull down the "Chart" list from the top menu bar and select "Add Trendline." Make sure that the "Linear" Trend/Regression type is selected.

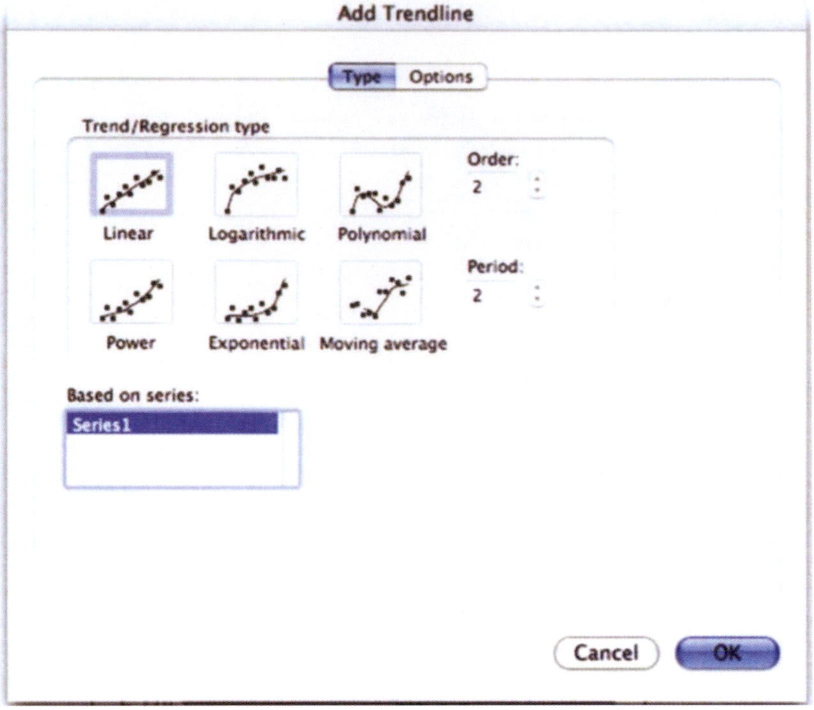

Note: The "Chart" pull-down menu is only available if the chart is selected (highlighted).

11. Click the "Options" tab in the "Add Trendline" window, and in the "Options" window that appears, check the boxes next to "Display equation on chart" and "Display R-squared value on chart." Click "OK."

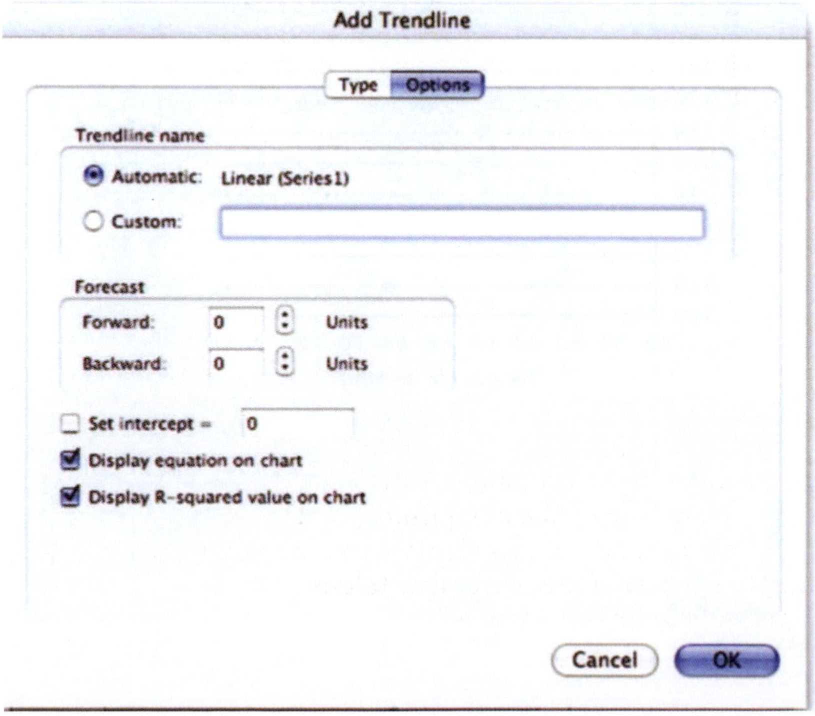

12. The best-fit line will be drawn through the points on your chart, and the equation for that line along with the R^2 value will appear on the graph. Record this equation in your laboratory notebook.

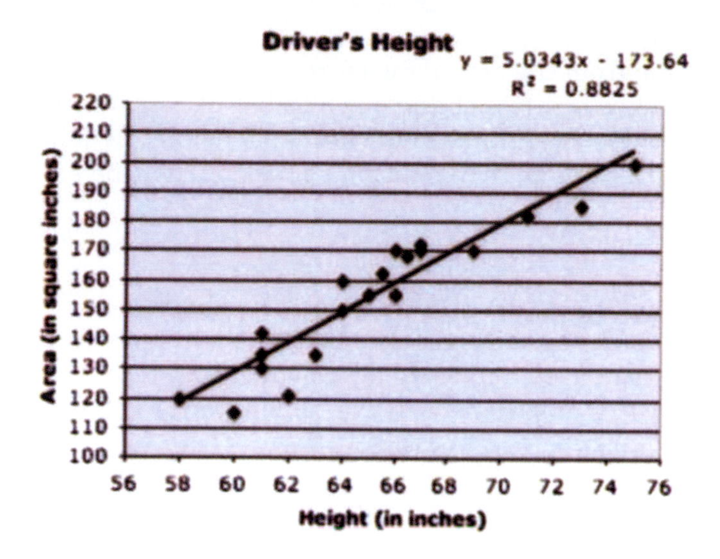

You can now use the linear regression line's equation to calculate the height (x) of the last driver in the Subaru station wagon. To do this, place the area you calculated based on Helen Chang's data (this will be your y value) and solve for x (the driver's height). Remember, as calculated from your equation, the height will be in inches. Convert the value you get into feet. For example, if you calculate the driver's height to be 68 in., this is equivalent to 5′8″ (not 5′7″ [68 in./12 in./1 ft = 5.67 ft] … no, no, no! Why not?).

You will no doubt have noticed that the points on your graph do not fall exactly on the regression line. In fact, some may be quite far removed from it. The degree to which the data points fall on the regression line is reflected in the R-squared value. The R^2 value is also known as the *correlation coefficient*. The further away from 1 (either positive or negative) that value is, the poorer the fit of the data to the line. Although some points might lie right on the line, most points probably do not. Because of that, we need to determine a mathematical value that indicates how far off the line the data points deviate. This value is called the *standard deviation*. Statisticians calculate its value using the formula

$$s = \sqrt{\frac{\sum (x - \bar{x})^2}{n - 1}}$$

where, in our case

s is the standard deviation
Σ is the symbol denoting summation
x is the height of a driver in the sampling
$\bar{x}$ is the height of each driver as calculated using the linear regression line corresponding to each area measurement taken
n is the number of samples measured

For your data, take each area measurement you made (each y value), and calculate the corresponding height ($\bar{x}$ value) using the linear regression line:

$$y = m\bar{x} + b$$

Subtract each $\bar{x}$ value from the actual measured height, square that value, add all of them together, divide by one less than your number of measurements, and take the square root. This will be the standard deviation. An example follows.

For the table later, the linear regression equation from the example date will be used. It is

$$y = 5.0343x - 173.64$$

To determine the $\bar{x}$ value for each measurement, we will substitute y with one of our actual measurements of area and solve for x (which will represent the $\bar{x}$ value). For example, the first area measurement in the table later is 120 in.^{2}. Using algebra to solve for x, we have

$$120 = 5.0343\bar{x} - 173.64$$

$$120 + 173.64 = 5.0343x$$

$$293.64 = 5.0343x$$

$$\frac{293.64}{5.0343} = \bar{x} = 58.3$$

Therefore, according to the regression line determined for the example data, a driver 58.3 in. tall would yield an area of 120 in.^{2} when the seat height is multiplied by its distance to the accelerator heel mark. We will use this as the $\bar{x}$ value to calculate the standard deviation of the sample data. Construct a table as exampled later.

5 Column × 22 Row Table of Area Measured in Square Inches (Row 1, Column 1)

Area Measured in Square Inches (y)	Actual Height Measured in Inches (x)	Calculated Height in Inches ($\bar{x}$)	$(x - \bar{x})$	$(x - \bar{x})^2$
120	58	58.3	−0.3	0.09
115	60	57.3	2.7	7.29
142	61	62.7	−1.7	2.89
130	61	60.3	0.7	0.49
135	61	61.3	−0.3	0.09
121	62	58.5	3.5	12.25
135	63	61.3	1.7	2.89
150	64	64.3	−0.3	0.09
160	64	66.3	−2.3	5.29
155	65	65.3	−0.3	0.09

162	65.5	66.7	−1.2	1.44
170	66	68.3	−2.3	5.29
155	66	65.3	0.7	0.49
168	66.5	67.9	−1.4	1.96
170	67	68.3	−1.3	1.69
172	67	68.7	−1.7	2.89
170	69	68.3	0.7	0.49
182	71	70.6	0.4	0.16
185	73	71.2	1.8	3.24
200	75	74.2	0.8	0.64
				Σ=49.75

We now have the sum of all the squared numbers. It is equal to 49.75. Our sample size is 20. Placing these values into the equation for standard deviation yields

$$s=\sqrt{\frac{\sum(x-\bar{x})^2}{n-1}}=\sqrt{\frac{49.75}{20-1}}=\sqrt{\frac{49.75}{19}}=\sqrt{2.6}=1.6$$

Therefore, for the example data, the standard deviation (s) is equal to 1.6.

Standard deviation describes how much variability there is in your data—the typical (or average) deviation from the ideal data represented, in this case, by points right on the regression line. Statisticians steeped in numbers accept that about 68% of the data should fall within one standard deviation of the regression line and that 95% of the data should lie within two standard deviations of the line. Any height calculated using the regression line, therefore, should be given as a range. For example, if a height of 5′8″ is calculated from the regression line using the example data, it would be reported as 5′8″ plus or minus 3.2 in. (for two standard deviations). In other words, the driver could be anywhere from about 5′5″ to about 5′11″.

Calculate a standard deviation for your data, and based on the measurements you collected and the regression line equation you determined, prepare an evidence report detailing the possible height of the last driver of the impounded Subaru station wagon within a range of two standard deviations.

Estimating the Height of the Last Person to Drive Erica Holmes' Vehicle: Pythagorean Theorem

Sadly, you may forget everything you ever learn in your geometry class. There is possibly one notable exception, the Pythagorean theorem. It is so beautiful and so elegant that it will probably stay with you throughout your lifetime, even if you don't become a mathematics teacher, an architect, or a building contractor. Discovered and proved to be true by the Greek mathematician Pythagoras, the theorem states that for a right triangle (Figure 3.3), the square of the hypotenuse is equal in length to the sum of the squares of the lengths of the other two sides. Expressed as an equation, the Pythagorean theorem is

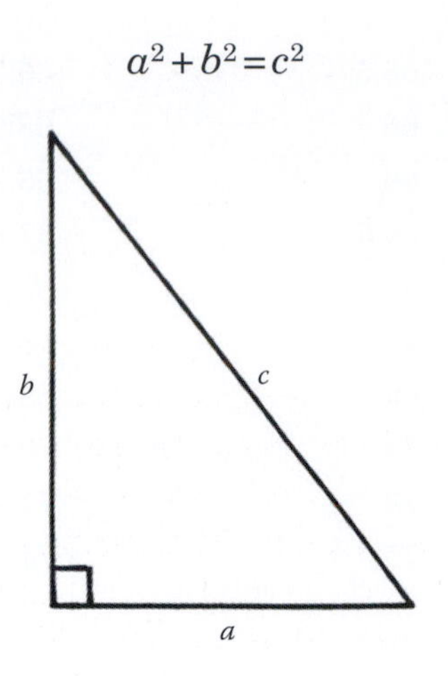

A right triangle.

If you can just remember that c is the hypotenuse and that the hypotenuse is the side opposite the right (90°) angle, you're in great shape! Then, if you know the length of any two of the sides of a right angle, you can calculate the third. For example, if you know the lengths of a and b, then c is calculated as

$$c = \sqrt{a^2 + b^2}$$

In this activity, working with a group of at least 10 students, you will estimate the height of the last person to drive Erica Holmes' vehicle by using the Pythagorean theorem and the following protocol.

Materials:

Instructor's or student's vehicle having a seat height of 11.5 in.
Measuring tape

1. Adjust the driver's seat so that the distance from the heel mark by the gas pedal to the front of the seat is 17.5 in. Measure the height of the driver's seat at its center facing the steering wheel. If it is not 11.5 in., use a blanket or other means to bring the seat to that height.

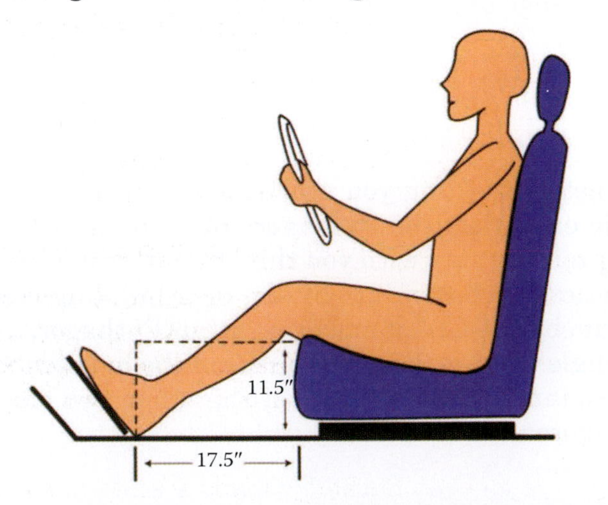

2. Prepare a table in your laboratory notebook having six columns designated student name, height (in feet and inches), height in cm, length of lower leg,

ratio of height to lower leg length, and seat setting (too close, too far, or just right). Your table should have as many rows as you have students in your group participating in the activity. Record each student's name and height in your laboratory notebook. Convert each student's height to a cm measurement using the conversion of 1 in. = 2.54 cm. *Show at least two sample calculations.*

3. Have each student take a turn at sitting in the driver's seat to determine if the seat position is too far, too close, or just right for them to comfortably and safely operate the accelerator without having to make any adjustment from the established 17.5 in.
4. Knowing that the distance from the heel mark to the front of the driver's seat (b) is 17.5 in. and the height of the seat (a) is 11.5 in., calculate *c* (the length of the driver's lower leg). Do this calculation in your laboratory notebook so that the result is recorded.

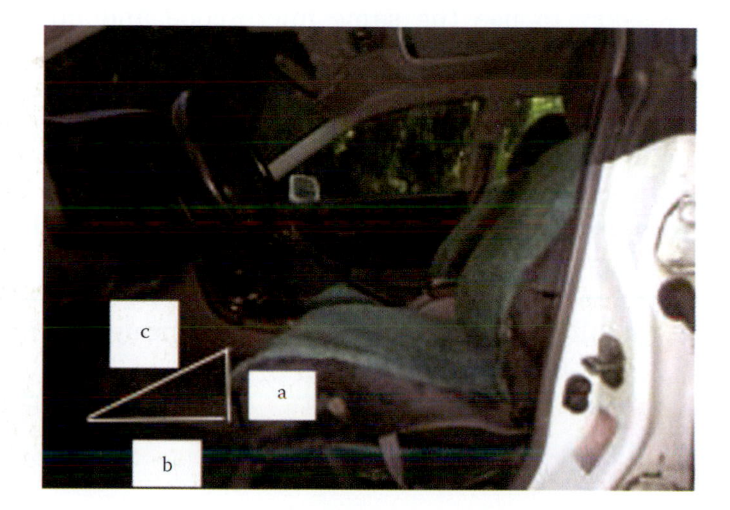

5. Have each student, while sitting with shoes on, measure the distance from their heel to the crease at the back of their knee (the crease formed when in a sitting position). Convert these measurements to cm and enter them into your table.
6. Using the cm values, determine the ratio of the length of the lower leg to overall height for each student in your sample. For example, for someone who is 168 cm (5′6″) tall with a lower leg length measurement of 47 cm (18.5″), the ratio of the length of their lower leg to their height is 47 cm/168 cm = 0.28.
7. Find the average ratio of lower leg length to height for your student sample, and record this value in your laboratory notebook.

8. In step 4, you calculated the lower leg length of the last person to drive Erica Holmes' vehicle. Using the average ratio of lower leg length to height calculated in step 7, determine the height of the last person to operate Erica Holmes car. Report the person's height in both cm and in feet.
9. Prepare an evidence report describing your findings. Consider these when preparing this report. Where could error be introduced in this methodology? What is the range in height of those people who found a seat 17.5 in. away from the accelerator pedal and 11.5 in. high to be a comfortable position? How does this result compare with that generated by using the rectangle method of Activity 3.3?

Review Questions

3.1 What does *trace evidence* refer to?
3.2 What is the medulla?
3.3 How would you go about finding the origin of any foreign object found on your clothing?
3.4 Why is trace evidence important to forensic scientists?
3.5 What is a fiber reference library?
3.6 Based on your observations, how can human hair be distinguished from nonhuman hair?
3.7 How can a synthetic fiber be distinguished from animal hair (human or nonhuman)?
3.8 When comparing a fiber taken in as evidence with your fiber reference library, why is it necessary to use the same microscope and microscope settings between them?
3.9 Cotton falls into which fiber classification (natural, manufactured, or synthetic)?
3.10 Give an example of a synthetic fiber.
3.11 What is the difference between accuracy and precision?
3.12 What does the standard deviation of a statistical analysis tell you?
3.13 What is the Pythagorean theorem?
3.14 What is the term applied to the *c* component of the Pythagorean theorem?
3.15 What are the medullary indexes for Figures 3.6 through 3.8?

Further Reading

Significant Fiber Evidence Recovered from the Clothing of a Homicide Victim After Exposure to the Elements for Twenty-Nine Days by R. Spencer in *Journal of Forensic Sciences*, Vol. 39, No. 3, pages 854–859, 1994.

Collection of Fiber Evidence Using Water-Soluble Cellophane Tape by J. Chable, C. Roux, and C. Lennard in *Journal of Forensic Sciences*, Vol. 39, No. 6, pages 1520–1527, 1994.

Hair and Fiber Transfer in an Abduction Case—Evidence from Different Levels of Trace Evidence Transfer by J.M. Taupin in *Journal of Forensic Sciences*, Vol. 41, No. 4, pages 697–699, 1996.

Gender Identification of Human Hair Using Fluorescence in situ Hybridization by J.A. Prahlow, P.E. Lantz, K. Cox-Jones, P.N. Rao, and M.J. Pettenati in *Journal of Forensic Sciences*, Vol. 41, No. 6, pages 1035–1037, 1996.

Forensic Palynology and the Ruidoso, New Mexico Plane Crash—The Pollen Evidence II by A. Graham in *Journal of Forensic Sciences*, Vol. 42, No. 3, pages 391–393, 1997.

The Retention and Recovery of Transferred Fibers Following the Washing of Recipient Clothing by R. Palmer in *Journal of Forensic Sciences*, Vol. 43, No. 3, pages 502–504, 1998.

Forensic Palynology: Variation in the Pollen Content of Soil on Shoes and in Shoeprints in Soil by M. Horrocks, S.A. Coulson, and K.A.J. Walsh in *Journal of Forensic Sciences*, Vol. 44, No. 1, pages 119–122, 1999.

A New Method for Fiber Comparison Using Polarized Infrared Microspectroscopy by L. Cho, J.A. Reffner, B.M. Gatewood, and D.L. Wetzel in *Journal of Forensic Sciences*, Vol. 44, No. 2, pages 275–282, 1999.

The Contribution of Forensic Geology and Other Trace Evidence Analysis to the Investigation of the Killing of Italian Prime Minister Aldo Moro by G. Lombardi in *Journal of Forensic Sciences*, Vol. 44, No. 3, pages 634–642, 1999.

A Validation Study for the Extraction and Analysis of DNA from Human Nail Material and Its Application to Forensic Casework by T.D. Anderson, J.P. Ross, R.K. Roby, D.A. Lee, and M.M. Holland in *Journal of Forensic Sciences*, Vol. 44, No. 5, pages 1053–1056, 1999.

Fibers Under Fire: Suggestions for Improving Their Use to Provide Forensic Evidence by M.C. Grieve and K.G. Wiggins in *Journal of Forensic Sciences*, Vol. 46, No. 4, pages 835–843, 2001.

Pollen on Grass Clippings: Putting the Suspect at the Scene of the Crime by M. Horrocks and K.A.J. Walsh in *Journal of Forensic Sciences*, Vol. 46, No. 4, pages 947–949, 2001.

DNA Profiling of Trace Evidence—Mitigating Evidence in a Dog Biting Case by P. Brauner, A. Reshef, and A. Gorski in *Journal of Forensic Sciences*, Vol. 46, No. 5, pages 1232–1234, 2001.

Is There a Real Danger of Concealing Gunshot Residue (GSR) Particles by Skin Debris Using the Tape-Lift Method for Sampling GSR from Hands? by A. Zeichner in *Journal of Forensic Sciences*, Vol. 46, No. 6, pages 1447–1455, 2001.

Recovery of DNA for Forensic Analysis from Lip Cosmetics by L.G. Webb, S.E. Egan, and G.R. Turbett in *Journal of Forensic Sciences*, Vol. 46, No. 6, pages 1474–1479, 2001.

Chemical Composition of Fingerprints for Gender Determination by K.G. Asano, C.K. Bayne, K.M. Horsman, and M.V. Buchanan in *Journal of Forensic Sciences*, Vol. 47, No. 4, pages 805–807, 2002.

Improving the Effectiveness of Fluorescence for the Detection of Semen Stains on Fabrics by H.J. Kobus, E. Silenieks, and J. Scharnberg in *Journal of Forensic Sciences*, Vol. 47, No. 4, pages 819–823, 2002.

Sub-Sampling and Preparing Forensic Samples for Pollen Analysis by M. Horrocks in *Journal of Forensic Sciences*, Vol. 49, No. 5, pages 1024–1027, 2004.

A New Method for Collection and Identification of Gunshot Residues from the Hands of Shooters by E.L.T. Reis, J.E. Souza Sarkis, O.N. Neto, C. Rodrigues, M.H. Kakazu, and S. Viebig in *Journal of Forensic Sciences*, Vol. 48, No. 6, pages 1269–1274, 2003.

The Forensic Analysis of Soils and Sediment Taken from the Cast of a Footprint by P.A. Bull, A. Parker, and R.M. Morgan in *Forensic Science International*, Vol. 162, No. 1–3, pages 6–12, 2006.

Towards a "Crime Pollen Calendar"—Pollen Analysis on Corpses throughout One Year by E. Montali, A.M. Mercuri, G.T. Grandi, and C.A. Accorsi in *Forensic Science International*, Vol. 163, No. 3, pages 211–223, 2006.

Hair as a Source of Forensic Evidence in Murder Investigations by P.E.J. Wiltshire in *Forensic Science International*, Vol. 163, No. 3, pages 241–248, 2006.

4
All about Blood

Vehicle Impound Lot, Monday 12:30 PM

"Did you see any bullet holes?" Helen asked.

"No," Jenkins replied, shaking his head slowly in thought.

"Then how did that bullet get in there?"

"I don't know."

Jenkins circled around to the back of the station wagon and, standing underneath the door, craned his neck around to examine the window and frame. "Nothing," he exclaimed.

"Maybe underneath the car," Helen suggested.

"An unusual place for a bullet entry. But it's possible."

"Anything is possible," Helen remarked. "Or maybe someone just picked it up and put it there." Jenkins shot her a sideways glance.

"Helen, put fresh gloves on." Jenkins did the same, then pulled the hood release lever underneath the console, walked to the front of the car, and popped the hood.

"Wow," said Helen. "What year is this car?"

"A 2001."

"My car's brand new and it doesn't look this good."

The engine was spotless. No dust on the battery poles. Not a hint of spilled oil. The fluids were all at their fill lines.

"Someone knows how to take care of a car," Jenkins remarked as he scanned the engine bay.

"Yeah, tight."

"What's this?" Jenkins asked.

"What? Where?"

"On the water reservoir," Jenkins said as he pointed toward the back of the engine bay.

"A drop of oil?" Helen suggested.

"It's red." Jenkins observed, shuffling to the side of the car and peering down.

"Rust then?"

"And there's something here, on this fluid reservoir. Looks like skin maybe or some kind of tissue, I don't know." Jenkins scanned to his right along the firewall. "Bingo! Look here! I think we've found our bullet entry point. Perfect. And there's blood around it."

"What are you talking about?"

"Blood. Here," Jenkins said pointing at tiny red pinpricks on the firewall around the cavity. "We'll need pictures and we've got to collect this stuff."

"What blood? You mean all those tiny dots? That doesn't look like any blood I've ever seen before. What can cause blood to look like that?"

"Trust me, Miss Chang, blood can look like that. But your point is well taken."

"I had a point?"

"We need to test whether or not this is blood."

"Don't we need to be in the lab for that?" Helen asked.

"No," Jenkins replied moving to his case and pulling out a small vial containing narrow strips of paper. "We'll use these."

"What's that?"

"Hemastix. You can get them at any drug store." Jenkins said, shoving them into his coat pocket. "But first, we've gotta document."

Jenkins and Helen placed numbered tents by the evidence positions and took digital photographs of each. Jenkins took a dowel, threaded it through the bullet's path, and photographed its angle of trajectory.

"We're ready for the blood test, Miss Chang. If you wouldn't mind, grab a cotton swab from my case. And that spray bottle of distilled water," Jenkins added.

Helen obliged.

"Spray a small amount of distilled water on it, dab the swab onto a small part of the stain, and then touch the swab to the end of this strip." They both watched the strip as Helen made the swipe. Jenkins heart shifted up a gear.

"You enjoy this, don't you, Lieutenant?"

"We're about to see something no one's ever seen before."

"No one's used Hemastix before?"

"Not for this case."

"So, how does this work?" Helen asked.

"I thought I just showed you," Jenkins responded. "You put some water on a swab, swab the stain, and then swab the Hemastix. If there's blood, it changes color."

"No, I mean the chemistry. It's a color change," Helen mused. "It must be enzymatic. Oxidation–reduction probably. Peroxidase activity of heme must react with some chromogenic compound."

"Yeah, whatever," Jenkins interrupted. "It tests for blood. We need to collect these for DNA."

Helen rolled the bloodstains on wetted swabs and placed them into collection tubes. They then circled around to the back of the vehicle to a position underneath the raised hatchback door.

"This is one helluva stain," said Jenkins, staring down at the large red blemish spread amoeba-like on the cargo bay liner. "We need to swab and photograph in several areas. See that braid pattern at the top of the stain? Make sure you get a good shot of that and swab it for DNA."

Helen went about the tasks as Jenkins kept a watchful eye.

"O.J.," Jenkins exhaled, delicately padding his forehead with a white handkerchief. The sun pelted down on balding real estate cresting the top of this head.

"Are you thirsty too? And I'm starving. Are we breaking for lunch?" Helen asked, exasperated.

"This blood," Jenkins replied, "reminds me of the O.J. Simpson case. That case was all about blood."

"At last a name I recognize. The football player, yeah? The guy's picture keeps turning up on the supermarket tabloids."

"Yes, a Heisman Trophy winner in college, then a star running back for the Buffalo Bills. Rushed over two thousand yards in a single season. He had fame, fortune, and a stunningly beautiful wife, Nicole. But the marriage broke up. O.J. was abusive and had a history of violence toward his ex-wife. It was Nicole's dog, a blood-soaked white Akita, howling in the middle of a summer's night in 1994 that first brought attention to her murder. Neighbors, responding to the canine's incessant barking, found Nicole Brown Simpson's slashed, nearly decapitated body sprawled in a pool of blood at the base of the stairs to her condominium."

"I've heard of this case," Helen remarked. "People still talk about it. There was another victim, a friend of hers, right?"

"Ronald Goldman. A waiter who had gone to Nicole's to return a pair of eyeglasses her mother had left at his restaurant. That act of charity, however, found him in the wrong place at the worst possible time. The LAPD discovered his body nearby when they arrived at the scene around midnight. Officers recovered a knitted watch cap and a bloody, left-hand glove near the bodies. Bloody shoe prints on the cement walkway led away from the victims toward the back gate. There was blood everywhere. DNA testing was to reveal who it all belonged to."

"So what happened? It's hard to argue with DNA, isn't it? How did it go south, 'cause he was acquitted, wasn't he?" Helen asked.

"Good question. The bloody shoe prints at the scene were Simpson's size—twelve. The unique sole pattern matched those made by Bruno Magli—Italian designer shoes. Shoes Simpson denied owning. A number of photographs surfaced later, however, showing him wearing that very type of shoe. Right alongside the bloody shoe prints on the walkway leading away from the murder scene were drops of blood. The murderer had apparently cut his left hand during the attack. By DNA, that blood on the sidewalk and blood found on the back gate matched Simpson's. Upon his arrest, a cut was found on O.J.'s left hand—a cut he claimed he acquired from a broken glass."

"And the jury bought that?"

"There's more. A right-hand glove, the complement to the one from the crime scene, was found on the grounds of Simpson's estate in Brentwood. Nicole, it came out in the trial, had given O.J. that type of glove as a gift several years earlier. The glove was smeared with blood from O.J., Nicole, and Mr. Goldman. The blood of all three was also found in his car. Hair in the watch cap found at the murder scene was consistent with Simpson's. Nicole's blood was on a pair of his socks found in his bedroom. Drops of blood lead from his car to his front door. And a limo driver, who was scheduled to take him to the airport, couldn't get Simpson to answer the front door when he arrived late that evening to pick him up. However, a bit later, the driver did see a dark figure matching O.J.'s description hurriedly enter the estate grounds from the side of the property and slip into the house at a time consistent with the murder timeline."

"A preponderance of evidence. Isn't that what you call it? So what happened? I don't get it. How did the jury find him not guilty?"

"A lot of things came into play. You couldn't know, but there were serious race problems at the time. Problems exploited by Simpson's defense team. Just a few years earlier, the LAPD had been caught on video brutally beating a black man over what was perceived as a routine traffic stop. LA's race riots of the 1970s were still in the collective memory. And O.J. Simpson was a sports hero and a celebrity. But, beyond that, the defense lawyers were able to expose one of the crime scene detectives, Mark Fuhrman, as a racist. They showed he had used racial epithets when referring to blacks. Unfortunately for the prosecution, it was Mark Fuhrman who found the right-hand glove on Simpson's estate. The defense argued, therefore, given Fuhrman's bent, that he could have planted that damning piece of evidence. And then there was the missing blood."

"Missing blood?"

"When O.J. was first questioned by the police, a nurse withdrew a vial of blood, which was taken into custody by Detective Philip Vannatter. He carried that blood vial back to the crime scene at Nicole's condo where it was finally booked into evidence. However, according to a calculation performed by the defense during the trial, taking into account the number of samples that had been withdrawn for DNA testing, they argued that some of its volume was missing. Not even considering the possibility of an innocent explanation…"

"Like whether or not the initial sample was accurately withdrawn, measured, and recorded and how carefully subsequent samples were withdrawn and accurately recorded?" Helen asked.

"For example. Yes. They implied the LAPD moved to a dark purpose—that members of the police force had sprinkled drops of O.J.'s blood at various incriminating locations around the crime scenes in an effort to frame Simpson for the murders. And then one of their expert witnesses claimed to have found traces of EDTA…"

"Ethylenediaminetetraacetic acid. A chelating agent and blood preservative," Helen interjected.

"Yes, Miss Chang. Their expert claimed to have found traces of EDTA in some of the blood evidence. That certainly bolstered the spirits of the conspiracy theorists."

"Yeah, but the presence of a chelating agent in blood evidence doesn't necessarily mean anything sinister, does it? Chelating agents are found in a lot of things. Laundry detergent, for example."

"A fact the defense team failed to mention," Jenkins added. "Subsequently, however, an expert from the FBI could find no trace of EDTA in the blood evidence. Dueling experts. Still, the attorneys for the defense went on to point out several evidence collection mistakes by the LAPD crime lab—failure to wear or change gloves during evidence handling, for example."

"So that's why you're so uptight about it," Helen said.

"Yeah, O.J. is probably the reason," Jenkins replied. "The O.J. Simpson case had a lasting effect on evidence collection procedures. Simpson's attorneys labeled the LAPD crime lab a 'cesspool of contamination.' That stuck in the minds of the jurors."

"Was there contamination of the evidence?" Helen asked. "That's easy to determine in DNA typing. Did the negative controls give a positive result?"

"No. But that didn't seem to matter. All evidence to the contrary, the accusation had been made and that seemed to be enough to cast doubt. And then there was Dr. Henry Lee, the famous forensic scientist hired on as part of Simpson's 'Dream Team.' After examining some of the blood evidence, he noted that a blood specimen wasn't as dry as he thought it should have been. I can still hear him saying it—'something's wrong,' he said. Something's wrong. What the jury didn't understand was that there was something wrong with his testimony. He said there was another bloody shoe imprint on the walkway by the bodies and so there must have been another assailant—undermining the prosecution's whole case that O.J. acted alone. It somehow didn't sink in with the jury in an argument by the prosecution that that imprint was a permanent cast in the cement made by one of the workers who laid down the walkway years earlier. Something's wrong. Those words just stuck in their minds. A predominantly black jury bought the conspiracy theory—a racist, inept, and bungling, white police force trying to frame an African-American hero. He was found not guilty."

"Justice and truth aren't necessarily the same thing, are they Lieutenant Jenkins?"

"O.J. had the best justice money could buy. At least in the subsequent civil trial brought to court by Nicole's and Ron Goldman's parents, the jury was unanimous in finding Simpson responsible for the murders. But let's get back to the task at hand. This looks like blood. But is it blood? Let's test it."

"There's something else I have to know," Helen said.

"What's that?" Jenkins asked.

"Well, there's a lot of blood here."

"If it's blood," Jenkins added.

"Yeah. Okay. If it's blood. And if it is blood, could we tell if the person to whom it belonged was either alive or dead while they were back here. I mean, you can only lose so much blood. Too much, you're dead, right?"

"You're quite right, Miss Chang. Here are some numbers. The typical human body carries 70 milliliters of blood per kilogram of body weight. Lose thirty percent of that, you'd find yourself in the morgue."

"I'll see if I can put that together," Helen said.

"And while you're doing that, I'm going to do some homework of my own," Jenkins said. "We need to start talking to some people."

"Is there a cafeteria in the building or a health food store nearby where I can get a salad?" Helen asked.

"No cafeteria. There's a coffee machine in the break room and a vending machine where you can get some chips. A health food store? I wouldn't know. You'll get back to me on that calculation soon?"

"I'll get right on it."

Blood Evidence

Saliva is sprayed, hair is yanked from its roots, skin is scraped off, and flesh is torn. Violent crime inevitably leaves a number of different types of biological materials behind as witness to the attack. With the possible exception of semen in the case of sexual assault, no type of biological fluid or tissue is consistently more revealing about the victim, the attacker, and the circumstances of the assault than blood. Blood can yield DNA that identifies the crime's participants. Its splash patterns can reveal the site and mode of the attack. Blood can make an attacker's fingerprints or shoeprints readily visible.

Presumptive Test for Blood

We can all recognize a bloodstain. If it's fresh, it's red. Older bloodstains are a reddish brown. But not all stains having the color of blood *are* blood. A number of liquids such as paint, rusty water, food coloring, salsa, and catsup can give the appearance of blood. Upon finding a suspicious-looking stain at a crime scene, a forensic scientist will need to make a determination as to whether or not it is really blood. This is done by performing a *presumptive test*, so called because, if the test is positive, the investigator can presume the stain is actually blood.

Most presumptive tests for blood show a positive result by changing color when exposed to *hemoglobin*, the iron-containing protein in red blood cells responsible for carrying oxygen from the lungs to the rest of the body. Unfortunately, some plants, such as horseradish and potatoes, contain enzymes that can also induce a color change during a presumptive test for blood. If these should be present at a crime scene, they could lead to a false-positive result. Nevertheless, these occasions are rare and the presumptive tests used by forensic scientists are reliable enough to have value. They almost all rely on a chemical process called *oxidation–reduction*.

Chemistry of Oxidation–Reduction Reactions

An *oxidized molecule* is one that combines with oxygen by a chemical reaction. So, oxidation can be considered as a reaction between an element or compound and an oxygen molecule. That's easy enough to remember. But when we're talking about the chemical process of oxidation–reduction, we're not necessarily referring to a reaction with oxygen. Not all oxidation–reduction reactions involve oxygen. To get a handle on oxidation, let's first get a grip on its counterpart, reduction.

From physics, recall that an atom is made up of charged particles called *protons* and *electrons* (neutrons, neutral particles also found in an atom, need not be part of this discussion). Protons are found in the nucleus of the atom and are positively charged. Electrons are found swirling around the atom's nucleus and carry a negative charge. A molecule is *reduced* if it has electrons to spare. More electrons means more negative charges. More negative charges means it's lessened or reduced. In an oxidation–reduction reaction, a reduced molecule (with electrons it can shed) becomes *oxidized* (loses electrons), and an oxidized molecule (one that can take on electrons) becomes reduced (gains electrons). Oxidation is the loss of electrons. Reduction is the gain of electrons.

Hemastix®

Hemastix, manufactured by Bayer Diagnostic, are narrow strips of plastic carrying a piece of filter paper attached to one end (Figure 4.1). The filters are treated with hydrogen peroxide and with a chromogenic reagent called TMB (3,3′,5,5′-tetramethylbenzidine). When exposed to hemoglobin, the filter changes from yellow to green.

Hemastix detects blood by an oxidation–reduction reaction. *Heme*, the major component of hemoglobin, has an activity characteristic of a class of enzymes known as *peroxidases*. A peroxidase reduces hydrogen peroxide (H_2O_2) to water (H_2O) while, in the process, oxidizing the molecule in the oxidation–reduction reaction that served as the electron donor. In the Hemastix reaction, the peroxidase activity of heme reduces hydrogen peroxide to water and changes TMB to its oxidized form, inducing it to change color from yellow to dark green (Figure 4.2). The test can detect as little as five red blood cells in a microliter of blood.

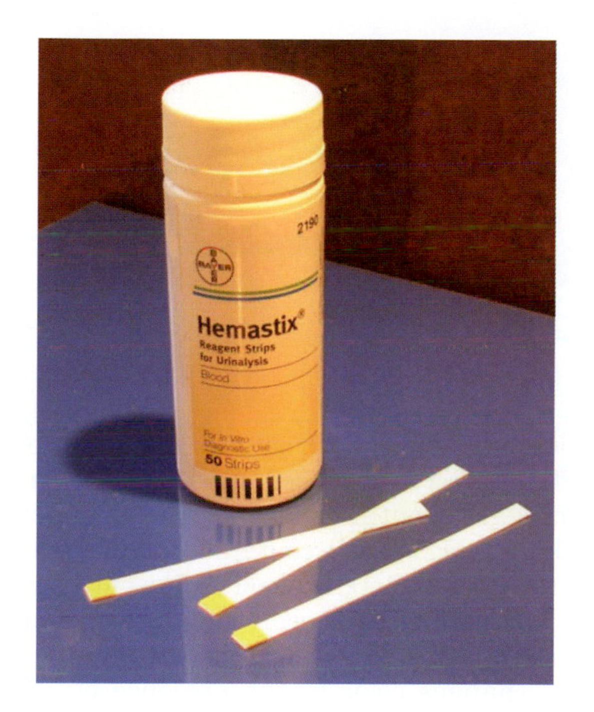

Figure 4.1 Hemastix strips.

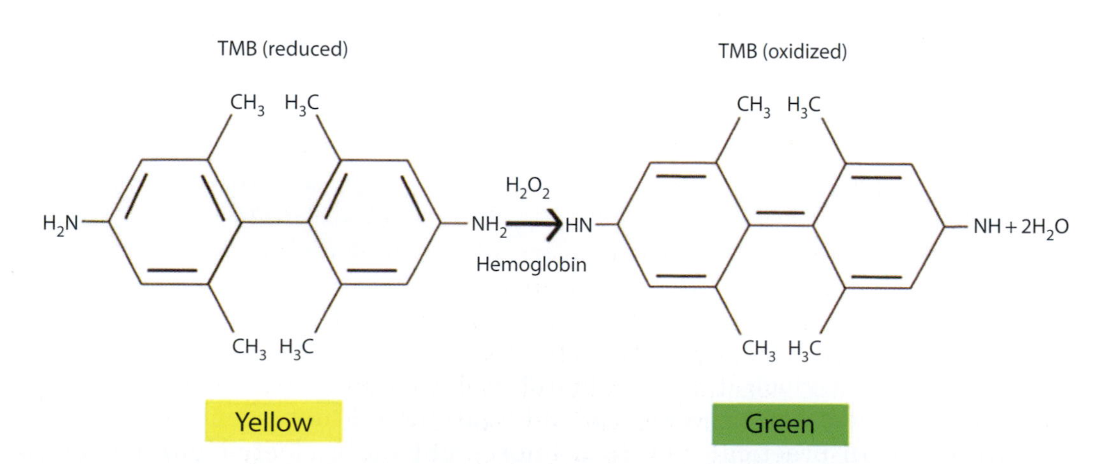

Figure 4.2 The oxidation–reduction reaction that leads to the TMB color change.

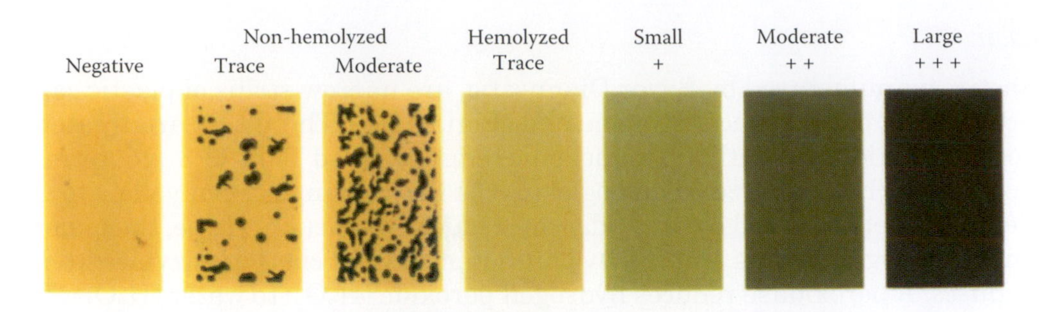

Figure 4.3 The Hemastix color scale. Hemolyzed blood refers to red blood cells that have been broken open. Nonhemolyzed blood refers to blood in which the red blood cells remain intact.

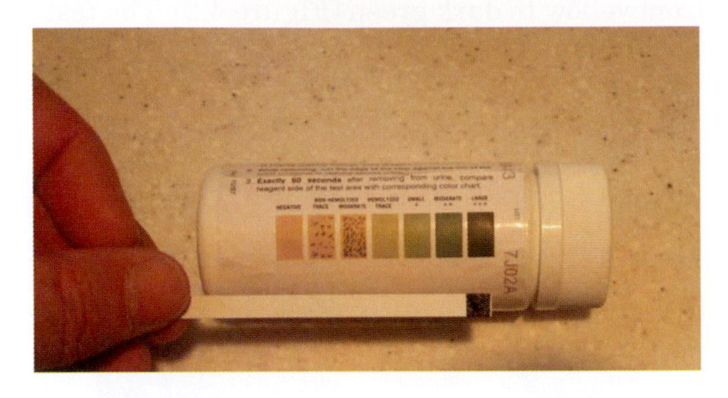

Figure 4.4 A Hemastix strip is held alongside the color scale to determine the relative amount of blood in a sample.

To test for the presence of blood, a drop of water is placed on the filter pad at the end of the strip. The strip is then placed into contact with the stain. If the stick turns from yellow to dark green within a few seconds, the stain could contain blood. A color scale on the side of the Hemastix container indicates the amount of hemoglobin in the stain (Figures 4.3 and 4.4). If blood is present, a color photograph of the reacted strip placed alongside the color scale should be taken and the strip placed into evidence.

Although Hemastix changes color in the presence of blood, other substances that have peroxidase activity like that of hemoglobin can also cause a color change. Contaminating bacteria, for example, produce peroxidases. As previously mentioned, peroxidase activity is also found associated with potatoes and horseradish. Chemicals such as hypochlorite having oxidizing activity will likewise cause false-positive results.

Luminol and Bluestar®

Everyone is familiar with the electric light bulb that passes an electric current through a thin metallic filament, thereby heating it to such a high temperature that light is emitted. Such bulbs are found in flashlights, automobile headlights, and throughout the office, schoolroom, and household. Fluorescent lights are also commonly found in practical use. In a fluorescent bulb, electric current excites a gas such as argon or neon, thereby leading to the production of visible light.

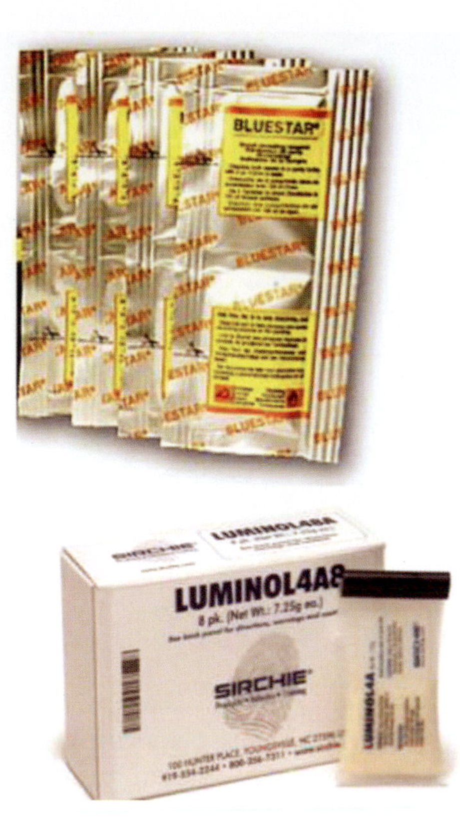

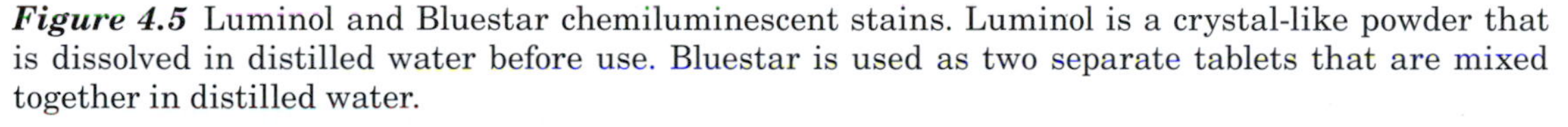

Figure 4.5 Luminol and Bluestar chemiluminescent stains. Luminol is a crystal-like powder that is dissolved in distilled water before use. Bluestar is used as two separate tablets that are mixed together in distilled water.

But some chemical reactions can also generate light. This is known as *chemiluminescence* and neither requires electricity nor generates heat. One of the best-known chemiluminescent reactions is that generated by the interaction of luminol with blood.

Luminol is a yellowish crystal (Figure 4.5). When dissolved in water and sprayed as a fine mist on a drop of blood, it glows an eerie bluish green. Luminol reagent is actually a mixture of three different chemicals, luminol powder, hydrogen peroxide (H_2O_2), and a hydroxide salt. Iron within the hemoglobin molecule of blood acts as a catalyst driving a chemical oxidation–reduction reaction between hydrogen peroxide and the luminol compound. Luminol is a reduced molecule. However, when it reacts with hemoglobin, it loses atoms of nitrogen and hydrogen and gains oxygen atoms becoming, in the process, a new, energized, and oxidized compound called 3-aminophthalate that quickly releases excess energy in the form of photons (visible light). The luminol reaction is fairly short-lived, however, and any glowing surfaces must be photographed quickly before all the reaction energy is lost and the bloodstain turns dark again. Luminol can reveal bloodstains that are months old and on surfaces that someone may have even tried desperately to clean.

Although luminol is a powerful tool for locating blood evidence, it is not without its drawbacks. Luminol reacts not only with blood but also with copper, urine, fecal matter, horseradish, and some bleaches leading to false-positive results. A savvy murderer could, in theory, wash down an entire crime scene with bleach and thereby camouflage any blood spatter. Because luminol's glow is most evident in complete

Figure 4.6 A black and white photograph of a bloody shoe print illuminated with Bluestar® forensic chemiluminescent stain.

darkness, a criminalist, if testing for the presence of blood in an outdoor location, may have to wait well into the night before they can perform the test. In addition, the glow given off by luminol is brief (only several minutes at most), it is difficult to get it to work properly, and it is potentially carcinogenic (can promote the development of cancer cells) and so must be handled cautiously.

A chemiluminescent compound known as Bluestar is similar to luminol but glows in the presence of blood (fresh or dried) for a longer period of time. It works by an oxidation–reduction reaction. In the presence of hydrogen peroxide, blood sprayed with Bluestar generates a bright blue chemiluminescent glow easily visible in the dark (Figure 4.6).

Is It Human Blood?

The reason a person can't have a kidney, a heart, a liver, or any other failed organ replaced by one from a goat, a cow, or a pig is because of molecules called *antigens* that coat the outside of all animal tissues. Humans have their own set of antigens as do mice, and elephants, and all other mammals. Molecules called *antibodies* bind antigens as part of their role in providing protection against invading microbes. If a goat liver is placed into a human recipient, the person's antibodies attack the antigen-covered foreign tissue causing its rejection. A human can only get a transplant organ from another human and maybe not even then. Individual humans have their own individual antigens. Many people, however, share similar antigens (they are said to be *compatible*), and those who do can safely exchange organs with limited fear of organ rejection.

Because humans have human antigens, human blood will react with antibodies taken from a different animal. This reactivity between human blood and nonhuman antibodies forms the basis for a simple test used to determine the source of a blood sample. A small amount of blood recovered from a crime scene is mixed with antibodies from a rabbit or, more recently, with antibodies made in a laboratory.

If the antigens from the blood react with the foreign antibodies, small clumps form and drop out of the mixture. Clumping signifies blood having a human origin.

Blood Type

Antigens are also critically important when transfusing blood into a patient recently injured or undergoing surgery. Blood cells carry two major antigens called A and B. Antibodies raised against those two antigens distinguish the different *blood types*: A, B, AB, and O. For example, if an antibody against the A blood antigen causes blood cells to clump, then the blood sample could be type A or type AB. If the blood also reacts with antibodies against B antibodies (anti-B), the sample must be type AB. If a blood sample only reacts with anti-A, it is type A. If the blood sample reacts only with anti-B antibodies, it is type B. If it doesn't react with anti-A or anti-B antibodies, it is type O.

Throughout much of the twentieth century, typing blood evidence was a standard forensic practice. However, because a person's blood type is not very informative (lots of other people will have the same type), almost all forensic laboratories now go straight to the newer methodology of DNA typing—a far more definitive test.

As we shall see in the next chapter, a protocol that can tell us how much DNA we've recovered from a blood sample can also tell us if it was spilled from a branch of the human family tree.

Blood Spatter

Drops of blood on the floor, speckles of blood on the walls, splashed blood on the ceiling, they all tell a story of assault or homicide. Where was the initial attack? Was it with a knife or a gun? If by a knife, how many strokes slashed the victim? Was the attacker left-handed or right-handed? Was the attacker over 6 ft tall or far shorter? Blood patterns can say a lot of things about a crime. The following photographs (Figures 4.7 through 4.15) show different types of blood spatter and the types of stories they might say about a crime.

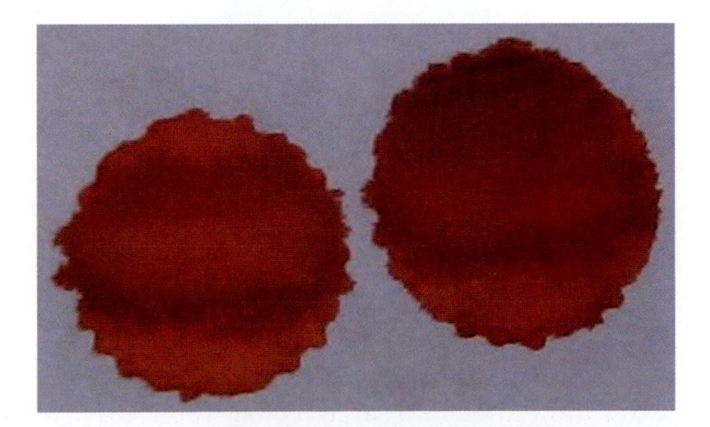

Figure 4.7 Large circular blood drops on a floor or countertop indicate their source was from a stationary object, a short distance straight above. Blood dripping from a fingertip, for example, would create this kind of stain.

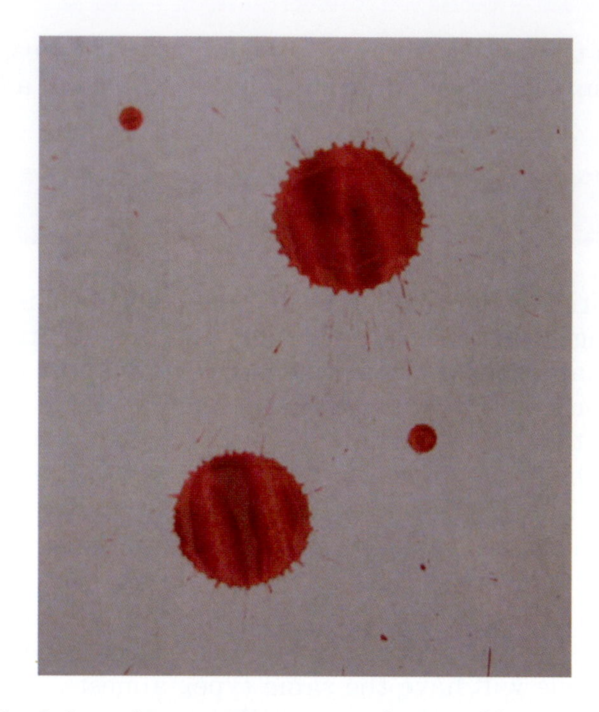

Figure 4.8 Circular blood drops (greater than or equal to roughly 4 mm in diameter) with thin spikes and fine droplets radiating outward indicate the blood dropped from a high distance straight above as might occur if drops of blood fell from a second-story balcony onto the floor or pavement below. These are examples of low-velocity blood spatter.

Figure 4.9 Blood drops running down in one direction result when blood flows at an angle such as might occur if it falls on a slanting surface or if a horizontal surface carrying fresh blood drops is moved to another location and if that surface is tilted when it is moved.

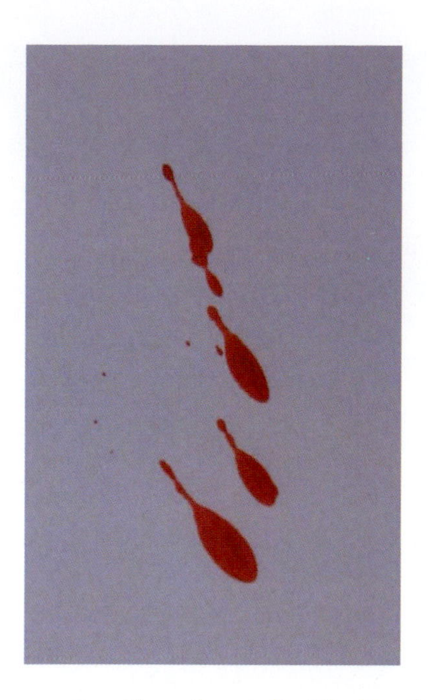

Figure 4.10 Blood splashed at an angle will produce tails. The blood spots point in the direction they were traveling. In this case, the blood was being sprayed toward the upper-left corner of the image. The more narrow and elongated the stain, the sharper the angle the blood was deposited.

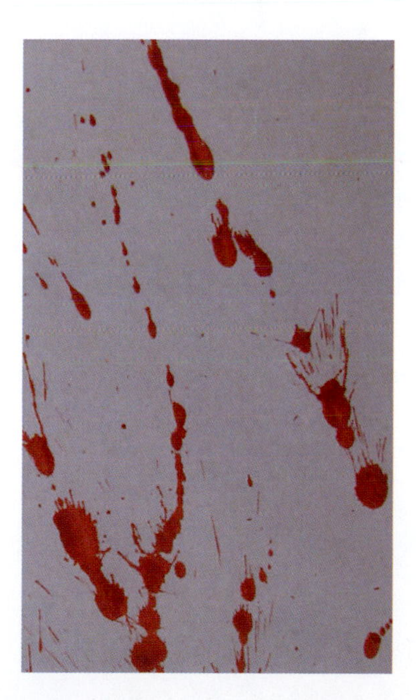

Figure 4.11 Cast-off spatter occurs when blood is flung as from a knife or blunt instrument such as a baseball bat or fireplace poker. The handedness of the assailant can be deduced from the curved track of the blood spots—does the track curve to the left or to the right? A knife leaves a narrower trail of blood than a baseball bat or tire iron. The number of blood trails and the amount of blood can indicate the ferocity of the attack. The more extreme the amount of blood, the more passion and emotion the assailant felt toward the victim. Repeated bludgeoning with a blunt weapon can cause a trail of blood such as this along a wall or ceiling. The first strike would not produce a blood spatter as this would be the strike that opens the wound. After a couple of seconds, blood would collect at the injury and a second blow would fling that accumulated blood from the weapon onto a wall or ceiling. Counting the separate paths of blood can tell an investigator how many additional blows fell onto the victim. Smaller blood drops between 1 and 4 mm in diameter represent medium-velocity blood spatter.

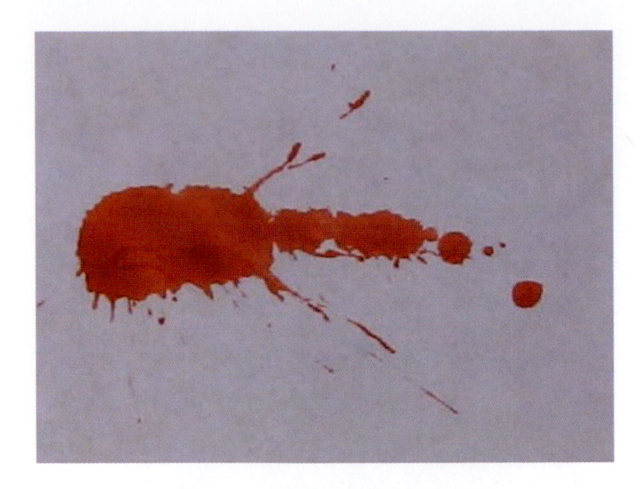

Figure 4.12 A spurt of blood can occur from a flung weapon or when blood bursts from a cut artery.

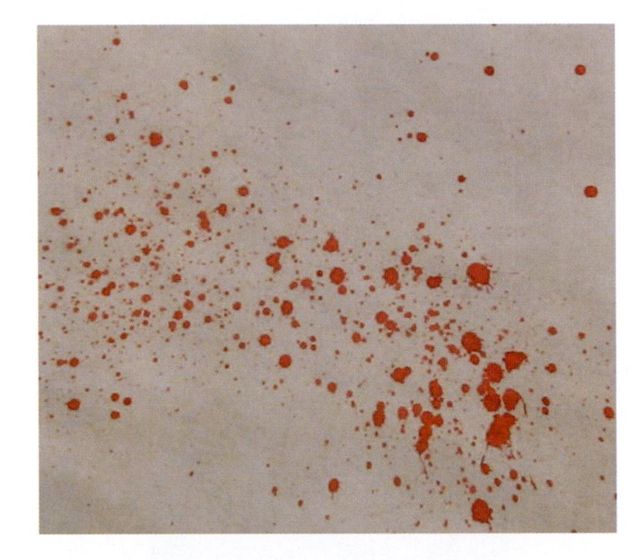

Figure 4.13 Multiple fine specks of blood occur when blood is sprayed at high velocity. Blood spots from high velocity are typically less than or equal to 1 mm in diameter.

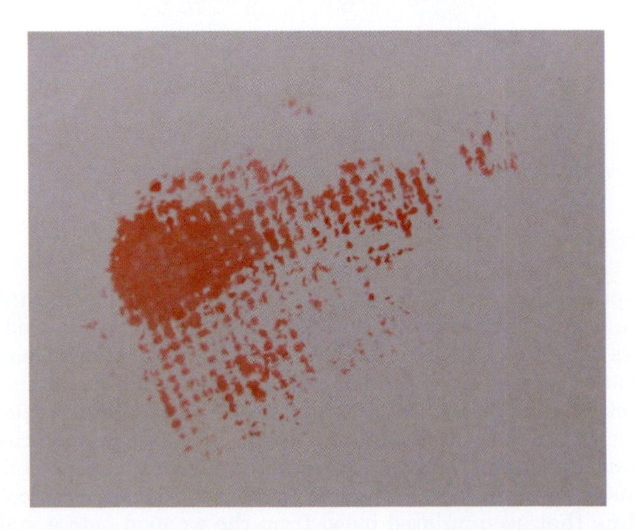

Figure 4.14 A transfer stain is formed when a blood-soaked fabric or article of clothing comes into contact with another surface.

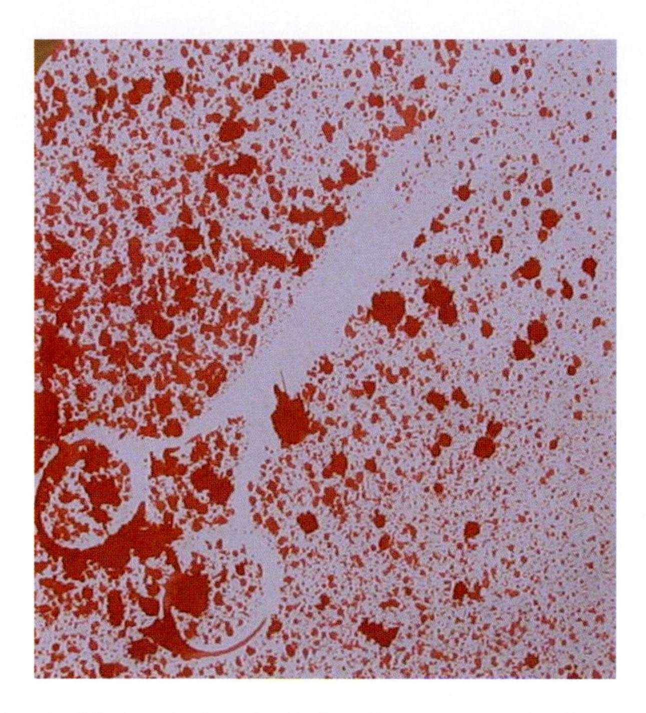

Figure 4.15 Shadowing (void) by a high-velocity blood spatter reveals that an object had been positioned between the victim and the surface on which the victim's blood was sprayed. To an investigator, it can reveal that an object may have been removed from the crime scene.

In the Crime Lab

Activity 4.1 Testing for the Presence of Blood with Hemastix

Is the stain at a crime scene paint, catsup, rust, blood, or something else entirely? A simple way to determine whether or not a stain contains blood is by using Hemastix manufactured by the Bayer corporation. Hemastix was developed as a means to test for the presence of blood in urine as might occur if the urinary tract is infected or diseased. In this activity, you will use Hemastix to determine if samples provided by your instructor contain blood.

Materials:

Hemastix strips (four per group)
Sterile water (if not available, use tap water)
Eyedropper
Bloodstains provided by your instructor
Lab glasses and latex gloves

Protocol:

Always wear safety glasses and protective gloves when handling blood products. Perform the following steps:

1. Your instructor will provide you with a sample of a bloodstain. Place a drop of sterile water onto the yellow patch of the Hemastix strip. Place this premoistened patch face down on an unstained area close to (but not within) the stain.

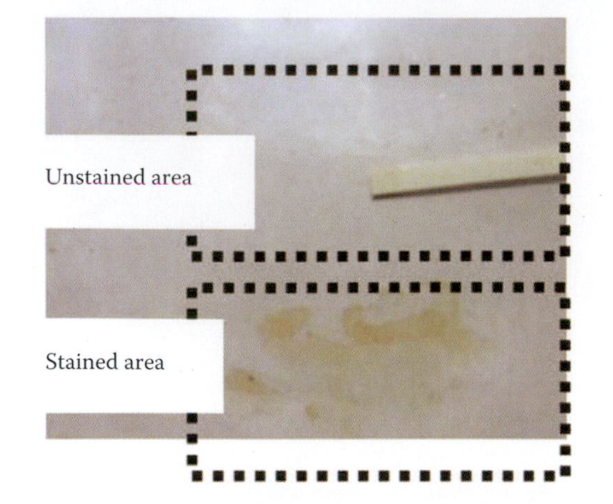

2. Turn the Hemastix strip right side up.

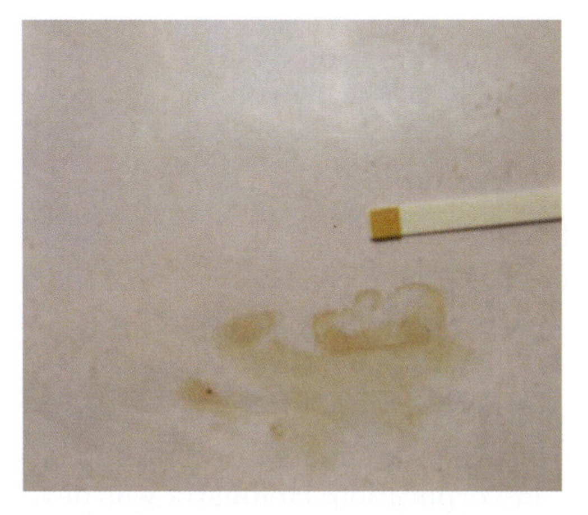

3. Compare the color of the Hemastix test pad on the end of the strip with the color guide on the side of the Hemastix container. Be sure to include both the qualitative and quantitative results. Record this information in your lab notebook.

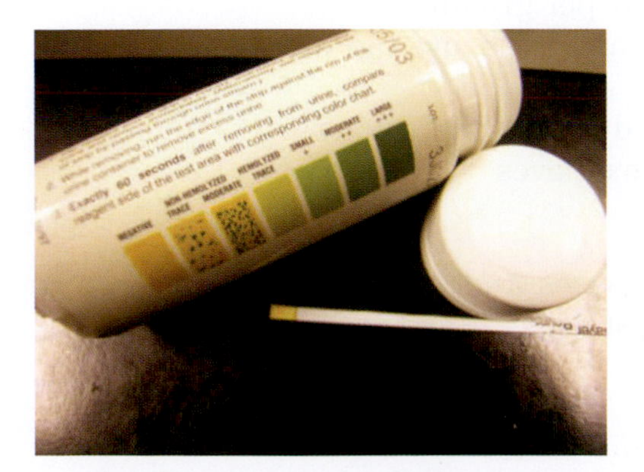

If a negative result is observed (no reaction—the test pad remains yellow for at least 30 s), proceed to the next step. If there is a positive reaction (the strip turns green or blue), repeat the step with a new Hemastix strip testing an area a little further from the stain. Repeat this test on an unstained area until a negative result is obtained. You may then proceed to the next step.

4. With a new, premoistened Hemastix strip, repeat the testing procedure directly within the stain.

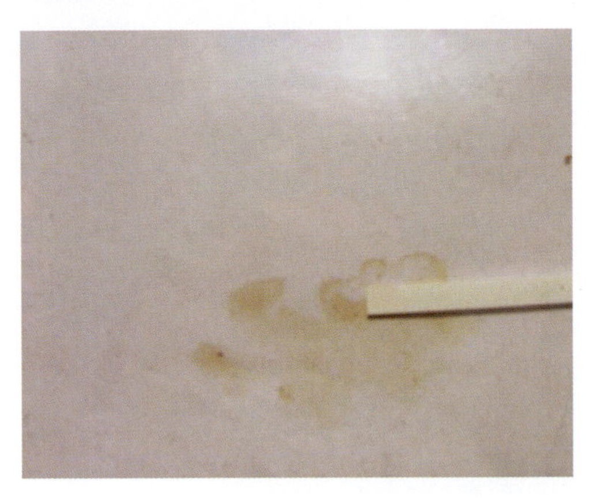

5. Turn the Hemastix right side up and note the color of the strip's test pad. Record this information in your lab notebook. Include both qualitative and quantitative results. Address these questions: (1) For a positive test, how long does it take for the color to change? (2) How long does it take for a negative control to look as if it is a positive test?

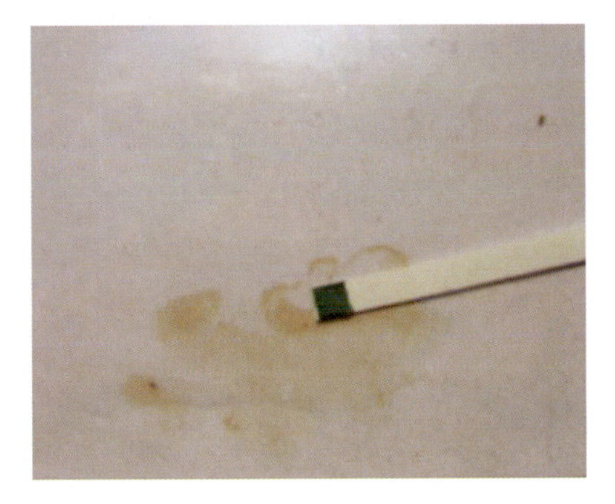

Activity 4.2 Relating Blood Drop Diameter to Drop Distance

Here, you will determine the relationship between the diameter of a blood drop and the distance from which it fell.

Materials:

Dropper bottle filled with food coloring solution (simulated blood)
Butcher paper or cardboard
Measuring tape
Caliper or ruler
Lab coat, gloves, and goggles

Protocol:

1. Cover yourself with a gown, gloves, and goggles.
2. Place a clean piece of butcher paper on the floor. Position the dropper bottle 1 ft (30.5 cm) from the floor and dispense one drop of simulated blood onto the butcher paper.
3. After the blood drop has been deposited onto the paper, make a note of its drop distance.

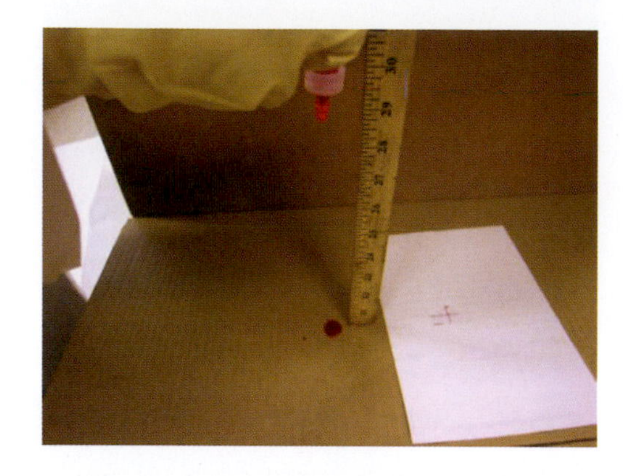

4. Repeat this process two more times from a height of 1 ft (30.5 cm).
5. Using calipers or a ruler, measure the diameter of each blood drop and record this measurement next to the stain.

Note: As the height from which the drop is made increases, the blood drop margins will form a "starburst" pattern. To obtain the true diameter, measure just inside the margin of the starburst pattern.

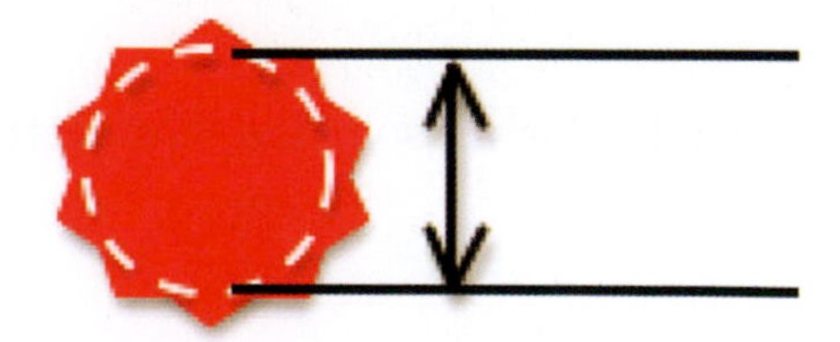

6. Using a fresh piece of paper, increase the distance to 2 ft (61 cm) and make three trial drops at this new height.
7. Repeat at distances of 4 ft (122 cm), 6 ft (183 cm), and 9 ft (274 cm), making three trial drops at each height.
8. Record your data as a table in your laboratory notebook. Within that table, record an average diameter for the three blood drops made from each height increment.
9. Create another table in your laboratory notebook in which you collect the averages calculated by your classmates for each set of measurements.
10. In your laboratory notebook, graph the class average blood drop diameter versus drop height.

Activity 4.3 Characterizing Blood Dropped on an Angled Surface

In this experiment, you will study the elliptical nature of the stains produced by drops of blood falling onto nonhorizontal surfaces and compare these to drops of blood deposited on a horizontal surface.

Materials:

Food coloring (simulated blood)
Cardboard or clipboard with paper or cardboard attached.
Protractor
Eyedropper
Tape measure
Caliper or ruler

Protocol:

1. Attach a sheet of white paper to a clipboard or to a flat piece of cardboard. Using a protractor, slant the papered surface against the top of a table or lab bench making sure that the vertex of the two flat surfaces is aligned with the vertex on the protractor. Your instructor will give you directions as to which angles should be measured.

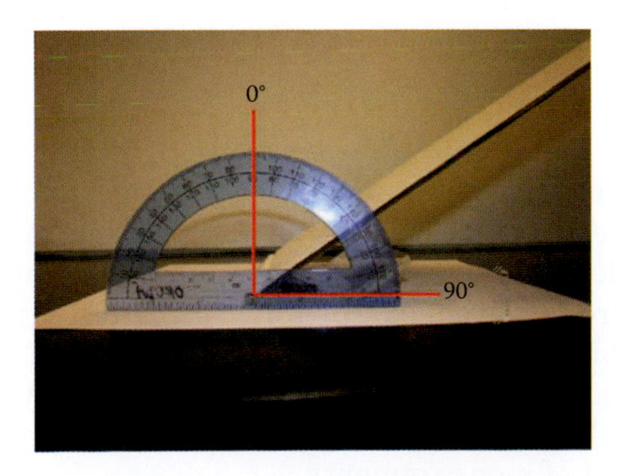

2. Holding an eyedropper containing simulated blood at a height of 30 cm above the slanted, papered surface, dispense one drop of liquid.

3. Reload the eyedropper and repeat this process for two more trials.
4. Note the *width* (its widest point) and *length* of each bloodstain for all three trials and record this information in your laboratory notebook.

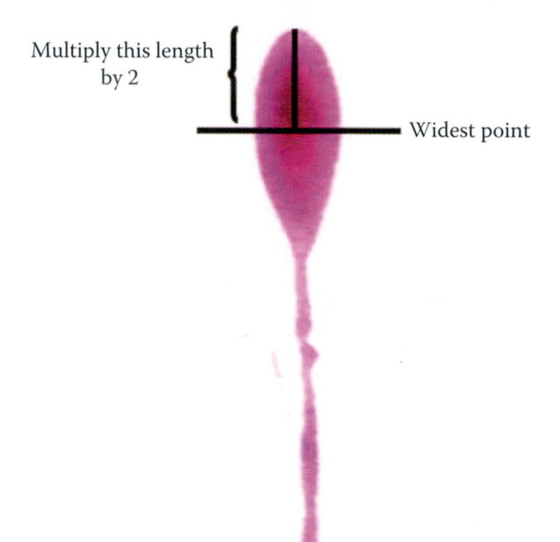

Note: As the angle decreases (becomes steeper), the shape of the blood droplet will become more elongated. To measure its true length, draw a line perpendicular to the widest point and measure the length from the perpendicular line to the blood drop's top edge. Multiply this distance by 2. This represents the length of the blood droplet.

5. Record the data in the form of a table in your laboratory notebook. Calculate the width/length (W/L) ratio for each measurement and then calculate the average for each set of measurements.
6. Prepare another table to tabulate the averages calculated from other groups in the class.
7. Graph the average W/L ratio calculated from the class data versus the angle of the surface for each set of measurements.
8. Make a comment in your notebook about the relationship between the W/L ratio and the angle at which the blood was dropped.

Activity 4.4 Characterizing Blood Dropped from a Moving Source

In this activity, you will determine the nature of blood spatter when liquid is dropped from a moving object.

Materials:

- Chemistry burette filled with food coloring (simulated blood)
- Butcher paper (about 15 ft long) or sheets of scratch paper taped together to span the length of approximately 15 ft
- Tape measure
- Stopwatch
- Calculator
- Ruler or caliper

Protocol:

You will perform this activity teamed with at least one other classmate. One person will pace the floor along the length of the butcher paper while dropping simulated blood. The other person will time the event.

Note: Food coloring can stain clothing. Wear a lab coat or use food coloring that's been diluted with water to minimize clothing damage.

1. Fill a chemistry burette with water or diluted food coloring.

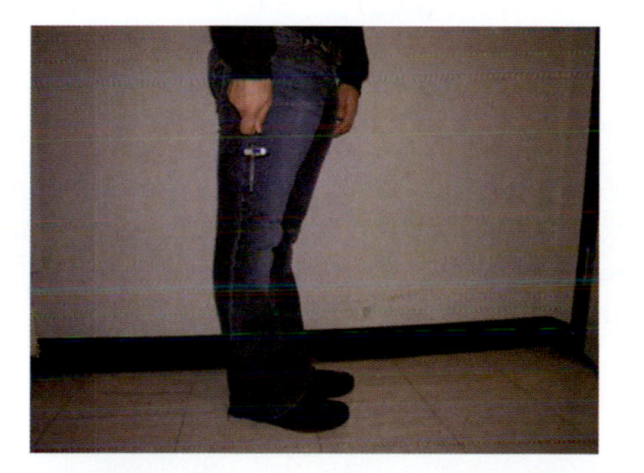

2. Measure out 15 ft of butcher paper along the floor.
3. Hold the burette at your side pointing down at the butcher paper. Measure the distance from the spigot end of the burette to the ground and record this information in your laboratory notebook.
4. Position yourself at the zero mark at one end of the 15 ft strip of paper.

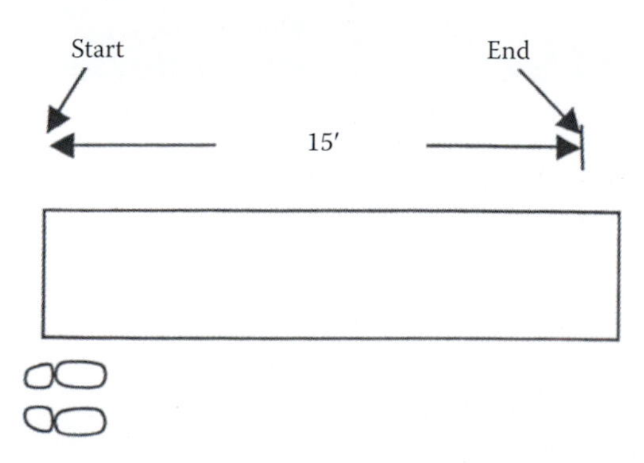

5. Designate a person in your group to keep time with a stopwatch. This person will tell you when to start walking alongside the butcher paper as you drop simulated blood.
6. Adjust the valve on the burette so that the drip rate is about one drop per second.
7. Once you have been given the "Go!" from the designated timer, walk at a slow pace while dripping the burette liquid over the distance of the butcher paper. Do not swing the burette; keep it at a 90° angle to the floor.

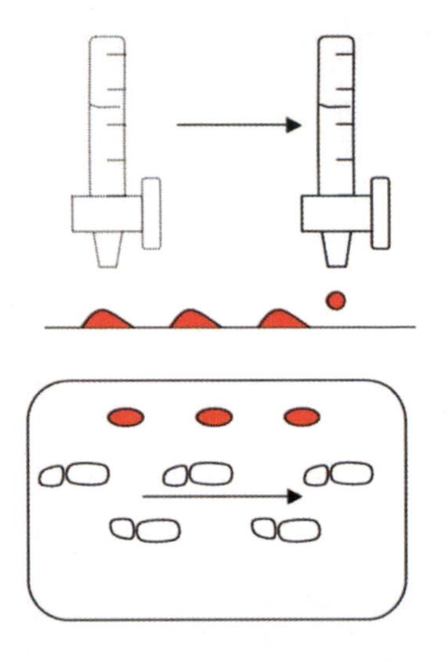

8. In your laboratory notebook, record the time it took to walk the 15 ft beside the butcher paper. Mark each drop on the butcher paper as *slow walk*.
9. Repeat this process but change the pace to a fast walk. Mark the drops made on the butcher paper during this pass as *fast walk*.

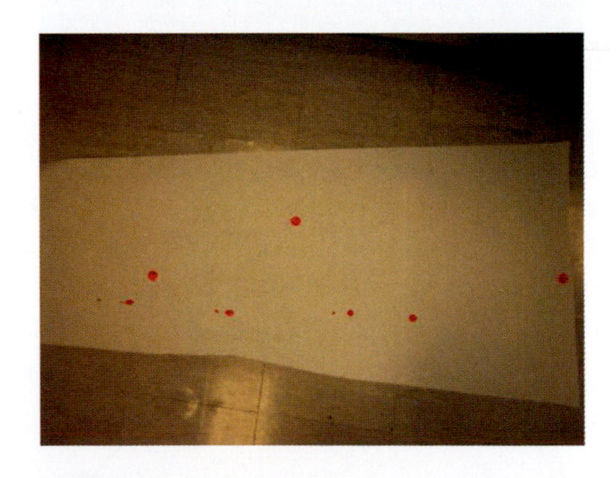

In your laboratory notebook, record the time it took to walk from one end of the paper to the other.

10. Repeat the procedure at a running pace. Be sure the blood drop height, drip rate, and distance are the same in all situations. Mark the drops made on the butcher paper during this pass as *running*.
11. Calculate the speed of the moving blood source for each trail and record these values in your laboratory notebook.

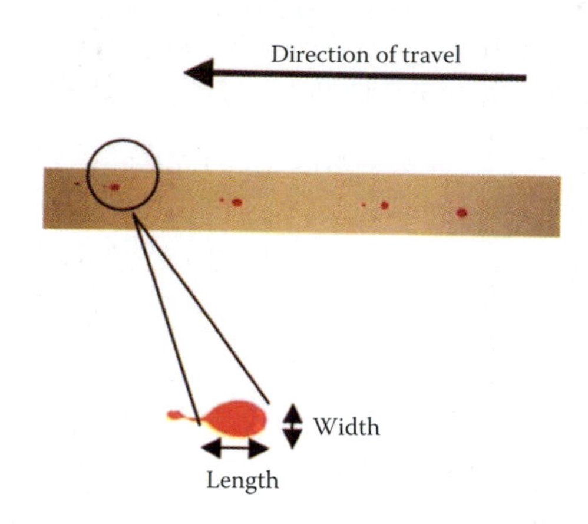

12. Measure the widths and lengths of all the blood drops at a given distance and determine the average W/L ratio for the different speeds.
13. Record the data (speed of blood source and W/L ratios of the blood drops) in your laboratory notebook. This can be represented as a table having six columns: pace of movement, distance (ft), time (s), speed (ft/s), direction (toward or away from a defined and fixed point), and average W/L ratio.
14. Prepare a graph of the group's average W/L ratio versus speed. What relationship do you observe between the W/L ratio and the speed of the moving blood source?

Activity 4.5 Making Blood Transfer Stains

In this activity, you will prepare examples of blood transfer pattern stains.

Materials:

Simulated blood
Various materials with the capacity to hold and transfer simulated blood
Scratch paper

Protocol:

1. Members of your group should bring in five different types of materials (swatches of cloth or carpet, shoes, etc.). Each item should have a duplicate—one that will be used in the initial transfer stain study and another that will be used by a second group to recreate the stains. The items should be capable of either absorbing simulated blood or of being coated with it such that a transfer from its surface is possible. Such items as Teflon-coated materials, plastics, glass, and smooth metals will not be effective in this exercise.

2. Soak a sample object in simulated blood and press the soaked item onto a piece of white paper.
3. Allow the liquid to dry. Label this pattern "Exhibit A."
4. Using a fresh piece of white paper, repeat this process with another item.
5. Make transfer pattern stains with all five items and mark them as Exhibit A, B, C, D, and E. Allow the stains to dry.
6. Exchange your transfer stain patterns with another group and provide them with the matching (but unused) set of items that were used to make your transfer stains.
7. Given the potential source materials and bloodstain patterns, recreate the patterns presented on the exhibits.
8. Report your findings back to the group from whom you received the exhibits.

Activity 4.6 Creating Cast-Off Blood Spatter

In this activity, you will determine the blood spatter pattern created by a moving blood source and study the consequences to that pattern when the source changes direction.

Materials:

Lab gown
Gloves
Goggles
Squeeze bottle with simulated blood
Butcher paper
Poster board

Protocol:

1. Cover yourself with a gown, gloves, and goggles.

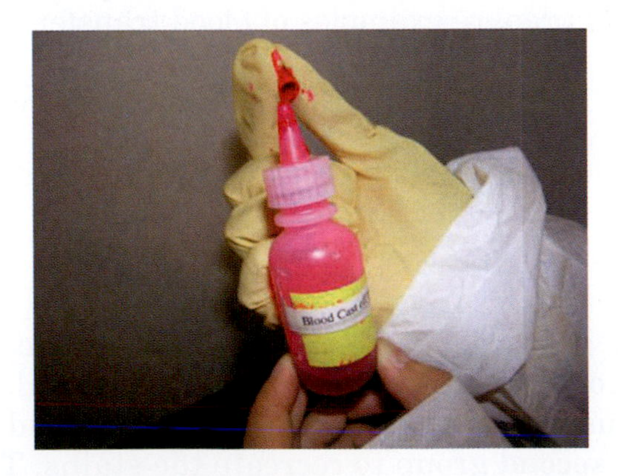

2. Tape butcher paper onto a poster board.
3. Obtain a squeeze bottle of simulated blood from your instructor.
4. Stand near the vertical surface of the poster board and, using a quick downward motion followed by a quick upward motion, allow the simulated blood

to escape from the squeeze bottle by the centrifugal force imparted on the bottle as you swing it. Document the sequence and direction in your lab notebook.

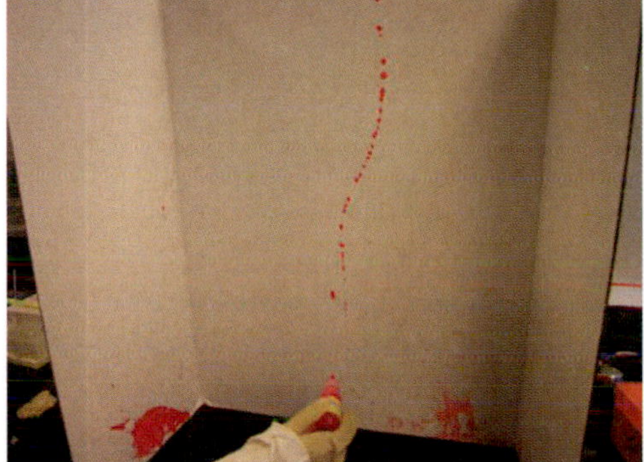

5. Add more cast-off patterns to the original surface, noting sequence and directional changes. Record this information in your laboratory notebook.
6. Once your blood cast-off patterns have been made and have dried, exchange your poster board with another group and process each other's blood spatter evidence.
7. In your laboratory notebook, record your observations regarding the relationship of the shape of the blood drops and the direction in which the blood was flung. Your report should include sketches of the bloodstain patterns.

Activity 4.7 Creating Impact Spatter

In this activity, you will recreate the type of blood spatter that might occur when a blunt instrument violently strikes a victim's head.

Materials:

Poster paint (diluted 1:1)
Cardboard box
Gloves
Goggles
Lab coat
Butcher paper
Sturdy flat and nonbreakable surface (such as a piece of tile)
Wet paper towels for cleanup

Protocol:

1. Cover yourself with a lab coat, gloves, and goggles.
2. Cut the top from a large cardboard box and tape butcher paper to cover its inside surfaces. Place a hard, nonabsorbent, nonbreakable surface close to one of the inside surfaces (a linoleum floor tile is shown here).

3. Place a small puddle of diluted poster paint (about the size of a quarter) on a nonabsorbent, nonbreakable surface near the vertical wall of the cardboard (a black marble tile is shown here).

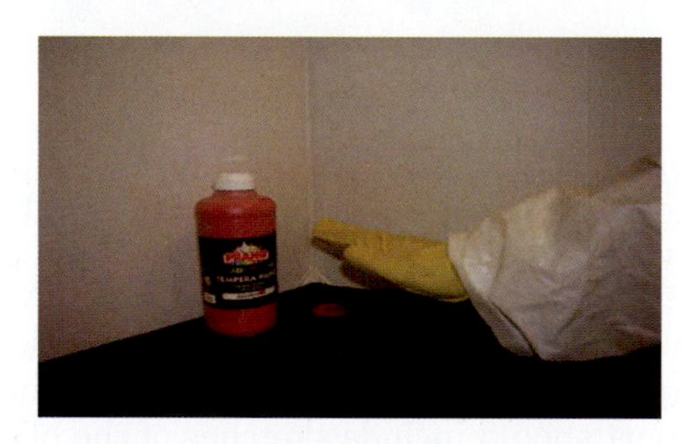

4. With an open and gloved hand, slap the pool of blood such that it splashes against the butcher paper taped against the cardboard backing.

5. Record your lab group name and the type of blood spatter (impact) on the butcher paper. Allow time for the spatter to dry.
6. In your laboratory notebook, draw the most common shapes created by this type of blood spatter.
7. Relative speed can be determined by the size of the blood droplets. Generally speaking, bloodstains less than 1 mm in diameter are considered high velocity. Bloodstain droplets in the range of 1–3 mm in diameter are considered medium velocity. Bloodstains exceeding 3 mm in diameter are considered low velocity. Measure several representative samples of the circular and elliptical bloodstains and record these in your laboratory notebook. Based on these measurements, what is the relative speed of the bloodstain?

Activity 4.8 Creating Blood Spatter with an Impact Device

In this activity, you will use an impact device to simulate the blood spatter created when a metal surface (such as a fire poker or baseball bat) hits a victim's skull.

Materials:

Impacting spatter device (ISD)
Two different colors of water-soluble poster paint
Cardboard box or science poster boards to simulate a vertical wall
Lab glasses, latex gloves, and lab coat
Measuring tape
Butcher paper or appropriate liner to protect lab bench
Paper towels

Protocol:

1. Put on safety glasses, latex gloves, and a lab coat. Line your lab bench with butcher paper beneath an ISD.

   Warning: Because this device can cause serious injury, please do not allow any body parts on, near, or around the impact zone or hinge area.

2. Remove two sides from a cardboard box and cover the inside surfaces with butcher paper. Each of the four exposed sides can now be used as impact surfaces to simulate a wall. (Alternatively, prepare a science fair poster board.)

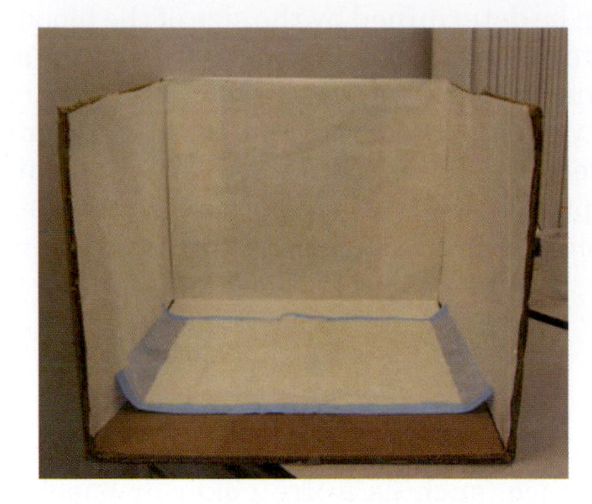

3. Place the ISD 2 in. from the wall. Record this distance in your laboratory notebook. Using a pencil, trace along the base near the impact zone so that the ISD can be placed back into the exact position again as needed.

4. Lift the handle of the ISD and deposit a 1 mm thick layer of poster paint along the width of the impact spatter zone. If needed, use your index finger to smooth out the film of paint. Make a note of the color of the paint in your laboratory notebook.

5. With the ISD in position, raise its arm to its maximum height (to 90°) and allow the arm to swing down toward the impact zone by gravity.
   Note: If no spatter presents itself on the wall, repeat the experiment again until a pattern is registered. If you repeat the test, make sure the ISD is in the same position relative to the wall as the first trial.

6. Wipe away any poster paint from the ISD's impact zone and bolt head. Move the ISD (4 inches away) from the covered surface inside the box. Using a

different color of poster paint, repeat the experiment in the same manner as that used in the original trial. Record this distance in your laboratory notebook.

Note: If no spatter presents itself on the box surface, repeat the experiment again until a pattern is registered.

7. When the paint is dry, analyze the impact spatter created under the two different conditions.

8. Record your observations in your laboratory notebook. Be sure to note the distance of the wall surface to the impact zone, the paint color, the swing arc (90°), and what velocity (low, medium, or high) the impact represents. Include in your description a drawing of the most common spatter shapes and patterns. Address these following questions: (1) What shape appears to be the most distinct and conspicuous? (2) What is the positional relationship between the droplets that are circular versus the droplets that are elliptical? (3) What difference in the blood spatter pattern occurs if the blood source is moved further away? Explain.

Activity 4.9 Determining the Characteristics of High-Velocity Blood Spatter

In this activity, you will characterize the size and shape of high-velocity blood spatter. You will also determine the maximum distance that high-velocity blood spatter can impact a vertical surface.

Materials:

Windex squirt bottle filled with colored water (simulated blood)
Tape measure or meter stick
Ruler or calipers for measuring diameter of simulated blood droplets
Vertical surface that can display simulated blood droplets
Butcher paper and tape with which to secure it to a vertical surface

Protocol:

1. Twist the nozzle on a spray bottle filled with simulated blood (or colored liquid) to the ON position.

2. Place the spray bottle approximately 3 ft (1 m) from a vertical surface covered with butcher paper.

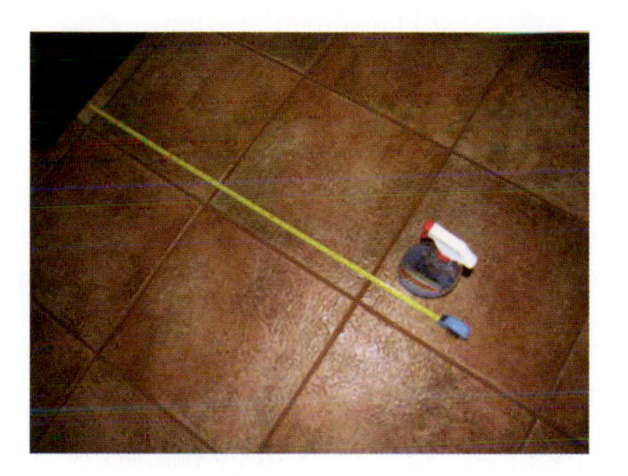

3. Press the spray bottle's trigger once and note if droplets of simulated blood reached the vertical surface. If no spatter appears on the butcher paper, move the squirt bottle approximately 12 in. closer to the target and squirt one time again. If droplets of simulated blood reached the vertical surface, replace the butcher paper, reposition the squirt bottle back 6 in., and squirt once.

4. Continue repeating this process until you find the distance where the droplets are just able to reach the vertical surface and note (a) the distance and (b) the average diameter of the droplets.

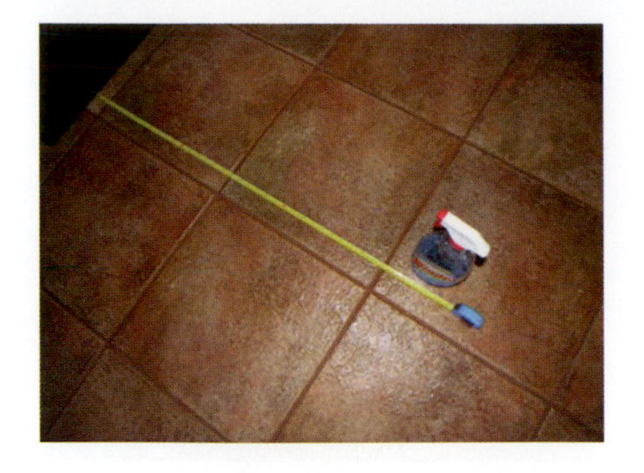

Record this information in your laboratory notebook.
Answer the following questions in your laboratory notebook:

1. What is the average shape of the water droplets that have made an impression on the vertical surface?
2. Based on the data collected, how would you characterize high-velocity blood spatter?
3. Based on your lab results, what is the maximum distance that the high-velocity blood source will impart an impression on a vertical surface?
4. What are some possible sources of high-velocity blood spatter?

Activity 4.10 Determining a Blood Stain's Address

Reconstructing the events of a crime that involved an assault or murder in which blood had been shed can entail investigating the source, in space, of that blood. Was the victim already fallen when they were struck a blow causing blood to fly? How close to a wall was the victim standing when they were shot? Was the victim facing the assailant or had they turned away? In this activity, you will determine where in 3D space a blood source was positioned at the time blood was shed.

This activity requires that we know something of geometry. We have seen that blood dropped from straight above (at a 90° angle) produces a circular bloodstain. When blood is dropped on an angled surface or when it is flung onto a horizontal surface from an angle less than 90°, an elliptical bloodstain is produced. With sharper angles, the length of the elliptical bloodstain increases in relation to its width. On a 2D plane, elliptical bloodstains can be traced back to their point of origin by drawing lines through their lengthwise axes to their *point of convergence* (the point where the lines intersect; Figures 4.16 and 4.17).

On a 2D surface, then, it's a fairly straightforward process to determine a bloodstain's point of origin. But what if you need to know how far off the floor the victim was when their blood was spilled (was the victim lying down or standing) or how close to the bloodstained wall the victim was when a bullet hit them? A 2D surface gives us an x and a y axis location. A 3D area requires a distance, denoted as z, from the plane that is defined by x and y. Fortunately, determining the distance of z is not tremendously difficult either. And that's all because of the direct relationship

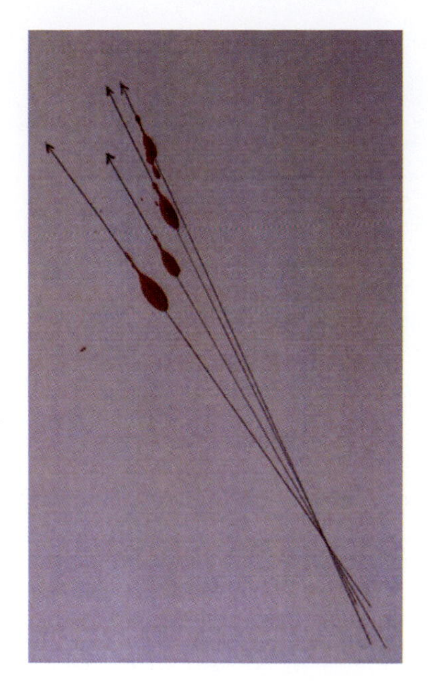

Figure 4.16 The origin of sprayed blood can be determined by drawing straight lines through the long axes of the individual bloodstains such that they intersect at the point of convergence. The arrows on the ends of these lines denote the direction of travel from the origin.

Figure 4.17 A bloodstain showing two points of convergence.

between a bloodstain's W/L ratio and its angle of impact. But, before we can get to z, we'll need to review a little geometry as concerns a right triangle.

A right triangle is a three-sided figure having a 90° angle at one of its vertices. The angle opposite the right angle can be designated by the symbol θ (*theta* from the Greek alphabet). The side opposite the right angle is called the *hypotenuse* and is the longest

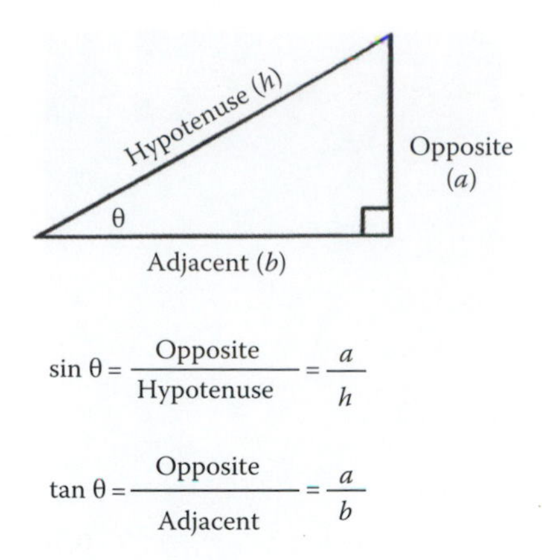

Figure 4.18 A right triangle has, as one of its angles, a right (90°) angle (represented as a box in the lower-right corner of the triangle). The angle opposite the right angle is designated as θ. The opposite side is that side of the triangle furthest from θ. The adjacent side is the side that, along with the hypotenuse, forms part of the θ angle. The sine of θ is defined as the length of the opposite side divided by the length of the hypotenuse. The tangent of θ is defined as the length of the opposite side divided by the length of the adjacent side.

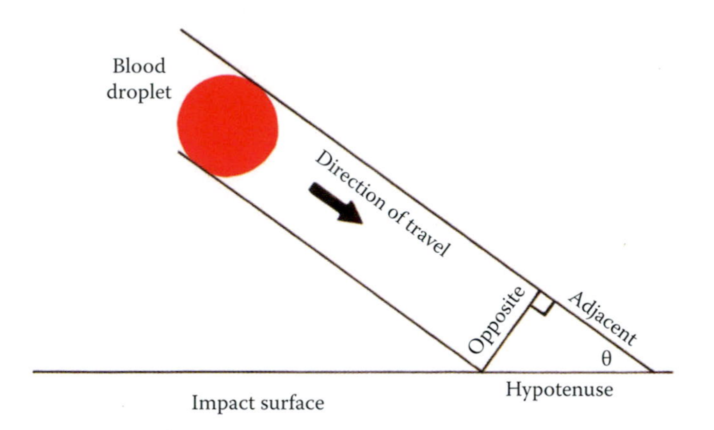

Figure 4.19 The angle of impact of a blood droplet defines a right triangle on the Impact surface.

side of the right-angled triangle. The *sine* (abbreviated *sin*) of the angle θ is the ratio of the length of the opposite side to the length of the hypotenuse. The *tangent* of θ is the length of the opposite side divided by the length of the adjacent side (Figure 4.18).

When viewed with the eye of a geometry student, a blood droplet traveling at an angle and hitting the surface of a plane traverses through a right triangle at the impact surface (Figure 4.19).

Interestingly, dividing the width of a bloodstain by its length [the W/L ratio] gives us the sine of the impact angle—an angle that can be found on a calculator or in a trigonometry table (Table 4.1). Let's suppose, for example, that we find a bloodstain that has a W/L ratio of 0.81. From Table 4.1, we find that that corresponds to an impact angle of approximately 54°. Notice, from Table 4.1, that a perfectly circular bloodstain (which would have a W/L ratio of 1), has an angle of impact of 90°.

Physically measuring the distance of the leading edge of the bloodstain to its point of origin (the convergence point) gives you the length of the adjacent side ("*Y*" in Figure 4.20).

You now know the angle of impact (θ) and the length of the adjacent side (*Y*). The height of the origin above the *x*, *y* impact plane, the *z* distance, can be determined

TABLE 4.1
Trigonometry Table for Sine and Tangent Functions

Angle	Sine	Tangent	Angle	Sine	Tangent
0	0.00000	0.00000	41	0.65606	0.86929
1	0.01745	0.01746	42	0.66913	0.90040
2	0.03490	0.03492	43	0.68200	0.93252
3	0.05234	0.05241	44	0.69466	0.96569
4	0.06976	0.06993	45	0.70712	1.00000
5	0.08716	0.08749	46	0.71934	1.03553
6	0.10453	0.10510	47	0.73135	1.07237
7	0.12187	0.12279	48	0.74315	1.11061
8	0.13917	0.14054	49	0.75471	1.15037
9	0.15643	0.15838	50	0.76604	1.19175
10	0.17365	0.17633	51	0.77715	1.23490
11	0.19081	0.19438	52	0.78801	1.27994
12	0.20791	0.21256	53	0.79864	1.32705
13	0.22495	0.23087	54	0.80902	1.37638
14	0.24192	0.24933	55	0.81915	1.42815
15	0.25882	0.26795	56	0.82904	1.48256
16	0.27564	0.28675	57	0.83867	1.53987
17	0.29237	0.30573	58	0.84805	1.60034
18	0.30902	0.32492	59	0.85717	1.66428
19	0.32557	0.34433	60	0.86603	1.73205
20	0.34202	0.36397	61	0.87462	1.80405
21	0.35837	0.38386	62	0.88295	1.88073
22	0.37461	0.40403	63	0.89101	1.96261
23	0.39073	0.42448	64	0.89879	2.05030
24	0.40674	0.44523	65	0.90631	2.14451
25	0.42262	0.46631	66	0.91355	2.24604
26	0.43837	0.48773	67	0.92051	2.35585
27	0.45399	0.50953	68	0.92718	2.47509
28	0.46947	0.53171	69	0.93358	2.60509
29	0.48481	0.55431	70	0.93969	2.74748
30	0.50000	0.57735	71	0.94552	2.90421
31	0.51504	0.60086	72	0.95106	3.07768
32	0.52992	0.62487	73	0.95631	3.27085
33	0.54464	0.64941	74	0.96126	3.48741
34	0.55919	0.67451	75	0.96593	3.73205
35	0.57358	0.70021	76	0.97030	4.01078
36	0.58779	0.72654	77	0.97437	4.33148
37	0.60182	0.75355	78	0.97815	4.80973
38	0.61566	0.78129	79	0.98163	5.14455
39	0.62932	0.80978	80	0.98481	5.67128
40	0.64279	0.83910	81	0.98769	6.31375

(Continued)

TABLE 4.1 (*Continued*)
Trigonometry Table for Sine and Tangent Functions

Angle	Sine	Tangent	Angle	Sine	Tangent
82	0.99027	7.11537	87	0.99863	19.0811
83	0.99255	8.14435	88	0.99939	28.6363
84	0.99452	9.51436	89	0.99985	57.2900
85	0.99620	11.4301	90	1.00000	Infinity
86	0.99756	14.4007			

These values can also be obtained from a calculator having trigonometric functions.

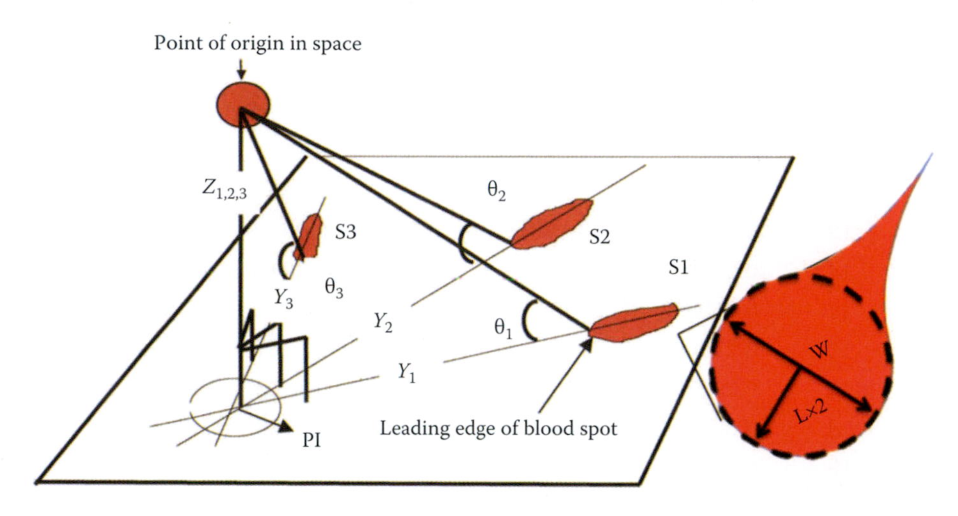

Figure 4.20 Three bloodstains (S1, S2, and S3) are mapped to their origin by determining the angle of impact (θ), the distance (*Y*) from their leading edges to their point of convergence (PI; point of intersection), and the distance, at a 90° angle, above the plane of impact (*Z*).

using the tangent function. The tangent of the angle of impact (θ) is equal to the length of the opposite side divided by the length of the adjacent side (tangent = $a/b = Z/Y$). Or z = the tangent multiplied by Y. For example, let's say that you measured Y (the distance from the leading edge of the bloodstain to the convergence point) to be 25 cm. Since we've already determined our impact angle to be 54°, the corresponding tangent (from Table 4.1) is 1.37638. Therefore, $z = 1.37638 \times 25$ cm = 34.4 cm. That is, the blood's point of origin is 34.4 cm at a 90° angle above the point of convergence.

A bloodstain's point of origin can also be determined by *stringing*—a technique in which a string, at one end, is fastened to the leading edge of the bloodstain and its other end is fastened to a rod secured at a 90° angle from the convergence point (Figure 4.21). The angle of the string at the bloodstain (as calculated using a sine function as described earlier) is adjusted with a protractor. The point of origin is where that string, with its impact angle maintained, meets the rod at the convergence point (Figure 4.22).

Since all falling objects under the force of gravity follow the path of an ellipse, the actual point of origin is lower than that determined by the methods described here. Nevertheless, calculating a bloodstain's origin will tell an investigator the position of the victim when they were attacked—were they standing, sitting, or lying down?

You will now use these techniques to calculate the origin of a bloodstain provided by your instructor.

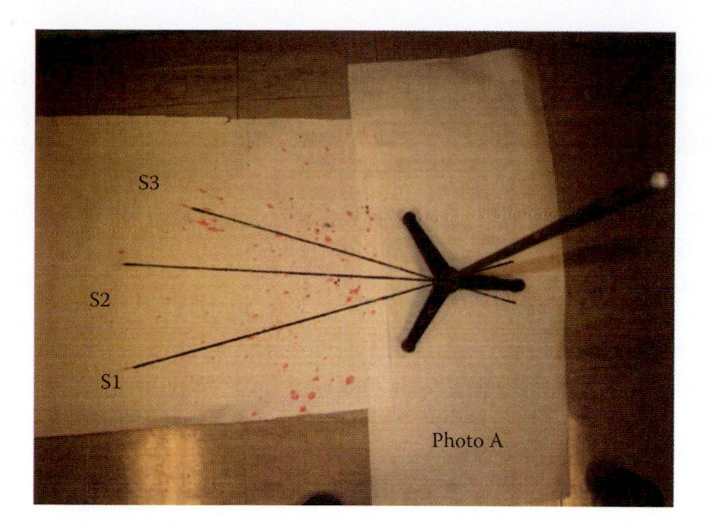

Figure 4.21 In the technique of stringing, a rod is placed at a 90° angle to the x, y plane of the convergence point.

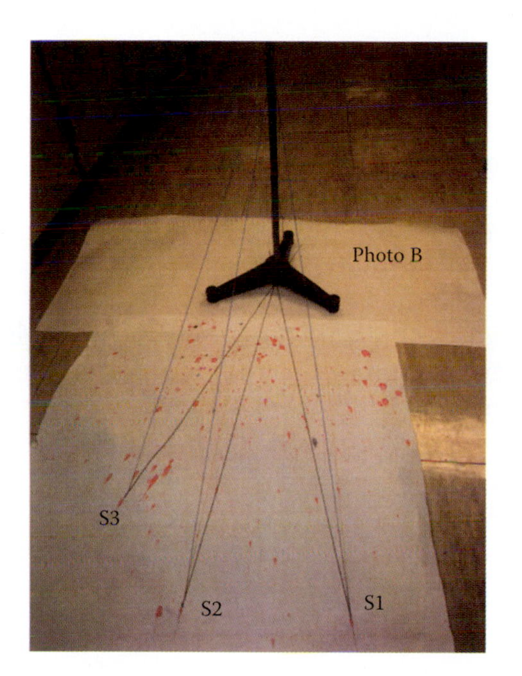

Figure 4.22 The point of a bloodstain's origin along the z axis is determined by strings maintained at the angle of impact reaching from the bloodstains to a securing rod placed at the convergence point.

Materials:

Ruler
Calculator
Ring stand with rod
String
Scotch tape
Protractor
Butcher paper with prepared blood spatter
Butcher paper
Simulated blood

Protocol:
By one of two means, you will be provided with a bloodstain similar to Figure 4.23 from which you will determine, in 3D space, the origin of the blood source. The bloodstain will have been prepared by your instructor or by another lab group.

1. Using a ruler, draw individual lines through at least three blood droplets so that each is bisected lengthwise. Extend these lines away from the direction of travel until all three lines intersect. This point of convergence is denoted as PI.
   If your lines do not all intersect at a convergence point (which is usually the case in the forensic examination of an assault or homicide), mark a point of origin that *averages* your initial result (Figure 4.24).
2. Using either calipers or a ruler, measure the width, length, and *W/L* ratio of each droplet identified in the previous step. Record your findings in your laboratory notebook in the form of a table having the following rows and columns:

Spot	*W* (cm)	*L* (cm)	*W/L*	Impact Angle (Sine)	Tangent (Impact Angle)	*Y* (cm)	*Z* (cm)
*S*1							
*S*2							
*S*3							

3. Using a calculator or Table 4.1, determine the angle of impact of each of the blood spots and record this angle in your data table.
4. Measure the length of Y_1, Y_2, and Y_3. The length (*Y*) is measured from the leading edge of the blood droplet to the PI. Record this information in your data table.
5. Determine Z_1, Z_2, and Z_3 using the tangent function multiplied by *Y* as described in the introduction to this activity. Enter these values in the table in your laboratory notebook.

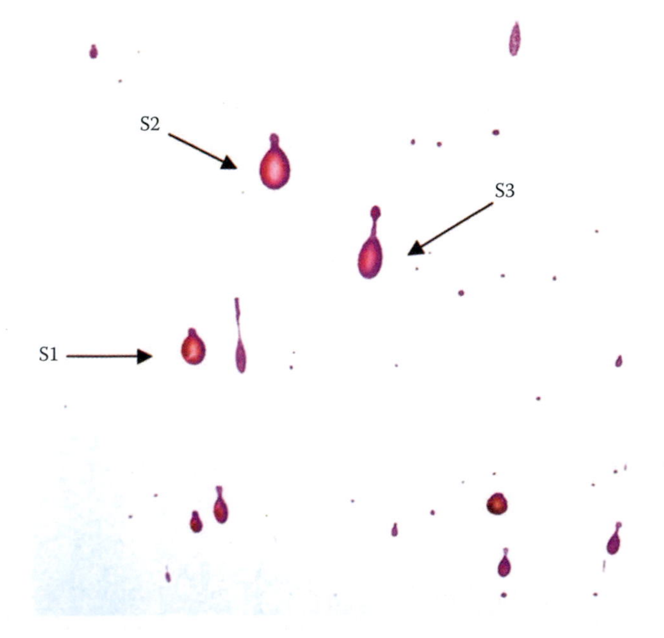

Figure 4.23 Blood spatter on a floor. S1, S2, and S3 are blood drops that can be used to trace back to the blood's origin. Their tails point in the direction of the bloodstain's path.

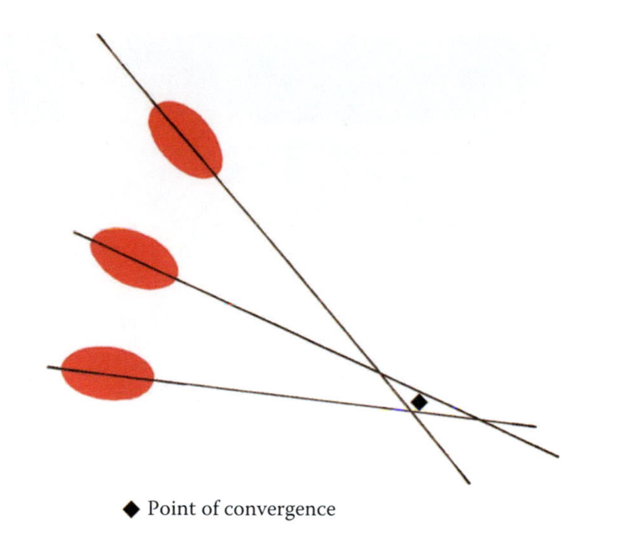

Figure 4.24 Lines drawn to bisect several bloodstains through their long axes do not intersect (solid lines). A point of convergence is derived that estimates an *average* intersection point (shown as a square within the triangle formed by the three lines bisecting the elliptical bloodstains).

6. Position the center of a ring stand over the convergence point (as shown in Figure 4.21). Tape one end of a length of string to the leading edge of a bloodstain. Using a protractor, elevate the string to the appropriate angle of impact. Tape the other end of the string to the rod portion of the ring stand corresponding to your calculated Z value. Repeat this process for the other blood spots. The point at which the strings converge is the approximate origin of the bloodstains.

Erica Holmes Missing Persons Case

Items of Evidence

Several stains were found within Erica Holmes' vehicle. These were marked with evidence tents and photographed (Figure 4.25) and are described in the following (Figures 4.26 through 4.31):

Are They Stains of Blood?

Lieutenant Jenkins used Hemastix strips to determine if the stains they photographed might be composed of blood. He used two strips for each stain. The first strip (a) was used to test whether or not an area close to the stain gave a positive result. A second strip (b) was exposed to a wetted swab lightly matted against the stain in question. The locations on which these tests were conducted are described in the following (Table 4.2).

The results of the Hemastix tests are shown in Figure 4.32.

Blood Loss

If it is assumed that the large stain on the cargo bay liner is blood, can a determination be made as to the volume of blood that would produce such a stain and whether or not a person could survive that much blood loss? Here, you will estimate whether or not a person the size of Erica Holmes could survive the loss of blood represented by this stain.

Figure 4.25 Frontal view of victim's engine bay showing *Evidence Item 1* (blood on windshield fluid reservoir), *Evidence Item 2* (tissue on engine block), and *Evidence Item 3* (apparent blood stain around bullet hole in firewall).

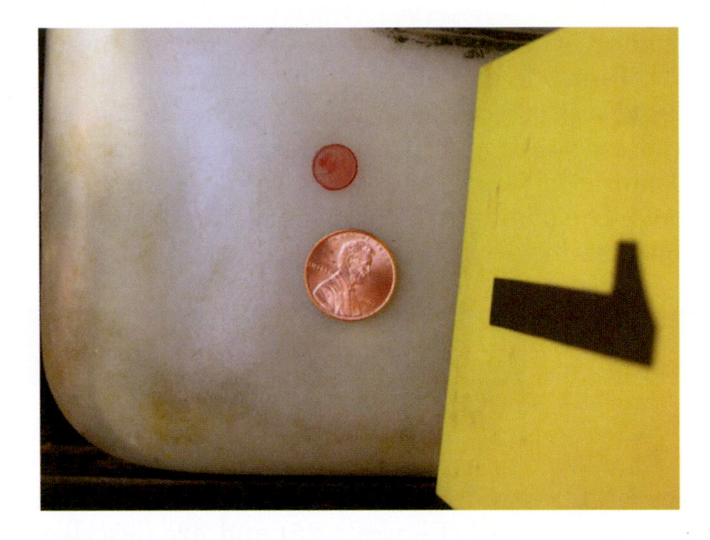

Figure 4.26 *Evidence Item 1* is a stain found on the water reservoir in the engine bay.

Protocol:

1. Figure 4.33 shows that the cargo bay liner has carpet grips (appearing as small dots) on its underside that are spaced approximately 1 in. apart horizontally and vertically. Using Figure 4.34, count the number of 1 in. squares fully covered by blood and record this information in your laboratory notebook.

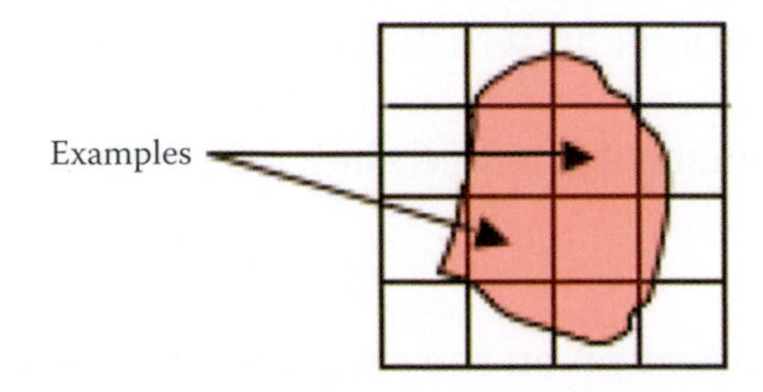

2. To account for the squares not completely covered by blood, match up those partially covered squares that would, if added together, be approximately

Figure 4.27 *Evidence Item 3* is the stain of small red droplets scattered around a hole in the engine bay's firewall.

Figure 4.28 *Evidence Item 3* is fine specks of apparent blood around what appears to be a bullet hole in the automobile's firewall (red arrow).

equivalent to one complete square. Continue this process until all the partially covered squares are accounted for and record this information in your laboratory notebook.

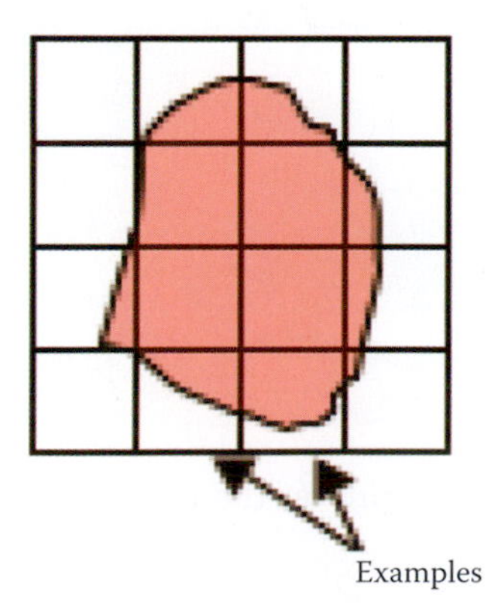

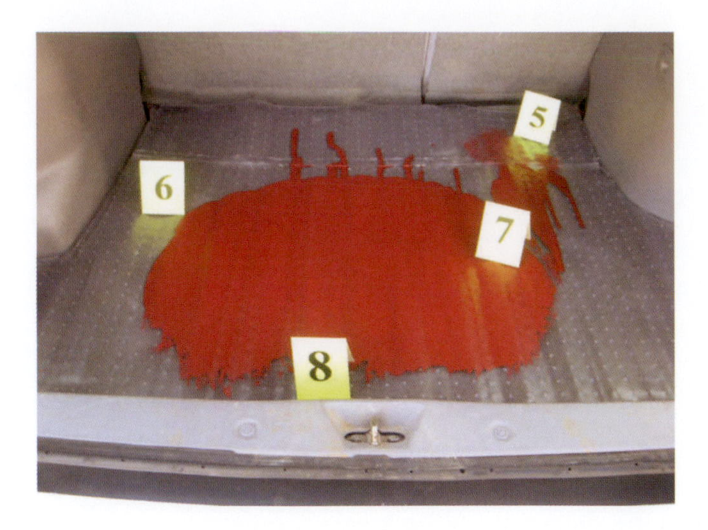

Figure 4.29 The large stain on the vinyl liner in the cargo bay of Erica Holmes' vehicle was divided into several areas marked with tents 5, 6, 7, and 8.

Figure 4.30 *Evidence Item 5* is a pattern stain adjacent to the large stain on the vinyl liner in the cargo bay of the vehicle.

Figure 4.31 *Evidence Item 9* is a fingerprint on the right side of the rear view mirror inside Erica Holmes' vehicle.

TABLE 4.2
Hemastix Tests Conducted on the Blood Evidence Found under the Hood of Erica Holmes' Vehicle

Evidence Item	Stain Location
18a (control)	Area on the water reservoir in the engine bay close to a stain that appears to be a drop of blood (marked with a tent as *Evidence Item 1*)
18b	Spot that appears to be a drop of blood on the water reservoir in the engine bay (marked with a tent as *Evidence Item 1*)
19a (control)	Area on the engine bay firewall adjacent to section showing specks of what may be blood surrounding an impact hole in the metal firewall (marked as *Evidence Item 3*)
19b	Small reddish specks around an impact hole in the engine bay firewall (marked with a tent as *Evidence Item 3*)
20a (control)	Taken from an area of the clear vinyl liner in the vehicle cargo bay near the pattern stain identified as *Evidence Item 5*
20b	Taken from within the pattern stain on the vinyl liner on the cargo bay identified as *Evidence Item 5*
21a (control)	Taken from an area of the clear vinyl liner in the vehicle cargo bay near the segment of the large stain on the cargo bay liner identified as *Evidence Item 6*
21b	Taken from within the large stain on the clear vinyl liner in the vehicle cargo bay identified as *Evidence Item 6*
22a (control)	Taken from an area on the clear vinyl cargo bay liner adjacent to that segment of the large stain identified as *Evidence Item 7*
22b	Taken from an area within the large stain on the clear vinyl cargo bay liner identified as *Evidence Item 7*
23a (control)	Taken from an area on the clear vinyl cargo bay liner adjacent to that segment of the large stain identified as *Evidence Item 8*
23b	Taken from an area within the large stain on the clear vinyl cargo bay liner identified as *Evidence Item 8*
24a (control)	Taken from an area on the interior rear view mirror adjacent to the fingerprint stain identified as *Evidence Item 9*
24b	Taken from an edge of the fingerprint stain identified as *Evidence Item 9*

In your laboratory notebook, calculate the volume of blood represented by the bloodstain using the following steps:

3. Calculate the total number of square inches covered by blood (squares completely filled plus the additive sum of the partially covered squares).
4. You will now need to determine the depth of a pool of blood spilled on a level surface. There are several ways this might be done. For example, layer several milliliter of simulated blood on a glass slide, hold the slide at eye level with a metric ruler behind it, and note the height of the liquid (see Figure 4.35). Alternatively, place a white or clear metric ruler vertically into several milliliter of simulated blood and note how far up the stain reaches on the ruler. If this approach is used, you will need to account for a meniscus (the curve of a liquid in contact with a solid surface). The degree to which a meniscus contributes to the measure can be roughly determined by measuring the height of the meniscus of water in a glass beaker. If measurements are determined in millimeters, they will need to be converted to inches. Remember that 1 in. is equivalent to 2.54 cm and that there are 10 mm/cm.

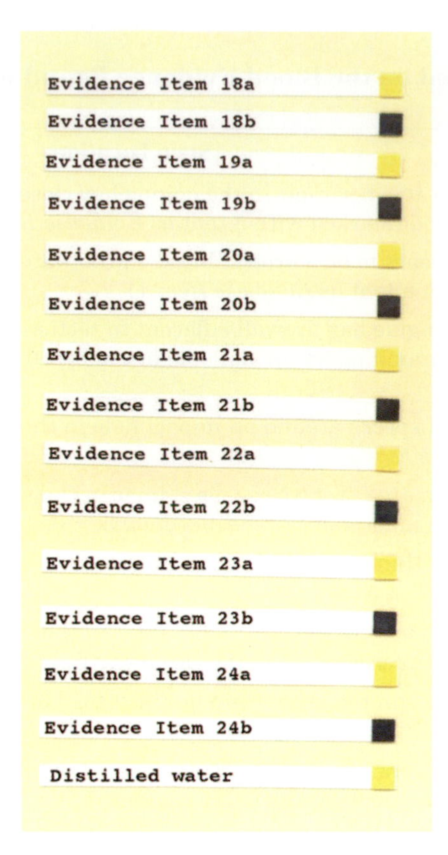

Figure 4.32 *Evidence Items 18 through 24* are the Hemastix presumptive blood test results for stains found within Erica Holmes' vehicle. Each evidence item consists of two samples marked "*a*" and "*b*." The "*a*" strip (the control), in each case, was made from a swab taken from an area close to the stain but not carrying any visible part of it. The "b" strip for each evidence item represents a direct sample of the stain in question. Also shown is a Hemastix strip dipped into a sample of the distilled water used in the testing process.

Figure 4.33 The ruler shown in Figure 4.35 taken as a close-up image to show that the carpet grips (the small dots in a regular pattern in this image) are spaced 1 in. apart in the vertical and horizontal directions.

Figure 4.34 The large bloodstain on the cargo bay liner from Erica Holmes' vehicle. A ruler is shown for scale. *Evidence Item 5*, a pattern bloodstain from which a sample was taken for DNA testing, is marked. The liner has been removed from the vehicle and placed on a white background for better contrast.

Figure 4.35 To estimate the depth of a spot of blood on a horizontal surface, a metric ruler is placed behind a glass slide carrying a small pool of simulated blood. The measurement is taken while holding the slide at eye level.

Once the depth of a pool of blood has been determined, calculate how many cubic inches of blood would have produced the stain on the cargo bay liner.

Jenkins stated that a typical human carries 70 mL of blood per kilogram (kg) of body weight, and if a person loses 30% of their blood, they are likely to die. If the bloodstain in the back of the vehicle came from Erica Holmes, might she still be alive? (Remember that 1 kg is equivalent to 2.205 lb and 1 mL is equivalent to 0.061 in.^{3}.)

Prepare evidence reports for Evidence Items 1, 3, 5, and 9 and for the large bloodstain on the cargo bay vinyl liner that includes the area tented with numbers 6, 7, and 8. Be sure to include the results of the presumptive blood tests and your speculation on what type of bloodstain the items represent (high velocity, transfer, etc.).

Bullet Angle of Entry

The following measurements were taken of the bullet hole found in the vehicle's firewall:

Width of bullet = 0.9 cm, Length of bullet hole = 1.0 cm

BD = the horizontal distance from the firewall (bullet hole) to the front edge of the bumper was measured at 109 cm.

BF = DE = the vertical distance from the firewall (bullet hole) to the ground was measured at 79 cm.

$\angle\theta$ = the downward entry angle of the bullet through the firewall at point "*B*" (refer to Figure 4.38).

Using Figures 4.36 through 4.38 and applying your understanding of a right triangle and sine/cosine/tangent functions, determine the approximate distance a shooter would from the bullet hole (assume a 6' tall shooter in an upright posture in front of the vehicle). Fill out an evidence report of your findings. Show your work.

Figure 4.36 Bullet hole position in the vehicle's firewall.

Figure 4.37 Aerial view of vehicle showing horizontal and vertical dimensions of the front of the vehicle where BD = distance from firewall to the front edge of the bumper (109 cm) and BF = vertical height from the firewall to the ground level (79 cm). *B* is the location of the bullet hole.

Figure 4.38 Side view front left quarter panel (driver's side) showing horizontal and vertical dimensions of the vehicle. Line AE represents the shoulder height of a shooter positioned in front of the vehicle. When calculating height of line AE, subtract 1' from the shooter's height to account for head height to shoulder distance.

Review Questions

4.1 When performing a presumptive blood test with Hemastix, why is it necessary to test an unstained area close to the bloodstain under examination as a control?

4.2 Describe the chemical reaction that changes a Hemastix from yellow to green in the presence of blood.

4.3 What is a false-positive test with Hemastix?

4.4 Give two reasons why a Hemastix control test (a swab taken of an area close to the stain under examination) might give a positive result.

4.5 What should you do if the control Hemastix test gives a positive result?

4.6 What is the relationship between the height from which a drop of blood falls and its diameter?

4.7 What information can blood drop diameter provide to the forensic scientist at a crime scene?

4.8 When studying blood drop patterns on a slanted surface, why is it necessary to keep the drop height distance the same as one changes the angle of the impact?

4.9 How can the information gained from the study of blood impact on an angled surface be used to evaluate a crime scene?

4.10 What is the relationship of the angle to the *W/L* ratio of a blood drop?

4.11 What is the difference between speed and velocity?

4.12 What is the formula for determining the velocity of a moving blood source?

4.13 When studying blood drops falling from a moving source, why is it important that the height of the blood source, distance traveled, and drip rate be the same for all the different velocities examined?

4.14 What feature of a blood drop can tell you what directions the source was moving?

4.15 What primary Newtonian law of motion explains the teardrop or elliptical shape of the blood droplet as the speed of the blood source increases?

4.16 A blood drop having a diameter of 1 cm falls at a 40° angle onto the floor. What is the length of the long axis of the elliptical bloodstain that results?

4.17 How does knowledge of the velocity of a moving blood source help the forensic scientist evaluate a crime scene?

4.18 What is cast-off?

4.19 How is the direction of a cast-off blood pattern determined?

4.20 What types of information can a forensic scientist derive from a cast-off blood pattern?

4.21 What is impact blood spatter?

4.22 What primary Newtonian law of motion is at work with impact blood spatter?

4.23 How does Newton's first law of motion explain the teardrop or elliptical shape of blood spatter against an angled surface?

4.24 What forensic information can be extracted from the *teardrop* shape of blood spattered at an angle?

4.25 What type of action or implements can cause a *teardrop* blood spatter pattern?

4.26 What information can be derived from impact spatter found on a wall?

4.27 What is the mathematical formula for deriving the volume of a cube?

4.28 What information can be gained by determining the volume of blood left at a crime scene?

4.29 What is the volume of blood loss from a 250 lb human that would prove to be fatal?

Further Reading

Blood Droplet Dynamics—I by P.A. Pizzola, S. Roth, and P.R. De Forest in *Journal of Forensic Sciences*, Vol. 31, No. 1, pages 36–49, 1986.

An Unusual Bloodstain Case by B.R. Burnett, J.M. Orantes, and M.L. Pierson in *Journal of Forensic Sciences*, Vol. 42, No. 3, pages 519–523, 1997.

A Novel Approach to Obtaining Reliable PCR Results from Luminol Treated Bloodstains by A.D. Manna and S. Montpetit in *Journal of Forensic Sciences*, Vol. 45, No. 4, pages 886–890, 2000.

Bloodstains by R. Platt in *Crime Scene: The Ultimate Guide to Forensic Science* (DK Publishing, New York), pages 84–85, 2003.

A Comparison Study of Hair Examination Methodologies by J.C. Kolowski, N. Petraco, M.M. Wallace, P.R. De Forest, and M. Prinz in *Journal of Forensic Sciences*, Vol. 49, No. 6, pages 1253–1255, 2004.

Deducing Drop Size and Impact Velocity from Circular Bloodstains by L. Hulse-Smith, N.Z. Mehdizadeh, and S. Chandra in *Journal of Forensic Sciences*, Vol. 50, No. 1, pages 54–63, 2005.

A Blind Trial Evaluation of a Crime Scene Methodology for Deducing Impact Velocity and Droplet Size from Circular Bloodstains by L. Hulse-Smith and M. Illes in *Journal of Forensic Sciences* Vol. 52, No. 1, pages 65–69, 2007.

Bloodstain Pattern Evidence: Objective Approaches and Case Applications by Anita Wonder, Elsevier-Academic Press, New York, 2007.

Evaluation of Six Presumptive Tests for Blood, Their Specificity, Sensitivity, and Effect on High Molecular-Weight DNA by S.S. Tobe, N. Watson, and N.N. Daeid in *Journal of Forensic Sciences*, Vol. 52, No. 1, pages 102–109, 2007.

Predicting the Position of the Source of Blood Stains for Angled Impacts by C. Knock and M. Davison in *Journal of Forensic Sciences*, Vol. 52, No. 5, pages 1044–1049, 2007.

5
DNA Quantification

Home of Sarah and Dwayne Holmes, Tuesday 3:14 PM

His eyes, intense and penetrating, stared front and center. No hint of a smile. Black hair shaved nearly to the skin arched above the ear and blended into his white frame cap. Three sharp hammer blows on granite could have made that chin. The dark uniform with red pin striping at the trim, the eagle, globe, and anchor emblem on the lapel, the stars and stripes draped beside him, he was all U.S. Marine. The government-issue headshot was mounted in a gold frame polished to the same glint as the brass buttons smartly spaced down the uniform jacket.

“First Combat Engineer Battalion, U.S. Marine Corp,” the burly voice with a smoker’s rasp to it rumbled behind him. Dwayne Holmes fell in line next to Jenkins who was surveying the fireplace mantel. As he came to a halt, the ice in his glass of scotch tinkled like empty shell casings splashing on concrete. The smell of alcohol rode like a knapsack on this breath. He was still of an imposing stature, a head above Jenkins at almost 6 ft, but otherwise, his resemblance to that man in the photograph was now only faint. The angular chin was gone. His face had become a weathered landscape having endured some 20 years of erosion. Furrows carved his cheeks like runoff trenches along a barren hillside. Gray hair had found a beachhead at his temples. The piercing, azure eyes had bleached a paler blue and had lost their urgency.

“The diamond with the three chevrons. What does that signify?” Jenkins asked.

“Company First Sergeant,” Mr. Holmes replied, his voice like tread rolling slowly over gravel. “You’ll never meet a finer group of men than you will in the U.S. Marine Corp. No sir. They’re the best. You sure I can’t get you a drink?”

“I’m fine, thank you,” Jenkins replied.

Mr. Holmes turned back to look at the couch where his wife, Sarah, and Helen Chang were sitting. “Miss Chang, was it? Can I get you something?”

“I’m cool. But thanks for asking,” Helen answered.

A gold-colored cat with faint white stripes sprung up from behind the couch and eased down into Sarah’s lap.

“A cat,” Jenkins said matter-of-factly. He pulled a handkerchief from his coat pocket and held it in his fist at the ready.

“Yes, this is Sasquatch,” Sarah said. “He’s Erica’s cat.” Sarah stroked him peacefully behind the ears.

A faint grimace involuntarily flinched across Jenkins’ face. “You saw combat?” Jenkins asked turning back to Dwayne.

“Operation Desert Storm—the first Iraqi conflict. We should have finished off Saddam right then and there. Marched right into Baghdad. There would have been no need for Iraqi Freedom. We would have had those damn Hajjis right where we wanted 'em. Now I watch 'em on CNN celebrating each time one of our own gets cut down. It's disgusting."

Jenkins turned his attention to the adjacent photograph on the mantle—a young woman in a red cap and gown. Her long, blond hair spilling out from beneath her tasseled cap like parade streamers. Her smile beamed radiance. "And this must be Erica?"

"Her high school graduation picture," Sarah Holmes said from her place on the couch. "Isn't she beautiful?"

"Very long hair," Jenkins observed.

"She's quite proud of it," Mrs. Holmes replied. "I don't know how she manages to keep it out of her dinner plate. She's always getting it caught in something—a button or a zipper."

"A good student?" Jenkins asked.

"Someday, I'm sure, she's going to go to college and have a fine career," said Mrs. Holmes.

"There's nothing wrong with being an auto mechanic," Dwayne cut in. "She had a knack for it."

"Erica is an auto mechanic?" Jenkins asked even though he knew the answer.

"Yep, I taught her everything she ever knew about fixing cars," Dwayne replied.

"Daddy's girl," Mrs. Holmes said with a smile.

Mr. Holmes swirled his glass of scotch, his eyes tracking the circular path of the ice cubes. He took a drink, quickly, as if it would yank him back to the moment.

"When was the last time you saw Erica?" Jenkins asked.

"We filed a missing persons report in January," said Sarah Holmes. "Nothing came of it then and nothing's going to come of it now, is it?"

"We have a heavy case load, Mrs. Holmes. I regret her disappearance didn't receive all the attention it deserved."

"January," said Mr. Holmes. "The last time we saw her was January. We filed the report the very next day."

"It was a Wednesday," said Mrs. Holmes. "I said goodbye to her that morning. Wednesday, I remember because it's Wednesday evenings that I practice with the church choir. I was home by 9:30. She's always home at least by then."

"You have choir every Wednesday night?" Jenkins asked.

"From 5:00 to 9:00," Sarah replied as she glanced back to her husband to catch the tail end of what Jenkins judged to be a scowl and the dissipating stain from an old and worn out argument between them. "Now Honey," she said to Dwayne, "you have your army buddies…"

"Marines," Dwayne corrected.

"Well, you guys stick together like glue," Sarah scowled playfully. "I have my choir."

"It was that Wednesday and you haven't seen or heard from her since then?" Jenkins asked, glancing back and forth from Sarah to Dwayne.

“No,” Mr. Holmes replied, taking another gulp of scotch.

“She’s run away before, but never for this long and never without some kind of word,” Sarah said.

Jenkins and Helen exchanged a glance.

“She’s left home before? Under what circumstances?” Jenkins asked.

“It was after a fight with her boyfriend,” Mrs. Holmes replied. “She spent two weeks with her uncle in Las Vegas during that one.”

“When was that, Mrs. Holmes?” Jenkins asked.

“Maybe about 10 months ago.”

“Have you spoken with her uncle?”

“Oh sure,” said Dwayne, “but he hasn’t seen her either.”

“Could I get his name and number from you? And her boyfriend’s name?” Jenkins asked flipping open a small notepad and retrieving a pen from his inside coat pocket.

“Sam O’Neill, that was her boyfriend,” she replied.

Jenkins paused a moment, slowly diverting his attention to the side, staring without purpose. He slowly closed the notepad and placed it back in his inside pocket.

“Did he and Erica fight often?” asked Jenkins.

“It wasn’t a match made in heaven, Lieutenant.” Mr. Holmes replied. “They were always one disagreement away from a breakup.”

“Had they had a fight the day of her disappearance?”

“The day before, yeah. They were barely speaking but still hanging on enough that Erica let him borrow her car for the day.”

“He took her car?” Jenkins asked.

“His was down for repairs at the garage.” Dwayne replied.

“And so how was Erica going to get around without her car?”

“Sam picked her up here.” Dwayne answered. “He said he was going to drop her off at the garage on his way to work. That was the last time we saw Erica. We reported her disappearance the very next day when she didn’t come home.”

“There was no phone call from her during the day?”

“No.”

“And you called her boyfriend, Sam?”

“Yeah. He said he hadn’t seen her.”

“And who made the call to report she was missing?”

“I made it,” Dwayne said. “I mean we both did. Sarah was afraid she might have run away again or something bad might have happened.”

“Why was that?”

“You know. All the troubles with Sam.”

"We have a cell phone record that shows you called Erica's service garage during the late afternoon of the day she disappeared."

"You've been checking up on me?" Mr. Holmes asked, irritated.

"I did some background work. The more I know, the better I can help you."

"Yeah. I was looking for her."

"But she wasn't there?

"Right."

"It was a completed call. Who answered the phone?"

"Who answered the phone?" Mr. Holmes said while moving to the opposite side of the sofa. He paused to swirl his scotch. "One of the help," he said and then took another gulp.

"Do you recall his name?"

"Uh, Jose or Juan or something like that. He's no longer there."

"No longer there?"

"Lieutenant, I'm not proud of this, being that I'm part owner, but we've had undocumented workers there from time to time."

"The garage has been hiring illegal immigrants?" Mrs. Holmes asked, surprised. "We're not going to get in trouble for that, are we Lieutenant?"

"I'm not ENS, Mrs. Holmes," Jenkins replied. "Let's just focus on Erica's whereabouts. Mr. Holmes, if I may. Your phone records also show that you received a call on the evening of Erica's disappearance. Around 5:30."

"I don't recall," Dwayne replied.

"It was from a public phone."

"Did you pick that up, Sweetheart?" Dwayne asked his wife.

"No. I would have remembered that," she replied. "Besides, I would have been at choir by then."

Dwayne shrugged.

"Records also show that a call was made from this residence to a Gary Furlong in Daly City."

"You called Furlough that night?" Sarah asked Dwayne.

"Furlough?" Jenkins asked.

"That was the name his buddies gave him," Sarah said quickly swatting the air. "You should hear the stories. Dwayne saved his life."

"How's that?" Jenkins asked.

"Furlough was shot and Dwayne carried him on his back a quarter of mile till he found a medic."

"He would have done the same for me," Dwayne said.

"You're being modest," Sarah chided. "He never would have made it back if not for you."

"So you called Mr. Furlong that night?" Jenkins continued.

"Could have, I suppose," Dwayne replied. "We talk all the time."

"Mr. and Mrs. Holmes," Jenkins said pausing a moment, "we've found Erica's car."

"What?" Dwayne asked.

"Erica's car. It's in the police impound lot."

"Can we get it back?" Sarah Holmes asked.

"Not right now," Jenkins replied. "It's been booked as evidence."

"Evidence. What do you mean? Why?" asked Mrs. Holmes, rising from the sofa, the cat spilling from her lap.

"We're doing some tests."

"Tests? What kind of tests?" Sarah asked.

"We just want to make sure we cover all the angles," Jenkins replied.

"Oh my God!" Sarah whispered. Her words seemed like a prayer, like dissipating smoke. With a slight tremble, she raised her eyes to her husband.

"Do you have any reason to believe that Mr. O'Neill would want to harm Erica?" Jenkins asked.

"That son of a bitch," Dwayne said. "He killed her didn't he? I tried to warn her about him. He was no good for her."

"What have you found?" Sarah pleaded. "Where's my girl?"

"We don't know where she is," Jenkins replied. "But we're doing all we can to find her. Do you know of anyone besides her boyfriend who might have wanted to harm Erica?"

"No, of course not," Sarah responded. "Everyone loved her."

"Mr. Holmes, do you ever drive your daughter's car?" Jenkins asked.

"Drive her car?" Dwayne responded.

"Oh heavens no," Sarah cut in. "That was her baby. I'm surprised she let Sam drive it. What women do for love."

"I'll need to speak with any of Erica's acquaintances," said Jenkins. "Do you know of anyone who might be helpful? Have you ever seen her argue with anyone besides her boyfriend?"

"You should talk to Chuck Beamer next door," Dwayne said emphatically. "If it could have been anyone other than Sam, it would be Chuck Beamer." Sarah glanced at her husband suspiciously. He looked back at her but she turned her head away quickly. Their eyes didn't connect.

"Thanks for the tip," said Jenkins. "If you should think of anything else that might be helpful, please don't hesitate to call me." Jenkins handed Dwayne his business card. "Helen, we should go."

Bending slightly at the waist to bring herself closer to Jenkins' ear, Helen whispered "DNA samples!"

"Excuse me?" Jenkins said in a low tone.

"We should collect DNA samples," Helen said, slightly louder.

"Oh yes, … of course," Jenkins stumbled. "Mr. and Mrs. Holmes, it would help the investigation if we could just take a sample of your DNA."

"You couldn't possibly believe we are suspects," Sarah said, aghast.

"No. No. Of course not," Jenkins replied. "This is just routine."

"I hate needles," Sarah exclaimed. "You don't need blood, do you?"

"No, not at all," Jenkins reassured her. "Helen, if you would do the honors."

Helen took a long cylindrical tube from her bag and withdrew a cotton swab held inside of it. "Say ahhhh," Helen asked of Sarah. Sarah complied and Helen swabbed the inside of Mrs. Holmes' cheek and placed the swab back into the vial. With a marking pen, she recorded the sample name and date on the side of the tube.

"And you, Mr. Holmes," Helen requested.

"Wait a minute, wait a minute," Mr. Holmes protested. "What's DNAhhhhhhh?" Helen teased his mouth open with a swab and swiped the inside lining of his cheek. She grimaced involuntarily from the smell of alcohol and tobacco carried on the exhaled vapors of his breath.

"That's good," Helen said. "You can close your mouth now." As she inserted the swab into its plastic vial, she shot Jenkins a glance that conveyed less than appreciation for being assigned the sampling task.

"Don't you need a warrant for something like this?" Dwayne asked impatiently. "What can you tell from DNA?"

"Ah, it's routine, Mr. Holmes," Jenkins said hesitantly. "It can help us find Erica. We'll also need you to come down to the station so that we can take your prints," Jenkins said.

"Prints too? Why fingerprints?" Dwayne asked.

"If we're able to recover prints from Erica's vehicle, we'll need to know whose is whose," Jenkins replied. "Thank you for your cooperation and we'll be in touch."

Helen and Jenkins moved to the front door with Sarah Holmes escorting closely. Dwayne retreated back to the fireplace.

"Lieutenant," Sarah Holmes said as Jenkins moved to follow Helen out the door. "Do you have children?"

"I have a daughter, Mrs. Holmes," Jenkins replied.

"Erica is my girl. My baby. There is nothing more important to a parent than their child." Sarah handed Jenkins a small scrap of paper on which was scrawled "David Epperson" and a phone number. It was a 702 area code.

"Your brother in Vegas?" Jenkins asked.

"Yes," Sarah replied. Jenkins slipped the paper into his pants pocket. "Lieutenant, bring her home."

Jenkins paused on the door stoop. "I understand," he said.

Sarah Holmes closed the door softly behind them.

"Are we going to talk to this Gary Furlong, now?" Helen asked.

"I already did," Jenkins replied. "I talked with him on the phone before we came over here but he didn't give much more than his name, rank, and serial number as it were. He admitted knowing Mr. Holmes. But you heard him in there, Furlong was in his unit. If he knows anything about this case, it'll take a subpoena, a prosecuting attorney, and a hand on the Bible to get anything out of him, and maybe not even then."

"Semper Fi," Helen murmured. "What is it with men? They just stick together, don't they? They'll keep their mouths shut no matter what the consequences—never snitching on one of their own. Oh no. You can't do that. Like some kind of unwritten but sacred commandment or something."

Jenkins drew a heavy breath. "I suppose so," he said on the exhale.

DNA Isolation and Quantitation

DNA, that beautiful spiral molecule twisting like the staircase in a lighthouse, carries all the information that was needed to make a complete you. Your gender, the color of your hair, your skin, your eyes, and even the ability, if you have it, to curl your tongue into the shape of a half pipe, you owe all to your DNA and the information it encodes.

In almost every crime of violence—assault, rape, or murder—DNA is left behind as a calling card to the participants of that violence. DNA is in the hair ripped out by an assailant. It's in the semen and saliva from the rapist. It's in the skin trapped under the fingernails of the victim who was trying to defend herself against attack. It's in the drops of blood splashed against the pavement from a gang slaying. It's a silent witness waiting in the bones of the dead and discarded. To get that witness to divulge its secrets, it must first be isolated in a pure form and its amount determined.

DNA is actually two molecules in one. It is *double-stranded*—made from two strands held together by weak chemical bonds, called *hydrogen bonds*, between complementary *bases*. An A base (adenine) on one strand always bonds with its complementary base T (thymine) on the other strand, and a C (cytosine) on one strand always bonds with a G (guanine) on the opposite strand (Figure 5.1). An A with a T and a C with a G are called *base pairs* (*bp*). When a base such as A, C, G, or T is also connected to a phosphate group (a phosphorous atom surrounded by four oxygen atoms) and a ribose sugar, it is called a nucleotide. DNA consists of two nucleotide chains. The hydrogen bonds between those two chains are weak and easily broken by heating or by chemical treatment under the right laboratory conditions.

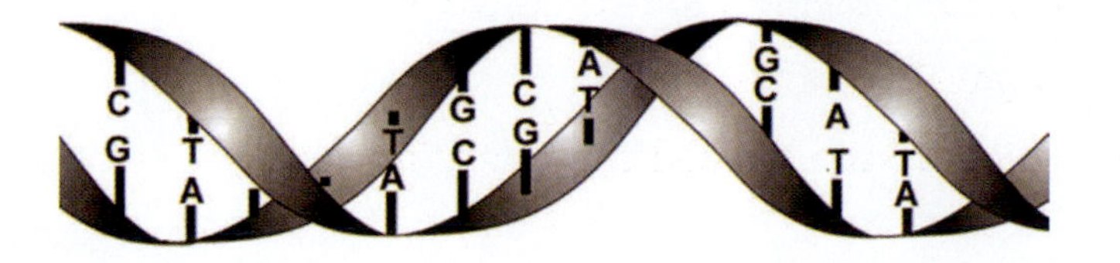

Figure 5.1 The DNA double helix consists of two strands wound around each other with bonds between complementary bases (A with T and G with C) on opposite strands holding the two strands together.

Each cell in your body (with some exceptions) carries 6,000,000,000 bp of DNA carried on 46 chromosomes. If you were to line your DNA up side-by-side with that belonging to any one of your friends, there would be a difference roughly once every couple hundred of bases. It is because of such differences, because each person's DNA is unique to them (with the exception of identical twins), that DNA has become such a valuable forensic tool in helping to identify the deceased and to discern the innocent from the guilty.

Identifying DNA Sources

DNA can be recovered from any tissue or bodily fluid that contains cells. Urine carries cells from the bladder and urethra, saliva carries cells from the cheeks and tongue, blood carries white blood cells (a red blood cell is without chromosomes), semen carries sperm cells, fecal material carries the cells of the intestines, bone carries cells from the marrow, and hair carries cells from the follicle—DNA can be isolated from all of them.

For many crimes, the sources from which DNA can be recovered are obvious. Pools of blood, skeletal remains, or flesh torn from the victim will be readily apparent at the primary crime scene. Less obvious, however, will be saliva, semen stains, dried urine, or drops of blood on a dark or red background. These may need to be visualized using special reagents such as luminol or by special light sources. Body fluids on skin can be visualized by the naked eye under UV light. Body fluids on clothing and other fabrics can be seen with a special blue light at a wavelength of 505 or 530 nm while wearing goggles having an orange filter. As most of the cases handled by a criminalist deal with sexual assault, tests have been developed for the forensic scientist that can be used to detect semen, not only by UV light, but also by the unique proteins semen contains (Figure 5.2a and b). These include acid phosphatase (AP) and prostate-specific antigen (PSA) that can react to produce a color change with special chemical tests.

A trained investigator will also know that cells can be recovered from articles of clothing at areas that rub against the skin. These would include the inside rim of a

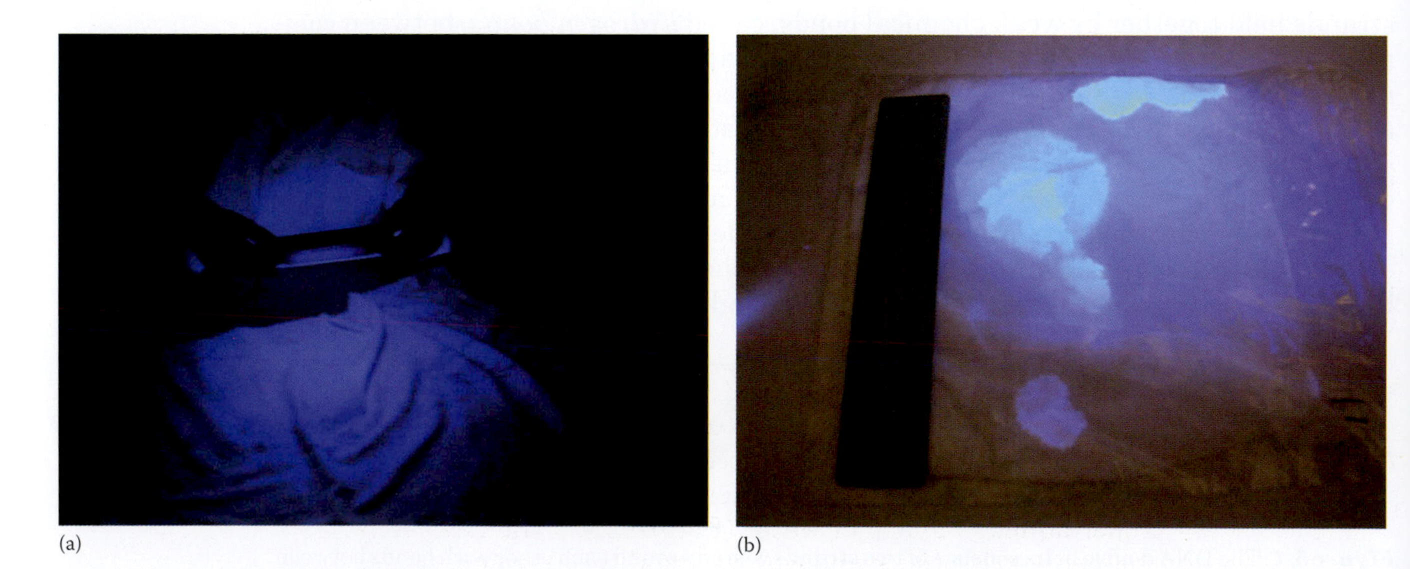

(a) (b)

Figure 5.2 (a) A UV light being used to help locate semen stains on bed linens. (b) A semen stain illuminated with UV light at 365 nm. (Photo courtesy of Dr. Steve Lee, Director of Forensic Science, San Jose State University, San Jose, CA.)

hat, the collar or cuffs of a shirt, and the nose bridge of a pair of glasses. In the cases of violent assault, investigators will also examine beneath the victim's fingernails to see if they can recover any of the assailant's skin cells that may have scratched off during the attack.

Isolation of DNA

No matter what type of cells the forensic analyst is dealing with, releasing the DNA from those cells requires breaking them open by destroying their cell walls. There are a number of ways to do this—heat, detergents, ultrahigh-frequency sound, enzymes, or protein-disrupting chemicals can all be used, some working better than others depending on the type of cell.

Cells contain a variety of molecules. When a cell is broken open and the DNA is released, tens of thousands of different proteins, carbohydrates, and fats will also spill out in the process. In addition, the biological sample itself may carry substances from the environment if, for example, the biological sample was recovered from the ground. These contaminating molecules can, depending on the DNA test, interfere or inhibit subsequent analysis and may need to be removed. *Heme* from blood can inhibit the enzyme used for DNA amplification, and *humic acid* from soil can destroy the DNA sample. It is usually the case, therefore, that more highly purified DNA yields a more reliable analysis.

Chelex

One of the simplest ways to recover DNA from human cells is by using the resin Chelex 100 from Bio-Rad Laboratories (Figure 5.3). Cells from blood, semen, or skin are placed into an alkaline (basic) solution of 5% Chelex and heated close to boiling for 10 min. At this high temperature, the cells burst open releasing their DNA. The Chelex resin binds to any *ions* (charged molecules) that might act to enhance the activity of enzymes called *nucleases* capable of degrading and destroying the released DNA. The DNA sample can then be used directly for quantification and analysis. Because heat is used to break open the cells, the DNA released is single-stranded.

Phenol–Chloroform Extraction

Extracting DNA by using a mixture of the chemicals phenol and chloroform has been practiced for decades and always, because of the caustic and dangerous nature of these chemicals, with a degree of trepidation. Phenol can quickly burn skin, and chloroform is a chemical that, prior to more modern methods, was, during the nineteenth and twentieth centuries, used for anesthesia. It is also a potential carcinogen (can cause cancer).

Phenol–chloroform reagent is prepared by mixing liquid phenol with an equal volume of 96% chloroform, 4% isoamyl alcohol. To this mixture is added an equal volume of cells resuspended in water or buffer. The entire solution is then mixed vigorously and centrifuged. The centrifugation step separates the two *phases*—an organic phase is made up of the phenol–chloroform–isoamyl alcohol and is below the upper aqueous phase of water (Figure 5.4). The DNA molecules collect in the aqueous phase. Proteins and cell wall materials from the disrupted cells collect as a whitish boundary between the two phases. The upper aqueous phase containing the DNA is removed and the extraction is repeated until

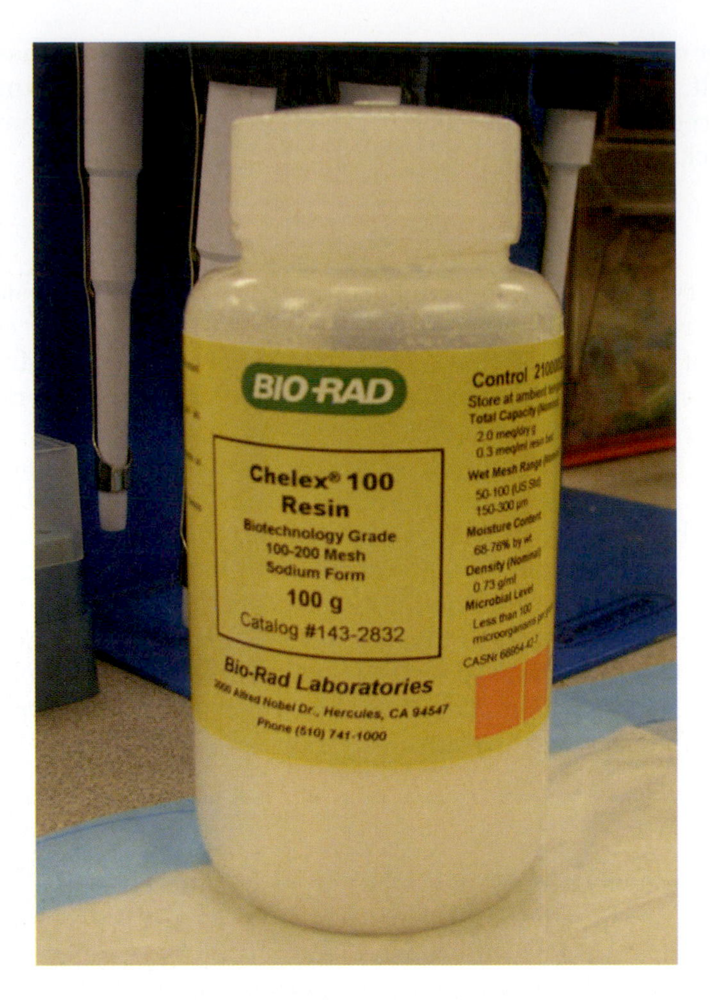

Figure 5.3 Chelex and heat are used to break cells open, and in the process, cellular enzymes that might destroy the released DNA are inactivated.

no white material collects between the two phases. The aqueous sample is then extracted with chloroform to remove any traces of phenol, and the final aqueous phase is precipitated by centrifugation in the presence of ethanol to remove any traces of chloroform. The pelleted DNA is resuspended in a buffer and stored in the refrigerator where it can be drawn upon for quantification and analysis. Since phenol–chloroform extraction of DNA does not require a heating step, the DNA molecules recovered from this procedure are double-stranded.

Differential Extraction: Cases of Sexual Assault

In cases of sexual assault, a vaginal swab can provide a sample of semen from which spermatozoa can be isolated and their DNA analyzed. However, that swab will also carry epithelial cells from the victim's vaginal wall. It is necessary in such cases, therefore, to separate the two types of cells—to separate the perpetrator's sperm cells from the victim's epithelial cells. Sperm have a hardy cell wall. This makes their separation possible.

Cells from a vaginal swab are washed off the cotton with a buffer. The epithelial cells are fairly fragile and will *lyse* (break open) in the presence of proteinase K (an enzyme that digests proteins) and a detergent such as sodium dodecyl sulfate (SDS). Sperm cells are resistant to such treatment. Following centrifugation to pellet the

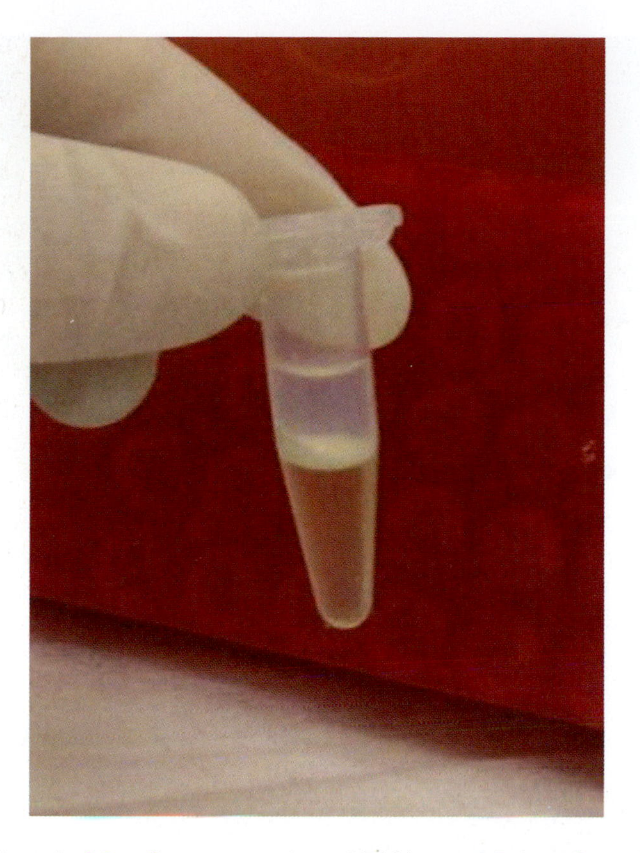

Figure 5.4 During phenol–chloroform extraction of DNA, two phases form following mixing and centrifugation—an upper aqueous phase containing the DNA and a lower organic phase consisting of the phenol–chloroform mixture. A thin, white flocculent layer of cell debris collects at the interface between the aqueous and organic phases following a brief centrifugation.

spermatozoa, the supernatant containing the victim's DNA is removed. The pelleted sperm cells are washed several times with buffer to remove any traces of epithelial DNA, and the remaining spermatozoa are treated with dithiothreitol (DTT), proteinase K, and detergent. In the presence of DTT, the sperm cells break open, releasing their DNA, which is then free of the victim's DNA.

Quantifying DNA

Before a criminalist can match DNA to a suspect, they have to know how much of the molecule they have. This knowledge will allow them to perform a more reproducible and accurate identification. DNA quantification is so critical to producing reliable results that it has been recognized as a necessary step to proper DNA analysis by both the Scientific Working Group on DNA Analysis Methods (SWGDAM) and the Technical Working Group on DNA Analysis Methods (TWGDAM), the two leading organizations involved in establishing the best practices for handling DNA evidence.

There are several methods for quantifying DNA. The most widely used general technique employed by most molecular biology and biotechnology laboratories is to measure the absorbance of a DNA solution at a UV wavelength of 260 nm. This is done on an instrument called a *spectrophotometer* (Figure 5.5). At the 260 nm wavelength, the concentration of double-stranded DNA is proportional to its absorbance by the following relationship:

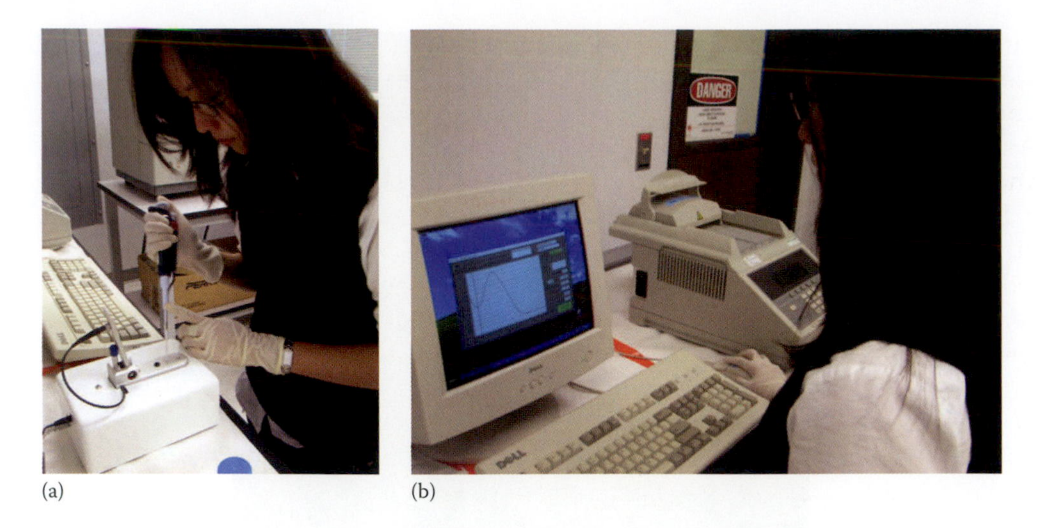

Figure 5.5 (a) Measuring the optical density (OD) of a DNA sample. On a NanoDrop spectrophotometer (NanoDrop Technologies), a 1 µL sample of DNA is carefully placed on the detector and its absorbance at 260 and 280 nm can be read. (b) The results are displayed on a computer connected to the spectrophotometer.

A solution of double-stranded DNA having an absorbance of 1.0 has a DNA concentration of 50 µg DNA/mL.

Double-stranded DNA can be split into two separate strands—the hydrogen bonds holding those two strands together can be broken—by heat. The Chelex procedure for DNA isolation uses a 10 min heating step at (or close to) boiling to break open the cells. DNA isolated by this procedure, therefore, will be single-stranded. To quantitate single-stranded DNA, the following relationship applies:

A solution of single-stranded DNA having an absorbance of 1.0 has a concentration of 33 µg DNA/mL.

Proteins are often copurified along with DNA isolated from biological material. Some proteins may act to degrade DNA. Others, such as hemoglobin, may inhibit the enzymes used to subsequently characterize the DNA's genetic markers. Therefore, knowing how much protein is present in a DNA sample can give a forensic scientist an indication of how it might perform in an enzymatic assay.

Whereas DNA absorbs maximally at 260 nm, protein absorbs at 280 nm. Forensic scientists will take the ratio of the absorbance at 260 nm (the "A_{260}" or "260") over the absorbance at 280 nm (the "A_{280}" or "280"). An A_{260}-to-A_{280} ratio of 1.8 is considered pure DNA. A 260-to-280 ratio of 1.5 or less may give poor results in an assay where enzymes are used to cut or replicate the DNA molecule.

Quantifying DNA by Real-Time PCR

A technique called *real-time polymerase chain reaction* (*PCR*) is gaining popularity as a means to quantitate DNA. It uses a sophisticated piece of equipment to monitor the amount of fluorescent light emitted when a specific segment of DNA is replicated over and over again.

PCR is a laboratory method for amplifying a defined segment of DNA. A PCR reaction is carried out in a small tube and requires only a short list of components. One of these is an enzyme, a protein, known as *DNA polymerase*. DNA polymerase can be found in your own cells. It is the enzyme that replicates DNA. It takes one strand of the DNA double helix and, using the base pairing rules (A across from T and C across from G), makes a new complementary strand across from it, linking one base to the next, thereby recreating the two-stranded helix.

As in standard DNA replication, the strand that's copied into a complementary strand during PCR is called the *template*. But DNA polymerase doesn't just make new DNA at any random place along the template—it needs a specific place to start. That starting place is provided by another piece of single-stranded DNA called the *primer* that binds to the template, again according to the base pairing rules. The primer is of a length, around 21 bases or so, such that, at the proper temperature, it sticks to only one place on the template strand (Figure 5.6). In PCR, two primers are used, one attaching to one strand of the double helix, the other primer attaching to the other strand. And, furthermore, the two primers are facing each other. That is, the building of new DNA chains onto those two primers is in the direction of one towards the other. In a PCR reaction, binding of primers to template and extension of those primers by the DNA polymerase enzyme is repeated many times.

The steps of PCR are controlled by shifting the temperature of the reaction. The first step, separating the template double helix into single strands, is accomplished by bringing the reaction temperature close to boiling. The next step in which the two primers bind to the separated template strands is controlled by lowering the temperature. The final step of a PCR cycle, in which DNA polymerase adds *nucleotides* onto the primers to make new DNA chains, is brought about by bringing the

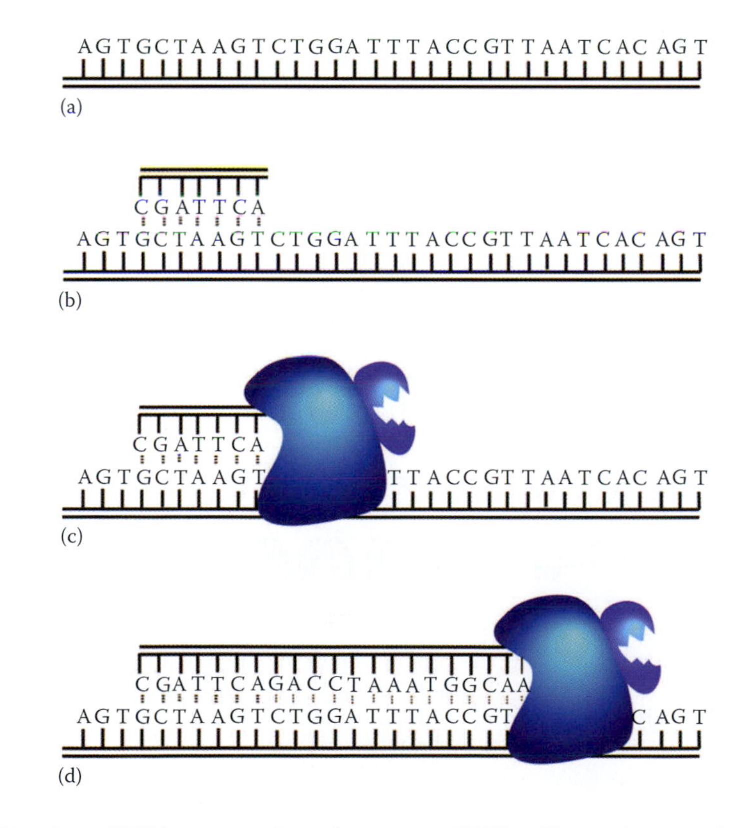

Figure 5.6 Replication of DNA occurs when the enzyme DNA polymerase extends a primer attached to a single-stranded template molecule. (a) A single strand of DNA. Double-stranded DNA can be converted to single strands by heating. (b) A primer attaches to the single-stranded template at complementary sequence. (c) The DNA polymerase binds to one end of the primer. (d) DNA polymerase extends the primer by attaching bases, one to the next, according to the complementary sequence of the template.

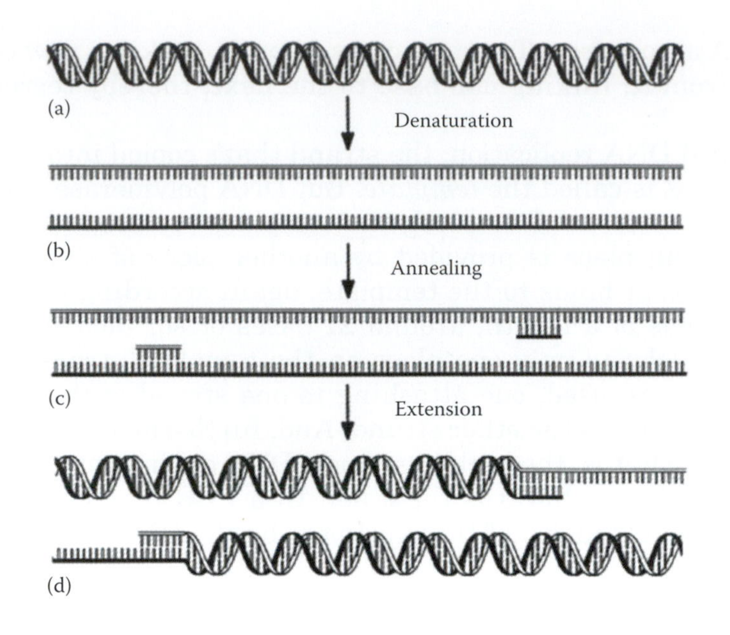

Figure 5.7 In the first cycle of PCR (known as denaturation), the double-stranded template DNA (a) is heated to produce single strands (b). During the annealing step, the temperature of the reaction is lowered so that two primers can attach to the opposite template strands (c). During the extension step (d), DNA polymerase adds bases onto one end of each primer.

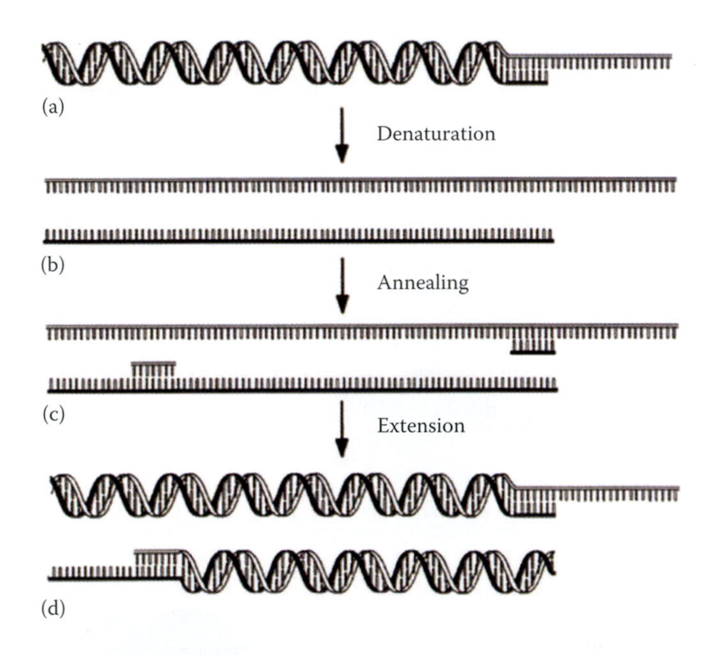

Figure 5.8 In the second cycle of PCR, the product made in the first cycle (a) is denatured at a high temperature to separate the strands (b). Primers anneal at a lower temperature (c), and DNA extends those primers (d). DNA polymerase only extends a primer out as far as the end of the template. DNA polymerase then falls off and is free to extend another primer.

reaction to an intermediate temperature. These heating and cooling steps are performed in an instrument called a *thermal cycler*. Most PCR reactions will be carried out anywhere from 25 to 40 cycles (Figures 5.7 through 5.10).

The primary function of the DNA polymerase enzyme is to extend a primer by linking one nucleotide onto the next as it copies a template strand. But the

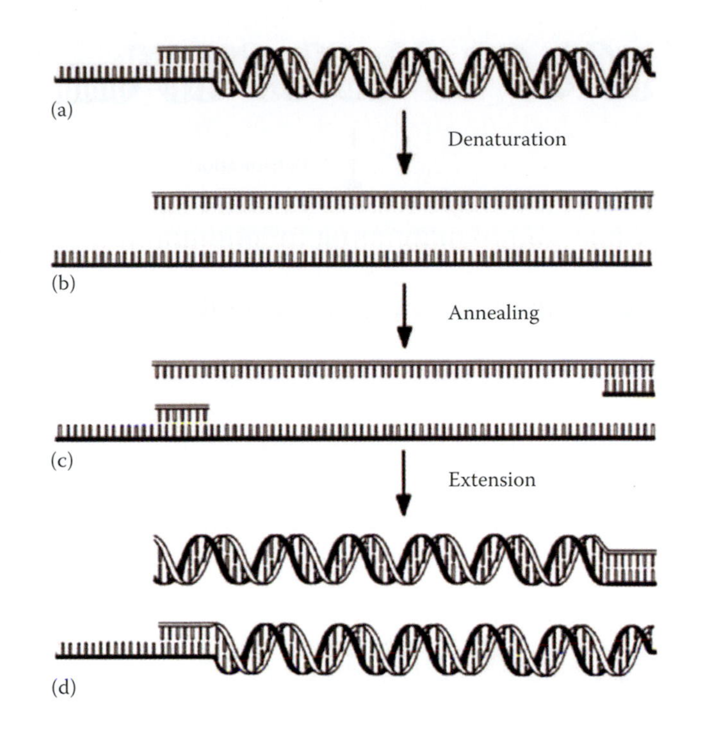

Figure 5.9 In the third cycle of PCR, the product made in the second cycle (a) undergoes denaturation (b), primer annealing (c), and extension (d). It is in the third cycle that a product appears with a length defined by where the primers sit and the distance between them (the upper of the two strands in step d).

enzyme engages in another activity as well—while it's extending a primer, it displaces and destroys any DNA strands it encounters that may be attached to the template it is copying (Figure 5.11). This function of the DNA polymerase is called its *5′–3′ exonuclease*.

In real-time PCR, DNA polymerase's 5′–3′ exonuclease activity is used to generate the production of fluorescent light. That light comes from a dye, called a *reporter dye*, attached to one end of a single-stranded piece of DNA called a *probe* (Figure 5.12) designed to sit down on the template by its complementary base sequence such that it is directly in the path of the DNA polymerase extending one of the PCR primers. The probe also carries, on its other end, a molecule called a *quencher* that, when in close proximity to the reporter and connected to it through the chain of bases making up the probe, prevents the reporter dye from glowing. However, when the DNA polymerase encounters the probe attached to the template strand it is copying and its 5′–3′ exonuclease activity chews it up, the reporter dye is released from the probe. As the reporter dye is separated from the quencher, it gives off fluorescent light that can be detected by the optics and camera of a real-time PCR instrument (Figure 5.13).

Real-time PCR is such an effective technique for quantifying DNA because the amount of fluorescent light produced is directly proportional to the amount of amplifiable template DNA added to the reaction. As amplification progresses, more template strands are produced to which the probe can bind. The more probe that binds, the more light that can be generated as that probe is broken down by an extending DNA polymerase. Eventually, enough light is produced that it becomes detectable by the real-time PCR instrument. The point at which the amount of fluorescence increases above background noise is called the cycle threshold (C_T).

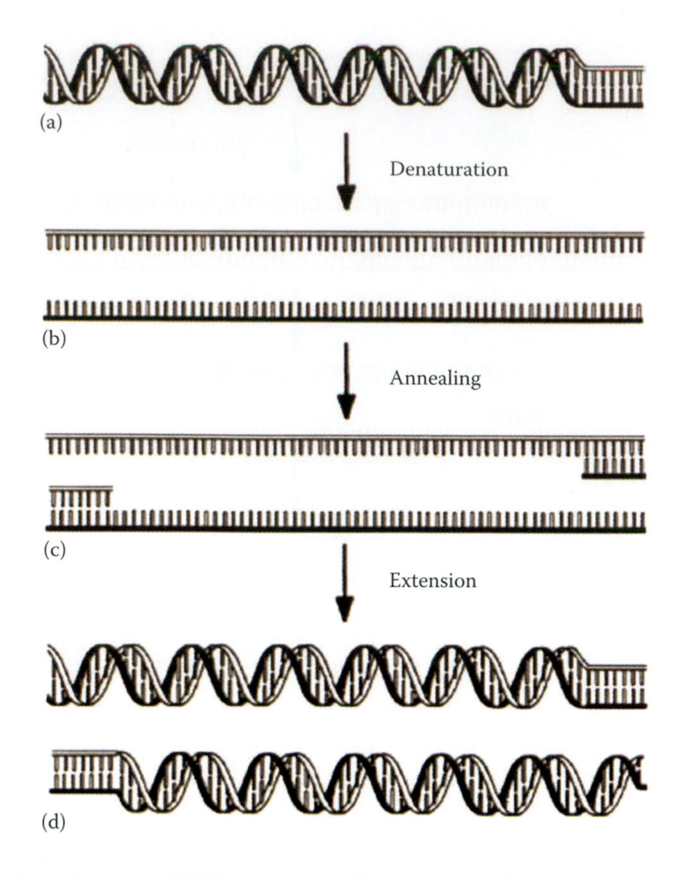

Figure 5.10 In the fourth cycle of PCR, the short fragment made in cycle 3 (a) is denatured by heat (b), primers are annealed to the separated strands (c), and two of the short products are made (d). From here on into subsequent cycles, the short product is amplified exponentially; one product makes two, two products make four, four makes eight, etc.

The more template DNA added to a real-time PCR reaction, the quicker fluorescence is detected and the lower the C_T value. When only small amounts of template DNA are put into a real-time PCR reaction, more cycles will be required to generate a detectable fluorescent signal and the higher will be the C_T value.

Another segment of DNA included as part of the assay is called the internal positive control (IPC). It has its own primer and probe set. Its function is to test for the presence of anything carried in the template DNA sample that might inhibit the reaction. For example, heme from blood and tannic acid from soil are powerful inhibitors of the DNA polymerase used in PCR. Amplification of the IPC will generate green fluorescent signal (the probe specific to human DNA glows blue). If the IPC amplifies in the real-time PCR assay, the experimenter knows that the reaction is working fine and that if no signal is generated from the DNA evidence sample, it's not because there is something wrong with the system.

The instruments used for real-time PCR carry within them a thermal cycler unit to shift the temperature between that needed to denature the template DNA and those needed to anneal and extend the primers. (Oftentimes, the annealing and extension steps are combined into a single step.) The instrument also carries the necessary optics to detect the increase in fluorescent light generated during the reaction.

Quantifying DNA by real-time PCR requires that the operator simultaneously runs DNA samples of known amount so that the software can construct a standard curve from which DNA concentrations of the unknown samples can be determined.

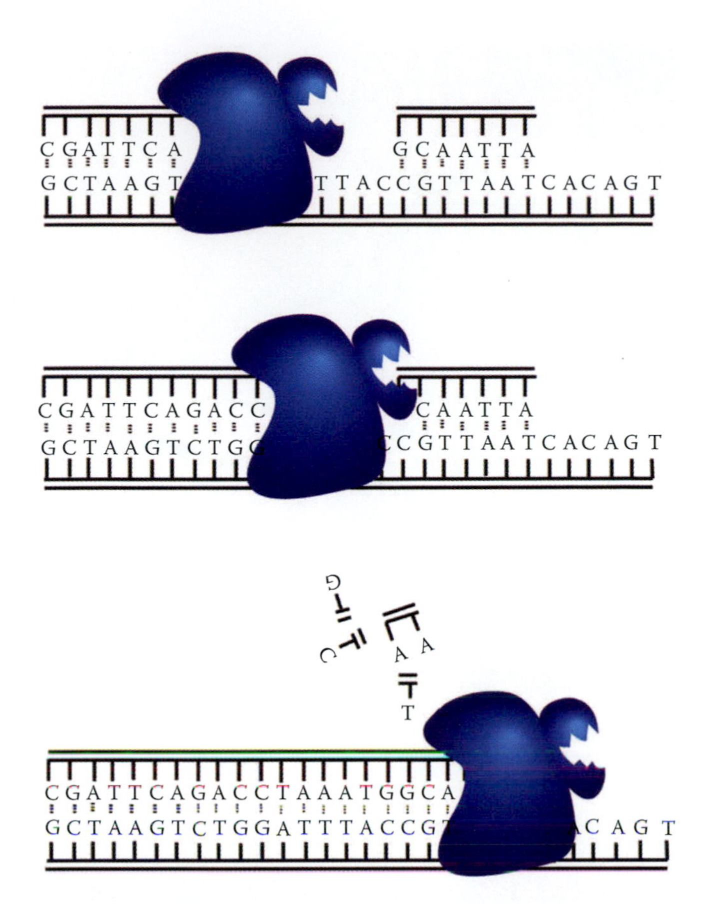

Figure 5.11 The 5′–3′ exonuclease function of DNA polymerase displaces and breaks down any strand attached to the template in its path. That strand, as it is displaced, is degraded into single and double nucleotides.

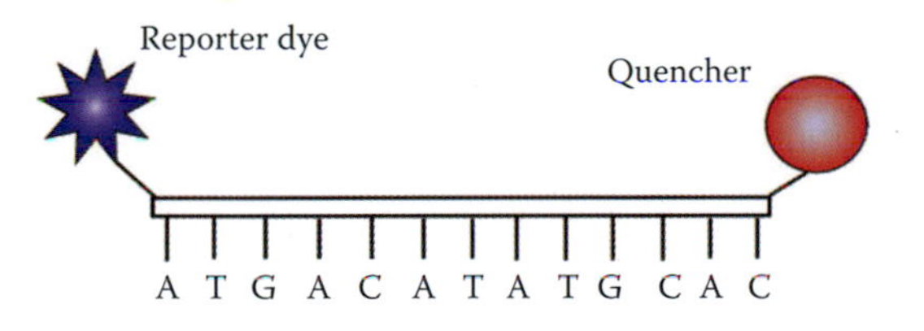

Figure 5.12 A TaqMan probe is a short, single-stranded segment of DNA complementary to a part of the template DNA strand between two PCR primers. It carries a reporter dye on one end and a quencher molecule on the other.

The Quantifiler kit marketed by Life Technologies (Figure 5.14) provides human DNA (the standard) of a known concentration that the operator dilutes into a series of tubes to produce lower and lower concentrations. Included in the Quantifiler kit are the primers needed to amplify a gene having only a single copy in the human genome. A TaqMan probe attaches to that gene during the PCR amplification and produces blue fluorescence during the assay. These primers and probe are specific for a gene found in humans and other primates. They will not produce a result for DNA recovered from nonprimate sources. Preparing real-time PCR reactions requires only a few steps (Figures 5.15 and 5.16).

Figure 5.13 A Life Technologies Model 7500 Sequence Detection System used for real-time PCR.

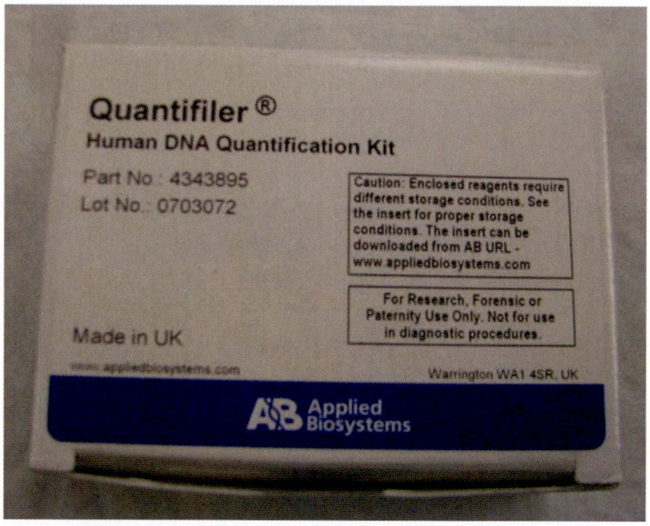

Figure 5.14 The Quantifiler kit from Life Technologies provides all the reagents needed to quantify evidence DNA samples by real-time PCR.

In the Crime Lab

Activity 5.1 Isolation of DNA from Strawberries

DNA can be isolated in fairly pure form from any fruit or vegetable using easily obtainable chemicals. The protocol described here for purifying double-stranded DNA from strawberries uses the following supplies:

Materials:

Dishwashing liquid
Table salt
Rubbing alcohol (chilled)
Sealable plastic storage bag

Figure 5.15 Real-Time PCR reactions are prepared in a microtiter plate—a plastic tray with 96 wells for individual assays.

Figure 5.16 The microtiter plate is covered with an optically clear adhesive so that the real-time PCR reactions will not evaporate during thermal cycling.

Wooden or bamboo shish kabob skewer
Clear plastic drinking cup
Cheesecloth
Funnel
100 mL distilled water
2 mL sterile water
1.5 mL microcentrifuge tube
Parafilm or 200 mL beaker for mixing
100 mL graduated cylinder
10 mL graduated cylinder or 10 mL pipette
Four strawberries

Protocol:

1. Prepare an extraction reagent by adding 2 g of table salt to a 100 mL graduated cylinder.

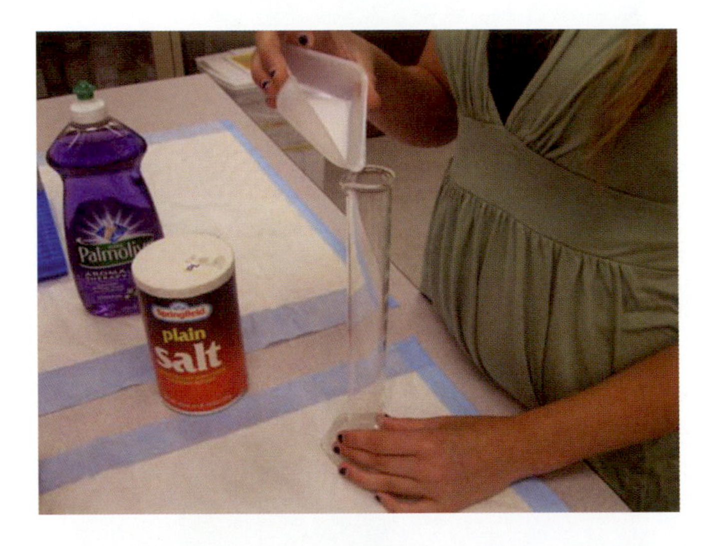

2. Add distilled water to the graduated cylinder to a volume of 90 mL.

3. Add dishwashing liquid up to the 100 mL mark.

4. Mix the extraction reagent by capping one end with Parafilm or by pouring the liquid back and forth several times between two containers.

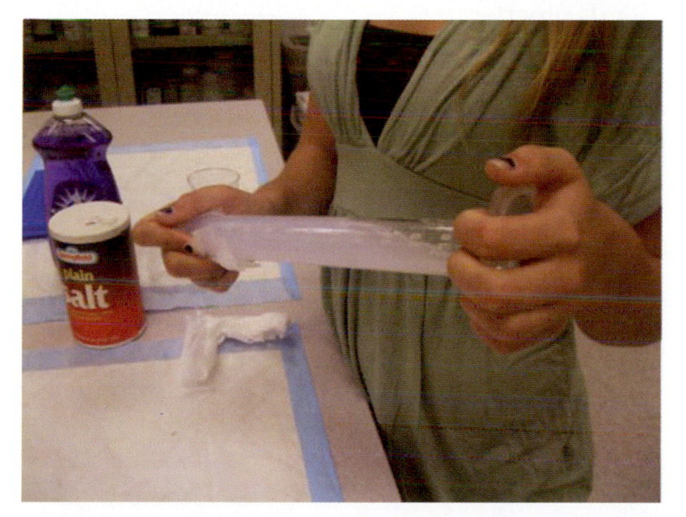

5. Place three to four strawberries into a sealable bag, remove as much air from the bag as possible, and then seal the bag tightly.

6. Squish the strawberries in the sealed bag until they are thoroughly smashed. This step should take at least 1 min.

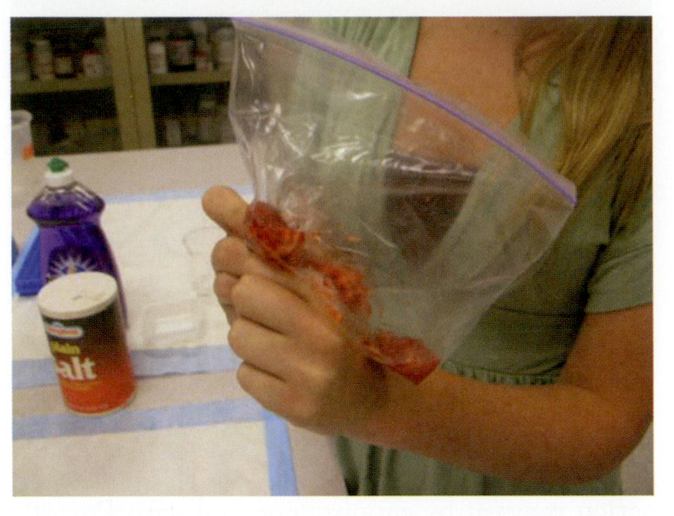

7. Measure 10 mL of extraction reagent prepared above into a graduated cylinder or into a 10 mL pipette.

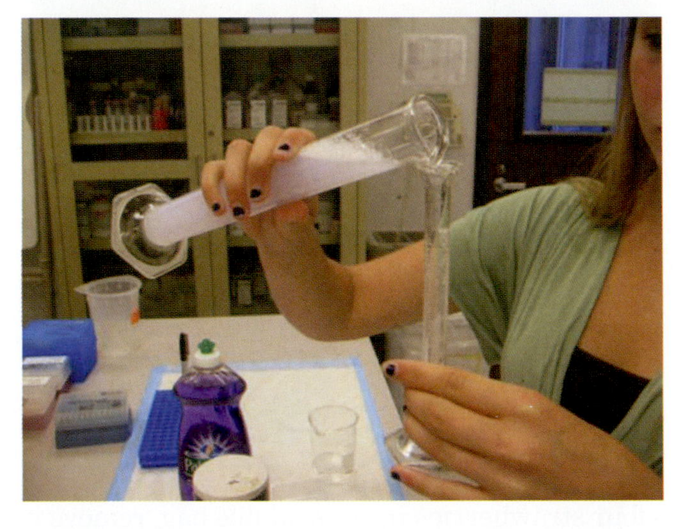

8. Add 10 mL of extraction reagent into the bag of squished strawberries and carefully reseal the bag.

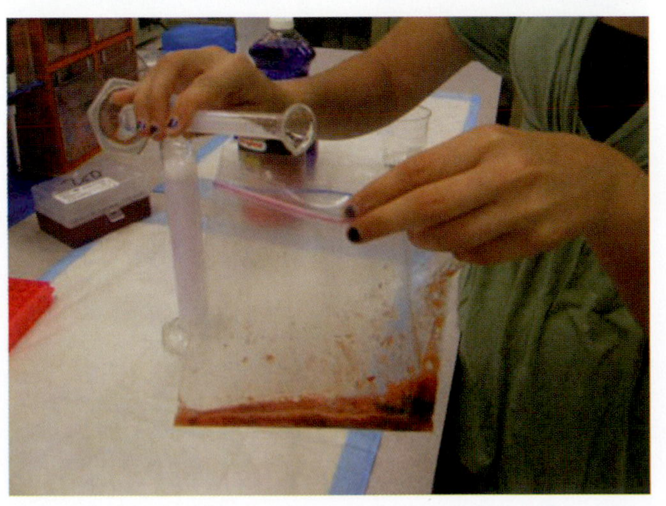

9. Squish the mixture together for approximately 1 min.

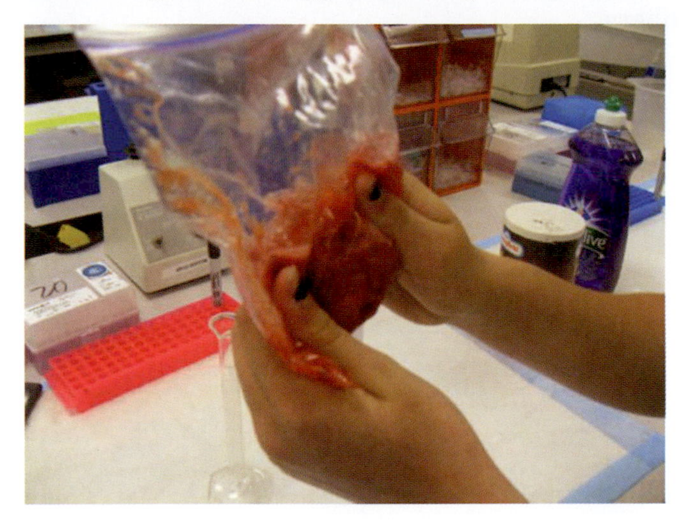

10. Pour the mixture through one layer of cheesecloth supported in a funnel held within a clear plastic drinking cup. Allow the liquid to pass through the cheesecloth into the plastic cup. Additional liquid can be recovered by wringing out the cheesecloth.

11. Slowly pour approximately 40 mL of cold isopropanol (rubbing alcohol) down the side of the cup into the strawberry extract.

12. Hold the drinking cup up to the light. DNA should become visible as stringy translucent fibers.

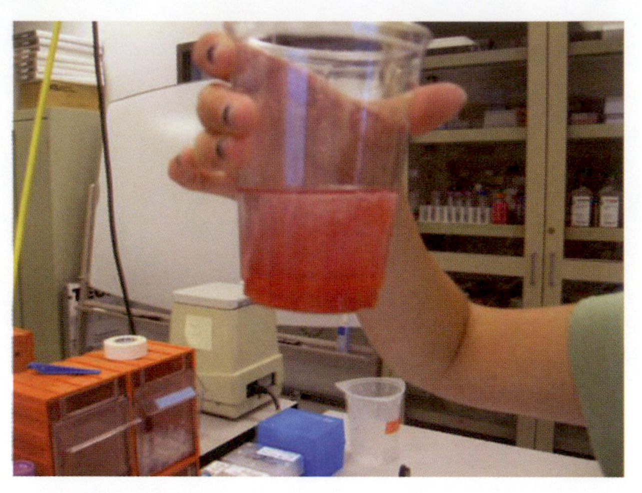

13. Slowly swirl a bamboo skewer into the mixture.

14. When the DNA has been spooled onto the skewer, gently withdraw the skewer from the liquid and press the collected DNA against an inner dry side of the drinking cup.

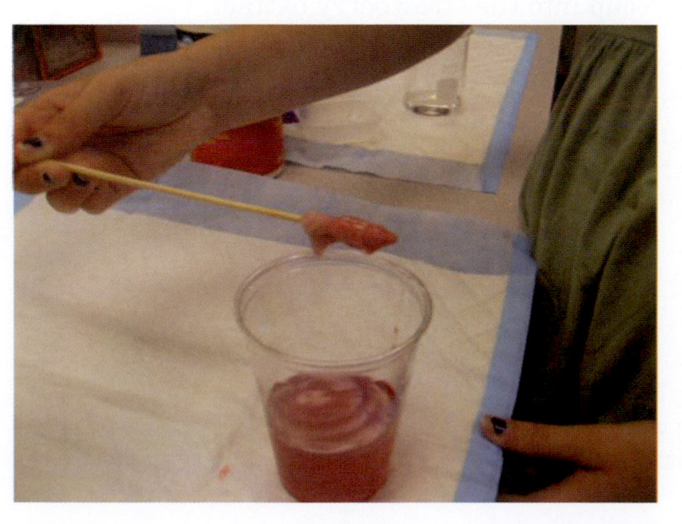

15. Scrape the spooled DNA into a 1.5 mL tube marked with "DNA" and the date.

16. Add sterile distilled water to bring up the volume to approximately 1.5 mL. Store the DNA sample in the refrigerator.

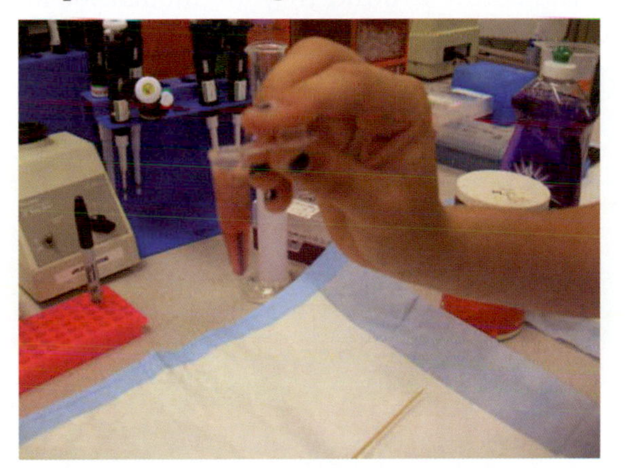

Activity 5.2 Isolating Buccal Cell DNA by Chelex Extraction

Most forensic samples are small… a hair, a drop of saliva, a spot of semen or blood, and, as such, require special handling for the extraction of their DNA. One popular approach to isolating DNA from forensic samples is by the use of a chelating resin called Chelex® manufactured by Bio-Rad Laboratories. Its chelating activity removes positively charged ions from a DNA sample, thereby rendering any nucleases (enzymes that destroy DNA, which rely on such ions for their activity) inactive. The following protocol describes the isolation of DNA from buccal (cheek) cells using Chelex. Since this protocol includes a heating step that helps to break open the cells, the DNA that is recovered will be in a single-stranded form.

Materials:

- 10 mL of sterile 0.9% saline
- Disposable drinking cup
- P1000 and P200 Pipetmen with tips
- 1.5 mL tubes
- 0.2 mL tubes (if using a thermal cycler for heating)
- Microcentrifuge rack
- Hot water bath or thermal cycler
- 200 µL of 5% Chelex

Protocol:

1. Without swallowing, pour 10 mL of 0.9% saline solution in your mouth.

2. Vigorously swish the saline around in your mouth for at least 30s. Spit the solution back into the cup.

Optional. Place a drop of the swish solution on a microscope slide, apply a cover slip, and observe the cells under the microscope. You will see individual skin cells as well as thin sheets of epithelial cells.

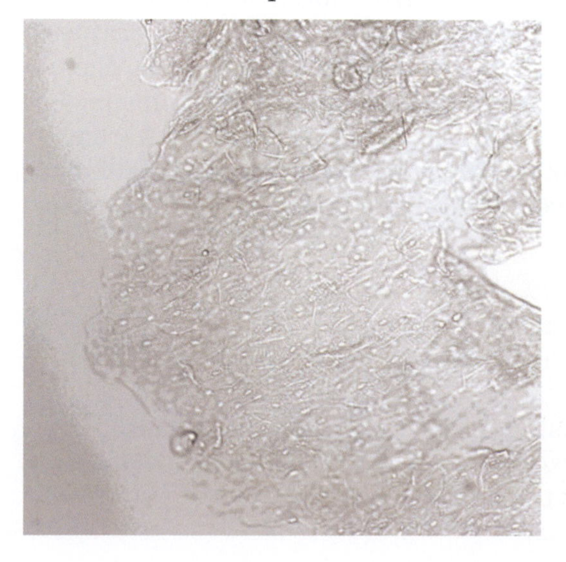

3. Using a P1000 pipettor (Rainin or equivalent) fitted with an appropriate pipette tip, withdraw 1 mL of swish solution.

4. Transfer the 1 mL of swish solution to a 1.5 mL tube.

5. Spin the cells in a microcentrifuge for 1 min at full speed to pellet the cells. At the end of this spin, you should see a white pellet of cells at the bottom of the tube.

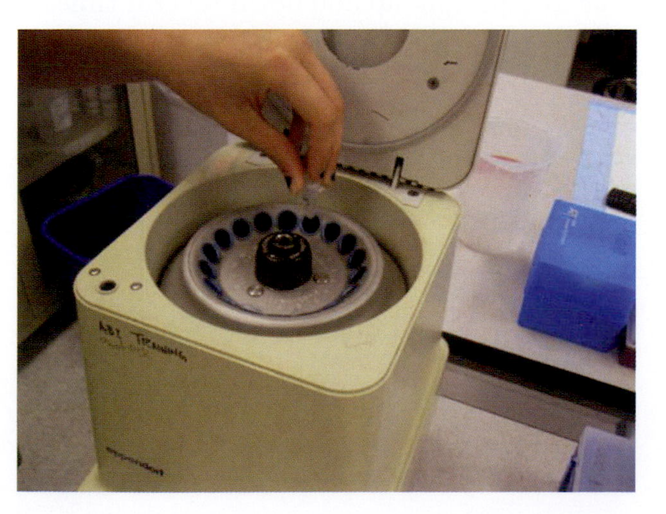

6. Pour the supernatant back into your cup. Try to remove as much liquid as possible.

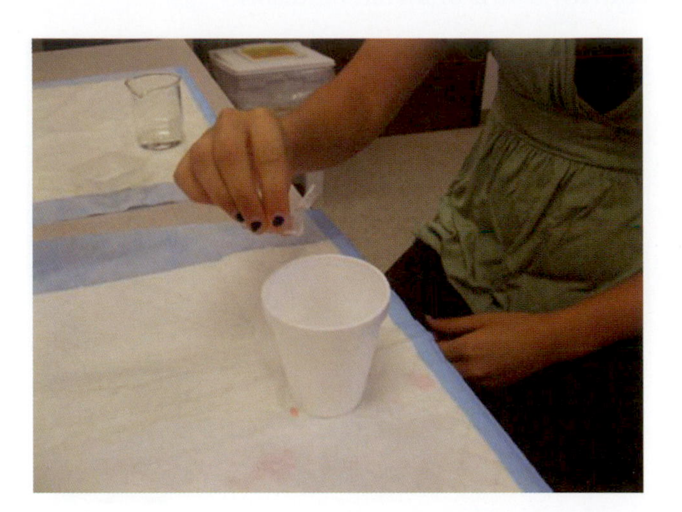

7. Add 30 µL of 0.9% saline solution to the 1.5 mL tube containing your cell pellet. Cap the tube tightly.

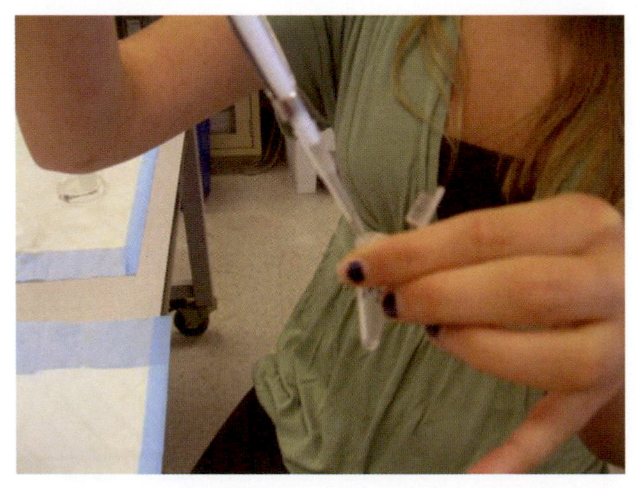

8. Resuspend the cell pellet in the saline by *racking* the tube (scraping the tube back and forth across the surface of a 1.5 mL microcentrifuge tube rack). Mixing can also be accomplished by holding the sample on a vortexer for several seconds or by pipetting up and down several times.

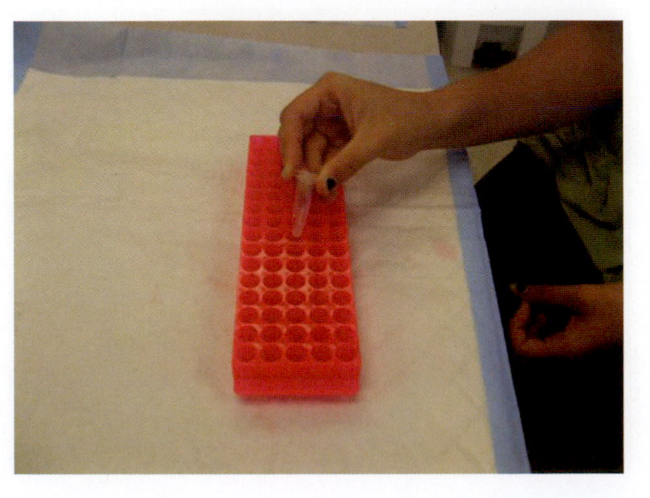

9. Transfer 30 µL of resuspended cells into 200 µL of 5% Chelex solution.

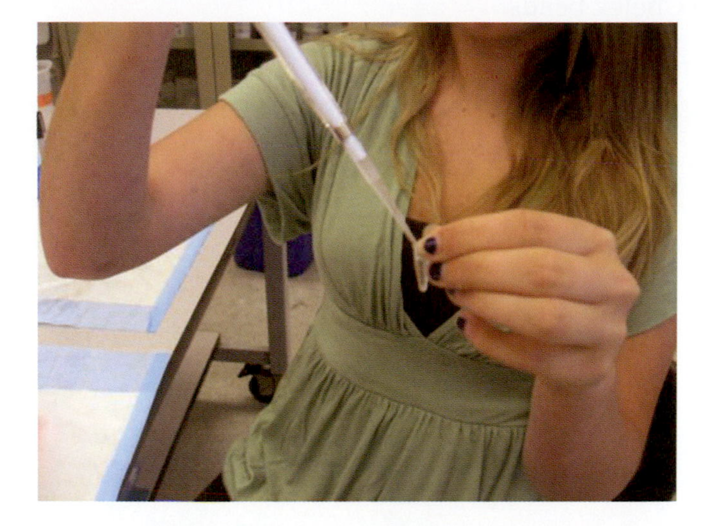

10. Mix the solution briefly by flicking the tube with your finger.

11. Either in a boiling water bath or in a thermal cycler set to 99°C, heat the Chelex solution containing cells for 10 min.

12. Mix the suspension briefly and spin in a balanced microcentrifuge for 1 min to pellet the Chelex beads.

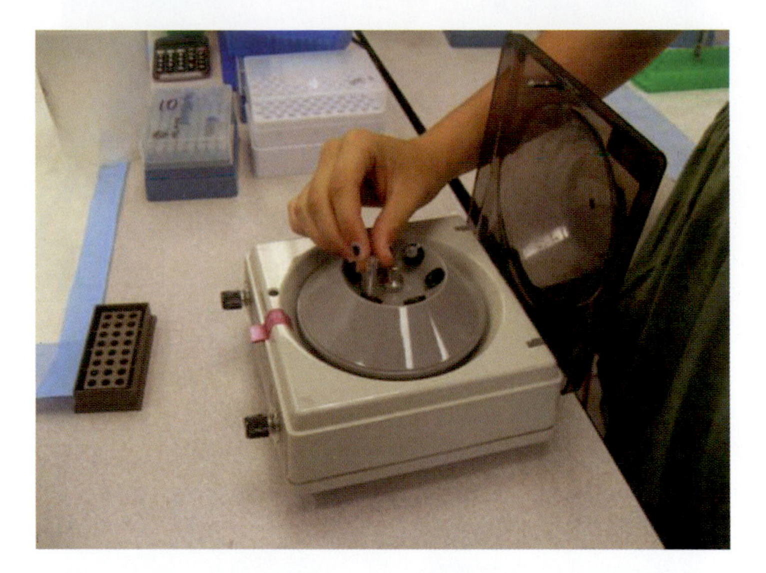

13. Being careful not to transfer any Chelex beads, withdraw 100 µL of supernatant from the top of the tube and place into a new 1.5 mL tube. Store the sample frozen.
This protocol yields single-stranded DNA at concentrations ranging from 2 *to* 50 ng/µL.

Activity 5.3 Creating a Standard Curve for Varying Concentrations of DNA

In this activity, you will create a dilution series of double-stranded DNA from 0 up to 250 µg/mL and read the absorbance of each dilution at 260 nm on a spectrophotometer. You will then plot the absorbance versus µg DNA/mL for these samples.

Materials:

3 mL calf thymus DNA at a concentration of 500 µg DNA/mL
Sterile, distilled water
P1000 pipettor
UV spectrophotometer
Six tubes that can hold at least 2 mL of volume
Quartz cuvette

Protocol:

1. Obtain six 1.5 mL tubes. Mark these tubes 0, 25, 50, 100, 150, 200, and 250 (corresponding to no DNA, 25 µg DNA/mL, 50 µg DNA/mL, 100 µg DNA/mL, etc.).

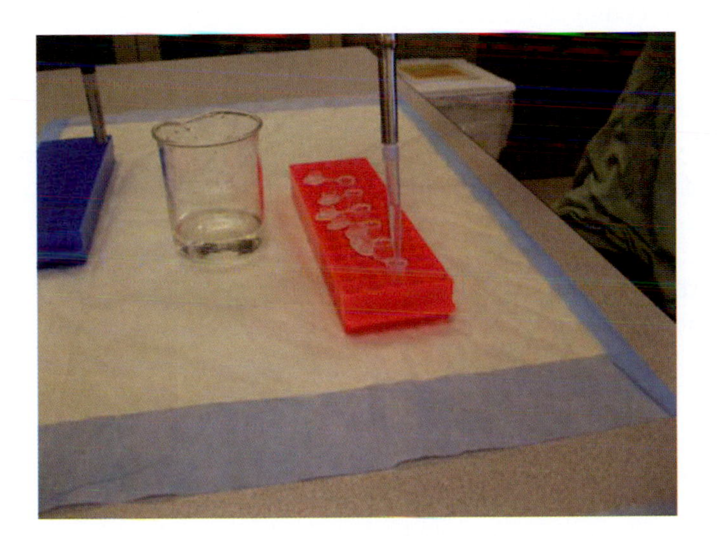

2. Using a P1000 pipettor, add the following amount of water to the corresponding tube as shown in the following table:

Tube	Water to Add (µL)
250	700
200	600
150	700
100	800
50	1200
25	500
0	1000

3. To the marked tubes, add the following volumes of 500 µg DNA/mL as shown in the following table:

Tube	Volume of 500 µg DNA/mL to Add (µL)
250	700
200	400
150	300
100	200

Take 0.3 mL from the tube marked 250 (now containing DNA) and add it to the 1.2 mL of water in the tube marked 50.

Take 0.5 mL from the tube marked 50 and add it to the 0.5 mL of water in the tube marked 25.

4. In a quartz cuvette, read 1 mL of each dilution at 260 nm. Also take a reading of 1 mL of your 500 µg DNA/mL stock solution at this wavelength.
5. In your laboratory notebook, plot µg DNA/mL on the x axis versus absorbance at 260 nm on the y axis for each of your samples. At what absorbance does the curve cease to be linear?

Activity 5.4 Measuring the Absorbance of DNA at Different Wavelengths

In this activity, you will measure the absorbance of the DNA you isolated from strawberries (Activity 5.1) at different wavelengths on a UV spectrophotometer.

Materials:

DNA from strawberries
UV spectrophotometer
Quartz cuvette

Protocol:

1. Allow the spectrophotometer to warm up on the UV setting for at least 10 min.
2. Blank the spectrophotometer with water.
3. Place 1 mL of the DNA you isolated in Activity 5.1 into a 1 mL quartz cuvette. (Note: This DNA may be too concentrated to pipette. When DNA has a concentration greater than roughly 1 mg/mL, its viscosity can prevent it from being drawn up into a pipette tip. If you find that your DNA is extremely thick and viscous, transfer a small amount into a 10 mL tube and add several mL of water or TE buffer. Allow the DNA to go completely into solution before proceeding to the next step.)
4. Measure the absorbance of your DNA sample at 200, 220, 240, 260, 280, 300, and 320 nm.
5. In your laboratory notebook, create a plot of your data in which the y axis represents absorbance and the x axis represents wavelength. Answer the following questions:
   a. What is the concentration of your DNA sample?
   b. What is the 260/280 ratio?

Erica Holmes Missing Persons Case

Helen took DNA samples from several areas of the blood-stained cargo bay liner (shown marked with tents in Figure 5.17). These areas are shown in greater detail in Figure 5.18.

Criminalist Helen Chang is using the Quantifiler kit (Life Technologies) to determine the DNA concentrations of the samples she has recovered from the crime scene and from individuals connected to the case. As a first step, she will serially dilute the kit's human DNA standard into lower and lower concentrations. The standard has a concentration of 200 ng/µL.

Problem 1 Helen wants a set of eight tubes, each having the following concentrations of DNA: 50, 16.7, 5.56, 1.85, 0.62, 0.21, 0.068, and 0.023 ng/µL. If she uses 10 µL of stock solution (200 ng/µL) to prepare the first tube, how much buffer must she dilute that 10 µL into to give the desired 50 ng/µL concentration?

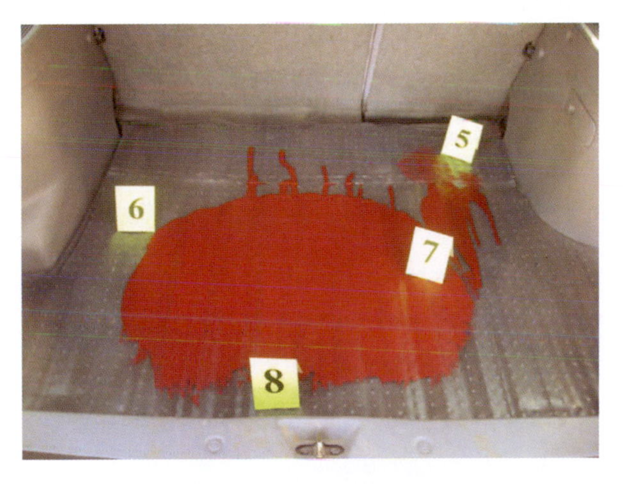

Figure 5.17 The cargo bay liner from Erica Holmes' vehicle with tents marking the areas from which DNA samples were taken.

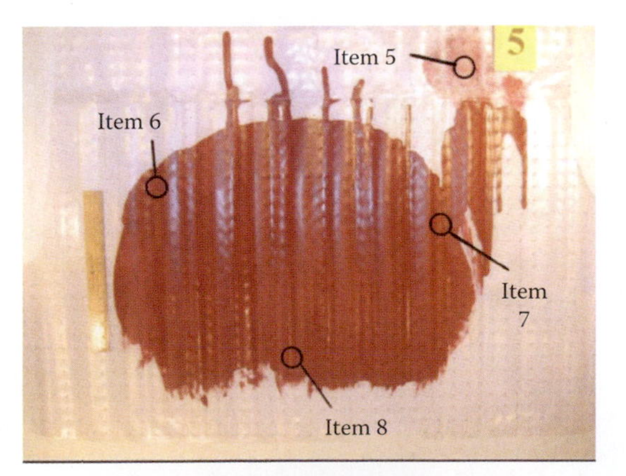

Figure 5.18 Detail of the areas from the large bloodstain on the cargo bay liner from which DNA was recovered. The areas sampled are circled on the photograph and their item number displayed.

Problem 2 If she uses 10 µL from that first dilution tube to make her second tube having a concentration of 16.7 ng/µL human DNA standard, what volume must she place that 10 µL into to obtain that desired concentration?

Problem 3 Assuming she will only transfer 10 µL from each tube into the next, how will she prepare the remaining dilution series to give her all eight tubes having the desired concentrations? In your laboratory notebook, draw a picture of the tubes showing their concentrations, the volumes they should contain, and how much is transferred from one tube to the next.

Once the dilution series is made, Helen places, in duplicate, 2 µL from each tube into the wells of a 96-well microtiter plate containing the primers, probes, and reagents (DNA polymerase, nucleotides, buffer, magnesium) needed to perform the real-time PCR assay. The final volume in each well is 25 µL. She also dedicates wells to her case samples and to a negative control. The negative control well carries all the reagents needed for the real-time PCR assay except DNA. In the place of DNA, she adds the buffer she used to make the dilution series of the standards.

Problem 4 In any type of PCR experiment, real time or otherwise, it is always important to run a negative control, a reaction void of any template DNA. What is the purpose of a negative control?

Having prepared the microtiter plate with all its samples, Helen seals it with an optically transparent adhesive film and places it within the Life Technologies real-time PCR instrument (Figure 5.19).

Helen opens the controlling software and fills out a new plate record where she enters the information about her samples (Figure 5.20).

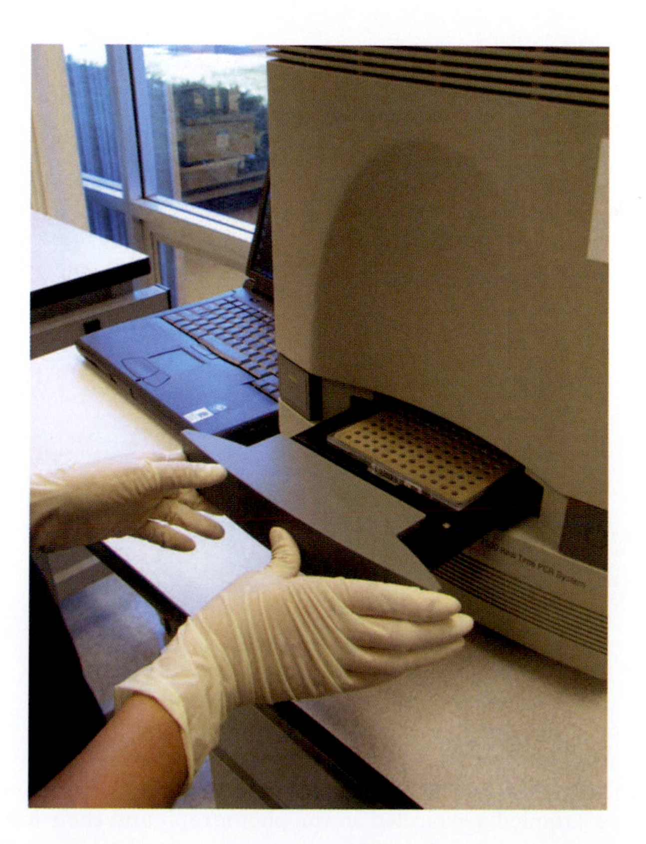

Figure 5.19 Placing the microtiter plate with Quantifiler reactions in a 7500 Real-Time PCR instrument from Life Technologies.

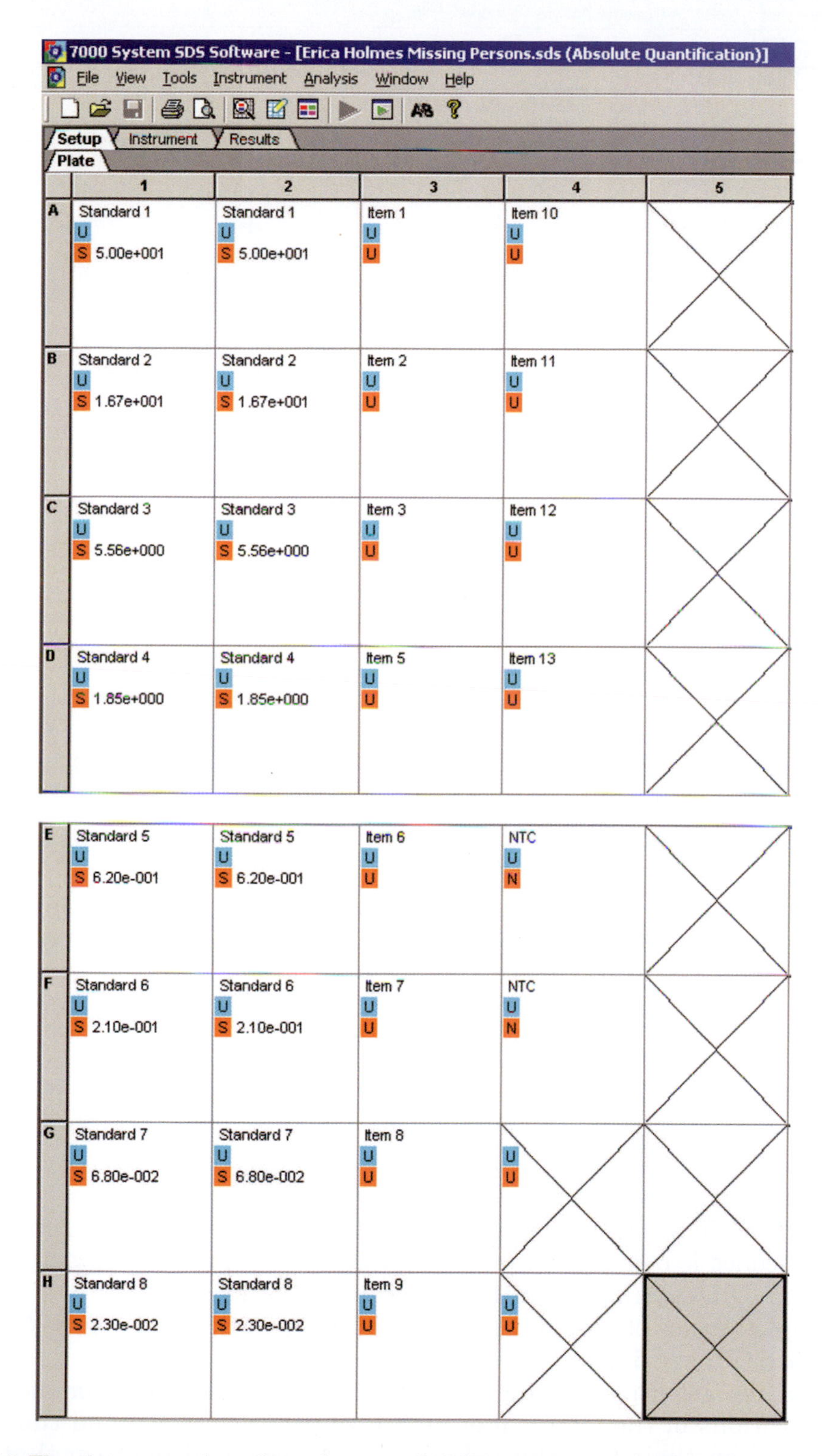

Figure 5.20 The plate setup describes what sample DNAs are in each well of the 96-well microtiter plate. The dilution series is run in duplicate for more accurate results. The human DNA standard has been diluted from 50 (aliquots placed in wells A1 and A2) down to 0.023 ng/μL (aliquots placed in wells H1 and H2).

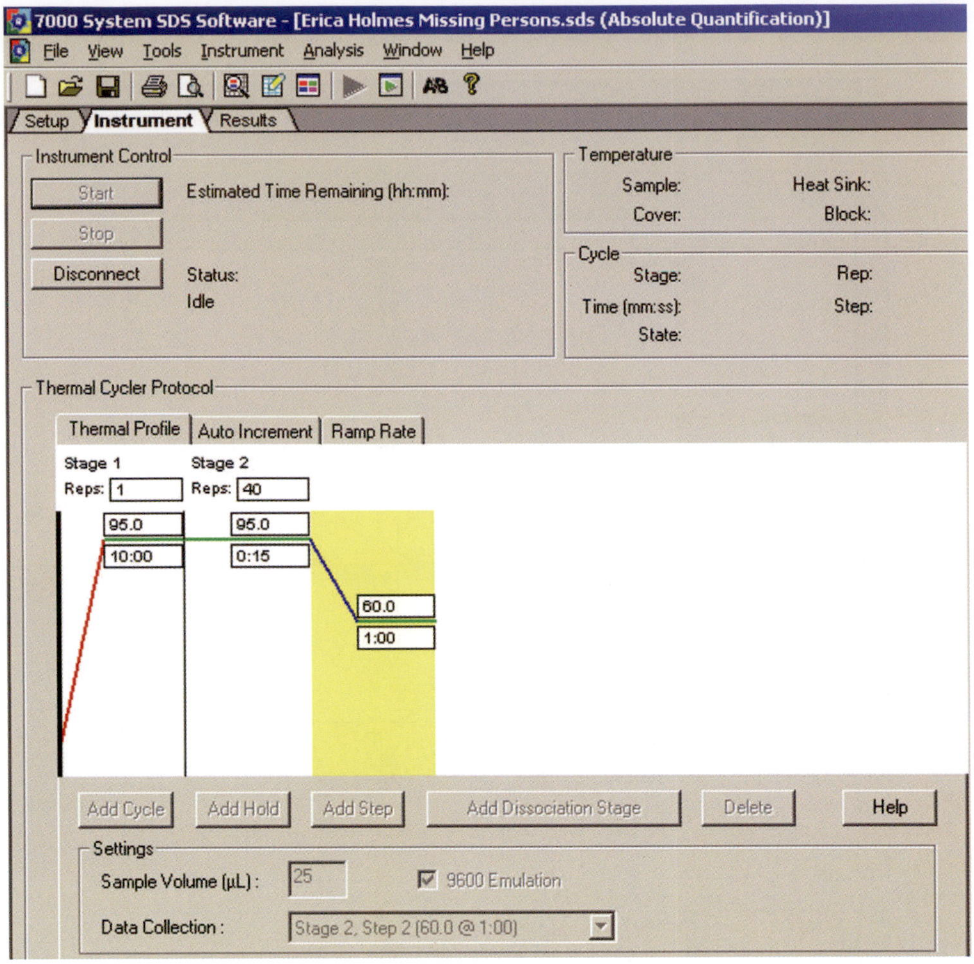

Figure 5.21 The real-time PCR TaqMan assay's cycling profile for quantitating DNA samples is carried out in three steps. An initial incubation at 95° for 10 min activates the DNA polymerase. The instrument then cycles the temperature between 95° and 60° 40 times.

Once Helen has filled out the setup plate field, she creates a cycling profile in which the temperatures used to amplify the template DNAs are defined and the sample volume is recorded (Figure 5.21). She then saves the information to the computer's hard drive and starts the run.

A real-time PCR assay can be monitored at any point during the run to see how much fluorescence is being generated at any cycle. Figure 5.22 shows the raw data for the human DNA standards at the end of the 40-cycle run.

Following 40 cycles of amplification, the instrument determines the C_T value for each standard (Figure 5.23).

Although the software for the real-time PCR instrument automatically calls the concentrations of the Quantifiler standard dilution series and the unknown samples based on their C_T values (Figure 5.24), you will perform that exercise here. Using Microsoft Excel program, you will first create a standard curve plotting the log of DNA concentration (on the x axis) versus C_T (on the y axis) for the known human DNA. Using linear regression and the equation for the best-fit line from the standard curve, you will determine the DNA concentrations of the evidence samples.

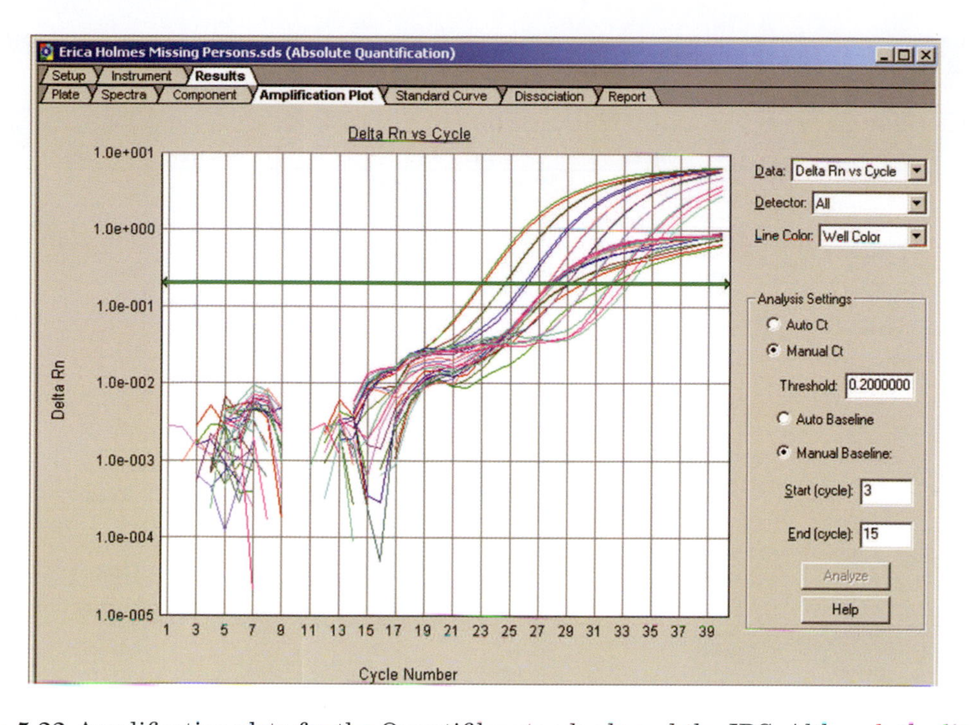

Figure 5.22 Amplification plots for the Quantifiler standards and the IPC. Although the lines are all different colors (this is user defined in the software), the TaqMan probe for the standards gives off blue fluorescence while that for the IPC gives off green fluorescence. The green horizontal line approximately two-thirds up the plot is the threshold from which C_T values are derived. The group of curves all collecting just below the "1.0e+000" line is generated by amplification of the IPC. The curves that stretch to the top of the plot are generated by the different dilutions of the human DNA standard. The higher the concentration of DNA, the lower the C_T value.

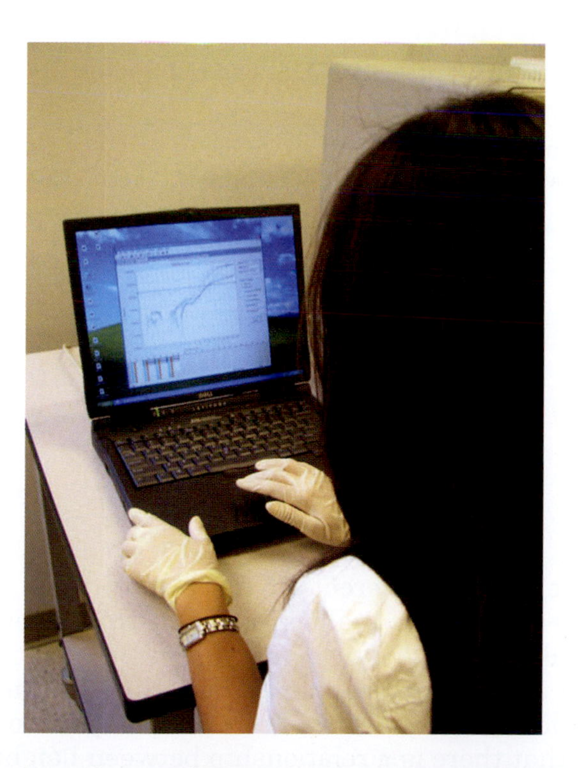

Figure 5.23 The results of a real-time PCR experiment are observed on the laptop connected to the instrument. Results are obtained within a couple of hours. The software automatically determines DNA concentration for each sample based on the PCR cycle in which its fluorescence above background is first detected.

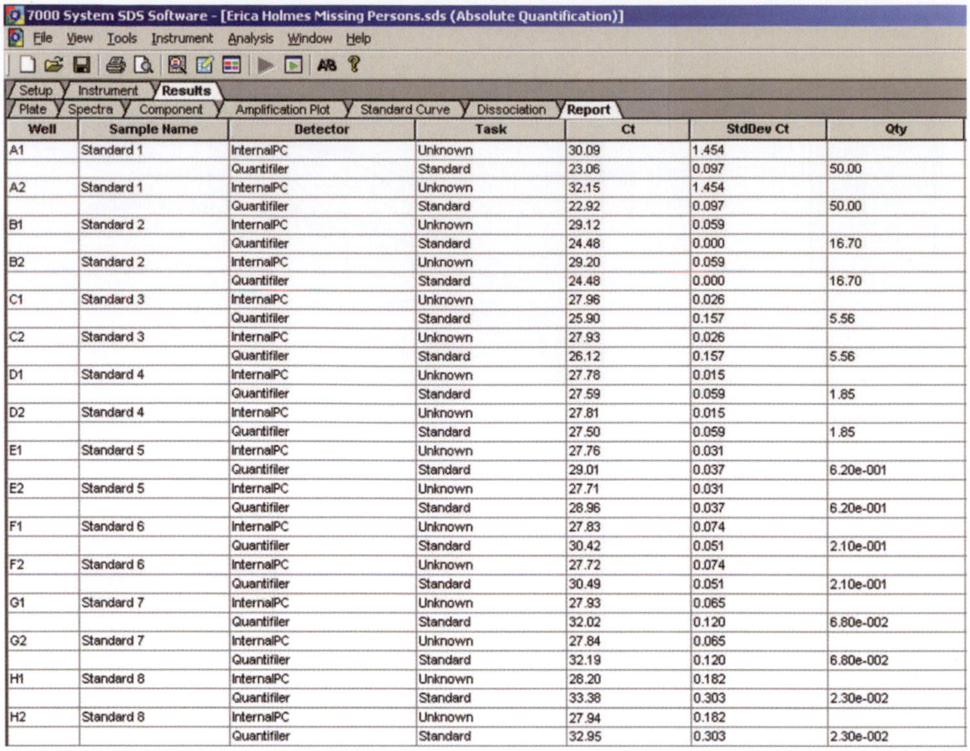

7000 System SDS Software - [Erica Holmes Missing Persons.sds (Absolute Quantification)]

File View Tools Instrument Analysis Window Help

Setup Instrument Results

Plate Spectra Component Amplification Plot Standard Curve Dissociation Report

Well	Sample Name	Detector	Task	Ct	StdDev Ct	Qty
A1	Standard 1	InternalPC	Unknown	30.09	1.454	
		Quantifiler	Standard	23.06	0.097	50.00
A2	Standard 1	InternalPC	Unknown	32.15	1.454	
		Quantifiler	Standard	22.92	0.097	50.00
B1	Standard 2	InternalPC	Unknown	29.12	0.059	
		Quantifiler	Standard	24.48	0.000	16.70
B2	Standard 2	InternalPC	Unknown	29.20	0.059	
		Quantifiler	Standard	24.48	0.000	16.70
C1	Standard 3	InternalPC	Unknown	27.96	0.026	
		Quantifiler	Standard	25.90	0.157	5.56
C2	Standard 3	InternalPC	Unknown	27.93	0.026	
		Quantifiler	Standard	26.12	0.157	5.56
D1	Standard 4	InternalPC	Unknown	27.78	0.015	
		Quantifiler	Standard	27.59	0.059	1.85
D2	Standard 4	InternalPC	Unknown	27.81	0.015	
		Quantifiler	Standard	27.50	0.059	1.85
E1	Standard 5	InternalPC	Unknown	27.76	0.031	
		Quantifiler	Standard	29.01	0.037	6.20e-001
E2	Standard 5	InternalPC	Unknown	27.71	0.031	
		Quantifiler	Standard	28.96	0.037	6.20e-001
F1	Standard 6	InternalPC	Unknown	27.83	0.074	
		Quantifiler	Standard	30.42	0.051	2.10e-001
F2	Standard 6	InternalPC	Unknown	27.72	0.074	
		Quantifiler	Standard	30.49	0.051	2.10e-001
G1	Standard 7	InternalPC	Unknown	27.93	0.065	
		Quantifiler	Standard	32.02	0.120	6.80e-002
G2	Standard 7	InternalPC	Unknown	27.84	0.065	
		Quantifiler	Standard	32.19	0.120	6.80e-002
H1	Standard 8	InternalPC	Unknown	28.20	0.182	
		Quantifiler	Standard	33.38	0.303	2.30e-002
H2	Standard 8	InternalPC	Unknown	27.94	0.182	
		Quantifiler	Standard	32.95	0.303	2.30e-002

Figure 5.24 The results for the Quantifiler standards are listed as their C_T values for each DNA concentration. The C_T values of the IPC (listed as "InternalPC" in the Detector column) should all be similar.

TABLE 5.1
C_T Values for the Human DNA Standard Series (See Figure 5.24)

DNA Concentration in Dilution Tube (ng/μL)	C_T Values for the First Set of Standards	C_T Values for the Second Set of Standards
0.023	33.38	32.95
0.068	32.02	32.19
0.21	30.42	30.49
0.62	29.01	28.96
1.85	27.59	27.50
5.56	25.90	26.12
16.7	24.48	24.48
50	23.06	22.92

As shown in Table 5.1, the different DNA concentrations gave the following C_T values (remember, there are two C_T values for each DNA concentration because each standard was run in duplicate):

Linear regression is a technique for creating a line that most closely describes the relationship between two variables. For example, you no doubt have a pretty good intuitive sense that there is a relationship between height and weight. In general, the taller the individual, the more they weigh. If you were to plot the height of various people in a sample population on one axis of a graph against their weight on the other axis, the points would probably scatter to various positions. You wouldn't be surprised to see either a short, overweight person or a tall, slender person within your sample. However, looking at those graphed points, you could probably discern a trend. Linear regression is used to draw a straight line of best fit through those points. By knowing the equation for that line, you could calculate the most likely weight of someone who is 5′9″, for example.

As described earlier, there is a relationship between C_T and DNA concentration. By plotting the values of C_T versus DNA concentration of the standards and by deriving a line of best fit and its equation for that data, we will be able to calculate the DNA concentrations of the evidence samples. We're going to use the Microsoft Excel program to do this:

1. On a computer equipped with Microsoft Excel, find the icon or program for Excel and click it open. A spreadsheet should appear.
2. In the column A, row 1 rectangle, enter "conc" (for concentration). In the column B, row 1 rectangle, enter "log conc." In the column C, row 1 rectangle, enter "Ct1." In the column D, row 1 rectangle, enter "Ct2."
3. In column 1 below "conc," fill down the concentration of the standards from lowest (0.023) to highest (50) (just the numbers, not "ng/µL").
4. Click on the first box under "log conc" in the second column to highlight it. Click the "*fx*" function in the toolbar at the top of the spreadsheet. This will call up the "Paste Function" box. Select "Math & Trig" in the "Function category:" list. From the "Function name:" list, select "LOG 10" and click "OK." The "LOG 10" dialogue box should appear.
5. Click within the "LOG 10" dialogue box and drag it out onto the workspace so that you can better see your column entries. Click on the A2 rectangle in your spreadsheet. This will place "A2" in the number box within the "LOG 10" dialogue box. Click "OK." The log value for the 0.023 concentration will appear in the highlighted box in the "log conc" column. Highlight all rectangles in that column from B2 to B9, and on the keyboard, press "Ctrl" and "D." All remaining log values will be filled in for that column.
6. In the third column under "Ct1," enter one set of C_T values for each DNA concentration (see Table 5.1). In the fourth column under "Ct2," enter the other set of C_T values for each DNA concentration (see Table 5.1).
7. Highlight all the values of both the "log conc" and the two "Ct" columns (not the header information). In the top menu bar, click on the Chart Wizard icon button (it looks like a small bar chart). This will bring up the Chart Wizard/ Chart Type window. Select the "*XY* (Scatter)" chart type. Click "Finish." A graph will appear over the spreadsheet displaying the plot of your data.
8. From the Chart pull-down menu at the top of the page, select "Add Trendline." In the popup menu that appears, make sure that the "Linear" plot is selected for the Trend/Regression type. The line can be based on either Series 1 (Ct1) or Series 2 (Ct2).
9. Within the "Add Trendline" window, click the "Options" tab (or button). Check the boxes next to "Display equation on chart" and "Display *r*-squared value on chart." Click "OK." The program will now draw the line of best fit through the plot and generate the regression line's equation. The *r*-squared value will also appear below the regression line equation indicating how well the line fits the data. The closer the absolute *r*-squared value is to one, the better the correlation between the two variables C_T and DNA concentration. You can use "Chart Options…" within the "Chart" pull-down menu to label

graph's axes and to give the graph a title. (*Note*: The "Chart" pull-down menu is only available if the graph on the spreadsheet is selected.) If you need to, the equation for the line of best fit can be dragged to an area where it can be read more easily by clicking on it and moving it with your mouse.

Problem 5 What is the equation for the linear regression line drawn to these data?

Problem 6 Based on the r^2 value, is there a strong linear correlation between C_T and DNA concentration?

The general equation for a line is $y = mx + b$, where m is the line's slope and b is the point where the line intercepts the y axis. Here, since y is C_T and x is the log of the DNA concentration, we'll rewrite the equation $y = mx + b$ as $C_T = m(\text{log conc}) + b$. Use the values you obtained in your regression analysis in Excel to replace m and b.

Problem 7 Rewrite the linear regression equation in terms of "log conc." You can now determine the concentrations of the evidence samples. All DNA samples were prepared by Chelex extraction. Two µL of Item 1 DNA, for example, gave a C_T value of 25.39 (Figure 5.25). In your equation, then, you need to solve for "log conc."

7000 System SDS Software - [Erica Holmes Missing Persons.sds (Absolute Quantification)]

File View Tools Instrument Analysis Window Help

Setup | Instrument | Results

Plate | Spectra | Component | Amplification Plot | Standard Curve | Dissociation | Report

Well	Sample Name	Detector	Task	Ct
A3	Item 1	InternalPC	Unknown	28.60
		Quantifiler	Unknown	25.39
B3	Item 2	InternalPC	Unknown	28.34
		Quantifiler	Unknown	26.38
C3	Item 3	InternalPC	Unknown	28.03
		Quantifiler	Unknown	26.79
D3	Item 5	InternalPC	Unknown	31.96
		Quantifiler	Unknown	24.62
E3	Item 6	InternalPC	Unknown	27.73
		Quantifiler	Unknown	Undet.
F3	Item 7	InternalPC	Unknown	28.84
		Quantifiler	Unknown	25.42
G3	Item 8	InternalPC	Unknown	27.87
		Quantifiler	Unknown	Undet.
H3	Item 9	InternalPC	Unknown	28.33
		Quantifiler	Unknown	26.63
A4	Item 10	InternalPC	Unknown	28.76
		Quantifiler	Unknown	25.36
B4	Item 11	InternalPC	Unknown	27.88
		Quantifiler	Unknown	28.90
C4	Item 12	InternalPC	Unknown	32.57
		Quantifiler	Unknown	24.60
D4	Item 13	InternalPC	Unknown	33.93
		Quantifiler	Unknown	24.59
E4	NTC	InternalPC	Unknown	27.79
		Quantifiler	NTC	Undet.
F4	NTC	InternalPC	Unknown	27.74
		Quantifiler	NTC	Undet.

Figure 5.25 Quantifiler results for evidence items collected during the Erica Holmes missing persons investigation. NTC stands for "no template control"—they are reactions that do not contain any DNA—water is used in place of DNA sample. "Undet." means undetectable—no fluorescence detected above background.

Once you have that value, you need to take its antilog to obtain the actual DNA concentration (see the following text).

To determine an antilog value in Excel, perform the following steps:

1. Click on the "*fx*" function in the spreadsheet's tool bar.
2. Select "Math & Trig" in the "Function category:" list of the "Paste Function" box.
3. Select "POWER" in the "Function name:" list.
4. Click OK. The "Power" box will appear.
5. Enter "10" in the Number box.
6. In the Power box, enter the value for "log conc" you calculated from the $C_T = m(\text{log conc}) + b$ equation.
7. Click OK. The number calculated is the concentration of DNA in ng/µL for that particular DNA sample.
8. Repeat this procedure for all the evidence items listed in Figure 5.25.

Problem 8 Show that 12 ng/µL is the same as 12 µg/mL.

Helen also measures the absorbance of each sample at 260 nm on a spectrophotometer and obtains the readings shown in Table 5.2.

Problem 9 Calculate the DNA concentration of each evidence item sample as determined by spectrophotometry (Table 5.2). Remember, all evidence item DNAs were isolated by Chelex extraction. Is the DNA, therefore, double-stranded or single-stranded? What calculation should be used to determine DNA concentration?

Problem 10 Helen wishes to put 1 ng of Sarah Holmes' DNA into a reaction that will analyze its genotype, and she will use 2 µL to do it so that she stays within the accuracy range of her pipettor. If she dilutes 2 µL from the DNA sample into TE buffer and then takes 2 µL of that dilution into her reaction, what volume of TE is needed for that dilution?

Prepare an evidence report to describe your DNA quantification results for the large stain on the vinyl cargo bay liner. Include information for those samples taken from this stain (Evidence Items 5, 6, 7, and 8).

TABLE 5.2
Absorbance at 260 nm for the DNA Samples of the Evidence Items

Evidence Item No.	*A*260
1	0.273
2	0.121
3	0.097
5	0.455
6	0.545
7	0.521
8	0.467
9	0.103
10	0.271
11	0.031
12	0.470
13	0.485

Review Questions

5.1 DNA recovered from cells by Chelex extraction is single-stranded. Why?

5.2 DNA is extracted from a suspect's blood by phenol–chloroform to determine if he was involved in a murder case. Twenty µL of the purified DNA is diluted in 980 µL of water (for a final volume of 1000 µL). That dilution is put into a quartz cuvette and its absorbance is read on a spectrophotometer at 260 nm. It gives a reading of 0.31. What is the concentration of DNA in the original sample?

5.3 A reference sample is needed from a victim of a sexual assault. Cells are recovered from a saline mouthwash procedure and the DNA is isolated by Chelex extraction. The DNA is diluted 50 µL into a total volume of 1000 µL and its absorbance is measured on a spectrophotometer at 260 nm. It gives a reading of 0.15. What is the concentration of DNA in the reference sample?

5.4 Ten µL of a suspect's reference DNA sample is diluted into 990 µL of water and its absorbance is read on a spectrophotometer. It gives an absorbance of 0.37 at 260 nm and an absorbance of 0.22 at 280 nm. What is its 260/280 ratio?

5.5 How much genomic DNA can be recovered from a single cell? Express your answer in picograms (pg). (To solve this problem, you need to know that there are approximately 6×10^9 bp of DNA per cell, that one mole of base pairs weighs 660 g, that there are 1×10^{12} pg/g, and that one mole of anything is 6.023×10^{23} [Avogadro's number] of that thing.)

5.6 If you recover 4000 cells from a saline mouthwash, how many µg of genomic DNA does that represent?

5.7 What percent of your body weight is made up of DNA? Assume that your body consists of 1×10^{14} cells. (1 lb = 453.6 g)

Further Reading

DNA Isolation

Chelex 100 as a Medium for Simple Extraction of DNA for PCR-Based Typing from Forensic Material by P.S. Walsh, D.A. Metzger, and R. Higuchi in *Biotechniques*, Vol. 10, pages 506–513, 1991.

Purification of Forensic Specimens for the Polymerase Chain Reaction (PCR) Analysis by A. Akane, H. Shiono, K. Matsubara, H. Nakamura, M. Hasegawa, and M. Kagawa in *Journal of Forensic Sciences*, Vol. 38, pages 691–701, 1993.

The Modified Method of Two-Step Differential Extraction of Sperm and Vaginal Epithelial Cell DNA from Vaginal Fluid Mixed with Semen by K. Yoshida, K. Sekiguchi, N. Mizuno, K. Kasai, I. Sakai, H. Sata, and S. Seta in *Forensic Science International*, Vol. 72, pages 25–33, 1995.

Improving the Effectiveness of Fluorescence for the Detection of Semen Stains on Fabrics by H. Kobus, E. Silenieks, and J. Scharnberg in *Journal of Forensic Sciences*, Vol. 47, No. 4, pages 819–823, 2002.

The Fingernails of Mary Sullivan: Developing Reliable Methods for Selectively Isolating Endogenous and Exogenous DNA from Evidence by R.E. Cline, N.M. Laurent, and D.R. Foran in *Journal of Forensic Sciences*, Vol. 48, No. 2, pages 328–333, 2003.

Using Hydrophilic Adhesive Tape for Collection of Evidence for Forensic DNA Analysis by R.C. Li and H.A. Harris in *Journal of Forensic Sciences*, Vol. 48, No. 6, pages 1318–1321, 2003.

A Simple Automated Instrument for DNA Extraction in Forensic Casework by S.A. Montpetit, I.T. Fitch, and P.T. O'Donnell in *Journal of Forensic Sciences*, Vol. 50, No. 3, pages 555–563, 2005.

Comparison of Five DNA Quantification Methods by Karsten Nielsen, Helle Smidt Mogensen, Johannes Hedman, Harald Niederstatter, Walther Parson, and Liels Morling in *Forensic Science International: Genetics*, Vol. 2, pages 226–230, 2008.

Molecular Study of Time Dependent Changes in DNA Stability in Soil Buried Skeletal Residues by Christina Kaiser, Beatrice Bachmeier, Claudius Conrad, Andreas Nerlich, Hansjürgen Bratzke, Wolfgang Eisenmenger, and Oliver Peschel in *Forensic Science International*, Vol. 177, Issue 1, pages 32–36, 2008.

Recovery of DNA and Fingerprints from Touched Documents by Jonathan Sewell, Ignacio Quinones, Carole Ames, Bryan Multaney, Stuart Curtis, Haj Seeboruth, Stephen Moore, and Barbara Daniel in *Forensic Science International: Genetics*, Vol. 2, pages 281–285, 2008.

Developmental Validation of the PrepFiler™ Forensic DNA Extraction Kit for Extraction of Genomic DNA from Biological Samples by Maxim G. Brevnov, Hemant S. Pawar, Janna Mundt, Lisa M. Calandro, Manohar R. Furtado, and Jaiprakash G. Shewale in *Journal of Forensic Sciences*, Vol. 54, No. 3, pages 599–607, 2009.

The Correlation between Skeletal Weathering and DNA Quality and Quantity by L.M. Misner, Andrea C. Halvorson, Jennifer L. Dreier, Douglas H. Ubelaker, and David R. Foran in *Journal of Forensic Sciences*, Vol. 54, No. 4, pages 822–828, 2009.

DNA Quantitation by UV Spectroscopy

Quantitation of Nucleic Acids by F.H. Stephenson in *Calculations for Molecular Biology and Biotechnology: A Guide to Mathematics in the Laboratory* (Academic Press, San Diego, CA), pages 90–108, 2003.

PCR

Polymerase Chain Reaction by the Dolan DNA Learning Center, Cold Spring Harbor Laboratory, Cold Spring Harbor, NY. Available at www.dnalc.org/ddnalc/resources/pcr.html. 1988.

Real-Time PCR to Quantitate DNA

Real-Time DNA Quantification of Nuclear and Mitochondrial DNA in Forensic Analysis by H. Andreasson, U. Gyllensten, and M. Allen in *Biotechniques* Vol. 33, pages 402–411, 2002.

Development, Characterization, and Validation of a Sensitive Primate-Specific Quantification Assay for Forensic Analysis by J.C. Fox, C.A. Cave, and J.W. Schumm in *Biotechniques*, Vol. 34, pages 314–322, 2003.

Developmental Validation of a Real-Time Quantitative PCR Assay for Automated Quantification of Human DNA by M.L. Richard, R.H. Frappier, and J.C. Newman in *Journal of Forensic Sciences*, Vol. 48, No. 5, pages 1041–1046, 2003.

Developmental Validation of the Quantifiler™ Real-Time PCR Kits for the Quantification of Human Nuclear DNA Samples by R.L. Green, I.C. Roinestad, C. Boland, and L.K. Hennessy in *Journal of Forensic Sciences*, Vol. 50, No. 4, pages 809–825, 2005.

A Duplex Real-Time qPCR Assay for the Quantification of Human Nuclear and Mitochondrial DNA in Forensic Samples: Implications for Quantifying DNA in Degraded Samples by M.D. Timken, K.L. Swango, C. Orrego, and M.R. Buoncristiani in *Journal of Forensic Sciences*, Vol. 50, No. 5, pages 1044–1060, 2005.

Development of a Human-Specific Real-Time PCR Assay for the Simultaneous Quantitation of Total Genomic and Male DNA by K.M. Horsman, J.A. Hickey, R.W. Cotton, J.P. Landers, and L.O. Maddox in *Journal of Forensic Sciences*, Vol. 51, No. 4, pages 758–765, 2006.

Simultaneous Determination of Total Human and Male DNA Using a Duplex Real-Time PCR Assay by J.A. Nicklas and E. Buel in *Journal of Forensic Sciences*, Vol. 51, No. 5, pages 1005–1015, 2006.

Developmental Validation of a Real-Time PCR Assay for the Simultaneous Quantification of Total Human and Male DNA by Benjamin E. Krenke, Nadine Nassif, Cynthia J. Sprecher, Curtis Knox, Melissa Schwandt, and Douglas R. Storts in *Forensic Science International: Genetics*, Vol. 3, pages 14–21, 2008.

Genetic Identification of Decomposed Cadavers Using Nails as DNA Source by M. Allouche, M. Hamdoum, P. Mangin, and V. Castella in *Forensic Science International: Genetics* Vol. 3, pages 46–49, 2008.

The Value of DNA Material Recovered from Crime Scenes by John W. Bond and Christine Hammond in *Journal of Forensic Sciences*, Vol. 53, No. 4, pages 797–801, 2008.

Developmental Validation of the Quantifiler® Duo DNA Quantification Kit for Simultaneous Quantification of Total Human and Human Male DNA and Detection of PCR Inhibitors in Biological Samples by Maura Barbisin, Rixun Fang, Cristin E. O'Shea, Lisa M. Calandro, Manohar R. Furtado, and Jaiprakash G. Shewale in *Journal of Forensic Science*, Vol. 54, No. 2, pages 305–319, 2009.

6 Expert Witness

Neighbors of the Holmes', Tuesday 5:02 PM

With her fingers poised on the door handle of Jenkins' Cutlass Calais, Helen waited for the click of the automatic door locks. It didn't come. Lieutenant Jenkins passed her with barely a glance and strolled out onto the street, taking the last bite of a Snickers bar.

"Are you coming, Miss Chang?" Jenkins asked, still chewing.

"Where are you going? And where did you get that? You realize I haven't eaten all day! I'm half starved."

Jenkins folded the candy bar wrapper into a one-inch cube and slipped it into his left coat pocket. "We'll stop at McDonalds on the way back to the station."

"Like I'd eat that!" Helen protested. "I'm a vegetarian."

"They've got salads."

"Yummy!"

"Come on," Jenkins said standing in the middle of the street. "We're going to talk to the neighbors. Look both ways when you cross the street."

"Stop that!" Helen said with a stomp of her foot.

"What?"

"That! I'm not a child."

"Just looking out for your safety."

"No you're not. You're patronizing me."

"You certainly have an awful lot of buttons, Miss Chang."

"And you just found one of them."

Jenkins took out his pen and notepad, flipping it open like Captain Kirk activating his communicator. He scribbled down a sentence.

"What are you doing?" Helen asked.

"One of Miss Chang's buttons; do not patronize (especially when she hasn't eaten)," Jenkins recited and made an exaggerated poke with his pen as if to accentuate a period.

"Thank you. Now, hold on," Helen protested as she navigated around the front of Jenkins' vehicle. "We're going to talk to the neighbors?"

"You'd be surprised what neighbors know about their neighbors," Jenkins replied. "Yours, for example, probably know quite a bit about you, Miss Chang. What time you wake up in the morning. What time you leave for work. What time you come home. What magazines and newspapers you subscribe to. Who your friends are. How often you see them. Who's your boyfriend. Are you cheating on him? With whom? Where you take your vacations and how long you're gone. When you shower. What you wear to bed. What arguments you've had and with whom. How often you see your parents or other members of your family. Your political affiliation. Are you patriotic. Have you concern for the environment. They've probably seen you naked."

"Okay. Okay. I get the picture."

They climbed the three steps leading up the porch to the front door of the house directly across the street from the Holmes' residence. Jenkins stalled there a moment, straightened his shoulders, and ran his left hand through his hair.

"Just ring the bell!" Helen urged.

"In just a moment," Jenkins said. Jenkins rarely used the doorbell. He didn't like the solicitor feel of them. Knocking seemed more definitive. It exuded more confidence. Even so, he always struggled with the level of force he should employ when knocking on a front door. It should be firm, he reasoned, signaling the importance of his arrival but yet without giving the impression that he was Gestapo. He paused a moment then gave the wooden door three sharp thumps with his knuckles.

Fifteen seconds elapsed. "No one's home," Helen said impatiently. "Let's get something to eat."

"Just a moment," Jenkins enunciated slowly and then pounded five more raps on the door, this time with more force than used on his first effort. Another fifteen seconds ticked by. "Miss Chang," Jenkins added, stalling, "we're going to need to talk about consent and taking DNA samples from people. As much as I admire your forthright approach to getting that swab into Mr. Holmes' mouth, there could be questions about its admissibility in a courtroom."

"Hey, I got the sample," Helen huffed. "Oh, this is too much," she said in exasperation and, with that, pressed her forefinger to the doorbell.

Chimes echoed within the residence—muted, like the bells of a cathedral on a far distant hill. Still no answer. Jenkins glanced over his left shoulder at the living room's plate glass window. There, from behind the drapes slightly parted, one eye from a half-hidden face scrutinized him. He had no idea how long he had been under observation. Upon discovery, however, their voyeur quickly disappeared behind the curtain and, within moments, they heard the sound of the front door's dead bolt retracting. The door creaked open a wedge, its swing restrained by a brass chain between the door and its frame. Peering out from the crack, a gray-haired woman with sunken green eyes scanned them head to toe. "You are?" she asked.

Jenkins withdrew his billfold and flashed his badge and ID card. "Detective Robert Jenkins, Ma'am, and Criminalist Helen Chang. If we could take a moment of your time, please."

"Is there a problem?" the woman asked.

"Not at all. If we could just ask you a few questions, Ma'am? We're investigating a missing person." Jenkins replied.

"This really will *only* take a moment," Helen stressed, giving Jenkins a sideways glance.

"I suppose so," the woman acquiesced. She closed the door, released the chain from its slide, and welcomed them in.

"Your name, Ma'am?" Jenkins asked.

"Charlotte. Charlotte Witherspoon."

"It's a pleasure, Mrs. Witherspoon," Jenkins said as he offered her his hand.

Suspiciously, slowly, she took Jenkins' hand and shook it cautiously.

"Oh, look!" Helen exclaimed as a dark and mottled calico cat slid along the side of her calf. She reached down to pick it up. "A tortie!" she said cradling the animal in her arms. "I've always wanted to own a cat."

"Miss Chang, please," Jenkins pleaded. "I have allergies."

"Noooo," Helen purred bringing the cat's face within inches of Jenkins' nose and gently waving it in front of him. Her lips pursed, cooing as if to an infant, "You can't possibly be allergic to something so cute."

Jenkins' eyes began to water and he felt on the verge of sneezing. He pulled out a handkerchief from his back pocket and quickly placed it over his face as if to shield against some contagion. Helen placed the kitten on the floor and leaned toward Jenkins. "This is a difficult case for you, isn't it?" she whispered with a half-concealed smile.

"You have no idea," Jenkins replied through the handkerchief. A sneeze burst from his lungs like the bark of a dog. The cat darted into the kitchen.

"It's a lovely home you have," Jenkins said with a sniffle, scanning the surroundings, taking several passes with his handkerchief across his upper lip, and returning the small piece of cloth to his pocket. "I've always liked these old ranchers. How long have you lived here?"

"About ten years," she replied. "My son bought it for me so that I'd be nearby. He lives two blocks down."

"That was very..." Jenkins, hearing a strange gurgling noise next to him, stopped mid sentence. Helen shifted her balance, squeezing her arms around her stomach. "That was very thoughtful of him," Jenkins resumed. "Do you know your neighbors well?"

"I keep to myself. I have my cats. And I have my church group on Sundays."

"Do you know the Holmes across the street?"

"We've met."

"So you know Sarah and Dwayne?"

"Yes. And they have a daughter, Erica. But I haven't seen her around much lately. Is she the missing person you're looking for?"

"In fact, yes, Mrs. Witherspoon. Have you ever seen any suspicious behavior going on near the Holmes' residence as regards to Erica?"

"No, she seems like a nice girl."

"Ever seen her engaged in an argument or any type of altercation with anyone?"

"No, not really."

"What do you mean 'not really'?" Jenkins asked.

"I don't wish to gossip," Mrs. Witherspoon said shaking her head, "but it's always seemed their neighbor, Mr. Beamer, has had an unhealthy interest in her?"

"Unhealthy?"

"He's a grown, well… older man. Much older, if you know what I mean," Mrs. Witherspoon said, rubbing her crucifix necklace between her thumb and forefinger. "I don't want to say he's a pervert or a child molester, or anything like that but there's just something about him. My son looked up the local molesters and pedophiles on the Internet and he isn't listed. But still, as I said, he just seemed to have an unnatural interest in Erica."

"In what way, if I may ask you to be more specific?" Jenkins asked.

"When she was about ten years old, he gave her a bicycle. A bicycle! That's a rather extravagant gift from a neighbor, don't you think? A man doesn't give a young girl something like that unless he wants something in return."

"So he was very nice to…"

"Overly nice."

"So he was overly nice to Erica?"

"Humm," Mrs. Witherspoon huffed indignantly.

"And did you ever see Mr. Beamer argue with Erica?" Jenkins asked.

"He's had strong words with her, yes," she replied.

"How often?"

"Just from time to time. Not when she was younger."

"Do you know for what reason?"

"No."

"Had Erica been trespassing on his property or had she damaged anything belonging to Mr. Beamer?"

"Not that I know of."

"You've been very helpful, Mrs. Witherspoon. I appreciate your cooperation. If you can think of anything else, don't hesitate to call me." Jenkins handed her his card. "Miss Chang, I believe we're done here." Jenkins dabbed his eyes with his handkerchief as he gave the woman one last nod.

Jenkins and Helen made their way out of the house and back onto the porch. They stopped there a moment as the front door closed behind them.

"It's been a long day," Jenkins said. "Why don't we hold off on interviewing Mr. Beamer and Sam O'Neill until tomorrow."

"I think that's an excellent idea," Helen said. "I've got to get home and get something in my stomach. I think I'm going hypoglycemic."

"Done, then," Jenkins said.

As they moved down the steps, he slowly glanced over his right shoulder and caught Mrs. Witherspoon peering out from behind the front curtains. “We're being watched,” Jenkins whispered as he fumbled in his right coat pocket for his keys. Finding them, he pointed the remote at his car across the street. Just then, a middle-aged man stepping out of the house to the right of the Holmes' residence caught Jenkins' eye. The man walked over to the side of the house and picked up a garden hose.

“Change of plans,” Jenkins said.

“Now what?” Helen asked, the will to live draining out of her.

“I think that's Mr. Beamer across the street. This'll just take a moment.”

Before Helen could lodge a protest, Jenkins had vaulted himself into something resembling a trot and was crossing the street.

“Mr. Beamer?” Jenkins yelled.

The man looked up at Jenkins coming toward him and adjusted his footing, his right leg back, in a more defensive posture—the garden hose at the ready.

“Mr. Beamer, is it?” Jenkins asked when he'd arrived in standard, socially acceptable orbit.

“Who wants to know?” the man replied.

Jenkins withdrew his badge and ID and, with one hand, flicked it open for display. The man lowered the hose to his side and adopted a more relaxed demeanor. Turning his back to Jenkins, he spooled the hose back up on its reel and shoved the reel between a stack of orange clay flower pots and a large bag of lawn fertilizer with the words “Beamer's Best – Super Lawn Fertilizer” written on its side. He turned around to Jenkins again. “Lieutenant Robert Jenkins, sir, and this is Helen Cha…,” Jenkins glanced to his left and right. She wasn't there. Pivoting around, he saw Helen back by the car draped over the hood like an abandoned marionette. Her arms dangled limp at her sides. Her head rested on the top of the vehicle as if it were buried in a pillow. “And that is Criminalist Helen Chang.”

“Mr. Beamer?”

“Yeah, what do you want?”

“Do you know Erica Holmes?”

“Of course, she's my neighbor.”

“How long have you known Erica?” Jenkins asked.

“Since she was born,” Mr. Beamer replied.

“A witness has told us that you have occasionally had harsh words with Erica.”

“Who told you that?”

“I'm not at liberty to say,” Jenkins replied.

“I never fought with Erica,” Mr. Beamer said dropping the hose. “I was stern with her, perhaps, if I believed she was making bad choices in her life.”

“Do you show that kind of interest in your other neighbors, Mr. Beamer?” Jenkins asked.

"Look, I..." at that moment, the door to the residence opened and an athletic, middle-aged woman in black Adidas running pants and a gray sweatshirt stepped out into the door frame. "What's going on here?" she asked wiping sweat from her forehead with a small white bath towel.

"This is Lieutenant Jenkins, Honey, asking about Erica," Mr. Beamer said, taking up a position next to his wife.

"How do you do, Mrs. Beamer," Jenkins said with a nod.

"Lieutenant, I've known Erica her entire life," Mr. Beamer continued. "I'd say she's very special to me. I'd never purposefully bring harm to her."

"No one's said she's been harmed," Jenkins cautioned. "We're just investigating a missing person at this point." Jenkins paused in thought for a moment. "Do you know of anyone who might want to harm Erica?" he asked.

"Did you talk to the Holmes'?" Mr. Beamer asked. "You talk about 'harsh words.' Dwayne has had plenty of those with Erica."

"Excuse me one second," Jenkins said holding up his hand. "My cell's vibrating. A call. If I may have just a moment to take this."

Jenkins grabbed his cell phone from its case attached to his belt. As he took some five paces away from the Beamers, he pecked at the icon for the hearing aid audio amplifier application. It opened. Facing at a right angle from the Beamers, he positioned the phone against his ear. "Hello," he said to no one. He waited and listened, occasionally saying either *yeah* or *no*.

It was Mrs. Beamer who spoke first. In a whisper, Jenkins could just make out her words. "It's because of you that the police are now investigating us. You brought this on us."

"Ssshhh!" Chuck whispered back. "He might hear us."

"Don't you Sshhush me!" she snapped back barely able to keep the sound of her voice below a naturally audible level. "I'm humiliated."

Mrs. Beamer crossed her arms and shifted her weight onto one hip, angling her glare away from her husband.

"Yeah. Yeah. That's fine," Jenkins said as convincingly as he could. "I'll talk to you when I get back." Jenkins folded the cell phone into its closed position and placed it back into its holster. "Sorry," he said walking back to the couple still standing on the front stoop. "Okay, I appreciate your help. If you could both come down to the station within the next day or so to provide prints." Jenkins shot a quick glance at his vehicle. Helen was staring back at him, her head resting against her elbow. "And a DNA sample," he added, "That would be helpful."

"Fingerprints and DNA?" Mrs. Beamer asked. "You mean we're suspects for something?"

"Just routine, Ma'am," Jenkins replied. "Have a good evening." And Jenkins walked away before they had time to protest.

"How'd that go?" Helen asked when Jenkins had returned to the car.

"Interesting." Jenkins replied. "Miss Chang, it's been a long day. What do ya say I buy you some dinner?"

"Do the police give badge-carrying detectives speeding tickets?" Helen asked.

Fast Food Eatery, Tuesday 7:15 PM

Helen could feel the glucose and insulin starting to trickle through her veins again. Life was seeping back into her.

"You know what I love about this place, Miss Chang?" Jenkins asked, his mouth full of a bite from a double cheeseburger.

"The artery-clogging transfats they cook the French fries in?" Helen replied, spearing another shred of lettuce with a white plastic fork.

"No."

"Maybe the intimate and refined ambiance," Helen suggested.

"Wrong again. It's the great meal at a good price," Jenkins affirmed, wrestling another French fry from its small cardboard shell.

"That's not all," Helen said.

"Huh?"

"Look in your bag."

Jenkins spread the rim of the bag open and peered down into it. Reaching in, he pulled out a black and white object wrapped in clear plastic. "Oh, look–a squad car!" he exclaimed.

"Ah, but it's no Cutlass Calais," Helen observed. Just then, she thought she might have caught a glimpse of a slight upward torque tugging at the corners of Jenkins' mouth.

Expert Witnesses: The Forensics Team

No one person can do it all. No one person has the knowledge, experience, and expertise in all the fields of science and psychology necessary to evaluate a crime and take it through to successful prosecution. The court must rely on an array of people each of whom may specialize in only one particular field and have been well schooled in all aspects of that subject matter. The court calls on them during a trial to help the judge and members of the jury better understand the aspects of a particular art or science that may be critical to the execution of a fair trial. These specialists are the expert witnesses.

Medical Examiner

An unexpected, unexplained, or suspicious death triggers a chain of events whose first link is often a specialist known as a *medical examiner*. When called to a scene to examine a body, the medical examiner is charged with identifying the individual and certifying their death. This official act must be carried out even if the body is obviously dismembered or decomposed. Was the death the result of natural causes, from an accident, by suicide, or from an act of homicide? It is the job of the medical examiner to make the determination—to give a medical explanation as to the cause of death.

A medical examiner is a doctor—a licensed physician—someone trained to heal the sick and comfort the dying. Not what you might expect for that member of the forensics team who works almost exclusively with the deceased. But a medical examiner's training also includes heavy doses of pathology—the study of how the human body succumbs to the agents of disease and injury. They use this training during the performance of their primary duty—to conduct autopsies for the purpose of determining the cause and manner of death.

Death can come swiftly from the tearing of flesh that a bullet or a knife blade brings. Severing of the pulmonary artery, for example, can bring a quick end to the victim's life. In such a case, identifying the cause of death during the autopsy might seem like an easy call. However, some other person may have been able to survive the exact same or similar injury. Why did this particular victim die? Did he also have a chronic disease or underlying infection that weakened him? Was he also the victim of poisoning by an estranged spouse or disgruntled employee? What was the time of death? Was he already dead before he was shot or stabbed? By drowning perhaps—any water in the airways? Was he a user of illegal narcotics or under treatment with prescription drugs? Could he have had a heart attack from fright prior to the assault? Was the death from natural causes? Was the death accidental? Was the death from suicide? Is the cause of death undetermined? The medical examiner is as much a detective as anyone on the police force.

One of the functions of the medical examiner, as just alluded to, is to estimate when death occurred. Determining the time of death can be crucial to placing a suspect at the crime scene and in eliminating the innocent. The most familiar way of estimating when a person died is by gauging the degree to which the body has succumbed to *rigor mortis*—the stiffening of the body brought on by a rigid interaction between the muscle proteins actin and myosin. Depending on the surrounding temperature (heat accelerates the process), rigor mortis usually sets in within 2–4 h after death, becoming first apparent in the lower jaw and neck muscles and then spreading downward. The entire body is usually completely rigid by 6–12 h. However, after roughly 48–72 h, the body becomes limp again as enzymes eventually break down the connection between the myosin and actin molecules.

A more reliable method of determining the time of death, at least within the first 24 h, is by measuring the body's temperature. From the moment of death, as metabolic processes cease, the body cools slowly, until it reaches the surrounding (ambient) temperature. The process of body cooling is called *algor mortis* and is measured by inserting a thermometer into the liver. Using the rate of algor mortis as a clock, the time of death can be estimated to within a couple of hours. As a rule of thumb, cooling occurs at roughly 0.75°F/h under warm ambient conditions and at a rate of roughly 1.5°F/h under colder ambient conditions.

A third method used to estimate the time of death relies on observations of *livor mortis*—the pooling of blood at the lowest parts of the body due to the pull of gravity. The collection of blood at the parts of the body closest to the ground causes a purplish discoloration of the skin and flesh. It usually begins within the first hour following death and is complete with roughly 12 h.

Forensic Odontologist

Before forensic DNA analysis became commonplace, bodies were routinely identified by their fingerprints and by their teeth. For the long deceased where bone may be all that's left of the corpse, teeth are still used as a way to help ID the remains.

Tooth enamel is the hardest, most enduring substance in the human body. When all other traces of flesh and bone have decayed or burned away, teeth may still survive. Their durability and their unique pattern make them a valuable source of forensic information. When the medical examiner is unable to attach a name to a body, therefore, the *forensic odontologist* may be called in to help make the identification. The forensic odontologist will use dental records to make a match with the dental patterns of the corpse. X-rays, dentals casts, and photographs are all sources of information for the odontologist.

Forensic odontology played a key role in the conviction of one of the most notorious serial killers in the history of the United States. A series of murders, spanning nearly a decade beginning with a 1969 homicide in California, stretched from the Golden State to Oregon, Washington, Colorado, Utah, and Florida. All the victims had a similar appearance—they were all young, attractive females with long dark hair parted in the middle. Investigators were able to make the connection that a young Seattle law student named Ted Bundy was in the vicinity when each murder occurred. However, they had very little physical evidence tying Bundy to the crimes—no fingerprints, blood, hair, or clothing. However, an autopsy of one of his victims, Lisa Levy, revealed a bite mark on her left buttock. A photograph of the bite mark taken alongside a measuring stick proved to be crucial. Bundy was finally taken into custody in Pensacola, Florida, in February of 1978 following the murder of a 12-year-old schoolgirl. Photographs and casts were made of Bundy's teeth. Expert testimony from a forensic odontologist convinced the jury at Bundy's murder trial that the bite marks discovered on Lisa Levy matched perfectly with the defendant's own unique crooked pattern of teeth (Figure 6.1). Bundy was convicted

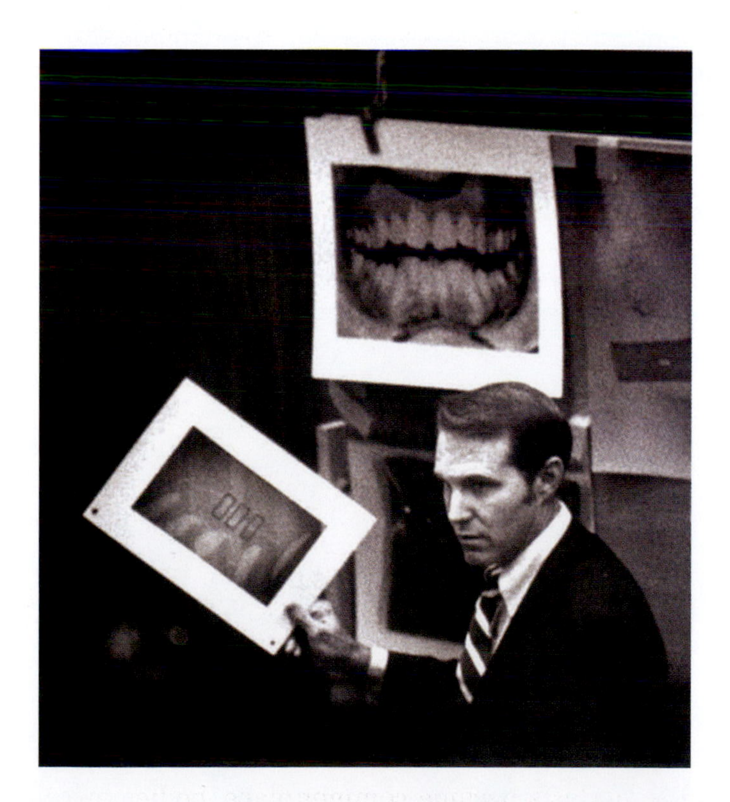

Figure 6.1 Dr. Richard Souviron presents bite mark evidence at Ted Bundy's appeal trial in Tallahassee, Florida. (From the Mark Foley Collection. Used with permission of the State Archives of Florida, Tallahassee, FL.)

of murder and executed for his crimes in 1989. His was the first case in the state of Florida that used forensic odontology in a conviction.

Forensic Entomologist

Determining the time of death can be critical to a homicide investigation as it helps to establish a timeline of events that can tie a suspect directly to a murder. For example, if a medical examiner called to the scene of a homicide determines that the victim has been deceased for 2 h, the police can compare that information with an apprehended suspect's account of his whereabouts. Does the suspect have an alibi that would place him elsewhere when the murder was committed? If not, then the suspect becomes far more interesting. But what of the decaying corpse discovered under a pile of leaves in the forest—a body long cold and lifeless? Knowing the time of death of that corpse can, for example, tie a serial killer to their presence in the area during the window of time when the body was disposed of. In such cases, it may be time to bring in the *forensic entomologist*—a scientist who knows bugs.

A blowfly (Figure 6.2) can detect a decaying corpse from miles away. The female lays her eggs, up to 200 of them, in the nose, mouth, or lacerated flesh of the decomposing body. In as little as 8–24 h, the eggs hatch into *larvae* (maggots). Within another 5–11 days, the maggots morph into their pupa stage. Within another 1–2 weeks, adult flies emerge (Figure 6.3). Knowing the life cycle of the blowfly and the conditions of temperature and daylight that affect it, the forensic entomologist can extrapolate the time of death (Figure 6.4).

Forensic Botanist

In 1959, a vacationing Austrian man disappeared while on a trip down the Danube River near Vienna. No body was found. However, the police, suspecting homicide, took a suspect in who had a strong motive for the missing man's murder. In searching the suspect's apartment for evidence that might link the suspect to the crime, a pair of muddy shoes were found and taken into evidence. Examined by an expert

Figure 6.2 The blowfly is a common corpse-inhabiting insect found throughout much of the world. Based on the stage of development of its eggs infesting a corpse, a forensic entomologist can estimate a time of death. (Image taken by Martin Pot, http://en.wikipedia.org/wiki/Image:Blowfly-head2.jpg.)

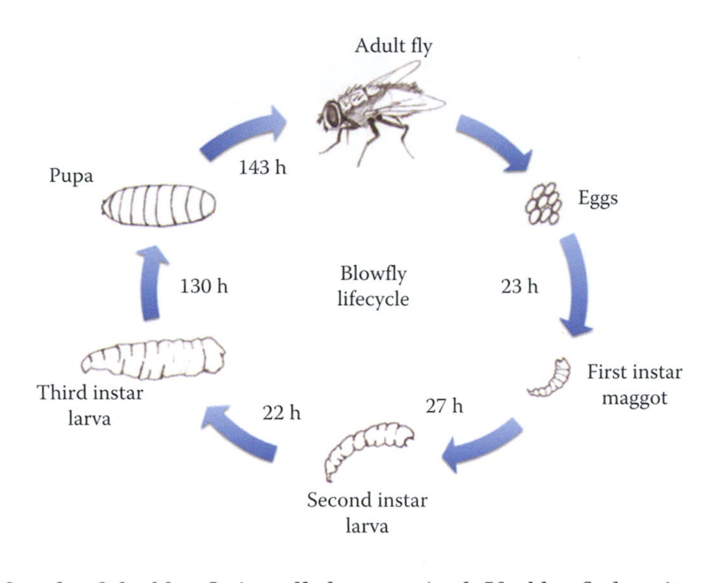

Figure 6.3 The lifecycle of the blowfly is well characterized. If a blowfly lays its eggs in a decomposing body, the time of death can be estimated by the lifecycle stage of the developing fly.

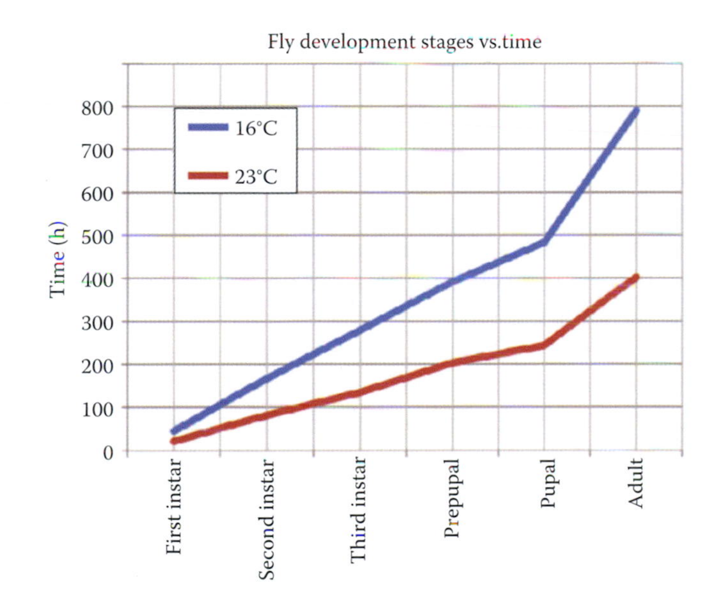

Figure 6.4 Flies and other insects go through multiple stages of development. This graph shows a very generalized representation of insect development and the effect that temperature has on its time course (development occurs faster under warmer conditions).

from the Austrian Geological Survey, the mud on the suspect's shoes was found to be imbedded with pollen grains from spruce, willow, and alder trees. It also contained the fossilized pollen of hickory that grew in the area during the Tertiary Period some 20 million years ago. It was determined that that particular combination of pollen only exists in a small area of the Danube Valley some 12 miles north of Vienna. When confronted with the findings, the suspect confessed to the murder and took the police to where he had buried the body—right in the Danube Valley as predicted by the pollen analysis.

Pollen (Figure 6.5) can be extremely valuable when recovered and used as *associative evidence*—placing a person at a unique location or in association with other people or objects.

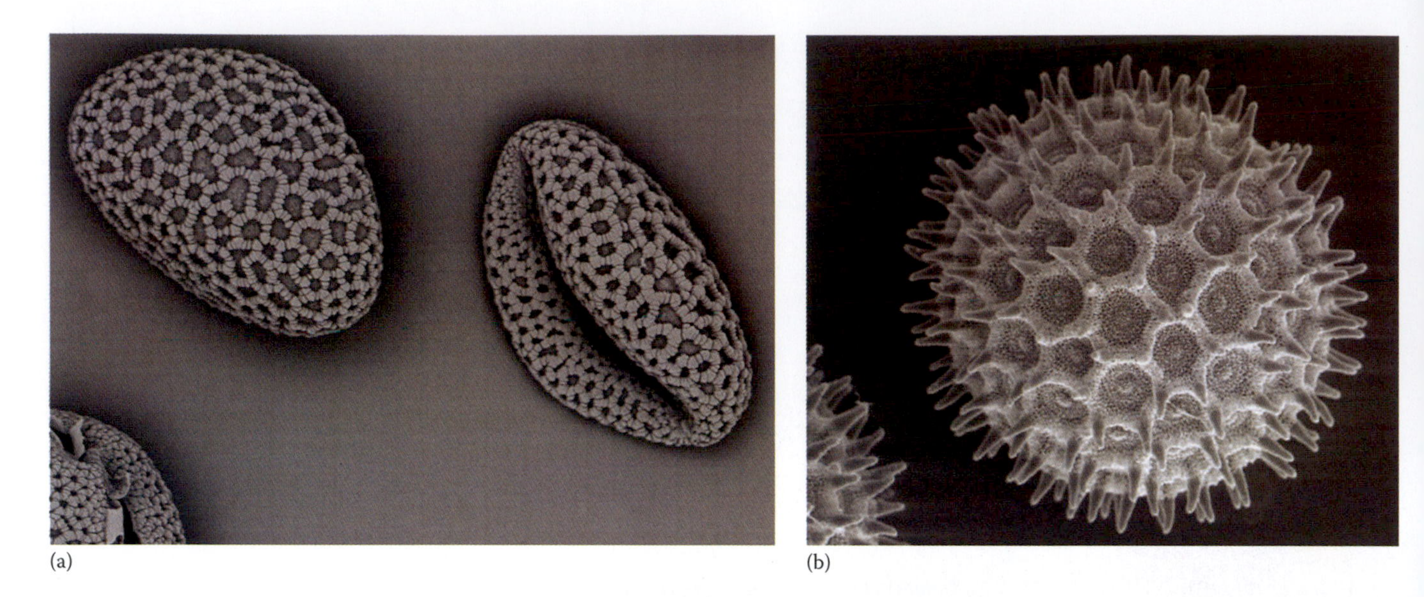

Figure 6.5 Electron microscope images of (a) pollen grains from *Lilium auratum* (the oriental lily) and (b) *Ipomea purpurea* (the heavenly blue morning glory). (Images from the Dartmouth Electron Microscope Facility, Dartmouth College, Hanover, NH.)

Forensic Toxicologist

Arsenic, mercury, morphine, ethylene glycol (antifreeze), benzodiazepine, 4-hydroxycoumarin (rat poison), and ricin have all been used to end lives whether by murder or by suicide. Even drugs such as acetaminophen and aspirin that we may be taking regularly because of their benefits for relieving mild pain and inflammation are deadly at an inappropriate dose. And what we assume to be absolutely harmless and benign, such as water or oxygen, can be lethal in excess. Even molecules having deceptively simple structures such as those of cyanide and arsenic (Figure 6.6a and b) can be quick and efficient killers.

A *poison* is anything that can harm or kill you when given at a sufficient dose. *Toxicology* is the study of how drugs and poisons alter the body's chemistry to cause illness. A forensic toxicologist will search for drugs and poisons in the blood, hair, urine, bile, and liquid of the eyes of the deceased.

But how can a forensic toxicologist identify one particular drug that may only linger in trace amounts within the complex soup of chemicals making up such biological fluids as blood or urine? Drug testing is performed by several different methods but they all rely on discerning the unique chemical characteristics inherent to each substance. In the widely used method of *gas chromatography* (Figure 6.7), for example, a forensic sample is vaporized by heat as it enters a narrow tube referred to as a *column*. The column is typically coated on its inside with a thin layer of a compound that binds different molecules with different affinities. The vaporized sample is sent through the column carried along on a stream of nitrogen gas. The molecules within the sample mixture interact with the column coating in ways that are dependent on their chemical and physical properties. Those molecules reacting very little with the column coating reach the detector at the column's other end more quickly than those molecules having a stronger interaction with the coating. The length of time it takes a molecule to pass through the column is called its *retention time*. Different molecules have different retention times. By comparing the retention times of the molecules in the forensic sample with those of known drugs, the components of the unknown sample can be identified.

$H{-}C{\equiv}N$
(a)

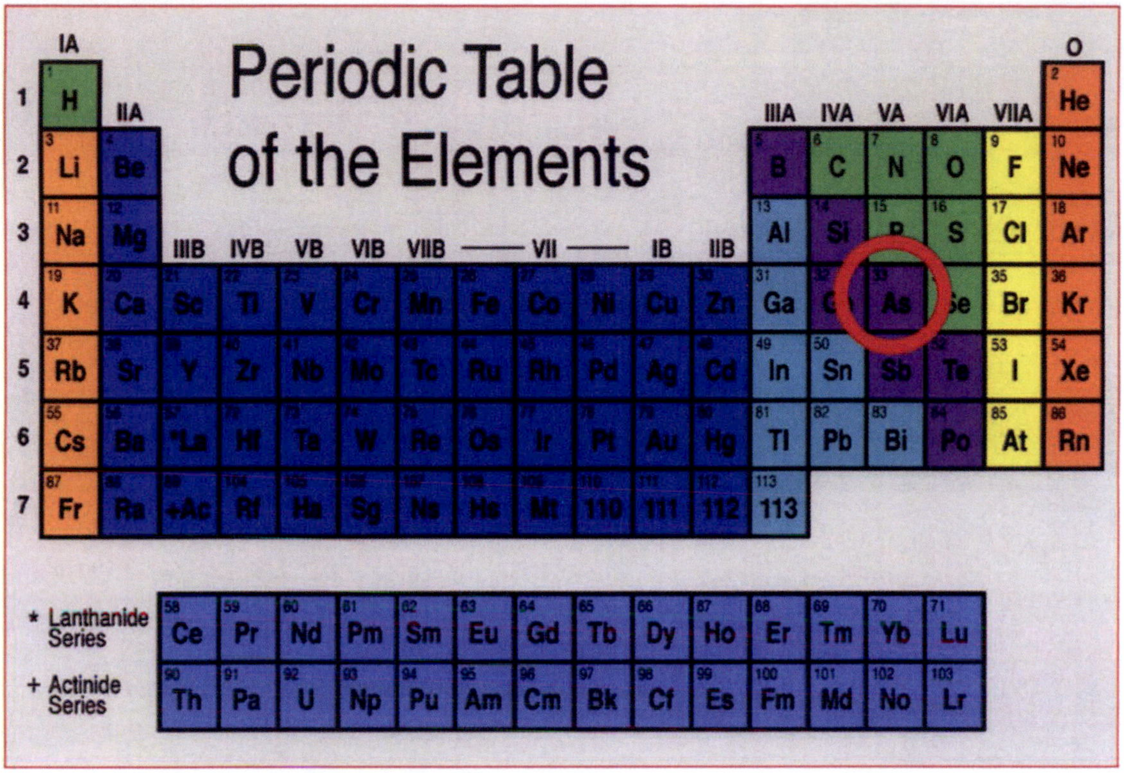

(b)

Figure 6.6 It's hard to believe that molecules consisting of just a few atoms can be so lethal. (a) Cyanide, one of the most lethal chemicals known, kills by inhibiting an enzyme known as cytochrome c oxidase necessary for the cell's production of the energy molecule ATP. Without ATP, the heart cannot beat and the central nervous system can no longer function. Many believe that Grigori Rasputin, the mystic confidant to the Russian Czar Nicholas II, was murdered by the use of cyanide. (b) Arsenic is a chemical element—a single atom. It inhibits an enzyme called pyruvate dehydrogenase that, like cyanide, disrupts the cell's ability to make ATP. The French emperor Napoleon Bonaparte may have been the victim of arsenic poisoning.

Another technique for identifying foreign compounds is called *mass spectrometry* (MS). A mass spectrometer (Figure 6.8), as its name implies, is an instrument that identifies molecules by their mass—by how much matter they contain.

In MS, the molecules to be analyzed are given a charge, either positive or negative, making them subject to movement in an electric field. The process of imparting a charge on a molecule is called *ionization* and a charged (ionized) molecule is called an *ion*. Most mass spectrometers are designed to analyze positively charged ions—those that have gained a proton (the positively charged particle found within the nucleus of an atom). As sample molecules are injected into a mass spectrometer, they are ionized and sent careening into the instrument where they travel through a unit of four equally spaced, cylindrical, gold-coated ceramic rods called a *quadrupole*. The rods of the quadrupole are set at a particular electric current and radio frequency such that only ions having a certain charge-to-mass ratio can travel down the center of the unit. All other ions either collide with the quadrupole rods or fly out between them and are lost. Those that make it through the quadrupole are detected at the other end of the instrument. Molecules are identified based on their relative charge-to-mass ratio as defined by their ability to make it through the quadrupole

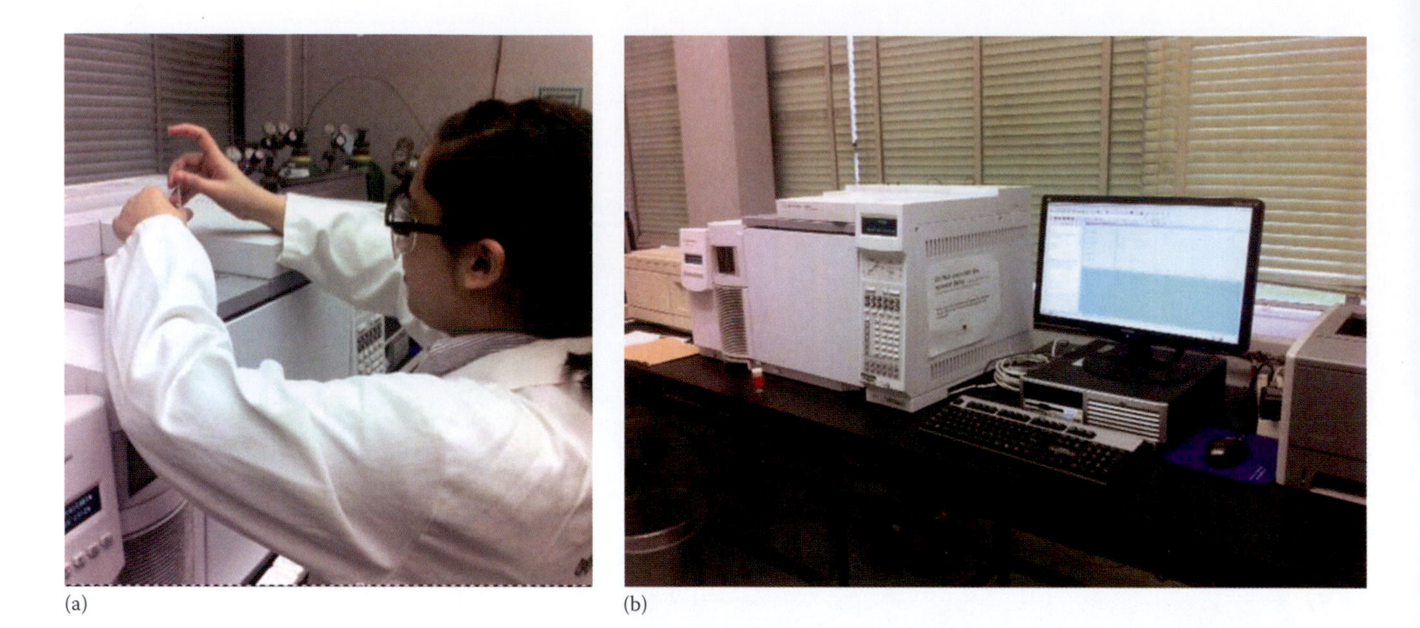

(a) (b)

Figure 6.7 (a) A crime lab toxicologist injecting a sample into a gas chromatography mass spectrometry (GCMS) and (b) GCMS workstation.

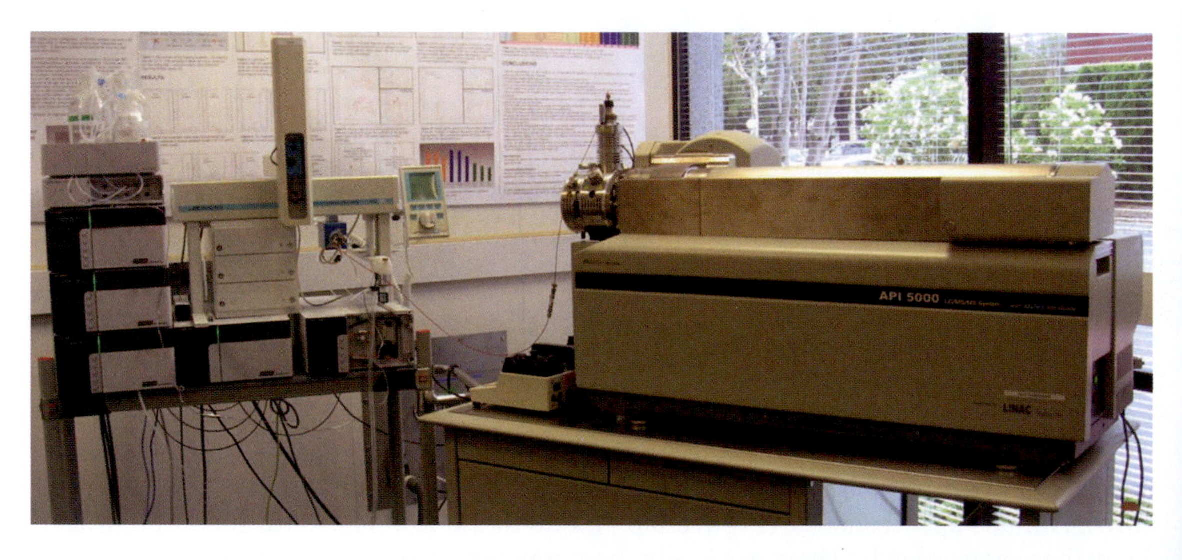

Figure 6.8 The Applied Biosystems API 5000 mass spectrometer can be used to identify trace and toxic compounds within biological fluids. High-pressure liquid chromatography (HPLC) equipment can be seen on the left side of the photograph. HPLC uses a liquid traveling through a column to provide an initial separation and purification of molecules from a complex mixture. The instrument on the right is the mass analyzer. The API 5000 is a triple-quad instrument (it carries three quadrupoles).

at a defined setting of current and radio frequency (Figure 6.9). Some mass spectrometers, known as *triple quads*, carry as many as three quadrupole units allowing for enhanced molecule identification and greater sensitivity (Figure 6.10).

Because of their unequaled power to identify a wide range of molecules when present even in only small amounts, MS is finding more uses in forensic science and is supplanting gas chromatography as the favored technology.

Although the use of poisons by an assailant wishing to remain anonymous was one of the favored methods of murder during much of history, that's not so much the

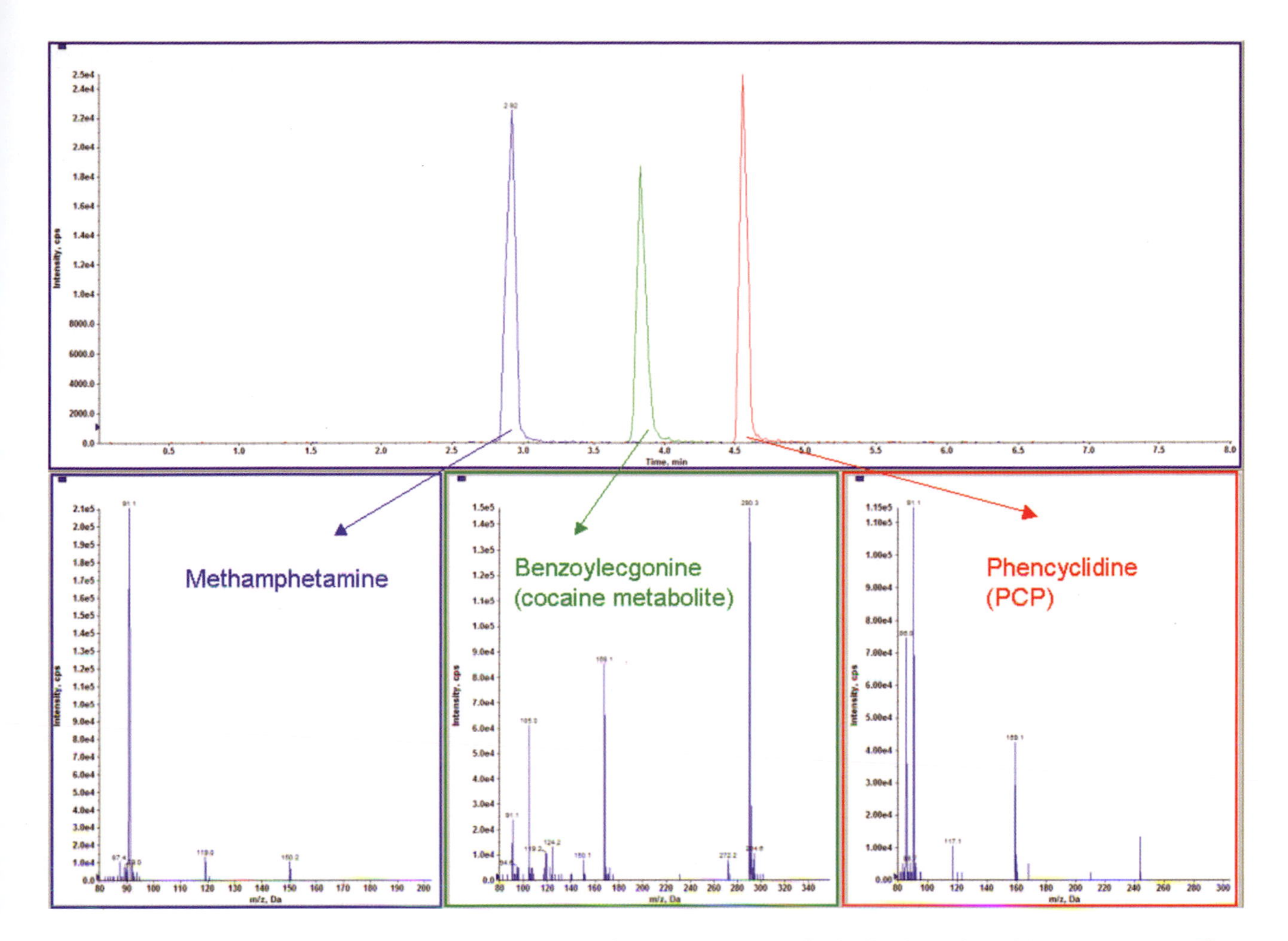

Figure 6.9 A mass spectrometer can identify the illegal drugs present in body fluids such as blood and urine. The top panel of this figure shows the separation of methamphetamine, benzoylecgonine, and PCP by HPLC prior to their injection into a mass spectrometer. The three substances are positively identified in the mass spectrometer by their molecular weight. Benzoylecgonine is formed in the liver by the metabolism of cocaine. These samples were analyzed on an Applied Biosystems instrument known as the 3200 QTrap hybrid triple quadrupole linear ion trap. (Image courtesy of Tania Sasaki, Technical Marketing Manager, Mass Spectrometry Group, Applied Biosystems, Foster City, CA.)

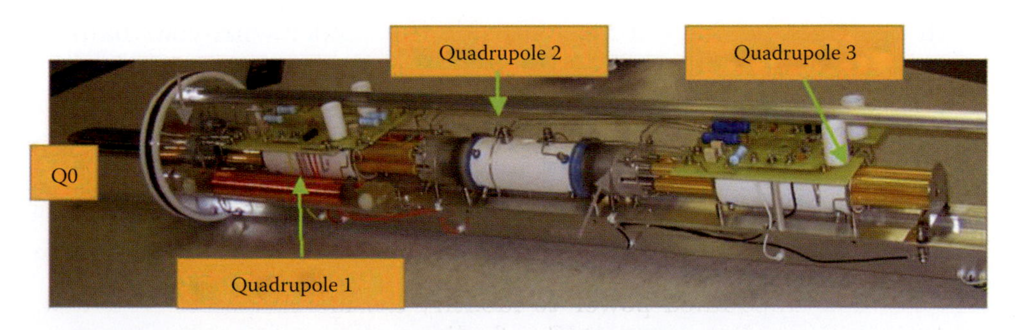

Figure 6.10 The "rail" taken from a triple quadrupole mass spectrometer. Three quadrupoles improve the instrument's sensitivity and resolution. Q0 is a quadrupole that uses radio frequency to focus ions into quadrupole 1. (Image courtesy of Tania Sasaki, Technical Marketing Manager, Mass Spectrometry Group, Applied Biosystems, Foster City, CA.)

case today. Undoubtedly that's because advances in toxicology can readily expose a poison in the victim's blood, urine, or body tissues. It's much more difficult to claim that a rival or estranged spouse died of *natural* causes when a few chemical and physical tests can make a poison so readily apparent and thereby rally a team of homicide investigators. And poison, as a murder weapon, is a little bit risky. If the victim realizes they're being poisoned, there's a fairly good chance that they'll survive if they can make a timely enough call to 9-1-1 or to the poison control center. No, the favorite weapon in the twenty-first century is the handgun. Though less discrete than poison, it's almost a sure thing.

But it's not as if the toxicologist will be out of work any time soon. Prescription drugs at too high a dose or in combination with other prescription drugs will continue to kill people even though quite unintentionally. And then there's heroin, cocaine, cleaning fluid, lighter fluid, methamphetamines, alcohol, marijuana, steroids, animal venoms, phencyclidine (PCP), and carbon monoxide, to name just a few, that can all find their way into the human body by one means or another. The forensic toxicologist is busier than ever.

Computer Forensics

The Internet has connected the people of the world in an unprecedented way. Anyone with access to the web can communicate with anyone else on the planet having similar access. With an Internet connection, you can view the treasures of the Egyptian pharaohs in the Cairo Museum or scroll through the paintings hanging on the walls of the Victoria and Albert Museum in London. Buy tickets to a Broadway show. Watch a video on YouTube of a daredevil in San Diego skateboarding off the roof of his house. Find a telescopic image of your home taken by an orbiting satellite. The possibilities are astounding. The Internet's power to reach out to a vast audience, however, has not escaped the attention of thieves, swindlers, flimflam artists, and sexual predators.

The two major scams floating in the electronic ether attempt to separate an unwitting victim from their money. You will find them far too frequently within your e-mail inbox. They're almost always rife with misspelled words, ill-conceived punctuation, and stark grammatical errors. They can originate from such unlikely places as Nigeria or Iran.

The first ploy describes either a fortune you've inherited from some wealthy benefactor or some grand prize you've won in a sweepstakes (Figure 6.11). To claim the fortune, you must send money to the person making the offer so that they can *release the assets* to you.

The second Internet ploy alerts you to some problem with your finances. In order to make things right again, you must provide the sender with your bank account

```
I AM MRS WENDY JONNES, I AM A BUSINESS OWNER I HAVE WILL MY OIL COMPANY AND MY
INVESTMENT TO YOU. I WOULD LIKE YOU TO CONTACT MY ATTORNEY HIS NAME IS
BARRISTER RODNEY
LEE HE WILL GUIDE YOU ON WHATEVER YOU NEED TO INHERIT THE COMPANY.YOU CAN
REACH HIM ON
(INFO.HARALDCHAMBER1@YMAIL.COM)+2348063843620. I AM GOING FOR AN OPERATION AND
I DONT
KNOW IF I CAN MAKE IT DUE TO MY MEDICAL EXPERT.I AM SORRY I KNOW THIS HURT. SO
CONTACT
MY ATTORNEY AND HE WILL GUIDE YOU ON WHAT TO DO.

REGARDS
MRS WENDY JONNE
```

Figure 6.11 In this e-mail swindle, you're required to make a payment to a "lawyer" so that you can claim the rights to the oil company you've supposedly inherited.

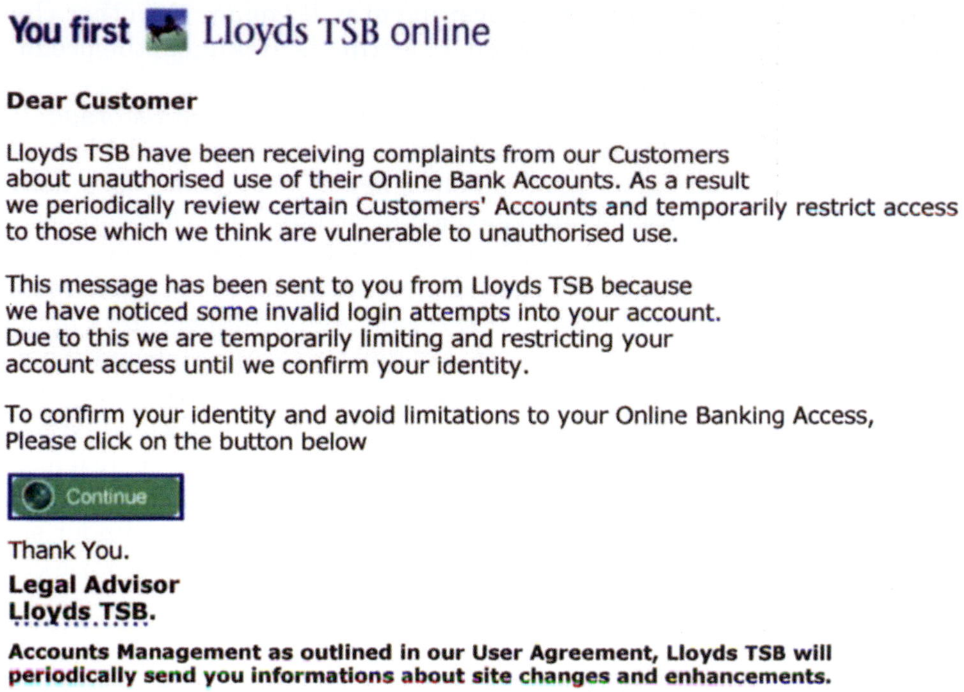

You first Lloyds TSB online

Dear Customer

Lloyds TSB have been receiving complaints from our Customers
about unauthorised use of their Online Bank Accounts. As a result
we periodically review certain Customers' Accounts and temporarily restrict access
to those which we think are vulnerable to unauthorised use.

This message has been sent to you from Lloyds TSB because
we have noticed some invalid login attempts into your account.
Due to this we are temporarily limiting and restricting your
account access until we confirm your identity.

To confirm your identity and avoid limitations to your Online Banking Access,
Please click on the button below

Continue

Thank You.

Legal Advisor
Lloyds TSB.

Accounts Management as outlined in our User Agreement, Lloyds TSB will periodically send you informations about site changes and enhancements.

Figure 6.12 A common e-mail ploy tries to gain access to your banking information, your log-in account name, and password. Once obtained, the thieves will transfer your money into their own accounts.

information, your personal identification number (PIN) or password to those accounts, your social security number, your mother's maiden name, or whatever else is necessary for the thieves to access your finances and drain you of your wealth (Figure 6.12).

Ruses to raid your finances are rampant on the Internet and, by their sheer volume, are difficult to police. The Internet user will need to rely on their better judgment to decide what looks to be a scam. But, in the words frequently attributed to the nineteenth century showman P.T. Barnum, "There's a sucker born every minute." That little adage, though cynical, seems true enough and Internet scams are likely to continue as long as there's an Internet and as long as the females of our species continue to give birth.

The Internet has also become the stalking grounds of sexual predators—those who entice children into sex. The predator (typically an adult male) usually makes contact with their victim in an Internet chat room where people, including minors, may electronically congregate to instant message each other on such topics as sports, computer games, celebrity gossip, or any number of other interests. There is a degree of anonymity in a chat room in that most people participate using the camouflage of some cute yet personally identifying screen name of their own invention. Posing as a minor, the predator engages individuals within the chat room participating as the others do. However, within a short period of time, they will subtly change the discussion, by innuendo and entendre, toward sex. A minor who is enticed by the bait will be invited to a private electronic chat where, usually, the language may become more explicit and arrangements are made by the predator for a meeting with the victim.

What most sexual predators are either unaware of or choose to ignore is that government police (such as the FBI in the United States) routinely patrol those chat rooms popular with minors. The undercover agent will engage the other chat room participants to identify the predator. When a meeting is arranged, the predator will be met with an arrest warrant.

What is remarkable about the Internet is its capacity for data storage. It's easy to believe that transactions through the electronic ether occur so quickly as to make them untraceable. And when we hit the delete key or drag some document or file to the trash, we think it dissolves into garbled electronic code, lost forever. Not so. When a file is deleted, it's still there on the hard drive. Its name was only changed to render it hidden from the user. So that deleted memo that first appeared as company e-mail between the CEO and the CFO regarding postdating stock options will appear later in the courtroom when they're indicted for securities fraud. That e-mail the chief scientist of a pharmaceutical company sent to his manager regarding the dangerous side effects of a drug just approved by the FDA will come back 2 years later in the class action lawsuit brought by the relatives of those who died from those sequestered side effects. And finally, the predator who downloaded the child pornography and then deleted those images when he realized he was under suspicion by the police confronts them again during his hearing after the forensic computer specialist had recovered those *deleted* files from the hard drive.

In the Crime Lab

Activity 6.1 Determining a Solution's Alcohol Content: The Breathalyzer Test Reaction

Every year in the United States, about 25,000 people are killed and 500,000 more injured as a result of drunk driving. Various organizations have stepped up efforts to educate the public about the dangers of driving while intoxicated, and stiffer penalties have been imposed for such offenders.

The police often use a device called a *breath analyzer*, or *breathalyzer*, to test drivers suspected of being drunk. The chemical basis of this device is a reduction/oxidation (redox) reaction. A sample of the driver's breath is drawn into the breath analyzer, where it is treated with an acidic solution of potassium dichromate ($K_2Cr_2O_7$)—a chemical having a yellowish-orange color. The alcohol (ethanol) in the breath is converted (oxidized) to acetic acid by the dichromate ion of potassium dichromate. Simultaneously, the orange-yellowish dichromate ion is reduced to a green chromic ion (Cr^{3+}) revealing, by the degree of color change, the level of alcohol in the driver's breath.

The reaction can be represented in two ways, by its complete molecular form or in its ionic form:

Potassium dichromate to chromic ion reaction

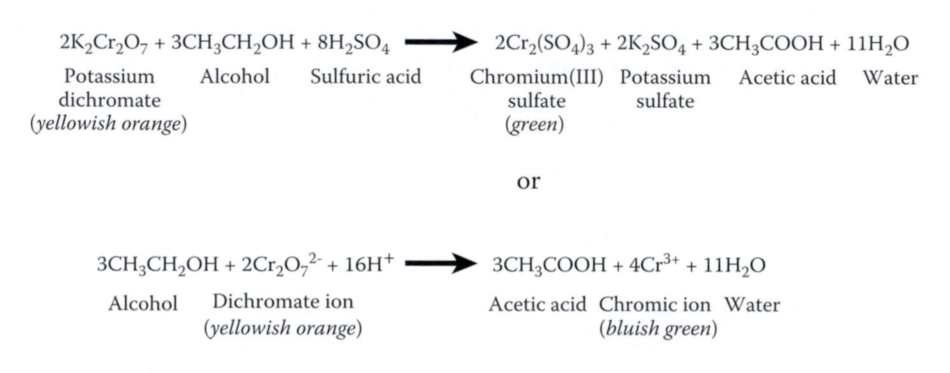

In this activity, you will perform the chemical reactions used to test for the presence of alcohol as used in the breathalyzer test.

Materials

Two spot plates with a minimum of 12 wells each
Four individual eyedroppers of the same type and size
Beaker of water
Beaker of 0.1% alcohol
Beaker of potassium dichromate ($K_2Cr_2O_7$)
Laboratory glasses
Gloves
Alcohol evidence sample
Laboratory marker (Sharpie)

Protocol

You will work in groups of three.

1. Using a laboratory marker, label 11 wells of a spot plate from 0.0% to 0.1% in increments of 0.01%. This will be your reference plate.
2. Using an eyedropper, dispense the appropriate number of drops of tap water into the labeled wells as shown in the following table.

Well Position (%)	Drops of Water	Drops of Alcohol	Drops of Potassium Dichromate
0.0	10	0	6
0.01	9	1	6
0.02	8	2	6
0.03	7	3	6
0.04	6	4	6
0.05	5	5	6
0.06	4	6	6
0.07	3	7	6
0.08	2	8	6
0.09	1	9	6
0.1	0	10	6

3. Using a different eyedropper, place the appropriate number of drops of 0.1% alcohol into the wells as shown in the table given earlier.
4. Using a third eyedropper, place the appropriate number of drops of potassium dichromate into the wells of the spot plate as shown in the table given earlier.
5. Using a fourth eyedropper, dispense 10 drops of the evidence sample into a well of your other spot plate and add 6 drops of potassium dichromate to that same well.

6. Slowly swirl the plates to mix the solutions. If alcohol is present, you should see the wells change color from yellow to a pale blue. The reactions have gone to completion when you can no longer see a color change.

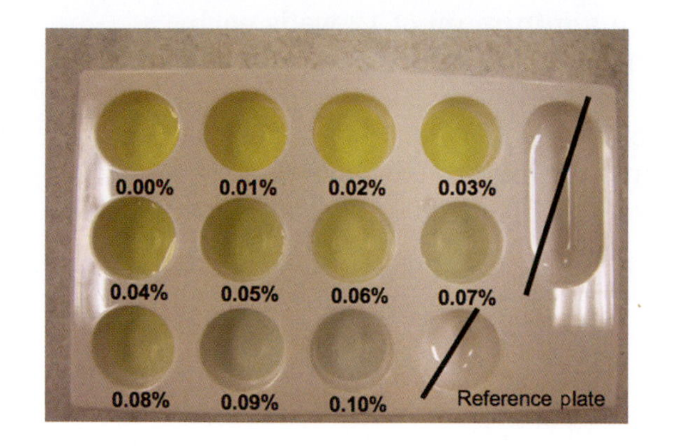

7. Move the evidence sample spot plate over the reference plate so that you can locate the best color match between the two plates.

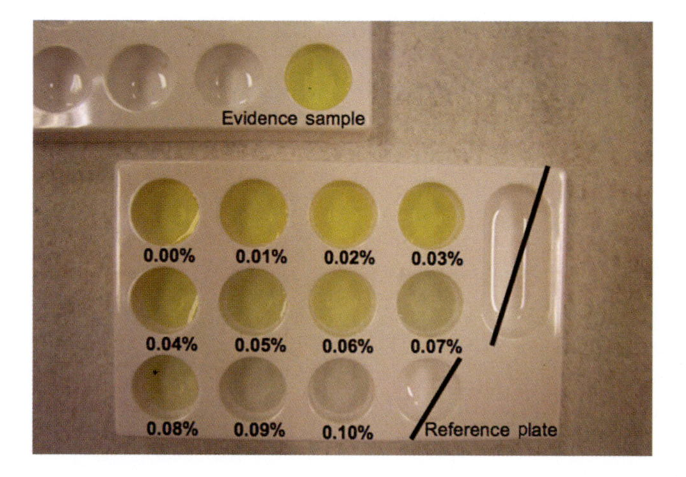

In your laboratory notebook, make a note of the alcohol concentration of the reference well having the closest match to your evidence sample.

Forensic Toxicology: Detecting Drugs Using Chromatography

Most countries patrol and secure their borders against drug smuggling. When suspicious substances are seized from an airplane, a boat, or from a person's luggage, the material must be identified to confirm that a crime has been committed. The technique called *chromatography* (Activity 6.2) is one of the methods used for that purpose. Chromatography is a method that separates different molecules within a mixture based on their physical and chemical properties. A *fingerprint* of those molecules is produced that allows for their identification.

These activities will introduce you to a technique called *thin-layer chromatography* (*TLC*) (Activity 6.3). It utilizes a silica gel matrix as a solid immovable platform through which your test sample, dissolved in a solvent such as water or alcohol, will pass by the force of capillary action. As it moves through the silica gel, the sample is separated into its component parts. The silica gel matrix is called the *stationary phase* and the alcohol, used as an organic solvent to carry your sample through the stationary phase, is called the *mobile phase*. Your dissolved sample is spotted onto a TLC plate that is then placed in a chromatographic chamber containing a small volume of solvent. Capillary action of the mobile phase (the solvent) moving up the stationary phase (the TLC plate) will separate the individual chemicals of the mixture. Each separated chemical is assigned an R_f value (retention factor) defined as the distance it traveled up the TLC plate divided by the distance traveled by the solvent. When a reference standard is run concurrently with evidence samples, the evidence sample's R_f number is used as a means to include or exclude the evidence item as being a possible match with one of the substances in the reference.

Activity 6.2 Using Chromatography to Separate the Components of Food Coloring

This activity will demonstrate the technique of chromatography. You will separate the components of food coloring using filter paper as a stationary phase and water as a mobile phase.

Materials

- Glass capillary tubes or toothpicks
- Beaker capable of holding a 10 cm piece of rectangular filter paper
- Filter or blotting paper
- Evidence sample(s)
- Prealiquoted food coloring (red, blue, yellow, or green)
- Epitube rack
- Calculator
- No. 2 pencil

Protocol

1. Fill a beaker with enough water to just cover the bottom.

2. Cut a piece of filter paper into a rectangle approximately 5 cm wide and 10 cm long. Using a dull No. 2 pencil, draw a line about 1 cm from the bottom (narrow) edge of the filter paper. This will serve as the line of origin. Place hatch marks along the line of origin where you will deposit your reference and evidence samples. These hatch marks should be equidistant from

the edges and from each other. Below each mark, write the numbers of the reference and evidence samples you will be analyzing.

Record this information in your lab notebook.

3. Using a toothpick or a glass capillary tube and being careful to keep the spot you make as small as possible, transfer a small amount of liquid from the source vials onto the line of origin of your cut filter paper.

4. Place the spotted filter paper into the chromatography chamber. Make sure that the water level in the chromatography tank does not cover or touch the line of origin. Do not move the TLC chamber once the solvent (the mobile phase) starts moving up the paper (the stationary phase).

5. Allow the water to run up the filter paper to least 80% of its length. Once this distance is reached, remove the filter paper from the beaker and mark the distance the water traveled with a No. 2 pencil.

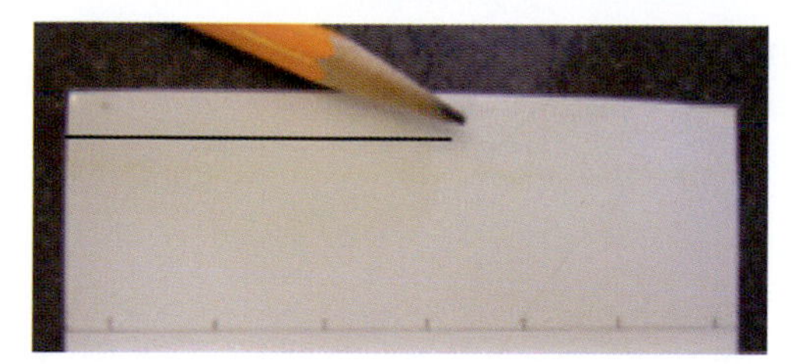

6. Using a ruler, determine the distance the solvent moved relative to the line of origin for each sample. This value can be denoted as d_s. Determine the distance each chemical component of each sample moved relative to the origin. This distance is determined by locating the most intense color region within the spot as your reference point. This value is designated as d_x. For each sample, divide the distance the chemical component moved (d_x) by the distance the solvent front moved (d_s). This value is the R_f (retention factor) value for that component. It is expressed as a decimal (e.g., 0.45). The value *0.45* means that the chemical component traveled 45% the length traversed by the solvent front.

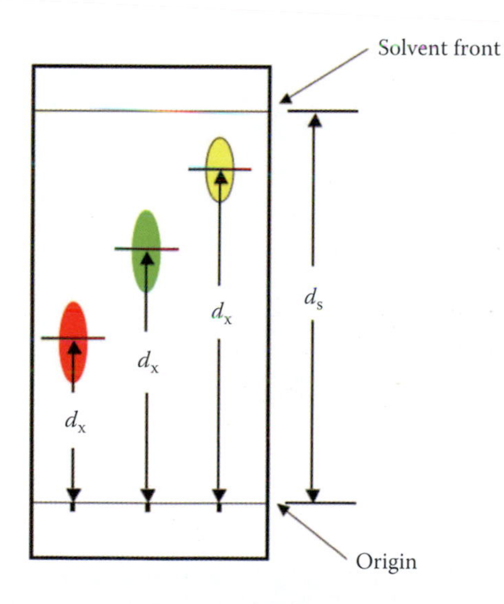

Record your observations in your laboratory notebook.

Activity 6.3 Using Chromatography to Identify a Drug

In the exercise, you will identify a drug based on its chromatographic properties. A TLC plate will serve as the stationary phase and alcohol will be used as the mobile phase.

Materials

Glass capillary tubes
TLC chamber or beaker with an aluminum foil cover
Alcohol
TLC plate (cut to the dimensions of the TLC chamber or beaker)

Drug reference standards in powder form contained in 1.5 mL epitubes (or equivalent type of container)
Evidence sample(s)
Epitube rack
254 nm UV light source
Lab glasses (UV blocking)
Gloves
Calculator

Protocol

1. Load a TLC chamber with enough alcohol to just fill the bottom of the container. Cover the chamber with its lid and allow the enclosed environment to become saturated.

2. Obtain the reference drug standards and evidence samples from your instructor.

Record the sample identification numbers in your laboratory notebook.
Add approximately 0.5 mL of alcohol to each sample. Agitate the tubes for approximately 1 min to dissolve the powders. Allow any undissolved residue to settle to the bottom of each tube.

3. Being careful not to press too hard, draw a line with a No. 2 pencil about 1 cm from the bottom edge of the TLC plate. This will serve as the line of origin. If white silica gel material is removed from the aluminum backing during this process, carefully draw another line slightly above it so that you can spot your samples on that line and onto the silica gel. Draw equidistantly spaced marks along the line of origin corresponding to the number of samples you will be testing. Mark each hatch mark with the same numbers as those used for the original evidence and reference samples.

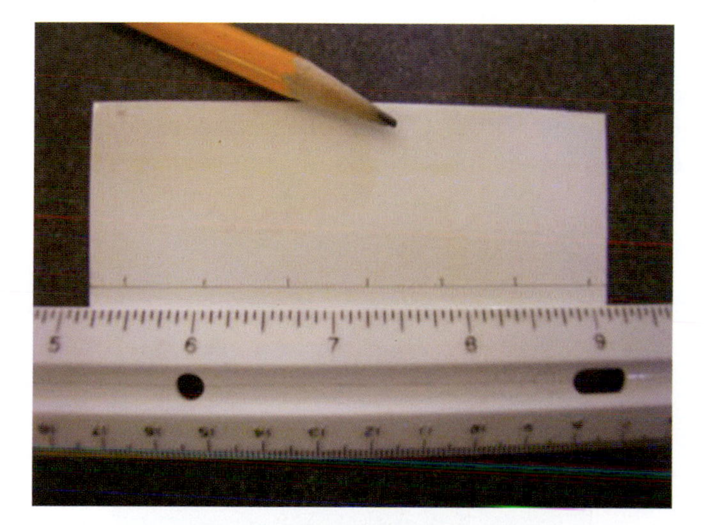

Record this information in your lab notebook.

4. Place one drop of each sample onto the premarked and corresponding spot on the line of origin. Use a different capillary pipette for each sample.

5. Wearing UV protective glasses, observe your spotted plate under UV short-wave (254 nm) light. Most of the spots should fluoresce a pinkish color.

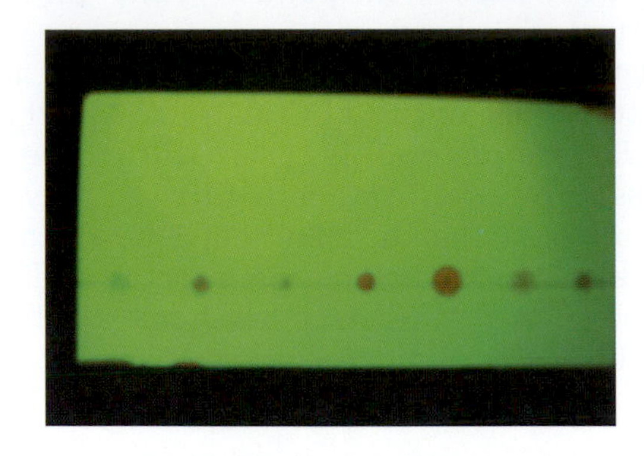

6. Place the spotted TLC plate into the chromatography chamber. Make sure that the solvent level in the TLC tank does not cover or touch the line of origin. Once the TLC plate is in place, do not move it.

7. Allow the solvent to run at least 80% of the available length of the TLC plate. Once this distance is reached, remove the plate from the chamber and, with a No. 2 pencil, mark the distance the solvent traveled (mark the solvent front).

8. While wearing UV protective glasses, illuminate the TLC plate with a short-wave UV light (254 nm). Using a dull No. 2 pencil, lightly circle the spot for

each sample. Draw a crosshair within the circle defining the darkest, most intense color zone within that spot.

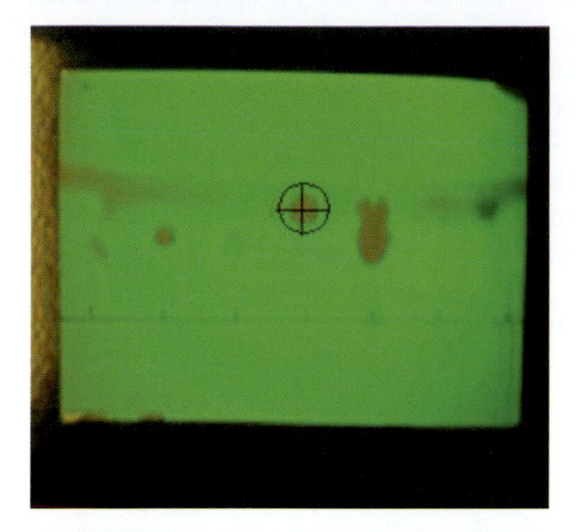

9. Measure the distance the solvent (d_s) moved relative to the line of origin for each sample. Determine the distance the chemical components moved (d_x) relative to the origin. Divide the distance the solvent front moved into the distance the chemical component moved (d_s divided by d_x). This is the R_f (retention factor) value for that component. It is expressed as a decimal (e.g., 0.45). The value *0.45* means that the chemical component traveled 45% the length of the solvent front. Identify the unknown sample by comparing its R_f value to the reference R_f values.

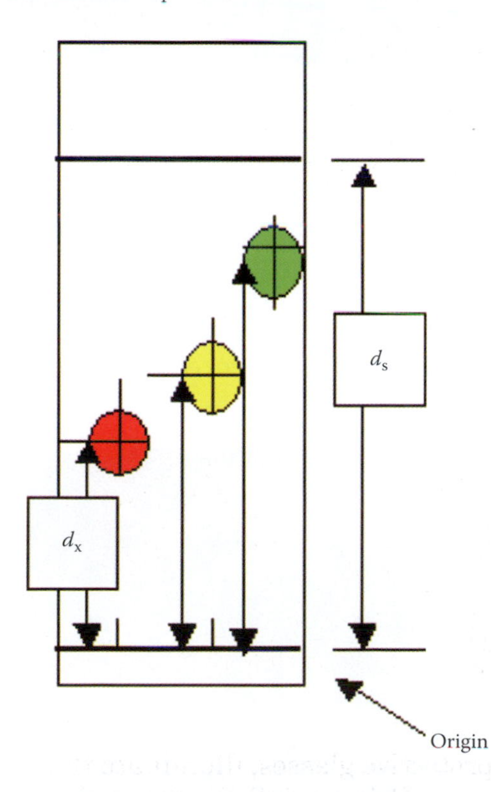

Record your results in your laboratory notebook.

Activity 6.4 Creating Bite Mark Impressions

Bite marks are unique. When left on a Styrofoam cup, a cigarette, or a pencil, they can lead an investigation to a suspect. This activity will guide you through the process of lifting a bite impression from a Styrofoam cup and determining whether it matches to a set of dental casts.

Materials

Styrofoam cup with a bite impression
Denstone or plaster of Paris
Dental extrusion putty
Putty knife
Flexible mixing bowl

Protocol

1. From your instructor, obtain a Styrofoam cup imprinted with a bite mark and record its identification number (or letter) in your laboratory notebook.

   Add a small amount of water to a rubber bowl containing Denstone (provided by your instructor) and mix with a putty knife. Continue adding small amounts of water until the mixture has the consistency of thick pancake batter. Check with your instructor to confirm the mixture is at the proper consistency.
2. Carefully layer the Denstone mixture over the bite mark on the Styrofoam cup. Once the bite mark is completely covered, apply several more layers of Denstone to give the cast some resilience. Allow the cast to dry overnight without movement.

3. Carefully peel the hardened Denstone cast from the surface of the Styrofoam cup. This cast represents a positive impression of the bite mark.

4. Your instructor will dispense a small amount of extrusion putty into your flexible bowl. Quickly (as the compound will set within a few seconds) mix the two types of putty together until the color is homogenous.

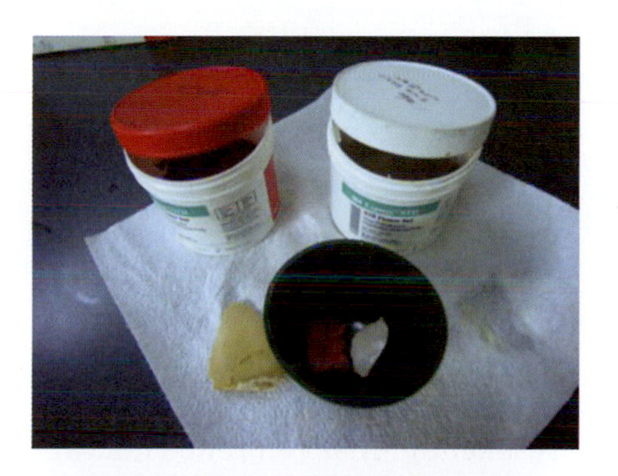

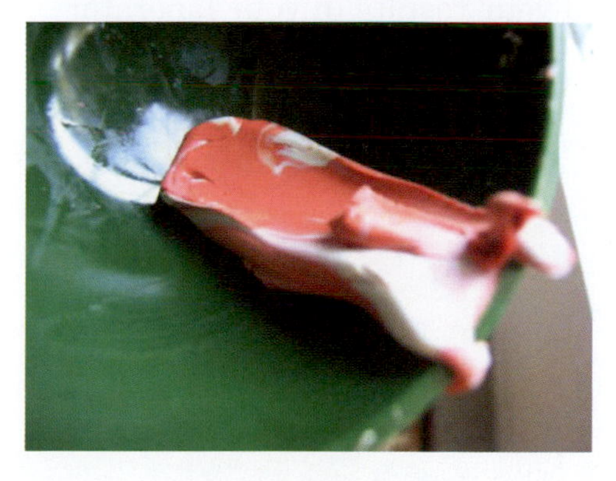

5. Using a spatula, apply and press the mixed extrusion putty onto the surface of the Denstone cast taken from the Styrofoam cup. Allow the putty to harden. Usually, within 5 min or less, the putty will have the consistency of a rubber eraser.

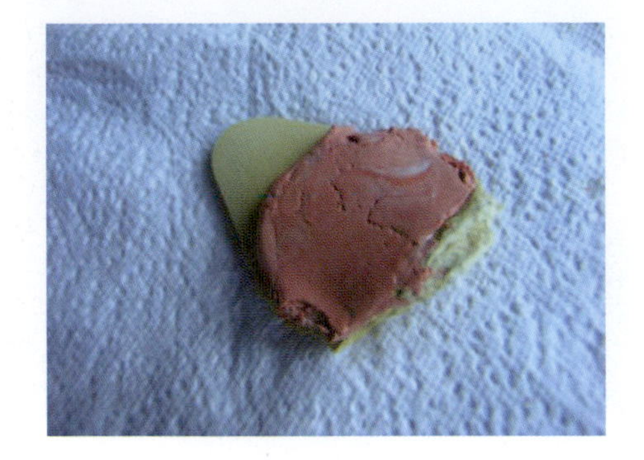

6. Carefully remove the extrusion putty from the Denstone bite mark impression. You have now created a negative impression of the bite mark.

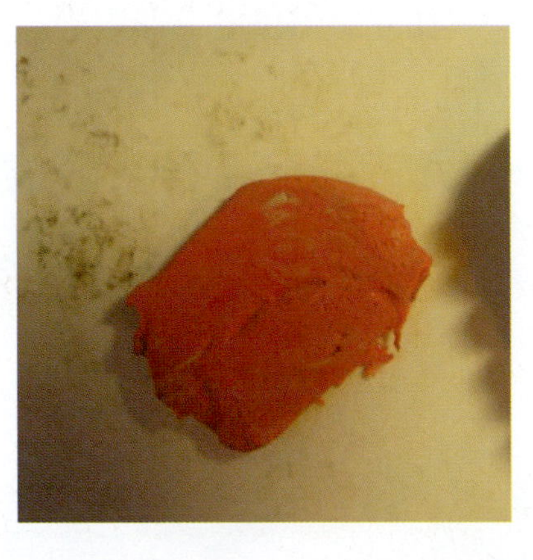

7. Match the putty impression against reference dental casts provided by your instructor and record your results in your laboratory notebook.

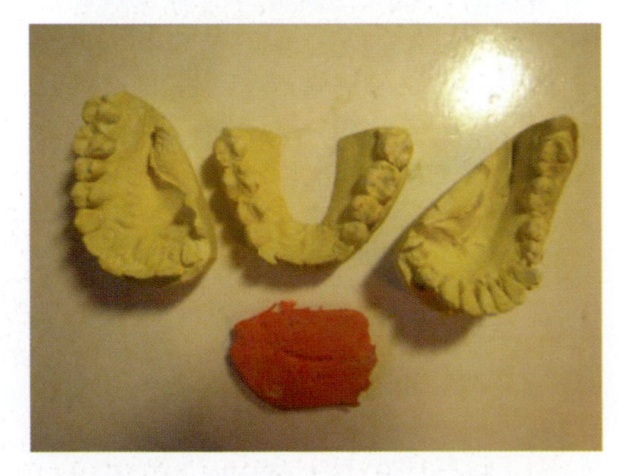

Activity 6.5 Collecting Local Flying Insects: A Study in Entomology

Entomology, the study of insects, can help investigators of a homicide determine the time of death by the maturity of insect eggs deposited on the corpse. An awareness of the local insect fauna can potentially place a death at a location other than where the corpse was discovered. In this activity, you will collect and catalog the various types of flying insects indigenous to your area.

Materials

Insect net
Small glass kill jar (cotton wad impregnated with ethyl acetate)
Computer with Internet access or appropriate insect reference chart
Aerial map of campus
Forceps
Dissection microscope and/or hand lens
Digital camera
Weather data on the collection day

Protocol

1. Your instructor will divide you into groups and assign each group to survey a designated area of the campus (refer to an aerial map of the campus to determine where you need to conduct your sampling). Before the instructor releases you from the classroom to conduct your insect survey, record the days' weather data to include (a) month, date, and year; (b) air temperature; (c) humidity; (d) wind speed; and (e) barometric pressure.

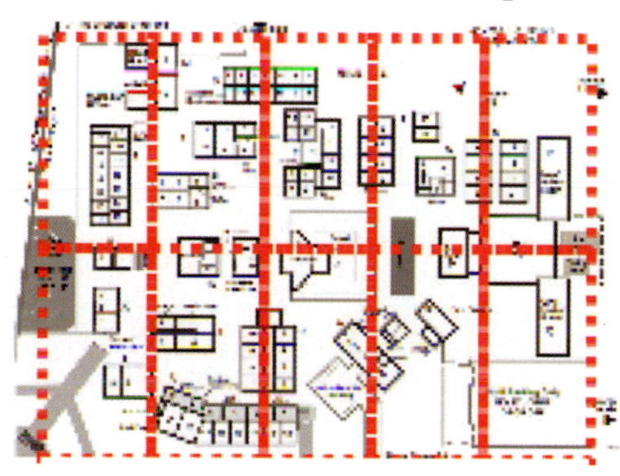

2. Obtain an insect net and a collection jar containing cotton saturated with ethyl acetate.* With your group, go to your assigned area and collect as many flying insects as you can during the time allotted to you. Avoid collecting bees, wasps, yellow jackets, hornets, or any such insects with stinging capabilities. When you return to the classroom and if the insects are dead, remove them from the collection jar and transfer them into an appropriate container labeled with the date and the name of your group.

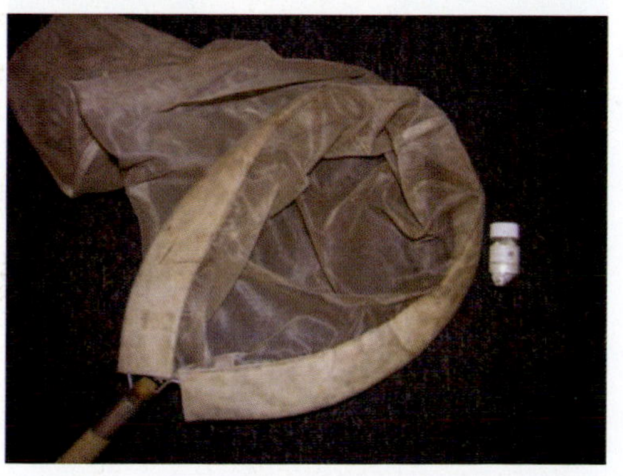

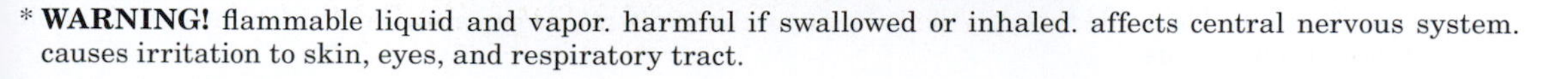
* **WARNING!** flammable liquid and vapor. harmful if swallowed or inhaled. affects central nervous system. causes irritation to skin, eyes, and respiratory tract.

3. Display your insect collection on a white sheet of paper on your laboratory table and make drawing of each variety in your laboratory notebook. Use a magnifying glass, hand lens, or dissecting microscope to improve the detail of your drawings. Also make drawings of other species displayed by the other groups in your class.

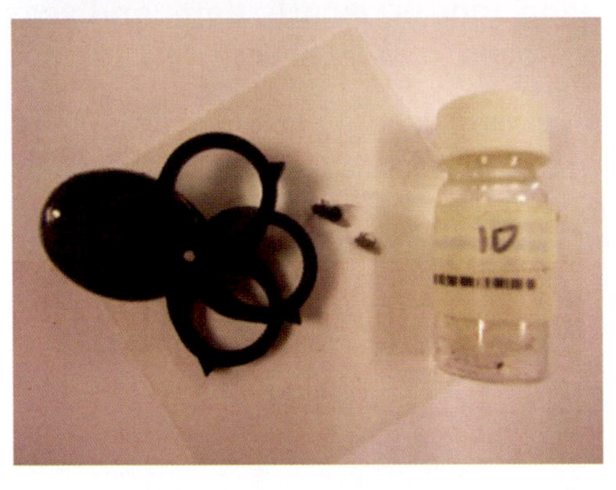

4. Using an insect identification book and/or computer with Internet access to an online insect identification key, identify the order and common name of the insect(s) your group collected.* Have your instructor verify that the identification of the insect is correct and input this data onto the front board so all students can inventory that day's total number and type of flying insects collected.

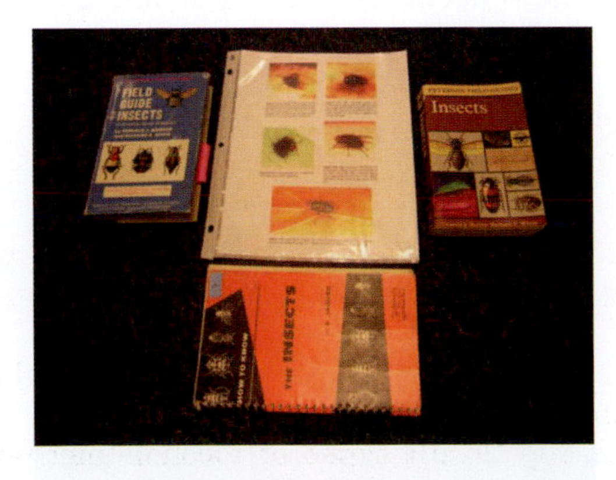

* Many insects can be identified through the following website: http://insects.about.com/od/onlineidentificationkeys/Online_Dichotomous.

Record the collated data in your laboratory notebook by date, order (and genus and species, if possible), common name, quantity, and weather conditions during the collection. This information can be prepared as a table. If specimens are collected over a time span of several months, prepare a graph of fly number (y-axis) versus month of collection (x-axis). Temperature at the time of collection can be plotted on the same graph using the second y-axis.

Activity 6.6 Categorizing Plants and Pollen

When a crime is committed, the perpetrator, the victim, and pieces of evidence may carry with them pollen and flora originating from the environments associated with the act. If these articles of trace evidence can be recovered and properly identified, they can provide valuable information about the location and circumstances of the crime. Forensic laboratories, therefore, will maintain catalogs of local plant and their pollen that can help them in unlocking the mystery behind a murder.

In this activity, you will create a reference library of local flowering plants and the types of pollen associated with them.

Materials

Flowers on your campus and/or store bought
Flower key
Compound microscope
Slides
Cover slips
Forceps
Clear fingernails polish
Taxonomic key to identify flowers
Taxonomic key to trees/shrubs

Protocol

Your class will be divided into groups and your instructor will assign each group to collect pollen from flowering plants in various parts of the school campus. Pollen can be collected on transparent tape and affixed to white index cards. Use the following websites to help you identify the varieties of pollen you've collected.
www.dnr.state.wi.us/org/caer/ce/eek/veg/treekey/index.htm
http://www.uwsp.edu/cnr/leaf/Treekey/tkframe.htm
www.cas.vanderbilt.edu/bioimages/tree-key/simple-leaf-trees.htm

Review Questions

6.1 A medical examiner uses a probe to measure the temperature of a murder victim's liver. He obtains a reading of 86.6°F. How long has the victim been deceased?

6.2 Draw the structural and chemical formula for ethanol (the form of alcohol in beer, wine, and hard spirits).

6.3 What chemical group do all types of alcohol (methanol, butanol, ethanol, isopropanol, etc.) have in common?

6.4 What is the percent alcohol in the evidence sample you tested?

6.5 What is an oxidation/reduction reaction?

6.6 By what chemical process does the dichromate ion change color in the presence of alcohol?
6.7 If the alcohol content of your unknown sample is off scale, how should that be reported in your lab notebook?
6.8 How does the body process alcohol?
6.9 In your state or country, what is the level of blood alcohol to be considered DUI?
6.10 Are the samples you tested for alcohol content under or over the state limit? Explain.
6.11 What is the function of a reference set of samples?
6.12 Differentiate between qualitative and quantitative analysis.
6.13 What is chromatography?
6.14 Why is it important that the line of origin be drawn with graphite pencil?
6.15 What does TLC stand for?
6.16 What is a reference standard?
6.17 Differentiate between the stationary versus the mobile phase.
6.18 What is the retention factor (R_f)?
6.19 What is the formula for determining R_f?
6.20 How can the R_f value be used to determine if an evidence sample is a match to the reference library?
6.21 Based on your R_f value calculations, do any of the evidence samples match with your reference standards?
6.22 What is the function of a forensic odontologist?
6.23 Why would it not be good practice to take place the dental cast directly onto the bite mark left on the Styrofoam cup?
6.24 Prior to making a bite mark mold with extrusion putty, what other potential biological evidence might be recoverable?
6.25 What is your analysis of the bite mark found on the Styrofoam cup?
6.26 How can insects determine the time of death?
6.27 How can insects assist law enforcement in determining the location of a death?
6.28 When an illegal drug shipment is seized at a coastal port or airport, how can insects assist federal agents in discovering its origin?
6.29 How can insects assist a forensic examiner in determining a cause of death?

Further Reading

The Medical Examiner and the Expert Witness

Unnatural Death. Confessions of a Medical Examiner by Michael M. Baden and Judith Adler Hennessee, Ballantine Books, Mississauga, Canada, 1989.

Corpse: Nature, Forensics, and the Struggle to Pinpoint Time of Death by Jessica Snyder Sachs, Perseus Publishing, Cambridge, MA, 2001.

Dead Reckoning: The New Science of Catching Killers by Michael Baden and Marion Roach, Simon & Schuster, New York, 2001.

Death's Acre: Inside the Legendary Forensic Lab the Body Farm Where the Dead Do Tell Tales by Bill Bass and Jon Jefferson, The Berkeley Publishing Group, New York, 2003.

Dissecting Death: Secrets of a Medical Examiner by Frederick Zugibe and David L. Carroll, Broadway Books, New York, 2005.

Forensic Science in Court: The Role of the Expert Witness by Wilson Wall, John Wiley & Sons, Ltd., West Sussex, U.K., 2009.
Bite to Byte: The Story of Injury Analysis by Persephone Lewin, Parrel Press, London, U.K., 2006.
Beyond the Body Farm: A Legendary Bone Detective Explores Murders, Mysteries, and the Revolution in Forensic Science by Bill Bass and Jon Jefferson, HarperCollins Publishers, New York, 2007.
Estimation of the Time since Death: Sudden Increase of Ambient Temperature by Paolo Bisegna, Claus Henßge, Lars Althaus, and Giusto Giusti in *Forensic Science International*, Vol. 176, No. 2–3, pages 196–199, 2008.
Time of Death of Victims Found in Cold Water Environment by Pekka J. Karhunen, Sirkka Goebeler, Olli Winberg, and Markku Tuominen in *Forensic Science International*, Vol. 176, No. 2–3, pages e17–e22, 2008.

Forensic Odontology

Forensic Odontologists Successfully Identify Tsunami Victims in Phuket, Thailand by P. Schuller-Gotzburg and J. Suchanek in *Forensic Science International*, Vol. 171, No. 2–3, pages 204–207, 2007.
When DNA Is Not Available, Can We Still Identify People? Recommendations for Best Practice by Jose Pablo Baraybar in *Journal of Forensic Sciences*, Vol. 52, No. 3, pages 533–540, 2008.
Three-Dimensional Comparative Analysis of Bitemarks by Allan J. Lasser, Allan J. Warnick, and Gary M. Berman in *Journal of Forensic Science*, Vol. 54, No. 3, pages 658–661, 2009.

Forensic Entomology

Use of Beetles in Forensic Entomology by Pankaj Kulshrestha and D.K. Satpathy in *Forensic Science International*, Vol. 120, No. 1–2, pages 15–17, 2001.
Factors Affecting Decomposition and Diptera Colonization by Carlo Pietro Campobasso, Giancarlo Di Vella, and Francesco Introna in *Forensic Science International*, Vol. 120, No. 1–2, pages 18–27, 2001.
The Utility of Mitochondrial DNA Sequences for the Identification of Forensically Important Blowflies (Diptera: Calliphoridae) in Southeastern Australia by J.F. Wallman and S.C. Donnellan in *Forensic Science International*, Vol. 120, No. 1–2, pages 60–67, 2001.
Dead Larvae of *Cynomya mortuorum* (L.) (Diptera, Calliphoridae) as Indicators of the Post-mortem Interval—A Case History from Norway by Morten Staerkeby in *Forensic Science International*, Vol. 120, No. 1–2, pages 77–78, 2001.
Medicolegal Relevance of Cadaver Entomofauna for the Determination of the Time of Death by M.I. Marchenko in *Forensic Science International*, Vol. 120, No. 1–2, pages 89–109, 2001.
DNA-Based Identification of Forensically Important Chrysomyinae (Diptera: Calliphoridae) by Jeffrey D. Wells and Felix A.J. Sperling in *Forensic Science International*, Vol. 120, No. 1–2, pages 110–115, 2001.
Genetic Relationships between Blowflies (Calliphoridae) of Forensic Importance by Jamie Stevens and Richard Wall in *Forensic Science International*, Vol. 120, No. 1–2, pages 116–123, 2001.
Flight Activity of the Blowflies, *Calliphora vomitoria* and *Lucilia sericata*, in the Dark by J. Wooldridge, L. Scrase, and R. Wall in *Forensic Science International*, Vol. 172, No. 2–3, pages 94–97, 2007.
The Use of *Megaselia abdita* (Diptera: Phoridae) in Forensic Entomology by J.D. Manlove and R.H.L. Disney in *Forensic Science International*, Vol. 175, No. 1, pages 83–84, 2008.

Use of *Lucilia* Species for Forensic Investigations in Southern Europe by S. Vanin, P. Tasinato, G. Ducolin, C. Terranova, S. Zancaner, M. Montisci, S.D. Ferrara, and M. Turchetto in *Forensic Science International*, Vol. 177, No. 1, pages 37–41, 2008.

Post-Feeding Larval Behaviour in the Blowfly, *Calliphora vicina*: Effects on Post-Mortem Interval Estimates by Sophie Arnott and Bryan Turner in *Forensic Science International*, Vol. 177, No. 2–3, pages 162–167, 2008.

Effect of Preservation Solutions on Preservation of *Calliphora augur* and *Lucilia cuprina* Larvae (Diptera: Calliphoridae) with Implications for Post-Mortem Interval Estimates by Donnah M. Day and James F. Wallman in *Forensic Science International*, Vol. 179, No. 1, pages 1–10, 2008.

Development of an Antigen-Based Rapid Diagnostic Test for the Identification of Blowfly (Calliphoridae) Species of Forensic Significance by Laura McDonagh, Chris Thornton, James F. Wallman, and Jamie R. Stevens in *Forensic Science International: Genetics*, Vol. 3, pages 162–165, 2009.

Internet Crime

Cybersex with Minors: Forensic Implications by Mark E. Jaffe and Kaushal K. Sharma in *Journal of Forensic Sciences*, Vol. 46, No. 6, pages 1397–1402, 2001.

Forensic Botany

Pollen Analysis Reveals Murder Season by R. Szibor, C. Schubert, R. Schoning, D. Krause, and U. Wendt in *Nature*, Vol. 395, No. 6701, pages 449–450, 1998.

Fine Resolution of Pollen Patterns in Limited Space: Differentiating a Crime Scene and Alibi Scene Seven Meters Apart by Mark Horrocks and Kevan A.J. Walsh in *Journal of Forensic Sciences*, Vol. 44, No. 2, pages 417–420, 1999.

Forensic Palynology: Variation in the Pollen Content of Soil on Shoes and in Shoeprints in Soil by M. Horrocks, S.A. Coulson, and K.A.J. Walsh in *Journal of Forensic Sciences*, Vol. 44, No. 1, pages 119–122, 1999.

Pollen on Grass Clippings: Putting the Suspect at the Scene of the Crime by M. Horrocks and K.A.J. Walsh in *Journal of Forensic Sciences*, Vol. 46, No. 4, pages 947–949, 2001.

Sub-Sampling and Preparing Forensic Samples for Pollen Analysis by M. Horrocks in *Journal of Forensic Sciences*, Vol. 49, No. 5, pages 1024–1027, 2004.

Forensic Botany: Usability of Bryophyte Material in Forensic Studies by Viivi Virtanen, Helena Korpelainen, and Kirsi Kostamo in *Forensic Science International*, Vol. 172, No. 2–3, pages 161–163, 2007.

Forensic Toxicology

The Elements of Murder: A History of Poison by John Emsley, Oxford University Press, New York, 2005.

Criminal Poisoning: Investigational Guide for Law Enforcement, Toxicologists, Forensic Scientists, and Attorneys by John H. Trestrail III, Humana Press Inc., Totowa, NJ, 2007.

Forensic Toxicology Widens Net for Drugs of Abuse: The Rise of LC/MS/MS for Toxicology Testing by Tania A. Sasaki in *Forensic Magazine*, October/November Issue, pages 20–25, 2007.

Two Fatal Cases of Selenium Toxicity by Henry A. Spiller and Eric Pfiefer in *Forensic Science International*, Vol. 171, No. 1, pages 67–72, 2007.

Markers of Chronic Alcohol use in Hair: Comparison of Ethyl Glucuronide and Cocaethylene in Cocaine Users by Lucia Politi, Alessandra Zucchella, Luca Morini, Cristiana Stramesi, and Aldo Polettini in *Forensic Science International*, Vol. 172, No. 1, pages 23–27, 2007.

Segmental Determination of Ethyl Glucuronide in Hair: A Pilot Study by B.M.R. Appenzeller, R. Agirman, P. Neuberg, M. Yegles, and R. Wennig in *Forensic Science International*, Vol. 173, No. 2–3, pages 87–92, 2007.

Differentiation between Drug use and Environmental Contamination When Testing for Drugs in Hair by Lolita Tsanaclis and John F.C. Wicks in *Forensic Science International*, Vol. 176, No. 1, pages 19–22, 2008.

Hair Analysis for Cocaine: Factors in Laboratory Contamination Studies and Their Relevance to Proficiency Sample Preparation and Hair Testing Practices by Virginia Hill, Thomas Cairns, and Michael Schaffer in *Forensic Science International*, Vol. 176, No. 1, pages 23–33, 2008.

A Controlled Study of the Time-Course of Breath Alcohol Concentration after Moderate Ingestion of Ethanol Following a Social Drinking Session by Jesus Barquin, Juan de Dios Luna, and Antonio F. Hernandez in *Forensic Science International*, Vol. 177, No. 2–3, pages 140–145, 2008.

7
Lies?

Menlo Park, Wednesday 8:57 AM

Jenkins wheeled right from Willow onto Middlefield Drive. Helen, obeying Newton's first law of motion, lurched to her left, straining to keep her cup of Starbucks in an upright, contained position.

"She corners like a dream, doesn't she?" Jenkins gloated.

"Oh yeah. Smoooooth," Helen replied, tugging at her inside seam with her free hand, her jeans having suddenly taken on the feel of something akin to dental floss.

"Someday, I'm going to live in Menlo Park," Jenkins mused. "The houses tucked away among the trees. It's so green. So shady. It just reeks of classy living."

"A little too close to Stanford for my taste," said Helen.

"You Berkeleyites need to get over it."

"Go Bears. Oh, Survey Lane, there on the left. Now take it slow," Helen pleaded.

Jenkins turned into the parking lot of the U.S. Geological Survey Western Regional Office and slid his Cutlass Calais between a Mercedes and a Lexus in front of the Visitors' Center.

"Do you think this is our man, Lieutenant?" Helen asked as she released her seatbelt.

"Love, hate, jealousy, revenge—they're all part of a continuum," Jenkins replied. "An object of soaring, unbridled love on one day can be despised with equal fervor on the next. I can't wait to hear what he has to say. But be prepared, Miss Chang. Most people are skilled liars."

"Men, in particular," Helen rejoined.

"Funny, I was going to say that women are the better liars," Jenkins countered.

"I guess we've both been burned."

Jenkins and Helen climbed the few steps to the Visitors' Center's double doors. Portraits of the president and vice president hung on the right wall of the entryway. *Our commander-in-chief*, thought Jenkins. *Politicians*, thought Helen.

"Excuse me," Jenkins said, grabbing the attention of the receptionist. "We're looking for Sam O'Neill." Jenkins withdrew his badge and held it up for her inspection. "Police business," he added.

"Let me page him for you," the receptionist said reaching for the phone.

"If you don't mind, we'd prefer to meet with him unannounced."

The receptionist placed the receiver back on its slot. "Building 2, second floor, room 214," she said glaring at him suspiciously. "But you'll need to sign in and put these on." The receptionist handed each of them a visitor's badge.

Building 2, a beige two-story structure on the opposite side of the parking lot, had wide pane windows showing desks and shelving stacked with books, pamphlets, maps, and loose papers. They entered through a glass door, lower level and found a stairway leading them to the second story. Room 214 was on the left side of the hallway.

"After you, Miss Chang," Jenkins offered at the room's doorway and he followed her in.

There was only one occupant. His back was to them. He had thick dark hair of medium length with a faint wave to it. Slight of build, not as tall as Jenkins, he stood approximately 5′6″, that with thick-soled hiking boots.

"Sam O'Neill?" Jenkins inquired.

The man turned to face them. Heavy eyebrows arched above dark brown eyes. His face was covered by a three-day growth of beard. He wore a plaid, flannel shirt and khaki pants. A card key name badge with his photograph was clipped onto his right pants pocket. "That's right," he said.

"Mr. O'Neill, I'm Lieutenant Robert Jenkins and this is Criminalist Helen Chang. If you have a moment?"

Sam shrugged.

"We've found your girlfriend's car."

"My girlfriend didn't lose her car," Sam replied surprised.

"A white Subaru station wagon?"

"My girlfriend drives a Honda Civic two-door."

"Erica Holmes?"

"Oh, Erica's car."

"So you know Erica Holmes?"

"Yeah, but we're over and I didn't know she lost her car. Was it stolen?"

"What was your relationship with Erica?"

"She was my girlfriend, once."

"That was when?"

"Up until about six months ago."

"Was it serious?"

"I'd say so."

"So you broke up?"

"Yeah."

"When was the last time you saw Erica?"

"That would have been six months ago."

"What do you remember about the last time you saw her?"

"I dropped her off at her work—her service garage on Geary in San Francisco."

“What car were you driving?”

“Actually, hers.”

“Why not your own?”

“It had a busted alternator. Erica was going to fix it for me. She lent me her car for the day.”

“So things were okay between you two at that time?”

“I can’t say that they were. We had been arguing again.”

“Regarding?”

“I can’t remember the exact topic—our work schedules, sex, her father’s hatred of me, commitment, finances, religion. Take your pick.”

“Do you mind if we sit down?” Jenkins asked gesturing to the chairs around a circular table at the side of the room.

“Back to your vehicle, Mr. O’Neill,” Jenkins continued as the three seated themselves. “Did Erica fix the alternator for you?”

“I presume. When I picked it up the next day, it was ready to go.”

“And your vehicle is...?”

“A Ford F150 truck.”

“So you borrowed Erica’s car, the white Subaru station wagon, and how did you get it back to her?”

“I didn’t.”

“Excuse me?”

“It broke down on Seaport Boulevard.”

“Let’s back up a bit. You dropped Erica off at her service garage using her vehicle?”

“That’s correct.”

“And then where did you go?”

“I came here to the USGS.”

“And so Erica’s car was parked here all day?”

“No, I took it up into the Santa Cruz Mountains. Up 17.”

“Why?”

“I was doing some survey work on the San Andreas Fault.”

“Mr. O’Neill, I see a number of government vehicles here and you even have a motor pool. Why didn’t you take a government truck?”

“They were all signed out.”

Helen nudged Jenkins with her knee underneath the table. Jenkins pretended not to notice.

“You weren’t having much luck with vehicles that day, were you?”

“I guess it happens,” Sam replied.

"On January twenty-fourth of this year, Erica's car was towed from Seaport Boulevard. Do you have any idea how it got there? That's a good distance away from the Santa Cruz Mountains."

Sam bent his head forward, placed both elbows on the table and rubbed his forehead with one hand and the back of his neck with the other.

"Mr. O'Neill?" Jenkins prodded.

Sam fidgeted in his chair.

"Would you be more comfortable with a lawyer present, Mr. O'Neill?" Jenkins asked.

"No. No. I'm okay," replied Sam.

"Alright. Then more to the point," Jenkins continued. "There's a large stain in the cargo bay of Erica's station wagon and we've found what appears to be blood under the hood. Would you know anything about that?"

Sam rose slowly from his chair and walked three paces to the side of the room covered by windows. He braced himself with one hand against a sill and stared out across the parking lot.

"Can you help us out here, Mr. O'Neill?" Jenkins insisted.

"You will find that stain in the cargo bay to be blood," Sam finally managed.

"Can you explain that?" Jenkins asked.

"It's from a mountain lion," Sam replied. Jenkins shot a quick glance at Helen in time to see her rolling her eyes.

"A mountain lion?" Jenkins asked incredulously.

"*Felis concolor*. Yeah, a mountain lion," Sam replied.

"And how did a bleeding mountain lion end up in the back of Erica's vehicle?"

"I shot it."

"Okay."

"I was surveying up in the Santa Cruz Mountains, as I said, and it was stalking me. I did what I could to discourage it. I yelled, made myself appear as large as I could. I threw a rock at it. It charged. I shot it and put it in the back of Erica's car."

"So you own a gun?" Jenkins asked.

"I always take one with me when I'm alone in a wilderness environment."

"Did you report the killing of the animal to your boss or to the Department of Fish and Game?"

"No. I screwed up. I was worried that I was in violation of the Endangered Species Act or the Sierra Club was going to come down on me or who knows what law I may have violated. They're beautiful animals. You can't imagine my guilt."

"When you shot the cat, was the animal between you and Erica's car?"

"No."

"Were you aiming towards or away from the vehicle?"

"It would have been away from the car."

"Are you sure?"

"Yeah, pretty sure."

"And how many shots did it take to down the animal?"

"Two. Maybe three. No, two."

"Not one shot?"

"No. It was two."

"May I see the gun?"

"I don't have it."

"Where is it?"

"I don't know. Up in the mountains, maybe. I haven't seen it since that day. For the life of me, I can't remember. I thought maybe I'd left it in Erica's car. But if I had, she would have returned it to me, no matter what her feelings about me. Wouldn't you think? There was a lot going on. That was one horrendously stressful day."

"So how does Seaport Boulevard figure into all of this?" Jenkins asked.

"I dumped the animal in the bay and, driving back here to work, Erica's car broke down."

"What was the problem?"

"I didn't know. I'm not a mechanic. I took a look under the hood in case it was something obvious but I didn't see anything."

"We found drops of blood in the engine bay. Do you know how they got there?"

"I could have had a nose bleed, I guess, when I was looking over the engine. I don't remember."

"Do you get nosebleeds often?"

"Yeah sometimes. Like when my sinuses are raw from a cold."

"Some of the blood spots look like they could have been sprayed."

"Maybe I sneezed. Look Lieutenant, I really don't remember."

"Alright. So you weren't able to get the car running?"

"That's right."

"Did you report that the vehicle was curbed and not functioning?"

"I tried to call Erica at the garage but she didn't pick up. But that wasn't surprising. I figured we were probably over."

"Did you use your cell phone?" Jenkins asked.

"No, I couldn't get reception. I used a phone at a Quick Stop or it was a 7-Eleven, you know, one of those, close by."

"Did you leave a message on the answering machine?"

"No. I called Erica's parents and let them know about it."

"What time was that?"

"Must have been sometime after five or so. It was dusk."

"Who answered the phone?" Jenkins asked.

"No one," Sam replied. "I think they screen their calls. I left a message on their machine. Told them where the car was."

"Did you assume that they would take care of the vehicle?"

"Yeah, they must have."

"Why do you say that?"

"The next day, a friend of mine took me to pick up my truck from Erica's garage and we drove down Seaport to see if the car was still there. It wasn't."

"How did you get home from Seaport after Erica's car broke down?" Jenkins asked.

"I called a cab," Sam replied.

"How?"

"By the pay phone."

"And no more contact with Erica after that day."

"No. She may have gone to her Uncle's or somewhere. I don't know. I haven't heard from her since."

"So you're seeing someone else now?"

"Yes."

"What is her name?"

"She works here. At the Visitors' Center. Farah Dawood."

"Is she here today?"

"Yeah. She is."

"Mr. O'Neill, is your truck outside?"

"Uh huh."

"Do you mind if we take a look at it?" Jenkins asked. "We could get a search warrant, but…"

"It's okay," Sam replied. "I can take you to it."

They walked down the stairs and out of the building into the adjoining parking lot. Sam directed them to the middle section of the second row of vehicles where his Ford F150 was parked. Jenkins circled around the vehicle, looking into the cargo bay as he moved to the passenger's door. He searched through the glove compartment. Finding nothing of interest beyond a map of the Peninsula, the vehicle registration, and a few gasoline receipts, he stooped over to examine the space underneath the seats. A dark metallic object caught his eye. Jenkins withdrew a pen from his inside coat pocket and began to poke and prod underneath the front seat. Within seconds, he pulled out a revolver skewered by its barrel on the end of his pen.

"Is this yours, Mr. O'Neill?" Jenkins asked.

"That's my gun! I thought I'd lost it," Sam exclaimed.

"Miss Chang, would you please hold this a minute?" Jenkins asked passing her the revolver balanced on the shaft of the pen. Helen took it cautiously and held it at arm's length, cringing as if it was soaked in the bacterium that causes plague. Jenkins pulled out a pair of latex gloves from his coat pocket and slid them on.

"Are you sure you don't want a lawyer present?" Helen said to Sam.

"Thank you, Miss Chang," Jenkins said as he carefully slid the gun up and off the pen. He tripped the cylinder release latch with his thumb and flicked the cylinder off the barrel. "Three bullets missing," he observed then slipped the revolver into a plastic evidence bag.

"I don't get it," Sam said, shaking his head.

"Here," Jenkins said, handing Sam his card. "Come down to the station for fingerprinting and DNA sampling. This afternoon, if possible," Jenkins advised. "Oh, and Mr. O'Neill?"

"Yeah?"

"Don't leave the state."

Jenkins held out his right arm in the direction of his car. "Miss Chang, we have another visit to make."

Jenkins and Helen left Sam there, his hands on his hips and staring at his truck.

"You're not going to *arrest* him?" Helen asked as they walked back across the parking lot. "That's whack! Isn't his story just all a little too tidy? Isn't there something called 'probable cause' or *corpus delicti* or some kind of legal thing that would let you to take him in?"

"We're not done with our investigation, Miss Chang," Jenkins replied.

"You know, Lieutenant," Helen said, "when I think of an 'O'Neill,' what comes to mind is maybe a guy with red hair, fair skin, and freckles who can throw a mean set of darts in an Irish pub."

"Not to stereotype, of course," Jenkins observed.

"Yeah, of course, not to stereotype," Helen responded. "But this guy doesn't look like an O'Neill."

"Did you see the name on his security badge?" Jenkins asked.

"No."

"His name is Samdeep O'Neill."

"Samdeep. What kind of name is Samdeep?" Helen asked.

"Middle Eastern. Iraqi perhaps."

Jenkins placed the revolver in the trunk of his car and he and Helen made their way back into the Visitors' Center. Finding the receptionist again, they inquired as to the location of Farah Dawood.

"She's in the back, in the conference room at the moment," the receptionist said. "Shall I page her for you?"

Jenkins gave her a look with a cock of his head.

"Oh yeah," said the receptionist in resignation, "you prefer to meet with her unannounced. The door on your right," she said, "and straight back."

They found Farah Dawood placing brochures and stapled copies of some report at each seat position along six rows of tables facing the front of the hall. She looked up when they entered the room and momentarily paused. She was a slender woman but curved. Thick dark hair was pulled back in a braid. As Jenkins approached, he could make out the color of her eyes. They were light brown.

"The first presentation isn't for another hour," she said in a voice that reminded Jenkins of wind chimes. "But you can wait in the library if you'd like."

"We're not here for the meeting," Jenkins replied. "You're Farah Dawood, correct?"

"Yes, how can I help you?"

"I'm Lieutenant Robert Jenkins and this is Criminalist Helen Chang. We're investigating a missing person and were hoping you might be able to help us out."

"I'll do what I can."

"How long have you worked here at the U.S. Geological Survey?" Jenkins asked.

"I started working here last year," Farah replied.

"And what do you do here?"

"I coordinate meetings and conferences. That's what I'm working on right now. We're hosting a national managers' meeting."

"It's a very nice facility."

"I'll take that as a personal compliment. Thank you."

"Do you know Sam O'Neill?"

"Yes, of course I know him. This is a missing person investigation?" Farah asked in reply.

"This is about Erica Holmes. Do you know her?"

"She used to be Sam's girlfriend."

"How long have you known Mr. O'Neill?" Jenkins asked.

"For about a year. Now, wait a minute." Farah said slightly agitated as if it had just occurred to her where this line of questioning was going and it was down a thorny and objectionable path. "Erica is missing and you think Sam had something to do with that in some kind of sinister way? Is that it? Not a chance. Sam is the sweetest man I've ever met."

"We're just trying to gather as much information as we can, Miss Dawood. The more we know, the better equipped we are to figure out where we might find Erica. Sam was one of the last people to see her before she was reported missing. So, you've known Sam for a about year?"

"Yeah, since I started working here."

"Did you ever work together on a project?"

"Yes, we have. I've helped him set up several conferences he was organizing."

"And did you know Erica Holmes, his girlfriend?"

“She came by here a few times.”

“And you and Sam are dating?”

“Yes, for about half a year now.”

“Do you own a gun, Miss Dawood?”

“Do I own a gun? Of course not!” Farah emphatically replied. “Are you now suggesting that I have something to do with Erica’s disappearance? That maybe I murdered her so that I could have Sam to myself? I think this ends our conversation. If you want to talk to me again, it’ll be with a lawyer present.”

“Thank you for your time, Miss Dawood,” Jenkins said. “Miss Chang,” he said motioning for them to rise. “Miss Dawood,” Jenkins continued, “I’m going to ask that you come down to the station for prints and a DNA sample. Here’s my card. If you fail to do so, I can get a warrant.”

Farah took the card and tossed it on the table.

“Thank you again for your time.”

“Well that could have gone better,” Helen remarked as they exited the building heading for Jenkins’ car. “But not bad there, Lieutenant. You think that either Sam killed Erica so that he would be free to pursue Farah or that Farah killed Erica to get her out of the way so that she could have Sam. Not bad at all.”

“A lot of people have lost their lives for being the unwilling participants in a love triangle, Miss Chang. Are you familiar with the Scott Peterson case?” Jenkins asked.

“It was several years ago,” Helen replied.

“Yeah. Peterson killed his pregnant wife, Laci, on Christmas Eve and discarded her body in San Francisco Bay. With her gone, he believed, he’d be free to devote his attention to his girlfriend Amber Frey, a woman he knew from Fresno. Beautiful women can make men do outrageous, ruinous, even unspeakable things.”

“Yeah, I don’t get that. Men will put everything at risk for a woman. Look at Bill Clinton.”

“Testosterone, Miss Chang. What’s your opinion on Farah? You think she had motivation enough?”

“It’s not likely,” Helen mused. “Women aren’t really into the whole violent homicide thing.”

“That’s what most people said about Lizzie Borden,” Jenkins observed.

“Who’s that?” Helen asked.

“Just a woman who killed both her parents with a hatchet. Such a sweet thing. Taught Sunday school. No one thought she could have possibly been capable of so horrific a murder. The jury let her walk. Lizzie Borden took an axe and gave her mother forty whacks. And when she saw what she had done, she gave her father forty-one.”

“Did you right that poem?” Helen asked.

“Oh no,” Jenkins replied. “I’ve written exactly one poem in my life, Miss Chang, and it had nothing to do with Lizzie Borden.”

"Can I hear it?"

"No. Miss Chang. We have two more visits to make today."

"Where's that?"

"Ever been out to Seaport Boulevard?" asked Jenkins.

"And the other?" Helen responded.

"Erica Holmes' last known location—her service garage. Are you up for a trip to the city?"

"Are you buying lunch?"

"You're a mercenary," Jenkins told her.

Getting at the Truth

Interviewing Witnesses

We're 100% certain we can recognize the faces of our family members. You know what your friend Nicole looks like—distinctly different from Steve or Michelle. Because of that belief, we also have confidence, a great deal of it in fact, that other people can tell the difference between individuals. Members of a jury typically place a large amount of trust, therefore, in the ability of witnesses to recognize the faces of an assailant. This trust often trumps any conclusions deductively drawn from the actual evidence studied in the case and can lead to unfortunate wrongful convictions.

Larry Fuller, a decorated Vietnam veteran, was sentenced to 50 years in prison for a 1981 aggravated rape at knifepoint of a 37-year-old Dallas woman after breaking into her home. The victim had picked Larry Fuller from one of two photo lineups even though in the photo the victim chose, Fuller had a beard and in an earlier statement to police, she had said that her assailant was clean shaven. Larry Fuller spent over two decades in prison before being released following DNA tests showing that he was not the assailant.

In August of 2003, charges were dropped against two Chicago men who spent 27 years behind bars for the 1976 rape and murder of a 9-year-old girl after DNA testing proved they could not have possibly committed the crime. Paul Terry and Michael Evans, both 17 years old at the time of their arrest, were convicted on the testimony of a single witness, even though no physical evidence ever linked them to the crime.

Thomas Doswell spent nearly 18 years in prison for the 1986 rape of a 48-year-old woman in a Pittsburg hospital. Doswell was 25 years old and the father of two children at the time of his conviction. He was denied parole four times because, in the eyes of the court, he was not rehabilitated; he insisted he was innocent. Witnesses, including the victim, had picked out Doswell's photo from a group of eight photos shown to them. It was standard Pittsburg police operating procedure at the time to place the letter "R" underneath the mug shot of anyone charged with rape. Doswell had been charged but acquitted of rape by a girlfriend at an earlier time. An "R" was written beneath his mug shot. Despite Doswell's objections that writing an "R" below his photo was so suggestive of guilt as to almost assure a false identification, he was, nonetheless, convicted of the crime and sent to prison. He served time until

DNA evidence examined by the nonprofit legal clinic, the Innocence Project, showed that someone else must have committed the assault.

In 2006, DNA evidence set free Connecticut man Scott Fappianno after he had spent 21 years in prison for the 1983 rape at gunpoint of a Brooklyn woman. The victim identified Fappianno as her rapist from police photographs of men who matched his general description. She also picked him out of a lineup even though he was some 5 in. shorter in stature and had shorter hair than the man she had told police was her rapist. He was sentenced to a 50-year term. After years of serving hard time, his parole board offered to reduce his sentence in exchange for an admission of guilt.

In 1985, Eddie Lloyd, a mental health patient, was convicted of the rape and murder of a Detroit teenager. Seemingly, it was an open and shut case. He had confessed to the crime. At the time, however, he also confessed to a number of other heinous crimes that police quickly proved he could not have committed. But with no other suspects and no way to show that he wasn't the murderer, the police had their man. In 2002, after spending 17 years in a prison cell, an exonerating DNA test set him free.

These several examples show the fallibility of eyewitness accounts and, conversely, the strength and power that juries attach to witness testimony. The number of cases where suspects were wrongfully sent to prison by false identification could fill volumes. There have been well over 100 of them in the United States where a defendant was freed because of postconviction DNA testing. Almost one-quarter of those cases involve a false confession.

For those crimes where the perpetrator is not literally caught in the act, the police and investigative team must ask the victim (if they survived) and any witnesses to provide a description of the offender. Standard procedure then has the witness pick out the perpetrator from mug shots of known criminals. Alternatively, the police may use a sketch artist or computer program to build a composite image of the perpetrator's likeness based on the witness' description. If a suspect has been brought in on suspicion, the police may have the witness identify the suspect when placed in a lineup of several *foils* all having an appearance similar to that of the apprehended suspect. Each of these paths to a suspect's identification, however, is only as good and trustworthy as the memory of the witness, which, as we've seen by the examples given earlier, can be atrociously and tragically flawed.

The Opposite of the Truth

At the moment a crime is committed, the worst is revealed about its perpetrator. He (or she) is ignoring the laws of society and is acting completely outside the bounds of honorable and acceptable behavior. After assaulting, raping, or murdering another individual, lying about it (a crime called *perjury*) is a trivial and dismissive act by comparison. Few criminals fess up to their crimes readily and willingly. They evade. They deceive. They may commit further criminal acts to cover up the first one. To solve a case, therefore, the investigator is left with the expensive, time-consuming, and laborious task of proving a suspect or accomplice's duplicity by examination of the available evidence. Imagine how much easier the job of solving crimes would be if there were a foolproof way to verify whether or not someone was telling a lie—if fact from fiction could be easily discerned?

Body language is the way we communicate without using words. For example, do you want to know if someone is attracted to you? Here are the signs: Are they holding eye contact longer with you than they do with other people? Do their pupils dilate when they look at you? Is there a lot of smiling going on? Do they mimic your body postures and gestures? When you're sitting next to them, are their feet pointing in your direction. Do they sit closer to you than to others? If a man is attracted to a woman, he may occasionally rub his ear lobe. When a woman likes a man, she will twirl a lock of hair with her finger or continually tuck it behind an ear. She may also touch her neck more frequently.

Although body language communicates signs of affection, it can also be used in the investigation of a crime. For example, an innocent person locked in a jail cell will pace up and down nervously. An injustice has been perpetrated upon them and they feel trapped, in a desperate situation, and are urgent for release. A guilty person will sit or lie down on the bunk bed in a relaxed manner; they know they're supposed to be there—they finally got caught. Oddly, it's a relief!

Whether we are readily aware of it or not, because humans are such social animals, we are all acute observers of body language. We generally have a pretty good idea when someone is nervous, relaxed, happy, or in grief. Those in law enforcement, by necessity, become experts in the study of reading body language. And nowhere is this skill more important than in judging whether or not someone might be lying.

Many humans start practicing deception at an early age. Whether it's to get out of trouble or to obtain something they want by manipulating those around them. Many people find lying to be a convenient tool and may practice and hone the art their entire lifetimes. Some become consummate artists of deception. Lawyers, politicians, and used car salesmen may come to mind as those most skilled in the art. For many of us, however, no matter how hard we practice, lying is an unnatural act and makes us feel uncomfortable. As we stray further away from the true north of our moral compass, our discomfort level increases, and no matter how hard we try, our body language, through seemingly involuntary gestures, can expose the deception and unmask us as liars.

The following changes in body language can signal that a lie is being told. It doesn't necessarily mean, absolutely, that a person is lying, just that it is a strong possibility. Sometimes, as the prolific Austrian psychiatrist Sigmund Freud once said, a cigar is just a cigar.

- A person telling a lie blinks more often.
- When lying, a person increases the number of times they touch their face. This can include stroking the chin, covering the mouth, rubbing the cheek or forehead, scratching the eyebrow, pulling the earlobe, grooming the hair, rubbing their eyes, or, the all-time favorite, touching or rubbing the nose.
- A person telling a lie will make more subtle shifts of their body weight than when telling the truth.
- Repeating a question asked even when it was asked perfectly clearly and loudly. For example, you girls, if you ask your boyfriend a question such as "Were you with Jessica in the library last night?" and he responds with "Was I with Jessica in the library last night?" before getting around to the actual answer, be prepared for an attenuated truth. This is a tactic many people use to stall the conversation so that they can allow their brains time to think up an answer that is a safe alternative to the actual facts. When that answer comes, however, beware—don't be surprised if it has some element of fable to it.
- When someone is telling a lie, they don't use hand gestures like they normally do.

- The liar will limit their physical expression.
- A liar is not likely to press an open hand to their chest or heart.
- A liar will avoid eye contact as much as possible and may turn their face or body away from the questioner.
- When telling a lie, a person may speak in a slightly higher-pitched voice or clear their throat before speaking.
- A liar might try to use humor or sarcasm to deflect a question.
- A liar will use more nonsense words like *uh* and *er*. Making up a lie is a lot to remember, what's true, what's not. Consequently, liars produce more errors in their speech and grammar. They may start a sentence, abandon it midway, and start another one.
- A liar may look up and to your left when telling a lie (if the person is right handed—a left-handed person telling a lie would look up and to your right; Figure 7.1a).
- A liar might place some object (a chair, coffee mug, broom, etc.) between themselves and the questioner (Figure 7.1b).
- A liar will give a broad answer with little consideration to finer detail. For example, a liar may tell you that he can't meet with you because he is going out to lunch with friends but he probably won't tell you where he's going for lunch or with whom. A deceptive person will be reticent to embellish their answer with much detail that might later be exposed as false. A truth teller will usually be happy to give you the details.
- A liar displays emotion out of sync with the conversation—an emotional display is delayed, may last longer than it should, and may stop suddenly. The classic example is the person receiving a fruitcake for the holidays, exclaiming how much they love it, and then smiling afterwards (rather than smiling while they are praising the gift).
- Liars are more formal speakers when lying and are therefore less likely to use contractions:

  Truth teller: "No, I didn't kill him."
  Liar: "No, I did not kill him."

(a)

(b)

Figure 7.1 The face of a liar. Someone telling a lie may rub their face or look up and to your left (if they're right handed) as seen in (a). While telling a lie, the liar may hide behind an object such as a coffee mug (b).

- A liar will reuse the words of your question in their answer:

  Questioner: "Did you take your father's car out Saturday night without his knowledge?"
  Liar: "No, I did not take my father's car out Saturday night without his knowledge."

- A liar or guilty person will feel relief when the subject in a conversation is changed abruptly. An innocent person will be confused by the change of subject and will want to finish the last topic before moving on to another one.
- A liar may perspire more.
- When telling a lie, the person might wrinkle their nose slightly, raise their shoulders, curl the corners of their mouth slightly downwards, or compress their lips.
- A liar may smile with their mouth but the smile will not include their eyes or the rest of their face as is the case with a genuine, feeling-good smile.
- A liar may play with their necklace or necktie while the lie is being told.

The Polygraph

Reading body language is a skill. It is also subjective—it requires interpretation by the observer. Science has come to the aid of the investigator of truth by an instrument called a *polygraph*, or more popularly referred to as a *lie detector* (Figure 7.2). The polygraph machine monitors a body's physiological reaction to stress. Telling a lie creates a stressful situation. Someone telling a lie sweats more. Perspiration lowers the skin's resistance to electric current. In a polygraph test, electrodes connected to the fingertips can monitor that change. Lying also increases the liar's pulse rate and their blood pressure—changes that can be measured by a sphygmomanometer wrapped around the upper arm (your doctor uses this device to measure your blood pressure when you have a checkup). The polygraph machine delivers a trace of the fluctuations in these measurements onto scrolling graph paper or onto a computer screen.

A polygraph test is administered by initially asking the subject a series of innocent questions that would not necessitate a falsified answer. This gives the examiner a baseline for the subject's physiological response to a nonthreatening conversation. The examiner will then ask questions about their involvement in the crime, usually intermingled with questions that do not require a lie. The examiner makes note on

Figure 7.2 A subject undergoing a polygraph exam. Sensors attached to the fingertips, chest, and arm monitor changes in a person's physiology as they undergo a series of questions related to a crime. (Image courtesy of John R. Patterson, American Polygraph Services, Fredericksburg, VA.)

the scrolling graph of when each question was asked and the subject's response to each question is compared to baseline.

The polygraph machine, for all its science, is not infallible. A subject's responses can fool the machine. If the subject is on medication, or illicit drugs, or tipsy from alcohol, or even hungry, their physiological response to telling a lie may not be that of a normal, sober person's. In addition, some people are just very good at lying. Telling a falsehood to a pathological liar means nothing. In addition, errors or bias by the examiner can taint the results, particularly if they have not established a consistent and representative background response from the subject.

Because of a polygraph's shortcomings, a failed test does not by necessity mean unequivocal guilt. Uncertainty of the polygraph's reliability usually casts a long shadow over the assumption of *reasonable doubt* and therefore such evidence is rarely admitted into the courtroom. Nevertheless, a polygraph machine has value in helping the investigator corroborate witness accounts, and because of its fearsome reputation as a *lie detector*, many suspects, when faced with a failed test or the threat of being subjected to the test, may change their stories to those closer to the truth or simply plead out altogether.

What the Evidence Reveals about the Perpetrator: Profiling

Evidence can tell an investigator quite a bit about a crime. If it's a homicide, how was the victim murdered? Were they drowned, bludgeoned, shot, poisoned, or electrocuted? What was the murder weapon? If the victim was shot, what was the caliber of the gun? Was the victim killed at a location other than where the body was found? How did the perpetrator gain access to the victim—through a window or by breaking through a door? Was the murder committed during a robbery?

Evidence collected from a crime scene is used to answer all these questions. Not surprisingly, however, physical evidence can also provide clues about the sex, age, personality quirks, lifestyle, and occupation of both the victim and the perpetrator—a study known as *profiling*. Understanding as much as you can about those involved in a crime can often tell you how they happened to all come together at the exact same place, at the exact same and unfortunate time. Profiling can give an investigator insight into what attracted the perpetrator to the victim and, with luck, can ultimately lead to motive that will further lead to the perpetrator's identity and arrest before they can commit another crime.

Profiling can be particularly important where a serial killer is being pursued for the murder of seemingly random individuals. Serial killers often commit their crimes following a recognizable *modus operandi* (*MO*) (or *method of operation*)—a pattern of behavior they follow when they kill their victims. Perhaps the victims were all murdered during a certain time of day, at or near a certain place, using the same type of weapon, and using the same means to gain access to the victim (e.g., through a bedroom window). Recognizing a pattern to the assaults can help identify the killer. By way of example, the serial killer Ted Bundy, whose killing spree lasted nearly a decade beginning in 1969, was responsible for the deaths of over 40 young women. Bundy, a law student from Seattle, always seemed to choose as his victim a young, attractive female with long hair parted down the middle. He liked to bite his victims (a peculiarity that eventually sealed his conviction), and he was meticulous about not leaving behind any fingerprints as evidence to any of his kills. Following a murder, he would usually dump the body in a deserted area far from the crime scene. Some victims were never found. But Bundy's MO helped the police to realize their relatedness.

Serial killers often share a common and tragic history. Many, for example, were abused as children—a misfortune that permanently damaged their psyche and nudged them down a road of cruelty toward other children, petty crime, and a disdain for adult authority. They may look for sexual gratification and for reestablishment of control and power in their own lives by the killing of others.

Most murders are not committed by serial killers but rather by someone close to the victim, by someone they know, and, usually, intimately, by a family member, lover, or close friend. Murder is most frequently an act of passion. Strangers do not usually evoke passion. Passion is the unbalanced offspring of love and can easily take the form of rage, jealousy, despondency, or revenge—the emotions that drive someone to murder.

The Sketch Artist

If a suspect is not immediately apprehended or identified but if witnesses are available who can provide a description of the assailant, the police may bring in an artist to render a *composite sketch*—a drawing based on an account of an individual's specific features (hairline, eye, nose, chin shape, etc.). The sketch may then be distributed to members of the police force within that jurisdiction and to other law enforcement agencies within the state and beyond.

During the commission of a crime, however, whether you're the victim or its witness, the stress of the moment's trauma can distort not only your mind's interpretation of the events but also the recollection of the visual characteristics of the perpetrator. Therein lies the problem. People react differently to stress. A man may have a different reaction than a woman. A man under attack, for example, may focus less on the face and more on the attacker's size and musculature—he's gathering the information as fast as he can as to whether or not he can beat him in one-on-one combat. A woman may look for some visual clue in the attacker's facial expressions or in their eyes that might reveal or betray their character. Quite often, the victims of violent assault may notice the assailant's face only briefly if at all. Instead, their attention may be riveted on the gun that's pointing at their chest or the knife the attacker has brandished and is flashing menacingly in front of them. The attack may happen so fast that the victim's mind is unable to process all the information needed to reconstruct the event.

There are over 7 billion people on the planet and, with the exception of identical twins, each has a unique face. The forensic sketch artist has to extract from a witness what makes the suspect's face different from every other face. The best starting place may be the *average* face (Figures 7.3 through 7.5). A sketch artist will then draw the features that deviate from the average. Are the eyebrows thicker or thinner than the average face? Is one eyebrow arched higher than the other? Where is the hairline? Are the lips fuller or thinner than the average? How do the ears differ from the average? How is the eye shape different—is one more narrow or wider than the other? Is the jaw square or soft? Is the nose wider or narrower? From these questions, a composite takes shape that defines the appearance of the suspect in more specific detail.

A sketch artist does not necessarily need to be gifted at the art of drawing. It may be more of a benefit that they possess an attention to detail and are capable of developing a rapport with the witness. Sketch artist Jeanne Boylan, for example, cannot boast to having any paintings hanging in the Louvre but her sketches of child murderer Richard Allen Davis and of the Oklahoma City bomber Timothy McVeigh played a large part in their capture and conviction (Figures 7.6a,b and 7.7a,b).

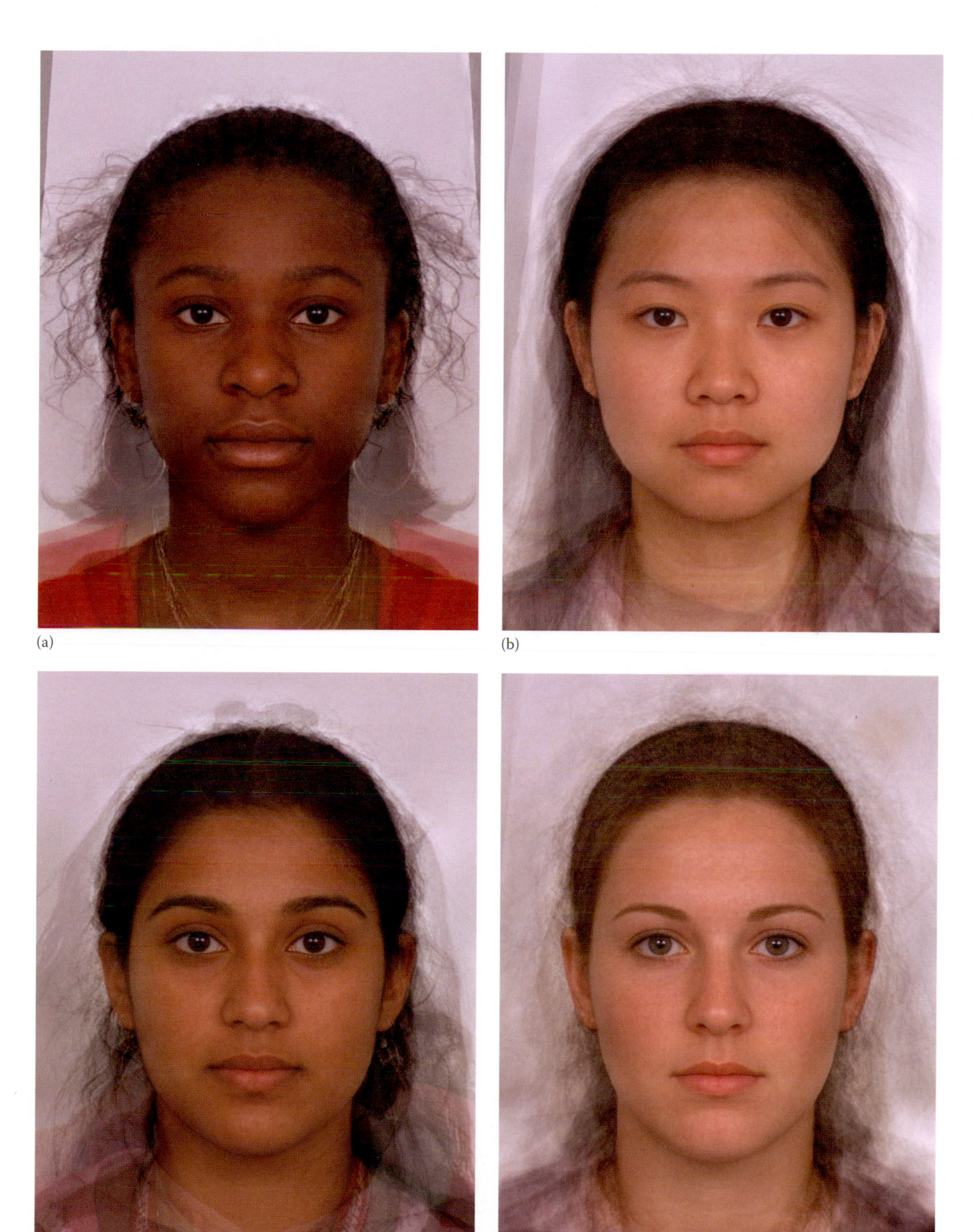

(a) (b) (c) (d)

Figure 7.3 Average female faces generated by a computer software program for (a) African female, (b) East Asian female, (c) West Asian female, and (d) Caucasian female. (Images used by permission and copyrighted by www. faceresearch.org. The images were made by a program described by Teddeman et al. [2001].)

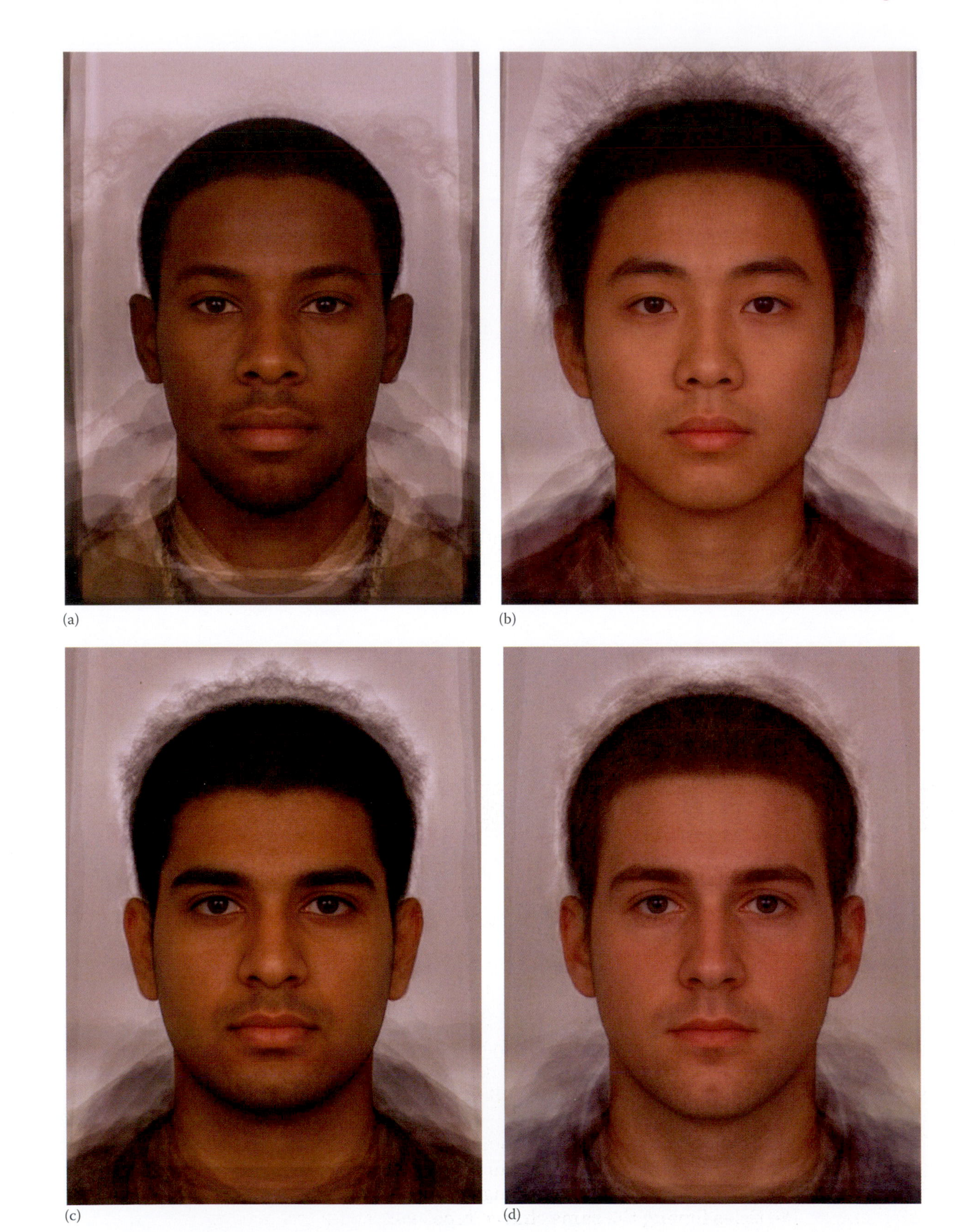

Figure 7.4 Average male faces generated by a computer software program for (a) African male, (b) East Asian male, (c) West Asian male, and (d) Caucasian male. (Images used by permission and copyrighted by www. faceresearch.org. The images were made by a program described by Teddeman et al. [2001].)

(a) (b)

Figure 7.5 Average multiracial faces generated by a computer software program for (a) a female and (b) a male. Try this for yourself at www.faceresearch.org/demos/average. (Images used by permission and copyrighted by www. faceresearch. org. The images were made by a program described by Teddeman et al. [2001].)

In the Crime Lab

Activity 7.1 Making a Lie Detector

Unless coming from a remorseless and pathological liar, the telling of a lie causes stress that leads to a direct physiological response, not least of which is an increase in the level of perspiration. Like seawater, the ion-filled liquid of sweat is an excellent conductor of electricity. That slight increase in perspiration that attends the act of lying can be detected electronically. In this activity, you will construct a *lie detector* from electronic components. When the device is placed in contact with a person's fingertips, a speaker, by a drop in its pitch, signals an increase in the skin's conductivity that can result from the perspiration produced when a lie is told.

Electricity is a form of energy that derives from the opposite charges of protons and electrons—the subatomic particles of the atom. Protons, found in the nucleus of an atom, have a positive charge. Electrons, whirling around the atom's nucleus, have a negative charge. Particles having the same charge repel each other, while particles of opposite charge are attracted to each other. Electrons, therefore, being negatively charged, are attracted to the positively charged protons. The flow of electrons to a

Figure 7.6 (a) Jeanne Boylan's sketch of a suspect who kidnapped and then murdered 12-year-old Polly Klaas in October of 1993 in Petaluma, California, led to the arrest and conviction of Richard Allen Davis (b). Details for the sketch were derived from two of Polly's friends who were at her house for a slumber party the night of the abduction. (Photo of Richard Allen Davis in Sonoma Municipal Court in Santa Rosa, California by Paul Sakuma/Associated Press, 1993.)

positive pole (or *electrode*) is called *electric current*. By directing electric current from a negative to a positive pole through a defined path, such as a copper wire, we create an electric *circuit*. The electronic circuits found in devices such as televisions, computers, and radios carry a variety of components that redirect, reduce, amplify, and store electric current. By controlling a current's path, we can harness the energy of electricity to accomplish a limitless number of tasks.

When constructing electronic circuits, several common terms will be encountered. These include the ohm (designated by the symbol omega: Ω), a unit of electrical resistance that a material or conducting substance exerts on an electric current. A resistance of 1 Ω results in a current of 1 A between two points along a conductor having a potential difference of 1 V. An ampere (or amp) is a unit of electric current and a *volt* is a unit of electric potential difference.

By convention, electronic components are given symbols that can be used to diagram their layout within a circuit or electronic device. The symbols for several of the most common components are given in Table 7.1.

Construction of the lie detector outlined in this activity is described on the website sciencetoymaker.org. Its electronic circuitry is shown as a diagram in Figure 7.8.

Materials:

Pushpin
2N3904 NPN transistor
2N3906 PNP transistor

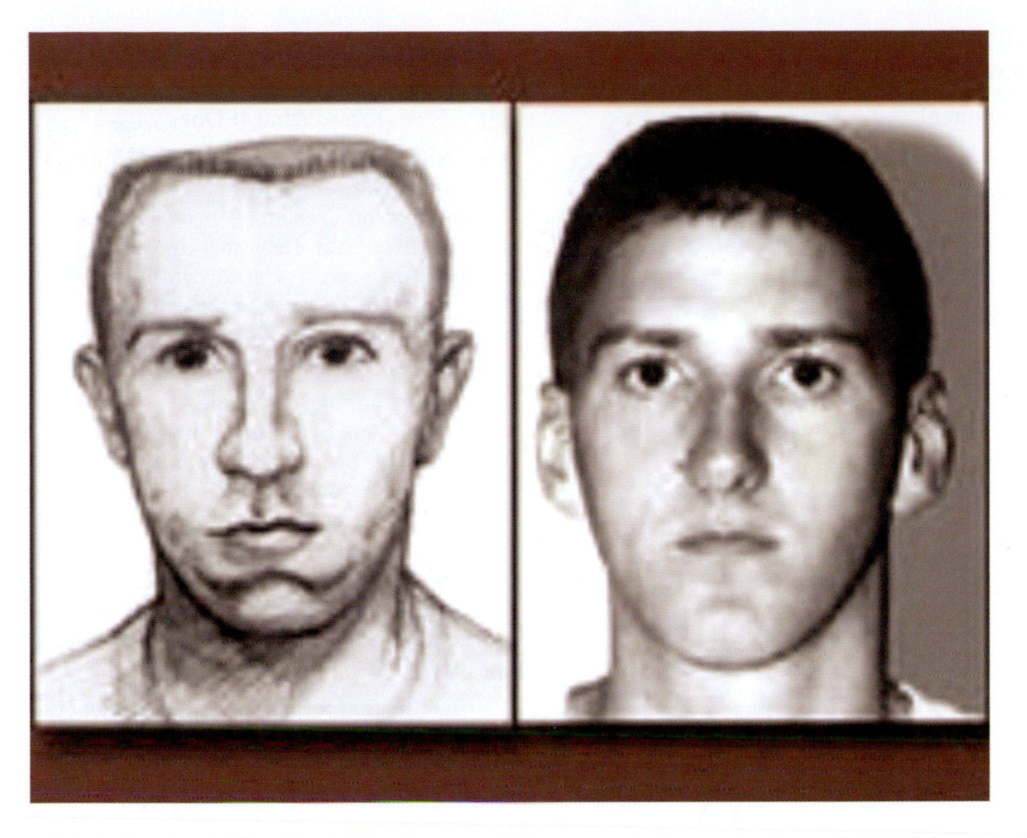

Figure 7.7 A sketch of Timothy McVeigh, one of the convicted conspirators of the Oklahoma City bombing that took place in 1995. The bombing targeted the Alfred P. Murrah Federal Building in Oklahoma City and took 168 lives. (Sketch is by Jeanne Boylan.)

4.7 K Ω 1/4 W resistor
82 K Ω 1/4 W resistor
9 V battery
9 V battery connector
22 gauge wire
Electrical solder, rosin core
30 W soldering iron
0.01 mfd ceramic disk capacitor
2 in. 8-Ω speaker
100% clear silicone caulk
18 gauge solid wire
Clear, flexible freezer bag
Ruler
Sharpie
Ruler
3″ × 2″ sheet of cardboard
White paper
Wire cutters/strippers
Masking tape
Sandpaper
Scissors
Forceps or needle-nose pliers
Safety glasses
Sponge

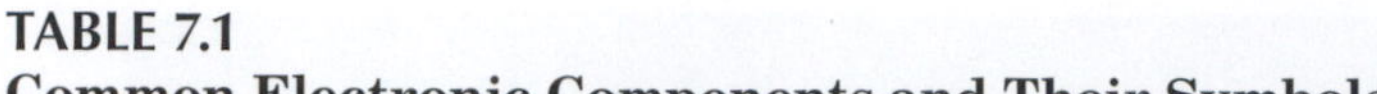

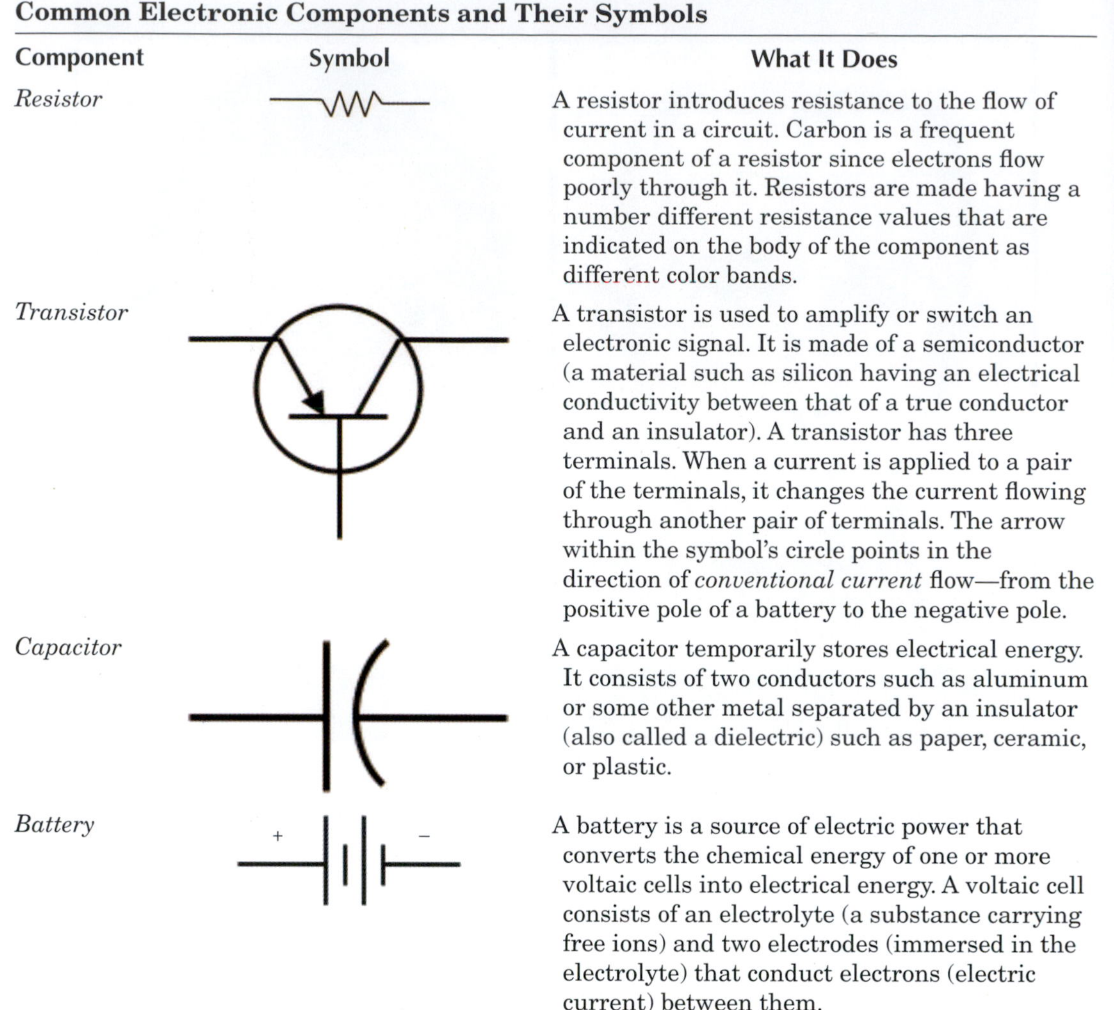

TABLE 7.1
Common Electronic Components and Their Symbols

Component	Symbol	What It Does
Resistor		A resistor introduces resistance to the flow of current in a circuit. Carbon is a frequent component of a resistor since electrons flow poorly through it. Resistors are made having a number different resistance values that are indicated on the body of the component as different color bands.
Transistor		A transistor is used to amplify or switch an electronic signal. It is made of a semiconductor (a material such as silicon having an electrical conductivity between that of a true conductor and an insulator). A transistor has three terminals. When a current is applied to a pair of the terminals, it changes the current flowing through another pair of terminals. The arrow within the symbol's circle points in the direction of *conventional current* flow—from the positive pole of a battery to the negative pole.
Capacitor		A capacitor temporarily stores electrical energy. It consists of two conductors such as aluminum or some other metal separated by an insulator (also called a dielectric) such as paper, ceramic, or plastic.
Battery	+ –	A battery is a source of electric power that converts the chemical energy of one or more voltaic cells into electrical energy. A voltaic cell consists of an electrolyte (a substance carrying free ions) and two electrodes (immersed in the electrolyte) that conduct electrons (electric current) between them.

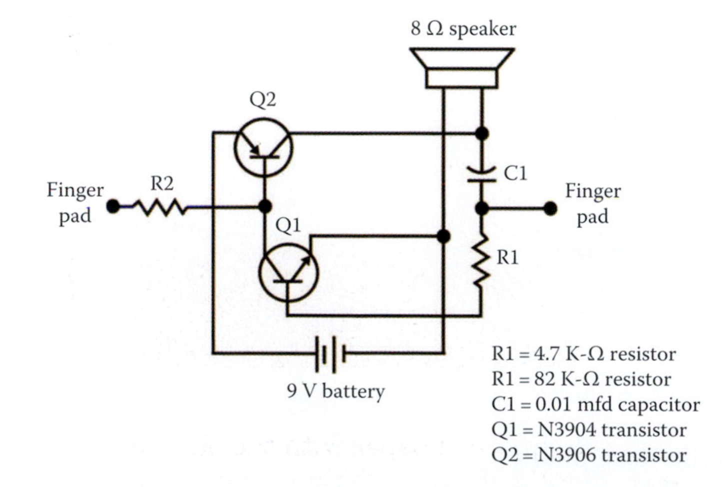

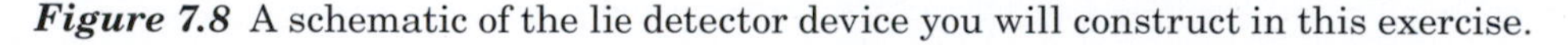

Figure 7.8 A schematic of the lie detector device you will construct in this exercise.

Protocol:

1. With a marker and on a sheet of white paper, draw eight parallel lines ¼ in. apart and 2 in. long.

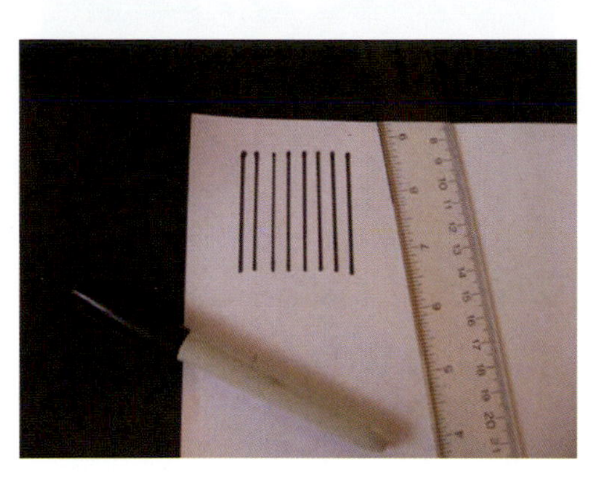

2. Centering the eight lines, cut a square 2.5 in. by 2.5 in. such that the lines are at least ¼ in. from any edge of the square.

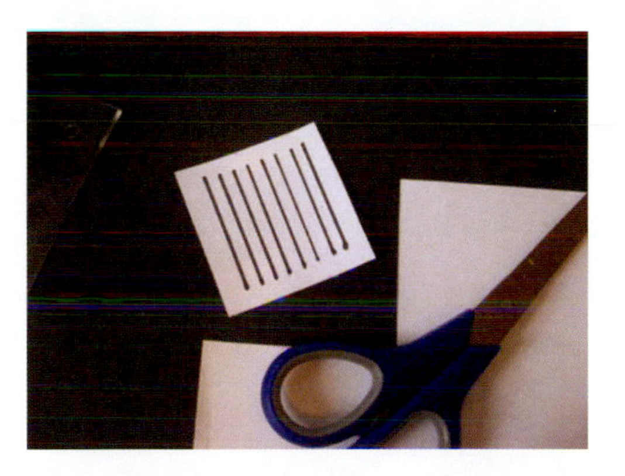

3. Cut a piece of clear plastic freezer bag into a 3″ × 3″ square.

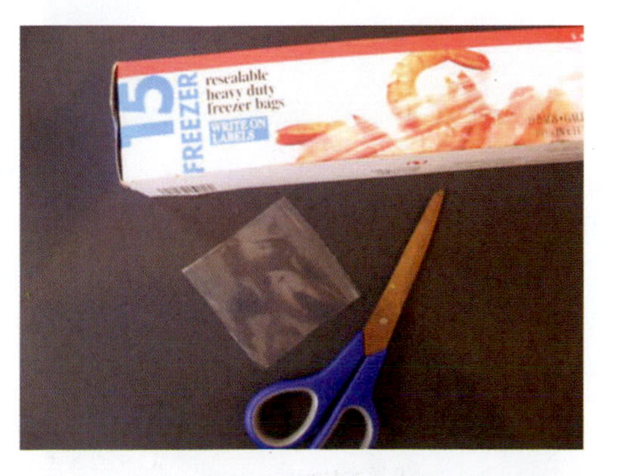

4. Using tape, secure the square of paper with the eight lines against the piece of freezer bag such that the lines are facing against the plastic. When taping the paper to the plastic, *do not* tape over and around the edges of the plastic.

Note: If the piece of clear plastic is too small such that the paper cannot be taped to it securely, cut another piece of plastic to a larger, more suitable size.

5. Using sandpaper, scuff the plastic over the area covering the eight-line pattern. Do not rub so hard that the plastic tears. This step is performed so that the silicone, applied in the next step, will adhere securely to the plastic.

6. Squeeze silicon in a zigzag pattern over the scuffed plastic.

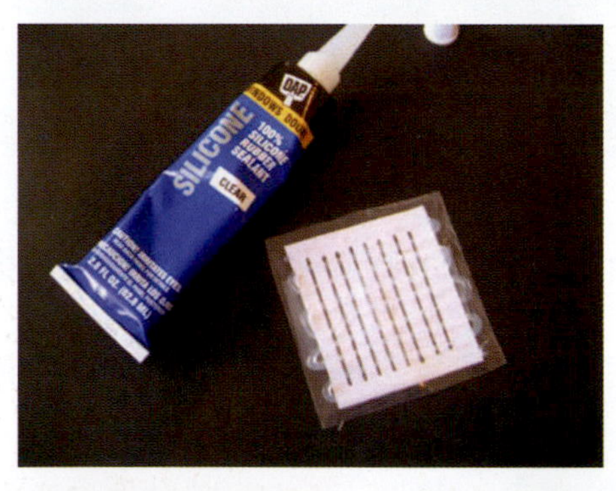

7. Using the edge of a small square of cardboard, spread the silicon evenly over the surface of the plastic.

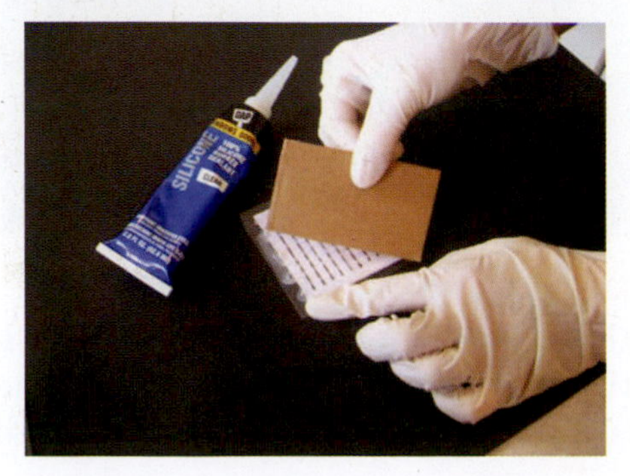

8. On top of the spread silicone, squeeze a row of silicone jelly stretching from the end of one of the lines to the end of the last one in the row, perpendicular to the pattern. In the same manner, deposit a row of silicone over the opposite end of the eight-line pattern.

9. Using strong scissors or a wire cutter, cut 22 gauge copper wire into eight, 2 in. sections. Make sure the pieces of wire are as straight as possible. If the sections are not straight, work with them as best you can to remove any kinks or curves.
   Note: If the wire you are using for this activity is insulated (has a colored coating on it), you will need to strip that insulation from the wire using a wire stripper. If you are not familiar with this tool, have your instructor help you.

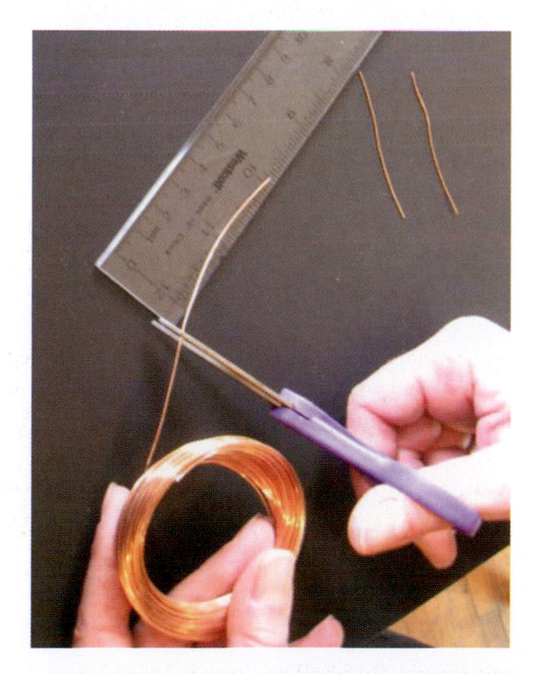

10. Using forceps or needle-nose pliers, place each of the eight, 2 in. long sections of 22-gauge copper wire above its own line of the eight-line pattern such

that each end of each 2 in. copper wire is sunk within the two mounds of silicone at the end of the pattern but suspended above the spread silicone on the plastic sheet. Allow the silicone with the embedded copper wires to dry overnight.
Note: Make sure the wires are lined up straight above the pattern. The copper wires should not touch each other.

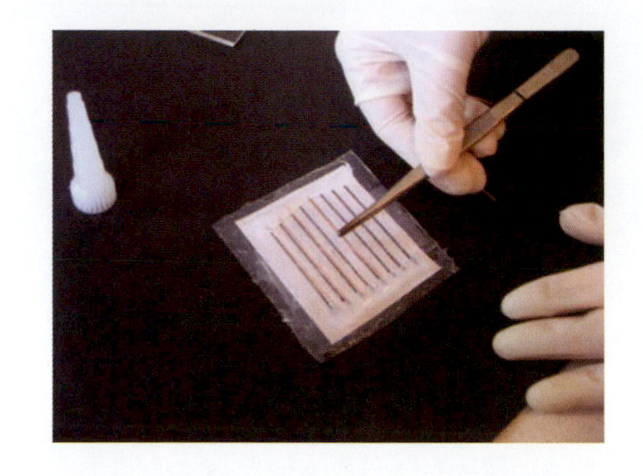

11. When the silicone is dry, remove the piece of paper with the eight-line pattern and the tape securing it from the plastic. On the smooth side of the plastic sheet (the side to which the paper with the eight-line pattern was taped), number the wires at one end 1 through 8 with a Sharpie or other permanent marker.

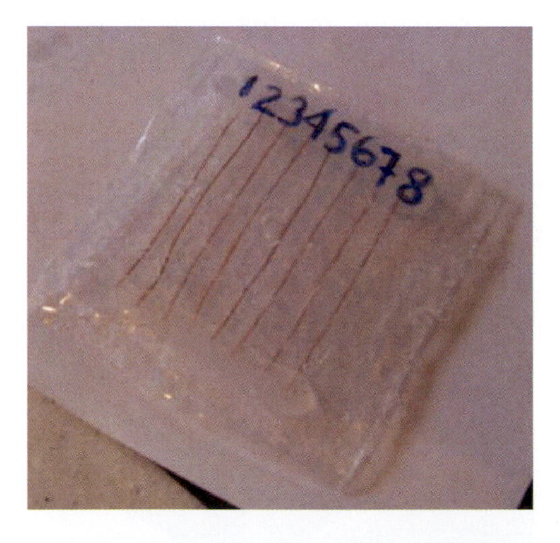

The steps that follow will detail how to assemble the electronic components as shown in Figure 7.9.

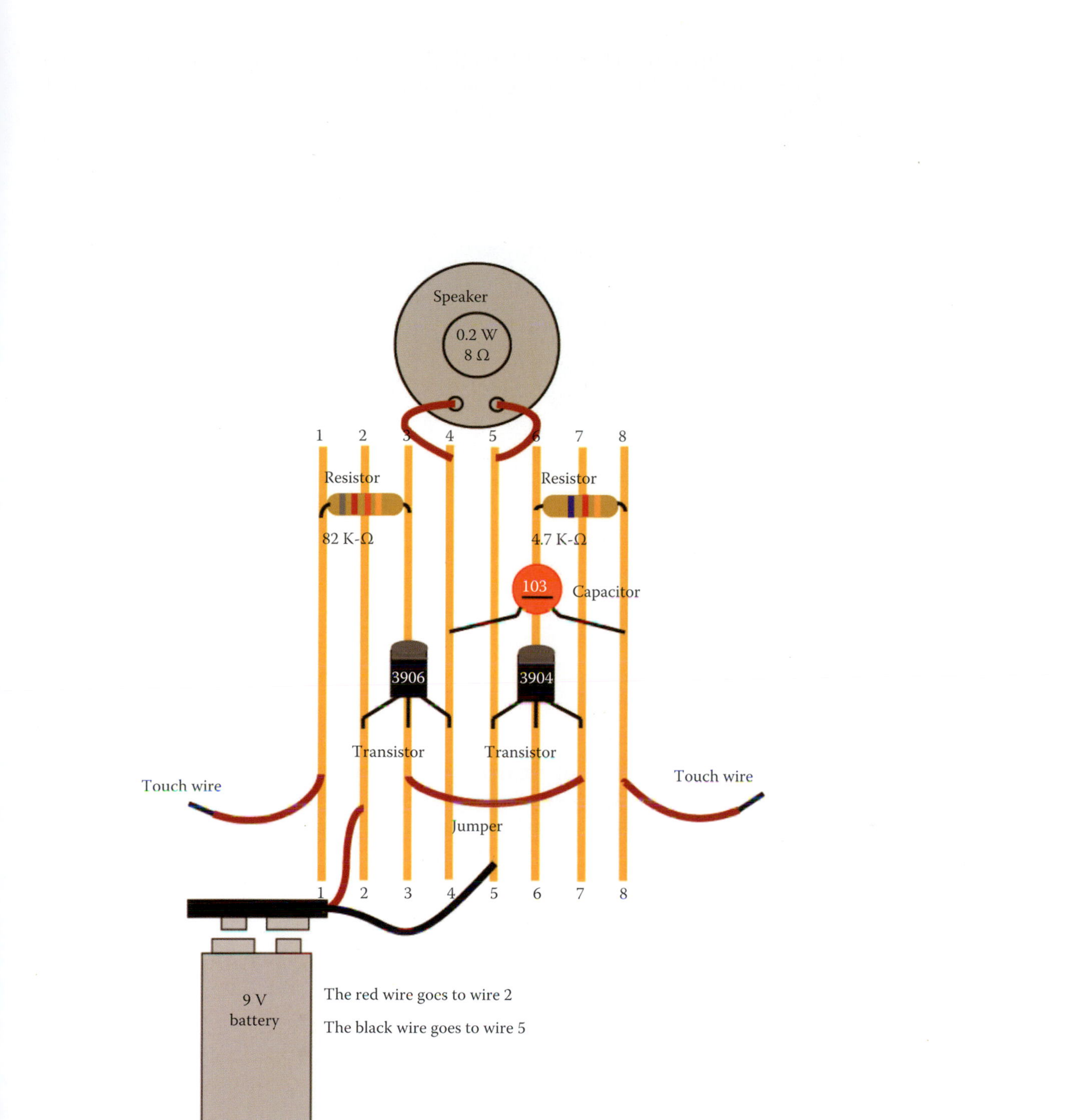

Figure 7.9 Diagram of the lie detector circuitry. Lines 1 through 8 represent 2 in. sections of 22-gauge copper wire. The 82 K-Ω resistor has the color bands gray, red, orange, and gold. The 4.7 K-Ω resistor has the color bands yellow, violet, red, and gold.

12. Using a pushpin, punch holes through the smooth side of the plastic (the side opposite to that with the silicone and wires) above wires 2, 3, 4, 5, 6, and 7 at positions approximately in the middle of the wires.
    Note: If you need to, the positions where you will make the holes can be marked with a Sharpie for better alignment. The holes should be punched as close as possible to the wires.

13. Bend each outside wire of transistors 2N3904 and 2N3906 at about 45° angles. Bend those wires again such that they are all facing in one (the original) direction. The wires' appearance should resemble a trident or pitchfork.

14. Push the leads of the transistors through the holes in the plastic such that they touch the copper wires on the opposite side of the numbered face. The flat, numbered surfaces of the transistors should be facing away from where you will attach the speaker and toward where you will attach the battery leads (see Figure 7.9).

Caution! You will be using a soldering iron that will become "*extremely hot.*" Under no circumstances should you touch the soldering end of the device. Touch the iron only by its handle. Keep the device away from anything flammable such as paper or clothing. "*Wear safety glasses.*"

15. Plug in the soldering iron and allow about 1 min for it to come up to temperature. Wipe the tip of the soldering iron on a moist sponge to remove any residue.

16. With the transistor lead in contact with the copper wire, position the end of the solder wire at their junction and carefully touch the tip of the soldering iron where the three objects meet. Rub the connection briefly with the soldering iron to make sure the solder flows between the copper wire and the transistor lead. Repeat this procedure for all six transistor leads.

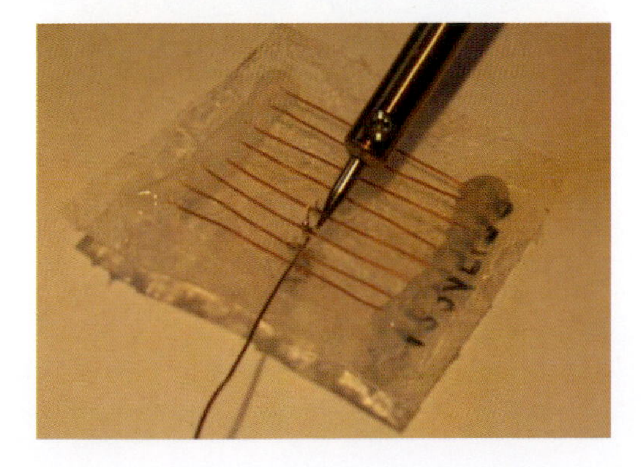

17. When the connections have cooled, wiggle the components to see if they are tightly attached. If a connection is not secure, resolder it. If the connections are secure, trim off any lead wire extending beyond the solder connection with scissors or wire cutters.
    Note: Excess leads should be trimmed so that they cannot touch any of the other wires causing a short.

18. Solder in the two resistors and the capacitor in a similar manner and as diagrammed in Figure 7.9. The 82 K-Ω resistor has a gray, red, orange, and gold band. The 4.7 K-Ω resistor has a yellow, violet, red, and gold band.
    Note: Do not punch holes through the areas where the ends of the eight wires are anchored into the silicone. The components cannot be soldered within the silicone.

19. Cut three 2 in. sections of insulated wire and, using wire strippers, strip approximately ¼ in. of insulation from each end of each wire. Use one of these as the jumper that connects wires 3 and 7. This wire should be soldered at its contact points with wires 3 and 7.

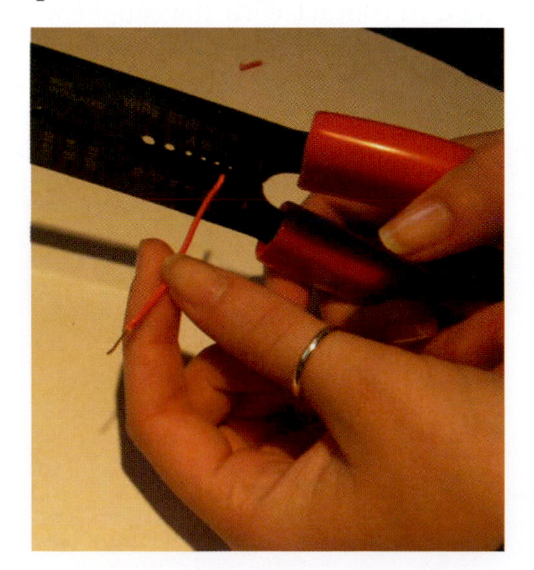

20. The remaining two sections of insulated wire from Step 19 are used to attach the speaker to wires 4 and 5. These wires should be soldered at their contact points. At the speaker, the ends can be hooked into the solder tabs and then soldered to secure the connection. It makes no difference which wire is soldered to which solder tab.
    Note: The speaker is magnetized and will attract the soldering iron's tip. You can avoid the soldering iron sticking to the speaker by holding the tip of the iron at right angles to the speaker.

21. Solder the battery snap wires such that the red lead goes to wire 2 and the black lead goes to wire 5. One touch wire should be soldered to wire 1 and another to wire 8.

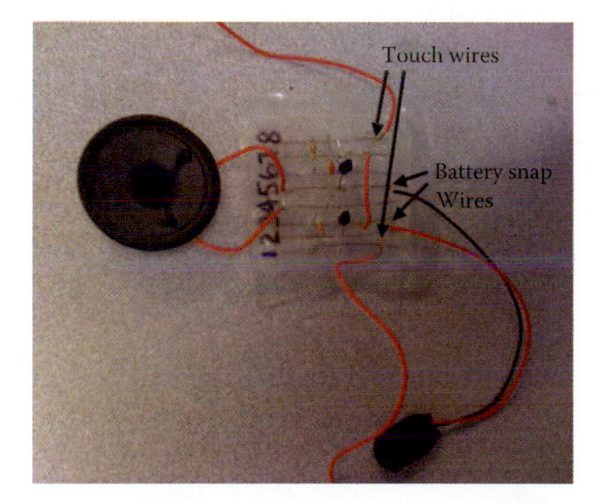

22. When all soldering has been completed, trim all leads sticking out past the solder points. One last time, make sure all solder joints are secure by gently wiggling each component.

23. Test the system by having a laboratory partner hold the touch wires while you touch the battery clip to the battery for less than a second. If no buzzing noise is produced, something is connected improperly. Recheck all the connections and make sure your device is configured as shown in Figure 7.9
    Note: Holding the battery clip to the battery on a dysfunctional system (one not producing a beep and therefore assembled incorrectly) can burn out the transistors.

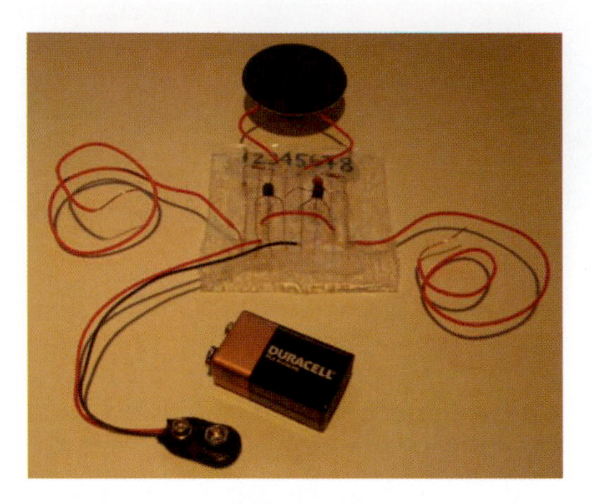

24. Wrap the end of each touch wire around a one end of a paper clip such that a finger can be inserted into each one. Solder the wires to the paper clips. When the battery is connected, the unit is ready for use.

Activity 7.2 Making a Portrait Sketch from a Witness' Account

In this activity, the class will be divided into two groups. Group one will be given the opportunity to view a picture of a person's face for 1 min. At the end of that time, you will be paired with a student in group two who will work as a sketch artist to recreate the face from your description.

Materials:

Photograph of person's face (provided by the instructor)
Pencil
Sketch pad or plain white paper

Protocol:

1. Your instructor will divide the class into two groups. Each person in the first group will play the role of a witness. The students in the second group will play the role of forensic sketch artist.
2. If you are a member of the first group, your instructor will provide you with a portrait photograph of a random person. You will be allowed 1 min to study the photograph after which time your instructor will collect it.
3. Your instructor will team you with a person from the second group of students. Your partner will play the role of a forensic sketch artist. During a 20 min session, the witness and the sketch artist will work together to create a composite drawing of the person in the portrait photograph.
4. At the end of the allotted time, turn the sketch into the instructor.
5. The roles will then be reversed. Your instructor will hand out a second portrait photograph to the student who acted as the forensic sketch artist for the first half of the class and the procedure for creating a sketch will be duplicated as described in Steps 2 through 4.
6. As a class, you will vote on which sketch goes with which photograph. You are not allowed to vote when the photograph you witnessed or sketched is being discussed.

Activity 7.3 Making a Portrait Sketch from a Witness' Account Using an Internet Portrait Software Program

You will repeat the procedure used in Activity 7.2 except rather than make a freehand sketch, you will use the Internet portrait software program available at http://flashface.ctapt.de/. (see Figure 7.10)

Materials:

Photograph of a person's face (provided by the instructor)
Computer with Internet access

Figure 7.10 The Flash Face program can be used to construct a composite image of a face. The user selects from a collection of features including hair, eyebrows, eyes, noses, mouths, and chins. Moving the cross within the graph in the lower right side of the window can control the width and height of each feature. The delete button to the right of that graph can be used to remove a feature just added (or any other feature by clicking on it and then hitting the delete key).

Erica Holmes Missing Persons Case

The following photographs show the slough area of San Francisco Bay near Seaport Blvd.

Further Reading

Detecting Lies and Deceit: The Psychology of Lying and the Implications for Professional Practice (Wiley Series in Psychology of Crime, Policing and Law) by Aldert Vrij, John Wiley & Sons, Ltd., West Sussex, U.K., 2000.

Stalking Following the Breakup of Romantic Relationships: Characteristics of Stalking Former Partners by K.A. Roberts in *Journal of Forensic Sciences*, Vol. 47, No. 5, pages 1070–1077, 2002.

Essentials of the Reid Technique: Criminal Interrogations and Confessions (Criminal Justice Illuminated) by Fred E. Inbau, John E. Reid, Joseph P. Buckley, and Brian C. Jayne, Jones and Bartlett Publishers, Sudbury, MA, 2005.

Some Thoughts on the Neurobiology of Stalking by J.R. Meloy and H. Fisher in *Journal of Forensic Sciences*, Vol. 50, No. 6, pages 1472–1480, 2005.

Gatekeeper: Memoirs of a CIA Polygraph Examiner by John F. Sullivan, Potomac Books, Inc., Dulles, VA, 2007.

The Lie Detectors: History of an American Obsession by Ken Adler, Free Press, Glencoe, IL, 2007.

Association between Personality Disorder and Violent Behavior Pattern by Daniel M de Barros and Antonio de Padua Serafim in *Forensic Science International*, Vol. 179, Issue 1, pages 19–22, 2008.

Effect of Two Types of Control Questions and Two Question Formats on the Outcomes of Polygraph Examinations by Frank Horvath and John J. Palmatier in *Journal of Forensics Sciences*, Vol. 53, No. 4, pages 889–899, 2008.

Stress and Deception in Speech: Evaluating Layered Voice Analysis by James D. Harnsberger, Harry Hollien, Camilo A. Martin, and Kevin A. Hollien in *Journal of Forensic Sciences*, Vol. 54, No. 3, pages 642–650, 2009.

Interviewing Witnesses

Preserving the Integrity of the Interview: The Value of Videotape by S.E. Pitt, E.M. Spiers, P.E. Dietz, and J.A. Dvoskin in *Journal of Forensic Sciences*, Vol. 44, No. 6, pages 1287–1291, 1999.

The Interview and Interrogation of Suspects by J.T. Dominick, S.A. Koehler, S. Ladham, R. Meyers, T. Uhrich, C.H. Wecht, and M. Welner in *Crime Scene Investigation* (Reader's Digest, Pleasanton, New York), pages 156–160, 2004.

The Forensic Sketch Artist

Mug Shots: A Police Artist's Guide to Remembering Faces by Douglas P. Hinkle, Paladin Press, Boulder, CO, 1990.

Facial Shape and Judgments of Female Attractiveness by D.I. Perrett, K.A. May, and S. Yoshikawa in *Nature*, Vol. 368, pages 239–242, 1994.

Computer Graphics in Facial Perception Research by B. Teddeman, D.M. Burt, and D. Perrett in *IEEE Computer Graphics and Applications*, Vol. 21, No. 5, pages 42–50, 2001.

Portraits of Guilt: The Woman Who Profiles the Faces of America's Deadliest Criminals by Jeanne Boylan, Pocket Star Books, New York, 2001.

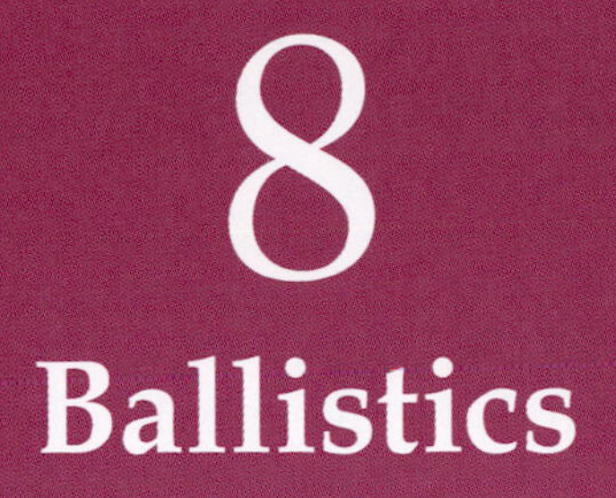

8 Ballistics

China Town, Wednesday 1:17 PM

"No. No. You hold them like this," Helen instructed. "The upper stick is held in place with the index and middle fingers pinched by the thumb. The other stick is held between the bottom of the thumb and the ring finger. Only the upper chopstick moves."

Down the street from the *Zhao Acupuncture Clinic* and directly across from *The Double Dragon Massage* and *Li Ly's Hair Salon*, *The Pot Sticker* on Waverly is tucked into the merchant buildings of Chinatown like another bead on a jade bracelet. Helen and Jenkins sat at a round, glass-covered table underneath a crystal chandelier by the watercolor of the three koi.

"Like this?" Jenkins asked holding up his chop sticks in his right hand and bracing it with his left.

"Yeah. Okay. Well almost. Oh, you're married!" Helen observed.

"What?"

"You're married. You wear a wedding ring."

Jenkins rolled his left hand over palm down and studied the gold band. "No," he said at last. "I was once married."

"How long ago was that?"

"Years ago," Jenkins replied. "I'm divorced."

"And you still wear a ring? Do you have kids?"

"A girl, not quite your age," Jenkins replied. "She's away at school."

"Where? Berkeley?" Helen asked, hopefully.

"No. She's down at UCLA."

"Well, nobody's perfect. But at least she's Pac-12. What's her name?"

"Cheyenne," Jenkins replied.

Helen grinned.

"What?" Jenkins asked innocently.

"Do you mean her name is Ann and she's shy?"

"No, Cheyenne, as in the Native American tribe, as in the city in Wyoming, rhymes with Cayenne, the spice."

"Parents always have to be careful how they name their kids, don't they," Helen observed. "I mean, you can't give a kid a name that their schoolmates can pervert into something embarrassing or obscene. Case in point, I was 'Helen, Helen, head like a melon'."

"I was 'Bob the slob'," Jenkins confessed rolling his eyes toward the chandelier.

"Bob the slob," Helen recited.

Jenkins tilted his head down like a bull before it charges, hooked an eyebrow skyward, and glared at Helen. "Excuse me, Miss Chang," he said, "that's Lieutenant Jenkins."

"Cheyenne," Helen remarked in an attempt to deflect any further stern warnings, "that's an unusual name."

"It's after where my wife was born."

"So your wife," Helen persisted, perhaps against her better judgment, "what happened?"

"She remarried and moved to Las Vegas."

"No. I mean why did you guys split up?"

"Ah, this looks good," Jenkins exclaimed as the waitress slid a plate of steaming food onto their table. "Now what is this stuff called again? And what are those little circular things?"

"This is tangcu youyu (*tahng tsoo yoe-yuu*) and those little circular things are suction cups."

Jenkins looked down at the serving plate, surveyed the culinary landscape, and slowly looked back up again. "Suction cups?" he asked incredulously. Raising his right arm in the air, index finger pointing to the ceiling, "Uh, waitress…"

Helen slapped his arm down. The waitress glanced over then returned to clearing dishes from a table by the doorway. "Yeah," Helen continued, "This is sweet and sour squid. I had them make it special."

"How considerate," Jenkins offered.

"Your wife?" Helen asked as she scooped several large spoonfuls onto her plate.

"Where do you put it all, Miss Chang?"

"I have a fast metabolism. Always have," she replied as she passed the plate to Jenkins while simultaneously reaching for the bowl of steamed rice. Jenkins, with surgeon-like precision, deftly teased the bell peppers and pineapple away from the squid and carefully scraped the vegetable matter onto his plate. "Oh no you don't!" Helen exclaimed when she realized what Jenkins was doing. "There," she said, transferring a slice of squid from her plate to his with her chopsticks. "You have to at least try it."

"Thank you, Miss Chang. It looks delicious," said Jenkins, rubbing a sudden itch on the left slope of his nose.

"So that's it?" Jenkins asked.

"What's it?" Helen replied.

"A fast metabolism?"

"Oh, well, I also take kick boxing classes at the *Y*," Helen confessed.

"Kick boxing, Miss Chang? You?"

"Oh no," Helen replied, realizing what Jenkins was suggesting. "I've never punched or kicked anybody in my life. It's really just aerobics. Kind of a dance class, really. It's to music."

A puff of air dismissively escaped Jenkins lips. Not a laugh but a prelude to one, perhaps. It brushed past Helen unnoticed. "Yeah. Okay. I myself will jog to the park at least once a year. You know, just to stay in shape."

Helen couldn't tell if that was supposed to be a joke and so let it go. "Your wife, Lieutenant?" she persisted.

Jenkins chased the slice of squid around his plate with his chopsticks. "I let her slip away," he replied. "Are you sure this fellow's no longer alive?" Frustrated, he dropped his chopsticks, grabbed his fork, and skewered the elusive piece of invertebrate. Reluctantly, he slowly placed it into his mouth. His tongue probed its texture and explored its anatomy. He rolled it over carefully several times against his palate as if he were feeling for a thorn or a stray sliver of bone. When he'd convinced himself it wasn't booby trapped, he slowly started chewing. "This is like gnawing on a rubber hose," Jenkins observed. He finally decided he was just going to take the bullet – he swallowed hard, a big, deliberate swallow so it would all go down in just one shot. The glug noise made as the bolus was forced past the epiglottis was audible. Helen glanced up.

"You're not hollow, Lieutenant. You've still got some life in you. You should get back out there."

"That's generous of you, Miss Chang, but I think, for some of us, there is just that one special person. Besides, I think I've forgotten how to swoon."

"No," Helen exclaimed waving her chopsticks horizontally back and forth. "You can never forget something like that. Can you? And you still wear your wedding ring after what, years did you say? I guess you still miss her, huh?"

"No. I still see her."

"How?"

"Every time I look at my daughter."

"You say that maybe there's just one right person for some of us?" Helen asked,

"Funny thing is, Miss Chang, they'll probably come along when you're least looking."

"I don't know if I'll ever find the right guy," Helen murmured. "Most guys don't go for smart girls. It's like they feel intimidated or something. And even if it does happen, I mean, it's so risky anyway, isn't it, laying it all on the line?"

"It is a risk," Jenkins agreed. "It's easy to get hurt."

"Or murdered!" Helen added, taking a sip of green tea. "Steamed rice?"

"Sure," said Jenkins, spooning a helping onto his plate. "I made some calls. Mrs. Holmes' brother in Vegas hasn't seen or heard from Erica in months. And Gary Furlong. Very tight-lipped. But I wouldn't expect to get anything out of him anyway."

"Any prints off that gun we found in Sam's truck?" Helen asked.

"The gun is registered to Mr. O'Neill all right but we couldn't recover any prints," Jenkins replied. "Nothing. It's clean."

"Guys just never turn out to be what you think they are at first blush."

"Sometimes, neither do crime scenes, Miss Chang."

"Well, to be honest, since I've taken this gig, I think my odds have slipped a notch. I don't know how it's going to go over me telling some hot guy that I study DNA from people's body fluids. That's not pillow talk. Care for another piece of squid?"

"Thanks, but I'm still working on the first one you gave me. Excuse me," Jenkins said to the waitress. "Could we please get some catsup at this table. Oh, and could you bring a hamburger with that?"

"No hamburger," she replied tersely.

The Nuts and Bolts of It Garage on Geary Blvd., Wednesday 3:52 PM

The Nuts and Bolts of It garage on Geary has two repair bays with hydraulic vehicle lifts and an office facing the street. Jenkins pulled his Cutlass Calais into a parking space along the side of the building and he and Helen walked to its front desk where a middle-aged woman greeted them from behind the counter.

"Good afternoon," she said, looking up from her computer display. "May I help you?"

Jenkins flashed his badge and ID.

"I was going to pay those parking tickets, honest," the woman responded. "I just needed a little more time to raise the spare cash and I was going to request an extension but I…"

"We're not here about parking violations," Jenkins interrupted.

"You must get that a lot," Helen whispered to Jenkins. He gave her a sideways glance.

"We're here about a missing person," Jenkins continued.

"Erica Holmes." stated the receptionist flatly.

"That's right," Jenkins replied. "Do you know her?"

"Yeah."

"When was the last time you saw her?" Jenkins asked.

"It was January. The day she disappeared."

"You were working here on that day?"

"Yeah."

"Did you see anything that was out of the ordinary? Did she argue with anyone… a customer or employee?"

"No."

"Did you see Erica go anywhere? Did she leave the garage that day?"

"Not that I saw. But I left before she did. I knock off a little after five."

"Erica was still here when you went home."

"Yeah."

"Was there anyone else working that day?"

"Yeah. one guy named Juan. But he left even before I did. He doesn't work here anymore."

"Do you know where Juan is now?"

"I have no idea."

"So, as far as you know, Erica was the last person here that evening?"

"Yeah."

"Did you receive a phone call from her father that day?"

"Not that I can remember."

"If you don't mind, we're going to take a look around."

"Knock yourself out," the receptionist said and went back to surfing eBay on her computer.

Jenkins and Helen exited the front office and turned right into the garage bay. "That's it?" asked Helen, glancing back at the door swinging closed behind them. "She may have been the last person to see Erica alive and you're not going to question her anymore?"

"She's of limited help other than to tell us that Erica was alone here on the evening of her disappearance," Jenkins replied.

One bay of the two-bay garage yawned empty. The other, furthest from the office, held a Ford Mustang elevated on the hydraulic lift. Jenkins noticed that Helen's attention was drawn to a mechanic, a young man in striped and grease-stained coveralls, standing underneath the vehicle. He was inspecting the brake pads on its right front wheel. Smudges of grease were brushed below each eye making him look, Jenkins thought, like a wide receiver. He was tan with sun-raked blond hair. Slender, but with a muscular build, Jenkins guessed him to be a surfer. He shot Jenkins a quick assessing look that collided in mid-air with Jenkins' own scrutinizing stare. "May I help you?" he asked.

"Police investigation," Jenkins stated.

The man shuffled a slow half pirouette as he fitted a brake pad with the caliper piston bringing him to a position facing Jenkins but still some fifteen feet away. "We use only genuine, manufacturer-certified parts," he said with a smile.

"How long have you worked here?" Jenkins asked.

"Two months," he replied, looking back up at the wheel rim. "What's this about?"

"Where were you before here?" Jenkins asked, ignoring the mechanic's query.

"San Diego," he replied.

Jenkins paced the perimeter of the bay. Helen stood by the bay entrance. "I'm hearing a noise coming from the front right side of my car—kind of a rattle," Jenkins said as he skirted around a red multidrawered tool cabinet.

"What kind of car you have?" the mechanic asked, not looking away from the wheel rim.

"A Cutlass Calais," Jenkins replied. He thought he heard what was either a chuckle or the stuttering scratch of a bolt grinding against metal coming from the mechanic's direction.

"Maybe a bearing or a loose manifold fitting," the mechanic offered. His smile was even bigger this time. It bordered on a laugh.

"If I bring it in later, could you take a look at it," Jenkins asked, stopping briefly to ponder a Snap-On wall calendar in which the March 2004 tool girl, barely blushing in a string bikini, prowled onto the hood of a white Corvette convertible as if she were about to slip into a Jacuzzi. March 2004. The calendar obviously wasn't functioning as a timepiece. Parts of a carburetor, various fan belts, a couple of hammers, and an assortment of screwdrivers and wrenches were strewn like shrapnel along the counter below the calendar. Jenkins rummaged through the metal but found nothing that shouldn't be part of a garage's paraphernalia.

Helen joined Jenkins by the back workbench. "What exactly are we looking for?" Helen asked, interrupting his search. She picked up a greasy timing gear, inspected it dismissively, and placed it back on the bench.

"I'm not sure, but I'll know it when I see it," Jenkins replied.

"See what?" Helen asked.

"It," said Jenkins.

Helen just sighed and walked over to the other side of the Mustang and thumbed through a Toyota truck repair manual.

"Are you with him?" the mechanic asked Helen.

"Him?" Helen blushed, glancing over at Jenkins who was now pacing in figure eights, his hands clasped behind his back with his eyes scouring the floor, searching the garage pavement as if he were a paleontologist at Oldavai Gorge looking for fossilized fragments of ancestral bone. "No……. Well,……. yeah,……. I am," Helen confessed.

"So you're police?" he asked.

"No. I'm a criminalist," Helen replied, closing the manual and turning to face the mechanic. She brushed a stray lock of hair behind her left ear. "We're investigating the disappearance of a woman who used to work here."

"Who?" he asked, finally taking his hands down and wiping them with a rag he had draped from a back pocket.

"Her name's Erica Holmes."

The mechanic pointed an index finger at his left cheek and motioned a couple strokes downward. "You have a…" he stammered, motioning again at his cheek and handing her his rag.

Helen grabbed the rag quickly and rubbed it against her cheek to remove the offending smudge. She only managed to make it worse. "Better?" she asked. Her face had flushed beneath the smear of black grease.

"Yeah," the mechanic lied. Helen handed the rag back to him with an embarrassed grin.

"Erica Holmes?" Helen continued.

"Don't know her, but then I haven't been here that long. Is that the same 'Holmes' that signs my paychecks?"

"Yeah, Dwayne Holmes is her father."

"What's your friend looking for?"

"He doesn't know."

"So what does a criminalist do?" asked the mechanic.

"I study evidence from a crime scene," Helen replied.

"That sounds cool. What kind of evidence."

Helen swallowed. "Biological," she replied hesitantly.

"Biological?"

"Yeah, you know, DNA from blood, urine, fecal matter, semen. That kind of thing."

"Oh," the mechanic winced, the smile melting off his face like heated wax. He returned to his study of the brake pads.

The sound of a low mournful groan diverted Helen's attention back over to Jenkins who had lowered himself onto all fours and, with a long pencil, was poking into a crevice between the back workbenches as if he was trying to tease a rodent from its den. Helen approached him from behind. "Lieutenant?" she said inquisitively. "Still looking for 'it'."

"Yes, and here 'it' is," he proclaimed triumphantly holding up a shell casing skewered on the end of his pencil. "Uuuhhhhhhggg," Jenkins exhaled as he rose to his feet.

"Is that what I think it is?" Helen asked.

"If you think it's a shell casing, then the answer is yes," Jenkins replied. "Excuse me," he said to get the mechanic's attention. "Know anything about this?"

"What is it?" the mechanic asked.

"A shell casing." Jenkins replied.

"Absolutely not," the mechanic said resolutely.

"I didn't think so," Jenkins muttered to himself as he placed the shell into a plastic evidence bag. "Let's get back, Miss Chang." Jenkins turned to leave.

"Do I have anything on my cheek?" Helen asked, grabbing Jenkins by the elbow and presenting her profile so that he could get a better look.

"Like what?" Jenkins asked, ignoring the obvious smear covering most of her left cheek.

"Oil."

"No, you look fine," Jenkins said managing to turn away in time that Helen couldn't catch his grin.

"Could we stop for a little bite on the way back to the office?" Helen asked.

"Monosodium glutamate," Jenkins said flatly. "I know this great place right off of 280 on Washington Street in Daly City. They make the French fries right there in front of you."

"Hamburgers?" Helen scowled. "What is it with you and those things?"

"I'm buying," Jenkins pronounced with an upward inflection to his voice meant to entice her.

"Let's go," Helen said in resignation.

"And Miss Chang?"

"Yeah."

"It's a very big ocean."

"I don't know what you're talking about."

Jenkins and Helen slipped back into Jenkins' car and buckled their seat belts. Jenkins pulled the bag with the shell casing out of his coat pocket and withdrew his revolver from his shoulder holster.

"For crying out loud," Helen exclaimed in horror, "what are you doing?"

"I just wanted to do a quick check of this bullet's caliber against the barrel of my revolver," Jenkins answered.

"Now? Can't it wait? I hate those things."

"Miss Chang, do you know anything about guns?" Jenkins asked.

"Not a thing," Helen replied. "And I don't care to know. Those things scare the bejeezes out of me. Would you please just put that away!"

"Quickly, then," Jenkins continued. "Maybe if you know more about it, you won't be as scared."

"I doubt it," Helen said sternly.

"This is the muzzle, the barrel, and the ejector rod," Jenkins said, moving his finger from one end of the revolver to the other. Helen felt like a rubber-necker passing an accident on the highway—she found herself unable to look away. "The cylinder holds the bullets. The hammer, when released, ignites the gunpowder in the shell casing which propels the lead bullet. The safety, also called the cylinder release latch, prevents the gun from accidental firing, the trigger, trigger guard, and the grip. There you go." Jenkins slipped the revolver back into his shoulder holster.

"I don't think that helped," Helen observed. "I still hate 'em."

Ballistics

To the assailant, murder is a risky business. Since we're all genetically endowed with a strong instinct for survival, when a person feels their life is in danger, that person will do anything and everything to stay alive. They will kick, hit, scream, claw, and bite—whatever it takes to preserve their life. Killing someone by the fist, club, or even by knife puts the murderer in close proximity to the victim and therefore at risk of injury. It's far safer for the assailant to draw on that uniquely human, technologically driven talent—the ability to kill from a safe distance—to kill with a gun.

Murder is a messy business too. Unless the victim was strangled by the assailant's bare hands or suffocated beneath a pillow while they slept, a number of different types of evidence including blood, trace, and DNA will be left behind at the scene. This is particularly true when a firearm is used in a killing. The bullet, the cartridge casing, and the gunpowder may all be left behind as calling cards pointing the way to the killer. If the police are able to recover the weapon, its serial number, and the records that follow that serial number, it may lead them directly to the killer.

A bullet's path and where it imbeds can give an investigator an idea of the nature of the crime. For example, in the case of a robbery in which the suspect is unexpectedly confronted, bullets may be flying in every direction. On the other hand, a single bullet to the back of a victim's head suggests a possible *execution style*, premeditated murder carried out by a professional hit man. By carefully examining the hole a bullet makes in the victim's body, in a wall, in furniture, or in any other physical obstruction, the bullet's trajectory—its path—can be deduced and the crime can be reconstructed. If the gun was fired at close range to the victim, the entry wound will be ringed with dark gunshot residue.

Because of the mechanism by which a gun is discharged, each firearm leaves its own signature on a murder. When the trigger is pulled, a firing pin strikes the primer cup at the back of the bullet's cartridge igniting the *primer*, a small shock-sensitive charge that detonates the gunpowder packaged behind the metal bullet. The force of the gunpowder's explosion propels the bullet out of the cartridge and sends it racing down the gun barrel toward the target. That barrel, machine drilled during the gun's manufacture, is marked by striated grooves that corkscrew down the inside of the barrel's length. These grooves impart a spin on the bullet as it exits the gun giving it stability and accuracy to the aim. (A football quarterback uses this same concept when passing the ball downfield to a receiver.) Because a bullet is made of lead or is jacketed with copper, the harder steel of the gun barrel etches striations into the bullet's softer metal. All these actions, taking place in a split second, leave a casing with a unique mark on the firing pin, a bullet with unique *rifling* marks, and the fine powder of gunshot residue on the shooter's skin and clothing. Forensic scientists can use these artifacts of a fired gun to make a match with the ballistics evidence gathered at the scene of the crime.

To determine if a firearm taken into evidence is the weapon that fired a bullet recovered from the crime scene, a criminalist will prepare a *reference bullet* obtained by firing the gun into a water tank (Figure 8.1). A reference bullet, since it's speed will be slowed by the tank water, will not be collapsed and distorted by impact as would happen if it was prepared by shooting at a solid surface. However, when the bullet is retrieved (Figure 8.2b), its markings can still be compared with

Figure 8.1 Firearms expert Richard Ernest with Alliance Forensics Laboratory and Consultants of Fort Worth, Texas, prepares a reference bullet from a handgun by discharging the weapon into a water tank.

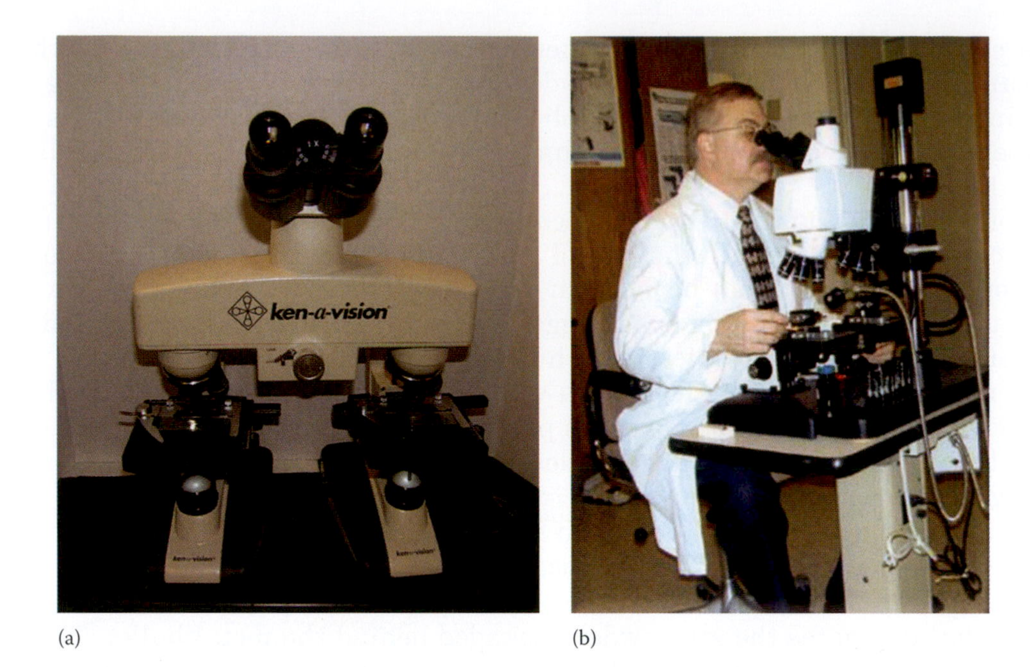

(a) (b)

Figure 8.2 (a) A comparison microscope consists of two stages that can be viewed simultaneously through a binocular eyepiece. Half of each stage will be presented in the image viewed through the eyepiece. (b) Firearms expert Richard Ernest with Alliance Forensics Laboratory and Consultants examines shell casings using a comparison microscope.

the evidence bullet. The shell casing from the reference bullet is also examined for any markings that might match a casing found at the crime scene.

A firearms expert will use a *comparison microscope* (Figure 8.2) to simultaneously examine markings on the crime scene bullet or casing with those on the reference set. The microscope has two stages on to which are placed the two items being matched. Both items are viewed through a single ocular device. Each image from each stage can be split in half and the two half images aligned within the eyepiece for easy, side-by-side comparison.

Three characteristic markings, called *lands*, *grooves*, and *direction of twist* (Figure 8.5), are used to determine whether or not two bullets were potentially fired from the same gun. Lands are furrows gouged into the bullet's metal that run down its length. Grooves are those areas of the bullet between the lands and represent the bullet's original surface. The designation of lands and grooves, therefore, seems counterintuitive. However, lands and grooves are opposites between the barrel of the gun and the bullet that passed through it (Figure 8.3). A land in the gun barrel will create a groove in the bullet. Likewise, a groove in the gun barrel will create a land on the bullet (Figures 8.4 and 8.5). A bullet's twist is created as it spirals down the gun barrel. A bullet's direction of twist can be determined by pointing it away, down the line of sight, and noting whether the lands and grooves angle to the right or to the left. Small scratches or striations within the lands and grooves can add additional features to a bullet's surface (Figure 8.6) and can assist in making a match with a reference. The task of matching bullets can be facilitated by the use of such database programs as DRUGFIRE maintained by the FBI in which digital images of bullets recovered from different crime scenes, even from different states, can be mathematically compared for similar distinguishing marks. Since each gun imparts its own unique pattern of markings on a fired bullet, a match with a reference can provide compelling proof that the recovered weapon is the one used in a crime.

Anatomy of a bullet

Land

Groove

Land

Groove

Right-hand twist

Figure 8.3 A bullet's lands, grooves, and twist direction are shown. The grooves, located between the lands, represent the bullet's original surface. This bullet shows a right-hand twist as the lands and grooves have a tilt to the right as they proceed up the bullet from the base toward the head. The head of this bullet was distorted by impact against a solid surface.

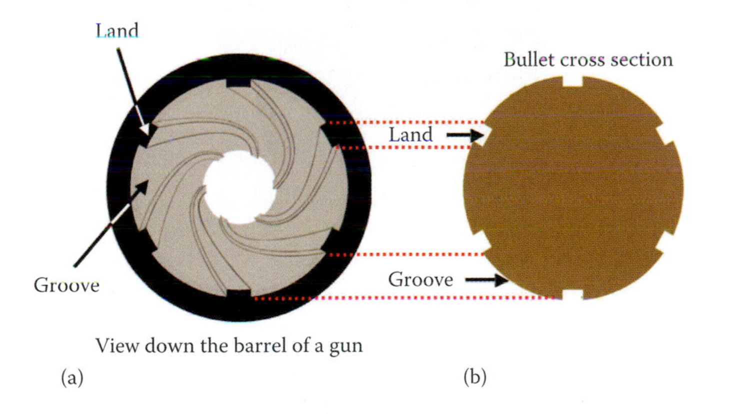

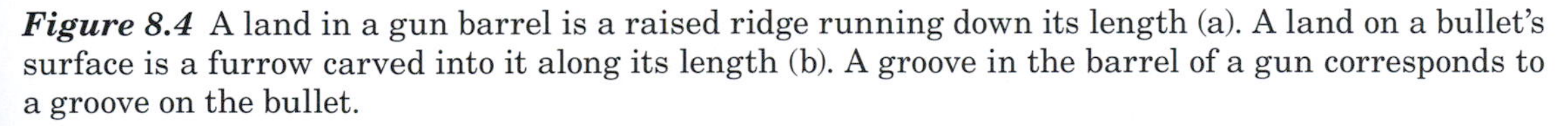

Figure 8.4 A land in a gun barrel is a raised ridge running down its length (a). A land on a bullet's surface is a furrow carved into it along its length (b). A groove in the barrel of a gun corresponds to a groove on the bullet.

A cartridge case found at a crime scene can tell an investigator the class and caliber of firearm used. The casing can also show markings on its metal surface that can tie it to a suspect's weapon. When placed into the barrel of a gun, the casing that holds the metal bullet is held against the firing mechanism's breech face (Figure 8.7). As the trigger is pulled and the gun is fired, a firing pin, located at the center of the breech face, impacts the primer cup at the bullet's rear. The primer ignites the gunpowder, and as the gunpowder explodes, the bullet is expelled from the casing and is sent hurtling down the gun barrel toward its target. The casing is then ejected from the gun barrel. All these events cause metal surfaces to clash

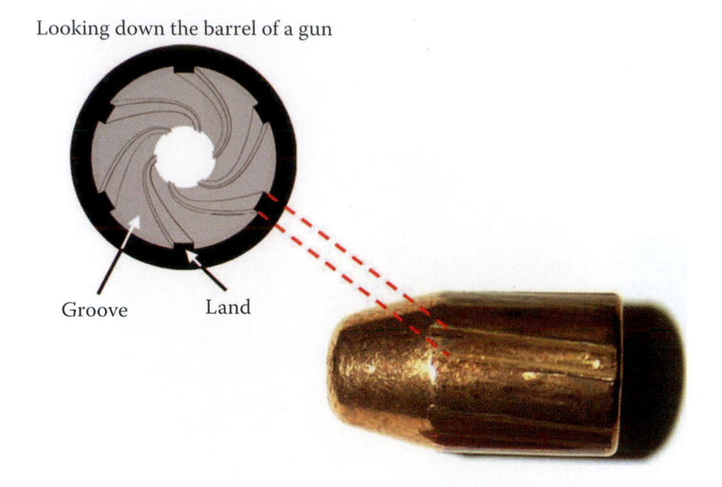

Figure 8.5 A land is a furrow gouged into the bullet's surface by a land in the gun barrel. Likewise, a groove in the gun barrel creates what is called the "groove" feature on a bullet.

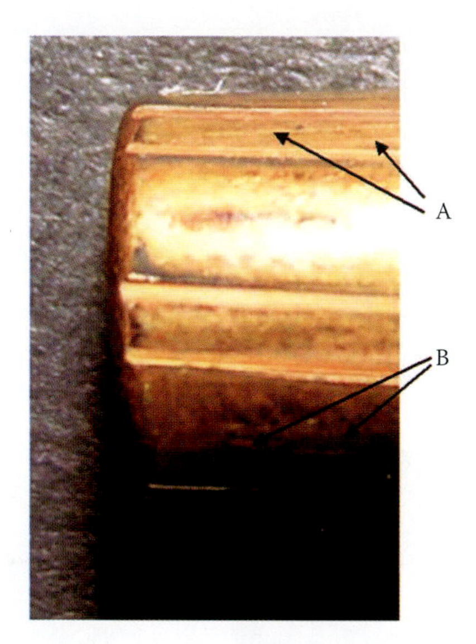

Figure 8.6 This figure shows the secondary characteristics of bullet markings. (A) Striations within a land can be used to individualize a bullet, as can (B) the striations within a groove.

or rub against other metal surfaces, each leaving their unique characteristic mark (Figure 8.8). The location in which the casing was found can indicate from where it was fired. Since most cartridges are ejected from the right side of the gun, an investigator can make a guess as to where the assailant was standing and in which direction they were facing when the gun was fired.

In the Crime Lab

Activity 8.1 Measuring Scale

There are a number of different professionals who may swarm into a crime scene once it is reported. Police officers, criminal investigators, criminalists, and members of the press may all descend upon the area, and each one of them, no matter

Figure 8.7 Anatomy of a gun's firing mechanism. The breech face (circled with a dashed red line) holds the casing when the bullet is loaded into the barrel. The firing pin (see red arrow) is in the center of the breech face. When the trigger is pulled, the firing pin impacts the primer cup containing the igniting powder. An impression of the firing pin is left on the primer cup surface. Other markings will be made on and around the shell casing when it presses back against the breech face as the bullet accelerates forward down the gun barrel. The direction of the bullet's path is indicated with a red arrow.

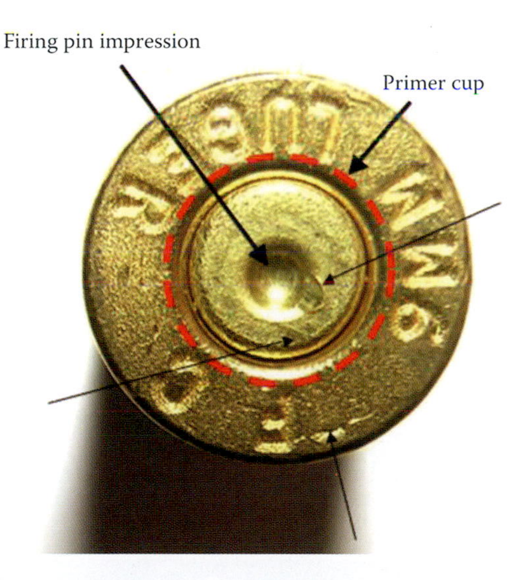

Figure 8.8 Markings on the rear of a bullet casing. The firing pin impression (indicated) is a concave indentation made when the firing pin strikes the primer cup (circled with a dashed red line). Other markings (scratches and indentations identified with fine arrows) may also form during the bullet's firing. A breech mark impression, for example, is created when the firearm's recoil forces the shell casing backwards against the breech face.

how careful they are, can potentially damage or contaminate important pieces of evidence. Careful photo documentation of the crime scene, therefore, completed as quickly and with as little disruption as possible, can be invaluable to officials investigating the crime as well as to those prosecuting it. A photograph of an object, however, does not necessarily tell its complete story.

Imagine you have a photograph of an object that has all the characteristics of the planet Mars. How do you know, however, whether it's a picture of the actual planet or of a marble, a cue ball, or a beach ball that's been meticulously painted to look like Mars? If you had another item of known dimensions, a marker, placed within the same plane as the object in question and equidistant from the camera, you would be able to make that determination. The crime scene photographer, therefore, will often place some familiar item, as a marker, within the photographic field to give scale to the object in question.

To determine the size of the object under examination, you can use the following relationship:

$$\frac{O_A}{O_P} = \frac{M_A}{M_P}$$

where
- O_A is the object's actual size
- O_P is the object's size in the photograph
- M_A is the marker's actual size
- M_P is the marker's size in the photograph

Using this equation, you solve for O_A. This exercise will give you the skills you will need to determine the size and caliber of firearm evidence encountered later in this chapter.

Materials:
- Quarter, US currency
- Ruler with centimeter scale
- Calculator

Protocol:
Use Figures 8.9 and 8.10 and the markers, a quarter and a ruler, respectively, to determine the dimensions of objects A, B, and C. Show your calculations in your laboratory notebook.

Activity 8.2 Using a Caliper

Precise measurements require precision instruments. When measuring critical items of evidence such as bones, bullets, and shell casings, for example, a standard

Figure 8.9 A quarter is used as a marker to help derive the dimensions of two pieces of paper marked A and B.

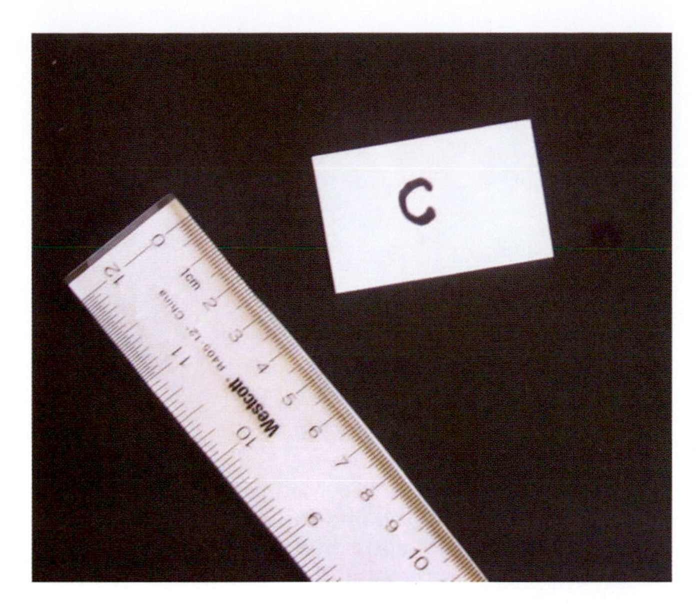

Figure 8.10 A ruler is used as a marker to help derive the dimensions of object C, a rectangular piece of paper.

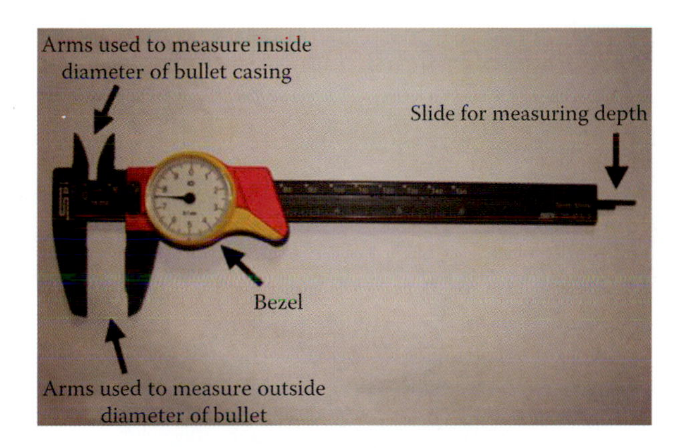

Figure 8.11 The arms (or "jaws") of the caliper widen and narrow to fit the object being measured. The bezel moves and rotates as the caliper arms are opened or closed. The movement of the bezel is synchronized with the needle that gauges the distance the arms move in increments of 0.1 mm. A 360° revolution of the bezel needle represents a distance of 10 mm (1 cm). A sliding extension (seen at the right end of the caliper in this figure) is used to measure the depth of an object.

ruler may not provide a level of precision that can withstand the rigors of scrutiny unleashed in a court of law. A measuring instrument called a *caliper*, however, can provide that level of precision. A caliper has two adjustable arms designed to measure the internal and external diameter of an object (Figure 8.11). As the arms move to fit the object being measured, a bezel dial indicates the distance between the arms in one-tenth millimeter increments (Figure 8.12).

This activity will instruct you on (1) the parts of a caliper, (2) ways a caliper can measure an object, and (3) how to use a caliper to measure the caliber of a bullet or shell casing.

Materials:

Calipers (one/lab group)
Various objects to measure

Figure 8.12 This caliper reads 24.0 mm. The bezel is positioned to the right of the 20 mm mark on the black straightedge (see red part of bezel) and the bezel needle is pointing to the 4 mm mark (20 mm + 4 mm = 24 mm). To determine the tenths place, note where the bezel needle lines up with the tick marks. Here, the needle lines up directly on the 4 mm mark. This coin, therefore, is 24.0 mm in diameter.

Protocol:

1. Before any measurements are made, close the arms of the caliper completely and check to see the bezel is reading 0.0 mm. If not, make appropriate adjustments by rotating the bezel gently until the needle lines up with the 0.0 mm marking.

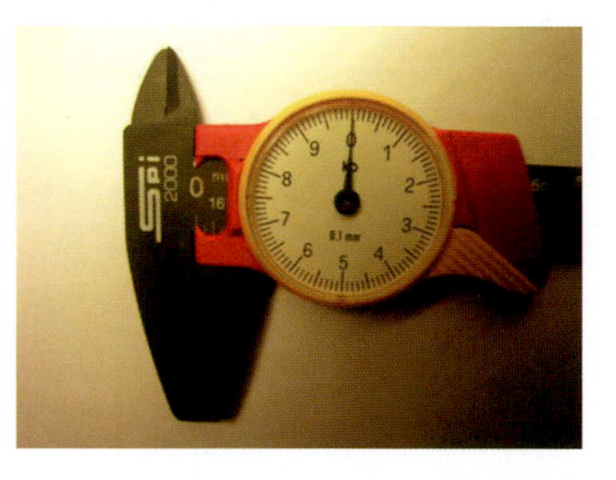

2. The outside dimension of an object is measured using the longer arms of the caliper.

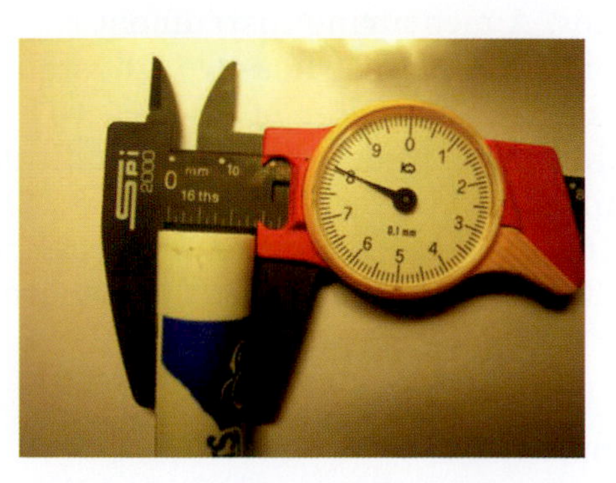

3. Determine the inside dimension of a hollow cylinder by placing the shorter arms on the caliper within the object and separating the arms until they make contact with the object's inner walls.

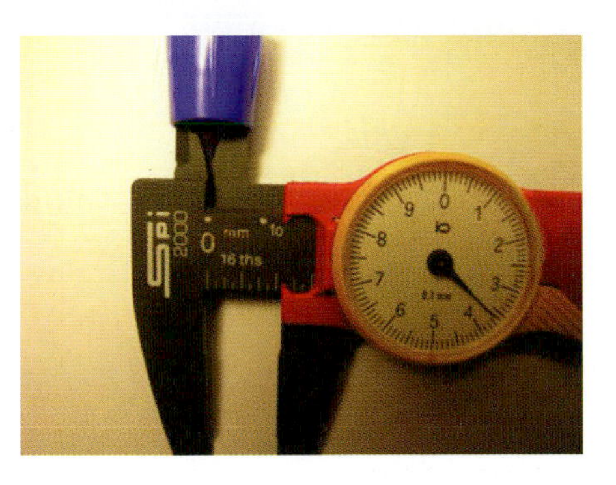

4. The depth of an object is determined by sliding the depth gauge until it touches the object's back wall. Here, a dry eraser cap is used. The bottom picture shows the appearance of the caliper when the cap is removed.

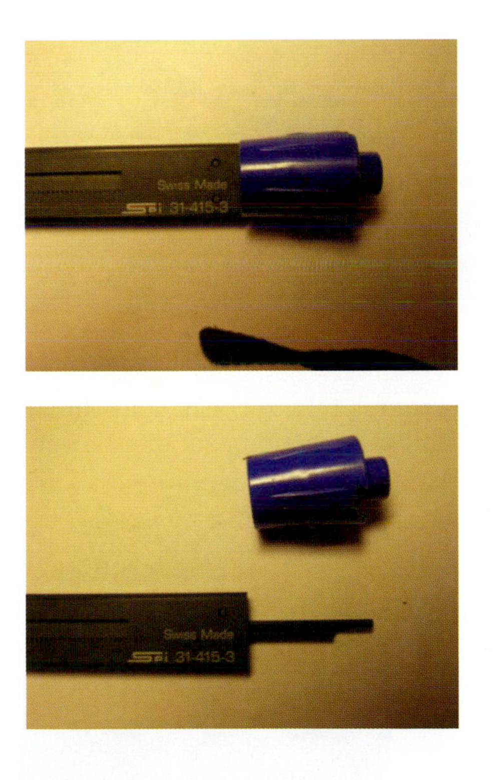

5. Your instructor will provide you with various objects that you will measure using a caliper. In your laboratory notebook, record the item being examined and the dimensions of its inside, outside, and depth. Convert all your measurements to inches. Show your calculations. Shown in the following text is an example of how you might organize your work.

Activity 8.3 Determining a Bullet's Caliber

In this activity, you will use a caliper to determine the dimensions of a bullet and shell casing.

Materials:
Spent bullets and shell casings
Calipers

1. Obtain a bullet and shell casing from your instructor.

2. Close the caliper arms completely to check that the bezel needle points to the zero mark. If it does not, adjust the bezel or ask your instructor to zero the instrument.

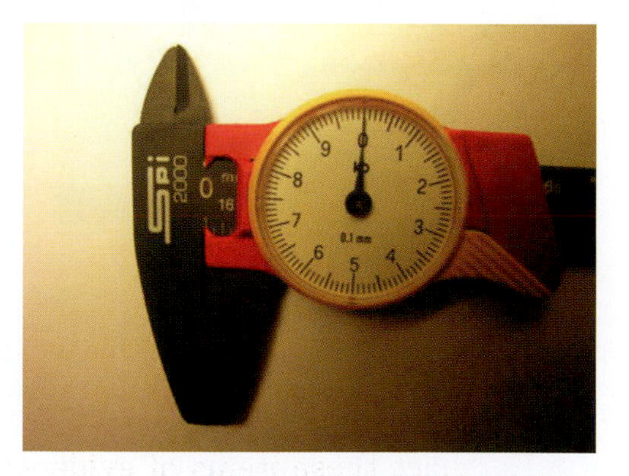

3. Measure the outside diameter of a spent bullet at its base. Record the measurement (in mm) in your lab notebook. Convert the caliper reading into inches using the conversion factor 25.4 mm = 1 in. The inch measurement gives you the caliber (e.g., 0.44 in. = 44 caliber bullet).

4. Repeat this process with a shell casing. However, for this object, use the caliper arms designed for measuring inside diameter. Record the measurement (in mm) in your laboratory notebook. Convert this measurement into inches. A measurement of 0.44 in. is recorded as a 44 caliber shell casing. Show your calculations.

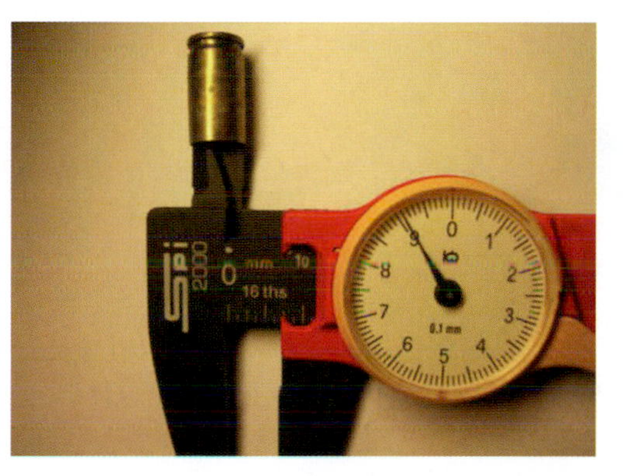

Erica Holmes Missing Persons Case

A bullet was found in the track of the driver's seat in Erica Holmes' vehicle while being inspected by Criminalist Helen Chang and Lieutenant Robert Jenkins. A handgun was found under the driver's seat of the Ford 150 belonging to Erica's ex-boyfriend Samdeep O'Neill. A shell casing was found in the garage bay of *The Nuts and Bolts of It* garage, Erica Holmes' former place of employment. It must be determined if these items are related—was the bullet recovered from Erica Holmes' vehicle fired from the gun recovered from Samdeep O'Neill's vehicle and is the casing recovered from the garage consistent in caliber with the recovered bullet?

Figures 8.13 through 8.16 depict these items of evidence. Fill out an evidence report of your findings. This report should include notes on the bullet's caliber, number of lands and grooves on the bullet and their direction of twist.

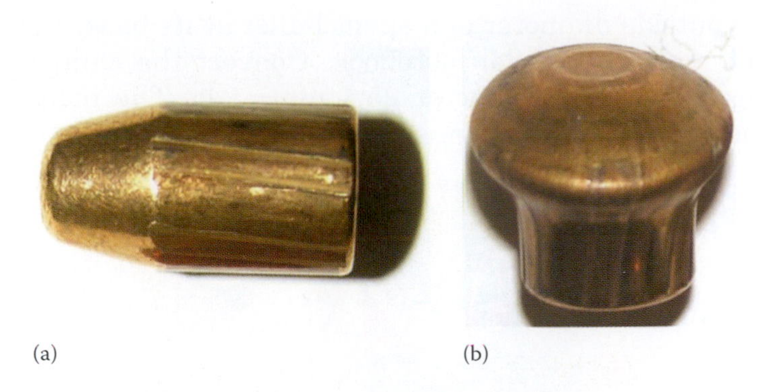

Figure 8.13 (a) Bullet fired from O'Neill's gun into water tank. (b) Bullet recovered from Erica Holmes' vehicle.

Figure 8.14 (a) Bullet recovered from Erica Holmes' vehicle. (b) Penny, US currency. (c) Bullet fired from O'Neill's gun into water tank.

Figure 8.15 (a) Test fired shell casing. (b) Shell casing recovered from Erica's work garage.

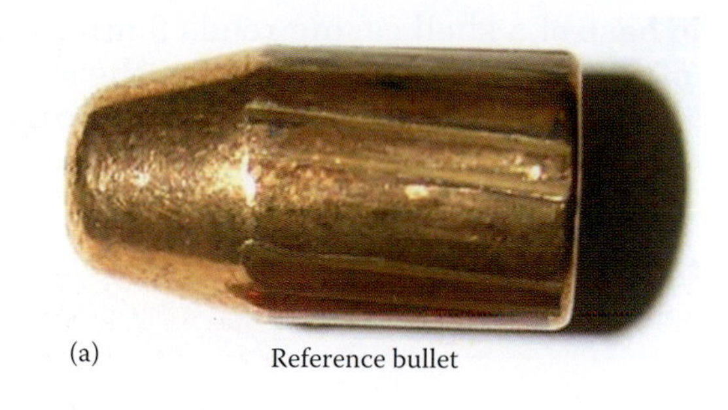

(a) Reference bullet

Longitudinal sections from crime scene bullet

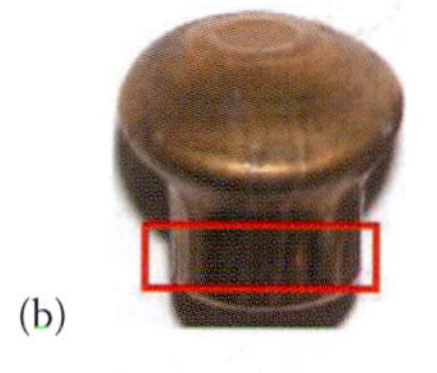

(b)

Figure 8.16 (a) Reference bullet that was test fired. (b) Spent bullet recovered from vehicle. Red rectangle represents the area where two different longitudinal sections are indicated above the spent bullet for comparative purposes to the reference bullet.

Review Questions

8.1 How are a reference bullet and casing prepared?

8.2 What are lands and grooves and how are they formed?

8.3 Why will a bullet travel farther and more accurately if it is rotating or spinning in space? (*Hint*: Apply Newton's laws of motion.)

8.4 What does the number "44" refer to in reference to a .44 magnum bullet?

8.5 What instrument is used to make a side-by-side comparison of two bullets?

8.6 Explain how a compound microscope works.

8.7 If a crime scene bullet and a reference bullet are found to have the same twist, lands, grooves, and caliber, can it be concluded that the two bullets originated from the same weapon? Explain.

8.8 What other characteristics besides lands and grooves might help to individualize a bullet to a weapon?

8.9 If a shell casing recovered from a crime scene and a reference shell casing are found to have similar diameters to each other and to the weapon in question, can one conclude that the shell casings are the same? Explain.

8.10 What other characteristics would help in matching a shell casing to another shell casing and to the weapon in question?

8.11 What is a caliper?

8.12 Define caliber.

8.13 What is the diameter of a bullet that is loaded into a .44 magnum firearm?

8.14 How many "mm" is a .44 magnum bullet/shell casing? (Show your calculation.)

8.15 The stamp at the base of a shell casing reads 9 mm. What does this mean?

8.16 Can the caliber of a bullet be determined from the size of its casing? Explain.

8.17 Why is it important that the diameter of a spent bullet be measured at or as close to the base of the bullet as possible?

Further Reading

Time Since Discharge of Pistols and Revolvers by J. Andrasko and S. Stahling in *Journal of Forensic Sciences*, Vol. 48, No. 2, pages 307–311, 2003.

Firearm and Toolmark Identification Criteria: A Review of the Literature, Part II by R.G. Nichols in *Journal of Forensic Sciences*, Vol. 48, No. 2, pages 318–327, 2003.

Time since Discharge of Shotgun Shells by J.D. Wilson, J.D. Tebow, and K.W. Moline in *Journal of Forensic Sciences*, Vol. 48, No. 6, pages 1298–1301, 2003.

NIST Bullet Signature Measurement System for RM (Reference Material) 8240 Standard Bullets by L. Ma, J. Song, E. Whitenton, A. Zheng, T. Vorburger, and J. Zhou in *Journal of Forensic Sciences*, Vol. 49, No. 4, pages 649–659, 2004.

Linking Crime Guns: The Impact of Ballistics Imaging Technology on the Productivity of the Boston Police Department's Ballistics Unit by A.A. Braga and G.L. Pierce in *Journal of Forensic Sciences*, Vol. 49, No. 4, pages 701–706, 2004.

9 Histology

Police Headquarters, Thursday 4:32 PM

"I took a molecular biology class at Berkeley," Helen said as she and Jenkins sat by the microscope in the evidence examination room, "where, for the final exam, the professor asked one question. Just one question… if you got it right, you got an A for the entire semester. Wrong, well, I guess it depended on how wrong you got it."

"What was the question?" Jenkins asked, intrigued.

"Here it is. One of the graduate students in a cell biology laboratory has been observing tissue cells in a culture flask under a dissecting scope. The graduate student goes to lunch and leaves the flask on the microscope's stage. When he gets back about an hour later, he looks at the flask under the scope and all the cells are gone. The graduate student can't find a single cell. What's the most likely explanation?"

"How did you answer?" asked Jenkins.

"I tried incorporating everything we'd learned in class that semester. I said that maybe the cells harbored a provirus that had become active during the one-hour period the graduate student was at lunch and that maybe the lab had gotten hot during that time or the cells were starved for oxygen and heat shock regulator proteins were transcribed, which could have turned on some other genes encoding proteolytic enzymes that digested the cell walls and…"

"Miss Chang, if I may interrupt. You've pretty much lost me here. Let's cut to the chase. What grade did you get?"

"It took me the full two hours to write my answer," Helen replied. "I thought I'd aced it."

"Your grade?" Jenkins asked again impatiently.

" I got a '*C*'!"

"Miss Chang," Jenkins said, unable to suppress a smile. "A '*C*'! You?"

"Yeah. I know. I thought I nailed it—an 'A' was in the bag. But then I saw this guy in my class a week after grades were out and he told me *he* got an 'A' on the test. I remembered him because he split about five minutes after the exam started. I figured he was clueless. I asked him how he answered the question. He told me he had written down just four words."

"What did he write?" Jenkins asked.

"Someone switched the flasks."

"Occam's razor," said Jenkins.

"Oh, no!" Helen exclaimed. "The professor talked about that."

"The most likely explanation for some mystery is the one that's simplest, makes the fewest assumptions, and doesn't invoke the spiritual world," Jenkins said. "Ghosts, UFO sightings, ESP, the paranormal, the supernatural, even the psychic detective lend themselves quite well to analysis using Occam's razor."

"Lieutenant Jenkins?" a voice said from the laboratory entrance behind him. Jenkins turned to see the department secretary at the door.

"Ms. Allen! Everything okay?" Jenkins asked.

"Those people from the Erica Holmes case you requested come in for fingerprints have been processed and released. But Mrs. Holmes has stayed behind to speak with you."

"About?" asked Jenkins.

"I don't know, but she seems distressed."

"Where is she?"

"In the waiting room," the secretary replied.

"Thank you Ms. Allen," Jenkins said as she departed. Jenkins' chest heaved as he filled his lungs with air and then slowly, almost imperceptibly exhaled out again. He stared at the floor as if his soul had become a casualty spread out beneath him.

"Lieutenant Jenkins?" Helen asked softly.

"I'm no good at this, Miss Chang," Jenkins muttered. "I don't have the talent… I have no gift for consoling people—trying to give them hope where perhaps there is no hope. I never know what to say. No one has ever taught me how to console the newly widowed, comfort the orphaned child, or lend solace to the bereaved parent. You should hope you never have to do it."

"I could go with you, Lieutenant," Helen offered, "but I don't know what I'd say either."

"Lieutenant Jenkins?" He looked up to find Sarah Holmes halfway through the door.

"Mrs. Holmes," Jenkins exclaimed, "you're not supposed to be in here. This is an evidence room."

"I'm sorry, Lieutenant," she said. "I followed the receptionist here. I know I shouldn't have but I'm desperate for some news. Have you found anything? Is my baby dead?"

Jenkins stood up and retrieved a chair from the other side of the room. He placed it close to his own. "Please, sit down Mrs. Holmes. You remember Miss Chang?"

"Yes," she replied. "Nice to see you again."

Helen nodded an acknowledgement. "You too."

"Lieutenant," Sarah Holmes said, trembling, "I can't eat. I can't sleep. Please, what can you tell me about Erica?"

Jenkins sat across from Sarah and studied her eyes. They flickered like a bulb whose filament was about to break. A drop of crystal liquid clung to the lower lash of her left eyelid like a desperate climber on a cliff face tethered to a group of anxious companions balanced on the ledge above. If it lost its grip, the others would be yanked down and doomed to follow it, one after the other, into the abyss.

"Mrs. Holmes," Jenkins said at last leaning slightly forward, his arms resting on his knees, his fingers interlocked, "do you have any reason to believe Erica is dead? Is there anything you haven't told me?"

Sarah disengaged the lock she'd had on Jenkins eyes and looked up at the wall beside her as if she was searching for some merciful distraction.

"Mrs. Holmes?"

"I fear the worst, Lieutenant," she replied.

"What's that?"

"Erica found out about her father and they'd been fighting for weeks about her boyfriend, Sam, and I fear that Erica, out of spite, may have confronted Dwayne with it and he could have lost it."

"What would Erica have confronted your husband with, Mrs. Holmes?"

Sarah rose from her chair to leave. "I shouldn't have come here, Lieutenant," she said. "I can't say any more. I'll show myself out."

"Wait. Please. Mrs. Holmes. Just one more moment," Jenkins said motioning her to sit.

Sarah reluctantly took the seat.

"Mrs. Holmes," Jenkins started but stopped himself. He caught her glance again and held it. He placed a hand on hers. "Sarah," he said continuing, "the most remarkable thing my daughter ever said to me, she was only eleven at the time, was that she hoped she died before I did. I was stunned. 'Why?' I asked her. 'If you died before me,' she replied, 'I couldn't bear life without you.' She could not have known how much deeper and even more profound the love of a parent can be. Part of a complete life, I believe, is to love someone so deeply and completely that you can never get over it. No parent should lose a child, ever. It is not the natural order. There can be no greater loss than the death of a son or daughter. I don't know how I could bear the death of my own daughter or how I'd possibly recover. But I do know, if she were truly gone, if I outlived her, she would be the one spared the pain, the sorrow, and the loss. She would never have to face it. It would be behind her."

Mrs. Holmes quickly wiped both eyes with one hand. "Thank you, Lieutenant," she said as she lifted herself from the chair. "Keep me informed. Won't you please?"

Jenkins nodded in the affirmative as she left the room.

"Lieutenant," Helen said softly when the door had swung closed, "I think you console people just fine."

Histology

You may find any number of metaphors for a cell. A cell is a factory. It is a fort. A cell is the building block of the organism. It is a machine. But no matter what you choose to compare its likeness to, that comparison should reflect its complexity, its central role as the basic unit of life, and it should even convey a sense of mystery. It is perhaps an irony that something so critical to life is yet so small that it can only be recognized and examined under a microscope.

Although each cell is equipped to function as a living entity, no cell is an island unto itself. Each cell in the human body will have hundreds of millions of other cells identical to it. Cells sharing a similar structure and a common function form the different *tissues*. Muscle, blood, and bone are types of tissues. *Organs*, such as the heart, liver, lung, and spleen, represent a collection of multiple tissues organized collectively to perform a specific purpose. For example, the tissues of the heart function to pump blood. The tissues of the lung work to exchange gases during the process of respiration.

Under a light microscope, the most distinguishing internal structure of a cell is its *nucleus*, the roughly spherical body (in the classic textbook sense) that carries the coiled chromosomes of DNA. Almost all cells, no matter what their source in the human body, carry a nucleus. The prominent exceptions are red blood cells and the enucleated cells of the outer skin. All cell types also contain *cytoplasm* (the gel-like fluid of the cell that carries nutrients and acts to support other organelles), *endoplasmic reticulum* (the membrane network where protein synthesis occurs), *mitochondria* (the organelles where the energy-rich molecule ATP is produced), *lysosomes* (where the cell breaks down waste products), and *Golgi apparatus* (where proteins are processed for secretion). Despite their commonalities, however, cells from different tissues—from the muscle, fat, liver, and lung, for example—have quite different appearances. The study of cells and tissues by microscope is called *histology*.

Skeletal Muscle

Each cell of the body, as an integral part of the tissue or organ it helps form, has a structure that makes it uniquely suited for its task. Cells of *skeletal muscle*, for example, are required to expand and contract as needed to move the limbs. Those muscles whose names you've heard bandied about in the gym—triceps, biceps, *quads*, and *glutes*—are all made from cells of skeletal muscle. These types of muscles are called *voluntary* since they can be controlled by conscious thought. Your brain, by the will of thought, sends a nerve impulse to your biceps commanding the muscle to contract and your arm to lift. In a healthy person, skeletal muscle makes up almost half of the body weight.

Under the microscope, the cells of skeletal muscle appear long and stringlike (Figure 9.1). The cells line up in parallel to each other along the tissue's long axis. A single muscle cell may be long enough to reach from one end of the muscle to the other. Skeletal muscle cells have two other striking features. (1) Each cell has anywhere from several to hundreds of nuclei (the cells are said to be *multinucleated*). The nuclei are found close to the cell's outer plasma membrane and are distributed along the cell's entire length. (2) The cells appear striated (Figure 9.2)—they carry regularly repeating bands of muscle fibers perpendicular to the long axis of the cell. These *striations* are filaments made of the proteins actin and myosin, which, upon interacting, cause the muscle to contract. Figure 9.3 shows skeletal muscle in cross section. The cells appear bundled and cylindrical.

Cardiac Muscle

The heart is an astonishing worker. It pumps almost 2,000 gallons of blood each day through some 100,000 miles of blood vessels. During an average human lifetime, it will beat some four billion times without taking a break. The tissue behind these phenomenal statistics is *cardiac muscle*. Unlike skeletal muscle, the muscle of the heart is involuntary.... You can't, by conscious thought, command your heart to stop beating.

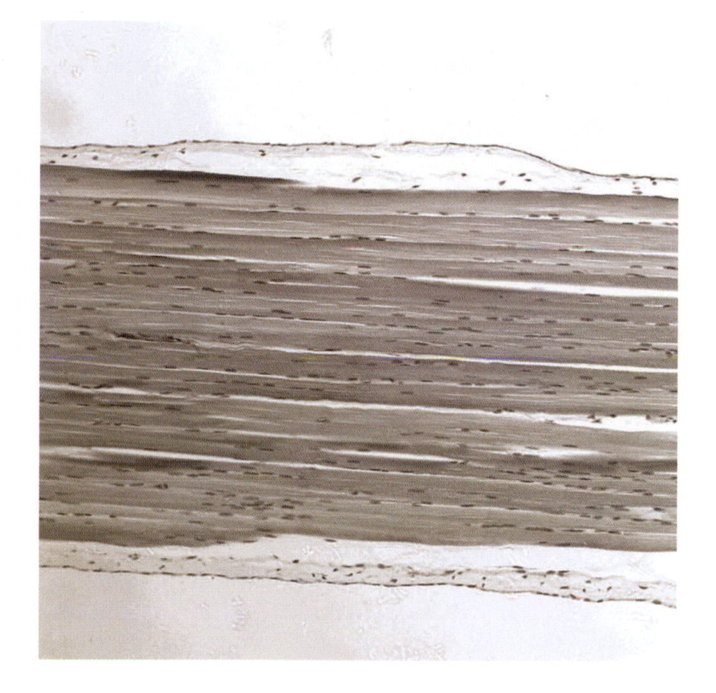

Figure 9.1 The cells of skeletal muscle are multinucleated and elongated and show striations running perpendicular to the long axis (longitudinal view).

Figure 9.2 Magnification of skeletal muscle showing striations and elongated nuclei.

Cardiac muscle cells (Figure 9.4) are elongated and multinucleated like those of skeletal muscle, and though also striated like their cousin, the striation is not as pronounced. In addition, unlike in skeletal muscle, the nuclei are located more in the center of the cell. The cells have the appearance of intertwining strings—each cell making contact with several other cells. A structure called an *intercalated disk* (Figure 9.5) running perpendicular to the cell's long axis marks the boundary between two cells touching end to end. The intercalated disk is responsible for the communication between adjacent cells that allows the sequential contraction of the heart's cells as needed to pump blood.

Smooth Muscle

A third type of muscle tissue, called *smooth muscle*, can be found in the uterus, bladder, intestine walls, and blood vessels. Though smooth muscle cells do contract (they

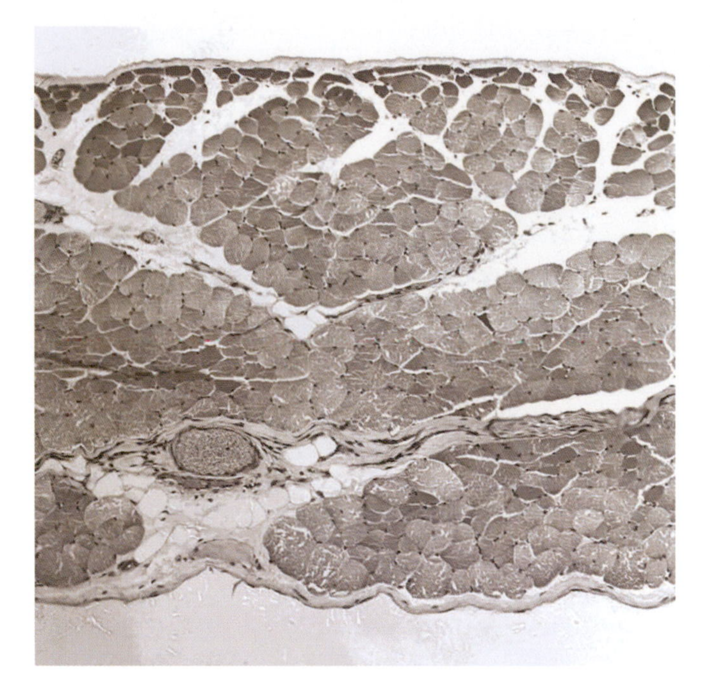

Figure 9.3 Skeletal muscle cells in cross section.

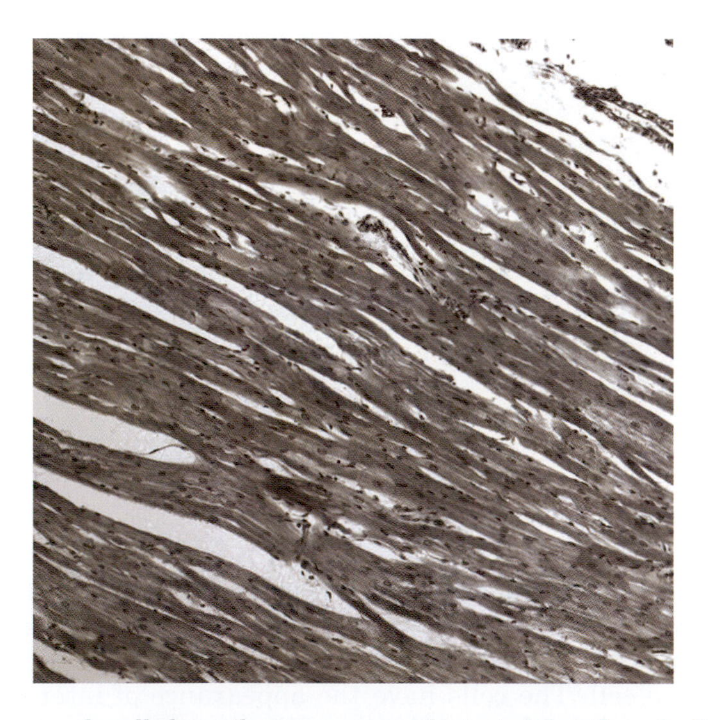

Figure 9.4 Cardiac muscle cells have the appearance of intertwining threads. The cells are multinucleated and have striations of actin and myosin fibers.

carry actin and myosin filaments), they do not show the characteristic striations of skeletal or cardiac muscle. The cells are spindle shaped—widest in the middle and tapered at each end. Their nuclei are elongated and centrally located (Figure 9.6).

Smooth muscle is called *involuntary* because it does not contract or relax by conscious thought. You have experienced this while sitting in class around 11 o'clock. Those groans coming from your stomach are the smooth muscles of your digestive system contracting and relaxing. When Humphrey Bogart's stomach was growling

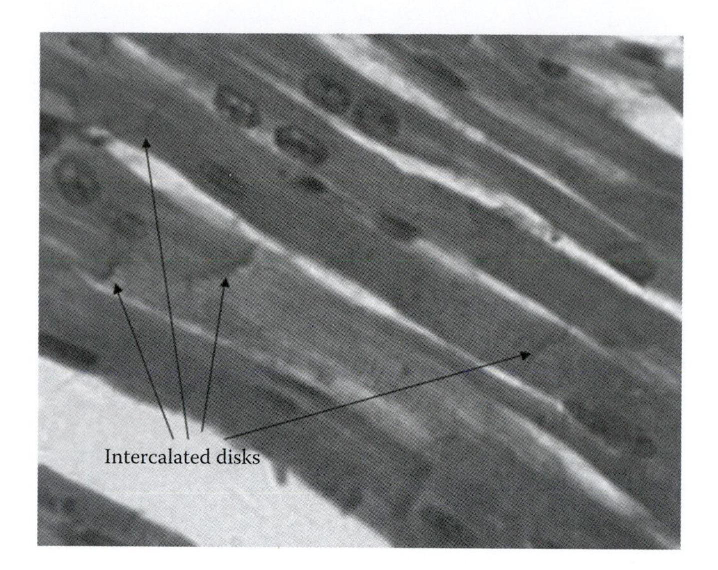

Figure 9.5 Intercalated disks mark the boundaries between adjacent cells of cardiac muscle.

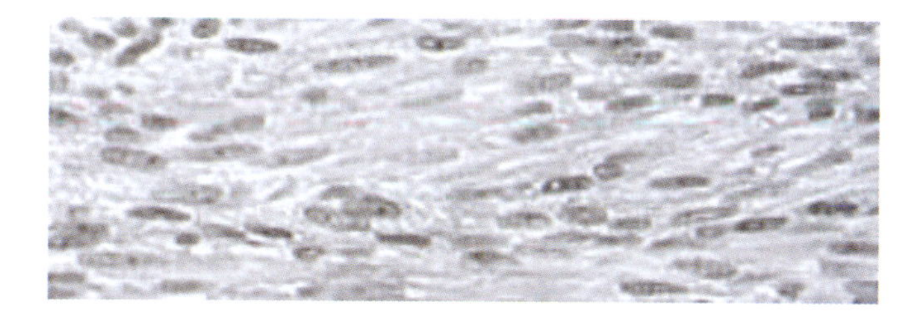

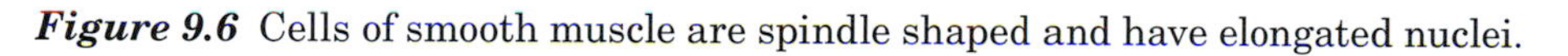

Figure 9.6 Cells of smooth muscle are spindle shaped and have elongated nuclei.

uncontrollably in the classic movie *The African Queen*, he was correct when he exclaimed to Katharine Hepburn, “Ain’t a thing I can do about it.”

Squamous Epithelium

It’s easy to think of *epithelial cells* as being those that make up the outer layer of the skin (also called the *epidermis*). However, the cells covering the surfaces of our body cavities and internal organs are also classified as epithelial. They protect and demarcate an organ from its external environment. They can also be involved in the trafficking of substances in and out of the organ they surround. Although the very outermost layer of the skin is composed of dead cells easily dislodged, just below this is a flat and thin layer of cells called the *squamous epithelium* (Figure 9.7). This type of tissue, also found lining the walls of the capillaries and the peritoneal

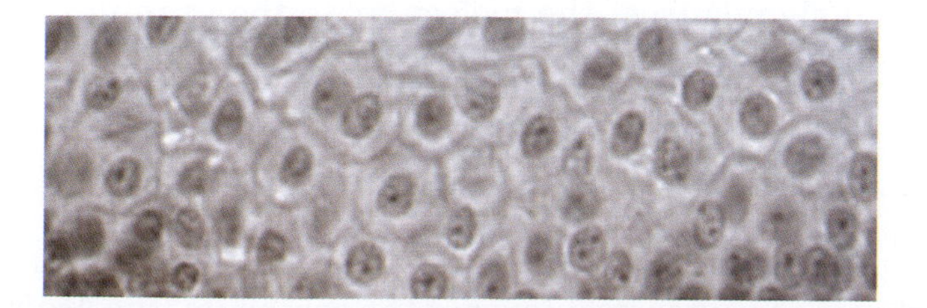

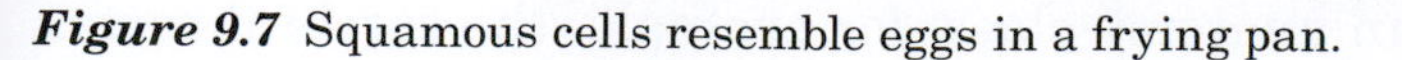

Figure 9.7 Squamous cells resemble eggs in a frying pan.

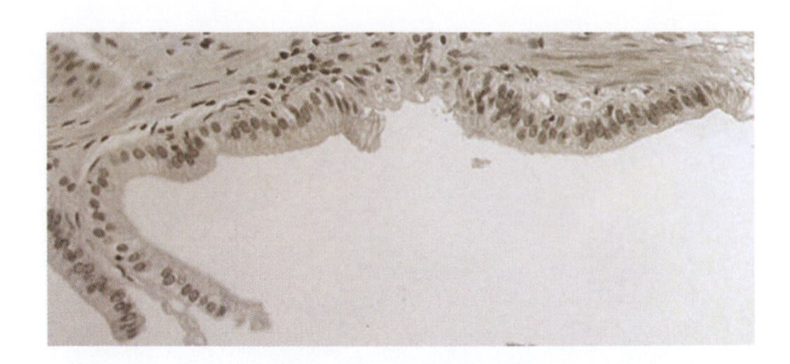

Figure 9.8 Columnar epithelium cells are almost rectangular and have the appearance of columns as shown here in a section of villi from the small intestine.

cavity, resembles many eggs cracked in a frying pan. They have a centrally located prominent nucleus and an irregular outline.

Columnar Epithelial Cells

Epidermal cells lining the intestine, stomach, fallopian tubes, and gallbladder have a column-like appearance and are called *columnar epithelium* (Figure 9.8). In the intestine, they function to pass nutrients to the blood in the process of absorption. Within their ranks, *goblet cells* can be found that secrete a protective mucous onto the tissue's surface that lubricates and prevents tissue damage from the enzymes that digest food. Under the microscope, the nuclei of columnar epithelial cells are oblong and are typically positioned at the base of the cells.

Cerebellum

If you place your hand at the back of your head where your skull meets your neck, you will have localized that part of the brain called the *cerebellum*. Latin for *little brain*, the cerebellum plays a critical role in coordination and motor control (body movement). The cerebellum is linked by many neural pathways to that part of the brain called the cerebral motor cortex that is responsible for sending the electrochemical signal to the skeletal muscles to move. The cerebellum is also involved in your ability to focus on an activity and in the processing of music and language.

Under the microscope, the cerebellum shows several characteristic features (Figure 9.9). The darker area seen in this photograph is the *granule cell layer*. Granule cells are small neurons, which, in the granular layer, are very densely packed and account for more than half of all neurons in the entire brain. *Axons*, very delicate threadlike fibers that transmit nerve impulses, ascend from the granule cell layer into the *molecular layer* (the less dense area in the upper left and lower right corners of this figure). The molecular layer has far fewer cells than the granular layer but is filled, primarily, with the many intertwining axons extending from the granule cells. Large neurons called *Purkinje cells* bridge these two layers and carry electrical signals from the molecular to the granular layer, which then transmits that signal on to the body. A close-up of the Purkinje cells is shown in Figure 9.10. These cells have long, branched fibers called dendrites that transmit the electrochemical signal of a nerve impulse.

Cerebral Cortex

The cerebral cortex is the outermost layer of the cerebrum (the *brain*). When a brain is preserved, as it would be for an anatomy class, for example, the cerebral cortex

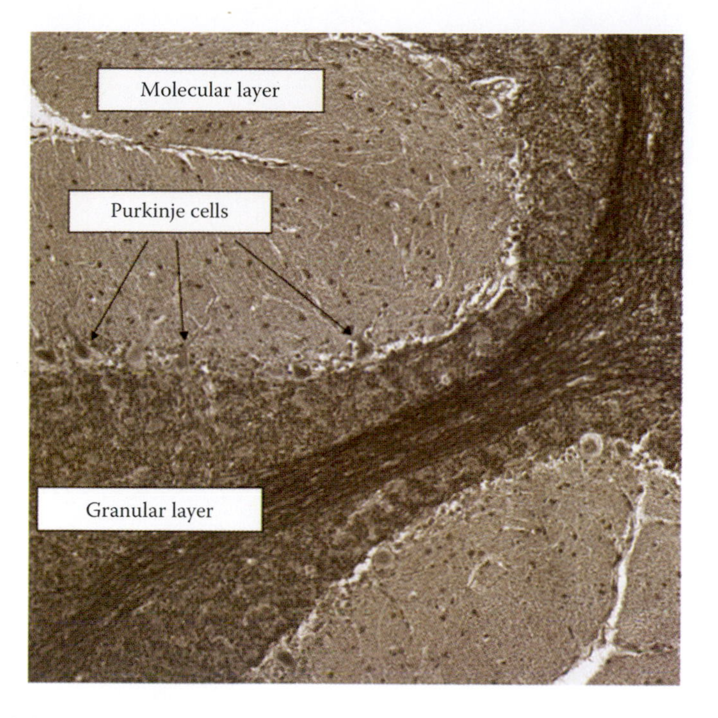

Figure 9.9 Cells of the cerebellum.

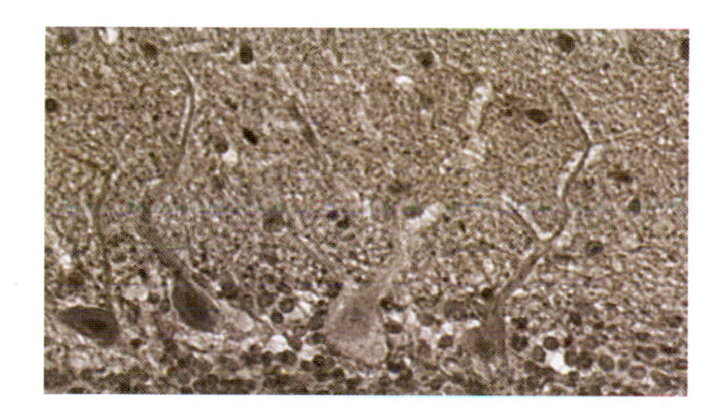

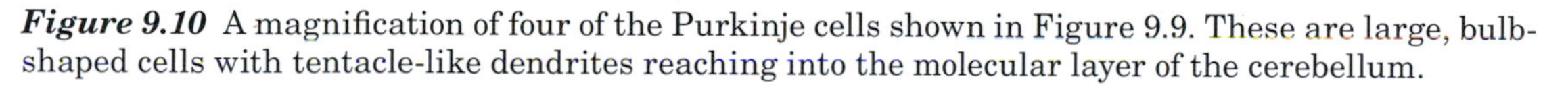

Figure 9.10 A magnification of four of the Purkinje cells shown in Figure 9.9. These are large, bulb-shaped cells with tentacle-like dendrites reaching into the molecular layer of the cerebellum.

takes on a gray color. From this artifact of preservation, this part of the brain is often referred to as *gray matter*. It functions in the processes of memory, thought, speech, vision, muscle movement, learning, and consciousness. The majority of the cerebral cortex is composed of neuron cells and their interwoven axons. The nuclei of these cells appear scattered randomly at a low density throughout the tissue (Figure 9.11).

Cerebrum

When most people refer to the *brain*, they, in fact, are referring to the cerebrum, that part of the brain that controls many of the unique human thought processes including speech, language, learning, and our social behaviors. It also controls the decisions to make movement. For example, the decision to lift this book from where it's lying on the desktop and to place it on your lap originates in the

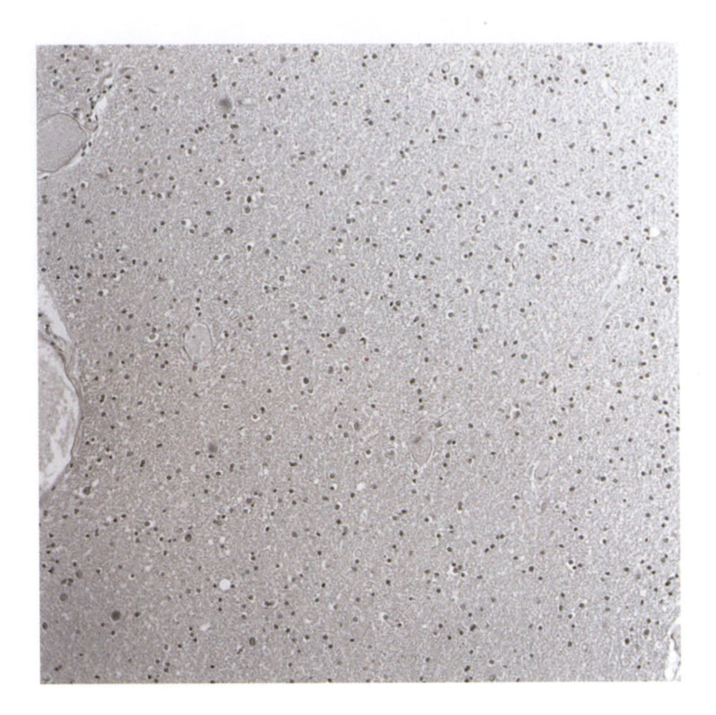

Figure 9.11 Cells of the cerebral cortex.

cerebrum, which then sends the proper motor commands to the correct muscles to accomplish the task.

Under the microscope, the cerebrum shows scattered nuclei and a very delicate mesh of neural axons barely visible at low magnification (Figure 9.12). Depending on the particular slice of tissue, it might be possible to see a granular layer and a molecular layer of neural cells as seen in cerebellum tissue. However, the demarcation

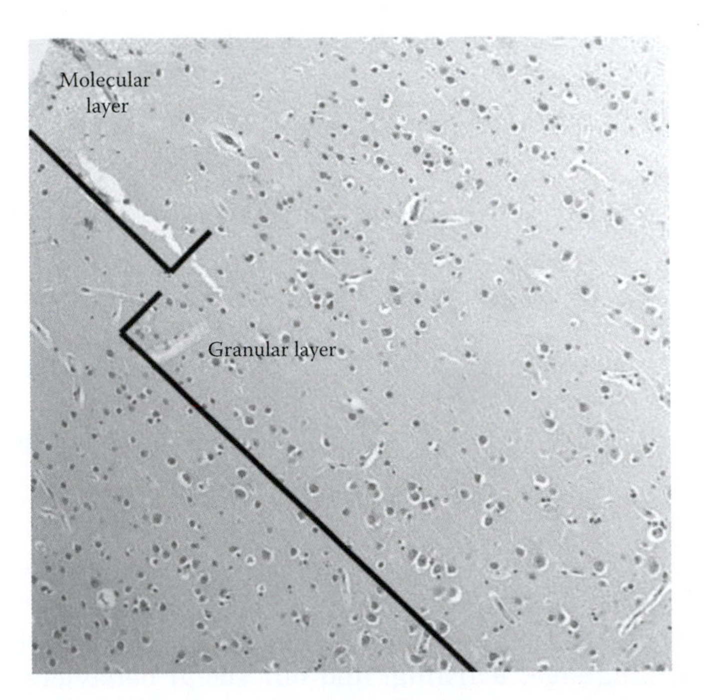

Figure 9.12 Tissue of the cerebrum showing the demarcation between the molecular and granular layers.

between the two layers in the tissue from the cerebrum is far less dramatic and there are no Purkinje cells.

Adipose

Fat, also known as *adipose*, is a unique kind of tissue providing insulation, energy storage, and protective padding for the organs. Under the microscope, adipose cells (called *adipocytes*) look like cobblestones (Figure 9.13). The nuclease and cytoplasm appear to be pushed to the periphery as almost all space within the cell is dedicated to holding fat. Since adipose is so jellylike, the cells are given support by a fine mesh of collagen fibers woven between the cells. Adipose tissue is found beneath the skin, in the bone marrow, between muscles, within the intestinal area, and around the heart. Its primary function is to store the triglycerides that can be converted to energy as needed.

Compact Bone

The tibia, fibula, femur, and all other bones of the skeletal system must support the weight of the body that gravity gives it. Bone tissue, called *compact bone*, is made up of cells called *osteocytes* (mature bone cells). These cells regulate the deposit of calcium salts within the bone *matrix*—an array of concentric ring structures called *lamellae* surrounding an opening called the *Haversian canal* (Figure 9.14) through which nerve cells and blood vessels are channeled. Calcium salts, along with the molecule collagen, help give compact bone its rigidity and strength.

Liver

The liver is the body's largest internal organ. As part of the digestive system, it produces enzymes and other compounds (such as *bile*) needed to break down food. In addition, it stores glycogen (a derivative of sugar and a source of energy), breaks

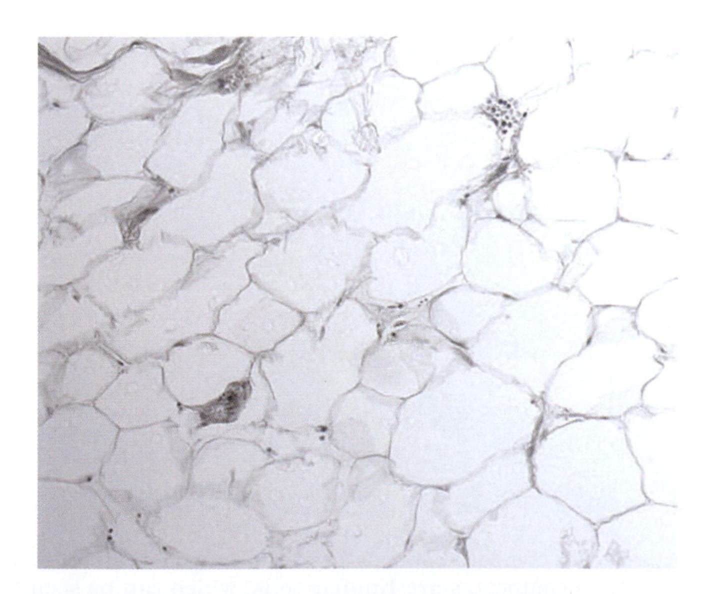

Figure 9.13 The cells of adipose tissue appear almost devoid of internal features other than a nucleus shoved up against the cell membrane.

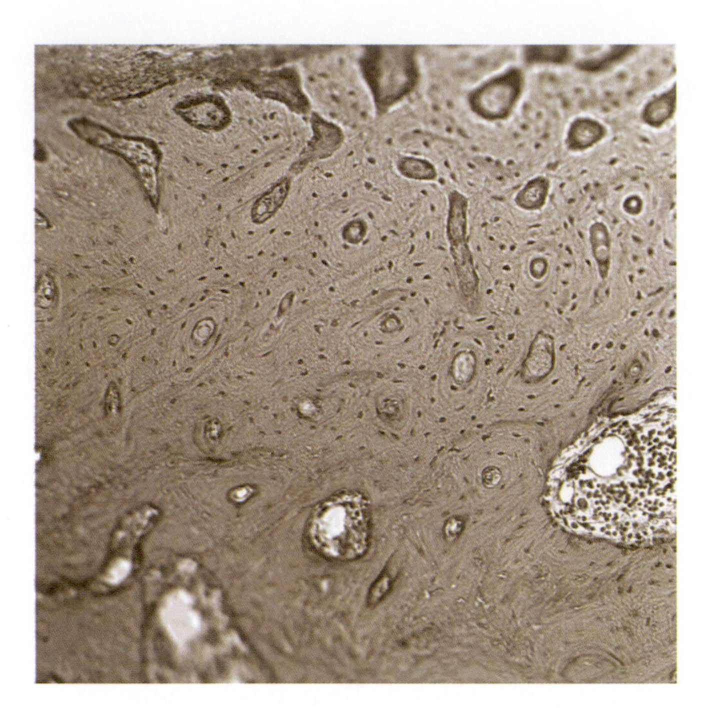

Figure 9.14 Compact bone appears to be a network of swirling cells.

down red blood cells for recycling, synthesizes plasma proteins, aids in the detoxification of harmful molecules, and manufactures hormones.

The primary cells of the liver are epithelial cells called *hepatocytes*. They have a large, circular, centrally located nucleus. A fraction of the hepatocytes are binucleated—they have two nuclei. Many of the liver's hepatocytes are arranged in rows called hepatic plates (Figure 9.15). Interspersed with the hepatocytes are cells

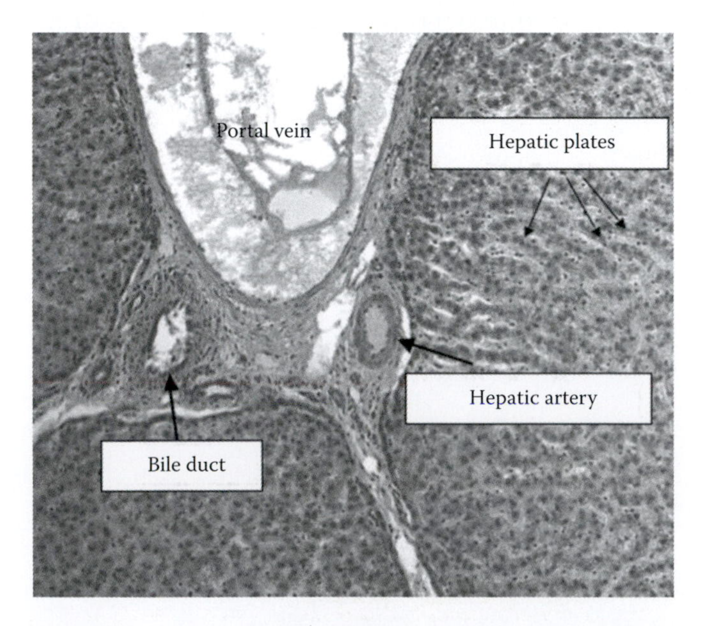

Figure 9.15 Much of the liver is composed of hepatocytes arranged as strings of cells called hepatic plates. Interspersed with the hepatocytes are Kupffer cells, which can be seen as the smaller dark dots (and seen in closer detail in Figure 9.16). This figure also shows a portal vein, hepatic artery, and bile duct. Characteristically, these three features occur together.

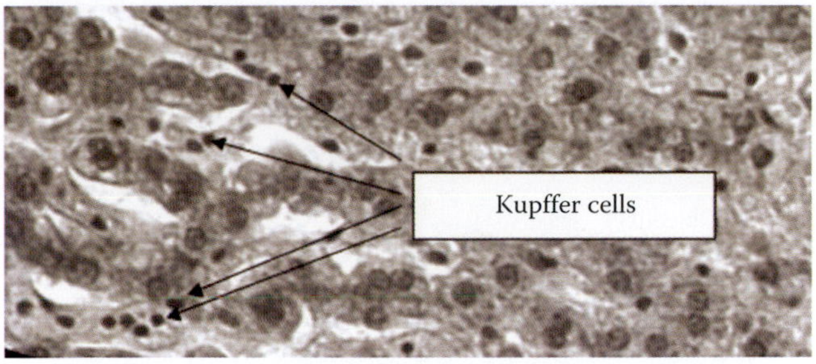

Figure 9.16 Liver cells as magnified from a section of Figure 9.15. The Kupffer cells are the small dark dots in this photograph.

called *Kupffer cells* (Figure 9.16), a type of *macrophage* whose function in the liver is to break down aged red blood cells and to destroy any invading microbes.

Lung

The lung is the organ through which, during the process of *respiration*, oxygen from the atmosphere is absorbed into the bloodstream and carbon dioxide is released back out. This gas exchange occurs at thin-walled hollow cavity structures called *alveoli* (alveolus, singular) honeycombed throughout the tissue (Figure 9.17). The alveoli are surrounded, often times, by only a single layer of squamous epithelial cells.

Compound Microscope

There isn't a more essential piece of equipment in a histology laboratory than the compound microscope. Without it, the human eye cannot possibly discern the characteristics of a cell that make it possible to assign it to a particular type of tissue. Figure 9.18 shows the compound microscope's major components.

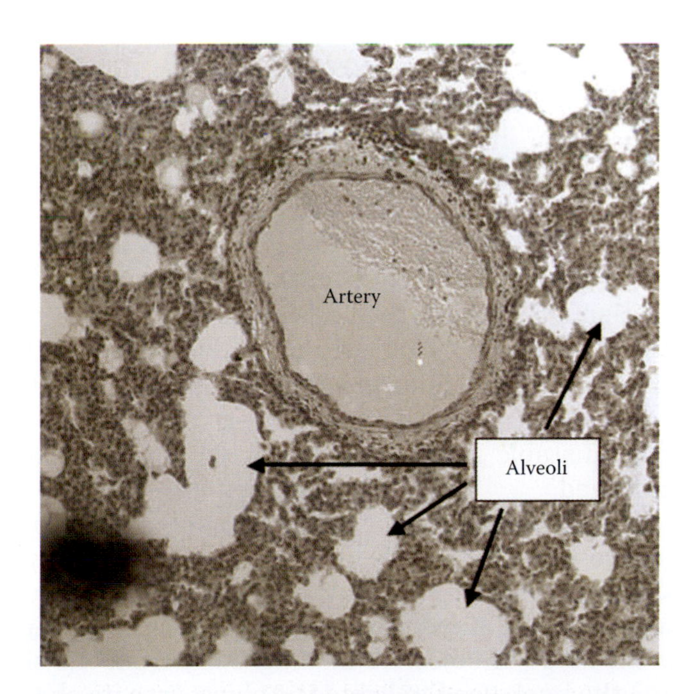

Figure 9.17 Lung tissue is made of squamous epithelium cells in thin layers around alveoli where blood exchanges carbon dioxide for oxygen during the process of respiration. The large circular structure in the center of this photograph is an artery.

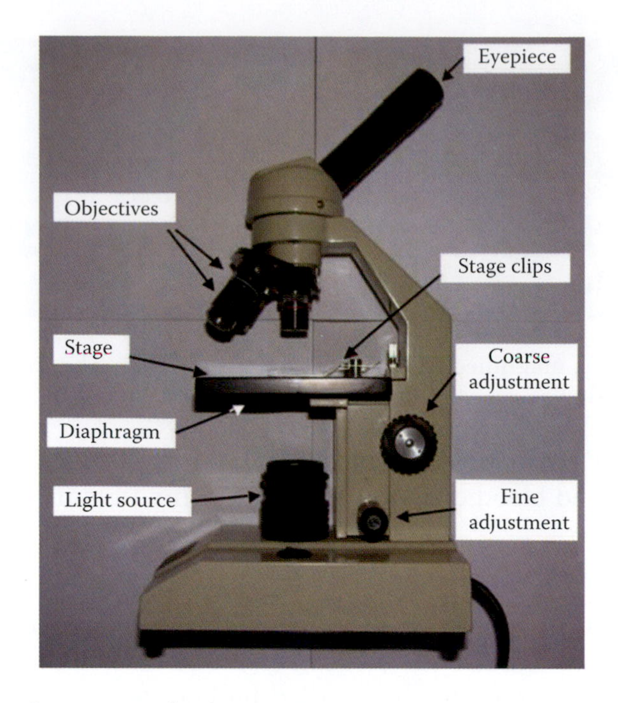

Figure 9.18 The parts of a compound microscope.

The compound microscope has several components.

Eyepiece—used to observe the object under examination. For most microscopes, the eyepiece carries a 10× lens. The degree of magnification is equal to the power of the lens within the eyepiece multiplied by the power of the objective lens. For example, if the eyepiece provides a magnification of 10× and the objective lens provides a magnification of 4×, the overall magnification is 40× (10× × 4× = 40×).

Objectives—a system of different lenses providing degrees of magnification. Most compound microscopes are equipped with a turret of three different lens systems providing levels of magnification at 4×, 10×, and 40× (or similar levels). The lowest magnification is usually used to locate points of interest within the object being examined. Once a feature of interest has been located, the operator will swing the objective lens turret to a higher magnification for more detailed examination. When moving the objectives from a lower power to a higher power, the object being viewed should be in the center of the field. When moving from low power (4×) to medium power (10×), the stage should be viewed from the side to ensure that the new objective coming into position does not hit the slide on the stage.

Stage—the platform on which the object is placed for viewing. That object almost invariably is mounted on a glass microscope slide, which is held in place by *stage clips*.

Diaphragm—the adjustable opening that directs light from the *light source* onto the object being examined.

Coarse adjustment—the knob used for initial focusing. After the object is secured to the stage of the microscope and before viewing it through the eyepiece, the coarse adjustment knob should be rotated so that the low power objective (4×) is positioned at minimum distance from the stage. This will ensure that the direction during the focusing phase has the stage or objective moving away from the slide.

Fine adjustment—the knob used to bring the object into its sharpest focus. When viewing is performed under medium or high power, only the fine adjustment should be used to focus the viewing area.

In the Crime Lab

Activity 9.1 Determining the Diameter of a Microscope's Field of Display

This activity will ask you (1) to know terms, function, and manipulation of a compound microscope and (2) to determine the diameter of the low-, medium-, and high-power field of vision.

Materials:

Compound microscope
Clear flat translucent plastic metric ruler
Calculator

Protocol:

1. The compound microscope is a delicate, precision instrument. Before starting, make sure you are properly instructed on its parts, function, handling, and operational use.

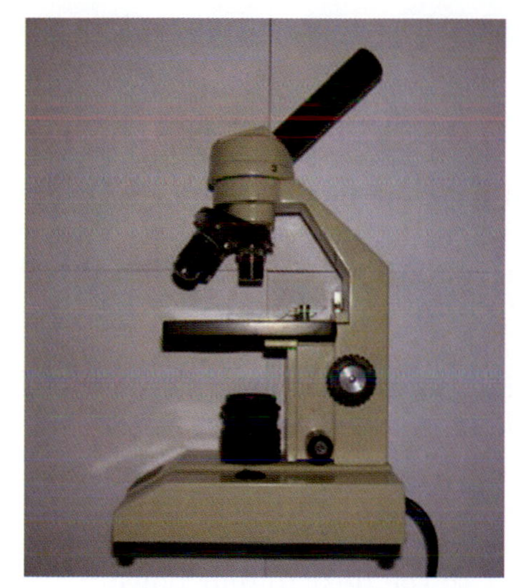

2. Set the microscope on its lowest objective. This is the shortest lens and is usually marked with "4×" or with a red ring around its circumference. Rotate the coarse adjustment dial so that the objective is at minimum distance from the stage.

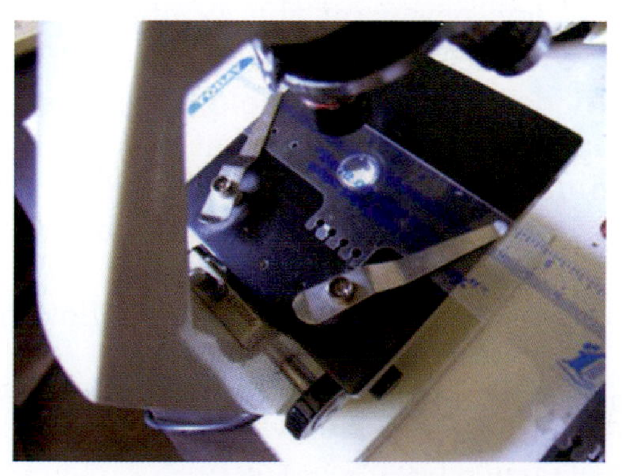

Note: During the focusing operation, the stage and objective will be moving away from the each other.

3. Place the flat translucent plastic ruler on the microscope stage so that the metric tick marks are centered over the stage's light portal.
4. While looking through the eyepiece, use the coarse adjustment to bring the ruler into focus. If necessary, turn the fine adjustment dial to achieve better focus.

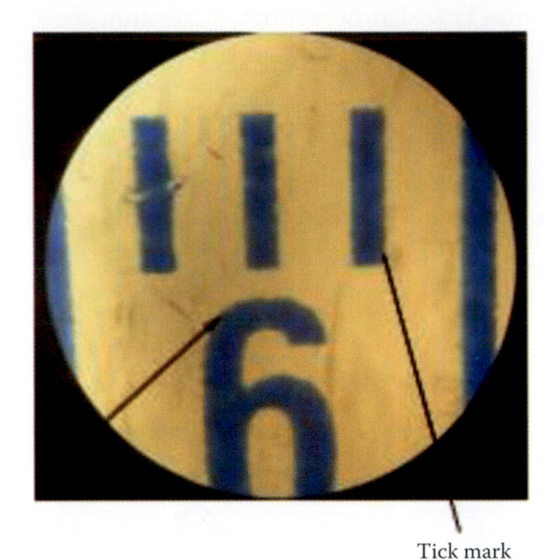

Tick mark

5. When the ruler is in focus, adjust its position so that one of the major tick marks is lined up with the left-hand margin of the field. Estimate the diameter (in mm) of the field at low power and record this value in your laboratory notebook.
   Note: Most likely, the right-hand margin of the field of view will fall somewhere between the tick marks (the next tick mark over will be out of the field of view). Slowly slide the ruler back and forth between the rightmost tick marks to estimate (interpolate) where the right-hand margin falls between them, for example, at 0.25, 0.50, or 0.75. The measurement might be, therefore, for example, 4.25, 4.50, or 4.75 mm.
6. Rotate the lens turret to the next higher power (that's usually a 10× objective). The higher magnification will reduce the field of display to the point where it will be more difficult to determine the diameter of the field of display. The following process can be used to estimate the diameter of the field of display at the 10× magnification. Suppose you measure the diameter of the field of display at low power (at the 4× objective) to be 3.5 mm. If the next objective is 10×, its field of display will be 0.4 times that obtained at 4× magnification (divide 4× by 10× to yield 0.4 [since $4/10 = 0.4$]). Therefore, if the field of display at 4× is 3.5 mm, at 10×, it will be 1.4 mm (since 0.4×3.5 mm = 1.4 mm).
7. Repeat this process for the next level of magnification.

In your laboratory notebook, provide answers to the following questions.

1. What is the diameter (in mm) of the field of view for the lowest power objective?
2. Express your answer to Question 1 in micrometers (µm) (1 mm = 1000 µm).

3. What is the diameter (in mm) of the field of view under the medium power objective lens? (Show your work and make sure your values have the proper units.)
4. Express your answer to Question 3 in micrometers (μm).
5. What is the diameter (in mm) of the field of view under the highest power objective lens? (Show your work and make sure your values have the proper units.)
6. Express your answer to Question 5 in micrometers (μm).
7. What is the relationship between the field of view's diameter and the level of magnification?
8. When moving from a lower power to a higher power, why is it important to have the subject positioned in the center of the field prior to rotating the higher powered objective into position?

Activity 9.2 Estimating the Diameter of a Cheek Cell's Nucleus

Materials:

Compound microscope
10% iodine solution
Eyedropper
Glass microscope slide
Cover slip
Flat wooden toothpick
Calculator

Protocol:

1. Gently slide the wider end of a toothpick back and forth along the inside of your cheek to collect a scraping of epithelial cells. Be careful not to apply too much pressure. You should not be damaging tissue during this exercise.

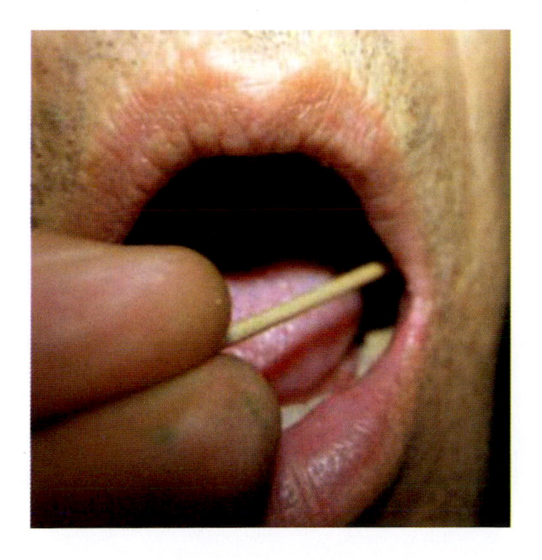

2. Place a drop of iodine solution onto a clean glass microscope slide.

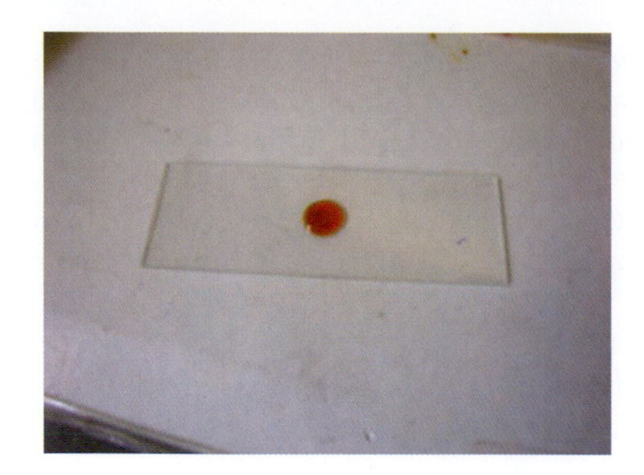

3. Swirl the wide end of the toothpick (carrying the collected cheek cells) several times in the iodine solution. This will release the cells into the solution.

Note: Iodine is used to stain the cells for easier viewing.

4. Cover the iodine cheek cell mixture with a cover slip.

5. Use the stage clips to secure the slide onto the stage of a compound microscope.

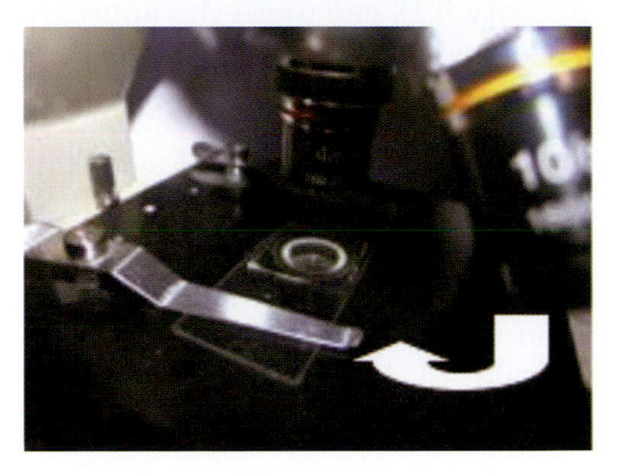

6. Rotate the lowest objective into place (usually marked with a 4×). Before you begin focusing, however, minimize the distance between the slide and the low power objective. (This will ensure that when you start focusing, the objective and the stage will be moving away from each other.)
7. Once you have managed to bring cells into focus under low power, move the slide so that several cheek cells are in the center of the field. Carefully, rotate the medium-powered objective (usually marked 10×) into position over the specimen.

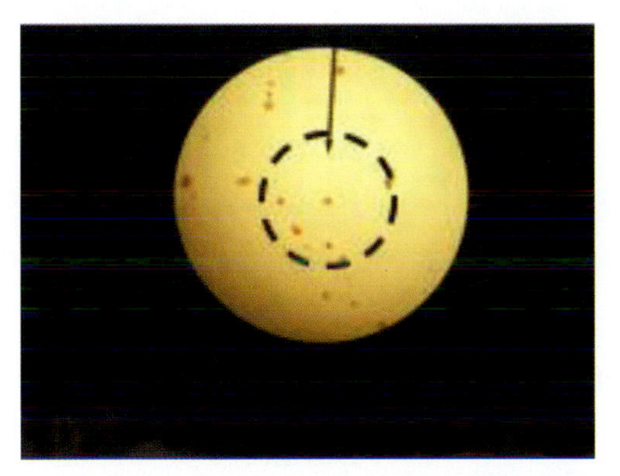

8. Bring the cells into focus using the fine adjustment. Estimate the number of cheek cells needed to span the diameter of the field of view. Record this information in your laboratory notebook.

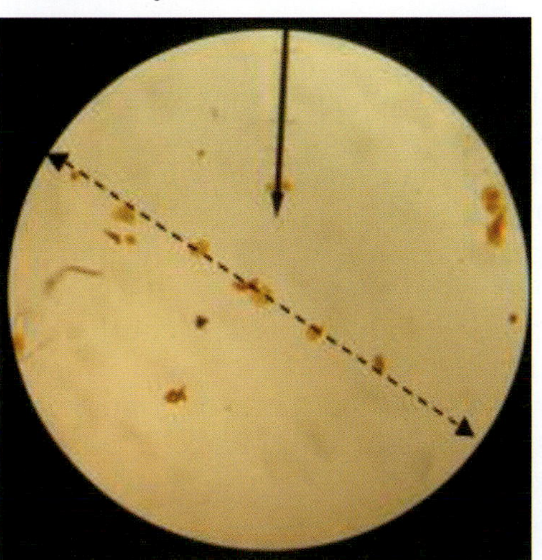

9. Knowing the power of the objective and the diameter (in mm) of the field of view (measured in Activity 9.1), calculate the approximate size of one cheek cell. Record your answer in both mm and in micrometers (microns) in your laboratory notebook.

$$\text{Diameter of one cheek cells} = \frac{\text{Field diameter}}{\text{Number of cheek cells to span field}}$$

10. At either medium or high power, locate a cell with a distinct nucleus (stained with a darker color and usually in the center of the cell). Approximate how many nuclei it would take to span the diameter of the cell in which it is found. Record this information in your laboratory notebook.

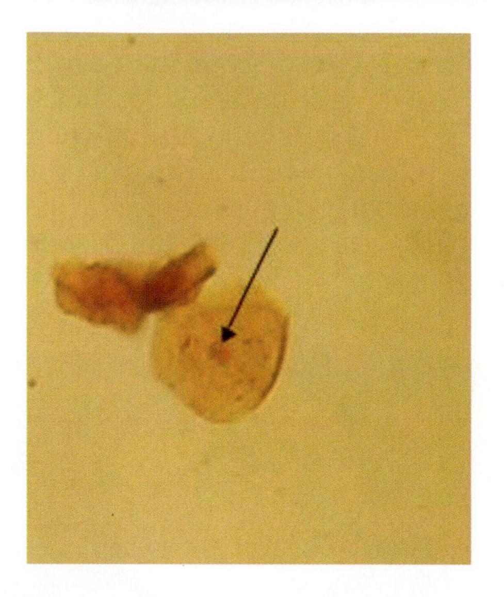

Calculate the approximate diameter of the nucleus and record your result in your laboratory notebook.

$$\text{Nucleus diameter} = \frac{\text{Diameter of one check cell}}{\text{Number of nuclei needed to span cell diameter}}$$

Analysis: Record the answers to the following question in your laboratory notebook.

1. What is the diameter of the field of view when examined under the lowest power objective (4×)?
2. What is the diameter of the field of view when examined under the medium power objective (10×)?
3. How many cells span the diameter of the field of view under the medium power objective (10×)?
4. What is the approximate diameter of one cheek cell? (Show your work and the units of measurement.)
5. Convert your answer to Question 4 into micrometers (μm).
6. How many nuclei span the diameter of a cell?
7. What is the approximate diameter of the nucleus of a cheek cell? (Show your work and the units of measurement.)

8. Convert your answer to Question 7 into micrometers (μm).
9. Convert your answer to Question 7 to meters (1 m = 1,000,000 μm).

Activity 9.3 Estimating the Scale of the Human Genome

We inherit our chromosomes from our parents. Each parent contributes a set of 23 chromosomes to our genetic makeup. Each cell with a nucleus, therefore, carries a set of 46 chromosomes. The human genome, the DNA that makes up our 46 chromosomes, is composed of approximately 6×10^9 bp. In this activity, you will (1) determine how tall a building must be to house a stack of papers on which are written the 6 billion bp of the human genome, (2) estimate the length of the DNA contained in a single cell, and (3) estimate the total length of all the DNA in your body. These calculations should be performed in your laboratory notebook. Be sure to show your work and to assign units to the values you calculate.

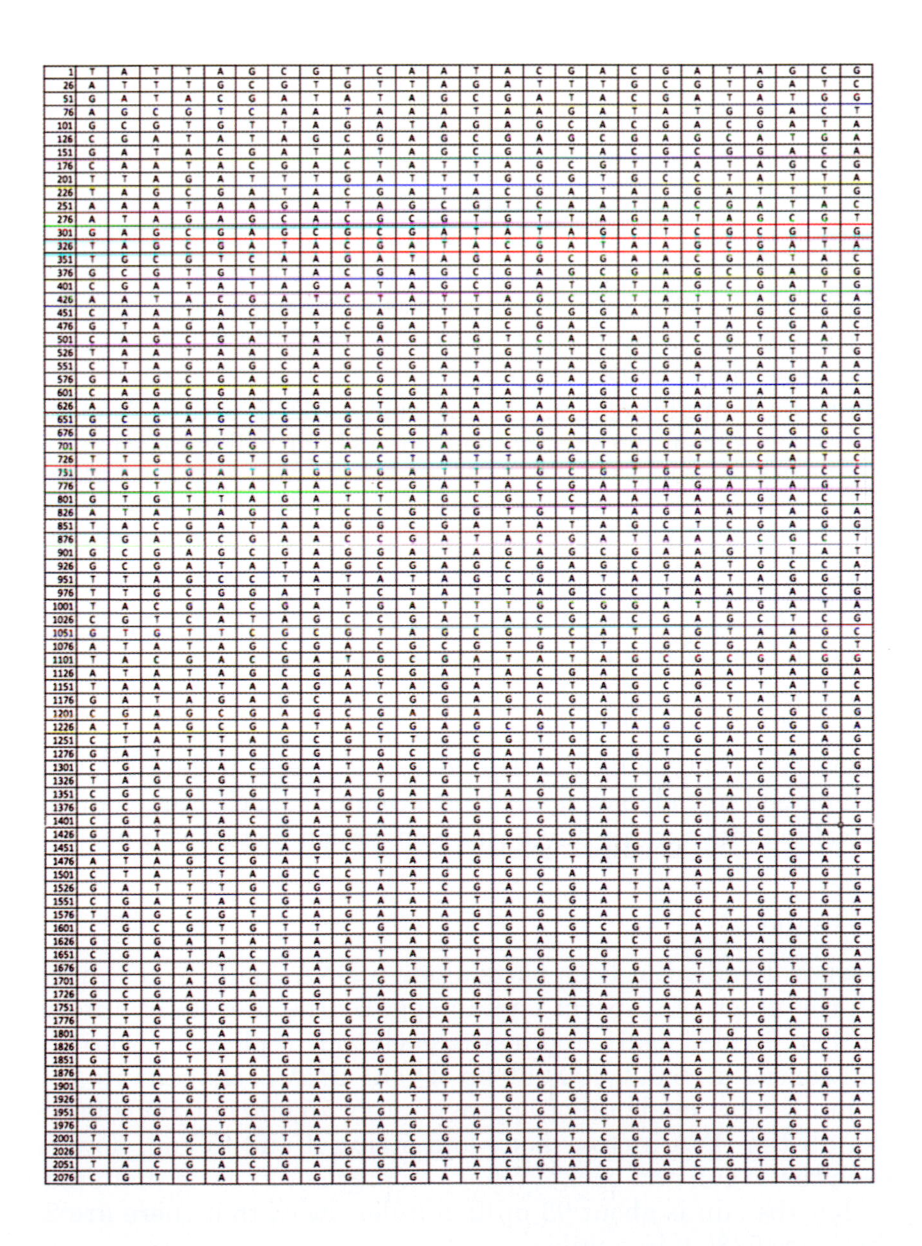

DNA and the Skyscraper

Here, you will determine how tall a building would need to be to house a stack of papers on which are written all the bases of the human genome.

1. Count the total number of bases written on the previous page. Each base on this page represents a base pair.
2. Determine the total number of pages (formatted like that of the previous page) required to carry the script of 6 billion bp.
3. There are 500 pages in a ream of paper. Determine how many reams of paper would be required to carry the script of the entire human genome.
4. A ream of paper is approximately 2 in. wide. Determine how tall (in inches) these reams of paper would be if stacked one on top of the other.
5. How many feet do this represent?
6. Assume one story of a skyscraper is 10 ft tall. How many stories tall would this stack of paper reams be if stacked one on top of the other?
7. How is a cell able to pack this much DNA into the small area of a cell's nucleus?

Length of DNA from a Single Cell

As we will examine in more detail in a later chapter, the base pair of DNA are strung along its chain at regular intervals like building blocks. Because the DNA molecule is so small, however, those distances between the bases are usually expressed in terms of angstroms—a unit used by physicists to measure the wavelengths of visible light. An angstrom is equivalent to 1×10^{-10} m. Only 3.4 Å separate one base pair from the next along the DNA chain.

Given that the human genome, in any somatic cell with a nucleus, contains 6×10^{9} bp, if the DNA from the chromosomes of a single cell were strung end to end, how long would the strand be?

1. How many angstroms long is the human genome?
2. How many meters long is one human genome?
3. Given that there are 2.54 cm in 1 in., how long is the human genome when measured in feet (12 in. = 1 ft)?

Your DNA Stretching to the Sun

Your body is made up of roughly 100 trillion (1×10^{14}) cells. If the DNA from all those cells was strung end to end, how many times would it reach from your classroom to the sun (93 million miles away) and back? Conversion factors you need to know are as follows:

5280 ft = 1 mile

Only 3.4 Å separate adjacent base pairs along a DNA chain. You started as out as a single cell, the union of a sperm and an egg. By the process of mitosis, that cell divided and then divided again and again, each time replicating your DNA so that each new cell carries all 6,000,000,000 bp of your DNA packaged into your 46 chromosomes. You are now made up of approximately 75,000,000,000,000 cells. If you were to take all the DNA in your body and string it end to end, how many times would it reach to the sun and back? (What you may not know is that an angstrom is 1×10^{-10} m, that the sun is about 93 million miles away, that there are 2.54 cm/in., and that there are 5280 ft in a mile.)

Your Genome in the Cell's Nucleus

In Activity 9.2, you calculated the diameter of the nucleus of a cell. Here, you will estimate, by rough approximation, how much area of the nucleus is taken up by the DNA of your genome.

1. Let's assume that the nucleus is a sphere. The volume of a sphere is given by the equation

$$\text{Sphere volume} = \frac{\pi d^3}{6}$$

   where d is the diameter of the sphere and π is the ratio of a circle's circumference to its diameter. We will take π, rounded off, to be equal to 3.14.

   What is the volume of the nucleus you examined? (Convert your diameter value to nanometers [1 nm = 1×10^{-9} m]. Your sphere volume should be in units of nm^3.)
2. We will treat the DNA molecule as if it were a cylinder, 6×10^9 bp in length. The volume of a cylinder is given by the relationship

$$\text{Cylinder volume} = \pi r^2 l$$

   where r is the cylinder's radius (one-half its diameter) and l is its length. Of course, your genome is not a long tube. It must twist and wind itself into a configuration that will allow it to fit within the nucleus. But for this calculation, we can pretend that it is.

   The DNA molecule has a radius of 1 nm. What is the volume of your genome? (Convert the value you obtained for the length of the genome [see previous text] into nm. Your answer for DNA's volume should be in nm^3.)
3. Your DNA takes up what percent volume of the nucleus?

Erica Holmes Missing Persons Case

The following photograph shows *Evidence Item 2* (material recovered from the engine block) under microscopic examination.

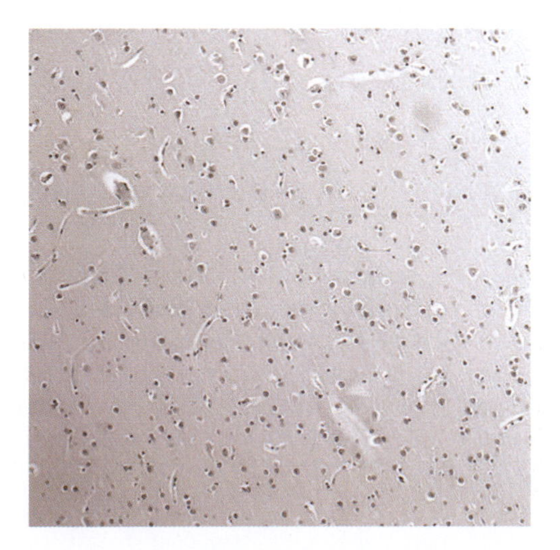

Fill out an evidence report detailing your findings regarding this photograph of Evidence Item 2.

Review Questions

9.1 The study of histology uses what primary piece of equipment?
9.2 A sirloin steak is mostly made up of what type of cell?
9.3 What types of cells have characteristic striations?
9.4 What type of cell lines are the walls of the intestines?
9.5 What structure inside a cell carries the DNA or the organism's genome?
9.6 Are the muscle cells of your biceps voluntary or involuntary?
9.7 Purkinje cells are found in what type of tissue?
9.8 You find a small piece of tissue at a crime scene. Within that tissue, you identify Kupffer cells under microscopic examination. What type of tissue is this?
9.9 In what type of tissue will you find Haversian canals?
9.10 Your body uses what type of tissue to store triglycerides?
9.11 What cells transmit nerve impulses?
9.12 In what type of cell will you find alveoli?
9.13 How is the amount of light that reaches the object on a microscope stage controlled?
9.14 A microscope's eyepiece contains a 10× lens. If looking through a 10× objective, what is the overall magnification?
9.15 If the diameter of the field of display at 4× magnification is 4 mm, what will be its diameter at 10× magnification?
9.16 A microscope, using a specific magnification, has a field diameter of 4 mm. One hundred sixty-seven cells can span that diameter. What is the diameter of one of these cells (in µm)?
9.17 The equivalent of eight nuclei can span the diameter of a cell examined in Problem 16. What is the diameter of the cell's nucleus (in µm)?
9.18 DNA from the nuclei of human cells is to be added end to end in a straight line. How many cells are required to provide enough DNA such that it stretches for one mile?
9.19 How many base pairs would stretch for one mile?
9.20 Let's say that a nucleus has a diameter of 0.005 mm. How long (in nm) would a DNA molecule need to be to completely fill up the nucleus? (Assume the nucleus is a sphere.)

Further Reading

Differences among Species in Compact Bone Tissue Microstructure of Mammalian Skeleton: Use of a Discriminant Function Analysis for Species Identification by Monika Martiniakova, Birgit Grosskopf, Radoslav Omelka, Maria Nondrakova, and Maria Bauerova in *Journal of Forensic Sciences*, Vol. 51, No. 6, pages 1235–1239, 2006.

Differentiating Human Bone from Animal Bone: A Review of Histological Methods by Maria L. Hillier and Lynne S. Bell in *Journal of Forensic Sciences*, Vol. 52, No. 2, pages 249–263, 2007.

A Novel Histological Technique for Distinguishing between Epithelial Cells in Forensic Casework by Claire E.V. French, Cynthia G. Jensen, Susan K. Vintiner, Douglas A. Elliot, and Susan R. McGlashan in *Forensic Science International*, Vol. 178, Issue 1, pages 1–6, 2008.

Histological Determination of the Human Origin of Bone Fragments by Cristina Cristina Cattaneo, David Porta, Daniele Gibelli, and Corrado Gamba in *Journal of Forensic Sciences*, Vol. 54, No. 3, pages 531–533, 2009.

10 Forensic Anthropology

Fisherman's Wharf, Friday, 10:12 AM

Fog hovered over Fisherman's Wharf like a beggar's blanket—cheap and ragged but thick. As Jenkins and Helen made their way down Taylor, a seagull screamed in the distance and the sea lions from Pier 39 barked their reply. The horn from Alcatraz Island moaned at intervals from somewhere to the North behind the mist curtain. Pedestrians along the waterfront seemed to glide like ghosts as they faded in and out through a vale of vapor—merely outlines of images without detail, without substance, and seemingly without purpose.

Jenkins, stepping from the curb onto Jefferson, was nearly clipped by an eastbound tour bus that disappeared like a phantom back into the fog. "Did you get that license plate?" he asked Helen as he climbed back onto the sidewalk.

"It's gone," she replied, unable to find focus on a target that seemed to dematerialize into gray static. "What do ya say we wait for the 'walk' signal this time? Ah, there it is. Now look both ways," Helen cautioned.

"Deja vu," Jenkins said crossing the street.

On the other side of Jefferson, quick-order cooks in stalls lining the sidewalk to their left ladled clam chowder into improvised bowls made from hollowed-out loafs of sour dough round. Soup was on the boil and crabs steamed in their kettles. Tourists posed for photographs beside anything unique. Despite the inclemency, the wharf was still breathing.

"Just smell that!" Helen said to Jenkins. "Isn't that wonderful? I just love seafood."

"Here," Jenkins pointed. "Down this alley."

Passing through a narrow opening between the Nonna Rose Restaurant and Nick's Lighthouse No. 5, they emerged at a railing above a marina lined with boats.

"This way," Jenkins said gesturing to his right toward a large sign on the side of a building that read *Fishermen's Grotto No. 9*. They walked out along a wood-planked dock as waves lapped rhythmically against the pilings and trawlers and purse seiners swayed at their moorings. These boats, in this section of the marina, were the gladiators of the fleet—not the brightly painted sprites that ferried the tourists around the harbor as drinks were served from a tended wet bar. No. These were the tough and rugged boats that had little use for cosmetic façade. Their paint was chipped, their hulls scarred, their rigging hurled everywhere, their cluttered decks warped and stained from the blood of a million mackerel, herring, and salmon. Somehow, strangely, these aging, decaying, crusty maidens of the sea were both repulsive and beautiful at the same time.

"It's freezing," Helen remarked crossing her arms and rubbing her shoulders as she walked along the right side of the dock furthest from the water.

“What do you expect?” Jenkins said, “It’s summer.” He stepped a pace in front of her, turned, and stopped in his tracks. “Wait a moment,” Jenkins said, shaking his jacket from his shoulders.

“I appreciate the gallantry,” she said when she realized what he was doing, “but now your concealed weapon is no longer concealed.”

Jenkins glanced down at his shoulder holster and revolver. “You’re right,” Jenkins sighed. “I guess you’re on your own.” Just then, the silhouette of a person back on the promenade behind Helen caught his attention. His eyes narrowed as if that would give them the power to see through the layers of fog.

“What is it, Lieutenant?” Helen asked when she saw the intent look on Jenkins’ face.

“Do you ever get the feeling, Miss Chang, that you’re being watched?”

“What? Who?” she asked, turning to find the object of Jenkins’ attention and momentarily obscuring his line of site. By the time Jenkins stepped to his side so that he could see around Helen again, the person had withdrawn deeper into the haze and had then disappeared altogether.

“Back at the parking garage and now again here behind us,” Jenkins muttered more to himself than to Helen.

“Whom are you talking about?” Helen asked.

“It’s hard to see anything in this pea soup, isn’t it?”

“Lieutenant?”

Jenkins watched the dock a moment longer but the apparition failed to reappear. “Never mind,” he muttered, “They’re gone. It’s probably nothing. Let’s get on with this.”

“Which boat are we looking for?” Helen asked, sighing in frustration as they resumed their march along the splintered timbers of dock.

“The *Blithe Spirit*,” Jenkins replied.

“This guy said he dragged up a bone while fishing?”

“That’s what he claims. Netting crabs by the Dumbarton.”

“Is it a human bone, Lieutenant?” Helen asked.

“That’s what we need to find out,” Jenkins replied.

They found the *Blithe Spirit*, a rusting excuse for a trawler, moored at the second slip from the end of the dock across from the Fishermen’s and Seamen’s Memorial Chapel. She was tied stern first. A man with a white beard wearing a grimy red parka; a blue watch cap; faded, grease-stained jeans; and black rubber knee-high boots coiled rope on the foredeck. He looked up when they approached and eyed the duo cautiously. The exposed skin of his face was like baked and wrinkled parchment.

“Ahoy there,” Jenkins hollered. “Permission to come aboard?”

“What’s your business?” the man asked.

“Detective Robert Jenkins and Criminalist Helen Chang,” Jenkins replied flicking his billfold open displaying his badge. “You called about a bone you hauled in?”

"Watch your step," the fisherman replied gesturing vaguely to the ladder leading from the dock down to the stern of his boat. "There's a bit of a swell running this morning. Wait for the crest then jump aboard."

"Thank you," Jenkins acknowledged. "After you, Miss Chang."

Grabbing an upper rail of the metal ladder with one hand, Helen swung around and descended. The *Blithe Spirit* rocked along her keel as she jumped onto the deck. Jenkins, arriving at the bottom of the ladder, placed one foot on the boat as she rose on a swell. The stern of the craft fell again before he'd made the transition and was caught straddled between boat and ladder.

"Need a hand?" asked Helen.

"No, no, I can get it," Jenkins replied as his legs began to wishbone at the trough of the swell. "Ah, Miss Chang?" he said trying to sound as calm as he could but still afraid a tone of desperation may have rubbed a tarnish on his veneer.

"Yeah?" Helen replied watching in amusement.

But the next swell began to rise under him and, as both feet were realigned with the horizon, he quickly made the jump to the deck.

"Lieutenant?"

"What?"

"You were going to ask me something?"

"Oh, ah, it's not important," Jenkins said dismissively.

"Here's what ya came for," the fisherman said skirting around the wheelhouse cabin carrying a long thin bone in his fist. He handed it to Jenkins who quickly slipped it into a plastic bag and then rolled it over in his palm several times.

"Where did you bring this in?" Jenkins asked.

"North of the Dumbarton," he replied. "Three days ago. Is it human?"

"It looks to be," Jenkins replied. "Thank you for calling us."

"No problem," the fisherman said. "Careful on the ladder," he muttered as he made his way back to the foredeck.

As Jenkins turned to ascend the ladder, he noticed, once again, the shadowy figure observing them from down the dock. "That did it!" he exclaimed. "Miss Chang, please hold this," he said, handing the bone to Helen as he rushed toward the ladder. Stumbling on the first rung, he regained his footing and climbed the remaining five rungs with no complications. The figure in the distance bolted, running back along the docks toward Jefferson. Jenkins gave chase but he could tell within the first 20 yards he was being outpaced. Huffing, he emerged from the docks onto Jefferson and stopped to catch his breath. Looking to the left. Nothing—pedestrians and cars but no disturbance in the normal flow of traffic. To the right, however, far down the block, he was just able to make out a figure parting the crowded sidewalk like leaves from a leaf blower. He ran, passing an In-N-Out Burger on his left—the irony momentarily coming over him, even then, that it was because of places like that that he wasn't as fleet of foot as perhaps he should otherwise be. Arriving at the bottom of the Aquatic Park amphitheater, he looked up to see his quarry just exiting an aisle at the top of the structure. But that was it for him—he couldn't take another step.

His heart, pounding in his chest, felt like it was being squeezed in a vice. He stopped and braced himself against a post.

"Hold this!" someone yelled behind him. He turned to see Helen rushing toward him. As if it were a baton being passed by a relay runner, she quickly shoved the bagged bone into his palm as she darted up the cement seats of the amphitheater. At the top row, she paused long enough to see the figure of someone at the corner of Beach and Larkin racing up the steps of Ghirardelli Square. The person disappeared into a fog layer as they turned to climb the second flight of stairs. Helen lurched into pursuit. Skipping up the stairway leading to the shops of Ghirardelli, she came to a sudden stop at Fountain Plaza. The area was crowded with tourists. No one looked more out of place than any other. A few were sitting on the edge of the fountain of the two mermaids. Shoppers came and went from the novelty shops. No one appeared to be panting from exhaustion or collapsed along the railing. She scanned the upper level but saw nothing extraordinary—just more tourists milling about. Helen knew this was the end of the line. Whoever it was had gotten away.

Forensic Anthropology

There are over 200 bones in the human body (Figure 10.1). They vary in size from the tiny stirrup bone of the middle ear (measuring only 0.07 in. [1.8 mm] in length) to the femur (measuring 20 in. [50 cm] long). The skeleton accounts for almost 15%

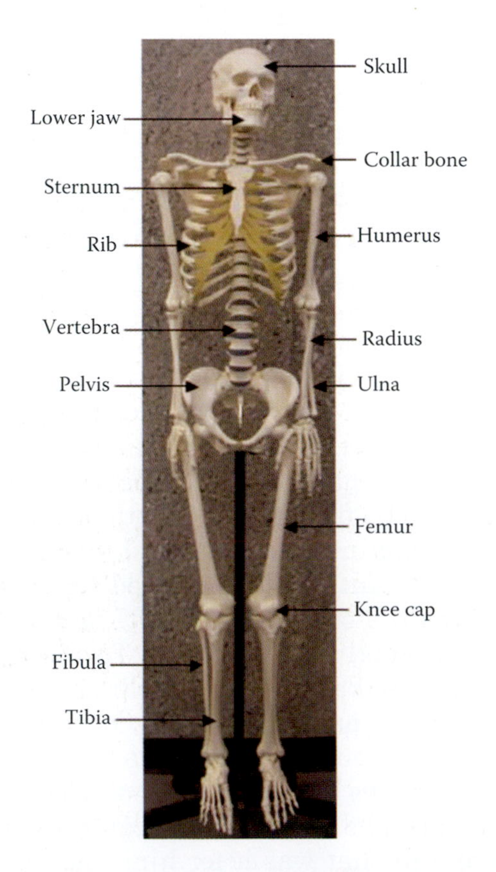

Figure 10.1 The human skeleton is made up of over 200 bones. The largest bones are labeled here.

of a person's weight. As the body's most durable tissue, bones can survive intact for thousands of years.

Forensic anthropology is the study of skeletal remains that are the evidence in a crime or legal dispute. Whether it's solving the mystery of how the young Egyptian pharaoh, King Tutankhamun, met his demise, piecing together the bone fragments of the skeleton found buried in a killer's basement, or making a first determination as to whether or not the bone the woman dug up in her backyard is even of human origin, the forensic anthropologist is a mix of archeologist, medical doctor, zoologist, and weapons expert.

The careful examination of bones can reveal the victim's sex, height, ethnicity, age at death, and the very means by which the life of the deceased was ended. In some cases, it can also give clues to the victim's occupation or lifestyle. The skeletal system of a construction or ironworker may show the effects of hard physical labor. The ballet dancer will show wear to the knees, ankles, and hips. If the forensic anthropologist gets lucky, the bones will reveal the actual identification of the victim by virtue of a unique injury or birth defect documented by medical records (Figure 10.2).

Recovering skeletal remains from any area, whether it's from deserted woods or from the backyard of an urban residence, should be carried out with all the care and attention to detail that any other type of crime scene should command. The area should be cordoned off and access restricted to all but those immediately essential to the investigation. The ground should be carefully sifted and all recovered bone fragments immediately bagged to minimize contamination. Careful notes should be

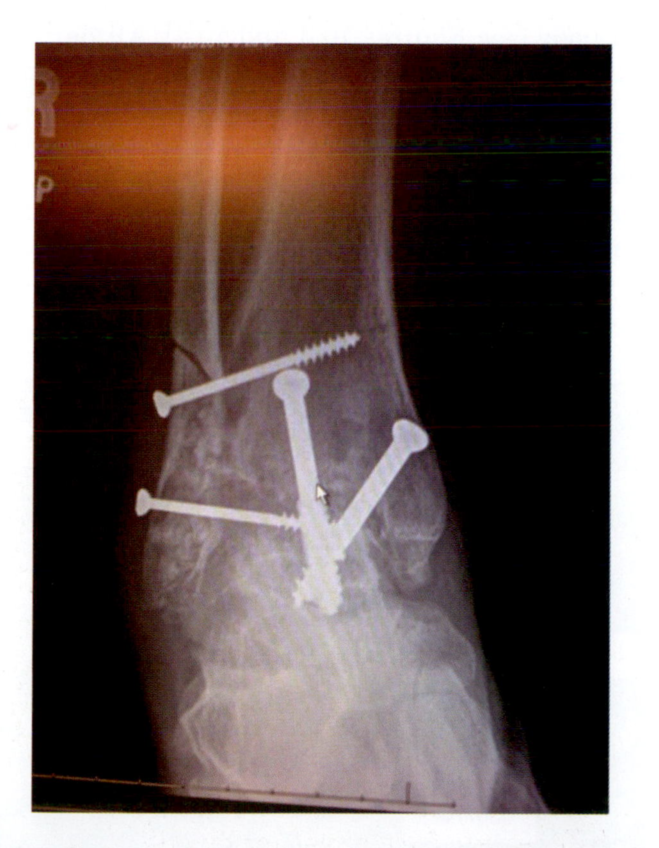

Figure 10.2 Dental or medical records can lead to a positive identification of a victim if the bones reveal characteristics unique to an individual. A broken bone, arthritis, or other injury, disease, or condition can aid in making a positive ID. This ankle of a gymnast under x-ray shows a unique and lasting medical intervention.

taken as to the conditions of the find, and the containers holding the bones should be marked immediately as to the location where they were discovered.

Determining a Victim's Age by Skeletal Remains

Interestingly, not all people have the same number of bones. The typical adult contains 206 bones. A newborn baby, on the other hand, has roughly 300. A baby's bones, however, in a predictable and well-characterized way, fuse to one another as the child grows. This process is called *ossification* and occurs as cartilage, that flexible, bone-like material found most often between bones hardens to connect one bone to another. Then, much later in life, as a person ages, their joints wear down, cartilage becomes thinner, and *osteoarthritic lipping* (the formation of a liplike bone mass at the edge of a joint) increases. Knowing these processes and at what times during development they occur can help the forensic anthropologist estimate the age of a homicide victim at their time of death.

A victim's age can also be estimated, of course, by their height. As a normal human being ages, they will increase in height in a predictable way. By the time a person has reached their 20s, they will have reached their maximum height. Much later in life, a person's stature will even decrease as osteoporosis and compression of the spine (caused by the constant assault of gravity) take their toll.

Bones of the Skull

As are all parts of the body, the different areas of the skull are defined by their orientation to the erect body (see Figures 10.3 and 10.4). All parts of the skeletal system are denoted in the same manner, and these directions and planes are described in Table 10.1.

The bones of the skull are responsible, in large part, for the features of the face. The teeth, the *zygomatic bone* (cheek bone), and the *mandible* (chin bone) all contribute to our outward facial appearance. What can be striking about the human skull is the apparent lack of a nose. Most of that feature, however, is made of cartilage, which will decompose more quickly than bone. All that's left of the ear is the

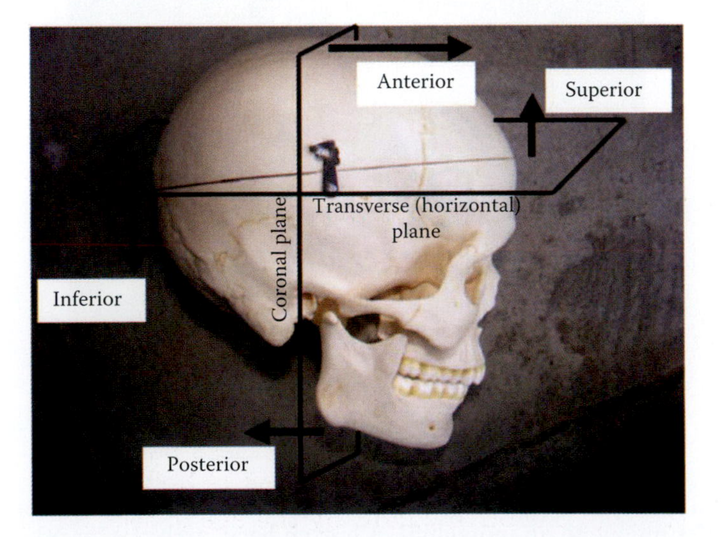

Figure 10.3 The directions and planes of the human skull. Anterior refers to the front, posterior to the rear, inferior to the below, and superior to the above.

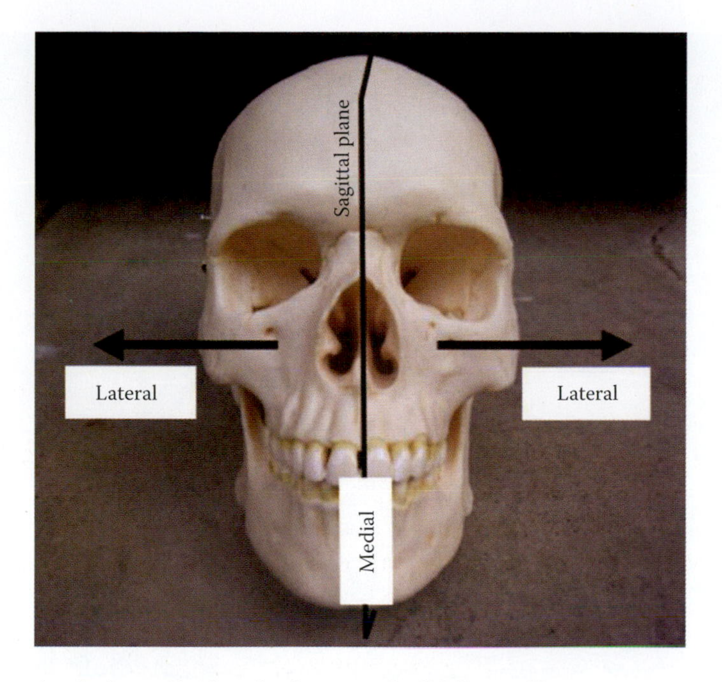

Figure 10.4 The sagittal plane divides the human skull bilaterally.

TABLE 10.1
Directions and Planes Used to Describe the Locations of Bones of the Skeletal System

Anterior	The front part of the body
Coronal	The plane that divides the body into front and back halves
Distal	Furthest from the body's trunk
Inferior	Lower than another point
Lateral	Away from the body's midline
Medial	Point lying closest to the body's midline
Posterior	Closest to the back of the body
Proximal	Closest to the body's trunk
Sagittal	The plane that divides the body into left and right halves
Superior	The higher point
Transverse	The plane that divides the body at the waist into upper and lower halves
Palmar	Relating to the palm of the hand
Plantar	Relating to the sole of the foot

external acoustic meatus, the external opening of the ear canal (Figure 10.5). Again, the ear owes its shape to cartilage.

The *cranium* protects the brain. What looks to be made of a single bone (excluding the mandible) is actually some twenty-seven bones knitted together forming structures called *cranial sutures*. The larger of these bones, the *frontal*, *occipital*, and *parietal* bones (Figure 10.5), are unconnected at birth allowing for easier passage of the child through the birth canal. By the age of two, however, the bones of the cranium, including the *temporal* bone forming the lower part of the braincase on the left and right side, come together and get sealed at their sutures. The sutures

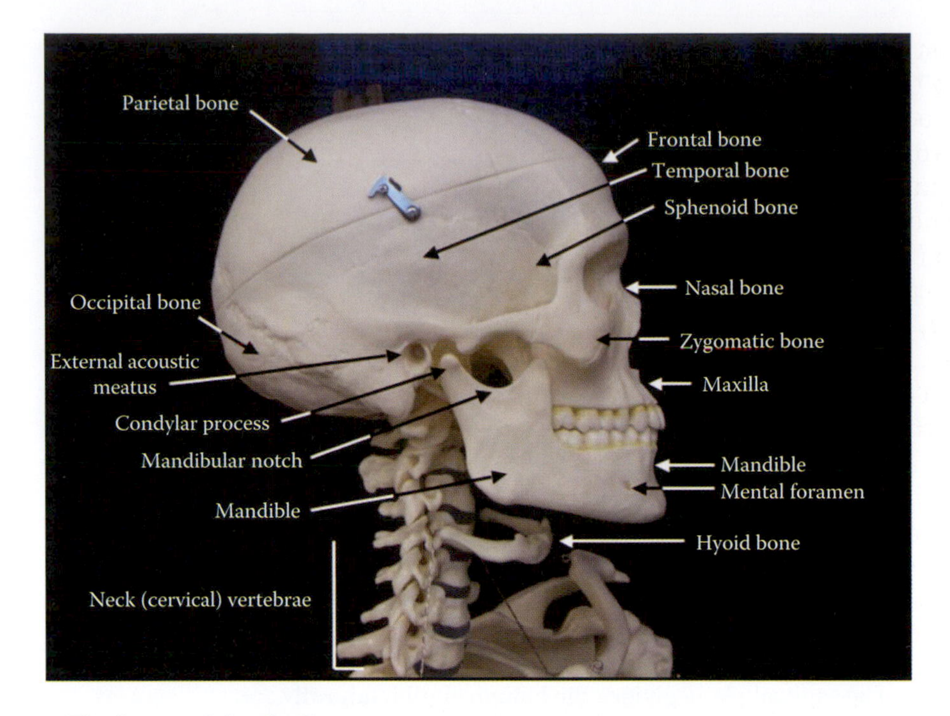

Figure 10.5 The bones of the skull.

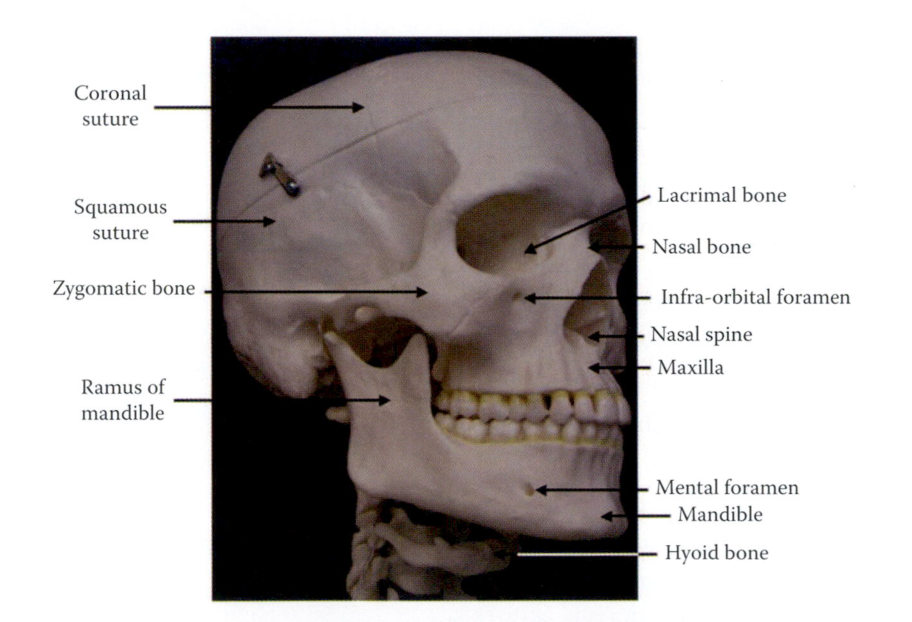

Figure 10.6 The bones and features of the human skull.

don't become completely fused, however, until after 40 years of age (the coronal and squamous sutures are identified in Figure 10.6). The age of a victim, therefore, can be estimated by the state of the cranial sutures.

The frontal, parietal, and temporal bones attach to the *sphenoid* bone that helps to connect the cranial and facial bones. The *frontal* bone gives shape to the forehead. The right and left *zygomatic* bones form the lateral walls of the eye sockets and give shape to the cheeks. The *maxilla* is the bone below the eye sockets around and below the nose that gives further shape to the cheeks and to the upper jaw. Within the front, inner wall of each eye socket is the *lacrimal* bone (Figure 10.6), the thinnest and most fragile bone of the human face. It functions to allow tears to pass from the eye into the nasal passage.

The occipital bone at the back and base of the skull has a large opening called the foramen magnum where it meets the neck. This opening allows the passage of the spinal nerves into the brain.

Of the bones that comprise the cranium, the *mandible* and teeth are the most durable (Figures 10.5 and 10.6). So much so, in fact, that these are the bones most often recovered by the paleontologists looking for fossils of our long-ago ancestors. At birth, the mandible is separated at the chin into two halves. By one year of age, however, the mandible has fused into a single piece.

From personal experience, no doubt, most people will have a pretty good idea of how teeth can indicate age. Though 32 teeth are found in the adult human (barring accident or the intervention of a dentist), that number can vary depending on age. By the time a person reaches their teenage years, they have lost their *deciduous* (baby) teeth and their permanent teeth have grown in. The two incisors (the front teeth) and first molars have grown in by age 7. During the following year, the second incisors will have grown in. By age 10, a person will have their first premolars and their canines by age 11 followed by the second premolars. The wisdom teeth (the third molars) will start to break the surface during the teenage years and, if they do not become impacted and are not surgically removed because of it, they should be completely in place by age 25.

Just below the mandible near the upper part of the neck is the *hyoid bone* (Figures 10.6 and 10.7). The hyoid bone is the only bone in the human body that does not directly attach to any other bone. Its function is to provide support to the tongue. You can feel the hyoid bone by placing your thumb and forefinger on the neck under the lateral sides of the mandible and by applying gentle pressure. This bone is almost always broken during strangulation and should be examined during autopsy for any signs of trauma. In children, the hyoid is made from three segments that fuse into a single bone during adulthood.

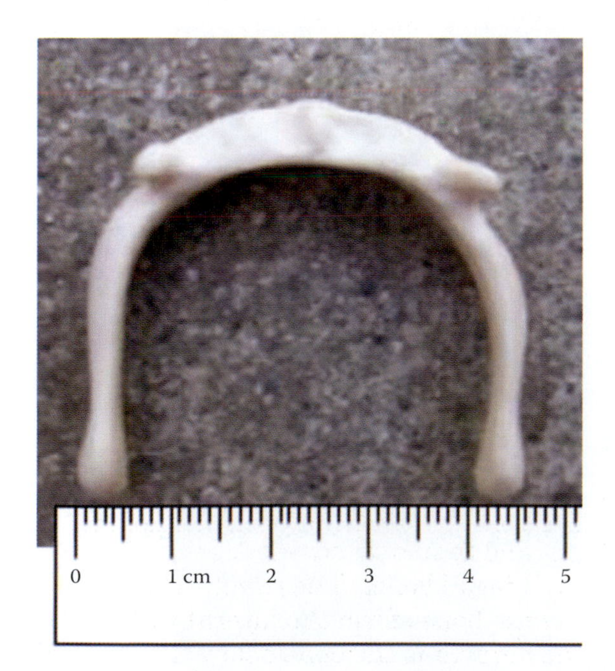

Figure 10.7 The hyoid bone is horseshoe shaped. This photograph shows the bone from the transverse, superior perspective.

Bones of the Upper Torso

The bones of the upper torso have the responsibility of protecting the vital organs that include the heart, lungs, and liver while also providing the strength and agility needed for locomotion and an upright stance. At the uppermost part of the torso, above the first rib, is the clavicle, which, along with the scapula, forms the shoulder (Figure 10.8). The clavicle connects the upper arm to the trunk of the body, and because it is close to the skin, it can be easily seen and felt. Being unprotected by muscle, the clavicle is prone to breaks and injuries particularly among athletes engaging in rough contact sports or those who suffer frequent traumatic falls. The clavicle exists as two bones at birth. However, by age 30, the bones have fused together at the sternum at the center of the chest.

Below the clavicle is the *rib cage* composed of 12 ribs on each side of the body. The upper 10 ribs attach to the *sternum* (breastbone) in the front of the chest and to the vertebral column at the back. The 11th and 12th ribs, though attached to the vertebrae at the back, do not attach to the sternum in the front. These two ribs are also known as the *floating ribs*. They are shorter and have ends that appear more pointed than the other ribs.

The *spine* runs the posterior length of the back. Its bones allow for an upright stance and for rotation of the upper torso. The vertebrae of the spine anchor the ribs in place and protect the *spinal cord*, the threads of nerves that run through an opening within each bone of the vertebrae sending electrochemical signals from the brain to the extremities. (A single bone of the vertebrae is referred to as a *vertebra*.)

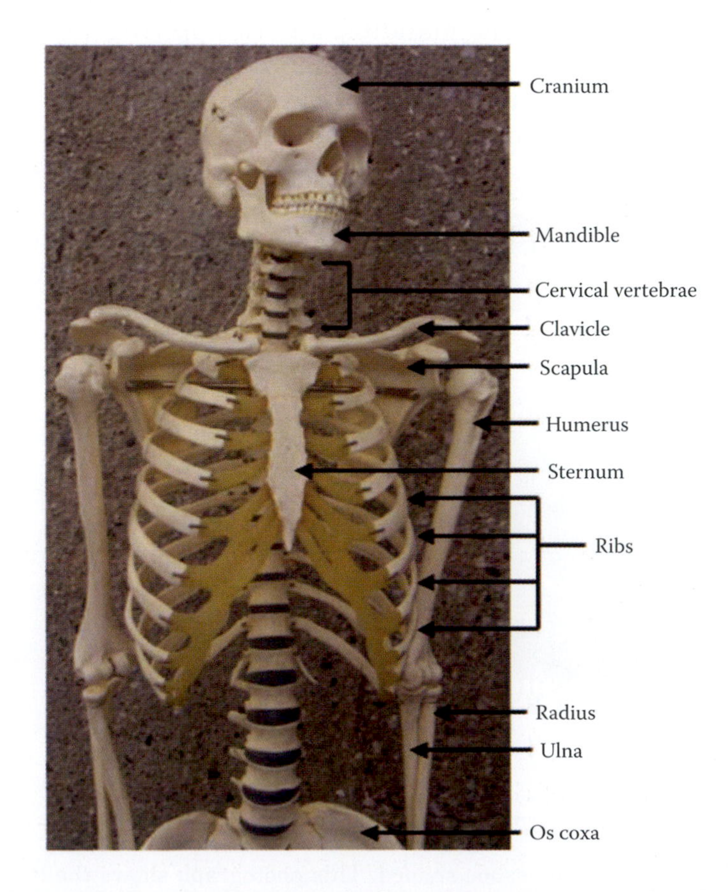

Figure 10.8 The bones of the upper torso include those that protect several of the vital organs.

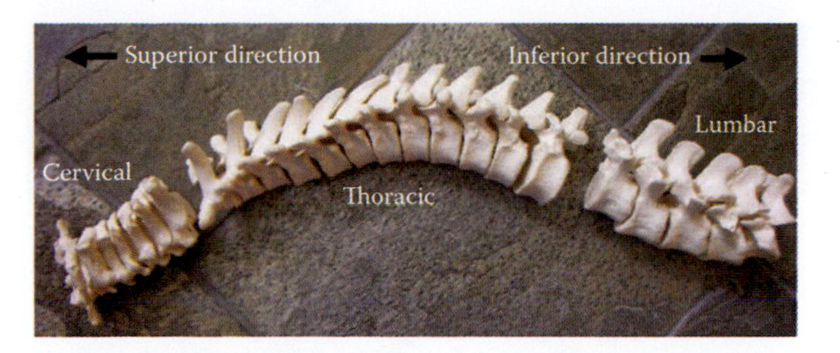

Figure 10.9 A lateral perspective of the left side of a sectioned vertebral column. The left section is the cervical vertebrae, the middle section is the thoracic vertebrae, and the section of bones on the right represents the lumbar vertebrae.

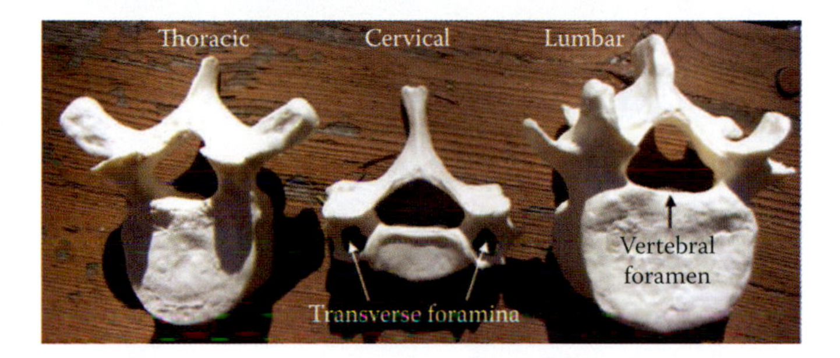

Figure 10.10 A cervical vertebra (center) is smaller than a thoracic (left) or lumbar (right) vertebra. The large, midplane openings in each type of the bone are the vertebral foramen. The thoracic vertebra (left) has a relatively small vertebral foramen when compared to the body of the bone. The thoracic and lumbar vertebrae lack the transverse foramina seen in the cervical vertebrae. This photo is taken from the superior perspective, transverse plane. Lumbar vertebra (depicted on the right) is the largest of the three types.

Humans have 33 vertebrae, 5 of which are fused to form the *sacrum* and 4 (called the *coccygeal bones*) are fused to form the *tailbone* (*coccyx*). The remaining 24 bones are divided into three groups by their location and morphology (Figures 10.9 and 10.10). The seven vertebrae at the top of spine (below the skull) are called the *cervical vertebrae* (Figure 10.10). They provide support to the head and neck. The 12 vertebrae to which the ribs are anchored are called the *thoracic vertebrae*. The five disks below the thoracic vertebrae comprise the *lumbar vertebrae*. Between each vertebra are *disks* made of cartilage that serve as shock absorbers and prevent the vertebrae from grinding against each other.

Each *vertebra* is made of two components, the vertebral body and the structure surrounding the *vertebral foramen*—that part of the bone that houses the spinal cord of nerve tissue extending from the brain to the rest of the body (Figure 10.10). The bumps you can feel running down the length of the center of your back are the spinous process of each vertebra (Figures 10.11 through 10.13).

The cervical vertebrae fit together in a way that allows your head the mobility to tilt up and down and to look right and left. Joint structures called *facets* (Figure 10.13) provide the means by which adjacent vertebra moves against each other and prevent the grinding of bone against bone.

The thoracic vertebrae of the midspine must also provide for some twisting and lateral movement and possess facets of a similar structure to those of the cervical vertebrae (Figure 10.14). The facets of the thoracic vertebrae also provide for articulation with the ribs.

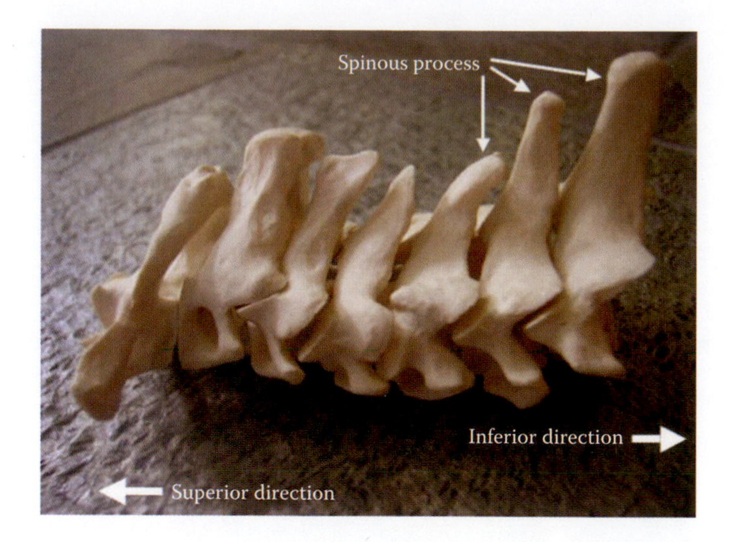

Figure 10.11 The cervical vertebrae showing the spinous process of each vertebra pointed upwards in this photograph.

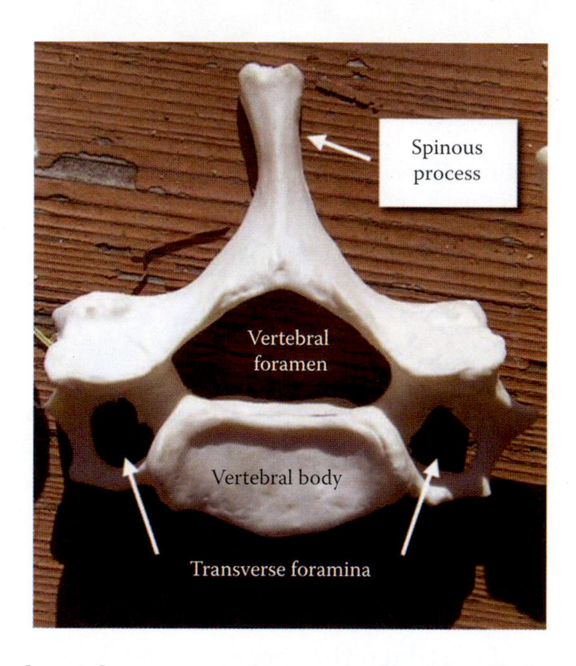

Figure 10.12 The cervical vertebrae possess transverse foramina that provide a conduit for veins, arteries, and nerves. These structures are absent in the thoracic and lumbar vertebrae. The spinal cord (the tissue, along with the brain, that forms the central nervous system) passes through the vertebral foramen. Vertebral foramen is large and wide relative to the size of vertebral body.

The bones of the lumbar vertebrae are thick and strong to support the weight of the upper body but are not structured for as much movement between them as are the cervical and thoracic vertebrae. Their spinous processes are broader (Figure 10.15) and their facets interlock for some side-to-side movement (Figure 10.16).

The *scapula* (shoulder blade) on the posterior lateral part of the back forms part of the shoulder. It articulates with the bone of the upper arm (the humerus, Figure 10.17). Though a fairly broad bone, it is relatively thin. It is easily punctured by a projectile and easily fractured during the process of recovering skeletal remains.

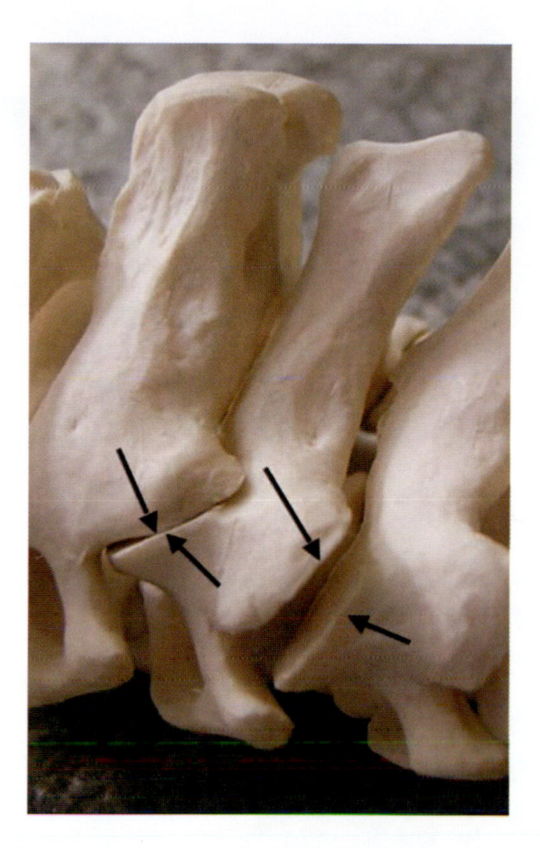

Figure 10.13 The articulating surfaces of the cervical vertebrae are shown with arrows. These are called facets and are usually cup shaped or planar.

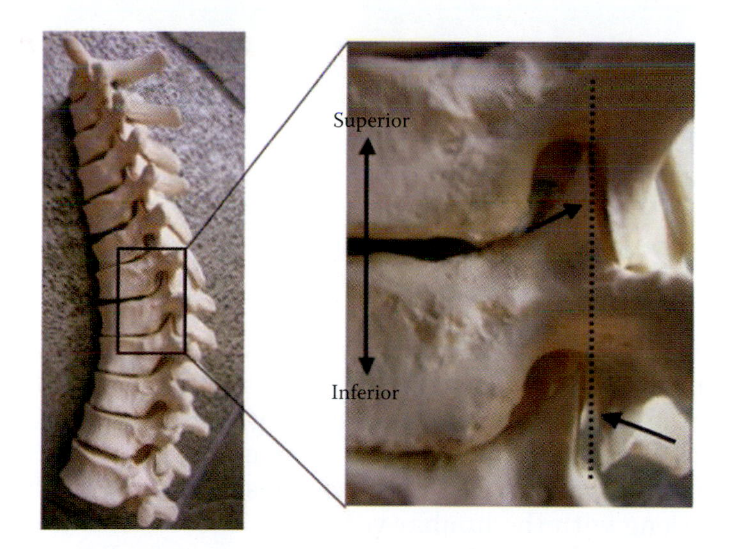

Figure 10.14 Facets along one thoracic vertebra are relatively planar (flat) and in line along the vertical axis. The dotted black line passes through a set of facets along one vertebra (arrows show the location of the facets common to the one vertebra).

Bones of the Lower Torso

The lower torso includes that part of the body that carries the intestines and reproductive organs. The major skeletal component of the lower torso is the *pelvis*—a word that derives from the Latin for *basin*, which is the general shape for that part of the skeleton that includes the hips, the *sacrum* (tail bone), and the pelvic area.

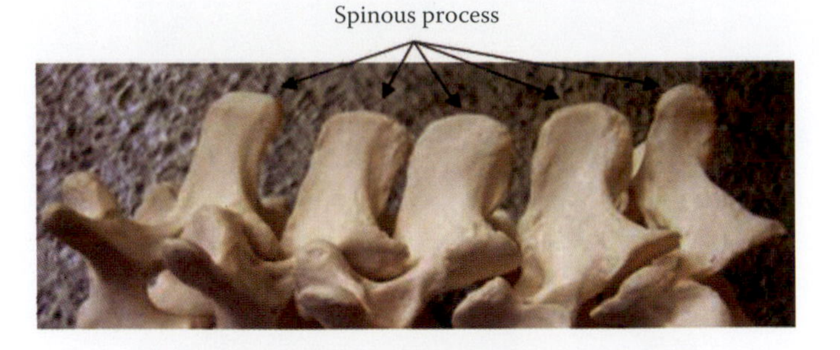

Figure 10.15 The spinous processes of the lumbar vertebra (shown with arrows) are relatively long and somewhat hatchet shaped.

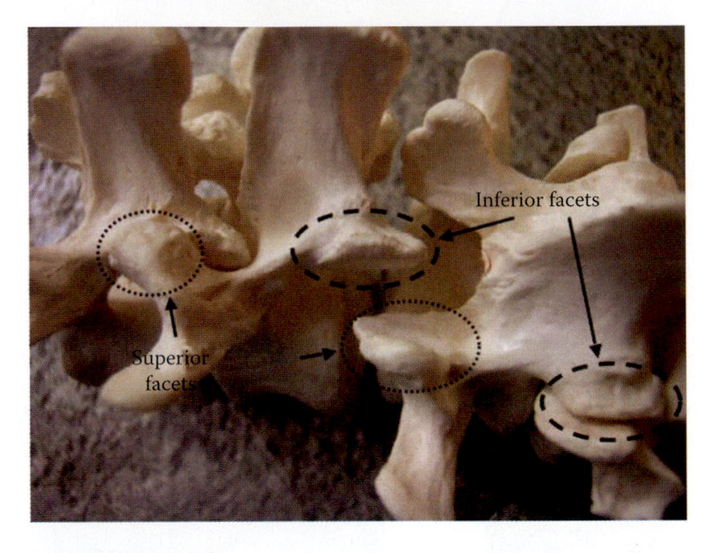

Figure 10.16 Superior facets of the lumbar vertebrae are concave (dotted circles) while the inferior facets are convex (dashed circles).

The pelvis serves several functions including providing protection for the urinary tract and internal reproductive organs, providing attachment for the lower limbs (the large femur bone of the upper leg attaches at hip socket), and providing support when the body is upright.

The posterior part of the pelvis is formed by the sacrum and the *coccyx* (Figures 10.18 and 10.19). The sacrum, attached to the bottom of the lumbar vertebrae, is made from five fused vertebrae making a single bone. These five bones, though separate at birth, fuse later in life to form a single structure. The coccyx at the very end of the spine is often referred to as the *tail bone*. It is made of four fused vertebrae. Along with the lumbar vertebrae, these bones work with the large muscle of the buttocks and upper limbs to provide power for lifting and motion. The *ilium*, *ischium*, and pelvic bone are separate bones in childhood but fuse together at puberty.

Bones of the Arm and Hand

The arm is composed of three bones, the humerus above the elbow and the radius and ulna below the elbow (see Figure 10.8). The bones of the radius and ulna (the forearm) articulate with the bones of the wrist at their distal end. Since the humerus undergoes an ossification process, it can be used to estimate age. It will ossify at the

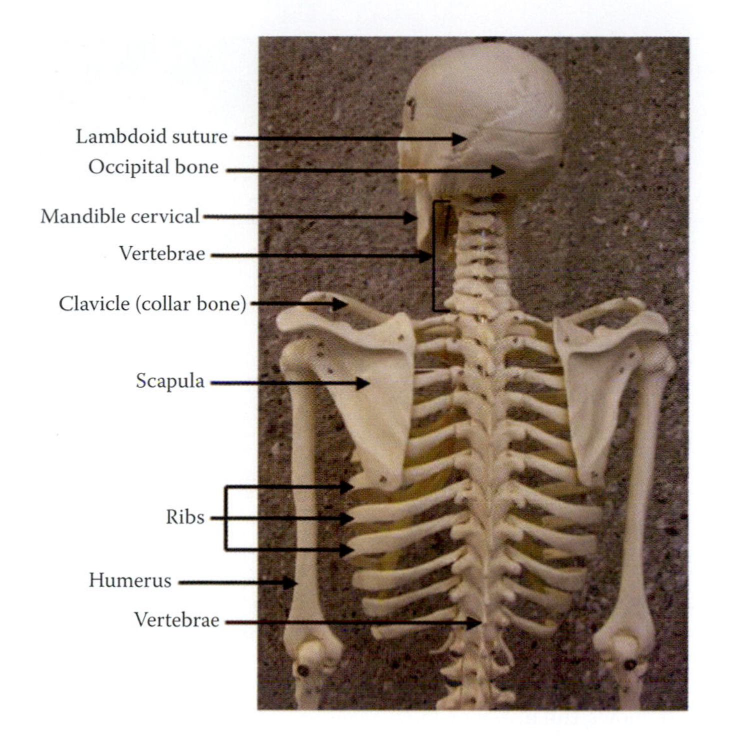

Figure 10.17 The posterior view of the upper torso shows the scapula, ribs, and vertebrae as prominent features.

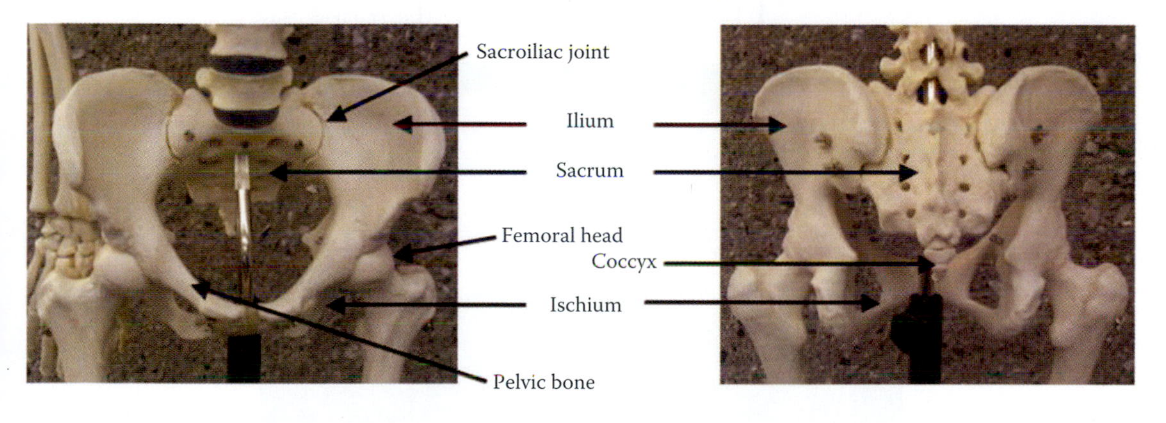

Figure 10.18 The bones of the pelvic area include the sacrum and the coccyx.

elbow by age 14 and at the shoulder by age 20. The bones of the wrist usually have ossified by the age of 19.

Each hand is made from 27 bones comprised of the carpals (8 bones), the metacarpals (5 bones), and the phalanges (14 bones) (Figure 10.20). All fingers have three bones, the proximal, middle, and distal phalange. The thumb has only two bones, a proximal and distal phalange—a middle phalange is missing.

Bones of the Leg and Foot

The femur is the longest bone in the human body. Having to support the weight of the body above it, it is also the strongest and most rugged. The distal end of the femur forms part of the knee (Figure 10.21). The patella, a small, triangular-shaped

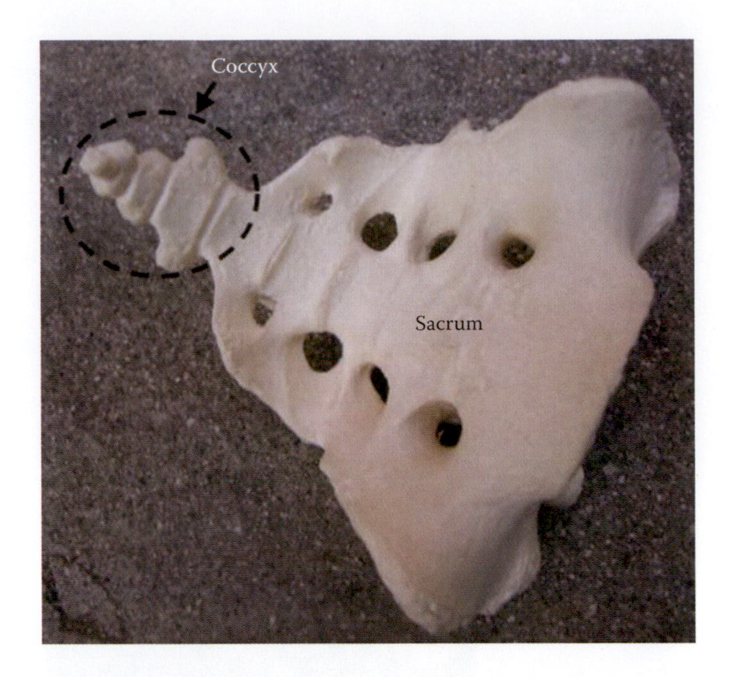

Figure 10.19 The coccyx (circled with a dashed line) and the sacrum form the posterior section of the pelvis. This photograph shows the anterior view.

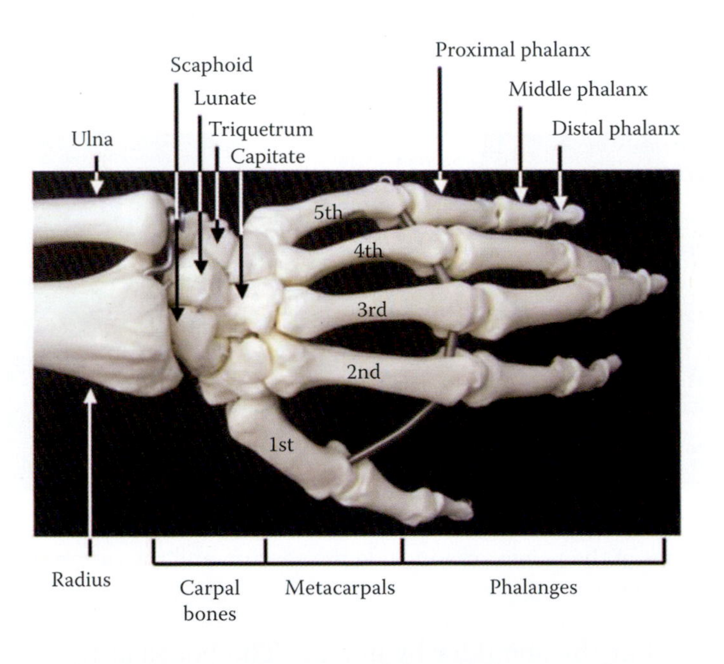

Figure 10.20 The bones of the hand include carpal bones of the wrist, the metacarpals of the palm, and the phalanges of the fingers. The left hand is pictured here.

bone at the knee, protects the joint where the femur meets the fibula and tibia of the lower leg. As do many other bones, the femur undergoes an ossification process during development and can therefore yield clues as to a victim's age. It ossifies at the thigh by 17 years of age and at the knee by the age of 18.

The tibia is the second largest bone in the body. The tibia and the fibula connect at their distal end to the talus (anklebone).

As is the hand that is built for movement in multiple directions, the foot contains a number of bones (over 20) that allow the activities of standing, walking, and

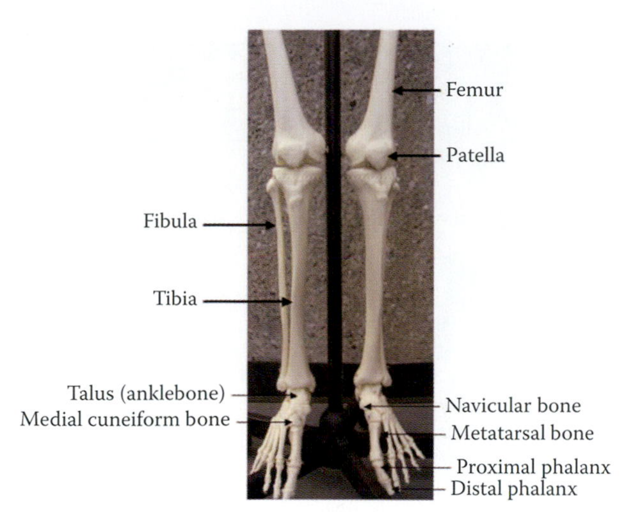

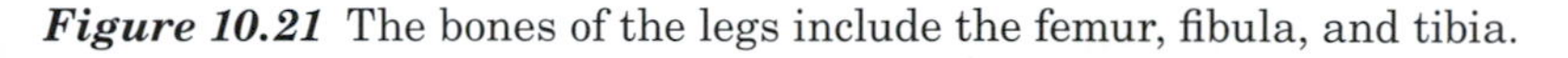
Figure 10.21 The bones of the legs include the femur, fibula, and tibia.

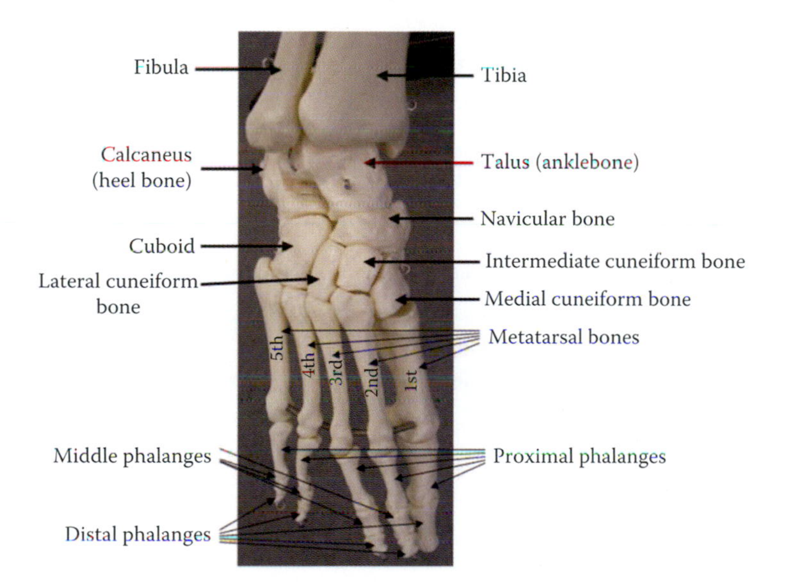

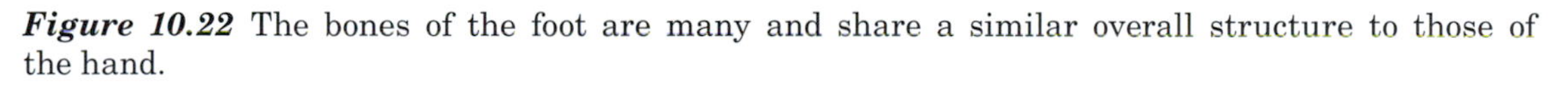
Figure 10.22 The bones of the foot are many and share a similar overall structure to those of the hand.

running. Each toe is made from three bones, except for the toe, which has only two (Figure 10.22).

Both the foot and the hand have metatarsals and phalanges. The wrist of the hand is made of bones known as carpals, whereas in the foot, the ankle (the wrist's counterpart) is comprised of a group of bones called tarsals (Figure 10.23).

Determining Stature from the Long Bones

The most accurate way to measure stature is to reassemble the skeleton and measure its length. The forensic anthropologist will then typically add 4 in. (10–11 cm) onto the height to compensate for the absence of flesh and connective tissue. Without a complete skeleton, as might be the case for disarticulated (disconnected) bones recovered in a wilderness area where scavenging animals might have dismembered and scattered the skeleton, stature estimates can still be determined from

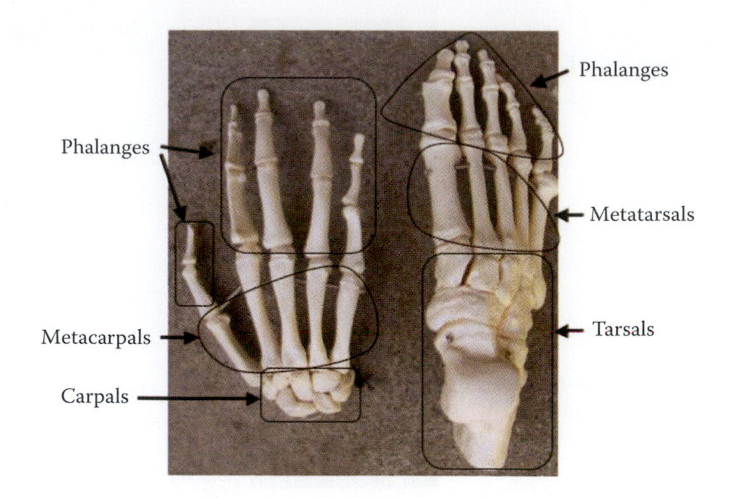

Figure 10.23 Bones of the right hand (carpals, metacarpals, phalanges; dorsal perspective) and of the right foot (tarsals, metatarsals, phalanges; dorsal perspective).

TABLE 10.2
Equation Used to Estimate Caucasian Female and Male between 18 and 30 Years of Age.

Bone	Bone Length Multiplied by	Add	Range
Caucasian Female			
Femur	2.47	+54.10 cm	±3.72 cm
Fibula	2.93	+59.61 cm	±3.57 cm
Humerus	3.36	+57.97 cm	±4.45 cm
Ulna	4.27	+57.76 cm	±4.30 cm
Radius	4.74	+54.93 cm	±4.24 cm
Tibia	2.90	+61.53 cm	±3.66 cm
Caucasian Male			
Femur	2.38	+61.41 cm	±3.27 cm
Fibula	2.68	+71.78 cm	±3.29 cm
Humerus	3.08	+70.45 cm	±4.05 cm
Ulna	3.70	+74.05 cm	±4.32 cm
Radius	3.78	+79.01 cm	±4.32 cm
tibia	2.42	+81.93 cm	±4.00 cm

measurements of the body's arm and leg bones (Table 10.2). Measuring the length of the femur (thigh bone) or the tibia or fibula (leg bones) will yield the best estimates. Measurement using the humerus, ulna, and radius of the arm may over- or underestimate actual height by as much as 4 cm.

Sexual Dimorphism and Sex Determination from Skeletal Remains

The male lion has his mane, the male moose his antlers, and the male peacock his magnificent display of tail feathers. Males and females, even though of the same species, can have markedly different appearances. This is called *sexual dimorphism* and it exists in humans too.

You probably recognized the most prominent difference between adult males and females even when you were a young child. A woman has breasts, wide hips, and a proportionately slimmer waist. Men have broad shoulders and facial hair. They just seem to have more hair everywhere (except as they age and it begins to disappear from the top of their heads). You may have noticed at a young age that you didn't see many females playing the position of left tackle on the Dallas Cowboys. Barring any rules against females playing in the NFL, women are, in general, of smaller stature than men. Males, on average, carry almost 15% more body mass and tend to be roughly 10% larger.

But talking about the physical differences between men and woman can be controversial. Engage in a conversation on that topic and you will hear such statements as "Yeah, well I know this girl who looks just like a guy" or "I know this girl who's taller than most guys." No doubt, we have all seen the exceptions that can blur the gender line. That is because, as members of the human species, our appearances span a continuous spectrum. There are no great gaps or stutters. By choosing the right examples, we can see a fluid melting of the female form into that of the male and vice versa.

The human pallet of our appearance is painted using hormones as a brush. Those hormones, primarily estrogen and testosterone, become active at puberty when they begin to change us into sexually active adults capable of parenting children. Males start shaving. Their voices change to a lower pitch. Females develop breasts and hips. Those same hormones shape the underlying bones of the skeletal system as well. In fact, prior to puberty, male and female skeletons are extremely difficult to tell apart. Hormones change that but to different degrees depending on the individual's genetic makeup and nutrition. In this section, therefore, when we discuss male and female differences, we will speak in generalities—to the first approximation of the truth.

But a skeleton's sex can also be determined by examination of the skull (Figure 10.24). Though less outwardly apparent, there are differences. Here's one that you can discover about your own. With two fingers, feel the back of your skull at its base. If you're a male, you might feel a bump. This is the nuchal crest. If you're a female, your skull will be smooth (Figures 10.24 and 10.25). The skeletal system uses this bump as a site of muscle attachment as is needed to support the usually more muscular physique of the male. In addition (and in general), a male's chin is squarer than a female's (Figure 10.26 and Figure 10.27) and has a broader mental eminence (Figures 10.24 and 10.27). The mastoid process (Figure 10.24 and Figure 10.28), the part of the jaw to which are attached the muscles needed for chewing, is larger in males (Figure 10.28). Looking slightly more brutish, males are more likely to have a more pronounced brow ridge (the supraorbital ridge, see Figures 10.24 and 10.29). The bone of the upper eye socket called the supraorbital margin tends to be thicker in males than in females (Figures 10.24, 10.30, and 10.31).

Males, typically, have broader shoulders than females as part of their wider, more musculature frame. Sexual dimorphism, therefore, of the scapula (shoulder blade, Figure 10.32) can be found. Particularly, noteworthy for the determination of sex is the glenoid cavity, that part of the scapula that articulates with the head of the humerus. In males, the glenoid cavity displays a larger area than that of the female (Table 10.3).

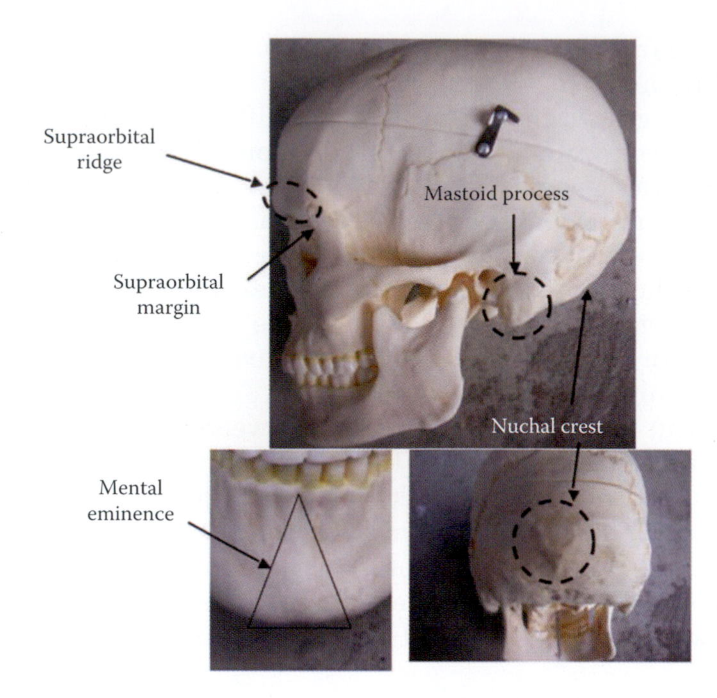

Figure 10.24 The features of the skull that display sexual dimorphism include the supraorbital ridge, the supraorbital margin, the mental eminence, the mastoid process, and the nuchal crest.

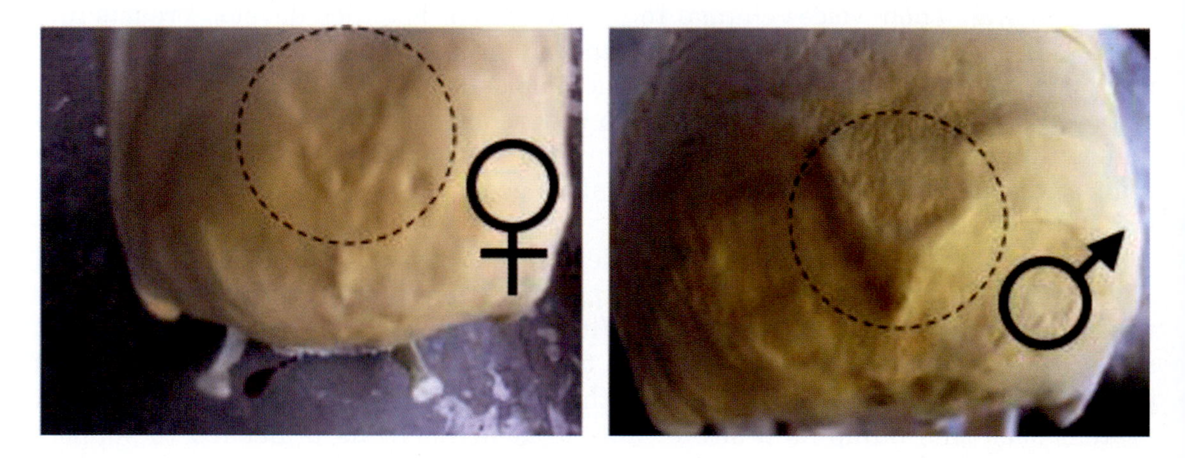

Figure 10.25 The nuchal crest (circled) is often a distinguishing feature between males and females. The male skull (right) has a more conspicuous (robust) protrusion. The photographs show the posterior view.

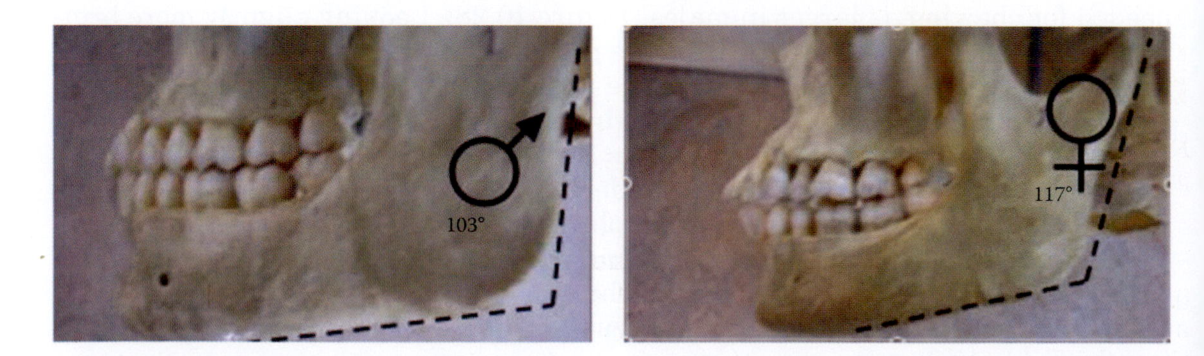

Figure 10.26 The angle of a male's jaw (left) tends to be closer to 90° than a female's jaw (right).

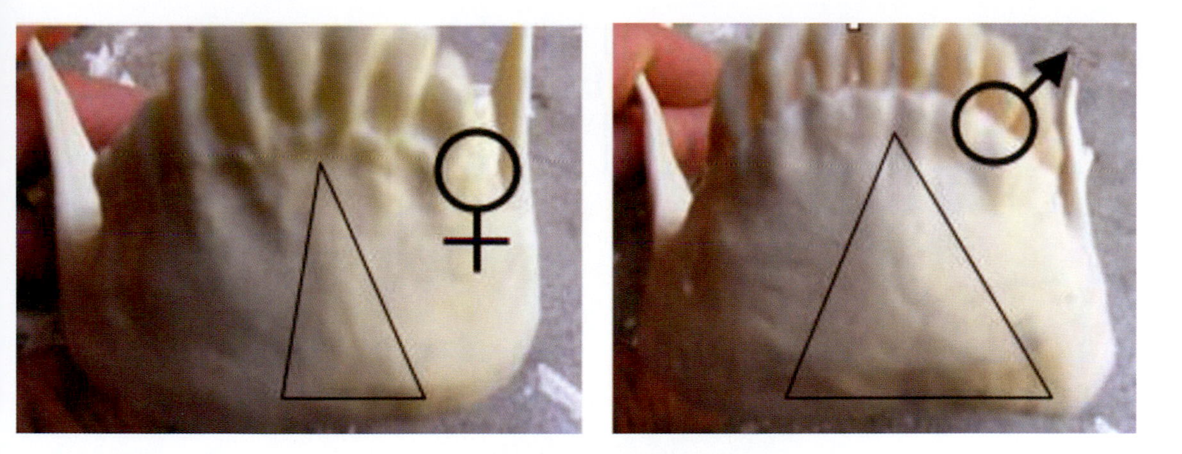

Figure 10.27 The mental eminence of the female (left) is not as broad as that of a male (right).

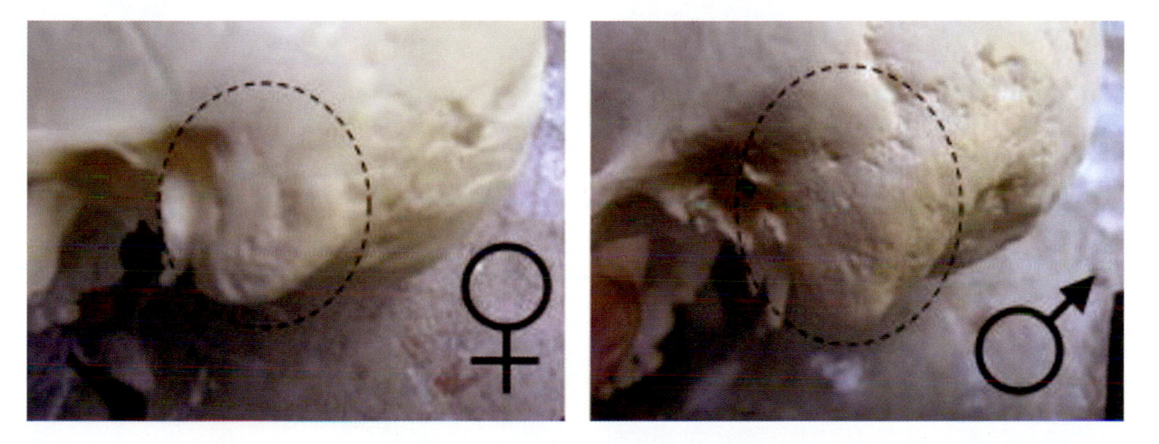

Figure 10.28 The mastoid process of the female (left) is less pronounced than that of a male (right).

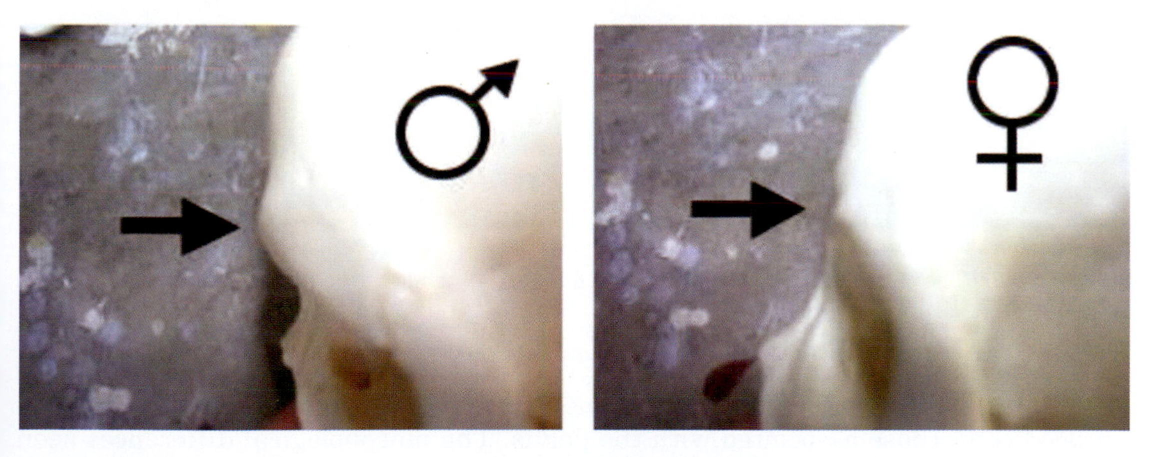

Figure 10.29 The supraorbital ridge of the male (shown with arrow, left) is more pronounced and protrudes further than that of the female (right). These photographs show the lateral view.

The long bones of the arm and leg (the humerus and femur) can be used as a means to determine the sex of skeletal remains. Again, with the bones of the male tending to wards the longer, thicker, and more robust. Table 10.4 shows the critical measurements for the humerus (see Figure 10.33) and Table 10.5 shows the critical measurements for the femur (see Figure 10.34).

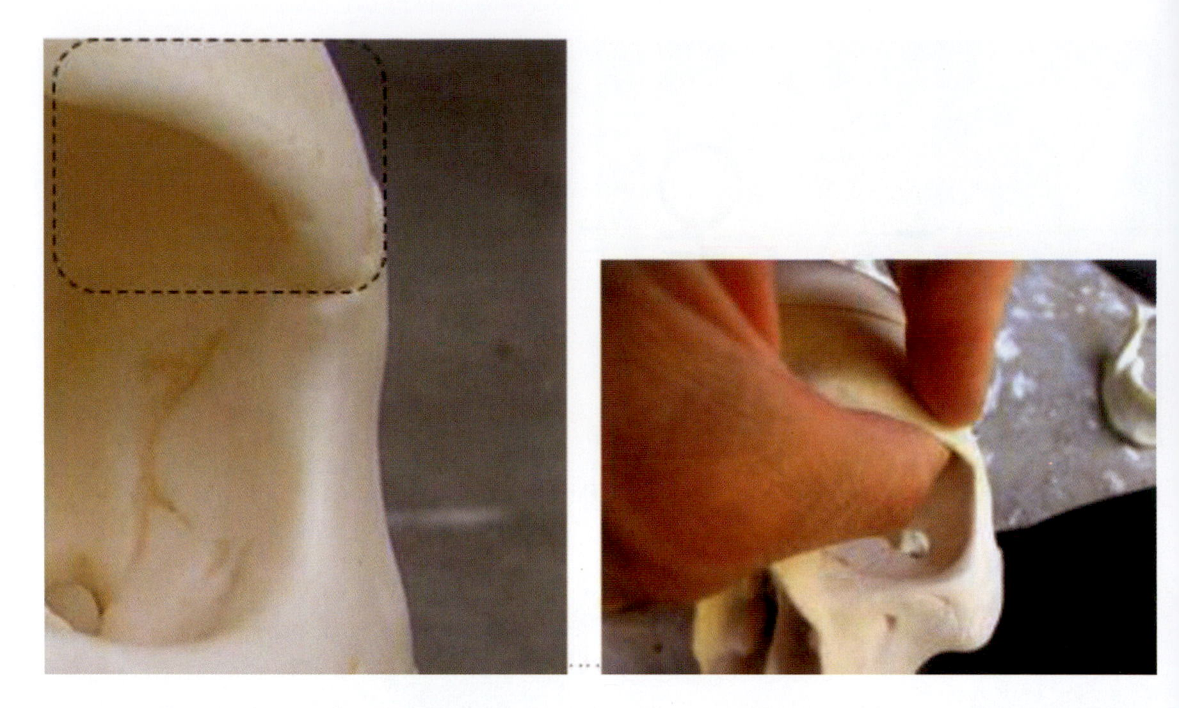

Figure 10.30 Frontal view of the left supraorbital margin (the area making up the upper region of the left orbital socket). Males (left) have a thicker supraorbital margin bone mass than females (right). The relative thickness can be roughly gauged by placing your thumb in the interior of the orbital and your index finger on the outer aspect of the orbital so that you are *pinching* the bone.

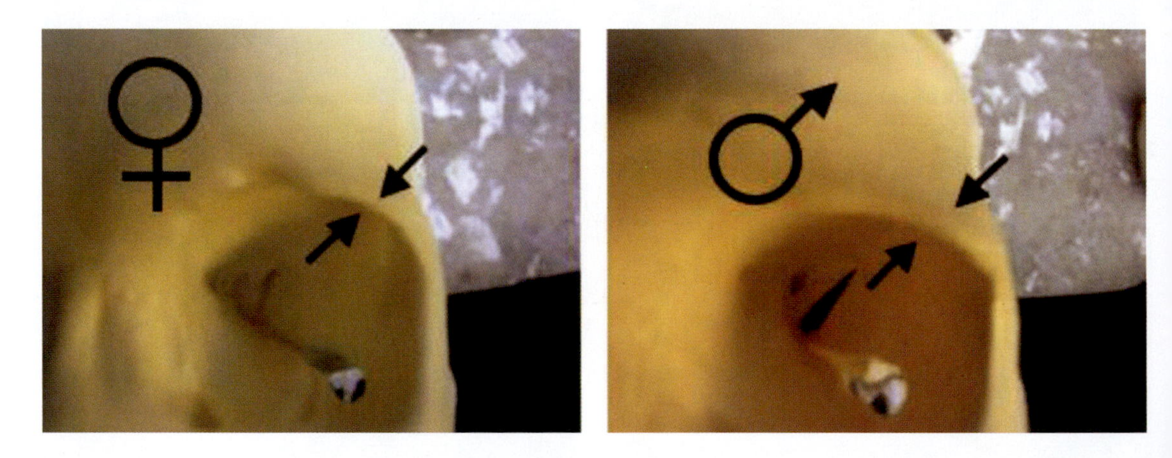

Figure 10.31 The supraorbital margin of the female (a) tends to be thinner than that of the male (right).

Of all the differences between the male and female skeletons, none is more pronounced than those associated with the pelvis. The morphological differences seen in the female from those observed in the male evolved so that a woman can accommodate the birth of a child. What makes childbirth particularly problematic, at least for our species, is the size of the human brain—it is distinctly larger than our other primate cousins'. Consequently, the female's hips have evolved to be wide enough to deliver a child and yet not so wide as to make walking a prohibitively difficult task. In addition, the center cavity of a woman's pelvis (the birth canal) is wider than that of a male's (Figure 10.35). The pelvis of the human male, on the other hand,

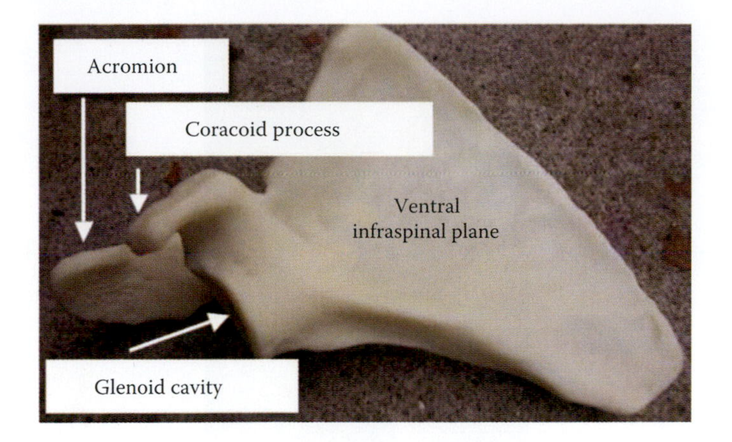

Figure 10.32 The scapula showing the glenoid cavity.

TABLE 10.3
Glenoid Cavity of the Male Shows a Larger Area than That of the Female

Sex of Individual	Glenoid Cavity Area (cm^2)
Male	≥9.57
Female	≤6.83
Indeterminate	>6.83 to <9.57

Note: If the area is greater than or equal to 9.57, it is consistent with a male. If the area is less than or equal to 6.83, it is consistent with a female. If the glenoid cavity is between 6.83 and 9.57 cm^2, then the bone is said to be indeterminate.

TABLE 10.4
Measurements of the Humerus Can Distinguish a Male from a Female

Anatomical Landmark	Female (mm)	Indeterminate Sex (mm)	Male (mm)
Transverse diameter (T_d)	37.0–39.0	>39.0 to <42.7	42.7–44.7
Vertical diameter of humeral head (V_d)	≤43	>43 to <47	≥47
Maximum length (M_l)	305.9 (avg.)	[a]	339.0 (avg.)
Epicondylar width (E_w)	56.8 (avg.)	[a]	63.9 (avg.)

[a] If the measured values are closer to the middle, the conclusion is indeterminate.

has evolved for efficient bipedal locomotion. It is narrower, taller, and more compact (no birth canal required). The female pelvis differs from that of a male by several other criteria including the more concave ventral arc (Figures 10.36 and 10.37), a wider pubic symphysis (Figure 10.38), a wider greater sciatic notch (Figures 10.39 and 10.40), a more concave subpubic region (Figures 10.36 and 10.41), and a broader pubic bone (Figures 10.36 and 10.42).

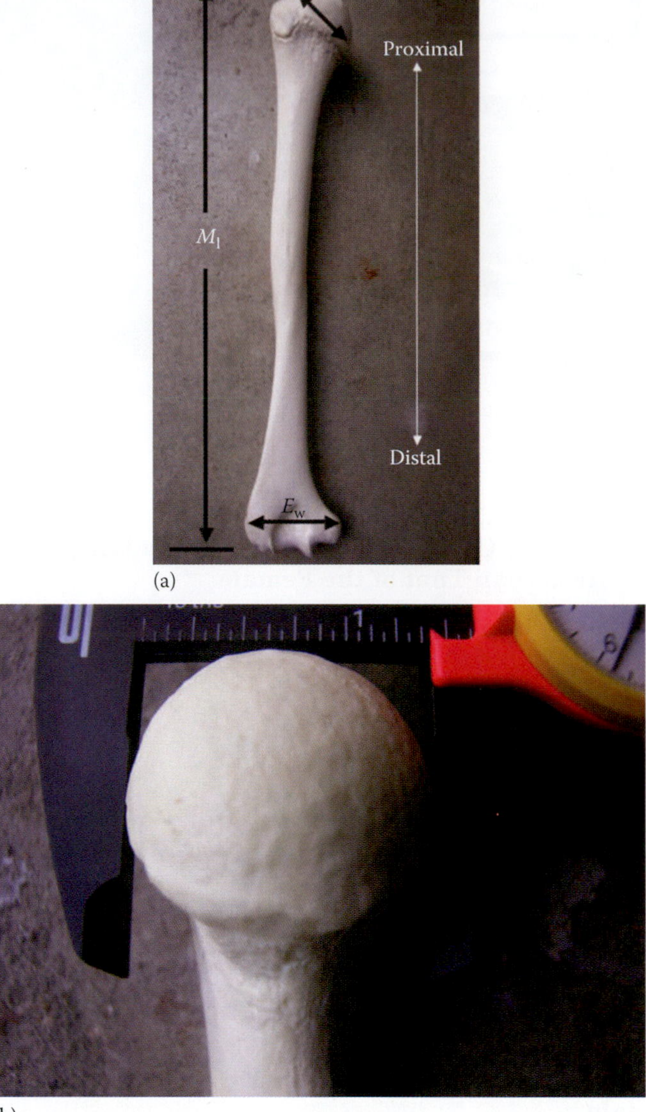

Figure 10.33 Measuring the humerus for sexual dimorphism studies takes several features into account including, as shown in (a), the maximum length (M_l), the vertical diameter (V_d, at the proximal end), and the epicondylar width (E_w). (b) Shows the act of measuring the humeral head with a caliper.

TABLE 10.5
Measurements of the Femur Can Be Used to Distinguish Male from Female

Anatomical Landmark	Female (mm)	Indeterminate Sex (mm)	Male (mm)
Vertical diameter of the femoral head (V_d)	<43.5	43.5–44.5	>44.5
Bicondylar width (B_w)	<74	74–76	>76
Maximum length (M_l)	<405	405–430	>430

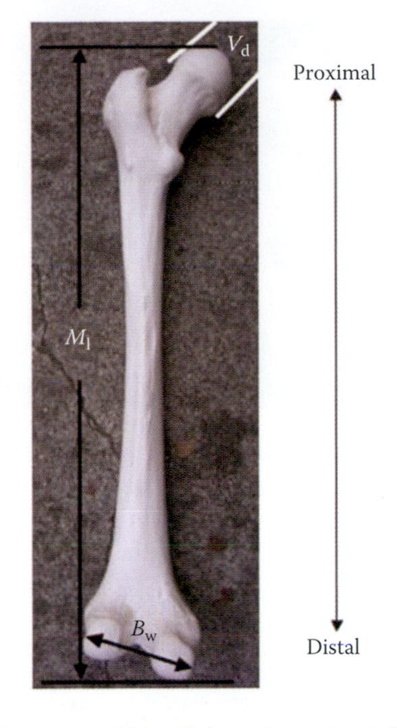

Figure 10.34 The anatomical features of the femur important for sex determination include the vertical diameter (V_d), maximum length (M_l), and the bicondylar width (B_w). SHOWN here is the left femur from the posterior perspective.

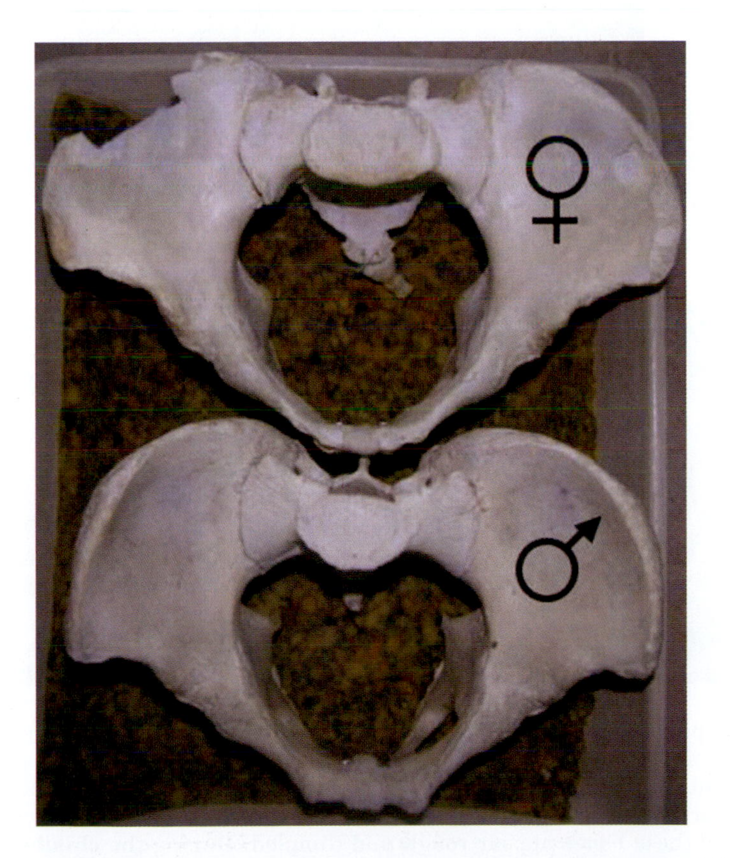

Figure 10.35 The female pelvic cavity (top) has a larger opening than that of the male (bottom). A normal-sized fist will more easily pass into the female pelvic cavity from the superior to the inferior direction along the coronal plane than it will into the male pelvic cavity. Photograph is taken from the superior, transverse plane.

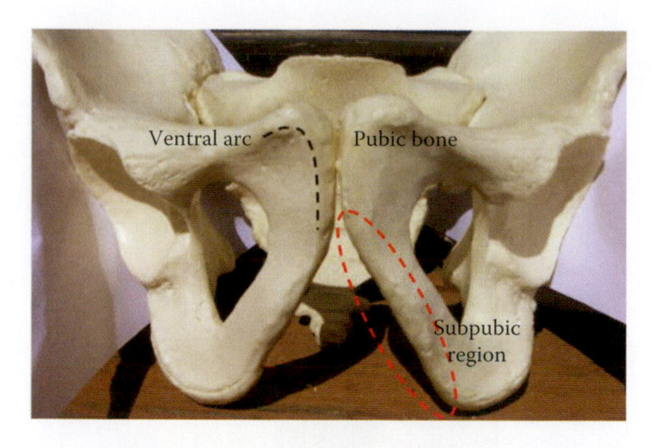

Figure 10.36 The features of the human pelvis that can be used to distinguish male from female include the ventral arc, the pubic bone, and the subpubic region.

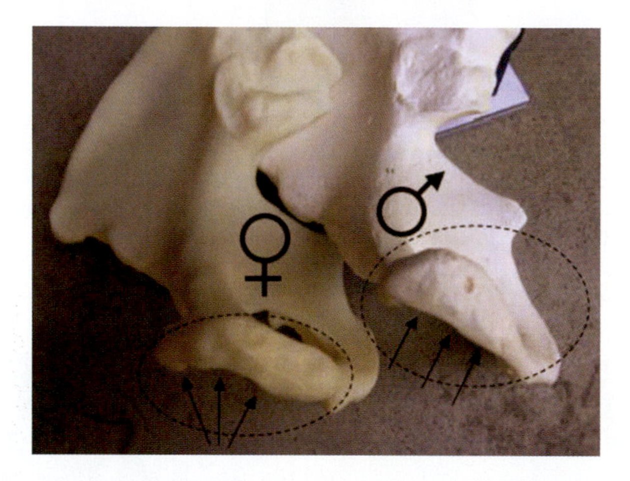

Figure 10.37 Right side of pelvis showing the ventral arc of the pubic symphysis (circled with dashed line). The female pelvis (left) exhibits a more concave profile than that of the male (right). Image is taken from the medial aspect.

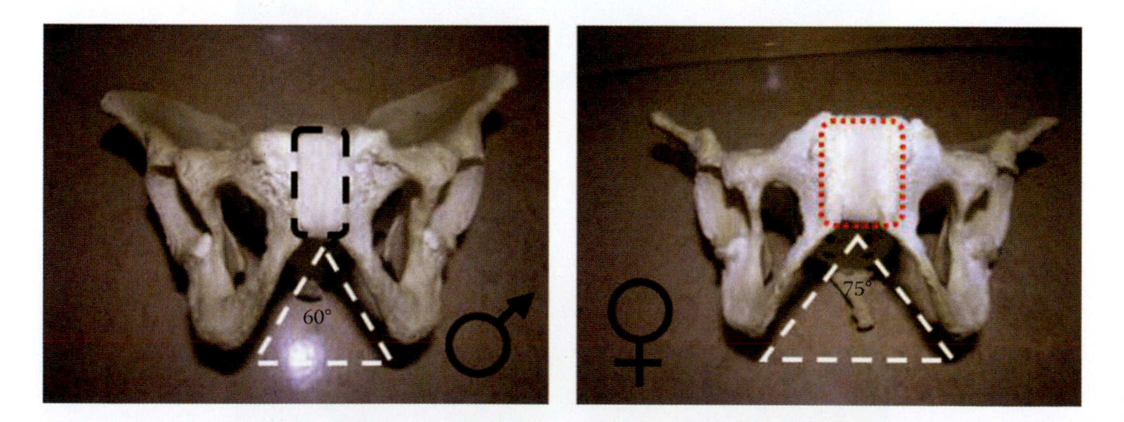

Figure 10.38 The pubic symphysis, a stretch of cartilage that joins the hipbones at the front of the pelvis (shown as dashed black lines in the photograph on the left and as dashed red lines in the photograph on the right), softens during pregnancy and allows the pelvis to spread during childbirth. After the baby is born, the pubic symphysis hardens again. This area wears down with age. In early life, the surfaces of these bones appear rough and dimpled. During the childbearing years, in the 20s and 30s, the bone smoothes over only to become bumpy again around age 40. The angle of pubic symphysis (apex of the isosceles triangle depicted with the white triangular lines) is more acute in males (usually less than 90°) and more obtuse in females (reaching over 100°). These photographs are taken from the frontal aspect.

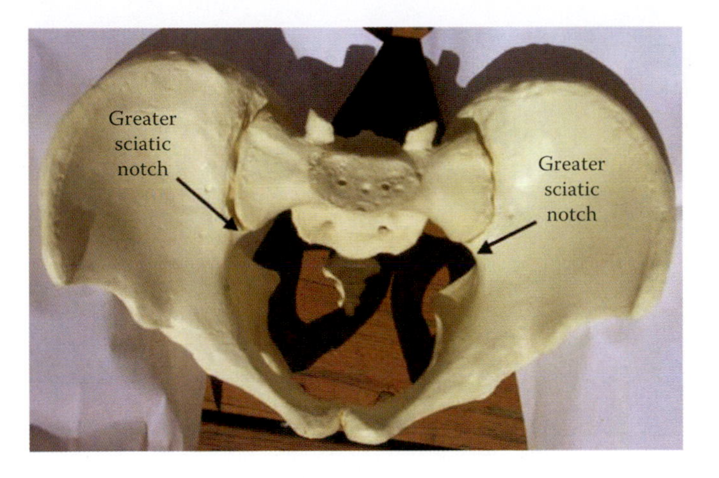

Figure 10.39 The greater sciatic notch of the pelvis is a feature that can be used to discriminate between male and female.

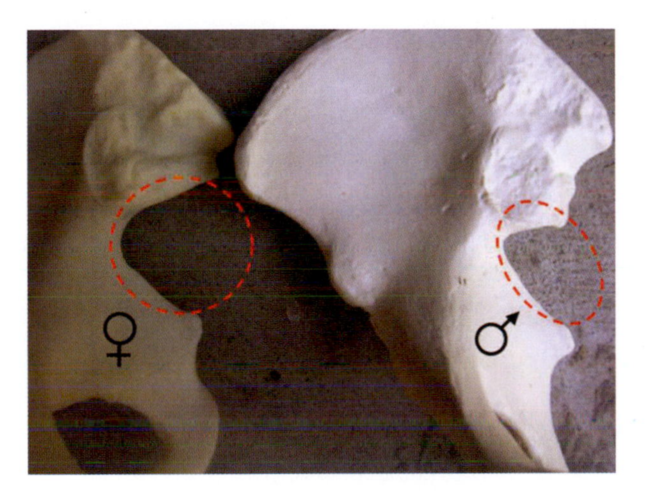

Figure 10.40 Right half of the pelvis showing the greater sciatic notch (circled with a red, dashed line) from the sagittal plane perspective. The female pelvis (left) exhibits a larger opening than that of the male pelvis (right). A simple *finger test* can help to distinguish the female from the male pelvis: more fingers can be wedged into the greater sciatic notch of the female pelvis than into that of the male pelvis.

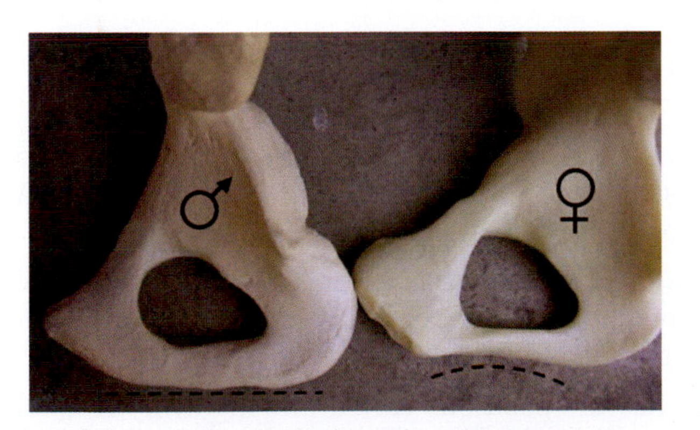

Figure 10.41 Right half of the pelvis showing the difference in concavity of the subpubic region between the male (left) and female (right) pelvic area. The outer edge of the subpubic region of the male is relatively straight. That of the female shows a slight arc. Images are taken from the sagittal plane perspective. The ridge of this section of the bone is called the *ischiopubic ramus*. The female pelvis exhibits a relatively sharper ridge than that of the male.

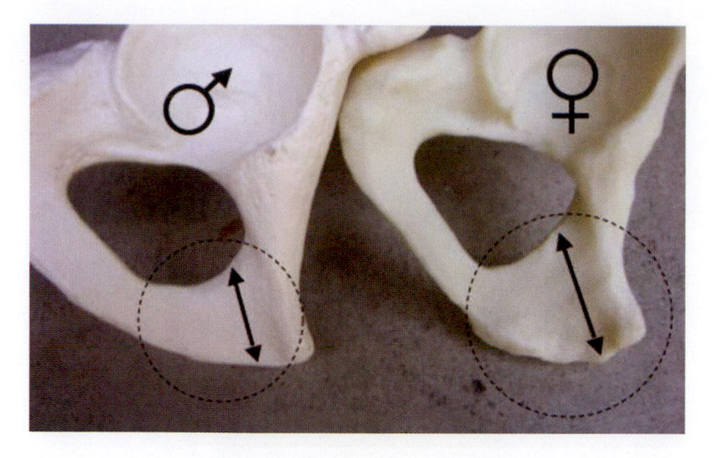

Figure 10.42 Right half of pelvis showing comparative widths of the pubic bone region (circled with dash line). The pubic bone of the male (left) displays less width than that of the female (right).

In the Crime Lab

Activity 10.1 Identifying Anatomical Directions and Planes

In this activity, your instructor will divide the class into groups of three students. Each group will dissect a pear (or other piece of fruit) as a means to study the directional planes of a body.

Materials:

Pear (or other piece of fruit)
Kitchen knife
Napkins and/or paper towels

Protocol

Direction Orientation

1. Obtain a pear and a cutting utensil from your instructor.
2. Carve the likeness of a human face into the upper region of the pear (near the stem area). Carve a set of eyes, a nose, and a mouth (see Figure 10.43).

Diagram and label the features described during this activity in your laboratory notebook. Record your answers to the following questions.

Question 1: If this pear now represents a human face, what is the side of the pear called that displays the face? What is the name of this plane? What is the name of the surface on the opposite side of the face?

Question 2: If you drew an imaginary line down the middle of the face, from the top of the pear to the bottom (N to S), that line would be referred to as the midline. What are the points lying closest to this line referred to as?

Question 3: What are the positions called moving away from the midline (moving in an E or W direction from that line)?

Question 4: The top region of the pear (relative to the bottom of the pear) is referred to as what?

Figure 10.43 A pear carved with a face. An apple will also work for this activity.

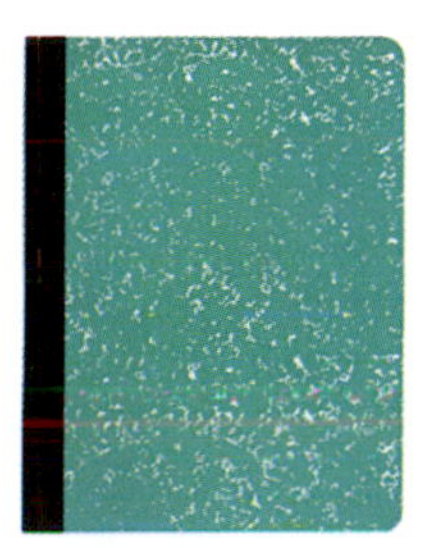

Question 5: Relative to the top region of the pear, what is the bottom region of the pear?

Question 6: Turn the pear sideways 90° so that you are looking at an ear. What is the name of this plane?

Question 7: If you were looking from a *bird's-eye view* at the top of the pear's head, what plane is this perspective?

Dissection Plane Orientation

In this part of the activity, the pear will be passed around the group with each member performing a different type of slice.

Student 1: Orient the pear so that the posterior surface is facing you. Cut a slice of the pear in the coronal (frontal) plane, and hand the pear and knife to the next person in your group.

Student 2: Orient the pear in the same direction used by the first student. Slice the pear in the sagittal plane in the lateral region near where the ear would be. Once this piece is removed, hand the pear and knife to the next person in your group.

Student 3: Slice the pear in the transverse plane in the inferior region near the bottom of the pear. Hand the pear back to Student 1.

Student 1: Cut what remains of the pear in the sagittal plane.

Student 2: Cut what remains of the pear in the transverse plane.

Student 3: Cut the main body of the pear in the coronal (frontal) plane. Hand the body of the pear back to Student 1.

Student 1: Cut the body of the pear in the transverse plane.

Student 2: Cut the body of the pear in the coronal (frontal) plane.

Student 3: Cut the body of the pear in the sagittal plane.

Activity 10.2 Determining Directional Terms and Planes of Skeletal Samples

Materials: 3D human skeleton models (articulated and disarticulated) or photographs

Protocol:
Your instructor will provide you with bone samples or photographs of parts of the skeleton.

In your laboratory notebook, draw a picture of each sample and record the following information for each bone.

- Distinguish between superior and inferior.
- Name and distinguish the three different planes.
- Distinguish between anterior and posterior.
- Distinguish between medial and lateral for a leg or arm bone.
- Distinguish proximal and distal points on a leg or arm bone.
- Distinguish between palmar and plantar.
- Using your own body or a fully articulated human skeleton, identify all of the directional terms and planes.

Activity 10.3 Identifying Bones of the Human Skeleton

This activity will help you learn the major bones of the human body.

Materials:
3D model of a fully articulated human skeleton
Anatomical wall charts of human skeletal system
3D models or digital images of a disarticulated human skeleton

Protocol

1. Your instructor will assign you to a laboratory station where a bone is displayed.

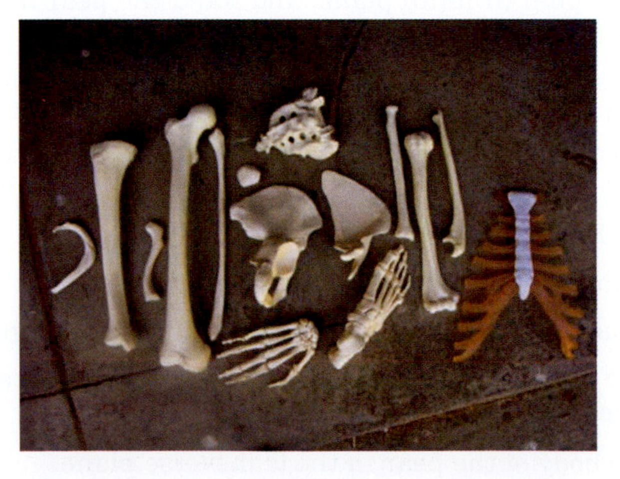

Check list of bones or skeletal landmarks you should know.

Lumbar	Fibula	Ulna
Thoracic	Clavicle	Humerus
Cervical	Femur	Sternum

Tarsals	Patella	Mastoid
Metatarsals	Hyoid	Nuchal crest
Phalanges	Sacrum	Supraorbital ridge
Carpals	Coccyx	Mental eminence
Metacarpals	Pelvis	Scapula
Ribs	Radius	Tibia

In your laboratory notebook, (a) name the skeletal bone or anatomical landmark and (b) draw the bone emphasizing distinguishing landmarks.

2. Visit all of the laboratory stations. You should prepare a complete set of notes identifying the major bones of the human skeleton.
   Notes: At the vertebrae station, you will (a) name, (b) draw, and (c) distinguish between the cervical, thoracic, and lumbar vertebrae. Be sure to make note of their unique features in your laboratory notebook.

Activity 10.4 Determining if Hand Length Can Predict Stature

In this activity, you will gather data from the class that includes student hand length and height. From this information, you will derive a formula to estimate a person's stature based on the length of their hand. You will then use a statistical test called *chi-square* to analyze the spread of the data and to thereby assess the legitimacy of the method for determining stature. The correlation between hand length and height will also be examined using linear regression and the correlation coefficient value (designated as R^2). (Linear regression was also used in Chapter 3 to determine if the driver's seat distance from the accelerator could predict the height of the driver.)

Materials

Ruler
Calculator

Protocol

1. Each student should measure the length (in cm) of one of their hands from the skin crease below the palm to the tip of the middle finger (see Figure 10.44). Each student should also have their height measured by the instructor or another student. Shoes should be removed for this measurement.

Using Chi-Square Statistics to Determine if the Hypothesis Is True

2. In your laboratory notebook, create a table with a column numbering each student starting with 1. Record each student's hand length in a second column and their height in a third column. These measurements should all be recorded in centimeters. (If you need to make a conversion, remember that there are 2.54 cm/in.)
3. Calculate the average hand length (the sum of all hand lengths divided by the number of students measured).
4. Calculate the average height of the students in your class.

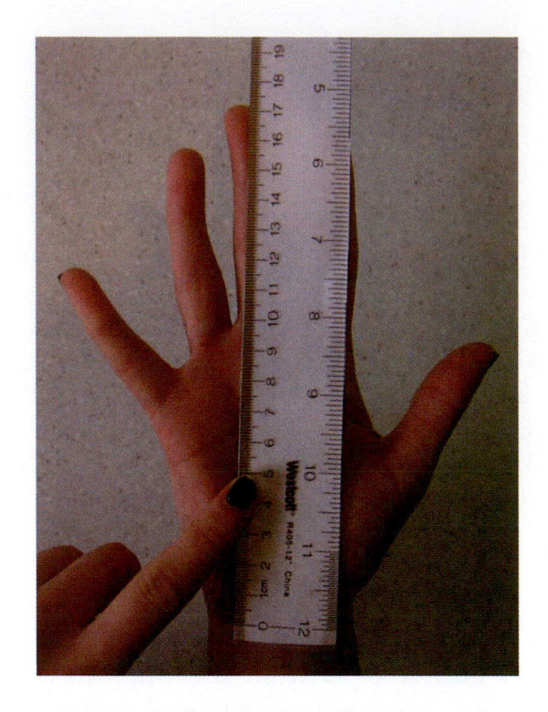

Figure 10.44 Use a ruler to measure the length of your hand from the crease at the wrist to the end of the middle finger. Take the measurement in centimeters.

5. Determine what value, when multiplied by the average hand length, will yield the average height:

$$\text{Average Hand length} \times n = \text{Average height}$$

Placing your data into the above equation, solve for n.

6. You will now use chi-square to test what is called the *null hypothesis* (H_0)—the idea that there is no difference between each person's stature (their *observed* height) and their *expected* stature as calculated using the equation you derived in step 5 earlier.

   To perform the analysis, set up a table having as many rows as there are students (plus one more for summing columns) and with the following headers:

   Activity 10.4 Step 6 Table

Student	Observed Height (O)	Expected Height (E)	Difference ($O - E$)	Square of Difference $(O - E)^2$	$(O - E)^2/E$

   The student column should contain the number of each student. The Observed Height column should contain the measured height of each student. The Expected Height column should contain the height of each student as expected when calculated using their hand length in the equation you derived in step 5 earlier. The Difference column contains the value obtained for each student when their expected height is subtracted from their actual, observed height. Each of these values is squared to fill in the fifth column. In the last column, each squared value is divided by the expected value.

7. Add the values in the last column. This number is called the *chi-square statistic* (χ^2) and is a measure of the degree to which the observed values diverge from those expected. It is given by the relationship

$$\chi^2 = \sum \frac{(\text{observed height} - \text{expected height})^2}{\text{expected height}}$$

8. If there is a large difference between the observed and expected values, the chi-square statistic will be large. The larger the statistic, the more likely the null hypothesis will be rejected... the more likely there actually is a difference between the observed and expected values.

   But at what value can we either accept or reject the null hypothesis and have some confidence in doing so? This value depends on two components, the *degrees of freedom* (*df*) and the *p-value*. The df will be one less than the number of students. For example, if you have 25 measurements (25 students), there will be 24 degrees of freedom. The *p*-value represents the level of significance under which the test is performed. Usually, this is at $p = 0.95$ or $p = 0.99$. At a *p*-value of 0.95, the test is performed at a 5% significance level. That is, there is less than a 5% chance that the null hypothesis will be rejected when it is actually true. Conversely, there is a 95% chance that the null hypothesis is true—there really is no difference between the observed and expected values.

   The expected chi-square value for given *p* and *df* values is provided in a chi-square distribution table (Table 10.6). If the chi-square statistic you obtain from your data is less than the chi-square value from Table 10.6, then there is evidence that the null hypothesis can be accepted—there is no difference between the observed and expected values. If you are examining the data at a *p*-value of 0.95, then there will be a 95% chance, if the null hypothesis is true, then your chi-square value will be less than the one in Table 10.6.
9. Your data set can also be analyzed for its *standard deviation (s)*, the degree to which the observed values vary from the expected values. It can be thought of as the average amount that the observed values deviate from those expected. It is given by the relationship

$$S = \sqrt{\frac{\sum (O - E)^2}{n - 1}}$$

   In this equation, the Σ symbol represents the sum. $\Sigma(O - E)^2$, therefore, is the sum of the square of the difference between the observed and expected value for each student (the total of the fifth column in your data table). The smaller the variation between the observed and expected values, the smaller the standard deviation.

   Calculate the standard deviation value for your data set and record this value in your laboratory notebook.

10. In your laboratory notebook, record your comments on the validity of using hand length to indicate stature.

TABLE 10.6
Chi-Square Distribution Table

df	$p=0.95$	$p=0.99$	*df*	$p=0.95$	$p=0.99$
1	3.84	6.64	18	28.9	34.8
2	5.99	9.21	19	30.1	36.2
3	7.80	11.31	20	31.4	37.6
4	9.48	13.27	21	32.7	38.9
5	11.07	15.08	22	33.9	40.3
6	12.59	16.81	23	35.2	41.6
7	14.07	18.48	24	36.4	43.0
8	15.51	20.09	25	37.7	44.3
9	16.92	21.67	30	43.8	50.9
10	18.3	23.2	40	55.7	63.7
11	19.7	24.7	50	67.5	76.2
12	21.0	26.2	60	79.1	88.4
13	22.4	27.7	70	90.5	100.4
14	23.7	29.1	80	101.9	112.3
15	25.0	30.6	90	113.2	124.1
16	26.3	32.0	100	124.3	135.8
17	27.6	33.4			

To find the chi-square value for your experiment, locate the df corresponding to your data set, and then locate its corresponding chi-square value to its right for a *p*-value of 0.95 or 0.99. If you do not find your exact *df* value corresponding to your data set, use the next highest value.

Using the Correlation Coefficient to Test How Strongly Hand Length Can Predict Height

In Activity 3.3 (Chapter 3, Trace Evidence), a statistical approach called linear regression was used to determine whether or not there was a correlation between a driver's height and the distance the driver's seat was adjusted away from the accelerator pedal. As part of that analysis, a correlation coefficient (R^2) value was calculated that gave an indication of how close the data points fell along the line of best fit. That statistical test can also be applied here to this analysis to assess if hand length can predict body height.

Let's say that when you plot your data of hand length versus body height, you get a result similar to that shown below in Figure 10.45. Linear regression analysis will yield an equation for the line of best fit and an R^2 value. The closer the R^2 value is to 1 (either +1 or −1), the tighter the data cluster along the line of best fit (Figure 10.46). A positive R^2 value will be obtained if the slope of the line of best fit is positive (slopes upward). That is, in this activity, if an increase in hand length correlates with an increase in body height. However, if it is seen that an increase in hand length correlates with a decrease in body height—if there is an inverse relationship between the two—the slope of the line will be negative (slopes downward).

For the data you have collected, follow the steps used in Activity 3.3 to determine a linear regression line and R^2 value using the Microsoft Excel software program.

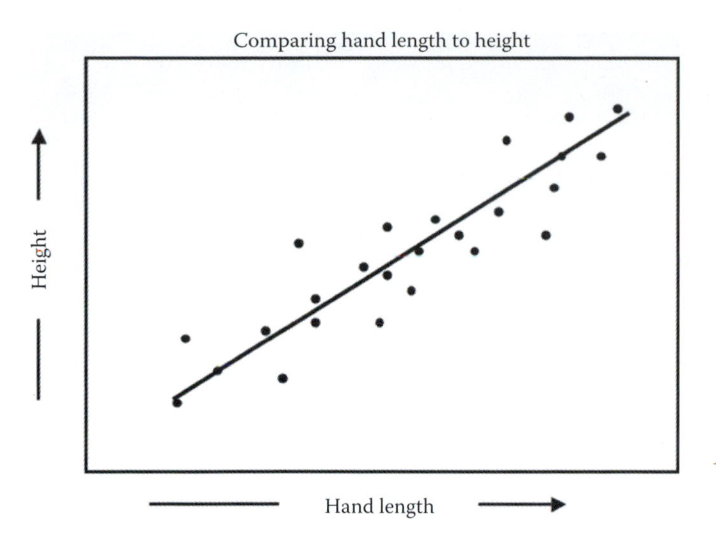

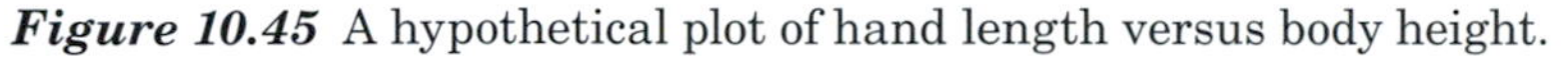
Figure 10.45 A hypothetical plot of hand length versus body height.

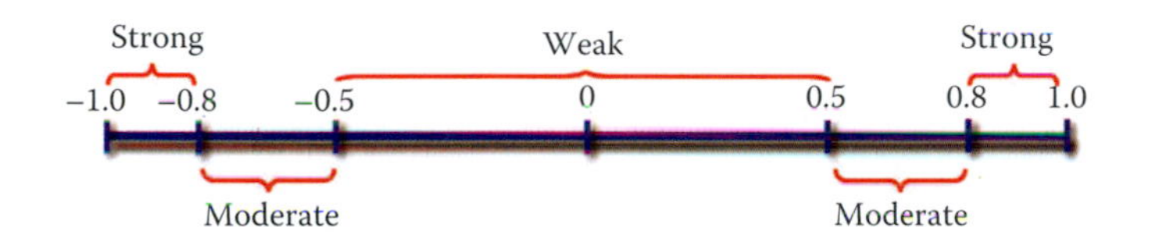

Figure 10.46 An R^2 value calculated by linear regression analysis gives an indication of the strength of the correlation between two variables (in this activity, between hand length and body height). The closer the value is to 1 (either positive or negative), the stronger the correlation. An R^2 value of 0 indicates no correlation—the points are random. R^2 values between 0.5 and 0.8 indicate a moderately strong relationship between two variables.

Place hand length on the x axis and body height on the y axis. With Figure 10.46 as a guide, make a determination as to how well hand length can predict body height. Record your results in your laboratory notebook.

Activity 10.5 Determining Stature from Skeletal Remains

Materials

3D model of human leg or arm bones
Osteometric board or metric ruler
Calculator

Protocol

1. Using the penny for scale, calculate the true length of the bone shown in Figure 10.47. Record (a) the type of bone, (b) its measurements (in cm) and the conversion into true length (cm), and (c) the final minimum and maximum height range for both male and female. Use Table 10.1 for the conversion of bone length to height. Record the height in centimeter, meters, and in feet and inches.

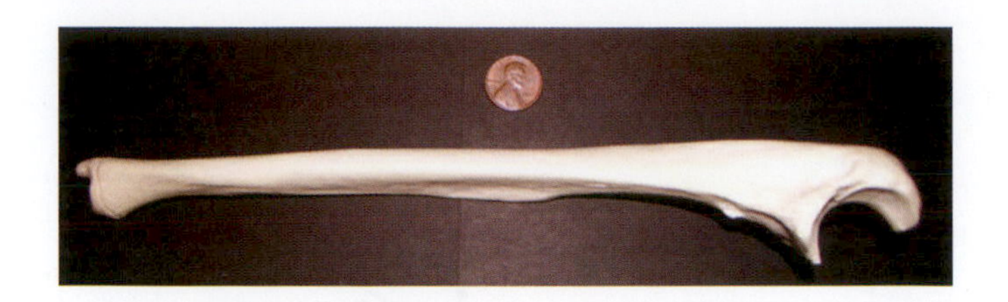

Figure 10.47 A digital image of a bone and penny (for scale) for Activity 10.5.

2. Identify a real arm and/or leg bone provided by your instructor, and using the osteometric board, measure its length. Derive the height of the individual in meters and in feet and inches. Show off your work in your laboratory notebook.

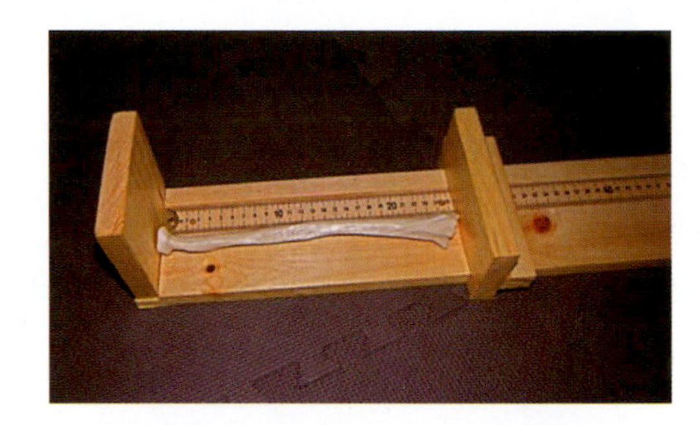

Activity 10.6 Identifying Sexual Dimorphism

In this activity, you will examine a human skull, pelvis, scapula, humerus, and femur and determine if they are from a male or female.

Materials:

3D models of a human male and female skull, pelvis, humerus, femur, and scapula
Osteometric board (substitute with metric rulers or meter sticks)
Calipers (substitute with metric rulers and meter sticks)
Dry erase pen
Calculator (if using digital images)
Graphing paper
Scissors

Protocol

1. Examine the bones provided by your instructor. In your laboratory notebook, create a data table that includes the bone type anatomical landmarks measured or qualitatively assessed, and a conclusion as to the sex of the bone provided.

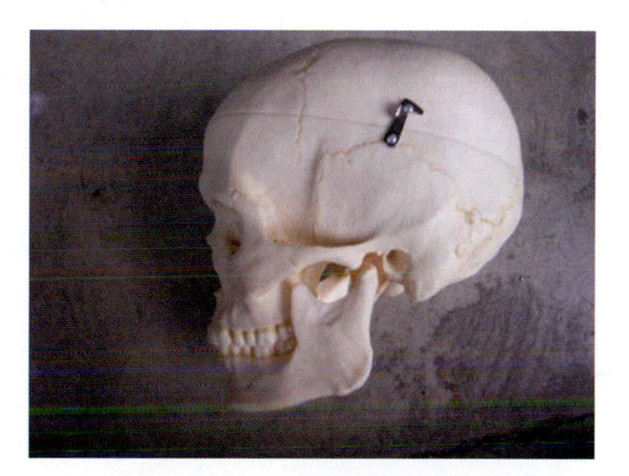

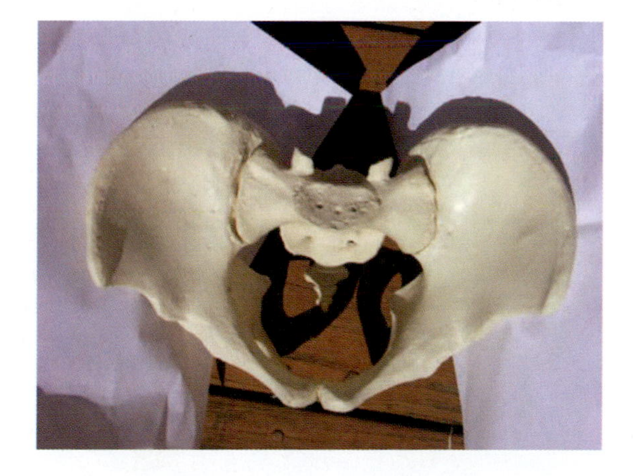

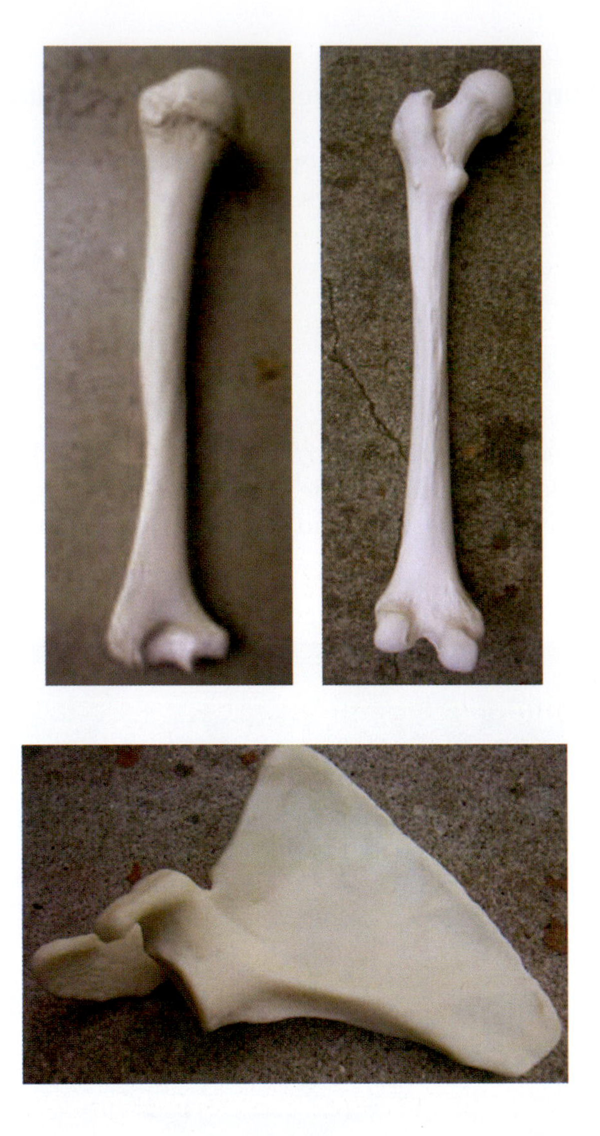

2. To determine whether the scapula is from a male or female, wrap a piece of paper around the glenoid cavity and press it against the rim of the cavity so that an impression of that cavity is imparted onto the paper.

3. With a marking pen, fill the area of the paper defined by the glenoid cavity's impression.

4. With a pair of scissors, carefully cut out the outline of the area you filled in with marker and place the cutout on graph paper. With a pencil, trace the outline of the cutout.

5. Determine the area within the outline by counting the full and partial squares. Record this information in your laboratory notebook and make your determination as to the sex of the bone.
   Note: *See the discussion of sexual dimorphism in this chapter for the critical measurements needed to differentiate between male and female.*

Erica Holmes Missing Persons Case

A fisherman using a trawl net (dragged behind a fishing boat to capture fish) collected what appeared to be a human bone. The location of his boat when he hauled in this bone was near Seaport Blvd. where the missing person's vehicle was last seen. The fisherman reported it to the authorities and it was delivered to the forensic laboratory.

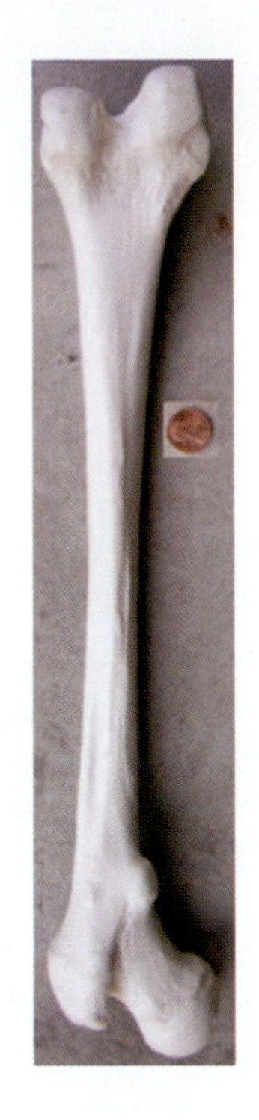

Prepare an evidence report describing your findings.

Review Questions

10.1 Distinguish between superior and inferior.
10.2 Name and distinguish the three different planes.
10.3 Distinguish between anterior and posterior.
10.4 Distinguish between medial and lateral.

10.5 Distinguish proximal and distal.
10.6 Define the word dorsal.

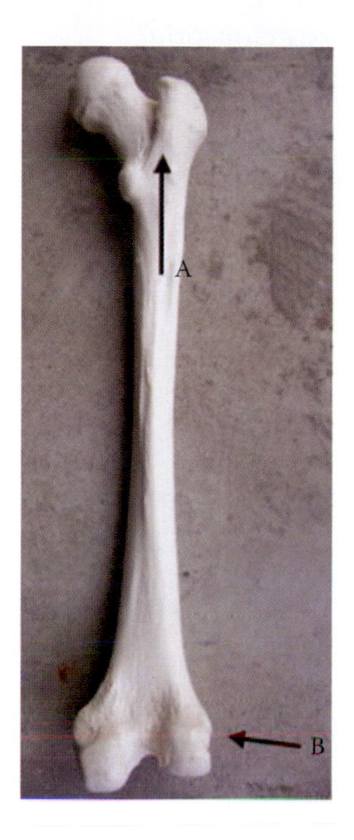

10.7 Which bone of the human skeleton is pictured here?
10.8 Was this photograph taken from the posterior or anterior perspective?
10.9 Is the arrow marked "*A*" pointing to the distal or proximal end of the bone?
10.10 Along which plane was this photograph taken?
10.11 Is the arrow marked "*B*" pointing to the lateral or medial aspect of this bone?

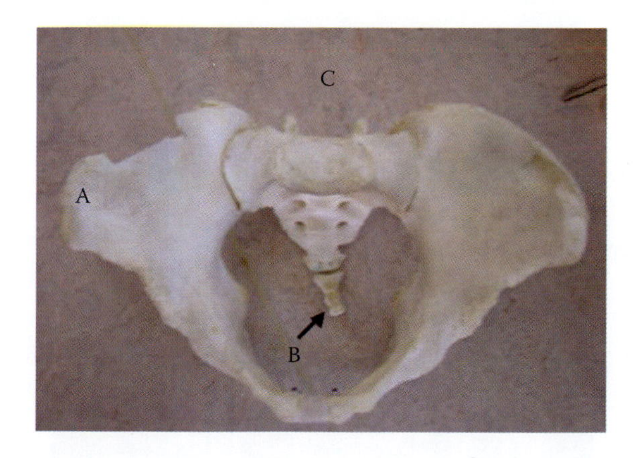

10.12 What part of the human skeleton is pictured here?
10.13 This photograph was taken from which plane?
10.14 Is "*A*" superior or inferior to "*B*"?
10.15 Is *C* on the anterior or posterior side?

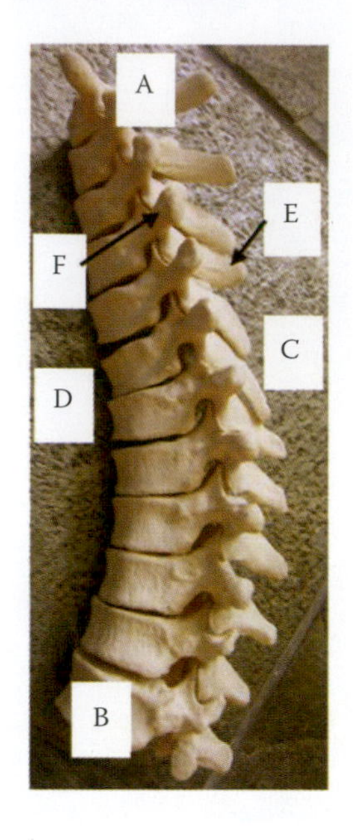

10.16 What is pictured here?
10.17 Was this photograph taken from a transverse, sagittal, or coronal plane?
10.18 Is "*B*" superior or inferior to "*A*"?
10.19 Is *D* the posterior or anterior position?
10.20 Is "*E*" medial or lateral relative to "*F*"?
10.21 Name the three types of vertebrae shown in the following photograph and describe what distinguishes them.

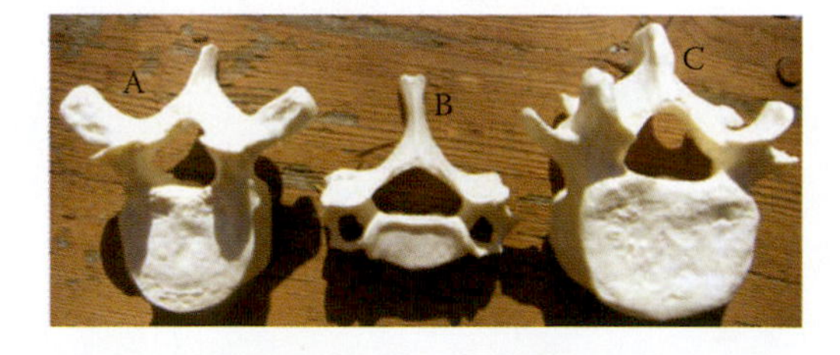

10.22 Name the bones depicted in the following photograph.

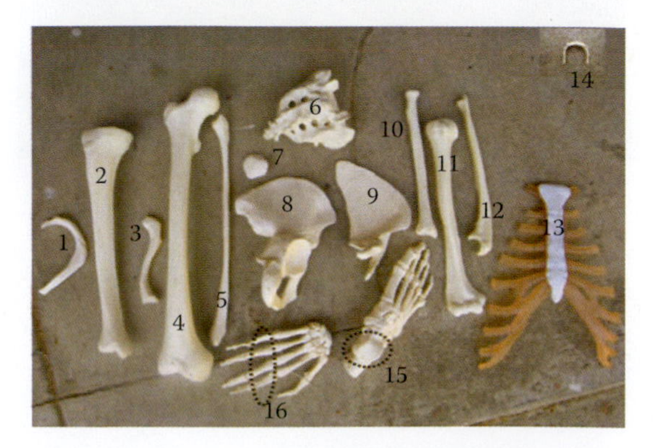

10.23 List the landmarks and distinguishing characteristics that differentiate between a male and female skull.

10.24 For the following photographs, identify skulls (a) and (b) as belonging to a male or female. What characteristic(s) did you use to make those determinations?

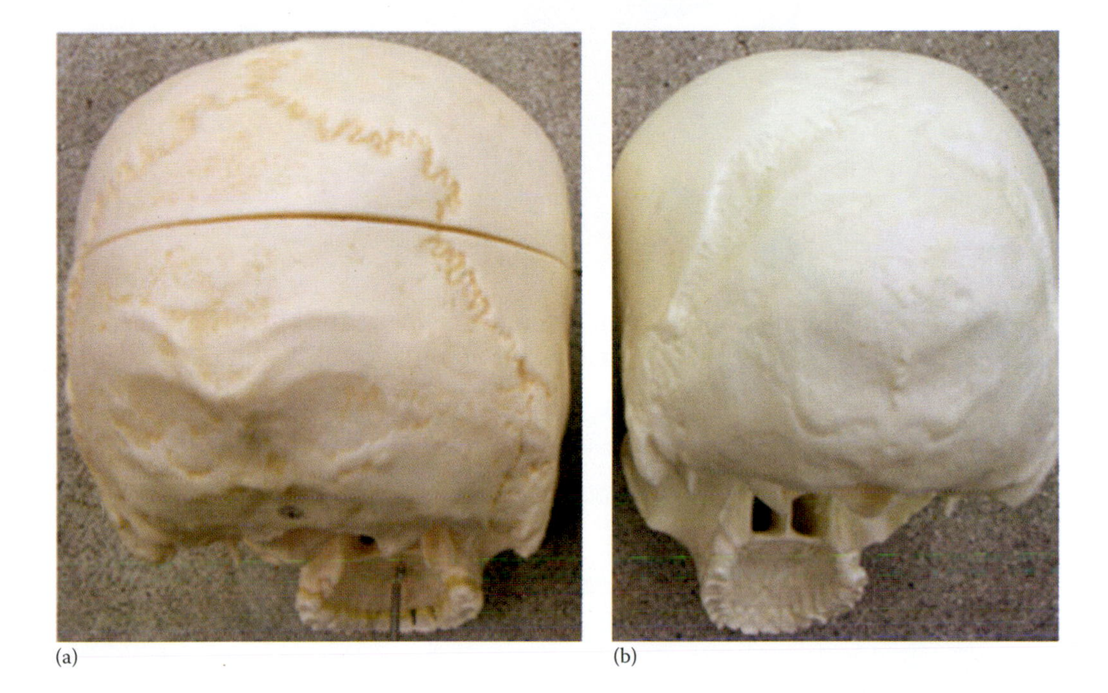

(a) (b)

10.25 For the following photographs, identify skulls (a) and (b) as belonging to a male or female. What characteristic(s) did you use to make those determinations?

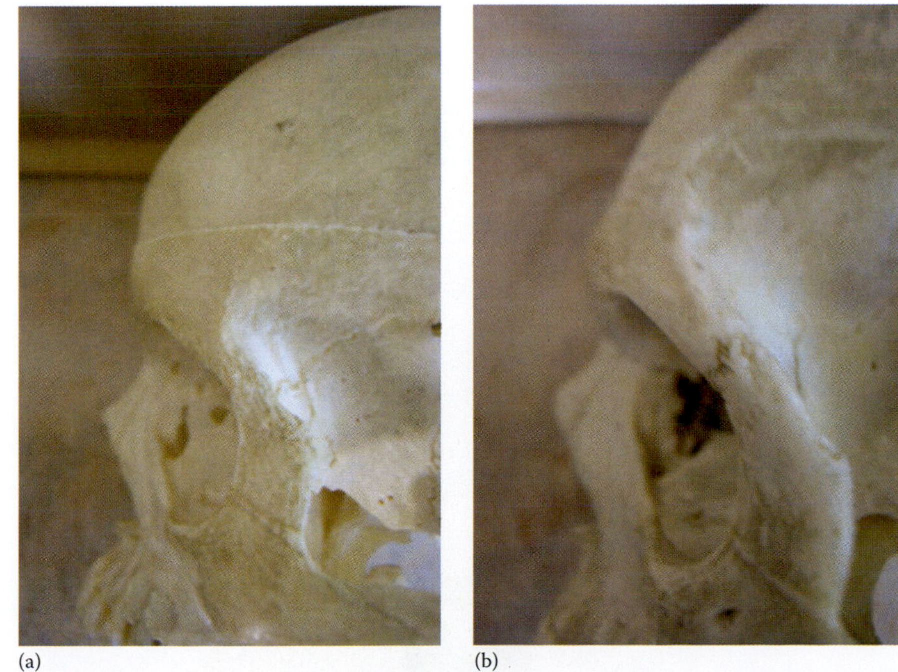

(a) (b)

10.26 For the following photograph, identify jaws A and B as belonging to a male or female. What characteristic(s) did you use to make those determinations?

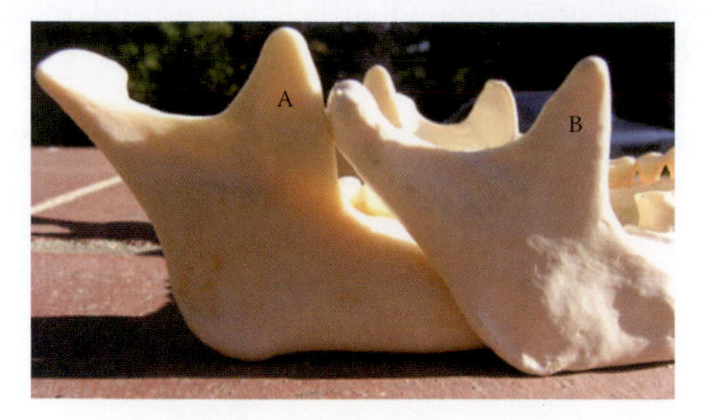

10.27 For the following photographs, identify jaws (a) and (b) as belonging to a male or female. What characteristic(s) did you use to make those determinations?

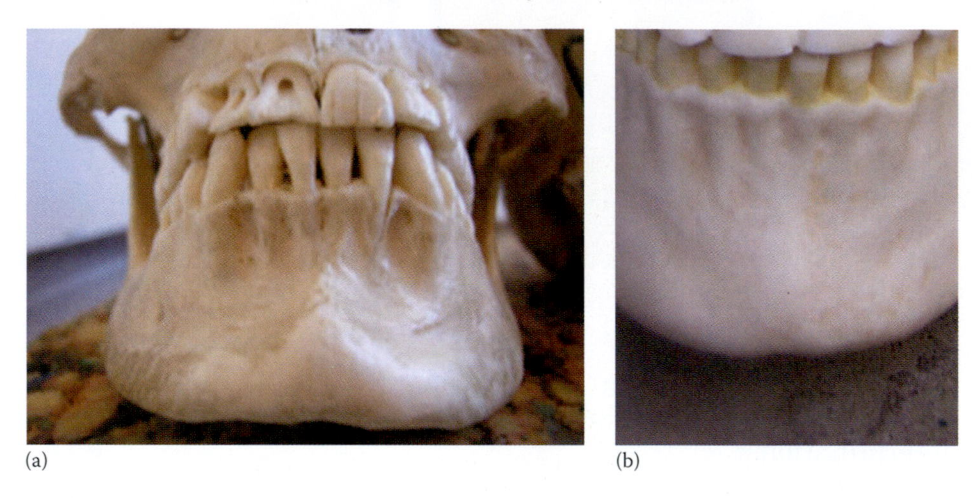
(a) (b)

10.28 Of the two skulls A and B shown in the following photograph, which is male and which is female? Why?

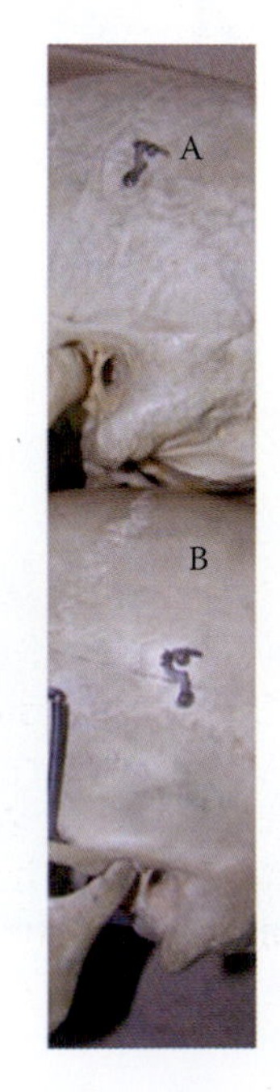

10.29 List the pelvic landmarks and describe how they can be used to differentiate between male and female.

10.30 Do the following photographs (a) and (b) show the pelvis of a male or female? Name the specific landmark you have chosen to justify your answer and explain why that landmark leads you to your conclusion.

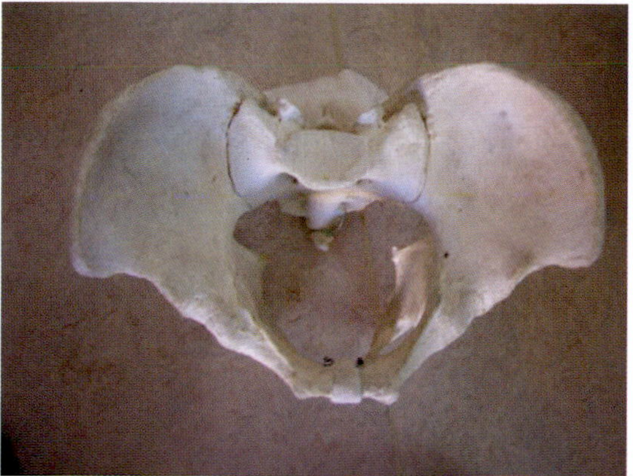

(a)

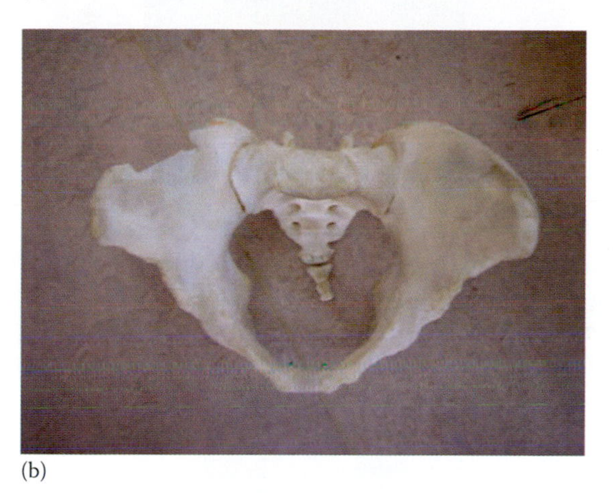

(b)

10.31 In the following photograph picturing pelvic bones marked "*A*" and "*B*," which is that of a male and which is that of a female? Describe what landmark(s) you used to make that assignment.

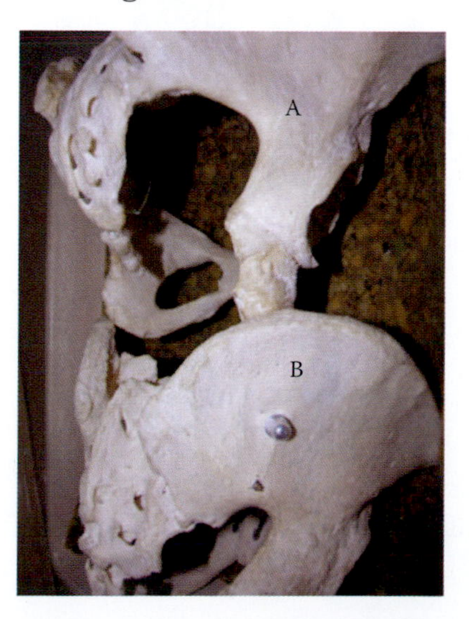

10.32 Determine if the humerus in the following photograph is from a male or female. The insert shows the proximal end of the bone from the medial perspective coronal plane. Use its associated penny for scale.

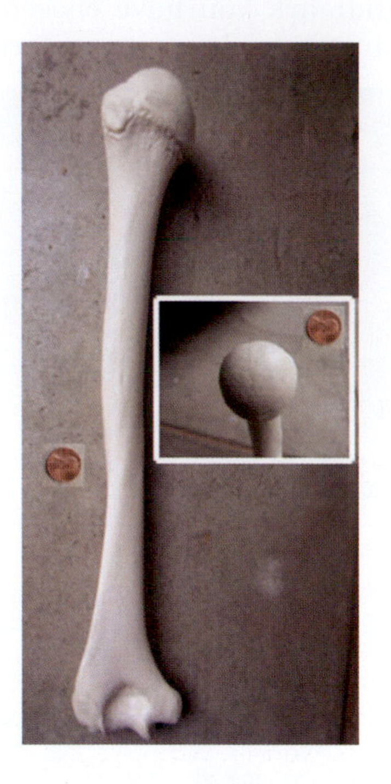

10.33 Determine if the femur in the following photograph is from a male or female. Use the photograph of the penny for scale.

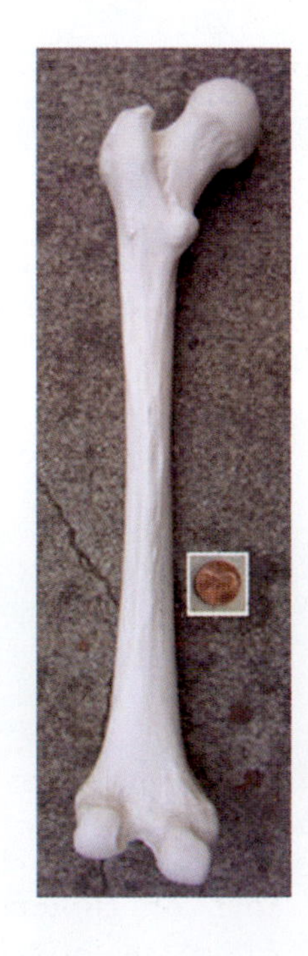

10.34 What is the limitation of stating the identity of anyone based on skeletal analysis?

Further Reading

Sex Determination with Fragmented Skeletal Remains by M.A. Kelley in *Journal of Forensic Sciences*, Vol. 24, pages 154–158, 1979.

Sex Determination from the Radius in Humans by J.C. Allen, M.F. Bruce, and S.M. MacLaughlin in *Human Evolution*, Vol. 2, No. 4, pages 373–378, 1987.

Quantitative Genetics of Sexual Dimorphism in Human Body Size by Alan R. Rogers and Arindam Mukherjee in *Evolution*, Vol. 46, No. 1, pages 226–334, 1992.

Estimation of Stature from Metacarpal Lengths by L. Meadows and R.L. Jantz in *Journal of Forensic Sciences*, Vol. 37, No. 1, pages 147–154, 1992.

Dead Men Do Tell Tales: The Strange and Fascinating Cases of a Forensic Anthropologist by William R. Maples, Broadway Books, New York, 1995.

The Bone Detectives; How Forensic Anthropologists Solve Crimes and Uncover Mysteries of the Dead by Donna M. Jackson, Little, Brown Young Readers, Boston, MA, 1996.

Evaluation of Seven Methods of Estimating Age at Death from Mature Human Skeletal Remains by E. Baccino, D.H. Ubelaker, L.A.C. Hayek, and A. Zerilli in *Journal of Forensic Sciences*, Vol. 44, No. 5, pages 931–936, 1999.

Bones: A Forensic Detective's Casebook by Douglass Ubelaker, M. Evans and Company, Inc., Publishers, New York, 2000.

The Bone Lady: Life as a Forensic Anthropologist by Mary H. Manheim, Penguin (Non-Classics) Publishers, Reissue edition, New York, 2000.

A Test of the Phenice Method for the Estimation of Sex by D.H. Ubelaker and C.G. Volk in *Journal of Forensic Sciences*, Vol. 47, No. 1, pages 19–24, 2002.

Silent Witness: How Forensic Anthropology Is Used to Solve the World's Toughest Crimes by Roxana Ferlini, Firefly Books, Ltd., Publishers, Buffalo, New York, 2002.

Testing the Validity of Metacarpal Use in Sex Assessment of Human Skeletal Remains by A.M. Burrows, V.P. Zanella, and T.M. Brown in *Journal of Forensic Sciences*, Vol. 48, No. 1, pages 17–20, 2003.

Age Estimation from Teeth in Children and Adolescents by M. Muller-Bolla, L. Lupi-Pegurier, G. Quatrehomme, A.M. Velly, and M. Bolla in *Journal of Forensic Sciences*, Vol. 48, No. 1, pages 140–148, 2003.

Reliability and Validity of Eight Dental Age Estimation Methods for Adults by H. Soomer, H. Ranta, M.J. Lincoln, A. Penttilä, and E. Leibur in *Journal of Forensic Sciences*, Vol. 48, No. 1, pages 149–152, 2003.

A Metric Method for Sex Determination Using the Hipbone and the Femur by J. Albanese in *Journal of Forensic Sciences*, Vol. 48, No. 2, pages 263–273, 2003.

The External Occipital Protuberance: Can it be used as a Criterion in the Determination of Sex? By I.N. Gülekon and H.B. Turgut in *Journal of Forensic Sciences*, Vol. 48, No. 3, pages 513–516, 2003.

Estimating Stature from Tibia Length: A Comparison of Methods by I.C. Pelin and I. Duyar in *Journal of Forensic Sciences*, Vol. 48, No. 4, pages 708–712, 2003.

Osteometric Sorting of Commingled Human Remains by J.E. Byrd and B.J. Adams in *Journal of Forensic Sciences*, Vol. 48, No. 4, pages 717–724, 2003.

Determining the Sex of Human Remains through Cranial Morphology by R.L. Rogers in *Journal of Forensic Sciences*, Vol. 50, No. 3, pages 493–500, 2005.

On the Non-equivalence of Documented Cadaver Lengths to Living Stature Estimates Based on Fully's Method on Bones in the Raymond A. Dart Collection by M.A. Bidmos in *Journal of Forensic Sciences*, Vol. 50, No. 3, pages 501–506, 2005.

The Distal Humerus—A Blind Test of Rogers' Sexing Technique Using a Documented Skeletal Collection by C.G. Falys, H. Schutkowski, and D.A. Weston in *Journal of Forensic Sciences*, Vol. 50, No. 6, pages 1289–1293, 2005.

Using the Acetabulum to Estimate Age at Death of Adult Males by C. Rissech, G.F. Estabrook, E. Cunha, and A. Malgosa in *Journal of Forensic Sciences*, Vol. 51, No. 2, pages 213–229, 2006.

Evaluating the Accuracy and Precision of Cranial Morphological Traits for Sex Determination by B.A. Williams and T.L. Rogers in *Journal of Forensic Sciences*, Vol. 51, No. 4, pages 729–735, 2006.

Estimation and Evidence in Forensic Anthropology: Age-at-Death by Lyle W. Konigsberg, Nicholas P. Herrmann, Daniel J. Wescott, and Erin H. Kimmerle in *Journal of Forensic Sciences*, Vol. 53, No. 3, pages 541–557, 2008.

DNA-Based Prediction of Human Externally Visible Characteristics in Forensics: Motivations, Scientific Challenges, and Ethical Considerations by Manfred Kayser and Peter M. Schneider in *Forensic Science International: Genetics*, Vol. 3, pages 154–161, 2009.

A Test of Three Methods for Estimating Stature from Immature Skeletal Remains Using Long Bone Lengths by Hugo F.V. Cardoso in *Journal of Forensic Science*, Vol. 54, No. 1, pages 13–19, 2009.

Estimation of Living Stature from Selected Anthropometric (Soft Tissue) Measurements: Applications for Forensic Anthropology by Bradley J. Adams and Nicholas P. Herrmann in *Journal of Forensic Sciences*, Vol. 54, No. 4, pages 753–760, 2009.

11
mtDNA Sequencing

Police Headquarters, Wednesday 10:40 AM

Jenkins sat at his desk shuffling three sheets of paper Helen had handed him some half hour earlier. These were the sequences, she told him, of mitochondrial DNA (mtDNA) from the bone recovered in the bay along with the mtDNA sequences of Sarah Holmes and another woman named Myla Graystone whose sister, Rita, was also a missing person. Each page was imprinted with four rows of small peaks highlighted in blue, green, black, and red strung together in an apparently random order, over one hundred peaks per row. Above each colored peak was one of four letters—either an A, a C, a G, or a T. He lined the pages up to compare them, shuffled them back and forth, and gave each its turn at the top of the stack. The noise, apparently, was an irritant to Detective Sanders whose desk was to Jenkins' left. Sanders began to fidget like a fifth grader just before the recess bell.

"How's the case coming, Jenkins?" Sanders asked dropping his pen and, with his fingertips, flicking the report he was working on toward the back of his desk. He swiveled his chair toward Jenkins.

"If you mean to ask, Jim, if Criminalist Chang is still working with me, the answer would be that she is."

"And how's she working out?"

"She's a credit to the department," Jenkins replied matter-of-factly. "And sorry about your bet. If you were hoping for some type of ineptitude on either of our parts, I'm afraid you're in for a disappointment."

"All is not lost," Sanders said, "We're now at double or nothing for the duration of the case." An inscrutable smile snarled his upper lip.

"Hence your interest in our progress," Jenkins said flatly.

"Ah, Jenkins!" Captain White said coming down the aisle from behind them. "How are things with the Holmes case?"

"I was just telling Detective Sanders that it's coming along. We should be able to wrap it up soon."

"Can we make an arrest yet?" the captain asked.

"There's still more evidence to look over," Jenkins replied.

"You'll let me know when you have something definite?"

"Of course, Captain." Jenkins said as the captain continued toward his office.

"Captain White!" Sanders called after him. Without missing a step, the captain turned around to look at Sanders. "May I have a word with you?" Sanders asked. Walking backward, the captain waved Sanders to follow.

Arriving in Captain White's office, Sanders closed the door behind them and waited for him to take his seat at his desk. "Captain," he said at last, "sometimes investigations are expedited by choosing the most compatible investigators to work on them."

"I agree with you," the captain said propping his elbows on the armrests and tilting back in his chair to study Sanders from a greater distance.

"I was just talking to Jenkins," Sanders said.

"And?"

"I probably shouldn't be saying this, but I want to look out for my coworkers."

"I appreciate that," the captain said.

"Well," said Sanders, "we were talking about his partnering with Criminalist Chang."

"Uh-huh."

"I think he may have been hinting that her inexperience was causing delays in the investigation. He used the word ineptitude, actually."

"What are you trying to say, Detective?"

"In the interests of the investigation, you may want to consider reassigning Criminalist Chang to a different mentor."

"I see," the captain said pausing in thought. He grabbed a pen and rolled it over in his hands end to end like a pinwheel. He leaned forward over his desk. His eyes narrowed. "Detective Sanders," he finally said, "if I so much as hear a word that you're meddling in Jenkins' case, if I hear a word that you're trying to screw things up for him, so help me, I swear I'll bust you down to meter maid. Do we understand each other?"

"Captain, I'm just trying to help the department."

"You can help the department by getting back to your desk and finishing that report on the City Hall burglary."

"Yes sir," Sanders said and quickly left the captain's office. Rather than returning to his desk, however, he made his way up to the DNA lab on the second floor where he found Helen Chang adding liquid to a round Plexiglas vessel on the ABI sequencer.

"Helen Chang?" Sanders asked peering through the half-opened door.

"That's right," Helen acknowledged turning from the instrument.

"Hi, I'm Detective Sanders. I sit next to your partner, Bob Jenkins."

"I've heard your name," Helen acknowledged.

"Is this it?" Sanders asked walking up to the instrument and placing a hand on its left panel. "Is this the DNA sequencing machine I've heard about?"

"I guess it is," Helen replied.

"It looks expensive," Sanders observed. "How does it work?"

"A laser causes fluorescent dyes on the ends of DNA fragments made in a sequencing reaction to glow as they're separated in an electric field. The different colors correspond to the different DNA bases on the ends of the fragments."

“Wow! You must have gone to school for a few years, huh?”

“Berkeley.”

“A great school! My parents always wanted me to go to Berkeley. I ended up at Baylor instead. Still, I always get tickets to the Berkeley/Stanford game. Does Jenkins know how this thing works?” Sanders asked.

“I think he’s more interested in what it tells him than how it operates. He hasn’t really asked.”

“That’s surprising,” Sanders said. “It seems fascinating. But then Jenkins is somewhat of a technophobe. He was the last one in the department to get a cell phone. So tell me, how does a young, attractive woman such as yourself end up in a crime lab doing DNA sequencing with a guy who doesn’t share your interest in it?”

“I’ve asked myself that very same question,” Helen replied with a half smile. “But without the young and attractive part,” she added as she returned to the task of pouring liquids into the elongated vials on the instrument’s stage.

“Are things going okay with Jenkins?”

“He’s not so bad once you get to know him.”

“I suppose,” Sanders acknowledged. “It’s just that the rest of us in the department are a little concerned for you.”

“Oh? Why’s that?” Helen asked.

“Don’t get me wrong, Jenkins is a competent detective, but he’s had issues with partners in the past.”

“Issues?”

“To be blunt,” Sanders said, “he’s not exactly known for sticking up for his buddies, you know, when the bacon’s in the pan.”

“Oh? I hadn’t noticed.”

“When you’re out there in the field, you’ve gotta be able to rely unconditionally on your partner. You back them up; they back you up. And you don’t bust their chops or rat on them if they happen to screw up.”

“Makes sense.”

“You’re a team. That kind of relationship, though, isn’t part of Jenkins playbook. I guess what I’m trying to say is that if you’d like me to help you out, you know, show you the ropes, I’d be happy to. I’m not sure why you were partnered with Jenkins in the first place. I suppose the captain had his reasons, but it’s beyond me what those reasons were. I’m sure Jenkins would be fine with it.”

“You think so?”

“Not to be discouraging but things he’s said about you. It doesn’t seem right him ragging on someone so new. Let me apologize for that on behalf of the department.”

“That’s not necessary,” said Helen,

“Well, maybe you could ask the captain to reassign you so that you and I can work together.”

"That's an interesting idea," Helen said stepping toward the laboratory door and taking Sanders drafting in her slipstream. She opened the door to let him out. "Let me think about it."

"You will think about it, right?" Sanders asked. "And just so there's no hard feelings anywhere, you probably shouldn't mention this conversation to Jenkins.

"Okay," Helen replied.

"Or Captain White," Sanders added.

"I won't," Helen replied as Sanders stepped past her. She closed the door quietly behind him. "And I was born yesterday," she said softly to herself as she walked back to the sequencer.

mtDNA Sequencing: Laboratory

Introduction

There are a number of methods used by forensic scientists to help them identify the participants of a crime. Eyewitness accounts, handwriting comparisons, hair analysis, shoe print castings, video surveillance, blood typing, and fingerprint analysis are all tools at a criminalist's disposal. But, ultimately, there is no more powerful and discriminating method of differentiating people than by examining their DNA at the base pair level—by DNA sequencing. (This does not apply to identical twins who, for all intents and purposes, have identical DNA. Identical twins can be distinguished, however and oddly enough, by their fingerprints.)

The power of DNA sequencing applied to forensic science draws from the variations in our DNA. If you were to align your DNA with the DNA from the person next to you, chromosome to chromosome, there would be a difference, on average, once every 1250 bp. Criminals can change their clothes, cut or dye their hair, grow a beard, shave it off, undergo plastic surgery, burn off their fingerprints, talk with a British accent, put on glasses, or practice any other deceptions you can think of, but they can't change their genetic makeup.

In any crime of assault, molestation, or murder, it is almost always the case that some type of biological material is left behind at the scene. It could be blood, saliva, skin, semen, or hair. They all carry DNA. Violence, therefore, lends itself well to DNA testing. The most widely used DNA test is STR (short tandem repeat) analysis (Chapter 12), a technique that requires relatively intact chromosomal DNA and looks at the lengths of PCR products generated by amplifying segments of our chromosomes containing variations in how many times a 4 bp segment is repeated. However, from some evidence samples, it can be difficult to isolate long, intact DNA as found in the nucleus and as needed for STR analysis. This is particularly true for tissue samples badly burned or extremely old or degraded. For those situations, forensic scientists may turn to another DNA source constituting a different kind of genome found within our cells, as they did to examine the charred remains of those killed in the September 11, 2001 terrorist attacks on the World Trade Center. They look to the mitochondria.

Here, we examine the technology of DNA sequencing in forensic science. DNA sequencing is DNA replication with a bit of a twist, and this is where we begin—by reviewing the mechanism by which DNA makes copies of itself.

DNA Replication

The DNA that makes up our chromosomes carries within it the information for constructing all the proteins a cell needs to carry out the various functions required for its survival and reproduction—functions that include fighting off invading microbes, communicating with other cells, breaking molecules down for energy, and building molecules up for its growth and division. Because of its central and critical role in the life of a cell, DNA must be faithfully and equally distributed during cell division—when one cell divides into two. Chromosomes must be duplicated into two identical copies so that each new cell carries the same amount of genetic information as the original cell from which it arose. The process by which DNA is duplicated is called *DNA replication*.

DNA replication is surprisingly easy to do in the laboratory—it takes only a handful of reagents. We have already encountered a number of the terms needed to understand the reaction (see Chapter 5 and the discussion of PCR). *Template*, you may recall, is the term applied to the strands of DNA being replicated. A *primer* is a short, single-stranded piece of DNA that *anneals* to the template by *complementary base pairing* (an A on one strand across from a T on the other strand and a C with a G on opposite strands). A primer serves as the starting point for replication. The enzyme *DNA polymerase* attaches *nucleotides* onto the end of a primer as a new strand of DNA, complementary to the template, is constructed.

One component of a nucleotide, the building block of DNA, is a type of sugar molecule called *ribose* (Figure 11.1). It has five carbon atoms. These carbons can be numbered clockwise around the molecule, starting from the oxygen atom at the top of the structure, 1′ (one prime), 2′, 3′, 4′, and 5′. Attached to all but the 4′ carbon atom is an oxygen atom connected to a hydrogen atom—a molecule called a *hydroxyl group*.

The sugar found in DNA is a slightly modified version of ribose—it's missing the oxygen at the 2′ carbon. It is therefore called a *deoxyribose* (more accurately, a 2′-deoxyribose, but at any rate, it is the reason for the "deoxy" in deoxyribonucleic acid; Figure 11.2).

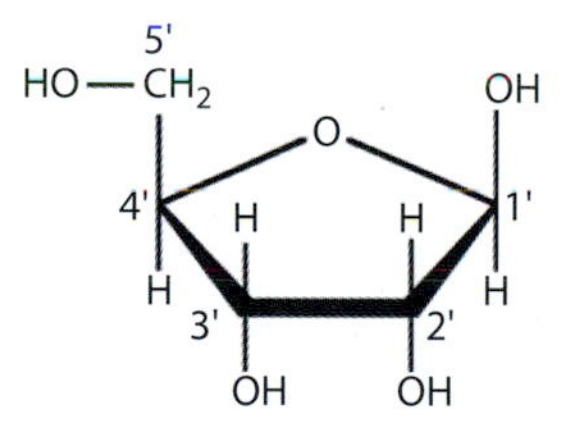

Figure 11.1 The sugar ribose has five carbon atoms (carbons are assumed to be at the vertices of the sugars' pentagon shape). The carbons are labeled clockwise from the penultimate oxygen atom 1′ to 5′.

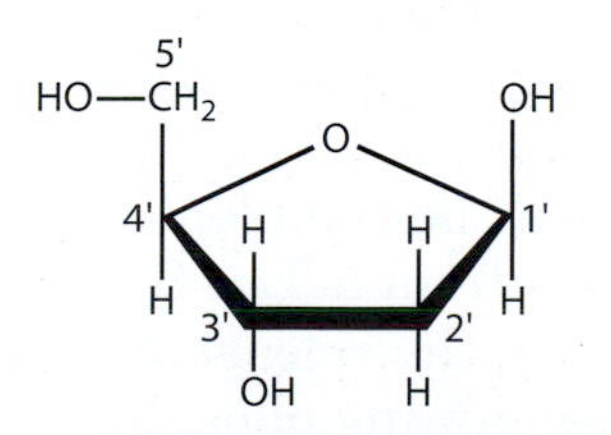

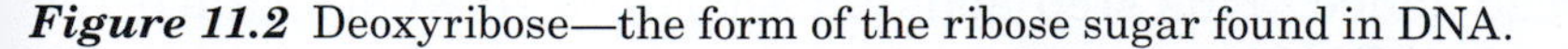

Figure 11.2 Deoxyribose—the form of the ribose sugar found in DNA.

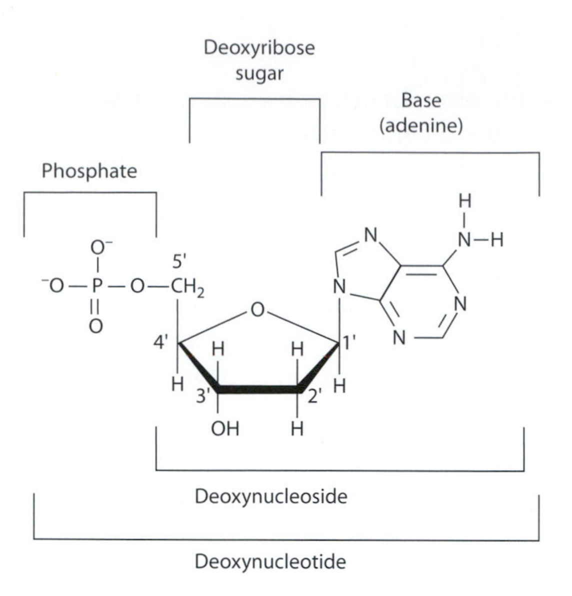

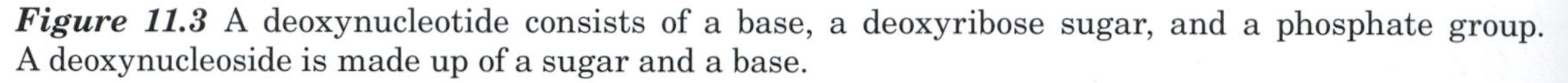

Figure 11.3 A deoxynucleotide consists of a base, a deoxyribose sugar, and a phosphate group. A deoxynucleoside is made up of a sugar and a base.

Another component of a nucleotide is a *base*. In DNA, there are four bases. They are adenine (A), cytosine (C), guanine (G), and thymine (T). Each base is attached to the 1′ carbon of the deoxyribose sugar. A molecule made up of a base attached to a sugar is called a *nucleoside*—it's still not a complete nucleotide, yet. That occurs when a third component, a phosphate group (a phosphorus atom with four oxygen atoms around it), is attached to the sugar's 5′ carbon (Figure 11.3). Normally, hydrogen atoms are attached to the oxygen atoms of a phosphate group. But, at the normal pH within a cell, these hydrogen atoms are donated to the water molecules surrounding the DNA strands. Having lost the positively charged hydrogen atoms to water, the oxygen atoms are left with a negative charge. It is because of the phosphate groups, therefore, that DNA has an overall negative charge. This fact is also why DNA is classified as an acid—a molecule that donates a proton (a hydrogen atom).

Four different deoxynucleotides are found in DNA. Figure 11.4 shows them as deoxynucleoside monophosphates (having a single phosphate group).

Although nucleotides are the building blocks found within a chain of DNA, they are not, directly, the raw components needed for DNA replication. For that process, the nucleotides must carry three phosphate groups (a *triphosphate*) attached to the 5′ carbon of the deoxyribose sugar. Such a molecule is called a *deoxynucleoside triphosphate* or dNTP, for short, where the *N* in dNTP can be any one of the bases A, C, G, or T. Therefore, there are four possible dNTPs needed to replicate DNA: dATP, dCTP, dGTP, and dTTP. DNA polymerase uses the energy inherent in the chemical bonds of a triphosphate to add one base onto the next as it builds a DNA chain (Figure 11.5). DNA polymerase adds a nucleotide onto the 3′ end of an extending chain (called the 3′ end because it is closest to the 3′ carbon of the deoxyribose sugar). The nucleotide it adds will be complementary to the base across from it on the template strand (an A across from a T, a C across from a G, etc.). The addition of a nucleotide is accomplished by the release of two of the phosphate groups from the dNTP and coupling of the remaining phosphate group to the oxygen atom at the 3′ carbon of the last base added. This step adds another link to what's called the *sugar–phosphate backbone* of DNA.

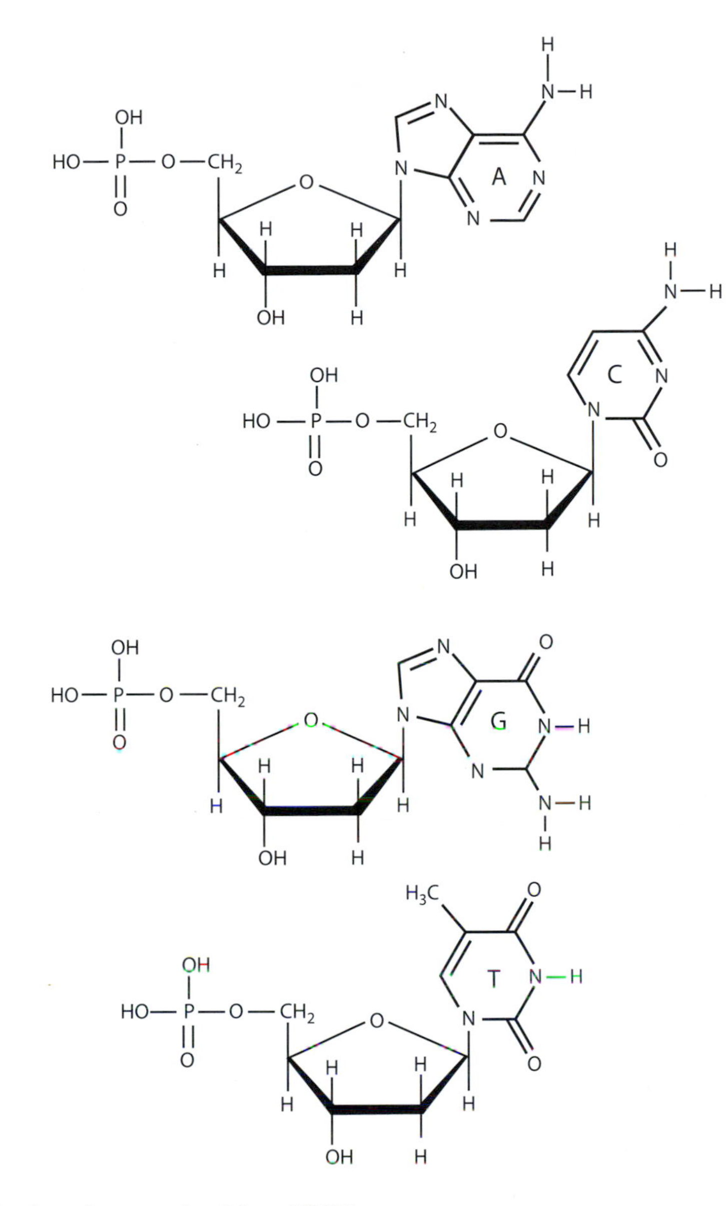

Figure 11.4 The four deoxynucleotides of DNA.

DNA Sequencing

During the mid-1970s, Frederick Sanger of Britain realized that by tweaking a replication reaction by just a little bit, it would be possible to sequence DNA—to tell the order of bases along a DNA strand. To do this, he set up four tubes and named them after the bases of DNA: A, C, G, and T. Into each tube, he added all the components needed to replicate DNA—he added primer, template, DNA polymerase, buffer, magnesium salt, and the four dNTPs. Into the *A* tube, however, he added a dATP nucleotide missing the oxygen atom from its sugar's 3′ carbon. Since such a molecule has lost its oxygen atoms from both the 2′ and 3′ positions, it is called a *dideoxynucleotide* (ddN). It is added to a replication reaction as a *dideoxynucleoside triphosphate* or ddNTP (Figure 11.6). When DNA polymerase added, by chance, a ddA onto the end of a growing strand, since that base lacks a 3′ oxygen, the chain was terminated—no nucleotides could be linked to it afterward. Into the *T* tube, he also added ddTTP. The *C* tube got ddCTP and the *G* tube got ddGTP.

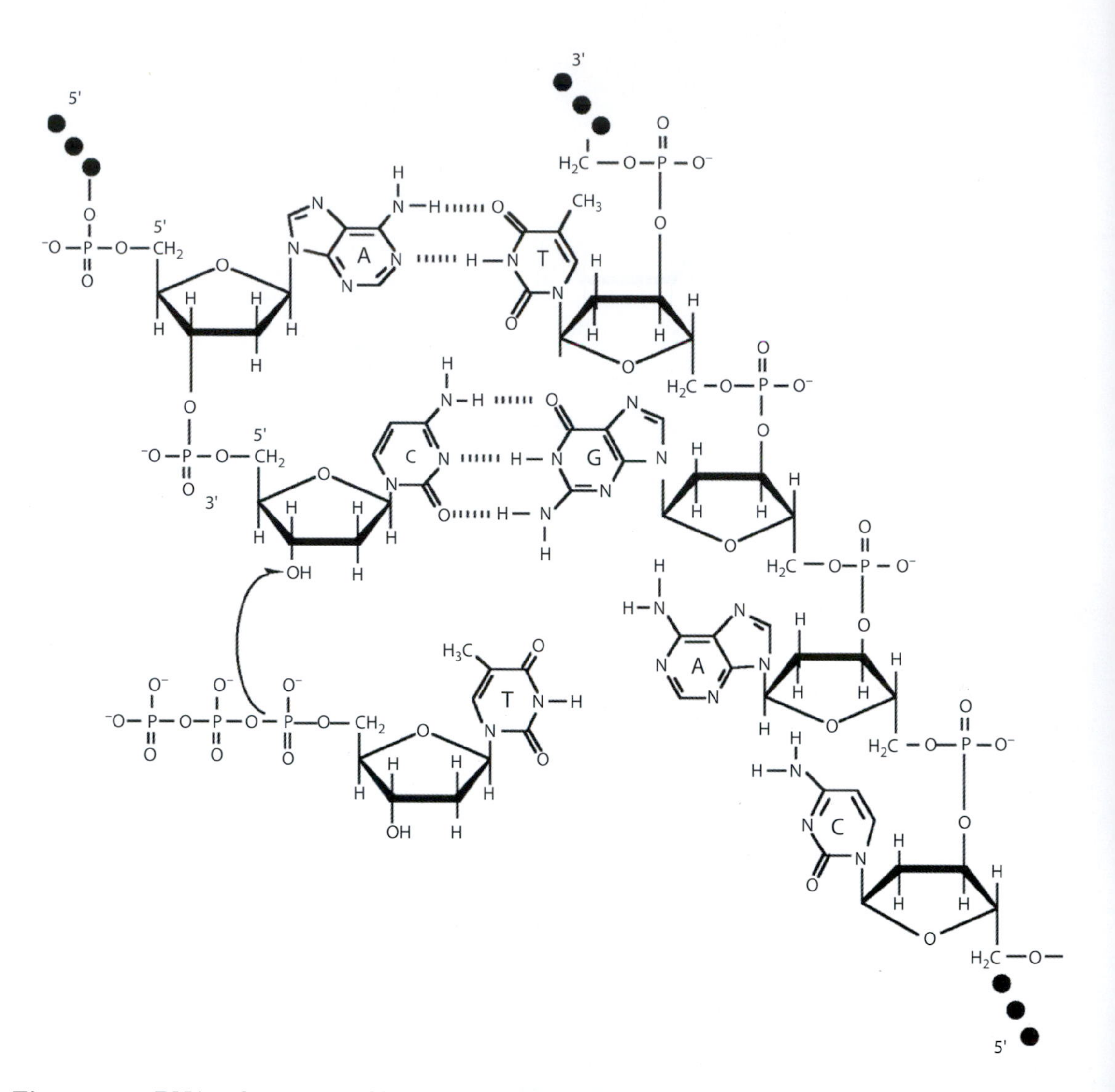

Figure 11.5 DNA polymerase adds another link to the DNA chain by creating a bond between the first phosphate group of a dNTP (here, dTTP is shown) with the oxygen on the 3′ carbon of the last base added to the chain (an arrow shows the atoms involved). The chain on the left represents the primer-extending strand. The chain on the right represents the template. Hatched lines between complementary base pairs represent hydrogen bonds.

The incorporation of the ddNs would be random—DNA polymerase could add either a dNTP or a ddNTP at any position. Since each tube had multiple copies of primed template, all possible termination events at all base positions would be represented. The *A* tube, for example, would have a collection of molecules of different lengths, and each fragment would be terminated in an *A* base. The *C* tube would have DNA chains terminated in a *C*, etc.

To determine DNA sequence, Sanger had to know the lengths of the DNA fragments made in the sequencing reactions. To do that, he took advantage of the fact that DNA is negatively charged. As such, in an electric field, it will migrate toward the positive pole (the anode). If the DNA fragments, on their way to the positive electrode, are also forced to travel through a Jell-O-like substance called a *polyacrylamide gel*, the shorter fragments, because they will find their way through the gel more easily, will move faster than the longer ones. This technique is called *electrophoresis*.

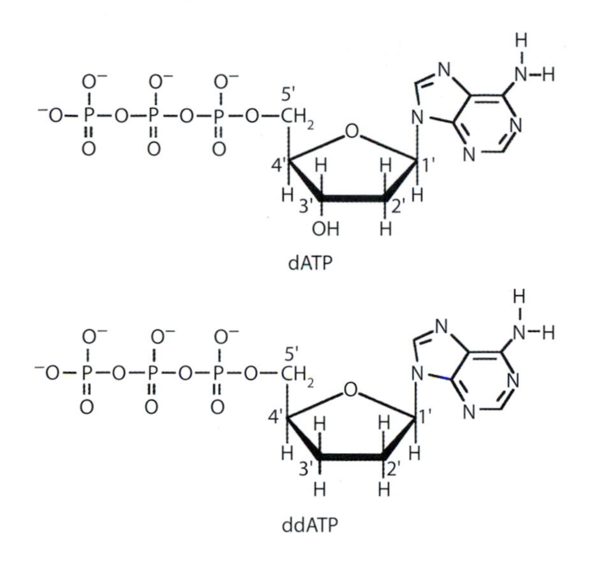

Figure 11.6 A dNTP (dATP shown) differs from a ddNTP (ddATP shown) by the oxygen atom at the 3′ carbon of the deoxyribose sugar.

Sanger electrophoresed the DNA fragments from each of his four reactions right next to each other on a polyacrylamide gel. To visualize the separated fragments, Sanger had included a radioactive molecule in the original sequencing reactions that was incorporated into the newly made DNA strands. Following electrophoresis, he placed *x-ray film* over the polyacrylamide gel, which, after several days of exposure, resulted in an image similar to that shown in Figure 11.7. DNA sequence is read by noting the order of bands from each lane (from each reaction), A, C, G, and T, reading from bottom (shorter fragments) to top (longer fragments). Each band up the ladder of bands on the x-ray film differs in size from the next one up the ladder by only one base.

The *Sanger method of DNA sequencing* (also called *the chain termination method*) using radioisotopes to tag the terminated fragments suffers from several drawbacks. Working with radioactivity is potentially dangerous, it's time consuming, and radioactive waste requires special considerations for its disposal.

Those shortcomings lead scientists at Caltech in Pasadena and at Applied Biosystems in Foster City to develop the technology for labeling DNA fragments with fluorescent dyes and for detecting those labeled fragments during their separation by electrophoresis. In 1986, Applied Biosystems' first automated DNA sequencing instrument made it to market. Called the Model 370A, the machine could generate roughly five times as much sequencing data as the *manual* Sanger method. The first fluorescent sequencing chemistry for use with the 370A employed the Sanger approach with ddNTPs as terminating bases, but in this case, the primers were labeled with blue, green, yellow, or red fluorescent dyes—each color corresponding to the terminating ddNTP added to the reaction. To prepare these reactions, the *A* tube contains ddATP and a primer labeled with a green dye. The *C* tube contains ddCTP and a primer labeled with a blue die. The *G* tube, with ddGTP, has a yellow-labeled primer, and the *T* tube with ddTTP has a primer labeled with a red dye. In addition, the DNA polymerase used to extend the primers is the same one used for PCR—*Taq*, an enzyme resistant to heat. At the end of a cycling process where the reaction is exposed to three different levels of heat, the four separate reactions are combined and electrophoresed in a single lane. A laser at the bottom of two glass plates sandwiching a polyacrylamide gel excites the fluorescently labeled terminated

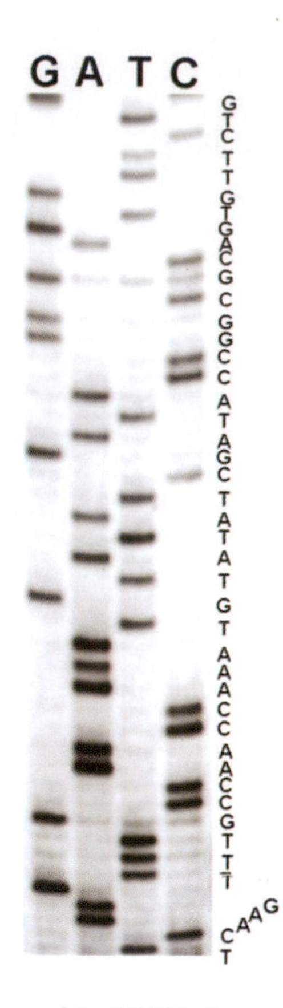

Figure 11.7 An x-ray film (autoradiograph) of DNA fragments generated in a Sanger sequencing reaction and electrophoresed through a polyacrylamide gel. Each sequencing reaction contains all the components needed to replicate DNA. Included in each tube, however, are radioactive dATP and an assigned ddNTP (ddATP in the *A* tube, ddGTP in the *G* tube, etc.). Truncated fragments are generated by the incorporation of a ddNTP—a random event that terminates chain growth. The terminated fragments are radioactive by incorporation of the labeled dATP. Following electrophoresis to separate the DNA chains smallest (bottom) to largest (top), x-ray film is placed over the gel and allowed to expose for up to 2 days (depending on the specific activity of the radioisotope). The film is then developed, and DNA sequence is read. Each lane contains the fragments generated by incorporation of the assigned ddNTP. For example, the *G* lane contains fragments ending in a G base. The fragments in the *A* lane all end in an A base and so on. DNA sequence is read from the bottom of the x-ray film (closest to the primer) to the top (farthest from the primer). A band produced by exposed film signifies a fragment ending in a G (leftmost lane), an A (second lane), a T (third lane), or a C (fourth lane).

chains as they migrate toward the anode. A computer interprets the color of each dye it detects passing the laser as a particular base along the DNA chain.

A number of innovations have been introduced since the first automated sequencer made its debut. Among these are the use of robotics; the use of long, polymer-filled *capillaries* for the electrophoresis step; and the use of alternate fluorescent dyes and reaction chemistries. One variation of the labeling protocol, called *dye terminator chemistry*, utilizes fluorescent dyes attached to the terminating bases (the ddNTPs; Figure 11.8). *Dye terminator sequencing* is easier to perform than the dye primer approach described previously since it needs only a single reaction tube. Sequencing is done with a template DNA, a primer, and a reaction mix containing magnesium, buffer, DNA polymerase, the four dNTPs, and fluorescently labeled ddNTPs. All terminated fragments generated in the reaction, since they will end in a ddNTP, carry fluorescent dyes on their 3′ ends. Electrophoresis of the fragments through a glass capillary filled with a polymer separates the different length chains by their size,

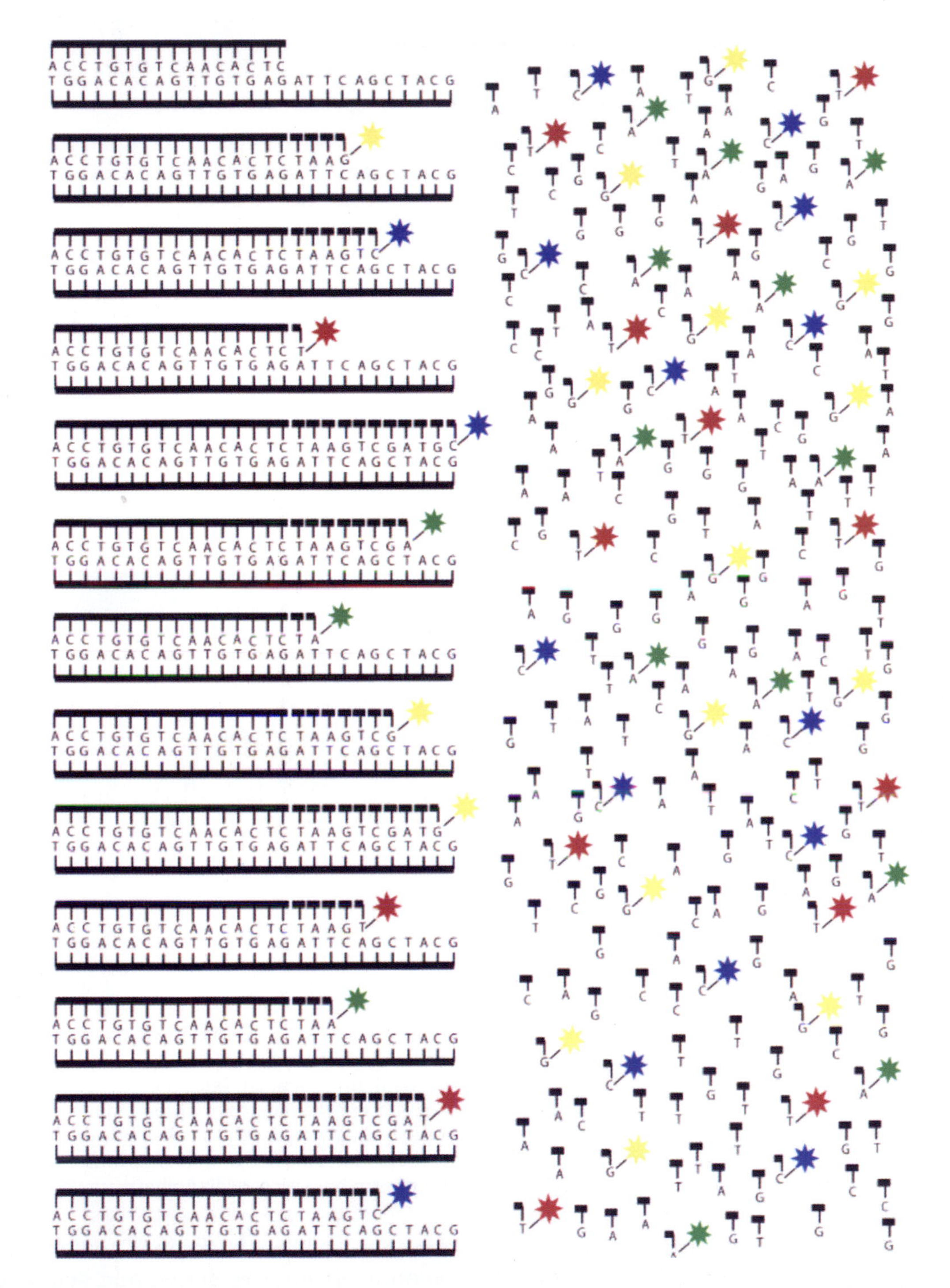

Figure 11.8 In a dye terminator DNA sequencing reaction, an unlabeled primer anneals to the template strand (the DNA complex pictured at the top of this figure). DNA polymerase adds nucleotides from a pool of dNTPs within the reaction mix. Included in that mix are fluorescently labeled ddNTPs. The position at which the polymerase incorporates a dye-labeled nucleotide is random. There will be many products of the exact same length terminated in the exact same color.

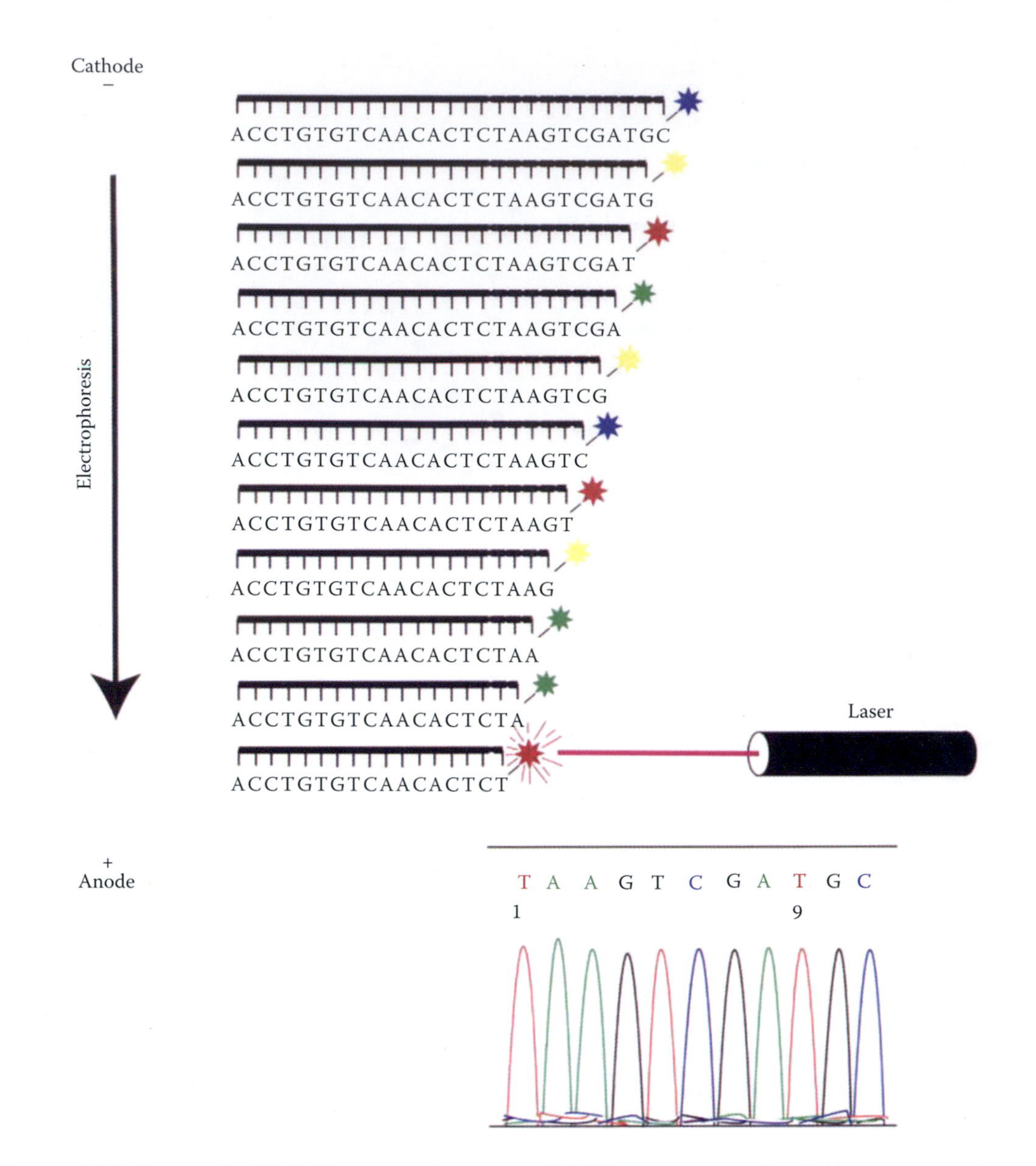

Figure 11.9 On an Applied Biosystems automated DNA sequencer, the fragments generated in Figure 11.8 are separated by electrophoresis shortest to longest. Since the DNA fragments are negatively charged, they will migrate toward the positive pole (the anode). Electrophoresis occurs in a glass capillary filled with a type of polymer that can resolve DNA strands that differ in length by only a single base. There will be hundreds of molecules of each defined length, but since they all terminated with the same ddNTP, they will all have the same color dye attached. An argon ion laser whose beam is directed at a position toward the end of the capillary excites the dyes on the ends of the fragment as they pass. Dye color is determined by a charge-coupled device (CCD) optics unit (not shown), and that information is interpreted by a software program as a base in the DNA chain.

shortest fragments running faster than longer ones. A laser positioned toward the far end of the capillary excites the dyes on the ends of the fragments, and sequencing software calls the base sequence according to the order in which the dyes are detected during their electrophoresis (Figures 11.9 through 11.13).

Mitochondria

You can move your arm. You can expand your lungs. Your heart beats. All these movements owe the energy used to make them small, intracellular, oblong organelles

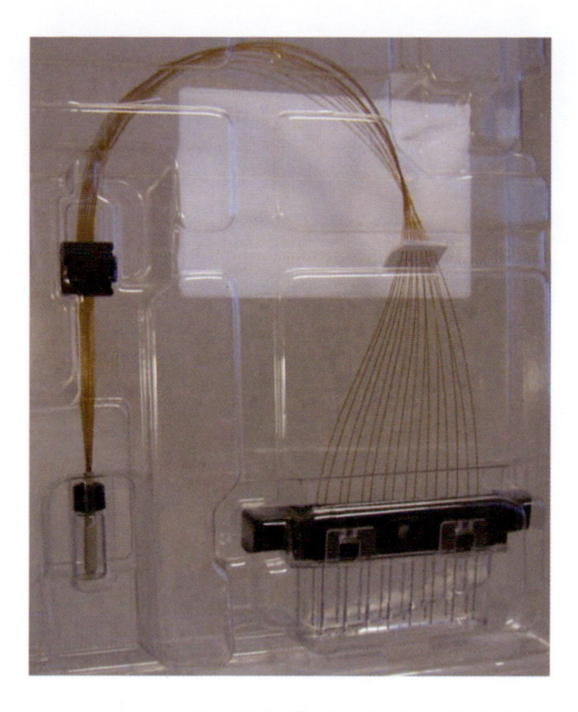

Figure 11.10 A capillary array run on the Life Technologies 3130xl Genetic Analyzer. The array consists of 16 hollow glass tubes that are automatically filled with a polymer gel between electrophoresis runs.

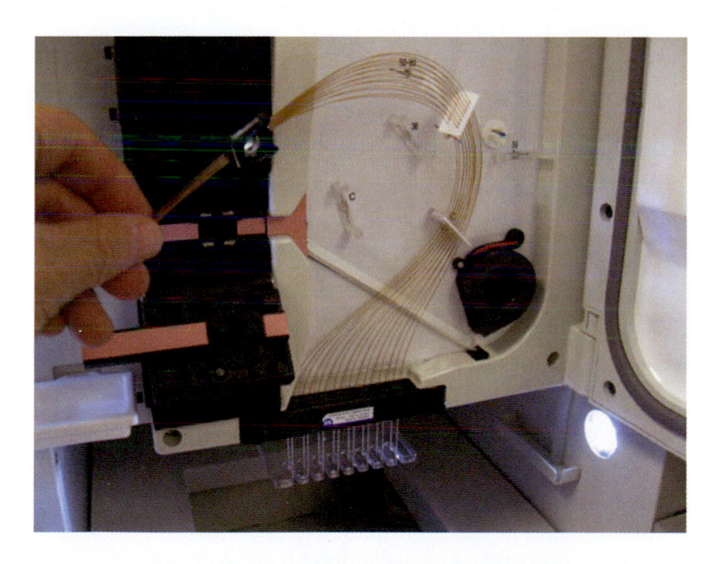

Figure 11.11 The capillary array is positioned within the sequencer.

called *mitochondria* (Figure 11.14). Mitochondria, it is generally accepted, were once free-living bacteria that took up residence inside eukaryotic cells (cells with a nucleus) perhaps 2 billion years ago. Their symbiotic relationship with eukaryotes provided them with protection and nourishment. The mitochondria provided their host with the chemistry set needed to produce ATP (*adenosine triphosphate*), the molecule all cells use for almost anything requiring energy. Over the long course of this relationship, the mitochondria eventually lost those genes redundant with those found on the chromosomes inside the nucleus of the eukaryotic cell. The mitochondria lost the characteristics of a free-living bacterium becoming, instead,

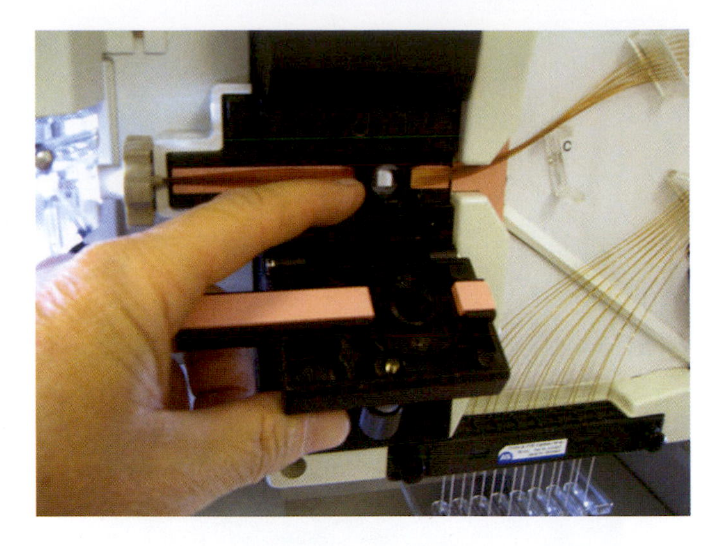

Figure 11.12 The optics chamber of the 3130xl sequencer. A split beam laser shines through the capillaries exciting the dyes on the ends of the DNA fragments generated in a sequencing reaction. Fluorescence signal is detected by a CCD camera.

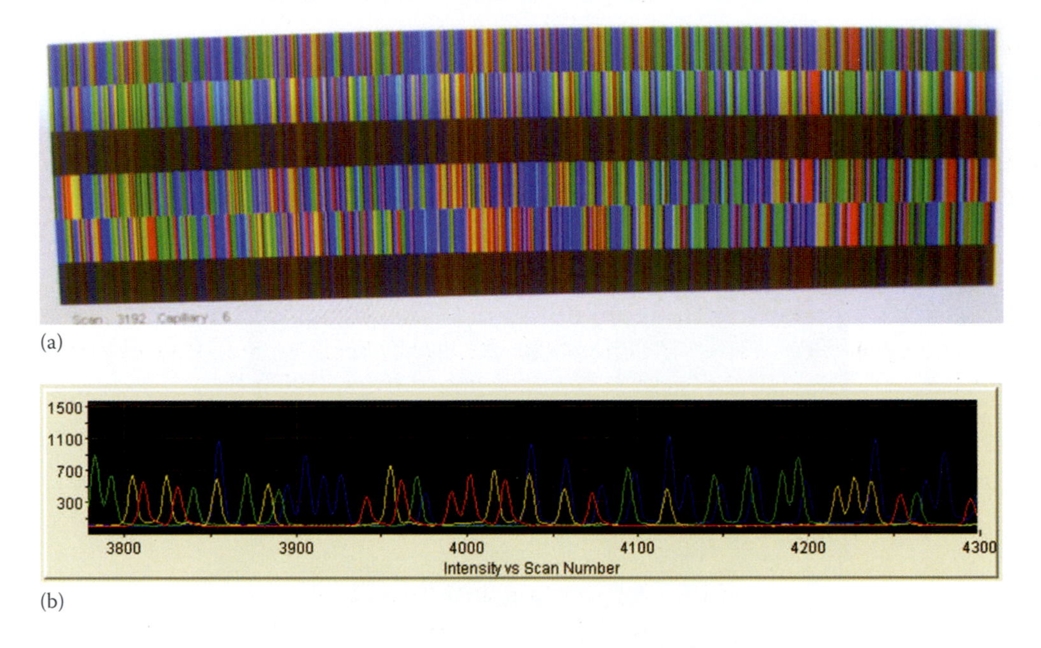

Figure 11.13 Raw sequencing data on an automated DNA sequencer consists of colored bands (a) that represent fluorescently labeled DNA fragments. These bands are viewed as peaks of fluorescent signal (b) that the instrument interprets as bases along a DNA chain.

a cellular organelle. What's left of the chromosome of the mitochondria is a circular piece of DNA some 16,570 bp in length encoding only 37 genes—those involved in the biosynthesis of ATP. What makes the mitochondria an attractive ally to the forensic scientist, however, is their abundance. There can be several mitochondrial chromosomes per mitochondrion and hundreds to thousands of mitochondria per cell. Because the mitochondrial genome is circular, small, and abundant, it can survive intact when the long, far less abundant DNA of the chromosomes has been lost. For example, mtDNA has been recovered and sequenced from the bones of Neanderthals over 30,000 years old.

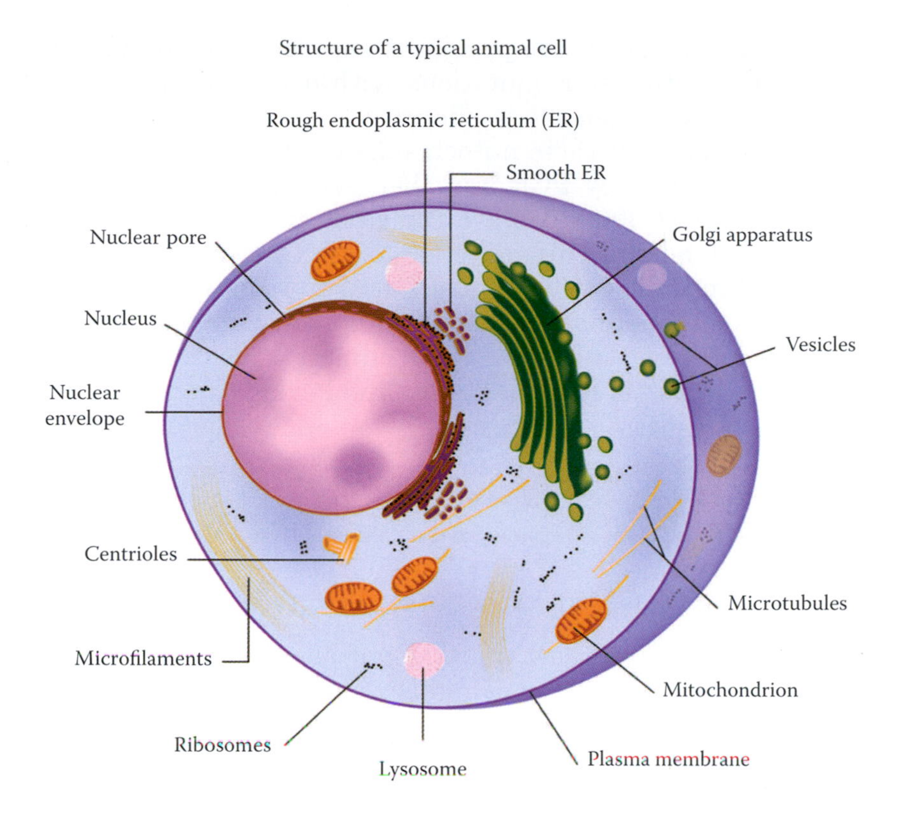

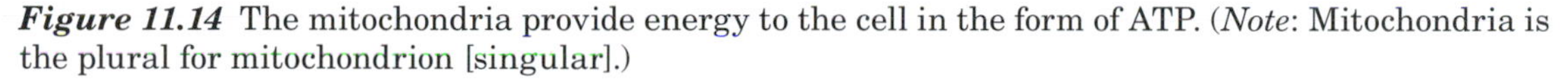
Figure 11.14 The mitochondria provide energy to the cell in the form of ATP. (*Note*: Mitochondria is the plural for mitochondrion [singular].)

Fertilization, when egg meets sperm, provides a female with a unique opportunity to assert a dominant role in determining the next generation's genetic makeup, at least when it comes to the mitochondria. Although a sperm cell has mitochondria, they are concentrated at the base of the tail, providing it with the energy it needs to propel the sperm up the vaginal canal. At fertilization, however, the tail is lost, and only the head of the sperm enters the egg, which is already filled with tens of thousands of mitochondria. All the mitochondria you have in your body, therefore, came from your mother.* The fact that mitochondria are maternally inherited provides the forensic scientist with a way to show relatedness between individuals. All relatives having a genetic line to your mother will have the same mitochondria—your mother's mother, her sister or brother, and your sister or brother. They all share the same mitochondria. This fact helped forensic scientists identify the remains of the victims of the September 11, 2001 attack on the World Trade Center in New York City where criminalists compared mtDNA from hairbrushes or tooth brushes recovered from the living quarters of the missing with the mtDNA from maternal relatives to assist in the identification of the victims.

Although the mitochondrial genome is tightly packed with the genes needed for ATP synthesis, there is a 1200 bp section of DNA called the *control region*, the *D-loop region*, or the *hypervariable region* that does not encode for any proteins. As such, it has been free to accumulate mutations without the burden of consequences that usually attends changes in the DNA molecule. That is, a mutation within a

---

* Some tissues may have mitochondria of different genetic sequences. This condition is known as heteroplasmy and can be the result of entry of the father's mitochondria into the fertilized egg.

gene can often spell disaster for the protein it encodes and, often likewise, for the organism containing it. However, mutations within noncoding regions will, more likely than not, trespass the genome in silence.

To identify individuals by their mitochondria, forensic scientists will amplify a part of the control region by PCR and then sequence that PCR product. Very roughly, two people out of 300 will have the same mtDNA sequence (Orrego and Clair King, 1990; Holland and Parsons, 1999). mtDNA sequencing was used in the Peterson case to aid in the identification of Laci Peterson who'd been murdered by her husband, Scott, on Christmas Eve of 2002 and was dumped into San Francisco Bay. Her body had remained in the water for almost 4 months before her remains washed ashore at Point Isabel Regional Shoreline Park.

In the Crime Lab

Activity 11.1 Simulating the DNA Sequencing Reaction: Part I

This activity will demonstrate how the order of bases along an unknown strand of DNA is determined by DNA sequencing. DNA polymerase in a DNA sequencing reaction, as it does in a PCR reaction, incorporates the four dNTPs, dATP, dCTP, dGTP, and dTTP, into a growing DNA chain as the template strand is copied. (In this activity, the dNTPs will be abbreviated as dA, dC, dG, and dT, respectively.) What differentiates a DNA sequencing reaction from PCR, however, is that for sequencing, the reaction also contains the four corresponding ddNTPs. (In this activity, these molecules will be designated ddA, ddC, ddG, and ddT.) These ddNTPs carry fluorescent dyes. Each ddNTP molecule has its own associated dye color. The ddATP molecule, for example, carries a dye that fluoresces green. Once the dye-labeled ddNTPs have been incorporated onto the end of a growing DNA chain, they terminate that chain and, because they are dye labeled, make the DNA strand *visible* to the laser and optics detection system of an automated DNA sequencer. As in PCR, a DNA sequencing reaction is cycled over and over again to allow for repeated replication of the template strand and to maximize incorporation of the ddNTPs, thereby increasing the amount of fluorescent signal. The DNA strands made during this process are electrophoresed through a long capillary in a DNA sequencing instrument, and the color associated with each piece of DNA passing the optics system is assigned a base depending on the color detected.

Protocol: Your instructor will provide an unknown DNA sequence written as a band of block letters A, C, G, and T in a random order.

1. Each student will be given one or more flash cards identified with the symbol dG, dT, dA, dC, ddG, ddT, ddA, or ddC.
2. The instructor will put a single-stranded four-base sequence (along with its 5′ and 3′ end designations for directionality) on the board.
3. You will play the part of the base shown on your flash card, and as that base, you will be part of a master mix solution from which will be drawn the bases needed for the extension of a DNA chain taking place during a DNA sequencing reaction. If, during the extension reaction (your teacher will instruct you as to when the activity begins), you recognize that your base should be the next one incorporated in the growing DNA chain, volunteer to go up to the displayed sequence and place your flash card at the appropriate position

above the strand being copied. For example, if the next base being copied on the given strand is an *A* and your flash card is either dT or ddT, place your card on the board above that *A*.

4. If, at any point, a ddN gets incorporated, the instructor will set aside the sequence of that terminated chain and a new reaction will be initiated. The template strand on the board will be copied over and over again in this manner until a ddN base has been incorporated at each position along the copied strand.
5. Once all possible terminated chains have been created, rearrange the DNA strands in the order in which they would migrate during electrophoresis on a DNA sequencing instrument. (If done properly, the ordered sequence should be complementary to the original sequence presented by the instructor.)
6. The instructor will put up a new DNA sequence on the board. Repeat the activity.

Simulating the DNA Sequencing Reaction: Part II

In this activity, you will sequence an unknown chain of DNA and determine its base content as the complement to randomly assigned dN and ddN bases.

1. Your instructor will place four blank squares on the front board to represent an unknown four-base sequence of DNA. The instructor will also distribute flash cards printed with individual dN or ddN bases.
2. With your fellow students, form a line facing the posted blank squares on the front board. Each student will place a base above a blank square according to the following guidelines:
    - The first student in line should place one of their bases above the first (leftmost) blank square on the board. This base can be either a dN or ddN. The first student then goes to the end of the line.
    - If a ddN is placed in the first position by the first student, no base can be placed immediately to its right. The chain is terminated. A new chain (string of bases) must be initiated above it. If the first student places a dN in the first position, the second student can place any base (a dN or ddN) to its right. The second student then goes to the end of the line.
    - If a ddN is placed in the second position by the second student, that chain is terminated, and a new chain must be initiated above the first blank square. However, the base sequence of the first two bases has now been set. For example, if the first student placed a ddG at the first position, that corresponding base of the unknown template must be a *C*, and only a dG or another ddG can be placed above it to initiate a new chain. Once set, the sequence cannot be changed during any subsequent rounds of copying.
    - After each student makes their contribution, they circle around to the end of the line.
    - If a student is unable to make a contribution to the sequence when it is their turn, they must cycle to the end of the line.
3. Repeat the above step until terminating (ddN) bases have been incorporated at the ends of all of the four possible chains.
4. Rearrange the terminated fragments in the order in which they would travel during electrophoresis.

5. In your laboratory notebook, record the sequence of all the terminated chains (in the order in which they would electrophorese through a capillary) and write down the sequence of the complementary template (representing the unknown sequence placed on the board by your instructor).

Activity 11.2 Aligning DNA Sequence Data

Activity 11.1 demonstrated the principles of chain termination DNA sequencing. As most genes (and chromosomes) are thousands (or many thousands) of bases in length, and as most sequencing reactions generate data only several hundred bases long, a typical sequencing study requires the alignment of a number of discontinuous but overlapping segments. Scientists make what is called a *contig* (for contiguous) from these overlapping fragments to decipher the complete sequence in its entirety.

In the following activity, you will take a fragmented English sentence (unknown to you at the beginning of this activity and written as a continuous series of letters) and, by aligning segments, re-create the complete sentence. The fragmented sentence can be thought of as being analogous to a series of sequenced DNA fragments. Keep in mind that there will be no spaces between words, no punctuation, and no capital letter to indicate the beginning of the sentence.

Protocol:

1. Your instructor will provide fragmented strips of paper that, collectively, spell out the words of an English sentence.
   Order these fragments into a coherent sentence and write that sentence in your laboratory notebook. Do not announce or discuss what it says, just raise your hand and have the instructor confirm your answer. Sit silently at your desk until the instructor gives the next set of instructions.
2. Your instructor will ask for a volunteer to write the sentence they constructed on the front board.
3. Repeat this process with another set of fragmented sentences and with strips of DNA sequence as provided by your instructor.

Analysis:
In your laboratory notebook, record your answer to the following question: What is the key aspect of this activity that allows one to order these fragmented sentences?

Activity 11.3 Determining Identity Based on mtDNA Sequence Comparison

In this activity, you will be provided with a reference sequence of mtDNA from a mother who lost two sons during wartimes. You will also be provided with mtDNA sequences extracted from remains recovered from two different burial sites where her sons were known to have fought. Your objective is to (1) determine all three mtDNA sequences and (2) perform a sequence comparison to determine if these skeletal remains are those of the two missing sons.

Materials:
Maternal mtDNA reference sequence
Two sets of mtDNA sequences from recovered burial remains

Protocol:

1. The instructor will provide you with three different colored sets of DNA sequences. One set represents the mother's known reference mtDNA sequence. The two other sequences represent those obtained from the mitochondria recovered from skeletal remains exhumed from two different burial sites. Align these sets of sequences to form contigs. (*Note*: In this activity, a contig will consist of a minimum of four overlap regions.)
2. In your laboratory notebook, re-create the data table below. In its squares, write out the contig sequence of the mother's DNA followed by the contig sequences from the two different burial remains as determined from step 1.

Data Table: Comparative mtDNA Sequences

Activity 11.3, Step 2, Comparative mtDNA Sequences

Base #	**1**	**2**	**3**	**4**	**5**	**6**	**7**	**8**	**9**	**10**	**11**	**12**	**13**	**14**	**15**
Ref.															
#1															
#2															

Base #	**16**	**17**	**18**	**19**	**20**	**21**	**22**	**23**	**24**	**25**	**26**	**27**	**29**	**29**
Ref.														
#1														
#2														

Ref. Known mtDNA sequence from mother of the two missing sons lost in battle
#1 mtDNA sequence sample from exhumed skeletal remains gravesite #1
#2 mtDNA sequence sample from exhumed skeletal remains gravesite #2

Analysis:
Write your conclusions in your laboratory notebook.

Erica Holmes Missing Persons Case

Helen Chang PCR amplified a 420 bp segment of the D-loop region from mtDNA isolated from Sarah Holmes, Rita Graystone (the woman who is trying to find her missing sister), and from the bone recovered in San Francisco Bay by the trawler fisherman. Given that mtDNA is maternally inherited, decide whether or not the bone is consistent with belonging to Erica Holmes. Fill out an evidence report with your analysis.

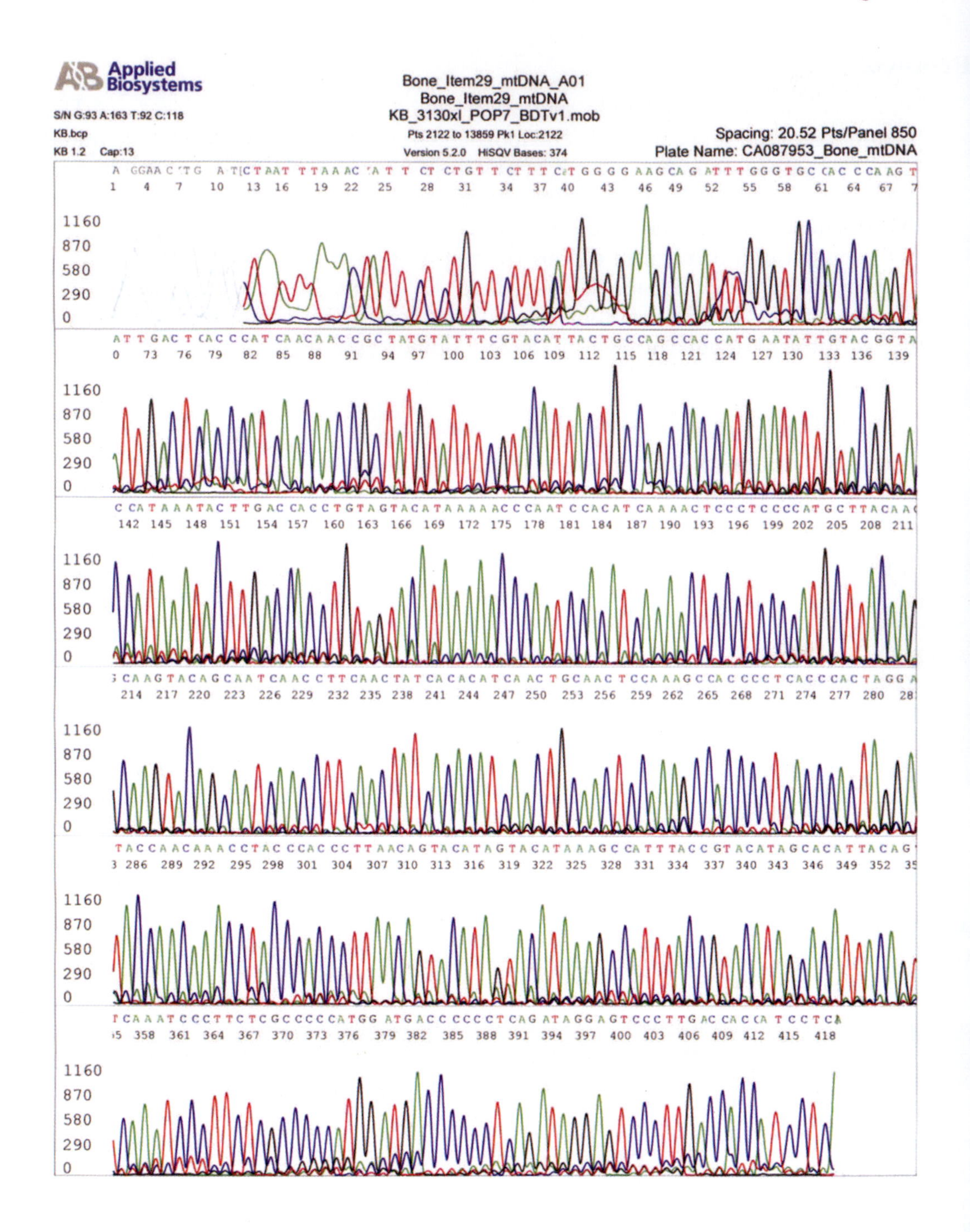
Applied Biosystems
Bone_Item29_mtDNA_A01
Bone_Item29_mtDNA
KB_3130xl_POP7_BDTv1.mob
S/N G:93 A:163 T:92 C:118
KB.bcp
Pts 2122 to 13859 Pk1 Loc:2122
Spacing: 20.52 Pts/Panel 850
KB 1.2 Cap:13
Version 5.2.0 HiSQV Bases: 374
Plate Name: CA087953_Bone_mtDNA
1160
870
580
290
0

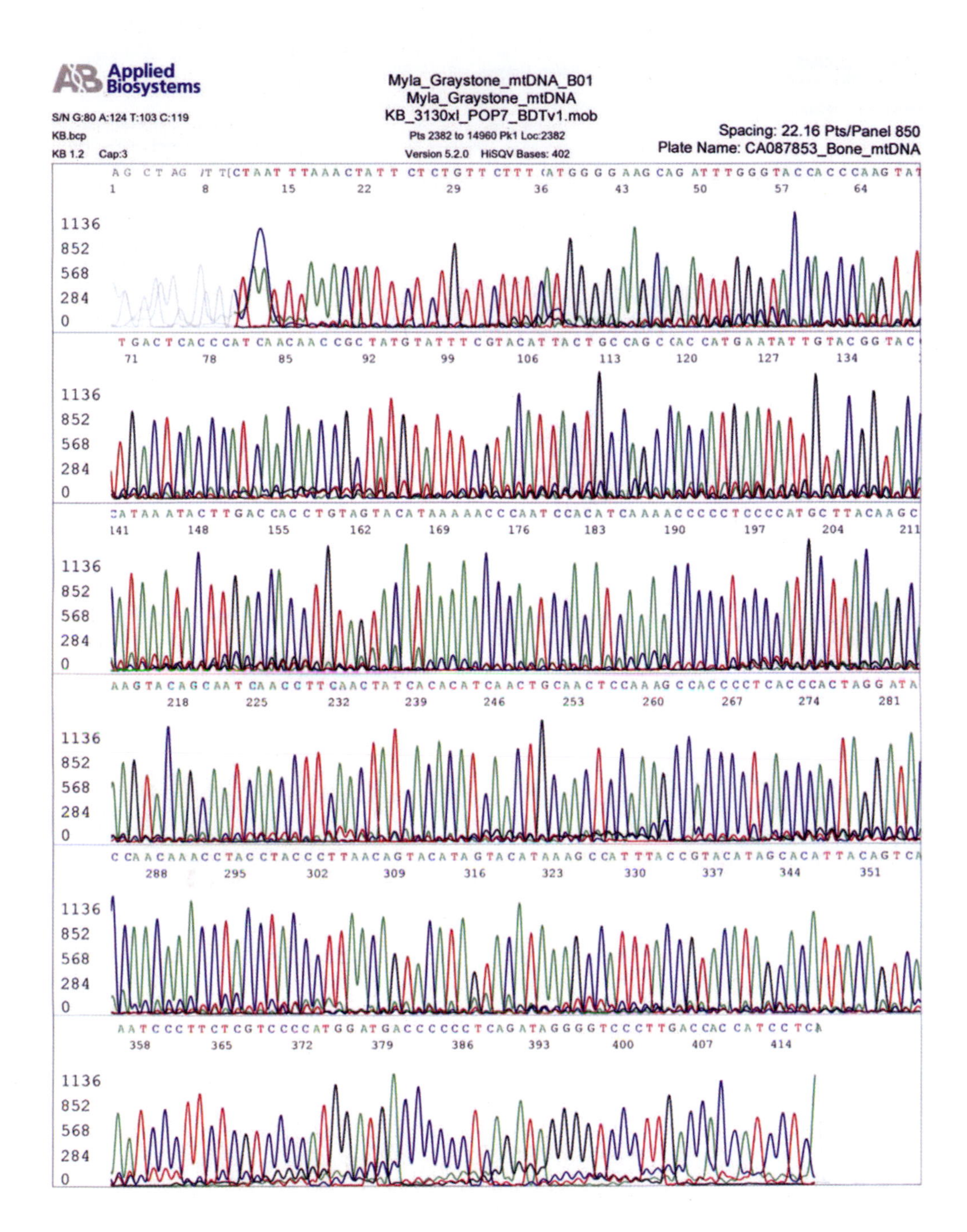
Applied Biosystems
S/N G:80 A:124 T:103 C:119
KB.bcp
KB 1.2 Cap:3
Myla_Graystone_mtDNA_B01
Myla_Graystone_mtDNA
KB_3130xl_POP7_BDTv1.mob
Pts 2382 to 14960 Pk1 Loc:2382
Version 5.2.0 HiSQV Bases: 402
Spacing: 22.16 Pts/Panel 850
Plate Name: CA087853_Bone_mtDNA

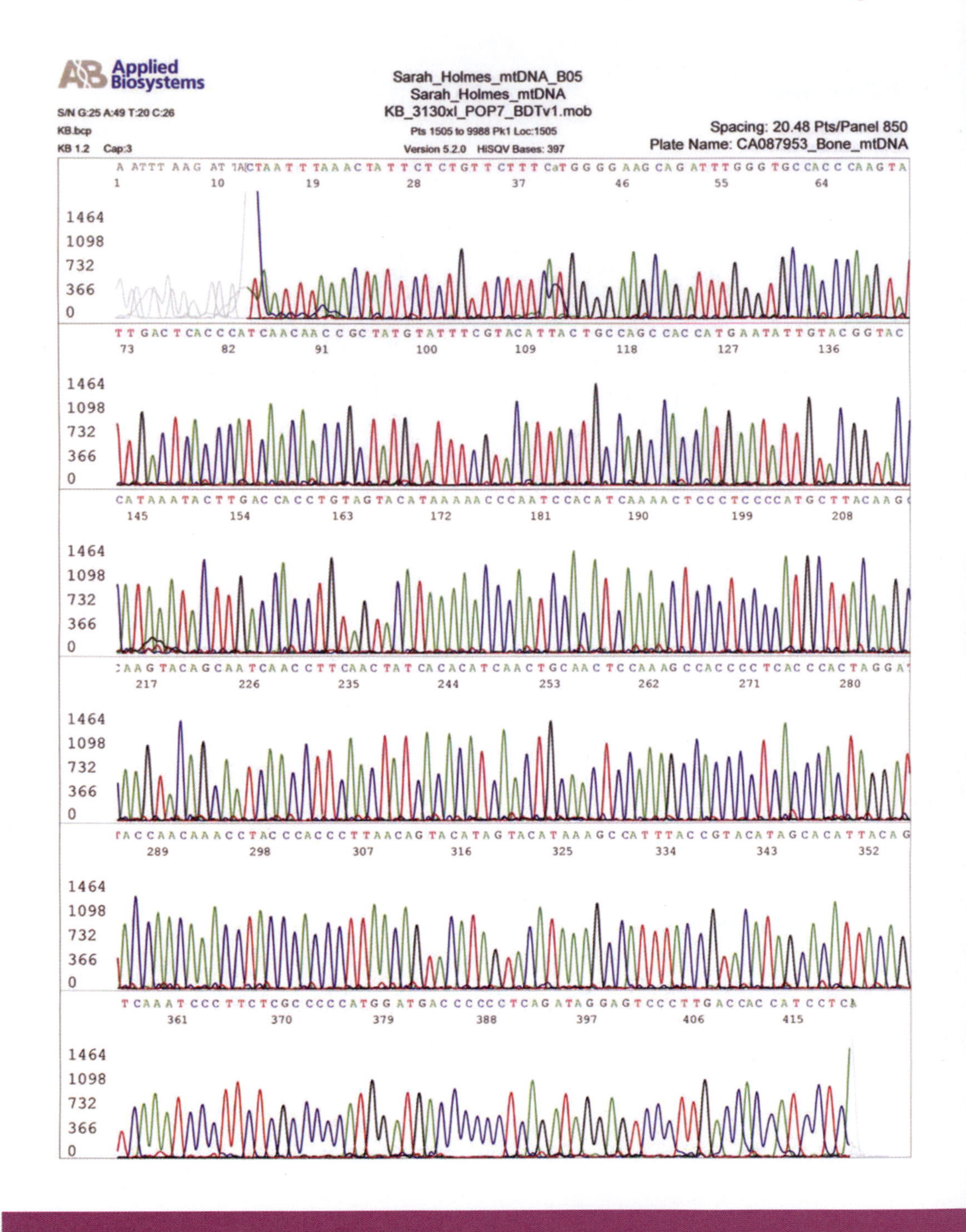

Review Questions

11.1 Explain the PCR process. Be sure to detail the three temperature steps.

11.2 In terms of chemical structure, what is a deoxyribose sugar?

11.3 The abbreviation often used for the building blocks of DNA is dNTP where *N* is anyone of the four bases. What is the full name for dATP?

11.4 What is the significance of the OH group on the 3′ end of the deoxyribose sugar?

11.5 If you remove the oxygen from the deoxyribose sugar at the 3′ end of the extending chain, what effect will that have on the extension phase of the PCR process?

11.6 What is a nucleotide called that is missing its 3′ OH group?
11.7 What does the abbreviation ddCTP stand for?
11.8 What is the relationship between DNA fragment size and rate of migration?
11.9 How does a DNA sequencing machine distinguish between a fragment ending in a dNTP and one ending in a ddNTP?
11.10 What is the function of mtDNA?
11.11 Explain the uniqueness of how mtDNA is inherited and compare this to the inheritance of nuclear DNA.
11.12 Can siblings from the same biological parents be distinguished from one another? Explain.
11.13 Which DNA source is more definitive when used for human identification, mtDNA, or nuclear DNA? Explain.

References

Determination of Familial Relationships by C. Orrego and M. Claire King in *PCR Protocols: A Guide to Methods and Applications* (Academic Press, London and San Diego, CA), pages 416–426, 1990.

Mitochondrial DNA Sequence Analysis—Validation and Use for Forensic Casework by M.M. Holland and T.J. Parsons in *Forensic Science Review*, Vol. 11, No. 1 pages 25–50, 1999.

Further Reading

Isolating DNA

A Simple Method for Preparing Human Skeletal Material for Forensic Examination by B.G. Stephens in *Journal of Forensic Sciences*, Vol. 24, pages 660–662, 1975.

A Simple Method for Extracting DNA from Old Skeletal Material by C. Cattaneo, D.M. Smillie, K. Gelsthorpe, A. Piccinini, A.R. Gelsthorpe, and R.J. Sokol in *Forensic Science International*, Vol. 74, pages 167–174, 1995.

Extraction, PCR Amplification and Sequencing of Mitochondrial DNA from Human Hair Shafts by M.R. Wilson, D. Polanskey, J. Butler, J.A. DiZinno, J. Repogle, and B. Budowle in *BioTechniques*, Vol. 18, No. 4, pages 662–669, 1995.

DNA Damage and DNA Sequence Retrieval from Ancient Tissues by M. Höss, P. Jaruga, T.H. Zastawny, M. Dizdaroglu, and S. Pääbo in *Nucleic Acids Research*, Vol. 24, pages 1304–1307, 1996.

Usefulness of a Toothbrush as a Source of Evidential DNA for Typing by M. Tanaka, T. Yoshimoto, H. Nozawa, H. Ohtaki, Y. Kato, K. Sato, T. Yamamoto, K. Tamaki, and Y. Katsumata *in Journal of Forensic Sciences*, Vol. 45, No. 3, pages 674–676, 2000.

A Simple and Efficient Method for Extracting DNA from Old and Burned Bone by J. Ye, A. Ji, E.J. Parra, X. Zheng, C. Jiang, X. Zhao, L. Hu, and Z. Tu in *Journal of Forensic Sciences*, Vol. 49, No. 4, pages 754–759, 2004.

Effects of Processing Techniques on the Forensic DNA Analysis of Human Skeletal Remains by J.L. Arismendi, L.E. Baker, and K.J. Matteson in *Journal of Forensic Sciences*, Vol. 49, No. 5, pages 930–934, 2004.

A Simplified Method for Mitochondrial DNA Extraction from Head Hair Shafts by E.A. Graffy and D.R. Foran in *Journal of Forensic Sciences*, Vol. 50, No. 5, pages 1119–1122, 2005.

Genomes for All by G.M. Church in *Scientific American*, January, pages 46–54, 2006.

DNA Sequencing

Cycle Sequencing by the Dolan DNA Learning Center, Cold Spring Harbor Laboratory. Available at www.dnalc.org/ddnalc/resources/cycseq.html.

Advanced Sequencing Technologies: Methods and Goals by J. Shendure, R.D. Mitra, C. Varma, and G.M. Church in *Nature Reviews / Genetics* Vol. 5, pages 335–344, 2004.

Emerging Technologies in DNA Sequencing by M.L. Metzker in *Genome Research*, Vol. 15, pages 1767–1776, 2005.

The Automated DNA Sequencer by A. McCook in *The Scientist*, Vol. 19, pages 15–17, 2005.

How It Works – Automated DNA Sequencer by A. McCook in *The Scientist*, Vol. 19, pages 18–19, 2005.

How Sequencing Is Done by the DOE Joint Genome Institute, U.S. Department of Energy, Office of Science, updated March 15, 2006. Available at www.jgi.doe.gov/education/how/index.html.

Mitochondria

Mitochondrial DNA and Human Evolution by R.L. Cann, M. Stoneking, and A.C. Wilson in *Nature*, Vol. 325, pages 31–36, 1987.

African Populations and the Evolution of Human Mitochondrial DNA by L. Vigilant, M. Stoneking, H. Harpending, K. Hawkes, and A.C. Wilson in *Science*, Vol. 253, pages 1503–1507, 1991.

A Nuclear 'Fossil' of the Mitochondrial D-loop and the Origin of Modern Humans by H. Zischler, H. Geisert, A. von Haeseler, and S. Pääbo in *Nature*, Vol. 378, pages 489–492, 1995.

Mitochondrial DNA Sequence Heteroplasmy in the Grand Duke of Russia Georgij Romanov Establishes the Authenticity of the Remains of Tsar Nicholas II by P.L. Ivanov, M.J. Wadhams, R.K. Roby, M.M. Holland, V.W. Weedn, and T.J. Parsons in *Nature Genetics*, Vol. 12, pages 417–420, 1996.

Neanderthal DNA Sequences and the Origin of Modern Humans by M. Krings, A. Stone, R.W. Schmitz, H. Krainitzki, M. Stoneking, and S. Pääbo in *Cell*, Vol. 90, pages 19–30, July 1997.

The Genome Sequence of *Rickettsia prowazekii* and the Origin of Mitochondria by S.G.E. Andersson, A. Zomorodipour, J.O. Andersson, T. Sicheritz-Ponten, U.C.M. alsmark, R.M. Podowski, A.K. Näslund, A.-S. Eriksson, H.H. Winkler, and C.G. Kurland in *Nature*, Vol. 396, No. 6707, pages 133–140, 1998.

A Chimeric Prokaryotic Ancestry of Mitochondria and Primitive Eukaryotes by S. Karlin, L. Brocchieri, J. Mrazek, A.M. Campbell, and A.M. Spormann in *Proceedings of the National Academy of Sciences*, Vol. 96, No. 16, pages 9190–9195, 1999.

Metabolic Symbiosis at the Origin of Eukaryotes by P. Lopez-Garcia and D. Moreira in *Trends in Biochemical Sciences*, Vol. 24, No. 3, pages 88–93, 1999.

Mitochondrial Evolution by M.W. Gray, G. Burger, and B.F. Lang in *Science*, Vol. 283, No. 5407, pages 1476–1481, 1999.

Mitochondrial Genome Evolution and the Origin of Eukaryotes by B.F. Lang, M.W. Gray, and G. Burger in *Annual Review of Genetics*, Vol. 33, pages 351–397, 1999.

The Origin and Early Evolution of Mitochondria by M.W. Gray, G. Burger, and B.F. Lang in *Genome Biology*, Vol. 2, pages 1018.1–1018.5, 2001.

mtDNA Sequencing

Automated Amplification and Sequencing of Human Mitochondrial DNA by K.M. Sullivan, R. Hopgood, B. Lang, and P. Gill in *Electrophoresis*, Vol. 12, No. 1, pages 17–21, 1991.

Identifying Individuals by Sequencing Mitochondrial DNA from Teeth by C. Ginther, L. Issel-Tarver, and M.C. King in *Nature Genetics* Vol. 2, No. 2, pages 135–138, 1992.

Strategies for Automated Sequencing of Human Mitochondrial DNA Directly from PCR Products by R. Hopgood, K.M. Sullivan, and P. Gill in *Biotechniques*, Vol. 13, pages 82–92, 1992.

Guidelines for the Use of Mitochondrial DNA Sequencing in Forensic Science by M.R. Wilson, M. Stoneking, M.M. Holland, J.A. DiZinno, and B. Budowle in *Crime Lab Digest*, Vol. 20, No. 4, pages 68–77, 1993.

Identification of the Remains of the Romanov Family by DNA Analysis by P. Gill, P.L. Ivanov, C. Kimpton, R. Piercy, N. Benson, G. Tully, I. Evett, E. Hagelberg, and K. Sullivan in *Nature Genetics*, Vol. 6, No. 2, pages 130–135, 1994.

Mitochondrial DNA Sequencing of Shed Hairs and Saliva on Robbery Caps: Sensitivity and Matching Probabilities by M. Allen, A.-S. Engström, S. Meyers, O. Handt, T. Saldeen, A. von Haeseler, S. Pääbo, and U. Gyllensten in *Journal of Forensic Sciences*, Vol. 43, No. 3, pages 453–464, 1998.

Forensic Applications of Mitochondrial DNA by J.M. Butler and B.C. Levin in *Trends in Biotechnology* Vol. 16, pages 158–162, 1998.

Mitochondrial DNA Analysis of the Presumptive Remains of Jesse James by A.C. Stone, J.E. Starrs, and M. Stoneking *in Journal of Forensic Sciences*, Vol. 46, No. 1, pages 173–176, 2001.

The Sequence of Structural Events that Challenged the Forensic Effort of the World Trade Center Disaster by E. Marchi and R.Z. Chastain in *American Laboratory*, Dec., pages 13–17, 2002.

Improved MtDNA Sequence Analysis of Forensic Remains Using a "Mini-Primer Set" Amplification Strategy by M.N. Gabriel, E.F. Huffine, J.H. Ryan, M.M. Holland, and T.J. Parsons in *Journal of Forensic Sciences*, Vol. 46, No. 2, pages 247–253, 2001.

Human and Insect Mitochondrial DNA Analysis from Maggots by J.D. Wells, F. Introna, Jr., G. Di Vella, C.P. Campobasso, J. Hayes, and F.A.H. Sperling in *Journal of Forensic Sciences*, Vol. 46, No. 3, pages 685–687, 2001.

Mitochondrial DNA and STR Typing of Matter Adhering to an Earphone by Y. Seo, T. Uchiyama, H. Matsuda, K. Shimizu, Y. Takami, T. Nakayam, and K. Takahama in *Journal of Forensic Sciences*, Vol. 47, No. 3, pages 605–608, 2002.

Correlation of Microscopic and Mitochondrial DNA Hair Comparisons by M.M Houck and B. Budowle in *Journal of Forensic Sciences*, Vol. 47, No. 5, pages 964–967, 2002.

Successful DNA Typing of a Urine Sample in a Doping Control Case Using Human Mitochondrial DNA Analysis by A. Junge, M. Steevens, and B. Madea in *Journal of Forensic Sciences*, Vol. 47, No. 5, pages 1022–1024, 2002.

Forensics and Mitochondrial DNA: Applications, Debates, and Foundations by B. Budowle, M.A. Allard, M.R. Wilson, and R. Chakraborty in *Annual Review of Genomics and Human Genetics*, Vol. 4, pages 119–141, 2003.

Evaluation of a Multicapillary Electrophoresis Instrument for Mitochondrial DNA Typing by J.E.B. Stewart, P.J. Aagaard, E.G. Pokorak, D. Polanskey, and B. Budowle in *Journal of Forensic Sciences*, Vol. 48, No. 3, pages 571–580, 2003.

Addressing the Use of Phylogenetics for Identification of Sequences in Error in the SWGDAM Mitochondrial DNA Database by B. Budowle, D. Polanskey, M.W. Allard, and R. Chakraborty in *Journal of Forensic Sciences*, Vol. 49, No. 6, pages 1256–1261, 2004.

Mitochondrial DNA Heteroplasmy Among Hairs from Single Individuals by S. Kazumasa, H. Sato, and K. Kasai in *Journal of Forensic Sciences*, Vol. 49, No. 5, pages 986–991, 2004.

Mitochondrial Genome Variation and the Origin of Modern Human Nature by M. Ingman, H. Kaessmann, S. Pääbo, and U. Gyllensten in *Journal of Forensic Sciences*, Vol. 50, No. 3, 2005.

mtDNA Investigations After Differential Lysis by K.D. Anslinger, B.R. Bayer, B. Rolf, and W. Eisenmenger in *Journal of Forensic Sciences*, Vol. 50, No. 3, pages 579–581, 2005.

Relative Degradation of Nuclear and Mitochondrial DNA: An Experimental Approach by D.R. Foran in *Journal of Forensic Sciences*, Vol. 51, No. 4, pages 766–770, 2006.

Extended Guidelines for mtDNA Typing of Population Data in Forensic Science by Walther Parson and Hans-Jurgen Bandelt in *Forensic Science International: Genetics*, Vol. 1, No. 1, pages 13–19, 2007.

Mini-midi-mito: Adapting the Amplification and Sequencing Strategy of mtDNA to the Degradation State of Crime Scene Samples by Cordula Berger and Walther Parson in *Forensic Science International: Genetics*, Vol. 3, pages 149–153, 2009.

The Use of Mitochondrial DNA Single Nucleotide Polymorphisms to Assist in the Resolution of Three Challenging Forensic Cases by Rebecca S. Just, Mark D. Leney, Suzanne M. Barritt, Christopher W. Los, Brion C. Smith, Thomas D. Holland, and Thomas J. Parsons in *Journal of Forensic Sciences*, Vol. 54, No. 4, pages 887–891, 2009.

12
STRs

DNA Lab, Police Headquarters, Friday 2:45 PM

A motive is like the trigger of a gun—it's the mechanism that gives movement to an action. It's what drives someone to steal a candy bar from the supermarket or cheat on an exam or lie to a parent about a poor grade in school. A motive may be petty. A motive may be irrational. A motive may be fleeting and subject to the mood swings of the motivated, but when it comes to murder, the motive behind that act can rarely if ever be called a justifiable excuse.

Helen sat in front of the DNA sequencer and watched as different colored bands scrolled across the computer screen like Christmas tree bulbs on a conveyer belt. She looked for motive in the glow of the blue, green, yellow, and red lights that passed in front of her in hope that they would illuminate the darker edges of her ignorance. If Erica Holmes was murdered, what was the motive? Why would anyone take the life of a woman poised at the cusp of adulthood so nearly realized?

The motive's partner in crime, Jenkins had once told her, is opportunity. A person may have motive to commit a crime, but without the opportunity to do so, the motive becomes irrelevant. Look first to motive, he told her. Hundreds may have opportunity, fewer have motive, and fewer still have both. Look first to motive and then work backwards.

Sam O'Neill had motive, Helen thought. But then, so did Farah Dawood. Erica could provoke passion in them both. If it was a love triangle, Erica's very existence might be a provocation. Spurned love is provocation. So is revenge. So is betrayal or the fear of it.

This was the second time she had processed these DNA samples. She was convinced after the first run that she had clumsily mislabeled a couple of them. This time, however, she went back to the original collection vials and worked with the samples separately.

The second run was coming to an end. The electric current dragging the fragments of DNA through the capillaries had shut down, and various prompts on the computer screen followed the automated process, whereby the raw data were flung into an analysis routine morphing the different colored bands into meaningful numbers. Bands of light became pieces of the DNA double helix with defined lengths and with specified numbers of 4 bp repeats within them. Helen looked at the chromatograms generated by the software and realized that she had not bungled the first experiment after all—she got the exact same results this second time. She was also convinced that within those colored peaks was a possible motive—one that still had the power to ruin lives—and she felt a sudden urgency to get the results into Jenkins' hands as quickly as possible.

The quickest way to get the chromatograms to Jenkins would have been by e-mail. Unfortunately, however, IT had not yet hooked her laboratory computer into the web. But she did have a printer lined directly into the DNA sequencer's computer and she used it to print out copies of the chromatograms. With the last one in hand, she hurried out of the laboratory, descended the stairwell, and rushed down the hallway to the central office where she found but one person at their desk, Detective Sanders talking on the phone. Jenkins was gone.

Sanders looked up as she approached. “Helen!” he said holding his right palm over the transmitter. “Have you thought about my offer?”

“It’s a very attractive one,” Helen replied, “but I need a little more time to think about it. Have you seen Lieutenant Jenkins?”

“We could do that, yes,” Sanders said back into the transmitter while holding up his right index finger to Helen. He covered up the transmitter again. “He left about 10 min ago,” Sanders said.

“Do you know where he went?” Helen asked. Sanders just shrugged. “Well, did he say anything?” Helen persisted.

“We’ll send someone over to take prints,” Sanders said into the phone. “Can you give me the address?” Helen sighed and stood there watching as Sanders wrote down an address on a small pad of white paper. “And do you have the vehicle identification number?” he asked the caller. “Yes, I can wait,” he said. He placed his palm back over the receiver. “All I know,” said Sanders, “was that he was talking on the phone with someone. It sounded like he was going to meet somebody who had some information to give him about the case.”

“That’s it? That’s all?” Helen asked.

“Yup,” Sanders replied. “He hung up and left in a hurry. Yes, Yes, that’s GH371 … ,” Sanders said back into the phone as he jotted figures on his notepad.

Helen stepped over to Jenkins’ desk but saw nothing that could give her a clue as to Jenkins’ whereabouts. However, there was a small pad of paper by his phone. Helen grabbed a pencil and, tilting it on its edge, rubbed the middle area of the top sheet. An address became visible.

She could just make it out—“2000 McKinnon, #418 @ Toland”. The streets, however, were unfamiliar to her. She pulled her cell from her back pocket and swiped her finger across it to bring it to life. The device flickered. She could just make out the message as it faded black, “Low Battery.” “Ahh jeeez,” she sighed. She sat down in Jenkins’ chair and swiveled it to her right so that she was facing his computer. She quickly pressed the “return” key and the computer came to life. However, a window, centered on its desktop, asked for the password. She left the field blank and pressed the “Enter” key.

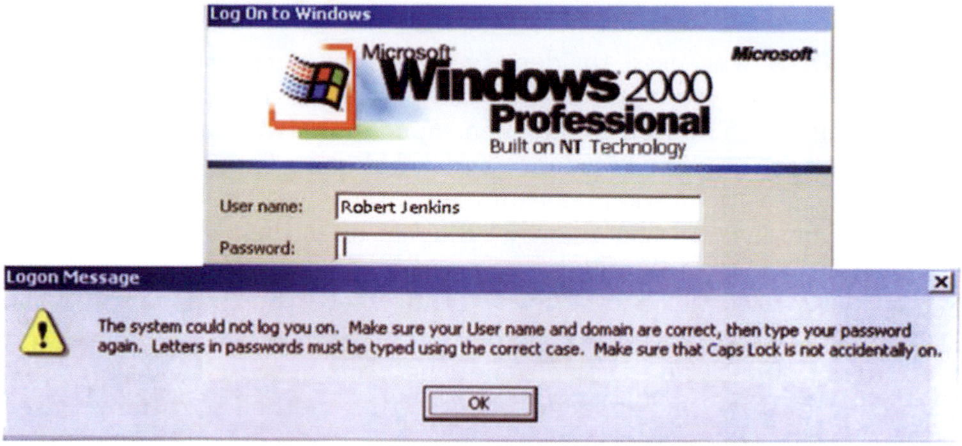

Error! She still had two chances to get it right.

This second time, she typed in “password” and pressed the “Enter” key. Again, an error message popped on the screen.

She had one more chance. If she failed this time, the computer would completely lock her out. *Jenkins’ daughter’s name—he’d use that as a password,* she thought. *But what was it? An American Indian name,* she remembered—*Apache, Cherokee, Chippewa. But it sounded like a spice and it was a city in one of the western states, Cilantro, Cinnamon, Cayenne—Cheyenne!* She typed in “Cheyenne” and pressed the “Enter” key. The Log On window dissolved. Access! She quickly navigated to Google Maps, printed out directions, and ran to her car as she fumbled through her purse of the phone charger.

DNA Typing

Introduction

DNA analysis of crime scene evidence has revolutionized forensics and, time after time, has proved to be one of the most powerful indicators of someone’s guilt or innocence. Even trace amounts of DNA—a small speck of blood, a stain of semen, or the remnants of a smear of saliva—can yield enough material to ID a criminal. The techniques used to identify the origin of a DNA sample has been referred to as *DNA fingerprinting* or *DNA typing.*

A number of DNA typing methods have been developed over the years, and each innovation has brought an improvement in the ability to discriminate between individuals within a population. All methods of DNA analysis reveal the contributor’s *genotype*—their particular genetic makeup or profile for the regions of their chromosomes being examined. If the genotype of the suspect does not match that obtained for the evidence sample, then that suspect is said to be *excluded* as a possible contributor of the biological evidence. If the suspect’s genotype is the same as that of the evidence sample, then the suspect is *included* as a possible contributor of the evidence sample.

RFLP

The first time DNA was used to identify a murder suspect dates back to 1983 when the body of a 15-year-old girl was discovered in a field near the village of Narborough, England. The victim had been raped and strangled. Criminalists were able to recover semen stains as evidence and could identify certain enzymes associated with specific genetic markers. Despite an intense search that spanned 2 years and grew to encompass 2 other nearby villages, her killer eluded the authorities long enough that he could take the life of a second 15-year-old girl. Her body, badly abused, was discovered not a mile away from where the first victim was found. Again, semen samples were recovered from the victim.

It was during this period that a geneticist from nearby Leicester University named Dr. Alec Jeffreys was experimenting with a method to differentiate people by their DNA profile (Figure 12.1). The technique he was developing, called *restriction fragment length polymorphism* (RFLP), is based on the fact that each of us, as odd as this may seem, has different amounts of genetic material in our chromosomes. Some people have more. Some have less. The regions responsible for these differences are said to be *polymorphic*—they have many different forms. To identify these areas, Jeffreys cut human DNA with a *restriction endonuclease*, an enzyme that recognizes a specific sequence of bases in a DNA molecule and then, like scissors to ribbon, cuts through both strands of the double helix. A restriction endonuclease known as *Hind*III, for example, recognizes the sequence AAGCTT and cuts between the two A's on both strands (notice that this sequence is a *palindrome*—given the rules of complementary base pairing, its sequence on one strand read in one direction is the same as on the other strand read in the opposite direction). The DNA fragments made by the cuts are then electrophoresed through *agarose* to separate the fragments by their size. The DNA bands are then transferred from the agarose onto a type of paper made from either nylon or nitrocellulose. A radioactive piece of DNA called a *probe* carrying DNA sequence similar to the polymorphic regions is then allowed to attach to the DNA fragments on the paper where they find homology. Any probe not attaching to the human DNA is washed away, and x-ray film is placed over the paper to produce an image similar to that shown in Figure 12.2.

Alec Jeffreys was called in to help on the case, and he applied the new RFLP technique to compare the evidence DNA with that of their primary suspect, an outpatient

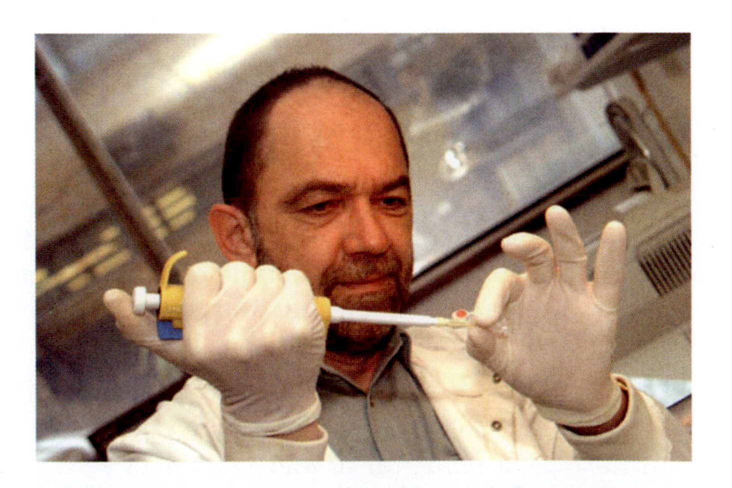

Figure 12.1 Professor Alec Jeffreys, the English molecular biologist who discovered the technique of DNA fingerprinting. (Photograph courtesy of Alec Jeffreys.)

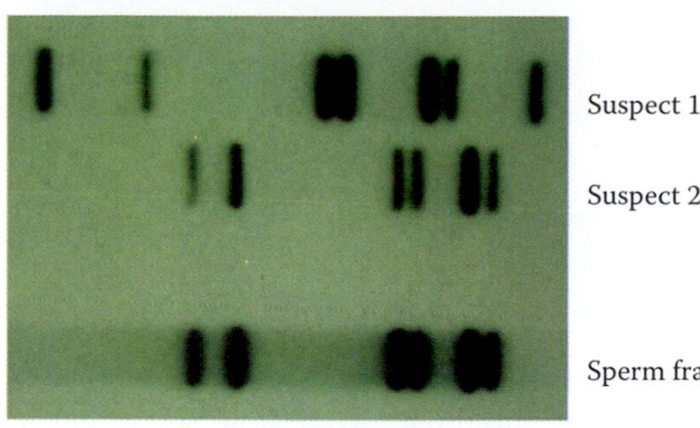

Figure 12.2 DNA fingerprinting used in a sexual assault case. The photo shows part of an x-ray film (or autoradiograph) of bands on an agarose gel separated by electrophoresis and hybridized to radioactive probe DNA. In RFLP analysis, the pattern of bands generated from DNA from a suspect is compared to the pattern of bands generated from a reference DNA. Here, the reference DNA was isolated from semen (the sperm fraction) recovered from the rape victim by vaginal swab. The pattern shown for suspect 2 matches the pattern of that from the sperm fraction, whereas the pattern from suspect 1 does not. We can therefore say that suspect 1 is excluded as a possible contributor of the biological evidence, while suspect 2 is included and should be subject to further scrutiny.

of a local mental health facility and a convicted exhibitionist. The suspect had confessed to the murder of both girls, and this DNA test was not much more than a formality. The DNA recovered from the semen of the victims matched each other—the same man had murdered both girls. The police were thrown off balance, however, when the test showed no match between their suspect and the semen DNA. The worst they could say about their suspect now was that he was a liar. The real killer was still at large.

The Narborough police cranked their investigation up a notch—they decided to test the DNA of every male in the local population! Beginning in early 1987, they started drawing blood from every man between the ages of 16 and 34. Over 4500 men were tested by RFLP analysis, but none of them came up matching the evidence. It was a chance conversation in a Leicester pub, however, that exposed the killer. It came to light that a man named Colin Pitchfork, an employee of a local bakery, had paid one of his coworkers to donate a blood sample for him—a revelation overheard by another employee who, after several weeks of anguish, notified the police. Colin Pitchfork was arrested and his DNA was found by RFLP analysis to be an exact match to that recovered from the crime scenes. Pitchfork was convicted and sentenced to life in prison.

RFLP had an advantage over previous tests that rely on identifying a handful of well-characterized enzymes in semen, blood, or saliva in that, with RFLP, many more of an individual's traits (now genetic rather than metabolic) could be examined. Scientists found a number of polymorphic genetic regions, also called *loci* (a single genetic site is called a *locus*), suitable for human identification—the more polymorphisms (*alleles*) at a genetic locus that can be examined, the more discriminating the test.

Reverse Dot Blot and Probe Strips

But even as RFLP was bursting into the field of forensics, another revolutionary technology, PCR, was already poised to supplant it. We have already seen that PCR is used to quantitate DNA (Chapter 5) and to amplify mtDNA for subsequent sequencing (Chapter 11). But PCR is also the cornerstone technology for identifying polymorphic DNA sites that also, like those used in RFLP, differ by their length.

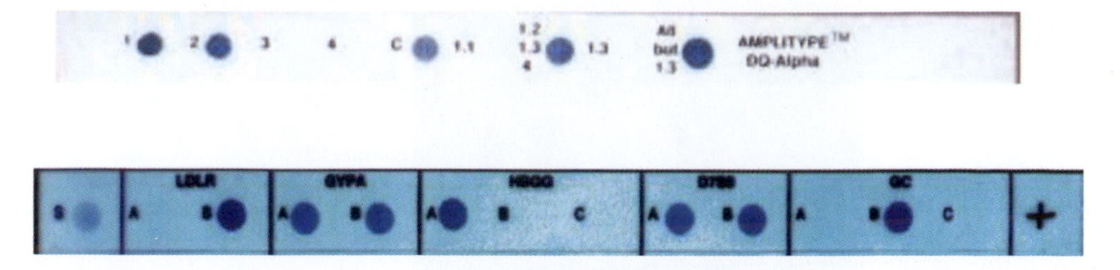

Figure 12.3 Probe strips used for DNA typing of the HLA DQα (top strip) and PM alleles (bottom strip). The HLA DQα probe strip can distinguish six possible HLA alleles (1.1, 1.2, 1.3, 2, 3, and 4). The PM probe strip carries probes to distinguish two alleles of the low-density lipoprotein receptor (LDLR gene), two alleles of the glycophorin A (GYPA) gene, three alleles of the hemoglobin G gamma-globin gene (HBGG), two alleles of a genetic locus known as D7S8, and three alleles of the group-specific component (GC) gene.

PCR, introduced in 1985, was almost immediately recognized as a potential boon to forensics because of its remarkable ability to turn a very small amount of DNA into an amount large enough to perform a meaningful analysis. Whereas the RFLP technique may require as much as 50 ng of nondegraded DNA, PCR can function with as little as 0.5 ng of evidence sample that has even been whittled down by environmental assault to pieces as small as a few hundred base pairs in length. Many cases beyond the reach of RFLP, therefore, could now be examined using PCR.

For at least a decade following its introduction to human identification, scientists struggled with the best way to use PCR to their advantage, searching for the most polymorphic genetic markers—those that would provide them with the greatest power to discriminate between people. One of the first commercial forensic PCR kits, the AmpliType™ DQα (DQ alpha) PCR Amplification and Typing Kit produced by the PerkinElmer, Inc., amplified the human leukocyte antigen (HLA) region containing the genes having notoriety for their role in tissue transplant rejection. At best, however, for this genetic locus, 7% of the time, two people chosen at random will share the same alleles.

The next commercially available forensic kit, the AmpliType PM® PCR Amplification and Typing Kit (also from Perkin-Elmer), examined the alleles at five different loci and offered a slightly better power to discriminate between random individuals.

Both of these early kits utilized *reverse dot blot* technology in which short, single-stranded DNA probes matching the different marker alleles are spotted onto strips of nylon paper. The forensic DNA sample in which the target loci have been amplified by PCR is allowed to anneal to the DNA on the probe strips. Following sufficient time to allow for annealing between probes and PCR products, any DNA that does not anneal is washed away. A color reaction is then performed to reveal those probe dots that have found and attached to PCR products generated in the forensic sample (Figure 12.3).

VNTRs

To augment the discriminating power of the HLA DQα and PM probe strips, forensic scientists also tapped into genetic markers called variable number of tandem repeats (VNTRs), regions of a chromosome in which a segment of DNA from 5 to 80 bases in length is repeated over and over again, one right next to the other. The nice thing about VNTRs is that it's fairly easy to call a genetic type. You simply PCR amplify the VNTR locus, electrophorese the fragments to separate them by

Evidence sample
Allelic ladder

Figure 12.4 DNA typing using the D1S80 VNTR. DNA recovered from a crime scene, from a reference sample, or from a suspect is PCR amplified targeting the D1S80 locus found on human chromosome 1. The amplified products are electrophoresed on a polyacrylamide gel capable of resolving DNA fragments differing in size by as little as 16 bp (the size of the repeating monomer). An allelic ladder containing the most common D1S80 PCR fragment lengths is loaded in an adjacent lane. The lowest band of the allelic ladder represents a fragment carrying 14 repeats. The second band from the bottom is made from a fragment carrying 16 repeats (15 repeats is extremely rare). Each band up the ladder from there differs from the one next to it by one 16 bp repeat up to a total of 41 repeats. DNA type is called by noting which bands of the allelic ladder the evidence sample bands migrate next to. In this figure, the evidence sample, a heterozygote (a homozygote would have only one band), is typed as an 18, 31 (read "eighteen comma thirty-one").

their size, and note the migration rate of the bands—that being an indication of how many repeats are present in the amplified product.

The best characterized and most widely used VNTR is known as D1S80 (it was utilized in the O.J. Simpson murder trial in 1995). Its name derives from both its location and its history. The "D" stands for DNA, the "1" because it is found on human chromosome number 1, the "S" means it is a single site—it's not found anywhere else— and the "80" because, historically, as genes and genetic loci were being mapped to their chromosomes, this was the 80th single (S) site found on chromosome 1.

The D1S80 VNTR carries a repeat 16 bp in length. The vast majority of people will have anywhere from 14 to 41 repeats on the two number 1 chromosomes they inherited from their parents (Figure 12.4).

STRs

As the Human Genome Project probed deeper into our genetic structure, we found other sites on our chromosomes called *STRs* even more suited for human identification than either VNTRs or the loci assayed by reverse dot blot probe strips. STRs are segments of DNA two to five bases in length, which, like VNTRS, are repeated multiple times along a region of a chromosome. To their great advantage, STRs are peppered throughout our genome, they have a high degree of variability, and, because they're shorter than VNTRs, they're amenable to analysis on an automated DNA sequencer—an instrument designed to look at short pieces of DNA. Their detection on a sequencer, however, requires that the PCR-amplified products be labeled with a fluorescent dye. This is accomplished by tagging one of the PCR primers (Figure 12.5).

Outside of the direct sequencing of long stretches of different chromosomes, STR analysis is the most discriminating DNA typing method yet developed. By amplifying multiple loci simultaneously in a *multiplex reaction* and by using multiple dyes, an extremely high discriminating power can be achieved. With the AmpFLSTR® Identifiler™ PCR Amplification Kit (Life Technologies) that looks at 16 different loci simultaneously, for example, it's calculated that only two people out of roughly 200,000,000,000,000,000 (200 quadrillion; 2×10^{17}) people will have the same STR peak pattern. Given that the world population is approximately 7 billion (7×10^{9}), your Identifiler STR profile is unique on planet Earth (unless, of course, you have an identical twin).

Although the number of repeats at any particular forensically interesting STR locus is variable, the number of repeats you have is stably inherited—you get the

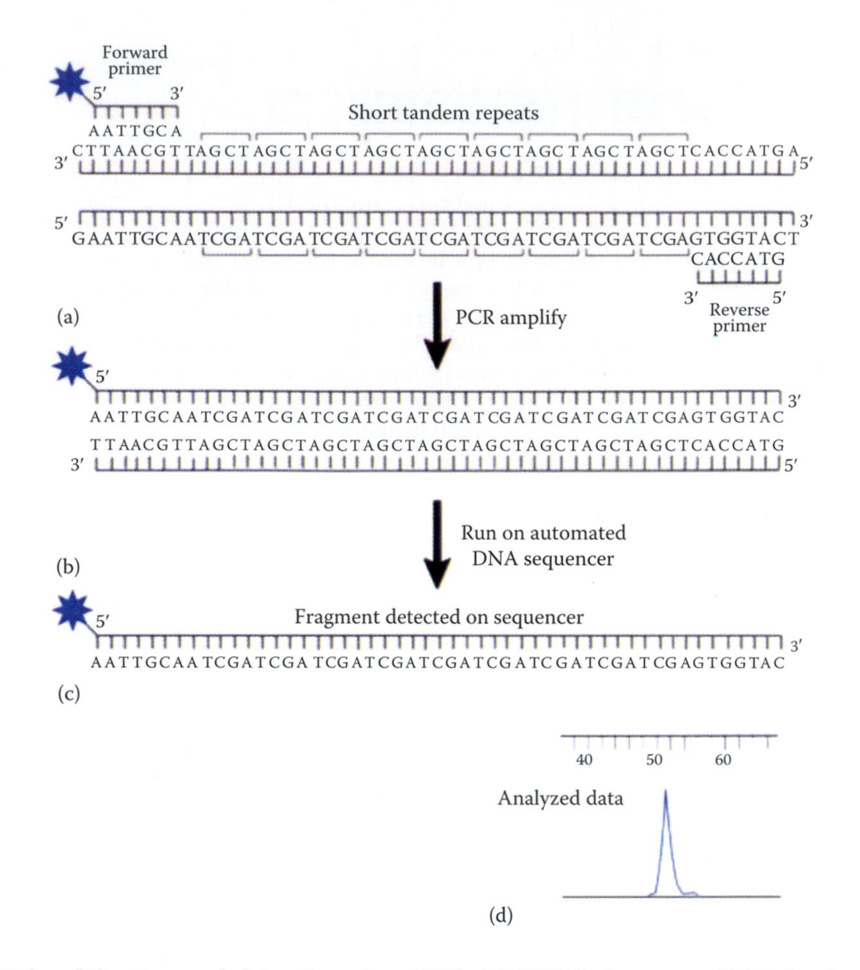

Figure 12.5 Amplification and detection of an STR. (a) STR loci are amplified by denaturing the DNA double helix and annealing primers (called *forward* and *reverse*) to the opposite strands flanking the repeat region. One of the primers carries a fluorescent dye on its 5′ end. (b) PCR amplification generates a double-stranded product in which one strand is fluorescently labeled (since the labeled primer is incorporated into the extended chain. (c) When electrophoresed on an automated DNA sequencer, the two strands are denatured, and only the fluorescently labeled strand is detected. (d) When analyzed, the software generates a blue peak whose size is calculated by extrapolation from a size standard and an allelic ladder coelectrophoresed with the evidence sample. The STR allele form shown here could be designated $[AGCT]_9$ to show its repeat sequence (AGCT) and the number of times it is repeated (9).

number of repeats you have from your mother and father. For any particular locus, if you get the same number of repeats from both your parents (you generate only one fragment size during amplification), you are said to be *homozygous*. If you get a different number (you generate two different-sized fragments during amplification), you are said to be *heterozygous*. Because STRs are stably inherited and because they are so discriminating, they are frequently used to determine *paternity*—who the father is in a dispute of custody, fidelity, alimony, or inheritance.

In the Erica Holmes missing persons case, Helen Chang uses the AmpFLSTR® Identifiler™ PCR Amplification Kit marketed by Life Technologies (Foster City, CA). The kit, amplifying 16 separate loci, requires a set of 32 different primers (2 PCR primers per locus). Fifteen of the loci are STR markers. The remaining marker is amelogenin, the gene responsible for tooth enamel. The amelogenin gene is found on both the X and the Y chromosomes, the chromosomes responsible for sex determination. Although the amelogenin gene is carried on both sex chromosomes, it is slightly longer on the Y chromosome than on the X chromosome. Consequently, a female, since she has two X chromosomes, will generate a single small PCR product. PCR amplification of amelogenin using DNA from a male will produce two product bands. In the Identifiler kit, the amelogenin-amplified products are labeled with a red fluorescent dye.

Thirteen of the STR loci targeted by the Identifiler kit are required markers for the CODIS (Combined DNA Index System) database maintained by the FBI Laboratory. CODIS, first introduced as a pilot program in 1990, provides federal, state, and local crime labs with the means to exchange and compare DNA profiles as an aid for the identification and conviction of violent offenders. All 15 STR loci of the Identifiler kit are tetranucleotide repeats (a 4-base segment of DNA repeated in tandem and in multiple iterations).

Four different fluorescent dyes (blue, green, yellow, and red) are used to label DNA fragments during amplification of the 16 targeted STR loci. An orange fluorescent dye labels a set of size markers used by the analysis software to help calculate the length of the amplified products.

An STR amplification is performed by combining 0.5–1.25 ng of sample DNA (recovered from a crime scene, a suspect, or a victim) with a mixture of fluorescently labeled primers, a DNA polymerase, buffer, dNTPs, and magnesium chloride. The reaction is cycled in a thermal cycler 28 times through denaturation, annealing, and extension steps (Figure 12.6). At the end of amplification, a small aliquot of the reaction is combined with formamide (to ensure the DNA strands remain denatured) along with the size standard (carrying its own unique dye), and the mixture is heated at 95°C for several minutes then quickly chilled on ice.

Amplified samples are electrophoresed on a Genetic Analyzer (Life Technologies) through narrow glass capillaries filled with a polymer that allows separation of fragments from smallest to largest (Figures 12.7 through 12.9) and detection of

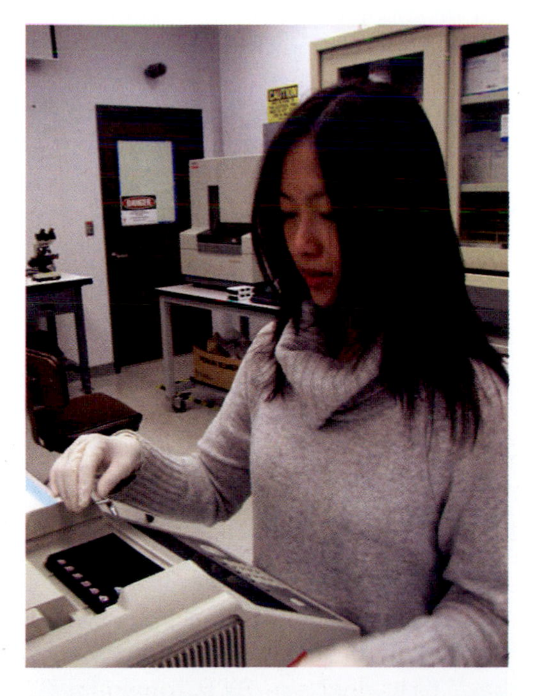

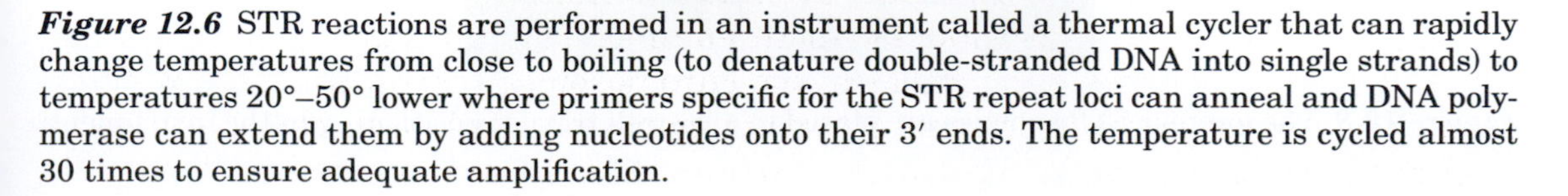

Figure 12.6 STR reactions are performed in an instrument called a thermal cycler that can rapidly change temperatures from close to boiling (to denature double-stranded DNA into single strands) to temperatures 20°–50° lower where primers specific for the STR repeat loci can anneal and DNA polymerase can extend them by adding nucleotides onto their 3′ ends. The temperature is cycled almost 30 times to ensure adequate amplification.

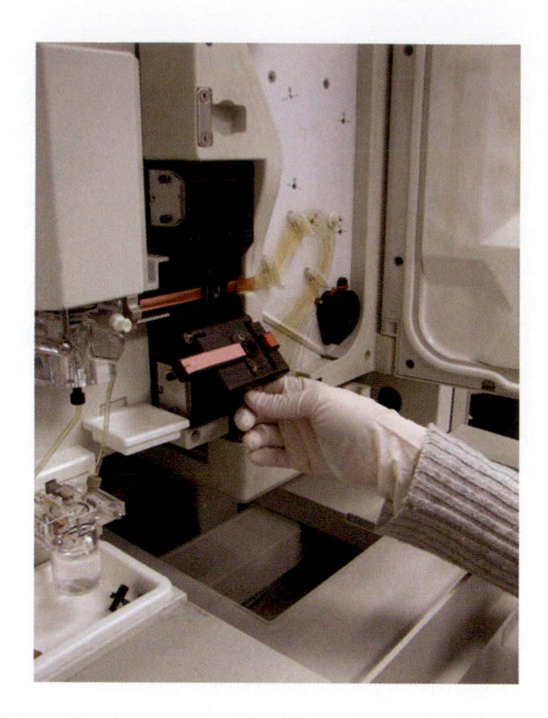

Figure 12.7 An array of 16 capillaries are fitted within the optics chamber of an Applied Biosystems Model 3130xl Genetic Analyzer. The capillaries are automatically filled with a special polymer that separates fluorescently labeled PCR fragments by their size. DNA fragments are injected into the capillaries by a brief jolt of electric current. As they migrate towards the positive pole, they pass and argon ion laser excites the dyes on their ends. A computer calculates their sizes, and a software program determines how many repeats are associated with each detected fragment. Buffer at each end of the capillary array completes the current flow.

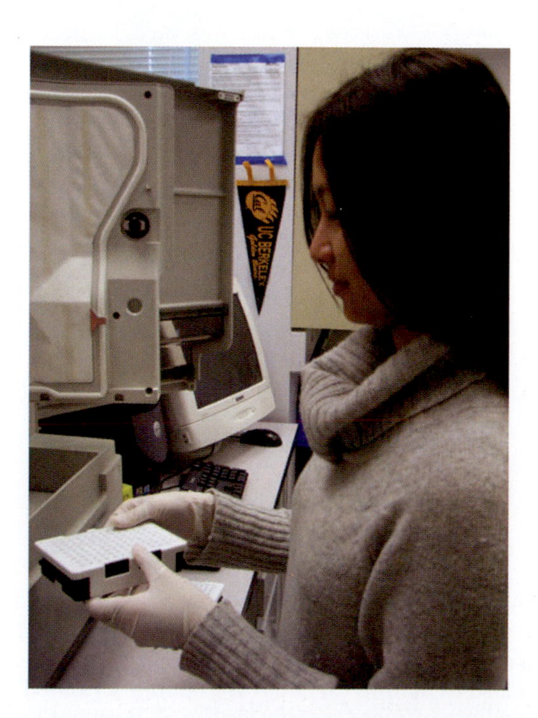

Figure 12.8 The forensic STR samples are placed in a 96-well tray for positioning in the instrument.

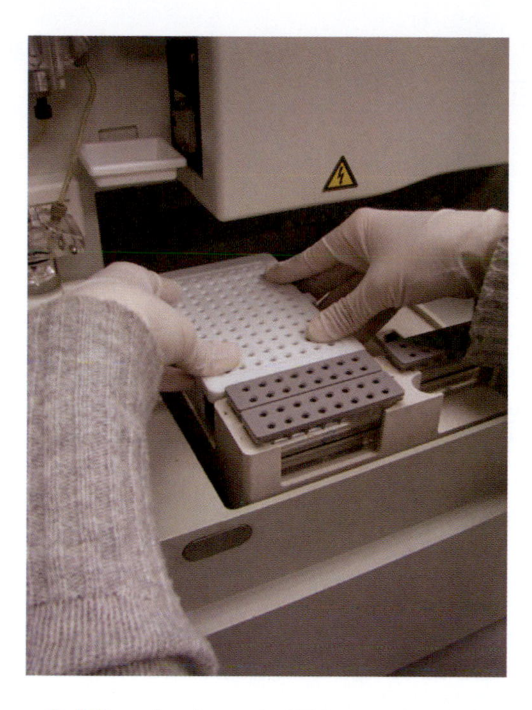

Figure 12.9 The 96-well tray holding the forensic STR samples in positioned on a robotic platform in preparation for electrophoresis and detection of the fluorescently labeled PCR-amplified products.

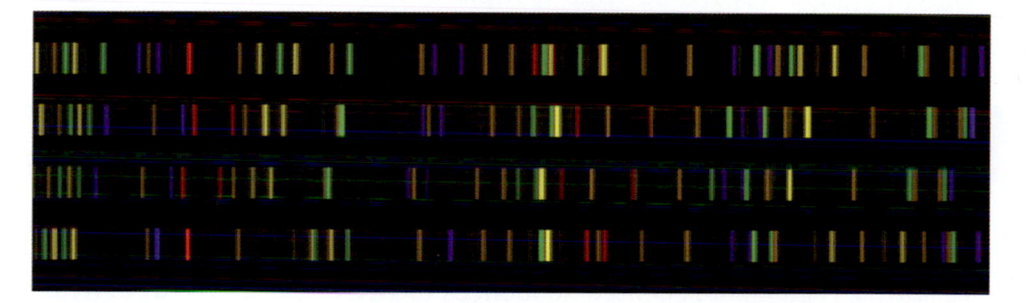

Figure 12.10 Separation of the amplified products along with a size marker and an allelic ladder allows the automated sequencer to call how many repeats are in each STR locus.

the different fluorescent dyes (Figure 12.10). DNA fragments are injected into the capillaries by a brief surge in electric current after which they are positioned into a container of buffer for the remainder of the run. Several capillaries are reserved for electrophoresis of an allelic ladder (all the possible fragments generated by human DNA). These are used to calculate the allele sizes (the number of four-base repeats) in the evidence samples (Figure 12.11).

MiniSTRs and Y-STRs

The two leading manufacturers of reagent kits for the amplification of STR loci are Promega (Madison, Wisconsin) and Life Technologies (Carlsbad, California). Both companies market kits for miniSTR analysis. These are shorter versions of the already well-characterized STR loci, but because they are shorter, they can be useful when analyzing DNA that has been badly degraded. The two companies also market amplification kits for Y-STR loci—STRs found only the Y chromosome.

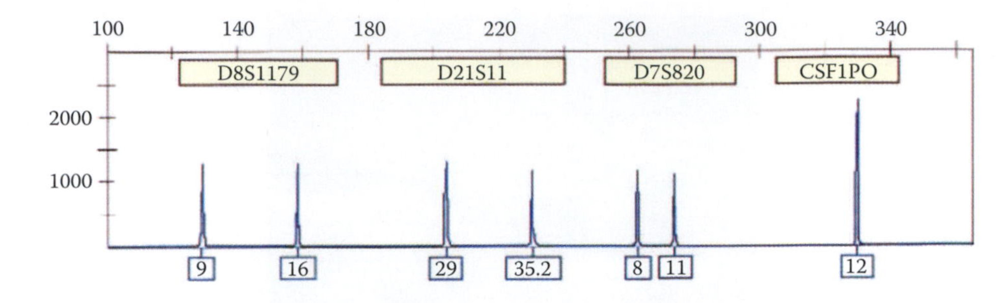

Figure 12.11 The analyzed data are presented as a chromatogram with each band of a specific color (blue, green, yellow, or red) having its own chromatogram (though the analysis software also allows for the display of all dye-labeled bands to be displayed in a single panel). Using the size standard and the allelic ladder, the analysis software calculates how many repeats are present in each band, and this is displayed as a boxed number beneath each peak. A repeat number 35.2 shown as an allele for the D21S11 locus means that that particular allele has 35 complete tetranucleotide repeats and half (2 out of 4 bases) of a tetranucleotide repeat. The numbers on the top x axis represent length in bases. The numbers on the y axis represent fluorescent signal intensity.

These kits have particular use for sexual assault cases where, in the recovery of DNA samples, the male DNA of the assailant can be mixed with the female DNA of the victim. Since the STRs being analyzed are found only on the Y chromosome and since only males carry a Y chromosome, only the male assailant's DNA will yield a result. Y-STRs obviate the need for careful differential DNA extraction of the biological sample recovered from a rape or other violent crime involving the two sexes.

In the Crime Lab

Activity 12.1 Locating an STR Locus

STRs are *stutter* regions of repeated sequences of DNA that are commonly used for human identification in forensics and paternity testing. Because these regions are highly polymorphic, they can be used to identify an individual with a high degree of discrimination.

The STR loci used by forensic scientists have four- or five-base repeats. (The repeat unit is called a *monomer*.) The number of those repeats in any forensic sample is specific to an individual. The STR monomer is designated by placing its sequence in brackets followed by a subscript number indicating how many times it repeats itself within the genetic locus. For example, $[GATC]_{24}$ indicates that the monomer sequence GATC is repeated contiguously (all in a row) 24 times.

In the following DNA sequence alignment, identify the STR repeat and answer the following questions.

```
                    10         20         30         40         50         60
a.GenBank  AACCTGAGTC TGCCAAGGAC TAGCAGGTTG CTAACCACCC TGTGTCTCAG TTTTCCTACC
b.forward  ---------- ---------- ----AGGTTG CTAACCACCC TGTGTCTCAG TTTTCCTACC
c.forward  ---------- ---------- ----AGGTTG CTAACCACCC TGTGTCTCAG TTTTCCTACC
d.rev-RC   AACCTGAGTC TGCCAAGGAC TAGCAGGTTG CTAACCACCC TGTGTCTCAG TTTTCCTACC
e.rev-RC   AACCTGAGTC TGCCAAGGAC TAGCAGGTTG CTANCCACCC TGTGTCTCAG TTTTCCTACC
                    70         80         90        100        110        120
a.GenBank  TGTAAAATGA AGATATTAAC AGTAACTGCC TTCATAGATA GAAGATAGAT AGATTAGATA
b.forward  TGTAAAATGA AGATATTAAC AGTAACTGCC TTCATAGATA GAAGATAGAT AGATTAGATA
c.forward  TGTAAAATGA AGATATTAAC AGTAACTGCC TTCATAGATA GAAGATAGAT AGATTAGATA
d.rev-RC   TGTAAAATGA AGATATTAAC AGTNACTGCC TTCATAGATA GAAGATAGAT AGATTAGATA
e.rev-RC   TGTNAAATGA AGATATTAAC AGTAACTGCC TTCATAGATA GAAGATAGAT AGATTAGATA
                   130        140        150        160        170        180
a.GenBank  GATAGATAGA TAGATAGATA GATAGATAGA TAGATAGATA GATAGATAGA TAGATAGATA
b.forward  GATAGATAGA TAGATAGATA GATAGATAGA TAGATAGATA GATAGATAGA TAGATAGATA
c.forward  GATAGATAGA TAGATAGATA GATAGATAGA TAGATAGATA GATAGATAGA TAGATAGATA
d.rev-RC   GATAGATAGA TAGATAGNNA GATAGATAGA TAGATAGATA GATAGATAGA TAGATAGATA
e.rev-RC   GATAGATAGA TAGATAGATA GATAGATAGA TAGATAGATA GATAGATAGA TAGATAGATA
                   190        200        210        220        230        240
a.GenBank  GGAAGTACTT AGAACAGGGT CTGACACAGG AAATGCTGTC CAAGTGTGCA CCAGGAGATA
b.forward  GGAAGTACTT AGAACAGGGT CTGACACAGG AAATGCTGTC CAAGTGTGCA CCAGGAGATA
c.forward  GGAAGTACTT AGAACAGGGT CTGACACAGG AAATGCTGTC CAAGTGTGCA CCAGGAGATA
d.rev-RC   GGAAGTACTT AGAACAGGGT CTGACACAGG AAATGCTGTC CAAGTGTGCA CCAGGAGATA
e.rev-RC   GGAAGTACTT AGAACAGGGT CTGACACAGG AAATGCTGTC CAAGTGTGCA CCAGGAGATA
                   250        260        270        280        290        300
a.GenBank  GTATCTGAGA AGGCTCAGTC TGGCACCATG TGGGTTGGGT GGGAACCTGG AGGCTGGAGA
b.forward  GTATCTGAGA AGGCTCAGTC TGGCACCATG TGGGTTGGGT GGGAACCTGG AGGCTGGAGA
c.forward  GTATCTGAGA AGGCTCAGTC TGGCACCATG TGGGTTGGGT GGGAACCTGG AGGCTGGAGA
d.rev-RC   GTATCTGAGA AGGCTCAGTC TGGCACCATG TGGGTTGGGT GGGAACCTGG AGGCTGGAGA
e.rev-RC   GTATCTGAGA AGGCTCAGTC TGGCACCATG TGGGTTGGGT GGGAACCTGG AGGCTGGAGA
                   310        320        330        340        350        360
a.GenBank  ATGGGCTGAA GATGGCCAGT GGTGTGTGGA A
b.forward  ATGGGCTGAA GATGGCCAGT GGTGTGTGGA A
c.forward  ATGGGCTGAA GATGGCCAGT GGTGTGTGGA A
d.rev-RC   ANGG-CT--- ---------- ---------- -
e.rev-RC   N-GGGCT--- ---------- ---------- -
```

1. Is the STR monomer unit a tetranucleotide (four-base) or pentanucleotide (five-base) repeat?
2. What is the base sequence of the STR monomer unit?
3. Determine which base position (see numbering at the top of each sequence panel) defines the beginning of the STR repeat region.
4. Determine which base defines the end of the tandem repeat region.
5. Determine the number of times it repeats.
6. What is the size of the repeat region in base pairs?

Activity 12.2 Characterizing STR Loci

An example of an STR locus is shown in Table 12.1. The sequence (only one strand is shown) has an embedded STR repeat at its base positions 14–20. The monomer sequence ATGC (written in italics) is repeated twice. The first column, bp, indicates the nucleotide number. For example, the number 1 base is an "a" and the 20th base is a "g." The second row of numbered bases (indicated by the number 21) indicates that the 21st base is a "c." The 5′ number indicates the direction the sequence is read (in a 5′–3′ direction).

The characteristics specific to this locus are summarized in Table 12.2.

TABLE 12.1
An Example of an STR Locus in Which the Monomer ATGC (Written in Lower Case Italics) Is Repeated Twice

bp	5′																			
1	a	t	c	t	a	c	c	c	t	g	t	a	t	*a*	*t*	*g*	*c*	*a*	*t*	*g*
21	*c*	t	g	t	a	g	t	a	g	t	a	t	a	g	t	c	g	t	a	g
41	a	c	g	t	a	t	g	c	c	g	t	t	t	t	a	a	g	c	g	g
51	g	a	a	t	t	a	c	t	g	c	g	t	g	g	g	g	t	t	a	g

TABLE 12.2
Summary of the Characteristics of the STR Shown in Table 12.1

Locus	Repeat Monomer	Number of Repeats	Start Point of Repeat	End Point of Repeat	Total Length of Repeat Regions
Example	ATGC	2	14	21	8

In this activity, your instructor will provide you with DNA sequences, which are embedded with an STR repeat. In your laboratory notebook, create a table like that shown in Table 12.2 in which you list the essential characteristics of the STR.

Erica Holmes Missing Persons Case

STR analysis was performed on the following evidence items:

- Evidence item 1: Stain on Subaru's water reservoir
- Evidence item 2: Tissue in engine bay
- Evidence item 3: High-velocity stain on Subaru's firewall
- Evidence item 5: Braided transfer stain on cargo bay liner
- Evidence item 7: Large stain on cargo bay liner
- Evidence item 9: Fingerprint stain on Subaru rear view mirror
- Evidence item 10: Sarah Holmes buccal swab
- Evidence item 11: Dwayne Holmes buccal swab
- Evidence item 12: Samdeep O'Neill buccal swab
- Evidence item 13: Chuck Beamer buccal swab
- Evidence item 28: Alice Beamer buccal swab
- Evidence item 30: Farah Dawood buccal swab

Prepare an evidence report of your findings.

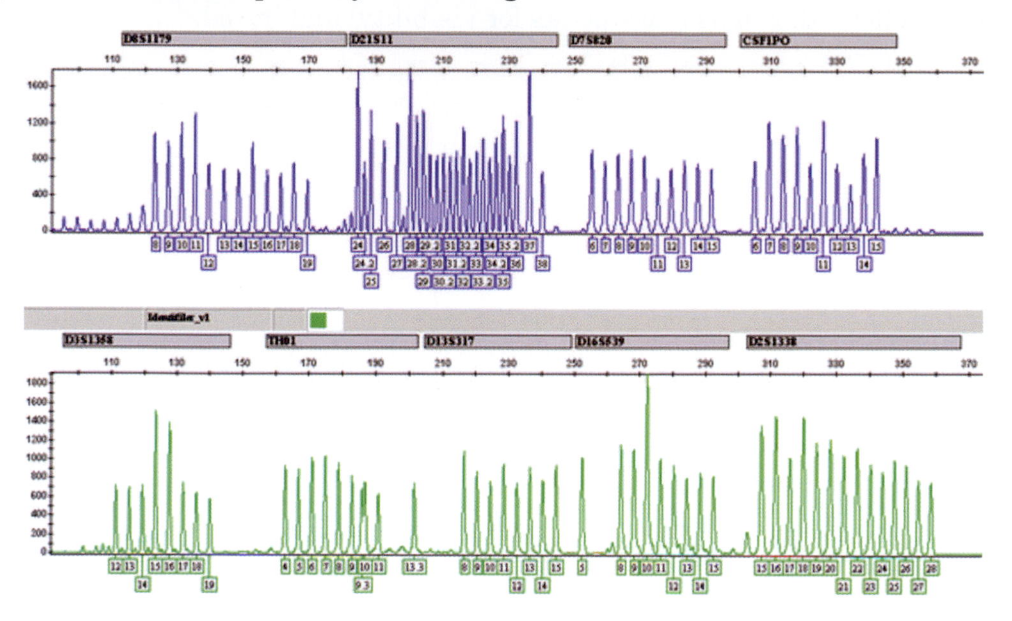

Shown in the two chromatograms previously are the allelic ladders for the loci labeled in blue and in green.

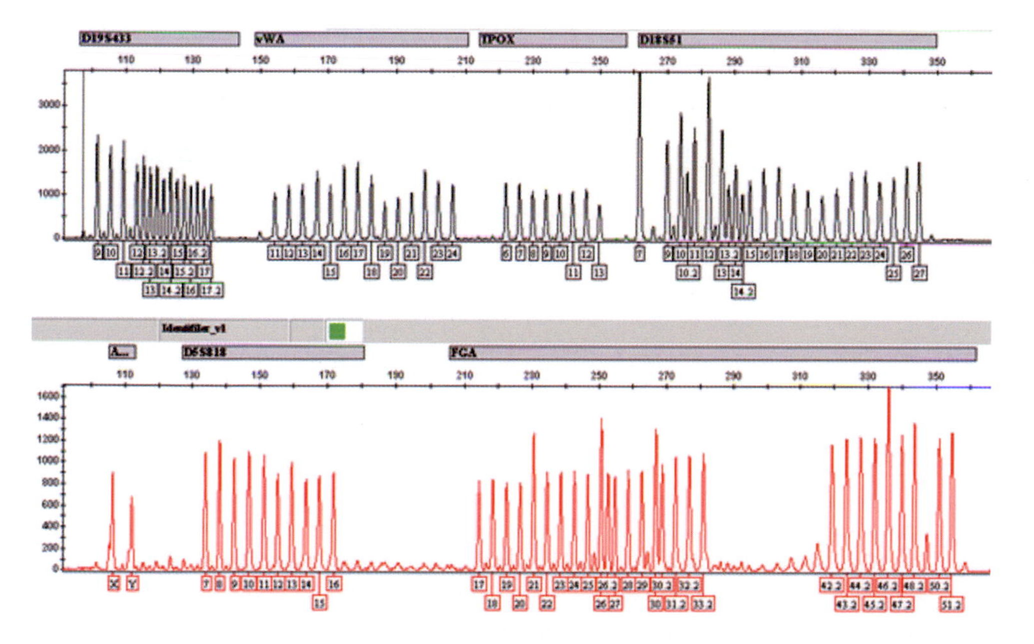

Shown in the two chromatograms previously are the allelic ladders for the loci labeled in yellow (shown as black peaks for visibility) and in red.

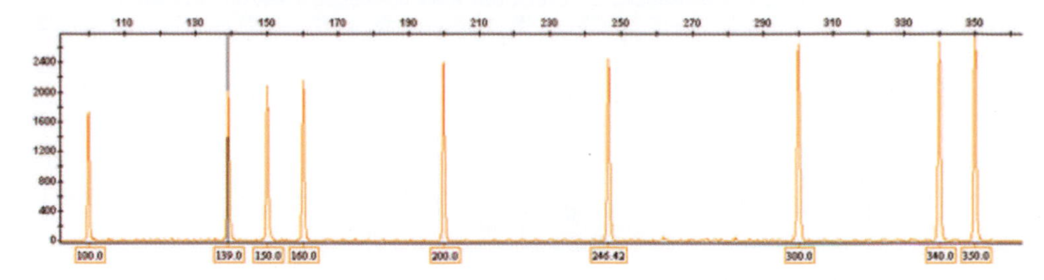

Shown previously is the size standard used by the STR analysis software to calculate the base pair size of the peaks generated from reference and unknown DNAs.

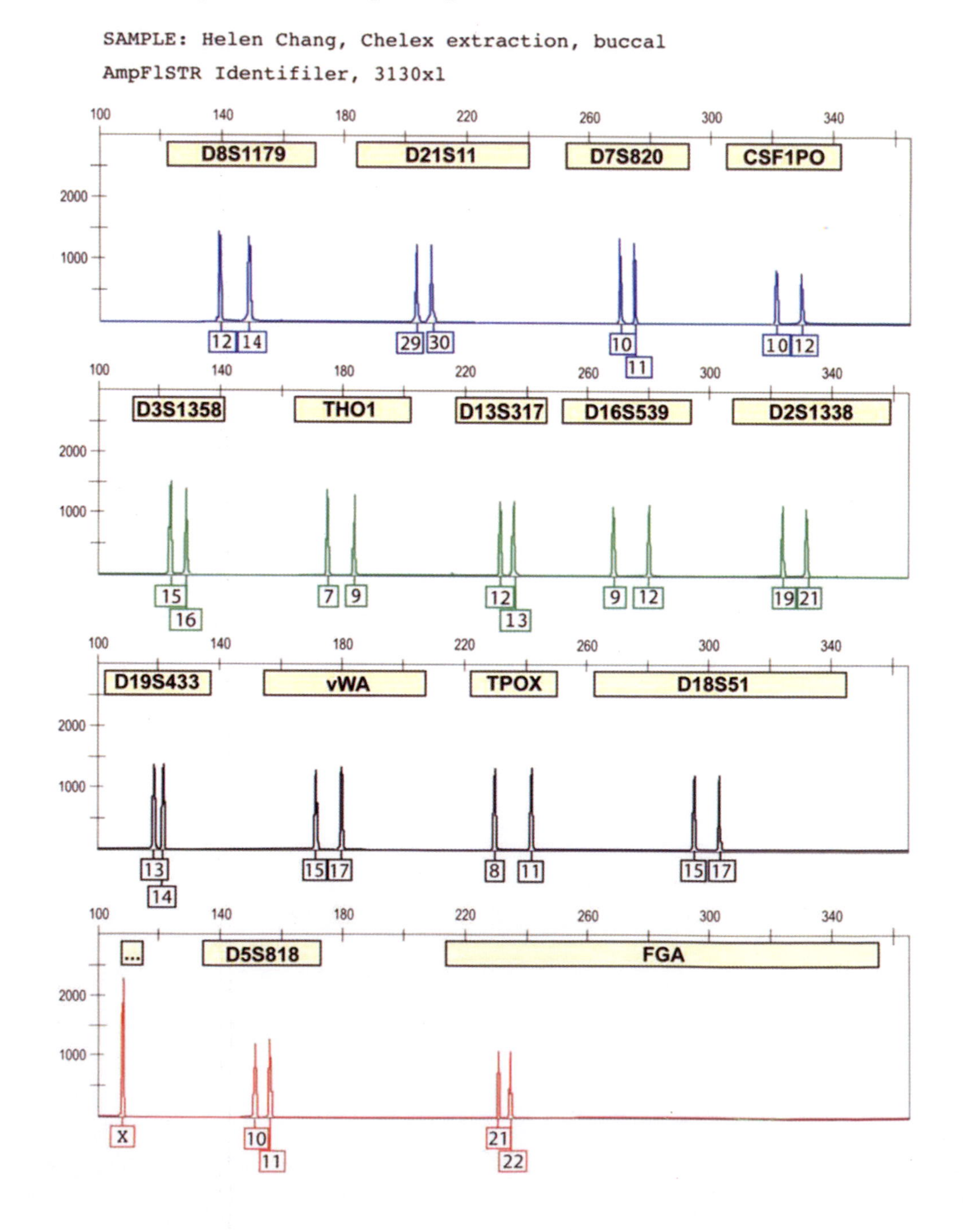

SAMPLE: CA087953, Evidence Item 1, Stain: Subaru's water reservoir

AmpFlSTR Identifiler, 3130xl

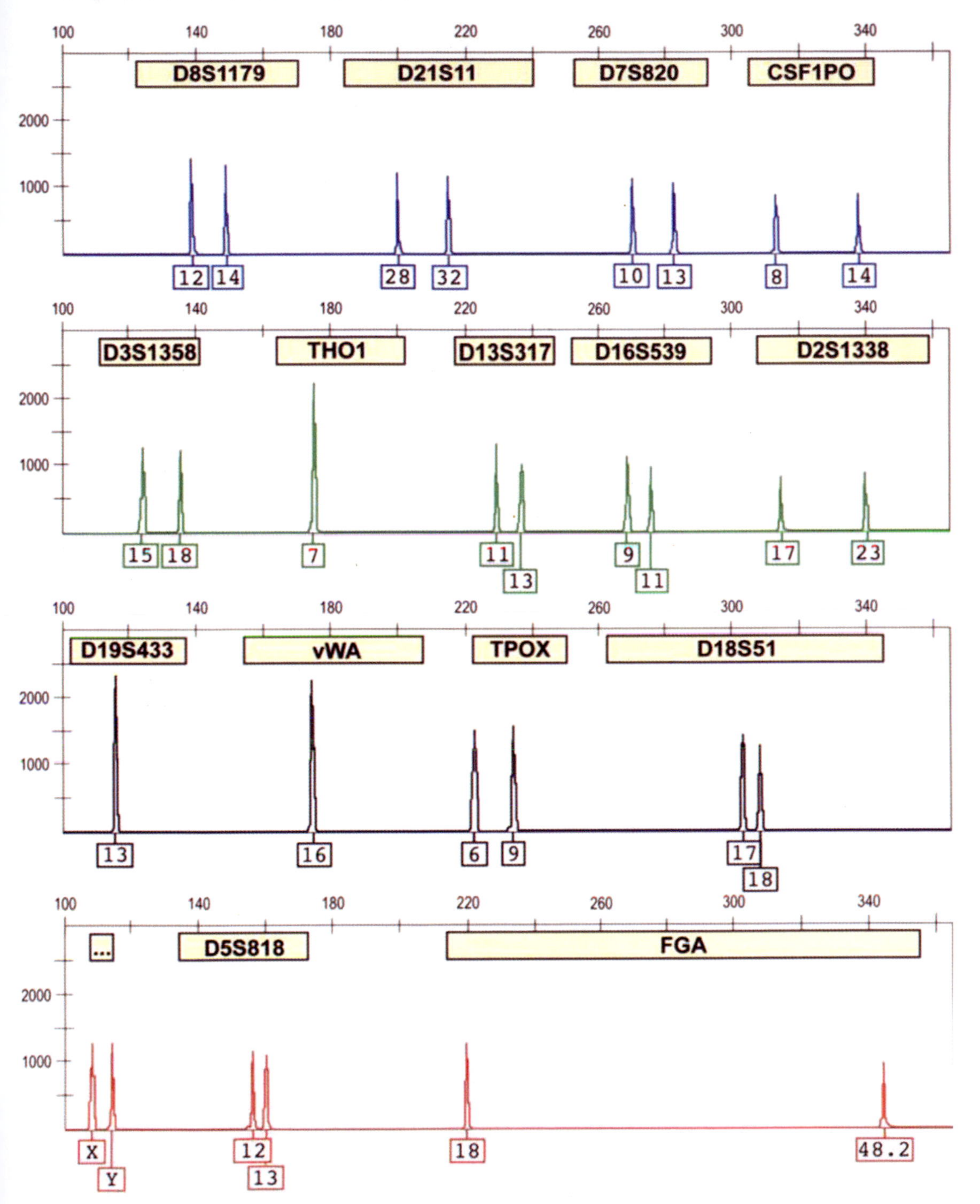

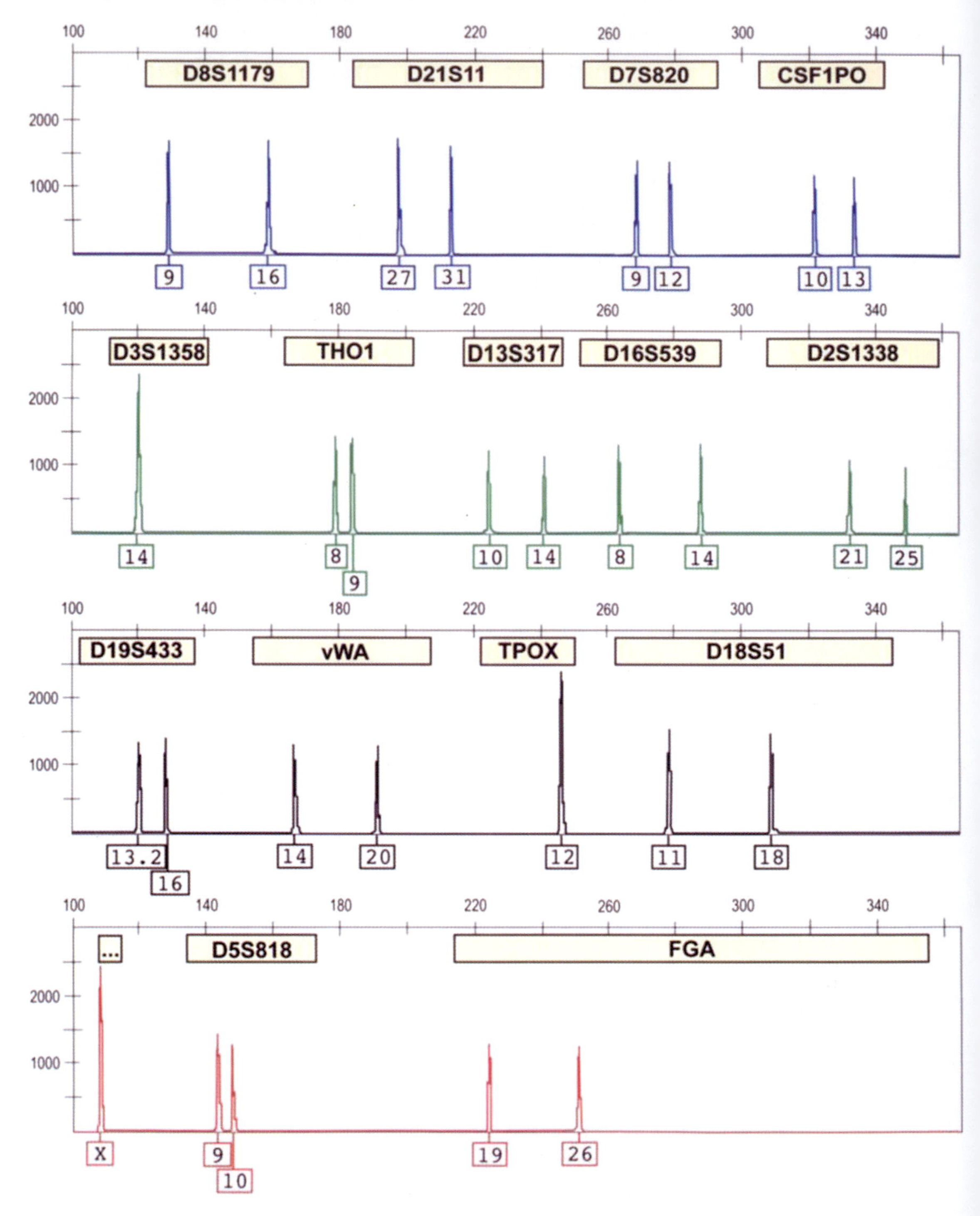
SAMPLE: CA087953, Evidence Item 2, tissue in engine bay
AmpFlSTR Identifiler, 3130xl
D8S1179
D21S11
D7S820
CSF1PO
9
16
27
31
9
12
10
13
D3S1358
THO1
D13S317
D16S539
D2S1338
14
8
9
10
14
8
14
21
25
D19S433
vWA
TPOX
D18S51
13.2
16
14
20
12
11
18
D5S818
FGA
X
9
10
19
26

SAMPLE: CA087953, Evidence Item 3, high velocity stain on firewall

AmpFlSTR Identifiler, 3130xl

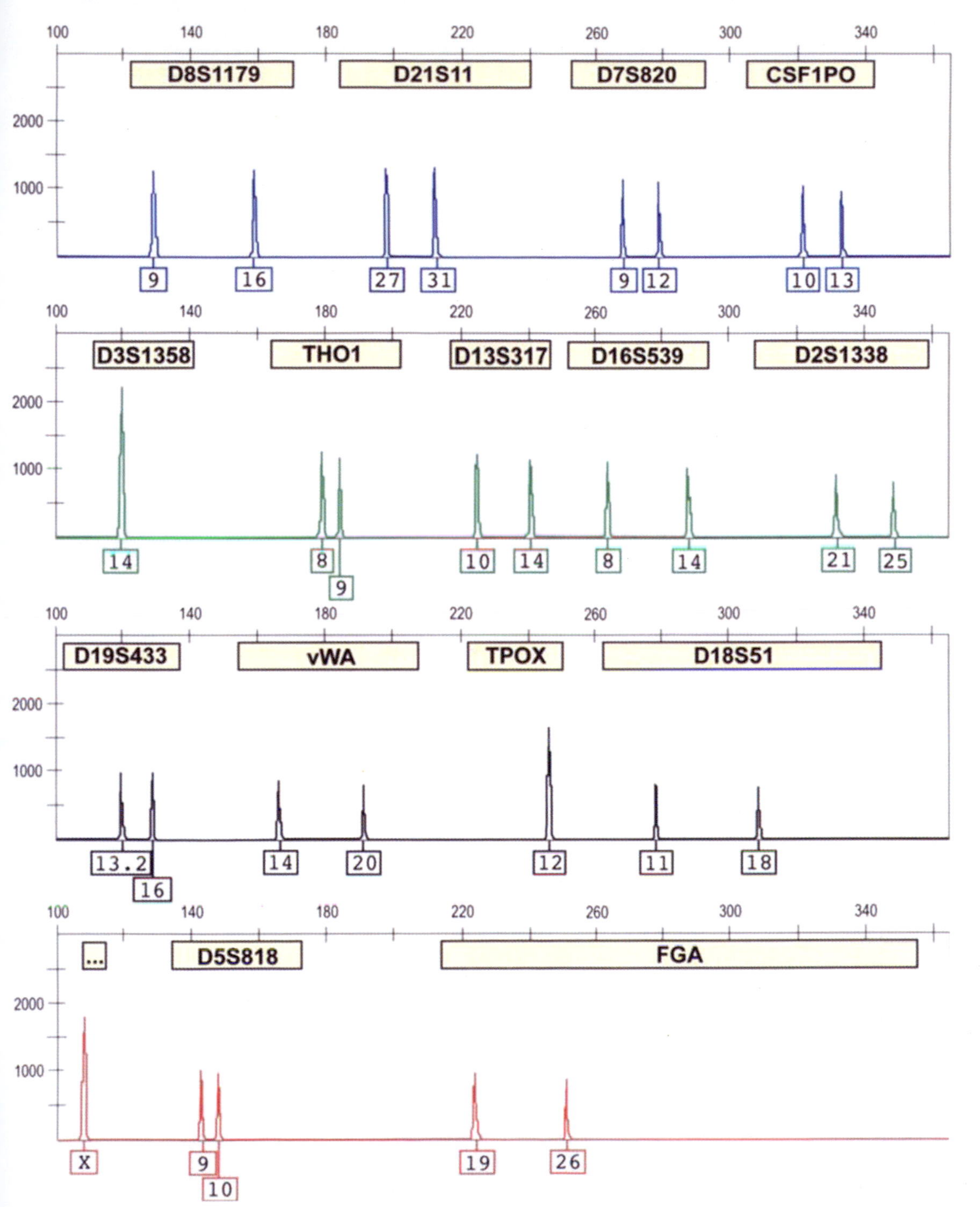

```
SAMPLE: CA087953, Evidence Item 5, transfer stain in cargo bay
AmpFlSTR Identifiler, 3130xl
```

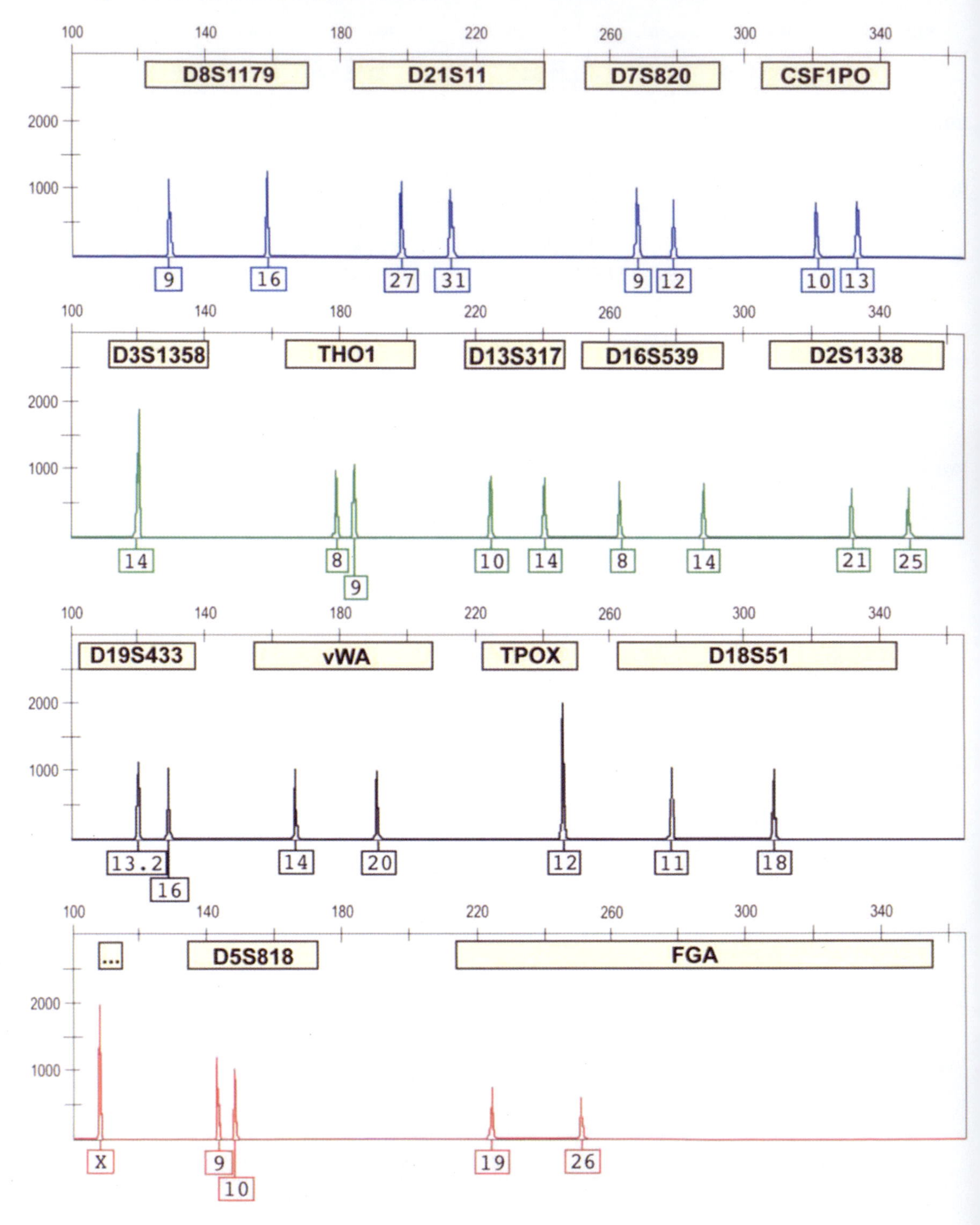

SAMPLE: CA087953, Evidence Item 7, stain in Subaru cargo bay

AmpFlSTR Identifiler, 3130xl

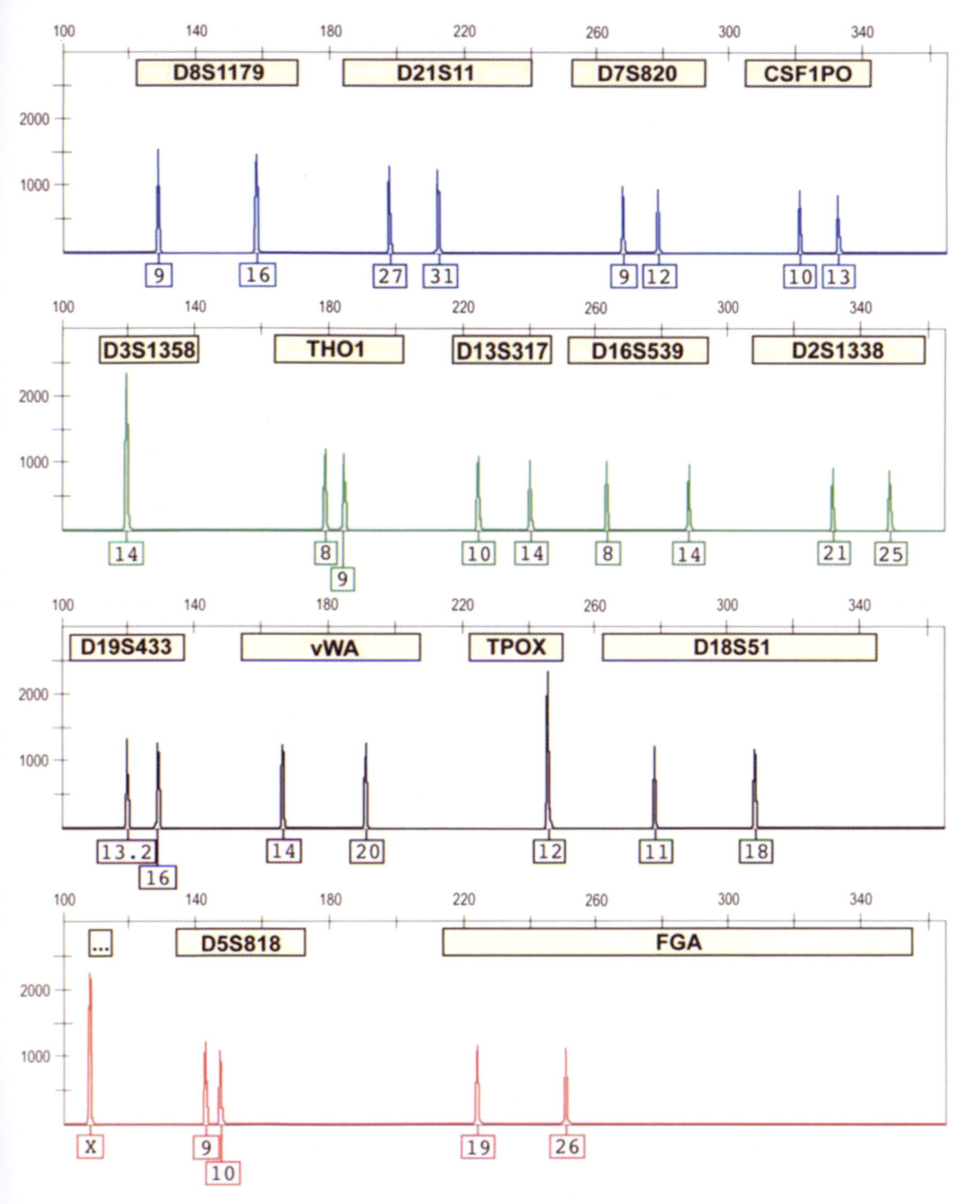

SAMPLE: CA087953, Ev. Item 9, rearview mirror bloody fingerprint

AmpFlSTR Identifiler, 3130xl

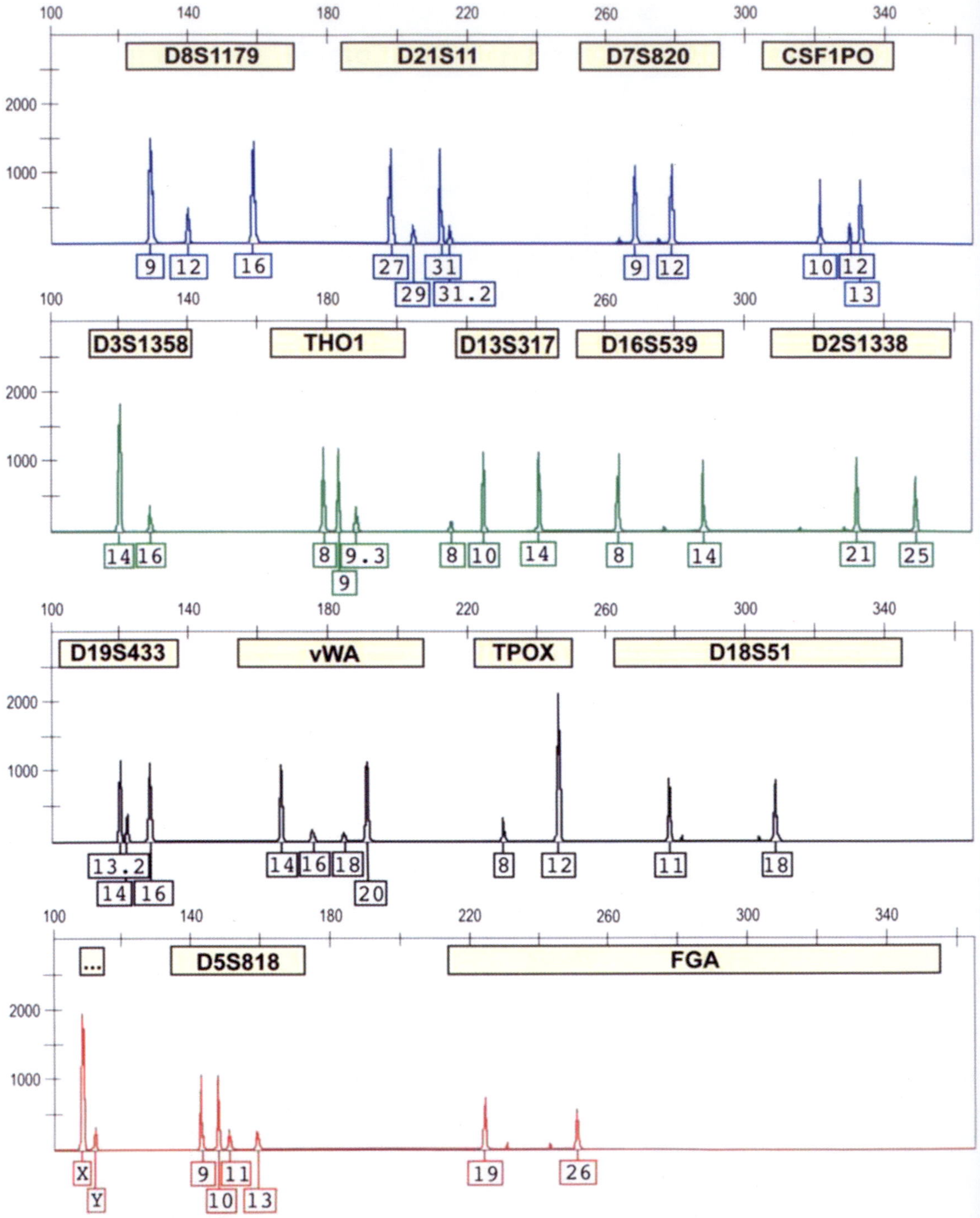

SAMPLE: CA087953, Evidence Item 10, Sarah Holmes buccal swab

AmpFlSTR Identifiler, 3130xl

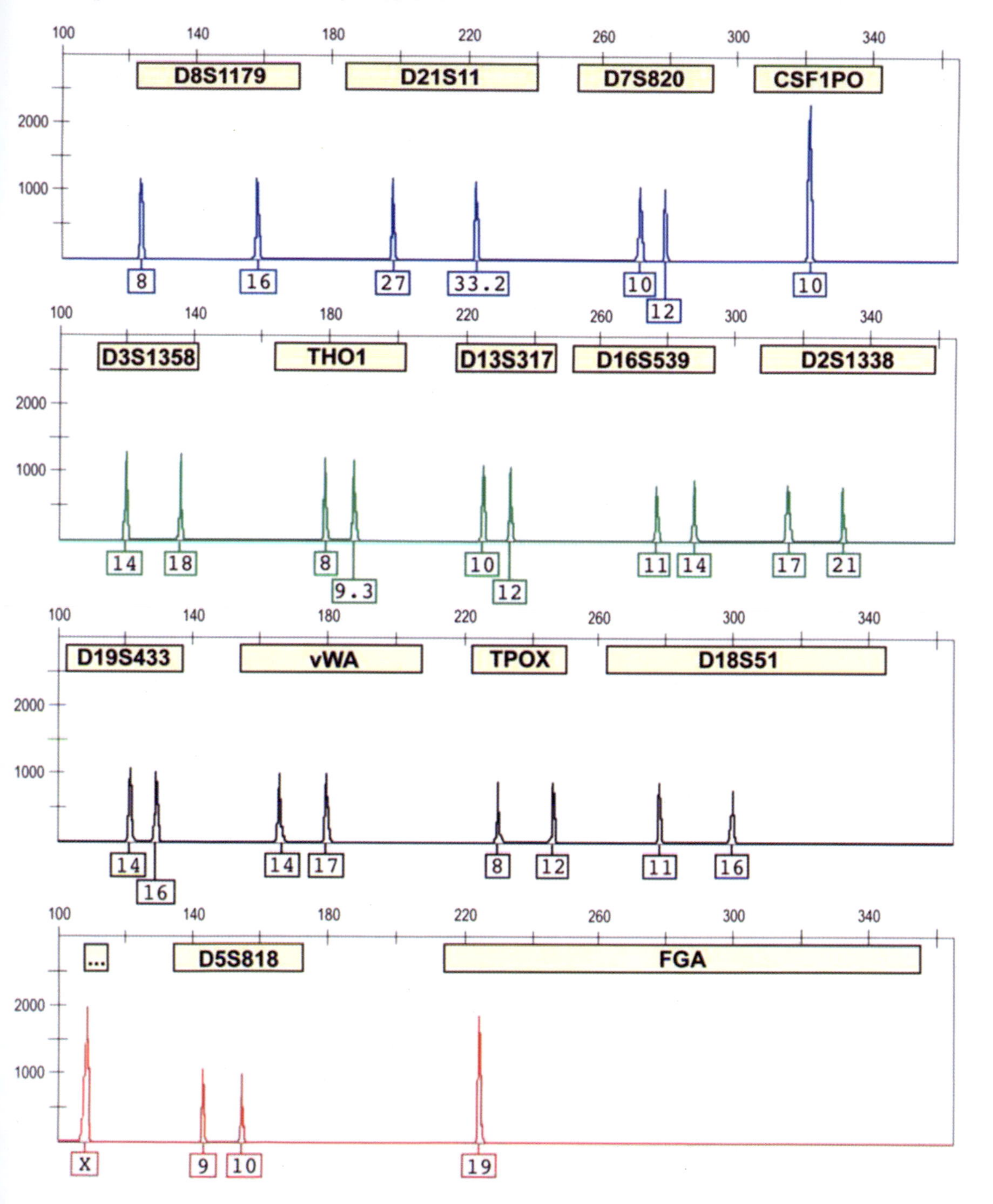

SAMPLE: CA087953, Evidence Item 11, Dwayne Holmes buccal swab
AmpFlSTR Identifiler, 3130xl

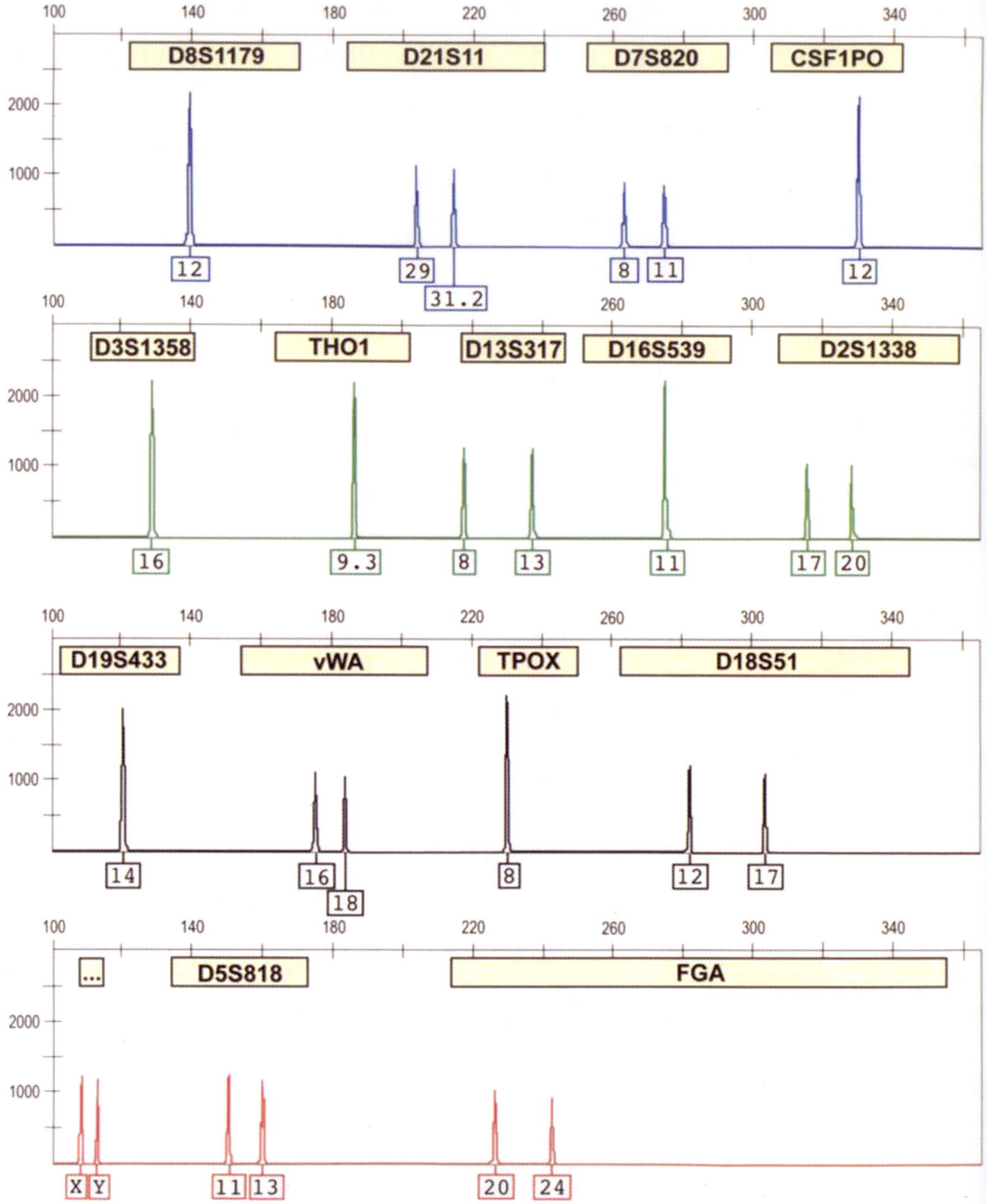

100 140 180 220 260 300 340
D8S1179 D21S11 D7S820 CSF1PO
2000
1000
12 29 31.2 8 11 12

100 140 180 220 260 300 340
D3S1358 THO1 D13S317 D16S539 D2S1338
2000
1000
16 9.3 8 13 11 17 20

100 140 180 220 260 300 340
D19S433 vWA TPOX D18S51
2000
1000
14 16 18 8 12 17

100 140 180 220 260 300 340
... D5S818 FGA
2000
1000
X Y 11 13 20 24

SAMPLE: CA087953, Evidence Item 12, Samdeep O'Neill buccal swab

AmpFlSTR Identifiler, 3130xl

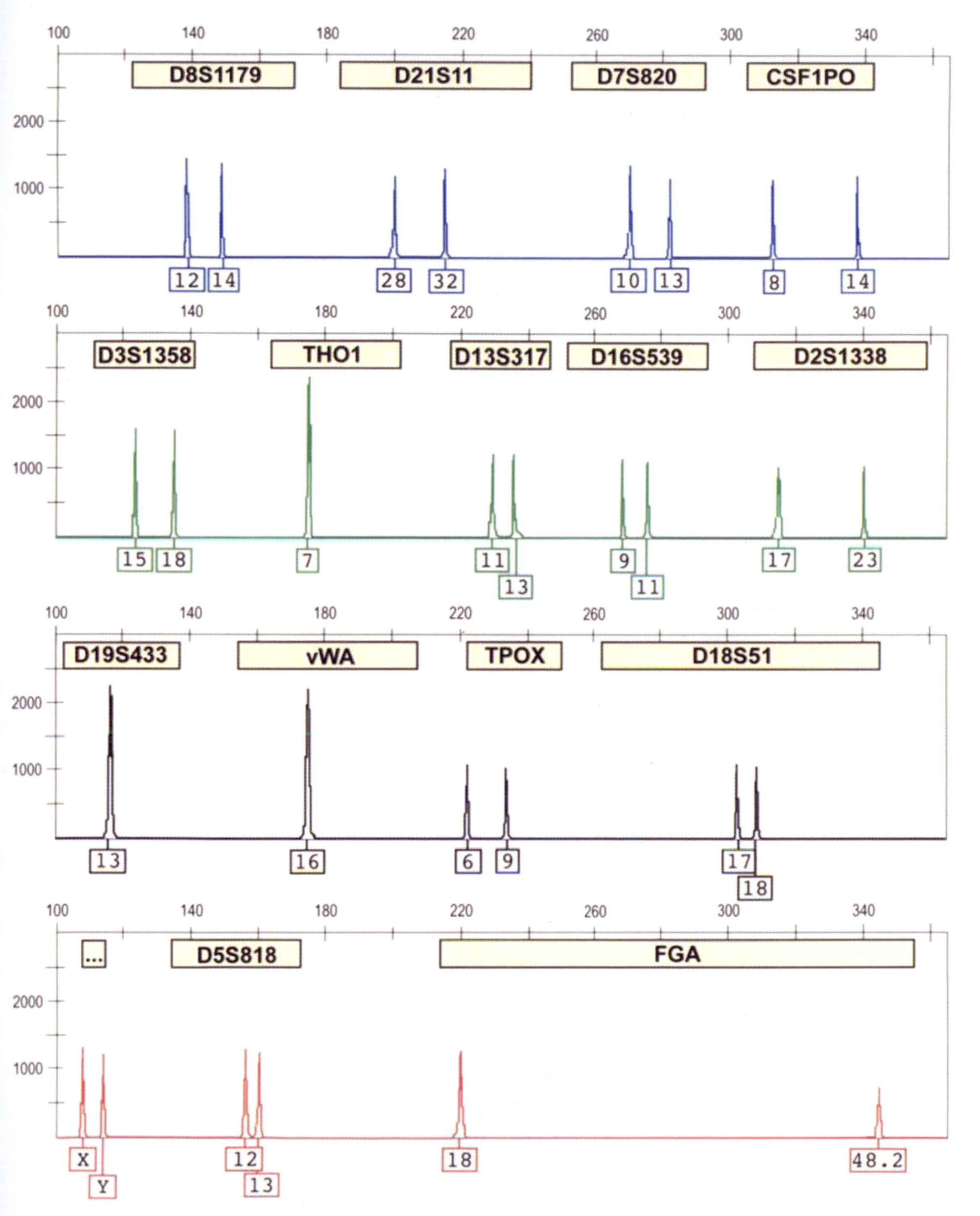

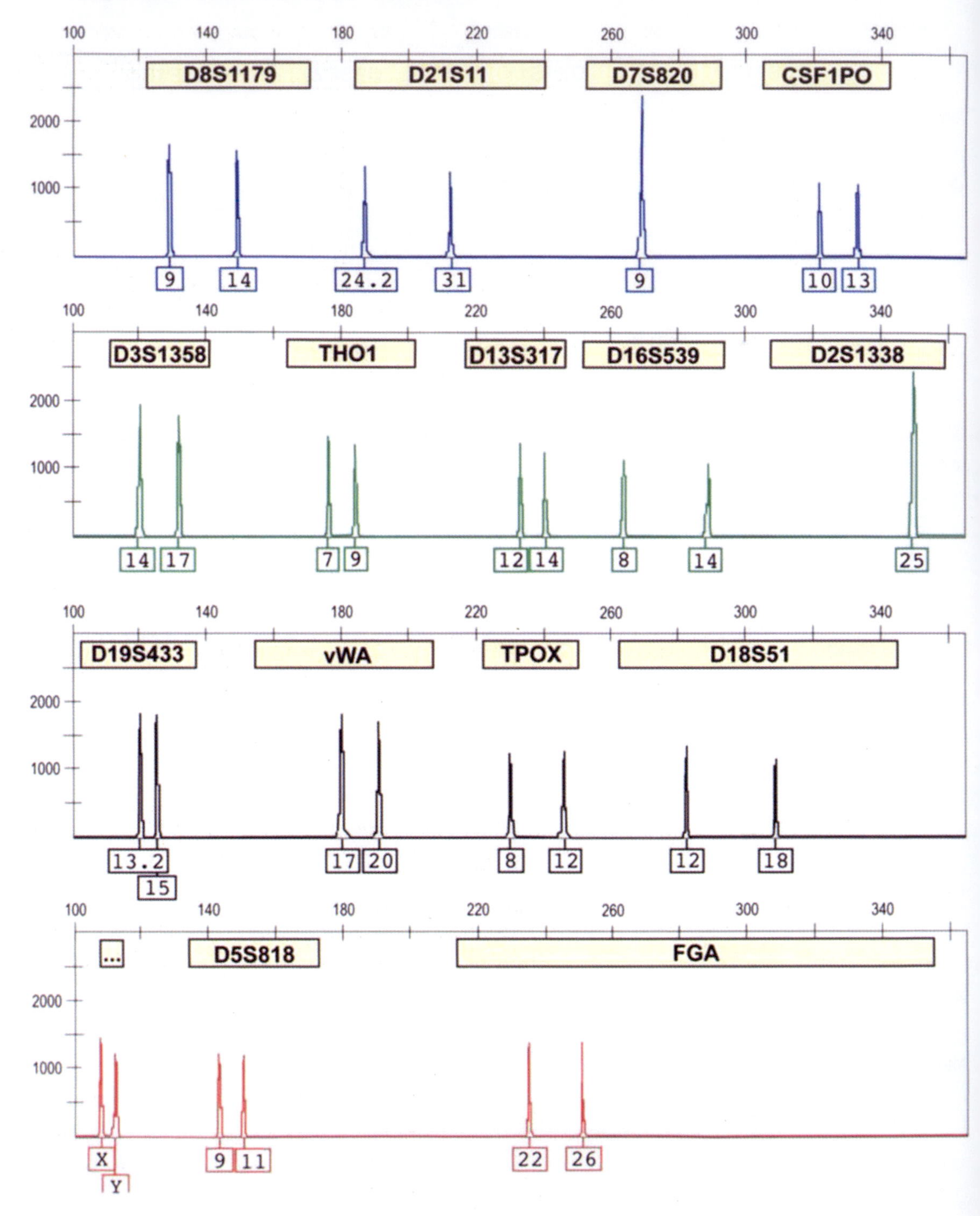
SAMPLE: CA087953, Evidence Item 13, Chuck Beamer buccal swab
AmpFlSTR Identifiler, 3130xl
D8S1179
D21S11
D7S820
CSF1PO
9
14
24.2
31
9
10
13
D3S1358
THO1
D13S317
D16S539
D2S1338
14
17
7
9
12
14
8
14
25
D19S433
vWA
TPOX
D18S51
13.2
15
17
20
8
12
12
18
D5S818
FGA
X
Y
9
11
22
26

SAMPLE: CA087953, Evidence Item 28, Alice Beamer buccal swab

AmpFlSTR Identifiler, 3130xl

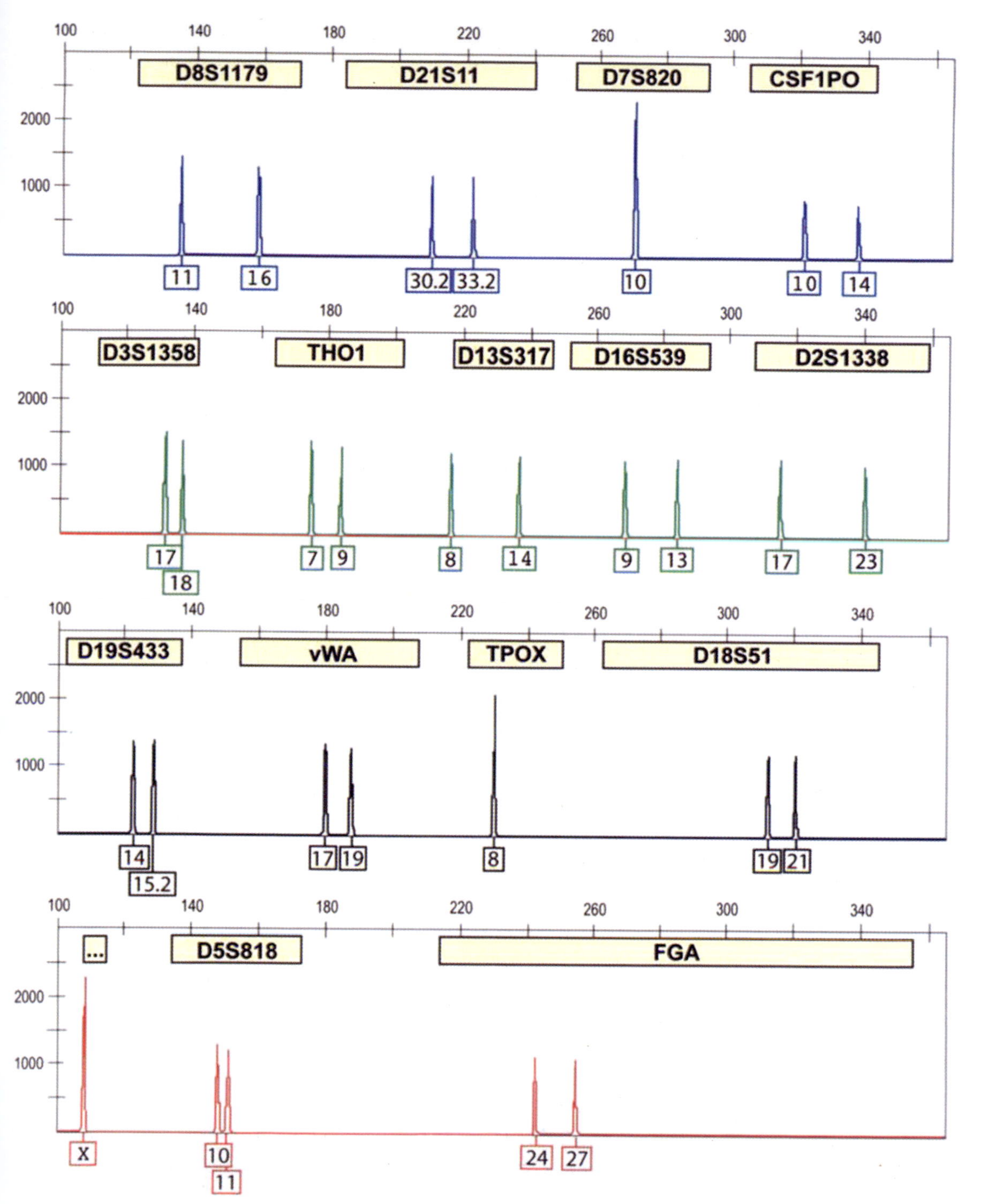

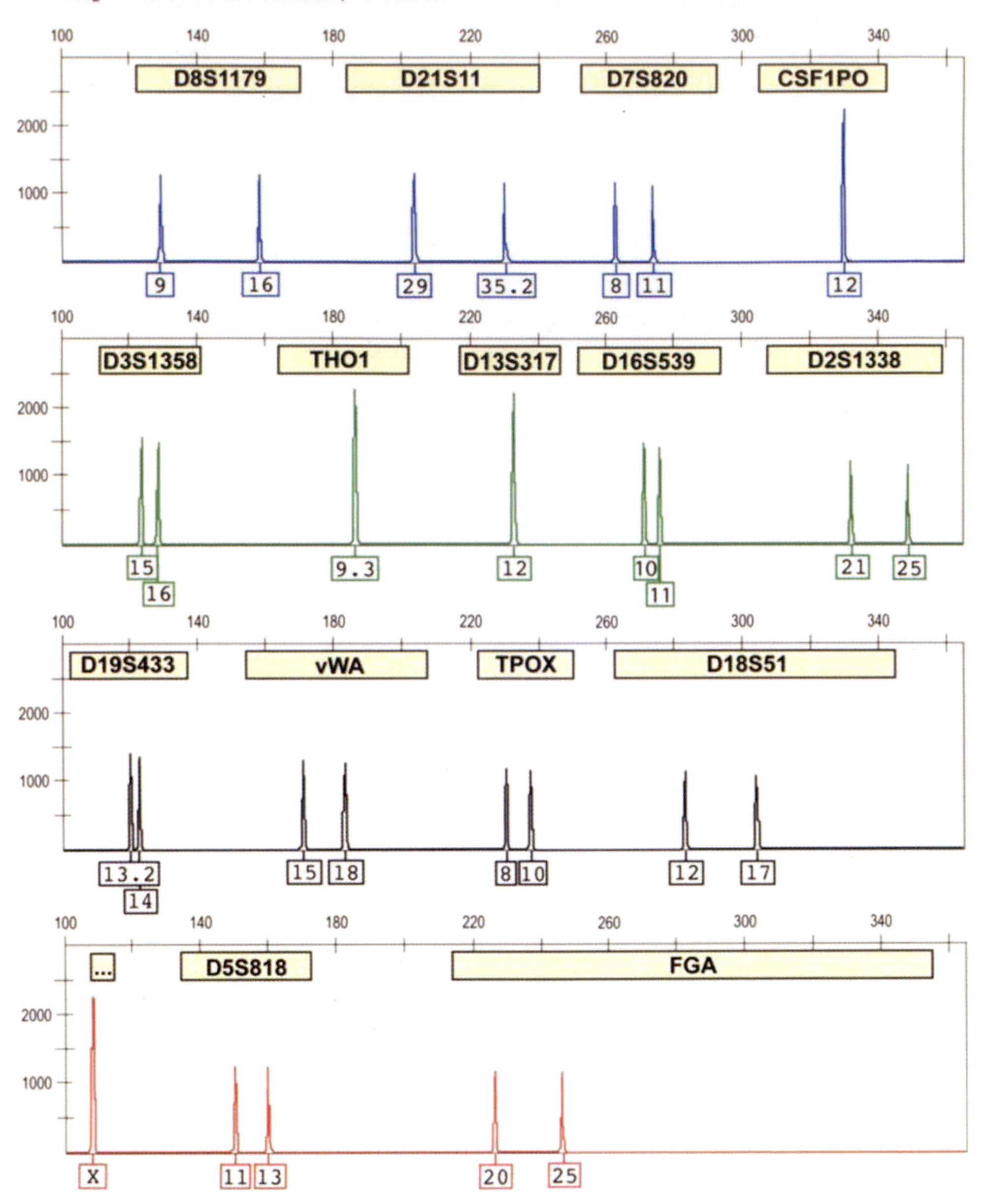
SAMPLE: CA087953, Evidence Item 30, Farah Dawood buccal swab
AmpFlSTR Identifiler, 3130xl
D8S1179
D21S11
D7S820
CSF1PO
9
16
29
35.2
8
11
12
D3S1358
THO1
D13S317
D16S539
D2S1338
15
16
9.3
12
10
11
21
25
D19S433
vWA
TPOX
D18S51
13.2
14
15
18
8
10
12
17
D5S818
FGA
X
11
13
20
25

Review Questions

12.1 Why is the analysis of STRs preferred when it comes to identification of biological evidence over analysis of functional genes (those encoding proteins)?

12.2 What advantages does the analysis of STRs have over RFLP analysis?

12.3 Within the sequence CCCGAACTACAGGAATTCAGGT, what might you suspect could possibly be a six-base sequence recognized by a restriction endonuclease?

12.4 What does the designation $[AATG]_5$, signify?

12.5 The following is a sample of a partial electropherogram showing the STR results at the D8S1179 and D21S11 loci. (a) What is the horizontal scale above the peaks represent? (b) What do the boxes with a number below the peaks represent?

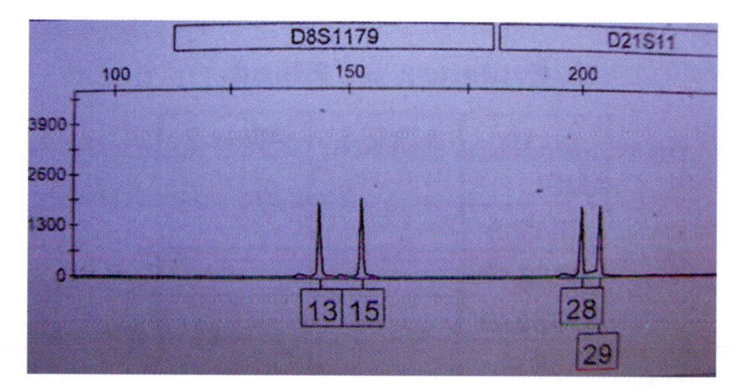

12.6 An allele of the STR locus D3S1358 has 15 tetranucleotide repeats. When amplified by PCR, this allele is approximately 123 bp in length. The D2S1338 locus has an allele that also contains 15 tetranucleotide repeats. However, its size when amplified by PCR is approximately 307 bp in length. How can two different loci have the same number of tetranucleotide repeats and yet their PCR-amplified products are of a different size?

12.7 On which human chromosome will you find the D13S317 STR locus?

12.8 Following differential extraction to isolate DNA specifically from spermatozoa obtained from a vaginal swab in a sexual assault case, the following result was obtained by amplification of the D1S80 locus.

Sperm fraction

Allelic ladder

Victim reference

Explain the result you see for the sperm fraction sample.

12.9 In a sexual assault case where Y-STRs are used to analyze DNA recovered from a vaginal swab, more than two bands are found at each locus position. Why might this be?

12.10 How many different primers would there be in an STR multiplex reaction in which 23 loci are amplified simultaneously?

Further Reading

Handwriting

Signature Authentication by Forensic Document Examiners by M. Kam, K. Gummadidala, G. Fielding, and R. Conn in *Journal of Forensic Sciences*, Vol. 46, No. 4, pages 884–888, 2001.

Individuality of Handwriting by S.N. Srihari, S.H. Cha, H. Arora, and S. Lee in *Journal of Forensic Sciences*, Vol. 47, No. 4, pages 856–872, 2002.

Writer Identification Using Hand-Printed and Non-Hand-Printed Questioned Documents by M. Kam and E. Lin in *Journal of Forensic Sciences*, Vol. 48, No. 6, pages 1391–1395, 2003.

Gelatin Lifting, a Novel Technique for the Examination of Indented Writing by J.A. de Koeijer, C.E.H. Berger, W. Glas, and H.T. Madhuizen in *Journal of Forensic Sciences*, Vol. 51, No. 4, pages 908–914, 2006.

Size Influence on Shape of Handwritten Characters Loop by R. Marquis, F. Taroni, S. Bozza, and M. Schmittbuhl in *Forensic Science International*, Vol. 172, Issue 1, pages 10–16, 2007.

On the Discriminability of the Handwriting of Twins by Sargur Srihar, Chen Huang, and Harish Srinivasan in *Journal of Forensic Sciences*, Vol. 53, No. 2, pages 430–446, 2008.

DNA Typing

DNA Fingerprints from Fingerprints by R.A.H. van Oorschot and M.K. Jones in *Nature*, Vol. 387, page 787, 1997.

Forensic Identification of a Rapist Using Unusual Evidence by C. Oz, J.A. Levi, Y. Novoselski, N. Volkov, and U. Motro in *Journal of Forensic Sciences*, Vol. 44. No. 4, pages 860–862, 1999.

Fingerprints and DNA: STR Typing of DNA Extracted from Adhesive Tape after Processing for Fingerprints by A. Zamir, E. Springer, and B. Glattstein in *Journal of Forensic Sciences*, Vol. 45, pages 687–688, 2000.

Trace DNA: A Review, Discussion of Theory, and Application of the Transfer of Trace Quantities of DNA through Skin Contact by R.A. Wickenheiser in *Journal of Forensic Sciences*, Vol. 47, No. 3, pages 442–450, 2002.

Fingerprints as Evidence for a Genetic Profile: Morphological Study on Fingerprints and Analysis of Exogenous and Individual Factors Affecting DNA Typing by F. Alessandrini, M. Cecati, M. Pesaresi, C. Turchi, F. Carle, and A. Tagliabracci *in Journal of Forensic Sciences*, Vol. 48, No. 3, pages 586–592, 2003.

VNTRs

Analysis of the VNTR Locus D1S80 by the PCR Followed by High-Resolution PAGE by B. Budowle, R. Chakraborty, A.M. Giusti, A.J. Eisenberg, and R.C. Allen in *American Journal of Human Genetics*, Vol. 48, pages 137–144, 1991.

Validation Studies for the Genetic Typing of the D1S80 Locus for Implementation into Forensic Casework by A.M. Gross, G. Carmody, and R.A. Guerrieri in *Journal of Forensic Sciences*, Vol. 46, No. 2, pages 1140–1146, 1997.

STRs

Fingerprint Enhancement Revisited and the Effects of Blood Enhancement Chemicals on Subsequent *Profiler Plus*™ Fluorescent Short Tandem Repeat DNA Analysis of Fresh and Aged Bloody Fingerprints by C.J. Fregeau, O. Germain, and R.M. Fourney in *Journal of Forensic Sciences*, Vol. 45, No. 2, pages 354–380, 2000.

Evaluation of an Alkaline Lysis Method for the Extraction of DNA from Whole Blood and Forensic Stains for STR Analysis by M. Klintschar and F. Neuhuber in *Journal of Forensic Sciences*, Vol. 45, No. 3, pages 669–673, 2000.

Fingerprints and DNA: STR Typing of DNA Extracted from Adhesive Tape after Processing for Fingerprints by A. Zamir, E. Springer, and B. Glattstein in *Journal of Forensic Sciences*, Vol. 45, No. 3, pages 687–688, 2000.

Validation of AmpFlSTR™ Profiler Plus PCR Amplification Kit for Use in Forensic Casework by W.E. Frank, B.E. Llewellyn, P.A. Fish, A.K. Riech, T.L. Marcacci, D.W. Gandor, D. Parker, R.R. Carter, and S.M. Thibault in *Journal of Forensic Sciences*, Vol. 46, No. 3, pages 642–646, 2001.

Validation of Short Tandem Repeats (STRs) for Forensic Usage: Performance Testing of Fluorescent Multiplex STR Systems and Analysis of Authentic and Simulated Forensic Samples by T.R. Moretti, A.L. Baumstart, D.A. Defenbaugh, K.M. Keys, J.B. Smerick, and B. Budowle in *Journal of Forensic Sciences*, Vol. 46, No. 3, pages 647–660, 2001.

Validation of STR Typing by Capillary Electrophoresis by T.R. Moretti, A.L. Baumstark, D.A. Defenbaugh, K.M. Keys, A.L. Brown, and B. Budowle in *Journal of Forensic Sciences*, Vol. 46, No. 3, pages 661–676, 2001.

TWGDAM Validation of the AmpF*l*STR Profiler Plus and AmpF*l*STR COfiler STR Multiplex Systems Using Capillary Electrophoresis by M.J. LaFountain, M.B. Schwartz, P.A. Svete, M.A. Walkinshaw, and E. Buel in *Journal of Forensic Sciences*, Vol. 46, No. 5, pages 1191–1198, 2001.

Role of Short Tandem Repeat DNA in Forensic Casework in the UK—Past, Present, and Future Perspectives by P. Gill in *BioTechniques*, Vol. 32, No. 2, pages 366–385, 2002.

Constructing Universal Multiplex PCR Systems for Comparative Genotyping by J.M. Wallin, C.L. Holt, K.D. Lazaruk, T.H. Nguyen, and P.S. Walsh in *Journal of Forensic Sciences*, Vol. 47, No. 1, pages 52–65, 2002.

TWGDAM Validation of AmpFlSTR PCR Amplification Kits for Forensic DNA Casework by C.L. Holt, M. Buoncristiani, J.M. Wallin, T. Nguyen, K.D. Lazaruk, and P.S. Walsh in *Journal of Forensic Sciences*, Vol. 47, No. 1, pages 66–96, 2002.

Skeletal Remains Presumed Submerged in Water for Three Years Identified Using PCR-STR Analysis by K. Crainic, J. Paraire, M. Leterreux, M. Durigon, and P. de Mazancourt in *Journal of Forensic Sciences*, Vol. 47, No. 5, pages 1025–1027, 2002.

Systematic Study on STR Profiling on Blood and Saliva Traces after Visualization of Fingerprint Marks by P. Grubwieser, A. Thaler, S. Köchl, R. Teissl, W. Rabl, and W. Parson in *Journal of Forensic Sciences*, Vol. 48, No. 4, pages 733–741, 2003.

The Development of Reduced Size STR Amplicons as Tools for Analysis of Degraded DNA by J.M. Butler, Y. Shen, and B.R. McCord in *Journal of Forensic Sciences*, Vol. 48, No. 5, pages 1054–1064, 2003.

Validation and Uses of a Y-Chromosome STR 10-Plex for Forensic and Paternity Laboratories by C.L. Johnson, J.H. Warren, R.C. Giles, and R.W. Staub in *Journal of Forensic Sciences*, Vol. 48, No. 6, pages 1260–1268, 2003.

Validation and Implementation of the PowerPlex® 16 BIO System STR Multiplex for Forensic Casework by S.A. Greenspoon, J.D. Ban, L. Pablo, C.A. Crouse, F.G. Kist, C.S. Tomsey, A.L. Glessner, L.R. Mihalacki, T.M. Long, B.J. Heidebrecht, C.A. Braunstein, D.A. Freeman, C. Soberalski, N. Bruesehoff, A.S. Amin, E.K. Douglas, and J.W. Schumm in *Journal of Forensic Sciences*, Vol. 49, No. 1, pages 71–80, 2004.

Erroneous Gender Identification by the Amelogenin Sex Test by A. Michael and P. Brauner in *Journal of Forensic Sciences*, Vol. 49, No. 2, pages 258–259, 2004.

Unusual Association of Three Rare Alleles and a Mismatch in a Case of Paternity Testing by C. Turchi, M. Pesaresi, F. Alessandrini, V. Onofri, A. Arseni, and A. Tagliabracci in *Journal of Forensic Sciences*, Vol. 49, No. 2, pages 260–262, 2004.

Enhanced Kinship Analysis and STR-Based DNA Typing for Human Identification in Mass Fatality Incidents: The Swissair Flight 111 Disaster by B. Leclair, C.J. Fregeau, K.L. Bowen, and R.M. Fourney in *Journal of Forensic Sciences*, Vol. 49, No. 5, pages 939–953, 2004.

Specificity of Sibship Determination Using the ABI Identifiler Multiplex System by T.M. Reid, C.A. Wolf, C.M. Kraemer, S.C. Lee, M.L. Baird, and R.F. Lee in *Journal of Forensic Sciences*, Vol. 49, No. 6, pages 1262–1264, 2004.

Developmental Validation of a Single-Tube Amplification of the 13 CODIS STR Loci, D2S1338, D19S433, and Amelogenin: The AmpF*l*STR Identifiler® PCR Amplification Kit by P.J. Collins, L.K. Hennessy, C.S. Leibelt, R.K. Roby, D.J. Reeder, and P.A. Foxall in *Journal of Forensic Sciences*, Vol. 49, No. 6, pages 1265–1277, 2004.

Characterization of New MiniSTR Loci to Aid Analysis of Degraded DNA by M.D. Coble and J.M. Butler in *Journal of Forensic Sciences*, Vol. 50, No. 1, pages 43–53, 2005.

Evaluation of Sieving Polymers for Fast, Reproducible Electrophoretic Analysis of Short Tandem Repeats (STR) in Capillaries by J.M. Bienvenue, K.L. Wilson, J.P. Landers, and J.P. Ferrance in *Journal of Forensic Sciences*, Vol. 50, No. 4, pages 842–848, 2005.

Development and Validation of the AmpFlSTR® Yfiler™ PCR Amplification Kit: A Male Specific, Single Amplification 17 Y-STR Multiplex System by J.J. Mulero, C.W. Chang, L.M. Calandro, R.L. Green, Y. Li, C.L. Johnson, and L.K. Hennessy in *Journal of Forensic Sciences*, Vol. 51, No. 1, pages 64–75, 2006.

Genetics and Genomics of Core Short Tandem Repeat Loci Used in Human Identity Testing by J.M. Butler in *Journal of Forensic Sciences*, Vol. 51, No. 2, pages 253–265, 2006.

Development and Validation of the AmpFlSTR® MiniFiler™ PCR Amplification Kit: A MiniSTR Multiplex for the Analysis of Degraded and/or PCR Inhibited DNA by Julio J. Mulero, Chien Wei Chang, Robert E. Lagace, Dennis Y. Wang, Jennifer L. Bas, Timothy P. McMahon, and Lori K. Hennessy in *Journal of Forensic Sciences*, Vol. 53, No. 4, pages 838–852, 2008.

Forensically Relevant SNP Classes by Bruce Budowle and Anglea van Daal in *BioTechniques*, Vol. 44, No. 5, pages 603–610, 2008.

Justice and Science: Trials and Triumphs of DNA Evidence by George Clark, Rutgers University Press, Piscataway, NJ, 2008.

The Prevalence of Mixed DNA Profiles in Fingernail Samples Taken from Couples who Co-habit Using Autosomal and Y-STRs by Simon Malsom, Nicola Flanagan, Colin McAlister, and Lindsay Dixon in *Forensic Science International: Genetics*, Vol. 3, pages 57–62, 2009.

Y Chromosomal STR Analysis using Pyrosequencing Technology by Hanna Edlund and Marie Allen in *Forensic Science International: Genetics*, Vol. 3, pages 119–124, 2009.

Maximizing DNA Profiling Success from Sub-optimal Quantities of DNA: A Staged Approach by Amy D. Roeder, Paul Elsmore, Matt Greenhalgh, and Andrew McDonald in *Forensic Science International: Genetics*, Vol. 3, pages 128–137, 2009.

Development of STR Profiles from Firearms and Fired Cartridge Cases by Katie M. Horsman-Hall, Yvette Orihuela, Stephanie L. Karczynski, Ann L. Davis, Jeffrey D. Ban, and Susan A. Greenspoon in *Forensic Science International: Genetics*, Vol. 3, pages 242–250, 2009.

13
Population Statistics

Warehouse District, Friday, 3:20 PM

The Potrero Avenue exit off of 101 led Helen abruptly into San Francisco's warehouse district. Sprawling, imposing buildings of dilapidated wood and corrugated metal siding posted signs for shipping materials, construction supplies, and rental storage space. The brown and dark orange warehouse on McKinnon stretched down an entire block. Its end on Toland was marked "418," and Helen found Jenkins' car parked by the gate of a chain-link fence barricading the property. The gate, she could see, was slightly ajar. She parked behind Jenkins' vehicle and walked quickly to the opening where she slipped through onto the warehouse grounds. A padlock on the warehouse door was unlocked, and she quietly moved to enter. The smell of cow manure spilled through the doorway. As she stepped over the stoop, a loud bang clapped in her ears. To her right, a woman was holding a gun, smoke still floating lazily off its barrel as if from a cigarette. Fifteen feet away, Jenkins, like a beaten prizefighter, had collapsed to his knees. His arms hung limp at his sides, his head drooped forward, and blood spread out on his white shirt from underneath the left lapel of his coat. Helen twirled around and kicked the woman's arm with such force that her weapon flew into the air. Helen rushed to a position behind Jenkins. When the gun met the concrete, it reeled end over end and came to rest just two yards in front of Jenkins. Helen dropped to her knees catching Jenkins as he collapsed backward against her. In a single motion, she reached under his coat, pulled his revolver from its holster, flicked the safety with her thumb and pointed it straight at the woman now scrambling to recover her weapon.

"Don't!" Helen screamed. "Stay right where you are!"

The woman, bending at the waist, her hand just inches from her gun, slowly straightened up.

"You're bluffing," the woman said in a mocking tone. "You don't know how to use that."

"You don't want to test that," Helen responded confidently. She held the gun like her arm was steel, unwavering, unflinching—resolved and with strength she thought herself incapable of. "Bob. Bob?" Helen prodded as if trying to wake him from sleep. Jenkins lay motionless against her. She could feel the warmth of his blood running down her left arm. "Bob," she coerced again.

"That's Lieutenant Jenkins," he managed in a whisper as he slowly opened his eyes.

"Why didn't you call me?" Helen pleaded. "Why didn't you tell me you were coming here?"

"I had a feeling in my gut," Jenkins murmured. "Something was out of place about this. I suspected it was her at Fishermen's Wharf—Mrs. Beamer."

Helen looked up at the woman. "Move back, turn around, and keep your hands pressed against the wall," Helen commanded.

"I'm going to close my eyes," Jenkins whispered. "I think I'll feel more comfortable that way."

"No, no, no, no, you do NOT close your eyes!" Helen commanded. "You stay with me. Right here!"

With Jenkins propped up against her and with Jenkins' revolver still pointing at her captive, Helen reached around, grabbed her cell phone, and dialed 911. "We have an officer down, building 418 at McKinnon and Toland," Helen said into the phone. "I need immediate medical assistance."

Two squad cars and an ambulance, sirens howling, arrived within minutes. Two officers placed Mrs. Beamer in handcuffs and guided her into the back of one of the black and whites. Jenkins, with an oxygen mask over his face and a compress on his wound, was strapped into a wheeled stretcher and rolled out to the ambulance.

"You be careful with him," Helen warned, slapping the arm of one of the EMT staff rolling the stretcher. The man flinched and jolted the stretcher. Jenkins groaned. "See! Be careful!" Helen said, slapping the man again and causing him to jolt the stretcher a second time.

Jenkins groaned again. "Miss Chang, please," Jenkins managed, "let them do their job."

The medical team slid Jenkins into the back of the ambulance and Helen moved to follow. One of the men, however, held his hand up motioning for her to stop. "Are you family?" he asked sternly.

"No," she replied, "closer than that—I'm his partner."

He motioned her to climb aboard.

Population Statistics and the Hardy–Weinberg Equation

Once a criminalist has made a match between the genotype of the evidence DNA and the genotype of a victim or suspect, it becomes important to know the significance of that match and to determine how rare a particular genotype is in the population. A court will want to know what the likelihood is that someone other than the victim or suspect left DNA at the crime scene. That type of estimate requires an understanding of population statistics.

Statistics was first applied to genetics during the 1860s by the Augustinian monk Gregor Mendel who, working with pea plants and a mathematical multiplication table called a *Punnett square*, was able to predict the proportion of offspring displaying a particular trait carried from the parental lines. Table 13.1 shows how a Punnett square can be used to calculate the ratio of offspring that will be tall from a cross of heterozygous pea plants.

In 1908, an English mathematician, Godfrey Hardy, and a German physician, Wilhelm Weinberg, working independently, described how the frequency of a trait within a population's gene pool remains constant over time—a relationship now called *Hardy–Weinberg equilibrium*. They realized that a Punnett square could be applied not just to a single cross as demonstrated by Gregor Mendel but to all the

TABLE 13.1
Punnett Square Showing That If a Pea Plant Heterozygous for the Tall Trait (*Tt* Where *T* Represents the Dominant Tall Trait and *t* Represents the Recessive Short Trait) Is Crossed with Another Heterozygous Plant, Three-Fourths of the Offspring Will Be Tall (*TT* or *Tt*), and One-Fourth Will Be Short (*tt*)

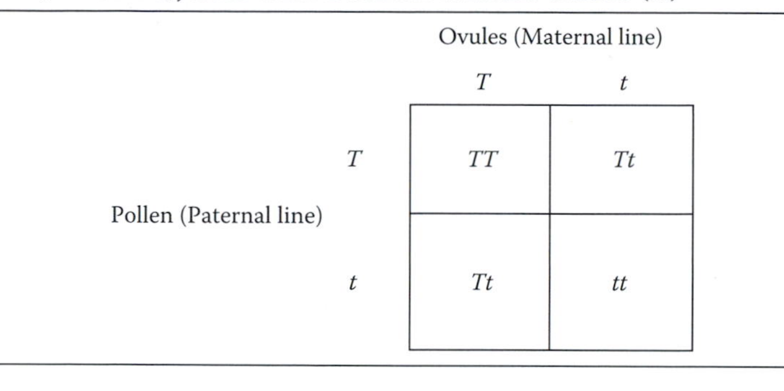

crosses occurring within an entire population, and, by so doing, the frequency of any particular genotype within that population could be calculated.

To understand Hardy–Weinberg equilibrium, we must first get a handle on the frequency with which *alleles* (forms of a gene or genetic site) are distributed in a population. Since alleles are inherited from both parents, each person will have two copies of a *locus* (a site on a chromosome) on their non-sex chromosomes. A person could get the same allele for a particular locus from both parents (in which case they would be homozygous), or a person could get different alleles from their parents (making them heterozygous). The frequency of any one allele in a population is calculated as the number of times an allele appears in a population of alleles. For example, let's say that an STR site carries either 12 repeats or 13 repeats and that in a population of 200 people, 4 people are homozygous 12, 12 (12 comma 12) repeats, 42 people are heterozygous 12, 13 repeats, and 154 people are homozygous 13, 13 repeats. The 12-repeat allele, therefore, is found 50 times, and the 13-repeat allele is found 350 times as shown in Table 13.2.

The frequency of the 12-repeat allele is then 0.125 (50, 12-repeat alleles divided by 400 total alleles). The frequency of the 13-repeat allele is then 0.875 (350, 13-repeat alleles divided by 400 total alleles. Notice that the sum of the allele frequencies is 1.0 ($0.125+0.875=1.0$). This is always the case. The sum of the allele frequencies for any particular locus must equal 1.0.

TABLE 13.2
Tabulating How Many Times the 12-Repeat and 13-Repeat Alleles Occur within a Population

Genotype	Number of Individuals	Number of Alleles	Number of 12-Repeat Alleles	Number of 13-Repeat Alleles
12, 12	4	8	$2\times4=8$	—
12, 13	42	84	$1\times42=42$	$1\times42=42$
13, 13	154	308	—	$2\times154=308$
Total	200	400	50	350

Note: Two hundred people carry 400 alleles since each person has 2 of each chromosome, 1 from their mother and 1 from their father.

TABLE 13.3
Punnett Square Representing the Distribution of Alleles in a Randomly Mating Population Where p Is the Frequency of the A Allele and q Is the Frequency of the B Allele

		All Mothers in a population	
		pA	qB
All Fathers in a population	pA	$pApA$	$pAqB$
	qB	$pAqB$	$qBqB$

The allele frequencies can now be used, with the help of a Punnett square, to calculate a genotype frequency—how frequently a particular genotype occurs within a population. For example, let's say that a certain allele we'll call A (which could represent an STR site having 12 repeats) has a frequency in the population of p. Another allele we'll call B (which could represent the 13-repeat allele at the same STR site) has a frequency of q. Table 13.3 shows a Punnett square in which the allele frequencies are multiplied to represent random mating events within an entire population.

In the Punnett square shown in Table 13.3, AA and BB represent homozygous individuals. The frequency of the AA homozygous genotype in a population would be p^2 since ($p \times p = p^2$). Likewise, the frequency of the BB homozygous genotype in the population is q^2 since ($q \times q = q^2$). The frequency of the AB heterozygous genotype is $2pq$ since $(p \times q) + (p \times q) = 2(p \times q) = 2pq$. The sum of all genotype frequencies should equal 1.0:

$$p^2 + 2pq + q^2 = 1$$

This relationship is known as the Hardy–Weinberg equation, and its great power in forensic science stems from its use in deriving a genotype frequency from allele frequencies. No matter how many alleles characterize a particular locus, the homozygote genotype frequency is always calculated as the square of the allele frequency (p^2), and the heterozygote genotype frequency is always calculated as two times the product of the individual allele frequencies ($2pq$).

By way of example, let's say that a person is homozygous for the 12-repeat allele. That allele has a frequency in the population of 0.067. The frequency of the 12-repeat homozygous genotype would then be $(0.067)^2 = 0.0045$. If we divide 1 by this number, we get 222. This tells us that one out of 222 people will have the 12, 12 homozygous genotype.

The ability to calculate a genotype frequency from allele frequencies using the Hardy–Weinberg equation relies on the underlying assumption that the population is in equilibrium, that is, that the allele frequencies in a population do not change over time. For that to occur, the population must be infinitely large, it's members mate randomly, no new mutations arise, there is no selection against any particular genotype, and no one leaves nor no one new enters the population. There is no population on Earth that can satisfy any of these requirements. But most large

TABLE 13.4
Genotype Frequencies for the STR Loci *A, B, C, D,* and *E*

Locus	Genotype Frequency
A	0.0761
B	0.0003
C	0.0225
D	0.1342
E	0.0057

populations come close enough to approximating them that forensic scientists feel confident that the Hardy–Weinberg equation can be used to give a satisfactory estimate of genotype frequency.

In almost all forensic cases, criminalists look at more than one locus to discern what alleles a suspect or victim carries. The more loci examined, the better the criminalist is able to discriminate between two individuals. An overall genotype frequency can be calculated when multiple loci are examined by using the *multiplication* (or *product*) *rule* whereby the genotype frequencies calculated for all loci are multiplied together. For example, let's say that a criminalist types a suspect at five different STR loci (A, B, C, D, and E) and determines the following genotype frequency for each locus as shown in Table 13.4.

The overall genotype frequency would be

$$0.0761 \times 0.0003 \times 0.0225 \times 0.1342 \times 0.0057 = 3.93 \times 10^{-10}$$

Therefore, the genotype frequency for the entire STR profile is 3.93×10^{-10}. This value can be converted to a "1 in" number by taking its reciprocal (by dividing it into 1):

$$1/3.93 \times 10^{-10} = 2.5 \times 10^{9}$$

Therefore, from a randomly sampled population, 1 in 2.5×10^{9} of its inhabitants will be expected to have this particular genotype combination.

In the Crime Lab

Flip a coin and the probability that heads will result is 50%. The probability that tails will result is also 50%. Let's say the first coin toss results in heads. Will the outcome of the second coin toss be affected by the results of the first coin toss? No, there is no reason why that should be the case. The probability of obtaining heads or of obtaining tails remains 50%. In fact, it doesn't matter how many times the coin is tossed; each toss has a 50% chance of coming up heads or coming up tails. We refer to this as an independent event—the outcome of the second event is not influenced by the outcome of the first (or any other) event. If we want to determine the probability of obtaining three consecutive heads when tossing a coin, we apply the product law. Because each toss is an independent event, we apply 50% to the first toss, 50% to the second toss, and 50% to the third toss and multiply all three events together:

$$0.5 \times 0.5 \times 0.5 = 0.125$$

Taking the reciprocal of 0.125 yields

$$1/0.125 = 8$$

Therefore, there's a chance of one in eight that if a coin is flipped three times, heads will come up each time.

In an ideal world, the best evidence is that which can be individualized—evidence that can be attributed exclusively to the criminal or object. Fingerprints, a DNA type, and a bullet are all types of evidence that are exclusive and individual. Unfortunately, an investigator may not be so lucky as to find such unique evidence at a crime scene. Evidence may have characteristics common to a group of similar objects. Fibers, paint, inks, and shoeprints are examples of such evidence. Although class evidence is not as powerful as individual evidence, the product rule can be used to strengthen it.

Activity 13.1 Using the Product Rule to Refine a Search for Suspects

The following activity will use the product rule to narrow the number of suspects down from hundreds to a handful.

Material:

Calculators

Protocol:

A person was seen leaving a high school administrative building at 6:00 in the evening. At 6:05 PM, a security vehicle responded to the silent alarm originating from that administrative building. Upon opening the building, the security officer smelled smoke. Quickly finding its source, a garbage can in the senior counselor's office, the security officer used the buildings extinguisher to put out the flames. The suspect was identified by a witness as a teenage female having blond hair, wearing an athletic jersey, blue jeans, and tennis shoes and carrying a backpack.

Using your class as a representative sample within the school population, answer the following questions:

1. How many students in your class are females?
2. What percentage does this represent?
3. Based on this percentage, calculate how many students in your entire school are females.
4. What percentage of the student body does this represent?
5. How many students in your class have blond hair?
6. What percentage of the class does this represent?
7. Calculate how many students in the entire school are females with blond hair.
8. What percentage of the student body does this represent?
9. How many students in your class are wearing an athletic jersey?

TABLE 13.5
Table for Summarizing the Data from Questions 1–16

Description	# of Students That Fit the Description in Your Class	# of Students in Your Class	% of Students That Fit the Description in Your Class	Student Body Population	# of Students at Your School That Fit the Description[a]	% of Students at Your School That Fit the Description
1. Female						
2. Blond hair						
3. Athletic jersey						
4. Blue jeans						
5. Tennis shoes						
6. Backpack						

This column is a cumulative analysis, which includes the previous descriptions, for example, description #2 blond hair includes female or #3 athletic jersey includes blond hair and female.

10. How many students in the school are females with blond hair and are wearing an athletic jersey?
11. How many students in your class are wearing blue jeans?
12. How many students in the school are females with blond hair and are wearing an athletic jersey and blue jeans?
13. How many students in your class are wearing tennis shoes?
14. How many students in the school are females with blond hair and are wearing an athletic jersey, blue jeans, and tennis shoes?
15. How many students in your class carry a backpack?
16. How many students in the school are females with blond hair, wear an athletic jersey, blue jeans, and tennis shoes, and carry a backpack?
17. Consolidate your data into a table like that shown for Table 13.5.

Analysis

1. What is the statistical probability trend when looking at one characteristic as opposed to six characteristics?
2. What is the advantage of knowing as many descriptors (sex, hair color, clothing, etc.) as possible about the suspect?
3. DNA profiling looks at multiple loci. In statistical terms, what is the advantage of looking at more and more loci?

Erica Holmes Missing Persons Case

The following tables provide the allele frequencies for the various STR loci used in the Holmes case.*

* Allele frequencies represent combined values from African American, US Caucasian, US Hispanic, and Native American populations described in the AmpF*l*STR® Identifiler™ PCR Amplification Kit User's Manual (Life Technologies). A total of 1187 individuals (2374 alleles) were examined. Where no allele frequency could be measured, a value was obtained by assuming the 1188th person assayed would carry that allele. The STR loci examined by the Life Technologies Identifiler Kit carry 4 bp repeats. Some loci, however, carry monomers with a repeat having less than 4 bp. For example, if a locus has ten, 4-bp repeats and one repeat that is only 2 bp in length, that allele is designated as a 10.2.

Loci Labeled with Blue Fluorescent Dye

D8S1179	
Allele (Repeat Number)	Allele Frequency
8	0.0097
9	0.0059
10	0.0640
11	0.0493
12	0.1293
13	0.3062
14	0.2666
15	0.1314
16	0.0303
17	0.0063
18	0.0008
19	0.0004

D21S11	
Allele (Repeat Number)	Allele Frequency
24	0.0004
24.2	0.0021
24.3	0.0008
25	0.0004
25.2	0.0008
26	0.0013
27	0.0324
28	0.1508
28.2	0.0004
29	0.1971
29.2	0.0021
29.3	0.0004
30	0.2527
30.2	0.0240
31	0.0708
31.2	0.1032
32	0.0126
32.2	0.0859
33	0.0025
33.2	0.0371
34	0.0038
34.1	0.0004
34.2	0.0046
35	0.0097
35.1	0.0004
35.2	0.0004

D21S11	
Allele (Repeat Number)	**Allele Frequency**
36	0.0025
37	0.0008
38	0.0004

D7S820	
Allele (Repeat Number)	**Allele Frequency**
6	0.0008
7	0.0101
8	0.1546
9	0.1213
10	0.2860
11	0.2296
12	0.1639
13	0.0295
14	0.0042
15	0.0004

CSF1PO	
Allele (Repeat Number)	**Allele Frequency**
6	0.0004
7	0.0152
8	0.0661
9	0.0320
10	0.2612
11	0.2599
11.3	0.0004
12	0.3336
13	0.0607
14	0.0105
15	0.0017

Loci Labeled with Green Fluorescent Dye

D3S1358	
Allele (Repeat Number)	**Allele Frequency**
<11	0.0017
11	0.0004
12	0.0021
13	0.0034
14	0.1116
15	0.3277
15.2	0.0004

D3S1358	
Allele (Repeat Number)	Allele Frequency
16	0.2713
17	0.1672
18	0.1040
19	0.0093
20	0.0008

THO1	
Allele (Repeat Number)	Allele Frequency
4	0.0004
5	0.0025
6	0.1824
7	0.3458
8	0.1251
8.3	0.0004
9	0.1293
9.3	0.2081
10	0.0059
11	0.0004
13.3	0.0004

D13S317	
Allele (Repeat Number)	Allele Frequency
8	0.0767
9	0.0939
10	0.0687
11	0.2570
12	0.3176
13	0.1167
14	0.0501
15	0.0013

D16S539	
Allele (Repeat Number)	Allele Frequency
5	0.0004
8	0.0202
9	0.1306
10	0.1125
11	0.3121

D16S539	
Allele (Repeat Number)	Allele Frequency
12	0.2620
13	0.1394
14	0.0219
15	0.0013

D2S1338	
Allele (Repeat Number)	Allele Frequency
15	0.0004
16	0.0400
17	0.1512
18	0.0569
19	0.1862
20	0.1104
21	0.0598
22	0.0939
23	0.1129
24	0.0973
25	0.0733
26	0.0168
27	0.0008
28	0.0004

Loci Labeled with Yellow Fluorescent Dye (Recorded in Black on the STR Electropherograms)

D19S433	
Allele (Repeat Number)	Allele Frequency
9	0.0008
10	0.0046
11	0.0257
11.2	0.0008
12	0.0754
12.2	0.0253
13	0.2426
13.2	0.0682
14	0.2810
14.2	0.0333
15	0.1150
15.2	0.0569
16	0.0362
16.2	0.0223

D19S433	
Allele (Repeat Number)	**Allele Frequency**
17	0.0025
17.2	0.0063
18.2	0.0029

vWA	
Allele (Repeat Number)	**Allele Frequency**
11	0.0013
12	0.0004
13	0.0055
14	0.0699
15	0.1239
16	0.2860
17	0.2405
18	0.1803
19	0.0695
20	0.0143
21	0.0017
22	0.0008
23	0.0004
24	0.0004

TPOX	
Allele (Repeat Number)	**Allele Frequency**
6	0.0215
7	0.0080
8	0.4478
9	0.1222
10	0.0573
11	0.2704
12	0.0729
13	0.0004

D18S51	
Allele (Repeat Number)	**Allele Frequency**
7	0.0004
9	0.0004
10	0.0059
10.2	0.0004

D18S51	
Allele (Repeat Number)	Allele Frequency
11	0.0072
12	0.1112
13	0.0990
13.2	0.0013
14	0.1512
14.2	0.0008
15	0.1584
16	0.1356
17	0.1491
18	0.0792
19	0.0476
20	0.0282
21	0.0139
22	0.0059
23	0.0034
24	0.0008
25	0.0004
26	0.0004
27	0.0004

Loci Labeled with Red Fluorescent Dye

D5S818	
Allele (Repeat Number)	Allele Frequency
7	0.0421
8	0.0181
9	0.0396
10	0.0556
11	0.3538
12	0.3222
13	0.1563
14	0.0097
15	0.0013
16	0.0004
17	0.0008

FGA	
Allele (Repeat Number)	Allele Frequency
16	0.0004
16.1	0.0004
17	0.0013

FGA	
Allele (Repeat Number)	Allele Frequency
17.2	0.0004
18	0.0135
18.2	0.0042
19	0.0720
19.2	0.0008
20	0.0998
20.2	0.0004
21	0.1449
21.2	0.0013
22	0.1735
22.2	0.0059
22.3	0.0004
23	0.1445
23.2	0.0029
24	0.1559
24.2	0.0008
25	0.1066
26	0.0425
26.2	0.0008
27	0.0147
28	0.0072
29	0.0017
30	0.0004
30.2	0.0004
31.2	0.0004
32.2	0.0004
33.2	0.0004
34.2	0.0004
42.2	0.0004
43.2	0.0004
44.2	0.0008
45.2	0.0004
46.2	0.0004
47.2	0.0004
48.2	0.0004
50.2	0.0004
51.2	0.0004

Prepare an evidence report detailing your statistical analysis of the STR evidence presented in Chapter 12. The following items should be addressed in this report:

1. What STR results require statistical analysis?
2. For each significant item, what is the chance that someone other than the suspect (or presumed victim) would have the same STR profile?

Review Questions

13.1 What mathematical device did Gregor Mendel use to predict the appearance of traits in the offspring of a cross between pea plants having different characteristics?

13.2 How many total alleles of a certain genetic trait will there be in a population sample of 300 individuals? (Assume the trait is not found on the X or Y chromosome.)

13.3 An STR locus carries three possible alleles, 7, 8, and 9 four base pair repeats. A random sample of 100 people in a population is found to have the following genotypes:

Genotype	Number of Individuals
7, 7	5
7, 8	15
7, 9	8
8, 8	30
8, 9	28
9, 9	14
Total	**100**

What are the allele frequencies for each of the three alleles?

Frequency of the 7-repeat allele = ______
Frequency of the 8-repeat allele = ______
Frequency of the 9-repeat allele = ______
Do the allele frequencies add up to 1.0?

13.4 Draw a Punnett square for a system having three alleles *A*, *B*, and *C* with allele frequencies *p*, *q*, and *r*, respectively.

13.5 As $p^2 + 2pq + q^2 = 1$ is the equation for the sum of all genotype frequencies for a two-allele system, what is the equation for the three-allele system in Problem 4?

Further Reading

How the Probability of a False Positive Affects the Value of DNA Evidence by W.C. Thompson, F. Taroni, and C.G.G. Aitken in *Journal of Forensic Sciences*, Vol. 48, No. 1, pages 47–54, 2003.

14
Fingerprint Analysis

Police Headquarters, Wednesday 11:48 AM

"Are you sure you don't need a few more days off?" Captain White asked Jenkins from behind his desk.

"I'm alright," Jenkins replied, rotating his left shoulder and rubbing his chest with his right hand, wincing slightly.

"They're going to need you to testify in this case," said the captain.

"I'll be ready," Jenkins said confidently.

"Lieutenant," Captain White said, fixing his gaze into Jenkins' eyes, "I've given this some serious thought, and I've decided to let you off the hook with Criminalist Chang. There's a murder cold case I want you to work on. You can do it solo."

"Thank you," said Jenkins.

"I'll have Lynn bring you the file."

"Yes, Sir," said Jenkins.

"Well then, you're dismissed. And could you get the light on your way out."

Jenkins turned to leave but stopped himself. "Captain," he said, turning to face Captain White again, "if it's all the same, I'd like to continue to work with Miss Chang. Actually," he said after a pause, "I won't take 'no' for an answer. Good day, Captain." And he left the room, intentionally ignoring the light switch and leaving the office door wide open.

"Jenkins!" he heard from behind him. "Jenkins!" the captain's voice boomed. Jenkins didn't look back. He kept walking toward his desk as a smile spread across his face.

Helen was sitting in his chair thumbing through the pages of his latest issue of *True Detective*. "Miss Chang," Jenkins said, "I'm hungry. May I take you out to lunch."

"Sure, I saw a couple of fast food burger places in the warehouse district" she replied with a tone of resignation in her voice.

"Actually," said Jenkins, "there's something I've always wanted to try."

"What's that?" Helen asked. "A burger *without* pickles?"

"Sushi."

Helen's jaw dropped. "There's hope for you after all, Lieutenant. It just so happens," she said, "I know a place where you can only use chop sticks, no forks allowed."

"Sounds perfect," Jenkins said agreeably. "Oh, and by the way, that kick to Mrs. Beamer in the warehouse, you learned that in your kickboxing class, right?"

"Lieutenant Jenkins," Helen said, "it's just a dance class."

"Right," he said as he held the exit door open for Helen to pass through.

Fingerprint Analysis

Fingerprint patterns fall into three classes easily remembered by the anagram *LAW* for *l*oops, *a*rches, or *w*horls. When ridgelines fold back on themselves, a *loop* results. A loop pattern is analogous to the path a car would take driving in and out of a cul-de-sac. Two types of loop patterns can be distinguished—a *left loop* where the loop pattern enters from the left (Figure 14.1) and a *right loop* in which the loop pattern enters from the right (Figure 14.2). Loops can also be classified as radial or ulnar. With a *radial loop*, the ridges of the loop point toward the little finger. With an *ulnar loop*, the loop ridges point toward the thumb. The terms radial and ulnar, therefore, are dependent upon from which hand the print was lifted.

All fingerprint patterns will also carry within them features called *minutiae* formed by the fingerprint ridges. A fingerprint ridge at its end is called a *termination*. A fingerprint ridge that splits into two is called a *bifurcation*. An *island* is formed when two bifurcations face each other and are relatively close together. A fingerprint ridge of very short length is called a *dot*. Two ridges can be joined by a *bridge* or can appear to form a *crossover*. A short ridge jutting out from a longer ridge is called a *spur*. A *delta* is a triangular shape buttressed against a loop or whorl. These various minutiae are labeled in the figures of fingerprint types

Figure 14.1 This fingerprint shows a several-layered loop pattern entering from the left. If this loop pattern is on the left hand, it is called an *ulnar loop*. If it's found on a finger of the right hand, it's called a *radial loop*.

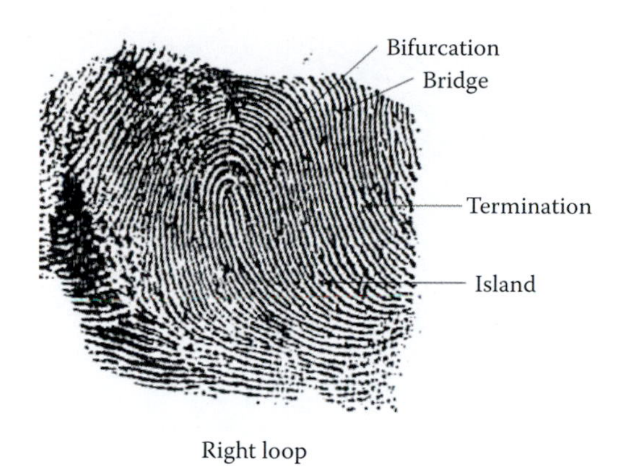

Figure 14.2 This fingerprint shows a loop pattern entering from the right. This fingerprint also shows several minutiae—a bifurcation, a bridge, a termination, and an island. If this pattern is seen on a finger of the right hand, it's considered to be an ulnar loop. If it's found on a finger of the left hand, it's considered a radial loop.

that follow. Keep in mind with these examples that every fingerprint has its own unique ridge formation. When identifying unknown prints, they will not look exactly like the ones shown in the following examples. The important thing is to remember the characteristics that LAW share in common—the presence or absence of deltas, the number of deltas, the shape of the pattern area, the direction of ridges, and the appearance of minutiae.

A fingerprint may also contain two loops, one swirling around the other as seen in Figure 14.3.

The ridgelines of an arch pattern appear as though they are stacked one on top of the next as they outline a small hump (Figure 14.4). A *tented arch* is an arch pattern fingerprint with a sharp steeple-shaped feature at its base (Figure 14.5).

The ridges of a whorl revolve around a central point, like a *bull's eye*. This pattern represents the most common type of fingerprint (Figure 14.6).

Visually comparing a fingerprint recovered from a crime scene with reference prints can be a laborious and tedious process. With the volumes of fingerprints collected, it is not surprising that computers have been enlisted to help in fingerprint matching. AFIS (automated fingerprint identification systems) used by the FBI has dramatically reduced the amount of effort required to match fingerprints. The AFIS program works by plotting the relative positions of landmark features of the crime scene print with those of prints in the database. The crime scene print is scanned into AFIS, which then identifies the print's minutiae points and compares

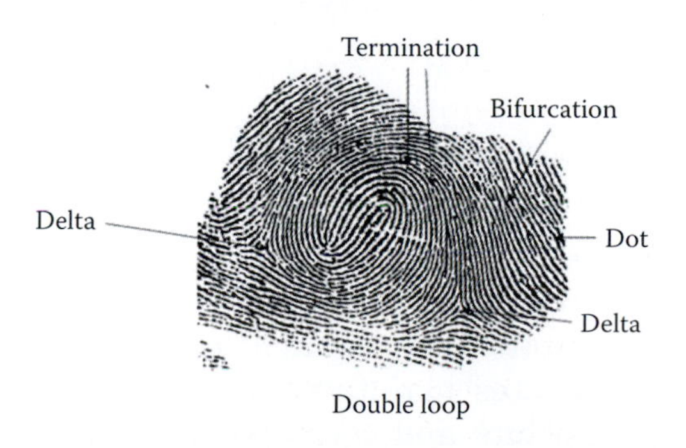

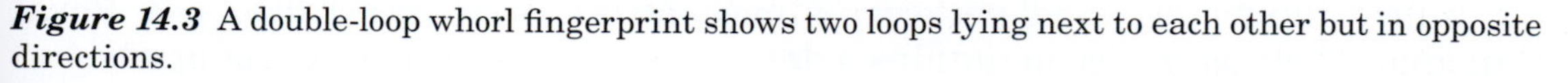

Figure 14.3 A double-loop whorl fingerprint shows two loops lying next to each other but in opposite directions.

Figure 14.4 An arch fingerprint shows stacks of ridgelines forming a hump shape.

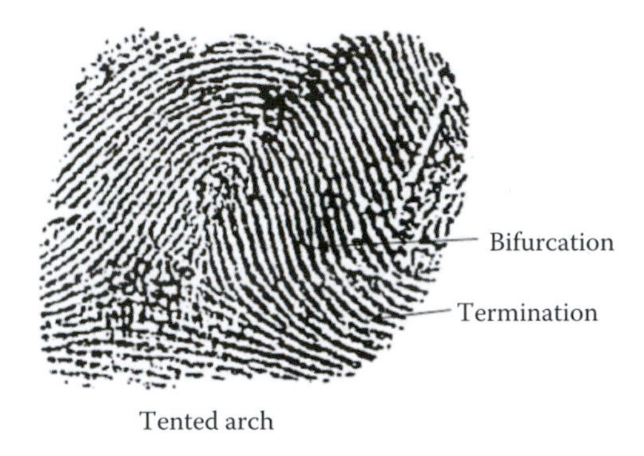

Figure 14.5 A tented arch fingerprint has a sharp triangle at the base of the arched ridgelines.

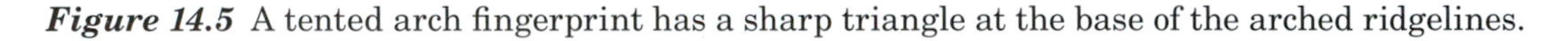

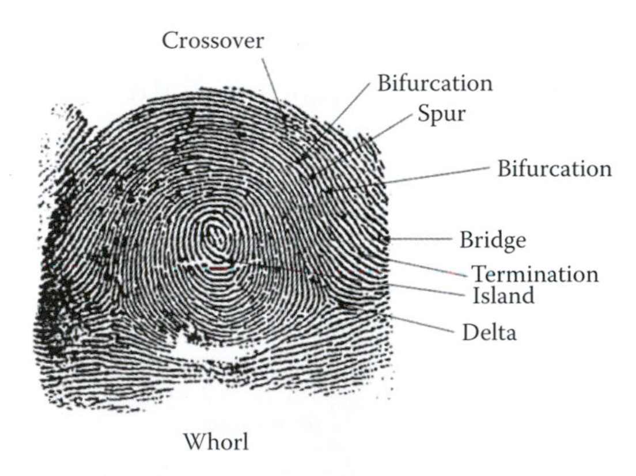

Figure 14.6 A whorl fingerprint looks like the top view of a vortex.

this information with that of prints in the database. The system returns the possible matches along with a score, or match probability, indicating the likelihood that each print identified by the software program is a match with the evidence print. Most states in the United States maintain an AFIS system. The FBI's criminal master file holds the fingerprints and corresponding criminal history on roughly 65 million individuals and performs almost 50,000 searches a day. The Royal Canadian Mounted Police maintains a database of over 4 million sets of prints.

In the Crime Lab

Activity 14.1 Identifying Fingerprint Type and Minutiae

In Chapter 2, you made a reference set of your fingerprints. In your laboratory notebook, identify the type of fingerprint each of your fingers carries. In addition, identify at least two minutiae for each print.

Activity 14.2 Comparing and Matching Fingerprints

This activity will give you practice in identifying fingerprints as to their type (loop, arch, or whorl) and as to the minutiae they may contain.

Materials:

Hand magnifier, dissection scope, or 8× slide magnifier
Scissors

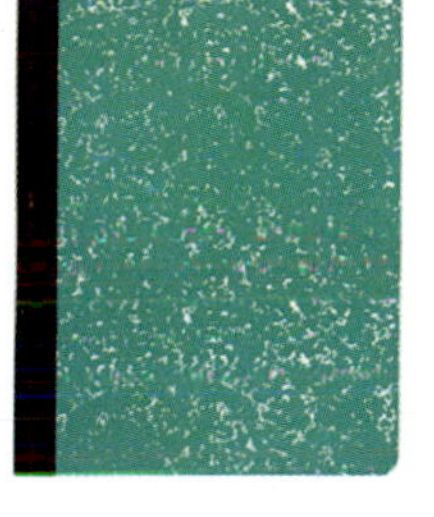

Protocol: Your instructor will assign you a fingerprint from the gallery of prints. Match the fingerprint you are assigned to another one (or ones) on the following plates. Some fingerprints may have no matches, while others will have one or more matches. For each fingerprint you are assigned, indicate the fingerprint classification (right loop, tented arch, or whorl, etc.). In addition, for those prints with matches, identify at least one minutia found in common between them. Record these results in your laboratory notebook.

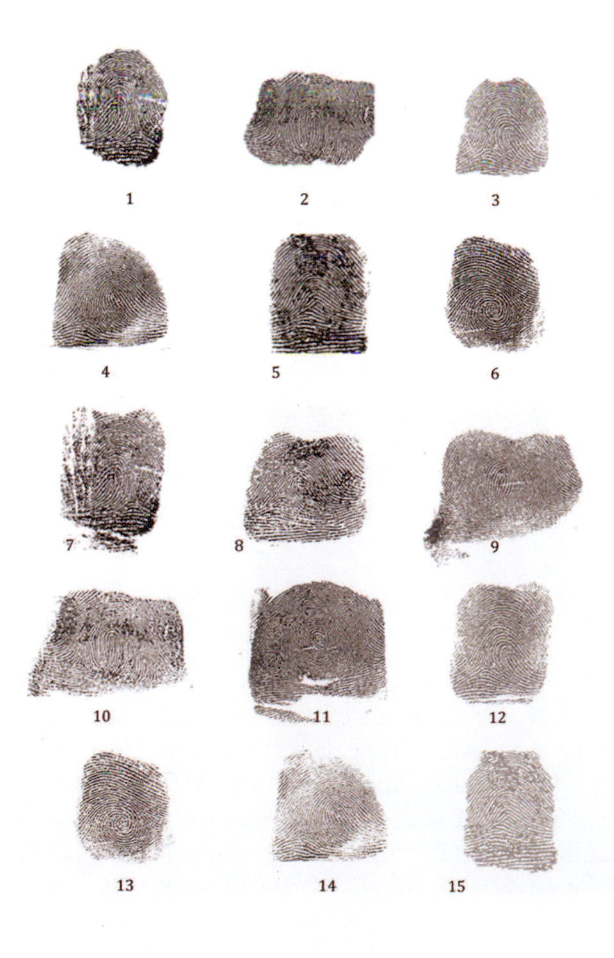

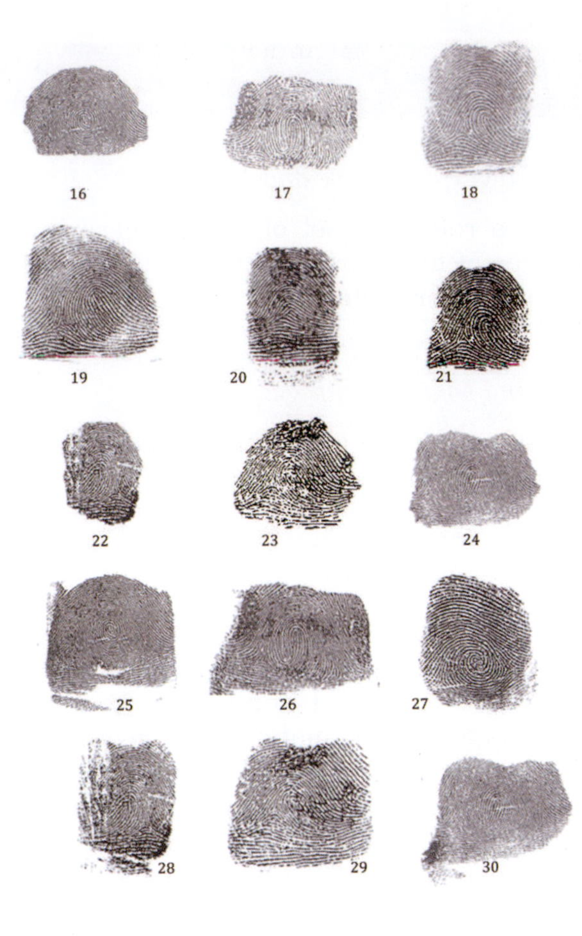

Erica Holmes Missing Person Case

The fingerprints of the suspects and the victim in this case are provided on the following pages. Prepare an evidence report of your findings. ("I" denotes a print recovered inside the vehicle. "X" denotes a fingerprint recovered from the outside of the vehicle.

I-6 is a fingerprint collected from the left side of the steering wheel.

I-7 is a fingerprint collected from the inner door handle on the driver's side.

I-8 is a fingerprint collected from the lower seat adjustment bar on the driver's side. This fingerprint proved positive for blood.

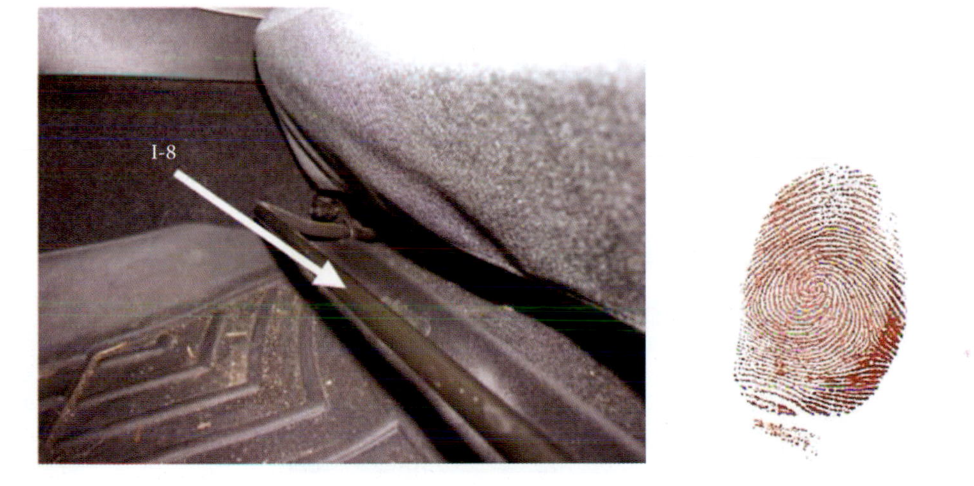

I-9 is a fingerprint collected from the backside of the rear view mirror. This fingerprint is Evidence Item 9 evaluated for STRs.

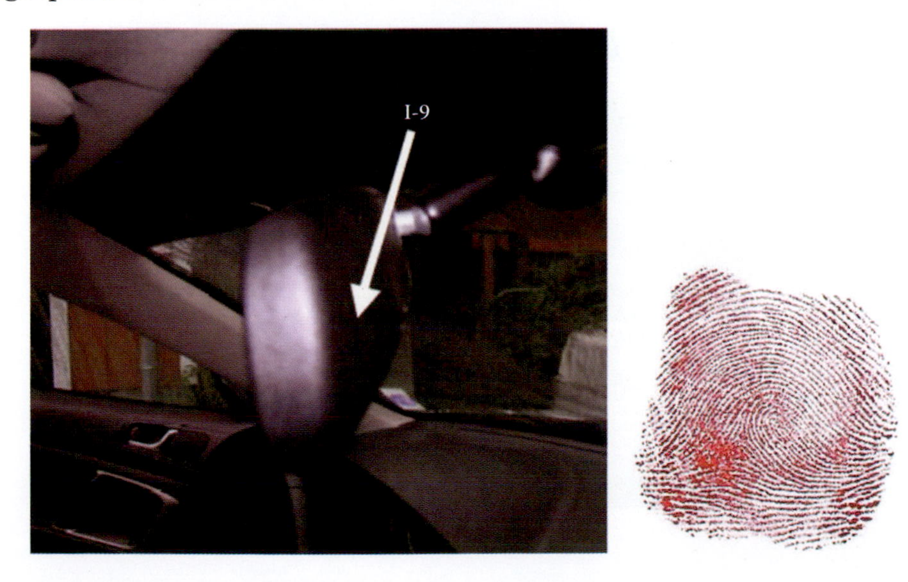

I-10 is a fingerprint collected from the rear hatchback inset used to grip the door when closing it.

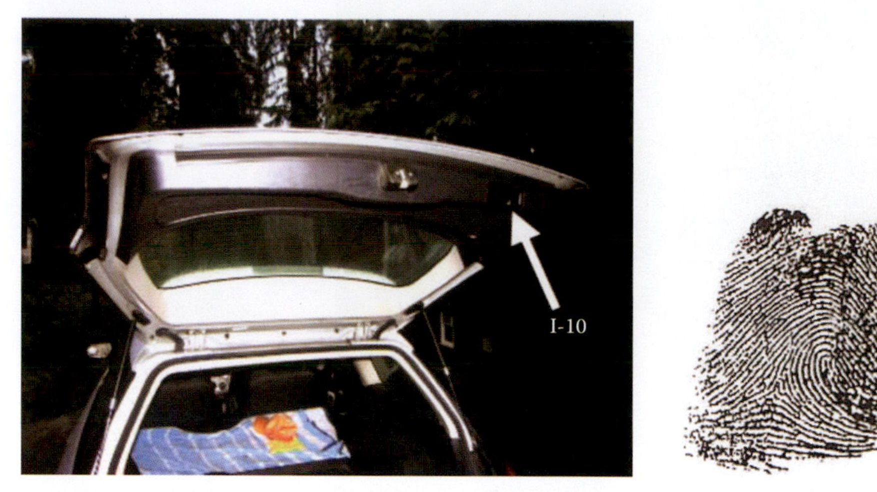

X-1 is a fingerprint collected from the middle front top of the engine cover proximal to the front grill and Subaru logo.

X-2 is a fingerprint recovered from the back right lower corner of the hatchback, below the Subaru logo.

X-3 is a fingerprint recovered from the driver's exterior door handle.

X-4 is a fingerprint recovered from the exterior surface of the side back window on the driver's side.

X-5 is a fingerprint recovered from the top of the black plastic air intake scoop entrance.

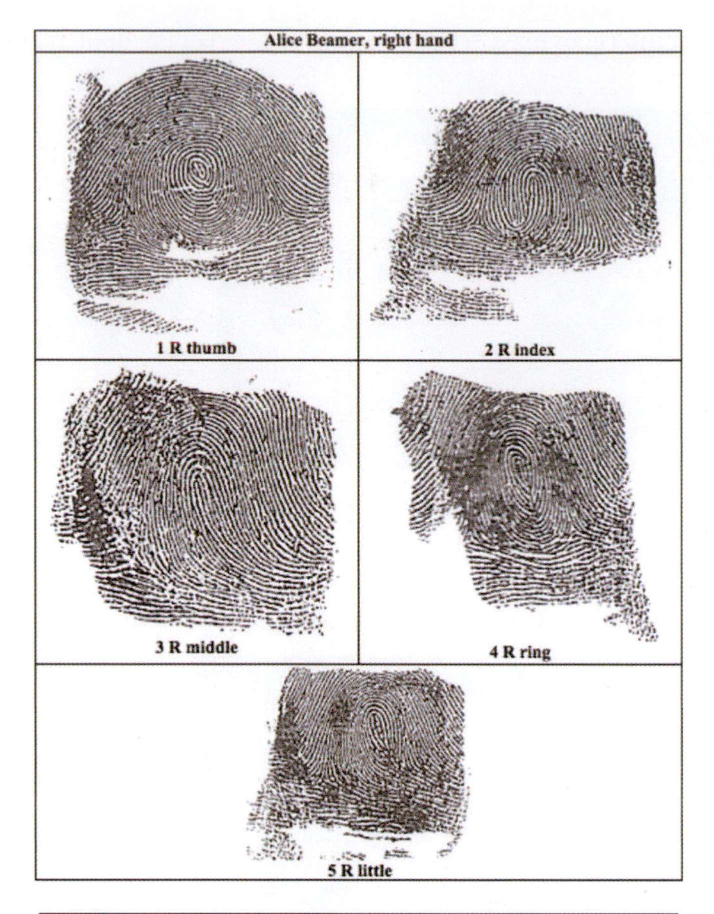
Alice Beamer, right hand
1 R thumb
2 R index
3 R middle
4 R ring
5 R little

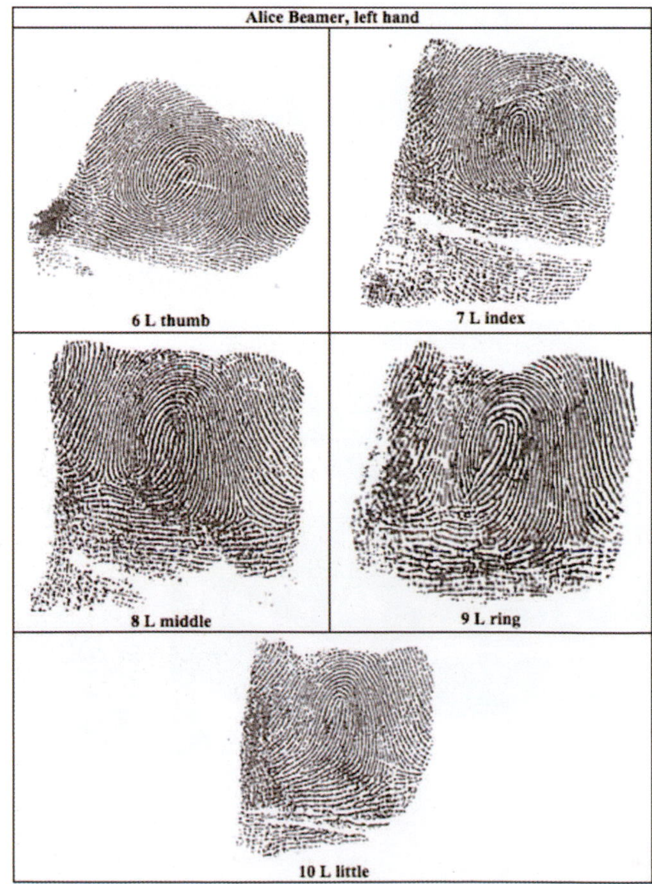
Alice Beamer, left hand
6 L thumb
7 L index
8 L middle
9 L ring
10 L little

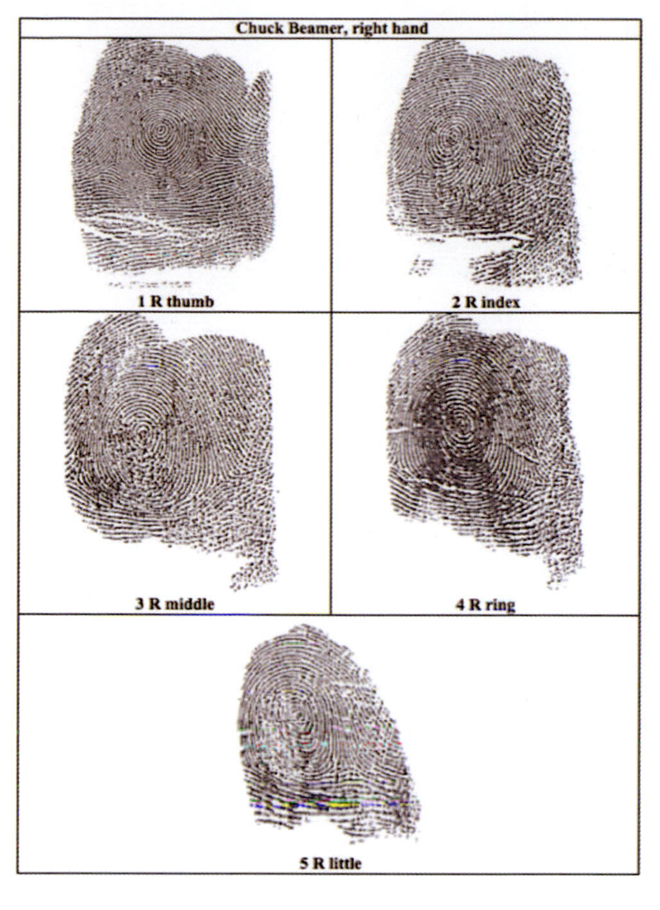
Chuck Beamer, right hand
1 R thumb
2 R index
3 R middle
4 R ring
5 R little

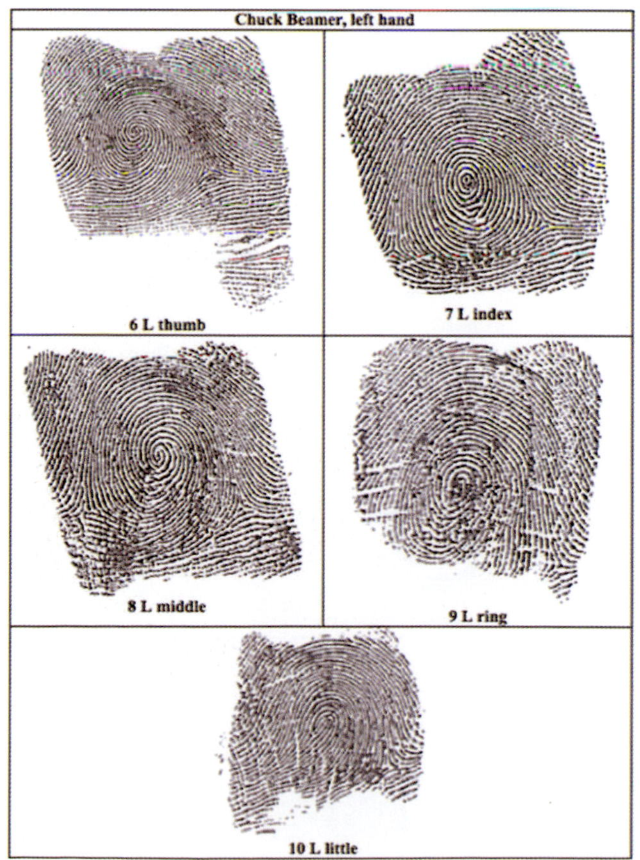
Chuck Beamer, left hand
6 L thumb
7 L index
8 L middle
9 L ring
10 L little

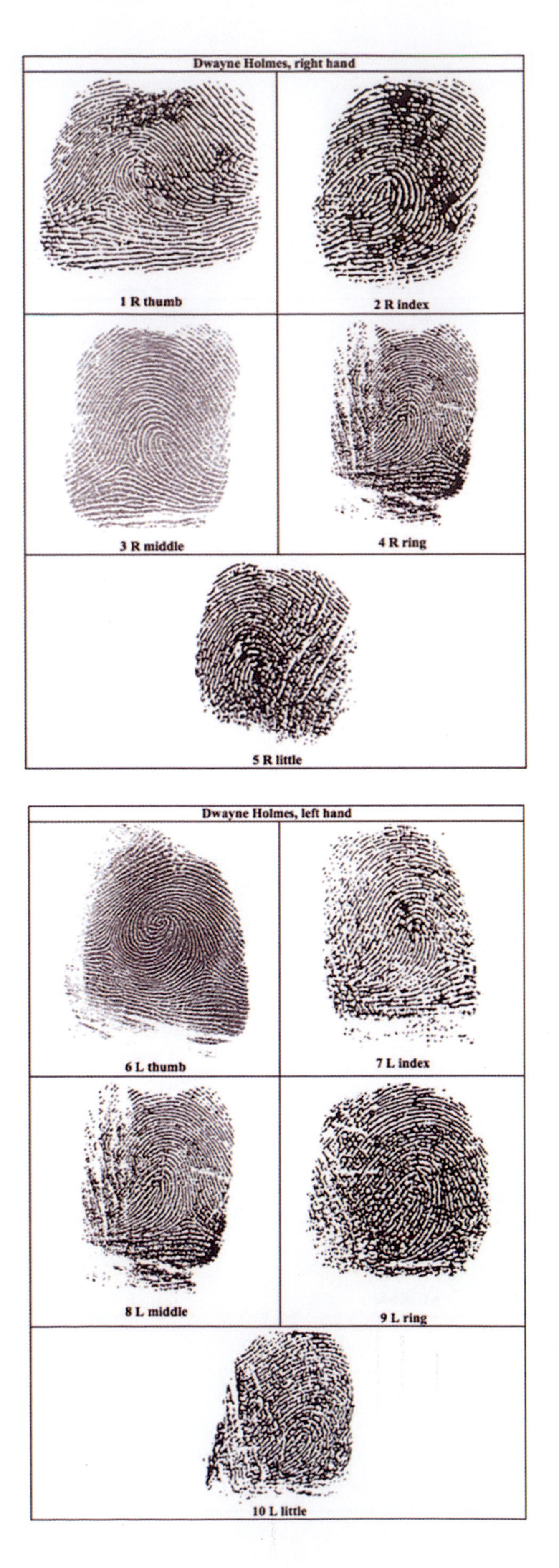
Dwayne Holmes, right hand
1 R thumb
2 R index
3 R middle
4 R ring
5 R little
Dwayne Holmes, left hand
6 L thumb
7 L index
8 L middle
9 L ring
10 L little

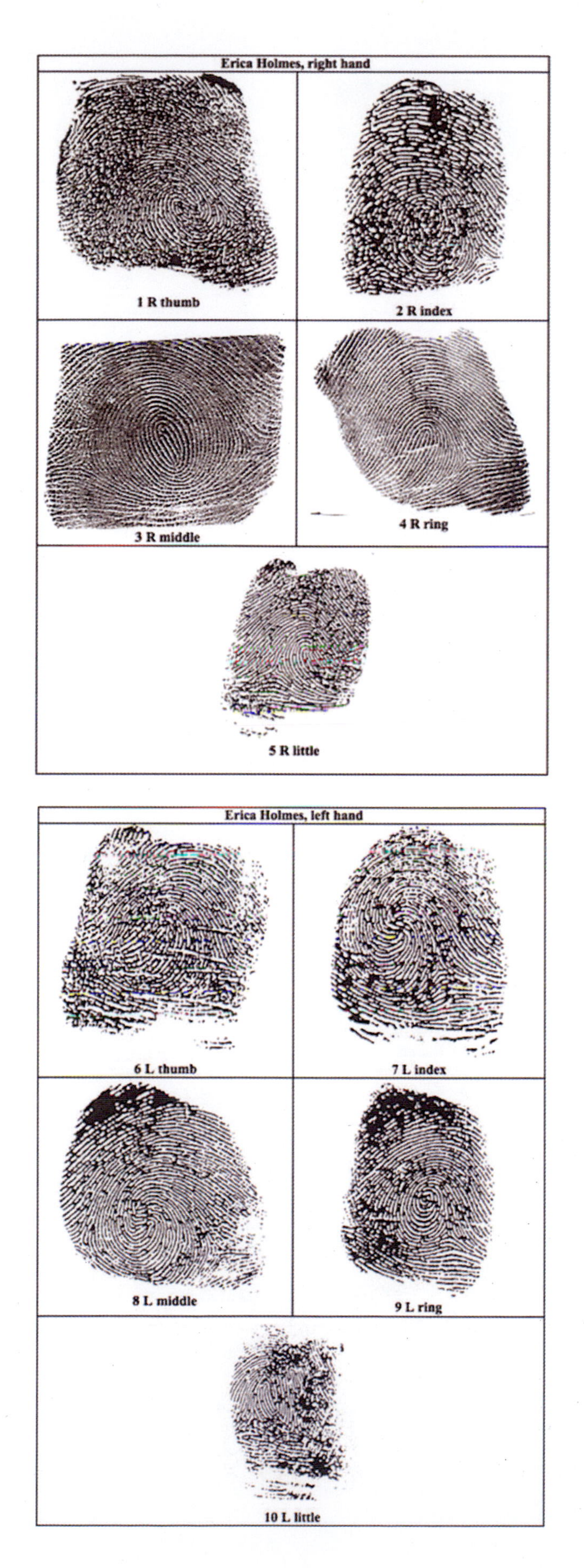
Erica Holmes, right hand
1 R thumb
2 R index
3 R middle
4 R ring
5 R little
Erica Holmes, left hand
6 L thumb
7 L index
8 L middle
9 L ring
10 L little

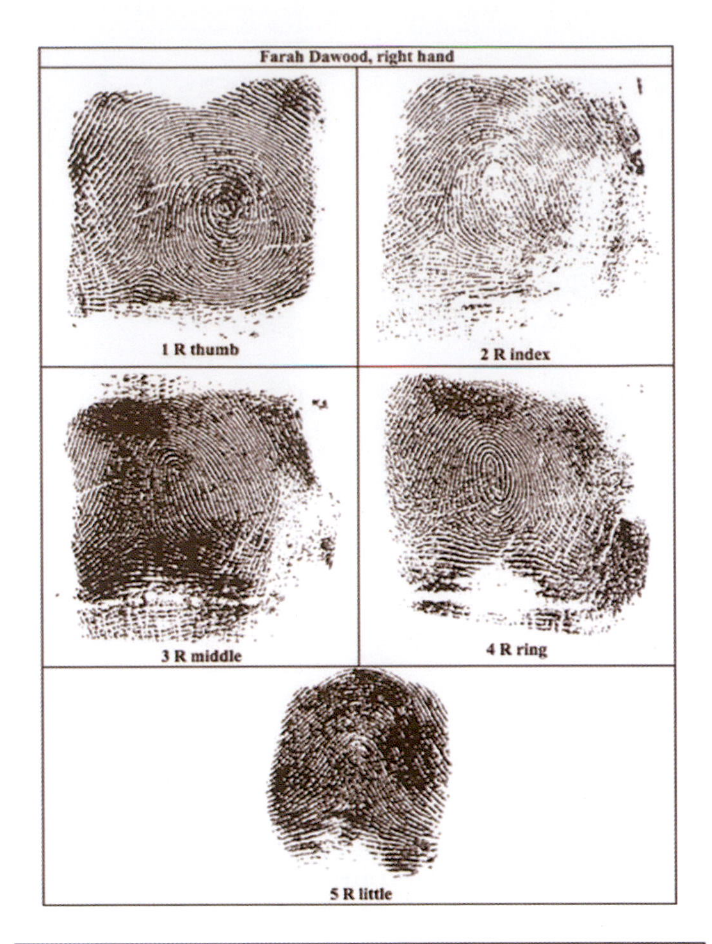
Farah Dawood, right hand
1 R thumb
2 R index
3 R middle
4 R ring
5 R little

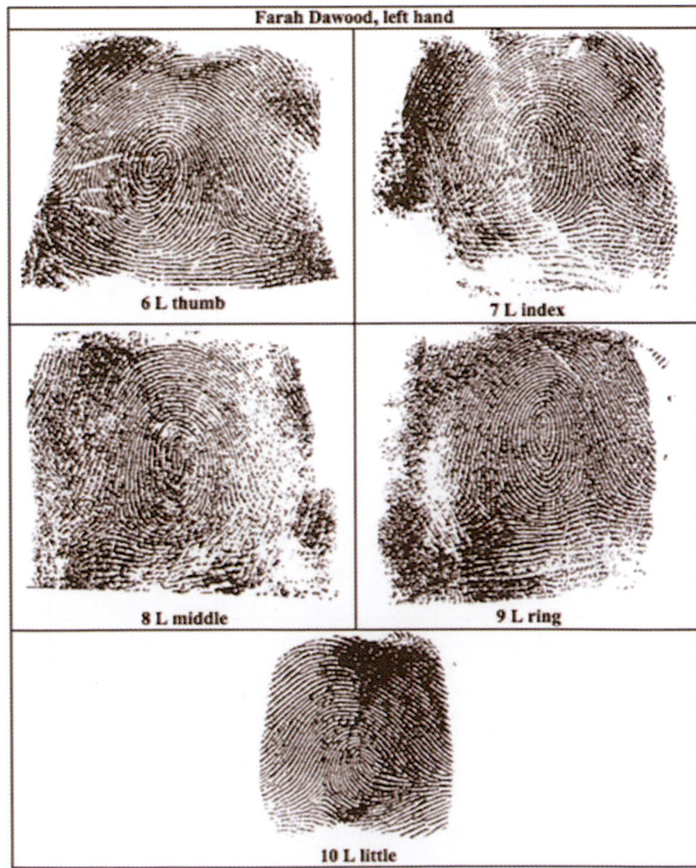
Farah Dawood, left hand
6 L thumb
7 L index
8 L middle
9 L ring
10 L little

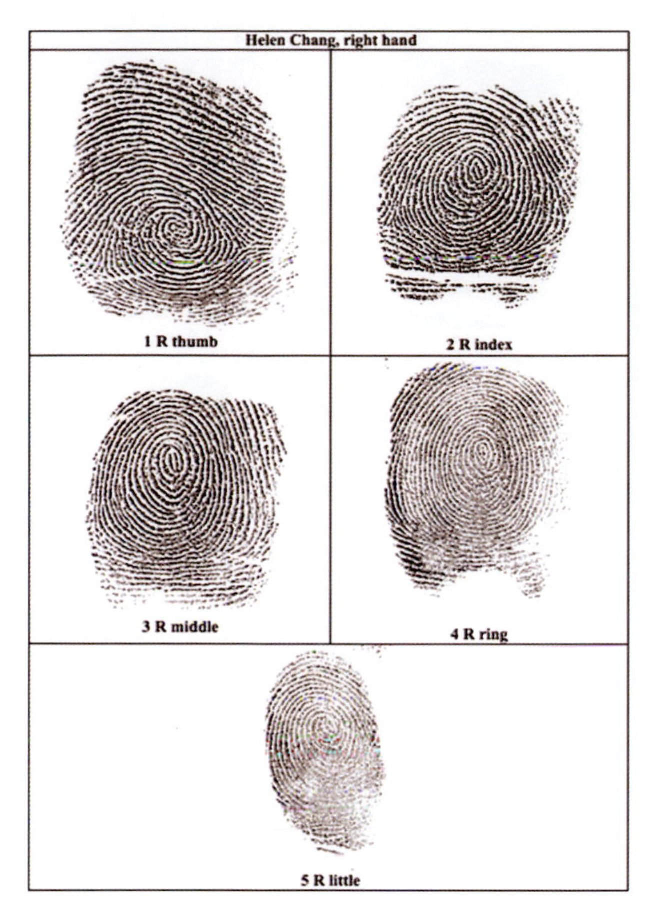
Helen Chang, right hand
1 R thumb
2 R index
3 R middle
4 R ring
5 R little

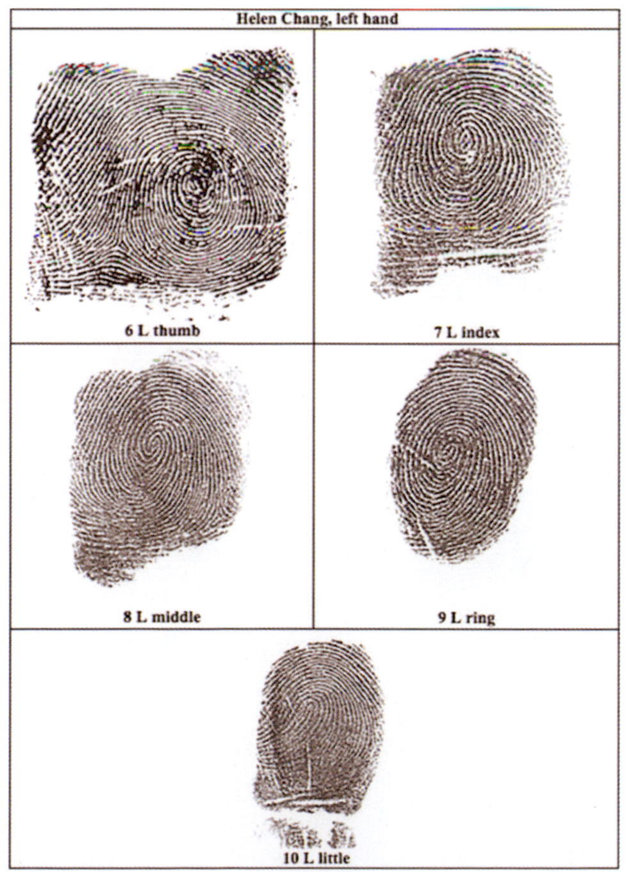
Helen Chang, left hand
6 L thumb
7 L index
8 L middle
9 L ring
10 L little

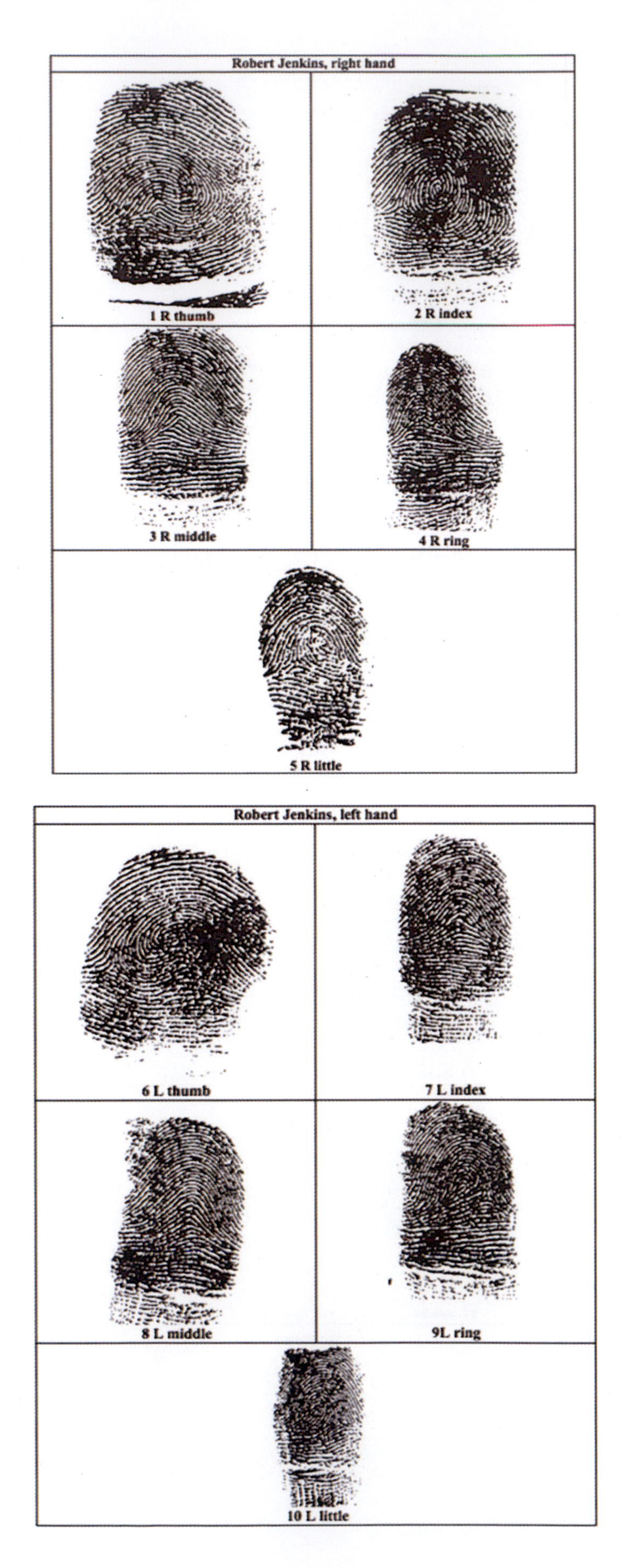
Robert Jenkins, right hand
1 R thumb
2 R index
3 R middle
4 R ring
5 R little
Robert Jenkins, left hand
6 L thumb
7 L index
8 L middle
9L ring
10 L little

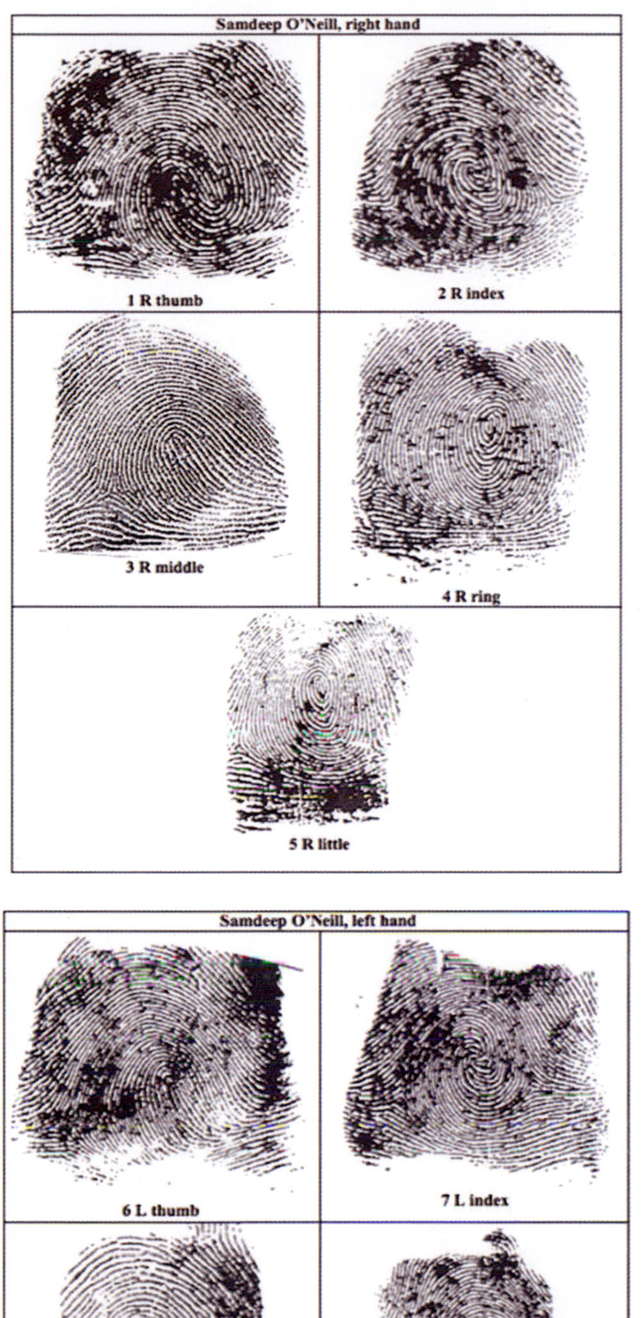
Samdeep O'Neill, right hand
1 R thumb
2 R index
3 R middle
4 R ring
5 R little

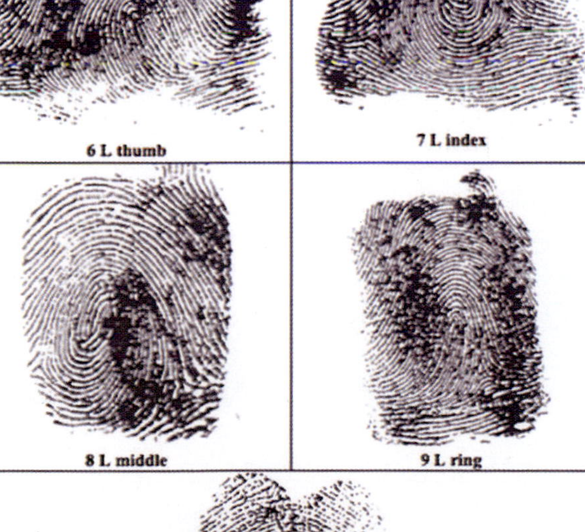
Samdeep O'Neill, left hand
6 L thumb
7 L index
8 L middle
9 L ring
10 L little

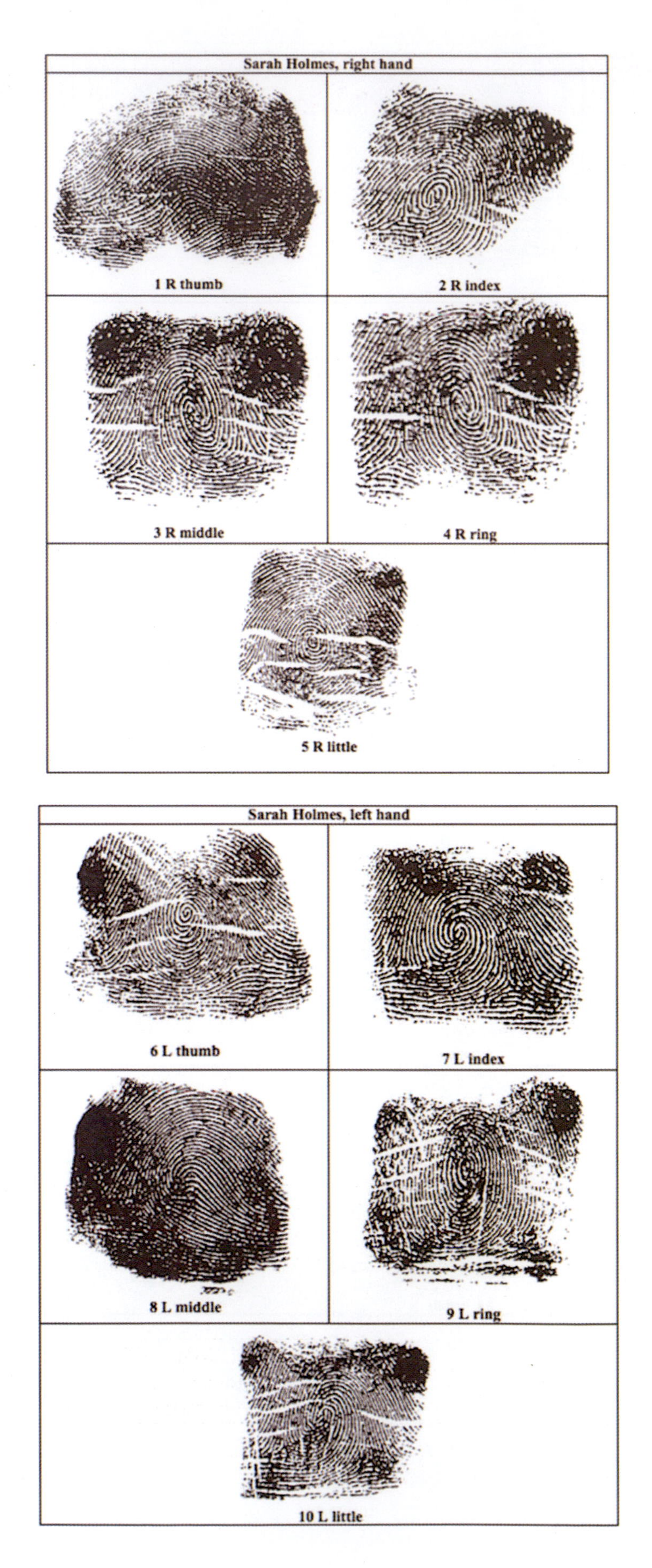
Sarah Holmes, right hand
1 R thumb
2 R index
3 R middle
4 R ring
5 R little
Sarah Holmes, left hand
6 L thumb
7 L index
8 L middle
9 L ring
10 L little

Further Reading

Fingerprint Analysis

Interpapillary Lines—The Variable Part of the Human Fingerprint by M. Stücker, M. Geil, S. Kyeck, K. Hoffman, A. Röchling, U. Memmel, and P. Altmeyer in *Journal of Forensic Sciences*, Vol. 46, No. 5, pages 857–861, 2001.

The Coming Paradigm Shift in Forensic Identification Science by M.J. Saks and J.J. Koehler in *Science*, Vol. 309, No. 5736, pages 892–895, 2005.

Computation of Likelihood Ratios in Fingerprint Identification for Configurations of Three Minutiae by C. Neumann, C. Champod, R. Puch-Solis, N. Egli, A. Anthonioz, D. Meuwly, and A. Bromage-Griffiths in *Journal of Forensic Sciences*, Vol. 51, No. 6, pages 1255–1266, 2006.

The Psychology of Murder

A Case of Suicidal Hanging Staged as Homicide by T.W. Adair and M.J. Dobersen in *Journal of Forensic Sciences*, Vol. 44, No. 6, pages 1307–1309, 1999.

Anger Experience, Styles of Anger Expression, Sadistic Personality Disorder, and Psychopathy in Juvenile Sexual Homicide Offenders by W.C. Myers and L. Monaco in *Journal of Forensic Sciences*, Vol. 45, No. 3, pages 698–701, 2000.

A Classification of Psychological Factors Leading to Violent Behavior in Posttraumatic Stress Disorder by J.A. Silva, D.V. Derecho, G.B. Leong, R. Weinstock, and M.M. Ferrari in *Journal of Forensic Sciences*, Vol. 46, No. 2, pages 309–316, 2001.

Spousal Homicide and the Subsequent Staging of a Sexual Homicide at a Distant Location by J.R. Meloy in *Journal of Forensic Sciences*, Vol. 47, No. 2, pages 395–398, 2001.

The Case of Jeffrey Dahmer: Sexual Serial Homicide from a Neuropyschiatric Developmental Perspective by J.A. Silva, M.M. Ferrari, and G.B. Leong in *Journal of Forensic Sciences*, Vol. 47, No. 6, pages 1347–1359, 2002.

Measures of Aggression and Mood Changes in Male Weightlifters with and without Androgenic Anabolic Steroid Use by P.J. Perry, E.C. Kutscher, B.C. Lund, W.R. Yates, T.L. Holman, and L. Demers in *Journal of Forensic Sciences*, Vol. 48, No. 3, pages 646–651, 2003.

Homicide Victim/Offender Relationship in Florida Medical Examiner District 8 by S.M. Drawdy and W.C. Myers in *Journal of Forensic Sciences*, Vol. 49, No. 1, pages 150–154, 2004.

A Research Review of Public Figure Threats, Approaches, Attacks, and Assassinations in the United States by J.R. Meloy, D.V. James, F.R. Farnham, P.E. Mullen, M. Pathe, B. Darnley, and L. Preston in *Journal of Forensic Sciences*, Vol. 49, No. 5, pages 1086–1093, 2004.

Drug and Alcohol Use as Determinants of New York City Homicide Trends from 1990 to 1998 by A.K.J. Tardiff, Z. Wallace, M. Tracy, T.M. Piper, D. Vlahov, and S. Galea in *Journal of Forensic Sciences*, Vol. 50, No. 2, pages 470–474, 2005.

Heterosexual Intimate Partner Homicide: Review of Ten Years of Clinical Experience by R.S. Farooque, R.G. Stout, and F.A. Ernst in *Journal of Forensic Sciences*, Vol. 50, No. 3, pages 648–651, 2005.

The Role of Psychopathy and Sexuality in a Female Serial Killer by W.C. Myers, E. Gooch, and J.R. Meloy in *Journal of Forensic Sciences*, Vol. 50, No. 3, pages 652–657, 2005.

Matricide by Person with Bipolar Disorder and Dependent Overcompliant Personality by M.D. Livaditis, G.S. Esagian, C.P. Kakoulidis, M.A. Samakouri, and N.A. Tzavaras in *Journal of Forensic Sciences*, Vol. 50, No. 3, pages 658–661, 2005.

The Motivation Behind Serial Sexual Homicide: Is It Sex, Power, and Control, or Anger? By W.C. Myers, D.S. Husted, M.E. Safarik, and M.E. O'Toole in *Journal of Forensic Sciences*, Vol. 51, No. 4, pages 900–907, 2006.

Violent Crime and Substance Abuse: A Medico-Legal Comparison between Deceased Users of Anabolic Androgenic Steroids and Abusers of Illicit Drugs by Fia Klotz, Anna Petersson, Dag Isacson, and Ingemar Thibilin in *Forensic Science International*, Vol. 173, Issue 1, pages 57–63, 2007.

15
In the Courtroom

Form and Substance of a Trial

The courtroom trial is where disputes are settled. Murder is a dispute. It is one between the state and the murder suspect. The state, in this case, is called the *plaintiff*—the one who initially brings the suit to seek a remedy for injury done to it by the *defendant* (the person charged with the crime). To resolve the dispute, the court enlists the help of the *trier of fact* who is represented by the judge and jury. *Trier of fact* is an interesting term, since the courtroom isn't actually trying to determine fact. It is trying to provide enough evidence to a jury that will allow them to reasonably decide guilt or innocence.

The US system of justice is said to be *adversarial* because two opposing sides attempt to convince the judge and jury that their theory of who committed the crime and the manner in which it was committed is closest to the truth. A *prosecuting attorney* attempts to show that the suspect is guilty of the crime. The *defense attorney* does everything within their power to show that their client, the defendant, is innocent of the criminal charges.

Witnesses are called to testify as to their knowledge relating to the case. They are only allowed, however, to address what they believe to be true as fact and must usually confine their testimony to concise responses to direct questions. If they should stray too far from that course, say by offering personal opinion as to what the various items of evidence mean to the case, the judge will undoubtedly cut them off and caution them to keep their replies to a minimum.

Often times, opinions that can provide weight to a witness' testimony may be sought from *expert witnesses*. To qualify as an expert witness, a person doesn't necessarily have to have a Nobel Prize in chemistry or physics. But they typically do, however, possess some unique skill, experience, or knowledge that goes beyond that held by the average person in the particular field in which they are asked to testify. When an expert witness takes the stand, they are usually asked questions by both sides as to their qualifications—what is it about their experience, training, and professional career that make them an expert in their field? Being an adversarial system of justice, an expert witness called to support the prosecution's case will be asked questions by the defense that attempts to show that they are not, in fact, qualified to provide testimony. The reverse is true for an expert witness called by the defense. In that case, the prosecuting attorney will try to downplay their qualifications.

Expert witnesses may be called into a case to provide their opinion as to the meaning of DNA evidence or how medications or other substances may affect behavior. Even though they may be experts in their unique field of science, they are rarely allowed to speak in terms of absolutes. An expert witness would not be allowed to say categorically that the use of anabolic steroids, for example, caused the defendant to murder his wife. He might say, however, that such behavior *is consistent with* that observed with abusers of anabolic steroids. Or that it might have contributed to his action. But not absolutely, definitively, that it was the reason the defendant killed his wife.

Each side in a criminal case attempts to provide enough evidence in court that will best support their version of the crime's events. Not all evidence collected, however, may be brought into the courtroom. Because it was illegally obtained, tainted, or overly prejudicial to the defendant, it can be ruled *inadmissible* by the judge.

Presumption of Innocence

Our criminal justice system is based on the premise that allowing a guilty person to go free is better than putting an innocent person behind bars. For this reason, the prosecution bears a heavy burden of proof. Defendants are presumed innocent. The prosecution must convince the judge or jury of guilt beyond a reasonable doubt.

Concept of Reasonable Doubt

A defendant may be found guilty *beyond a reasonable doubt* even though a possible doubt remains in the mind of the judge or juror. Those hearing and deciding the case must rely on their best judgment to decide what is *reasonable*. It is possible to argue, for example, that aliens from another planet came to Earth, committed the crime, and then flew back to their own galaxy. There might be a suspicion in a juror's mind that such a thing could be possible, but is it really reasonable, given the evidence presented, to make that conclusion? Conversely, a jury might return a verdict of not guilty while still believing that the defendant probably committed the crime.

Jurors must often reach verdicts despite the presentation of contradictory evidence during the trial. Two witnesses might give different accounts of the same event. Sometimes a single witness will give a different account of the same event at different times. Such inconsistencies often result from human fallibility rather than from intentional lying or the bearing of false witness. A jury member applies his or her own best judgment in evaluating inconsistent testimony.

A guilty verdict may be based upon circumstantial (indirect) evidence. However, if there are two reasonable interpretations of a piece of circumstantial evidence, one pointing toward guilt of the defendant and another pointing toward innocence of the defendant, the jury member is required to accept the interpretation pointing toward the defendant's innocence. On the other hand, if a piece of circumstantial evidence is subject to two interpretations, one reasonable and one unreasonable, the jury must accept reasonable interpretation event if it points toward the defendant's guilt. It is up to the jury to decide whether an interpretation is reasonable or unreasonable.

Role Descriptions

Trial Attorneys

Trial attorneys control the presentation of evidence at trial and argue the merits of their side of the case. They do not themselves supply information about the alleged criminal activity. Instead, they introduce evidence and question witnesses to bring out the full story.

The *prosecutor* presents the case for the state against the defendant. By questioning the witnesses (in our mock trial, it will be the scientific experts—the criminalists), you will try to convince the judge or jury that the defendant is guilty beyond a reasonable doubt. You will want to suggest a motive for the crime and will try to refute any defense alibis. The burden of proof is on the prosecutor—they must prove the guilt of the accused.

The defense attorney presents the case for the defendant. In this role, you will offer your own witnesses to present your client's version of the facts. You may undermine the prosecution's case by showing that the witnesses they have called to testify cannot be depended upon or that their testimony is seriously inconsistent with the evidence. The defense is not obligated to prove the innocence of the suspect. They strive to establish reasonable doubt.

Trial attorneys will

- Conduct direct examination
- Conduct cross-examination
- Conduct redirect examination, if necessary
- Make appropriate objections
- Make opening statements and closing arguments

Court Bailiff

The court bailiff calls the court to order and swears in the witnesses (Figure 15.1). The bailiff watches over the courtroom proceedings to protect the security of the courtroom.

Opening Statement

The opening statement outlines the case as the two parties, the prosecution and the defense, intend to present it. The prosecution delivers the first opening statement.

Figure 15.1 Expert witnesses are sworn in by the court bailiff.

A good opening statement should

1. Explain what you plan to prove and how you will do it
2. Present the events of the case in an orderly sequence that is easy to understand
   An opening statement may include the following phrases:
   - "The evidence will indicate that...."
   - "The facts will show...."
   - "The scientific experts will be called to tell...."
   - "The defendant will testify that...."
3. Suggest a motive or emphasize a lack of motive for the crime

Direct Examination

Prosecuting attorneys conduct direct examination of their own witnesses to bring out the facts of the case. Direct examination should

1. Elicit explanations for the meaning of the pieces of evidence presented in the case
2. Reveal all of the facts favorable to your position
3. Make the witness seem believable
4. Keep the witness from rambling about unimportant matters
5. Ask questions of the witness that will reveal the story of the crime. Questions that just call for *yes* or *no* answers should be kept to a minimum.

Cross-Examination: Defense

Cross-examination follows direct examination of the opposing attorney's witness. Attorneys conduct cross-examination to explore weaknesses in the opponent's case, test the witness' credibility, and establish some of the facts of the cross-examiner's case. The cross-examination should elicit information based on the witness' previous statements and should use leading questions designed to get *yes* and *no* answers. Questions used in cross-examination may include the following phrases:

- "Isn't it a fact that...?"
- "Wouldn't you agree that...?"
- "Don't you think that...?"

Redirect: Prosecution

Following cross-examination, the counsel who called the witness may redirect examination. Attorneys conduct redirect examination to clarify new (unexpected) issues or facts brought out in the immediately preceding cross-examination *only*. They may not bring up any issues brought out during direct examination.

If the credibility or reputation of a witness had been attacked on cross-examination, the attorney whose witness had been damaged may wish to *save* the witness during redirect, reestablishing that witness' veracity.

Closing Arguments

A good closing argument summarizes the case in the light most favorable to the presenter's position. The prosecutor is the first to present their closing arguments.

The defense will follow with their closing arguments. The prosecution closes their case with their rebuttal to the defense's argument.

A good closing argument should

1. Be spontaneous, synthesizing what actually happened in court rather than appearing as a prepackaged monologue
2. Be emotionally charged and strongly appealing
3. Emphasize the facts that support the claims of your side
4. Attempt to reconcile inconsistencies that might hurt your side

A closing argument may contain the following phrases:

- "The evidence has clearly shown that…."
- "Based on this testimony, there can be no doubt that…."
- "The prosecution has failed to prove that…."
- "The defense would have you believe that…."

Rebuttal

The rebuttal is that time allowed to the party who gave the first closing argument to refute any arguments given by the other party's closing argument, which followed. Only issues that were addressed in the opponent's closing argument may be rebutted—no new issues can be raised.

Mock Trial

Thus far, this course has taken you through two of the three major activities a forensic scientist would engage themselves in (1) crime scene documentation and (2) laboratory analysis of physical evidence. The last responsibility of a forensic scientist is to present the results of the evidence in a court of law either on behalf of the prosecution or the defense. It is important to remember that it is not the job of the scientist to determine the guilt or innocence of a defendant but rather to present the evidence in an unbiased manner applying rigorous and thorough scientific principles and methodology. It is the job of the prosecuting attorneys to sift through the physical evidence and piece together those parts of the scientific analysis that point to the guilt of the defendant. By the same token, it is the job of the defense attorneys to seek out the scientific data supporting the innocence of the defendant and that potentially creates reasonable doubt in the minds of the judge and jury.

The following instructions will guide you through the legal process of how to conduct a simulated (*mock*) trial in the classroom. It will include all of the standard proceedings that take place in the courtroom from the opening statements made by the respective lawyers, to testimony of the scientific experts, to closing arguments, to jury deliberation, and, finally, to the penalty phase (if the defendant is found guilty). Your instructor will assign roles to be played by each student. You may be assigned to be a prosecuting attorney, a defense attorney, an expert witness, a court bailiff, or the judge. All those not given a specific role to play will serve on the jury.

The following is an overview of the sequence of events for the mock trial simulation. This schedule is based on a 50-min class period with two scientific groups presenting each day.

First Day of Trial

1. The bailiff introduces the judge
2. Judge gives opening remarks and instructions to the court
3. The prosecution presents their opening statement
4. The defense presents their opening statement
5. Scientific expert testimony (team #1) representing state's evidence on behalf of the prosecution (includes both cross-examination and redirect)
6. Scientific expert testimony (team #2) representing state's evidence on behalf of the prosecution (includes both cross-examination and redirect)

Second Day of Trial

1. The bailiff introduces the judge
2. Judge's instructions (modified)
3. Scientific expert testimony (team #3) representing state's evidence on behalf of the prosecution (includes both cross-examination and redirect)
4. Scientific expert testimony (team #4) representing state's evidence on behalf of the prosecution (includes both cross-examination and redirect)

Scientific expert testimony (steps 3 and 4 earlier) will be continued until all of the teams have presented. Most criminal trials avoid having the suspect take the witness stand, but if the instructor elects to do so, this testimony should take place on the next to the last day of the trial prior to closing arguments.

Court room proceedings repeat itself until all teams have presented.

Last Day of Trial

1. Closing arguments by the prosecution
2. Closing arguments by the defense
3. Closing rebuttal by the prosecution
4. The judge provides instructions to the jury
5. Jury deliberation
6. Verdict
7. The judge renders penalty (if the defendant is found guilty). If a hung jury, the judge determines if the case warrants a retrial or the case is dismissed

Post-Trial Discussion Moderated by Instructor

Your instructor will provide analysis of the trial and elicit commentary from the class.

You on the Witness Stand

You will be asked to present your findings in front of the court (Figure 15.2). You should prepare a PowerPoint presentation that addresses the key pieces of physical evidence needed by the jury to evaluate your testimony. This will be a collaboration between your team of scientists and the prosecuting attorney who has hired you to

Figure 15.2 Expert witnesses being sworn in and testifying at the front of the courtroom.

testify on your findings. Because you are speaking to a jury of nonscientists, you should keep the PowerPoint presentation very visual with minimal text. It should be basic yet meaningful in a way that audience members can understand what the evidence was, how it was analyzed, and what information could be derived from it. A presentation that is too complex and peppered with too much scientific jargon will be difficult for the jury to understand. For example, if you are asked by the attorney to explain the process of the PCR, rather than go into details of the chemical and physical dynamics of the instrumentation, you might provide the analogy that it works similar to a Xerox machine.

In addition, you should collaborate with your attorney on the questions that will be asked of you on the witness stand. Keep in mind that your time on the witness stand will be limited—you will have a finite amount of time to present your pieces of evidence. Also be aware that you will be cross-examined by the defense attorney so anticipate questions that may be posed to you. It is their job to create reasonable doubt and to discredit your testimony. Don't take their questions as a personal attack; it is just the way the legal process works. Make sure your team is fully prepared to defend your analysis and the scientific principles behind what you performed in the lab. After cross-examination, your attorney will have the opportunity to redirect. During redirect, the prosecution will only ask questions posed by the defense attorney. Once redirect is completed, the judge will dismiss you from the witness stand.

Classroom Setup for the Mock Trial

The classroom can be set up in either configuration *A* or *B* (Figures 15.3 and 15.4). The teacher will be positioned in the back of the classroom and, for the purposes of student evaluation, reserves the right to interject questions of any party during the proceedings.

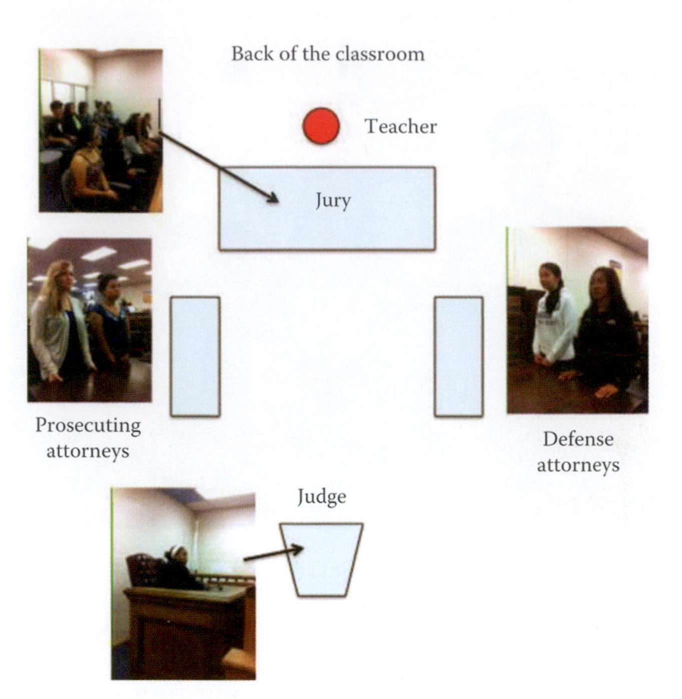

Figure 15.3 Classroom setup *A*. In this configuration, swearing in by the court bailiff as well as direct and cross-examinations of the expert witness occurs at the front of the classroom. The jury box is positioned in the center of the classroom. The prosecuting attorneys and expert witnesses are seated off to the side facing the jury. The defense attorneys are positioned on the opposite side of the classroom but also facing the jury. Your instructor is positioned in the back of the classroom with the team's rubric and answer sheet (turned in the week before the start of the trial). Your instructor may, at their discretion, interrupt the attorneys' line of questioning during examination of the expert witnesses to verbally evaluate the team's testimony.

Courtroom Logistics/Time Line: First day of trial

A time line for the courtroom trial is presented later. A narrative (to follow) will guide you through a suggested script pertinent to each role. During the entire trial, the instructor will be evaluating the testimony (see rubric) and, at any time, may interject with questions designed to assess the team members' knowledge of the science behind the evidence presented.

0:05 minutes: The members of the court are seated in the appropriate parts of the room. The judge enters. The judge reads directives.
0:01 minutes: The prosecution presents their opening statement.
0:01 minutes: The defense presents their opening statement.
0:02 minutes: The court bailiff swears in the first expert witness. The prosecution asks each member of the forensics team to state their educational and occupational experience before direct testimony begins.
0:15 minutes: The prosecution begins questions on direct (the attorneys ask preassigned questions). At any point during the direct examination, the defense may object.
0:05 minutes: The defense conducts their cross-examination. At any point during the cross-examination, the prosecution may raise objections.

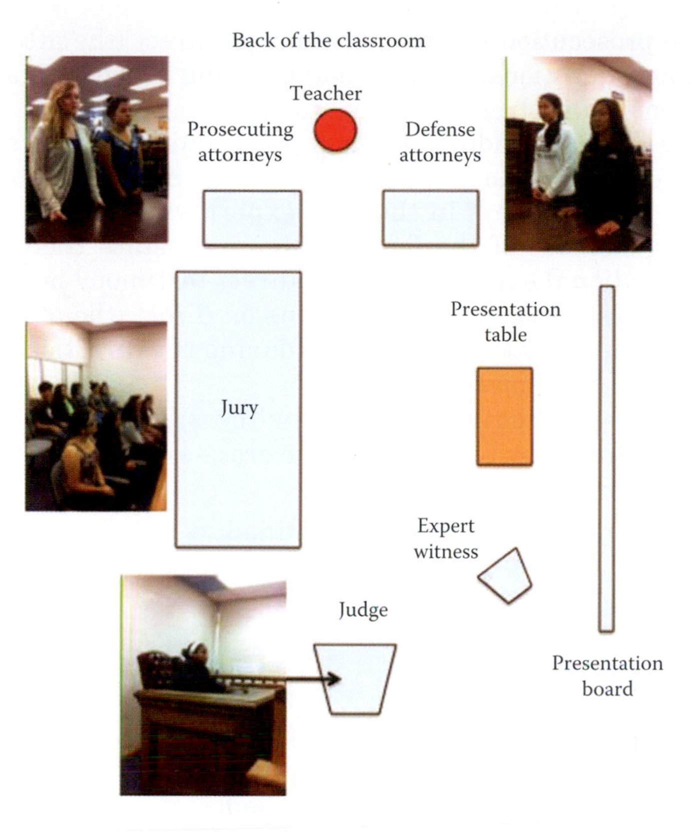

Figure 15.4 Classroom setup *B*. In this configuration, attorneys for the prosecution and the defense are seated side by side across the room from the judge with the jury to the side of the room. The expert witness is positioned in the court equidistant from the jury and the attorneys. The expert witness is provided a board to project their PowerPoint presentations. The expert witness may also be allowed a table for a projector and for displaying physical evidence.

0:02 minutes: The bailiff swears in the next expert witness. The prosecution asks each member of the forensics team to state their educational and occupational experience before direct testimony begins.
0:15 minutes: The prosecution begins questions on direct (the attorneys ask preassigned questions). At any point during the direct examination, the defense may object.
0:05 minutes: The defense cross-examines the witness. The prosecution may raise an objection at any point during the cross-examination.
0:51 minutes: Total elapsed time.

Courtroom Logistics/Time Line: Second day of testimony*

0:05 minutes: The members of the court are seated in the appropriate parts of the room. The judge enters. The judge reads directives.
0:02 minutes: The court bailiff swears in the first expert witness. The prosecution asks each member of the forensics team to state their educational and occupational experience before direct testimony begins.

* This schedule should be used for all the days required to complete expert witness testimony up to, but not including, the last day of the trial.

0:15 minutes: The prosecution begins questions on direct (the attorneys ask preassigned questions). At any point during the direct examination, the defense may object.
0:05 minutes: The defense conducts their cross-examination. At any point during the cross-examination, the prosecution may raise objections.
0:02 minutes: The bailiff swears in the next expert witness. The prosecution asks each member of the forensics team to state their educational and occupational experience before direct testimony begins.
0:15 minutes: The prosecution begins questions on direct (the attorneys ask preassigned questions). At any point during the direction examination, the defense may object.
0:05 minutes: The defense cross-examines the witness. The prosecution may raise an objection at any point during the cross-examination.
0:49 minutes: Total time elapsed.

Repeat this process until all experts have testified.

Courtroom Logistics/Time Line: Last day of trial: Reading of the verdict and posttrial discussion

Repeat this process until all experts have testified.

0:05 minutes: The members of the court are seated in the appropriate parts of the room. The judge enters. The judge reads directives.
0:03 minutes: The prosecution presents their closing arguments.
0:03 minutes: The defense presents their closing arguments.
0:02 minutes: The prosecution presents their rebuttal arguments.
0:01 minutes: The judge reads instructions to the jury.
0:10 minutes: The jury deliberates. (This is a criminal trial so the jury must be unanimous in its decision. If a unanimous decision cannot be reached, the foreperson returns a *hung jury*.)

At this point (and depending on the logistics of the courtroom and building), all those involved in the case (judge, attorneys, expert witnesses, etc.) except the members of the jury should leave the room so that the jury, remaining behind in the courtroom, can deliberate. The instructor will randomly select 12 jurors to decide the final verdict but all jury members will be asked to participate in the decision-making process. The members of the jury should select a foreperson who should call for a vote on guilt or innocence before any discussion takes place. If the decision is unanimous, then there is no need to deliberate. If the vote is not unanimous, then deliberation should begin. When the allotted deliberation time is reached, the foreperson should take an official vote. The results of that vote and final verdict should be recorded by the foreperson.

0:01 minutes: When a decision has been made, the bailiff will escort all role players back into the classroom.
0:01 minutes: After the judge seats everyone (with the words, "You may be seated"), the Judge says, "Foreperson, have you reached a verdict?"

0:01 minutes: The jury foreperson stands and recites, "We have your honor." (before reciting the jury's decision, foreperson hands the verdict to the Bailiff who in turn will give the verdict to the judge. Allow a short period of time for the judge to read the verdict silently to him/herself). "We the jury …" (refer to courtroom narrative).
0:01 minutes: If the jury has found the defendant guilty, the judge will be asked to render the penalty phase.
0:28 minutes: Total elapsed time.

The instructor will moderate a post trial discussion in which the decision-making process of the jury will be discussed.

Courtroom Narration

Day 1

1. *Bailiff*
   - "Hear ye, hear ye, the court is now open and in session. The Honorable Judge ____________ presiding. All persons having business before the court come to order. This is the case of the ____________ *(name of the state and/or country)* versus ____________ *(name of the person)*. Would you all rise, please." (Judge walks in.)

   Swears in jury
   - "Do you swear to serve as a juror in this trial to the best of your ability, honestly and conscientiously?" (*Pause for jury to respond*). "Be seated."
2. *Judge*
   - "Good morning/afternoon, The people of the ____________ *(name of state and or country)* versus ____________ *(last name of suspect)*. Are the people ready?"
3. *Prosecuting attorney*
   - "Good morning/afternoon, your Honor. ____________ *(Name of law firm)* appearing for the people. We are ready to proceed."
4. *Defense attorney*
   - "____________ *(Name of law firm)* appearing for the defense, your Honor. We are prepared to proceed."
5. *Judge*
   - "Ladies and gentlemen of the jury. You are now about to participate as jurors in a trial in which the defendant is accused of committing the criminal act of ____________. Prosecution, would you please present your opening statement."
6. *Prosecuting attorney*
   - "Yes, your Honor." (Prosecuting attorney makes opening statement.)
7. *Judge*
   - "Defense, you may make your opening remarks."
8. *Defense attorney*
   - "Yes, your Honor." (Defense attorney makes opening statement)
9. *Judge*
   - "____________ *(name of law firm)* you may call your scientific experts."

10. *Prosecuting attorney*
    - "Your Honor, I would like to call ________________ (*name of crime lab*) to the stand."
11. *Bailiff* (swears in scientific experts)
    - "Raise your right hand(s). Do you swear to tell the truth, the whole truth, and nothing but the truth in this case under penalty of perjury?" (*Pause for response.*) "State your name and educational and occupational experience."

Attorneys: During direct/cross-examination/redirect, you may object to the line of questioning posed by the opposing lawyer and/or may ask to approach the bench by saying "Judge, may I approach the bench?"

Judge: If objections are posed by the opposing attorney(s), you must make a decision of "*objection sustained*" or "*objection overruled*." If an objection is sustained, the objection is acknowledged and the questioning attorney must restate or stop the line of questioning. If an objection is overruled, the objection is disregarded, and the questioning attorney may continue to 12.

Prosecuting attorney (direct)

On direct, refer to the questions in the scientific experts' research notebooks.

12. *Judge*: "Defense, you may cross-examine."
13. *Defense attorney*: When finished with cross-examination say, "I have no further questions, your Honor."
14. *Judge*: "Prosecution, you may redirect." (Redirect is rebutting an argument that the defense has posed during cross-examination that you need rectified.)
15. *Prosecuting attorney*: Upon completion during redirect, respond by saying, "I have no further questions, your Honor." Or if there are no questions on redirect, respond by saying, "I have no questions, your Honor"
16. *Judge*
    - "If there are no further questions, you may step down."
    - "________________ (*name of law firm*), you may call your next client".
    - Repeat steps #10–#16.
17. *Judge*: At the completion of the last group for that day, say, "The court will be in recess until tomorrow."

Attorneys: During direct/cross-examination/redirect, you may object to the line of questioning posed by the opposing lawyers and/or may ask to approach the bench by saying, "Judge, may I approach the bench?" at which time both attorneys will be in a sidebar discussion out of ear witness of the courtroom audience.

Judge: If objections are posed by the opposing attorney(s), you must make a decision of "*objection sustained*" or "*objection overruled*". If an objection is sustained, the objection is acknowledged, and the questioning attorney must either restate or stop the line of questioning. If an objection is overruled, the objection is disregarded, and the questioning attorney may continue with the line of questioning, and/or the witness must answer the question.

Day 2: Courtroom Reconvenes

1. *Bailiff*
    - "Hear ye, hear ye, the court is now open and in session. The Honorable Judge ____________ presiding. All persons having business before the

court come to order. This is the case of the ____________ (*name of the state and/or country*) versus ______________ (*name of the person*). Would you all rise, please." (Judge walks in.)

- *Swears in jury*
- "Do you swear to serve as a juror in this trial to the best of your ability, honestly, and conscientiously?" (*Pause for jury to respond.*) "Be seated."

2. *Judge*
   - "Good morning/afternoon. The people of the _____________ (*name of state and or country*) versus ______________ (*last name of suspect*). Are the people ready?"
3. *Prosecuting Attorney*
   - "Good morning/afternoon, your Honor. ______________ (*name of law firm*) appearing for the people. We are ready to proceed."
4. *Defense attorney*
   - "______________ (*name of law firm*) appearing for the defense, your Honor. We are prepared to proceed."
5. *Judge*
   - "______________ (*name of law firm*) you may call your scientific experts."
6. *Prosecuting attorney*
   - "Your Honor, I would like to call ________________ to the stand"
   - (*name of crime lab*).
7. *Bailiff* (swears in scientific experts)
   - "Raise your right hand(s). Do you swear to tell the truth, the whole truth, and nothing but the truth in this case under penalty of perjury?" (*Pause for response.*) "State your name and educational and occupational experience."
8. *Judge*: "Defense, you may cross-examine."
9. *Defense attorney*: When you are finished with cross-examination, say, "I have no further questions, your Honor."
10. *Judge*: "Prosecution, you may redirect." (Redirect is rebutting an argument that the defense has posed during cross-examination that you need to rectify.)
11. *Prosecuting attorney*: Upon completion of redirect, respond by saying, "I have no further questions, your Honor." Or, if there are no questions on redirect, respond by saying, "I have no questions, your Honor."
12. *Judge*
    - "If there are no further questions, you may step down."
    - "__________ (*name of law firm*), you may call your next client".
    - Repeat steps #5–#11.
13. *Judge*: At the completion of the last group for that day, say, "The court will be in recess until tomorrow."

Last Day of Trial: Assume No Further Expert Testimony

Judge: "The prosecution followed by the defense may now make closing arguments."

Prosecution (closing arguments).

Defense (closing arguments).

Prosecution (rebuttal).

Judge

"Ladies and gentlemen of the jury, you have heard the facts presented in this case in which it is charged that the defendant" (name of suspect and what the charge is, e.g., Harvey Oswald for the murder of John Kennedy).

"Generally, you must first determine on the basis of the facts presented to you whether or not the defendant is guilty of the charges or not guilty of the charges. If you feel there is a reasonable doubt that the defendant is guilty of any crime, return a verdict of not guilty. If you feel there is sufficient evidence to justify a finding of guilt for the crime, return a verdict of guilty. In your decision as a jury, you must be unanimous in your agreement; the bailiff will escort you to a room where once assembled the foreperson will lead the group in the ensuing discussion and decision-making process. When you have reached a decision, return and report them to the court. The bailiff will lead the jurors from the courtroom."

Bailiff
When the jury has reached a decision, the bailiff will escort the jury back into the courtroom.

Judge: "Foreperson, have you reached a verdict?"

Foreperson: "Yes we have your honor." (before you announce the decision, hand the final verdict to the bailiff, who it turn will hand this to the judge. Allow a short period of time for the judge to read the verdict silently to him/herself). At which point read Line #1, #2, or #3.

Foreman of the jury

If a hung jury, quote line #1.
If a guilty verdict is reached, quote line #2.
If an not guilty verdict is reached, quote line #3.

Line #1 "We have, your honor. We, the jury, based on the evidence and testimony given here today, are a hung jury."

Line #2 "We have, your honor. We, the jury, based on the evidence and testimony given here today, find the defendant guilty.

Line #3 "We have, your honor. We, the jury, based on the evidence and testimony given here today, find the defendant not guilty."

Judge: If there is a hung jury, decide whether the case warrants a retrial or a dismissal (meaning the defendant is acquitted of all charges).

Judge: If the jury returns a *guilty* verdict, you will render the penalty phase (life imprisonment without parole, or 15 years in the state penitentiary with a possibility of parole in seven years, etc.).

Common Trial Objections

When an attorney objects to a line of questioning by the opposing attorney, they say, "Objection, your Honor, the question is ..."

That question may be objectionable if it is as follows:

1. Ambiguous—it can be taken to have more than one meaning.
2. Argumentative—its intent is to influence the judge or jury rather than to actually bring out new information. An argumentative question may also try

to get the witness to agree to inferences drawn from previously aired proved or assumed facts.
3. Already asked and answered—a similar question posed of the witness has been previously asked by the same attorney.
4. Assumes facts not in evidence—it presumes unproved facts as being true.
5. Compound—it combines two questions into one.
6. Too general—it invites the witness to respond with testimony that may be irrelevant and cover ground outside of information that is pertinent to the case.
7. Hearsay—it invites the witness to draw on conversations or statements that occurred out of the courtroom to prove the truth of their court testimony though such statements are not part of the testimony examined by the court for the case being tried.
8. Irrelevant—it invites the witness to provide testimony not related to the case.
9. Leading—it influences the witness to give a response expected and desired by the examining attorney.
10. Misstates the evidence—it incorrectly quotes previous testimony.
11. Speculative—it invites the witness to speculate or answer on the basis of conjecture.

Mock Trial Final Points Rubric

Title of Case: ____________ v. ____________ Class: ____________ Period: ____________

Team members: A. ________________ (Self-assessment) ____________% ____________

B. ________________ (Self-assessment) ____________% ____________

C. ________________ (Self-assessment) ____________% ____________

Self-assessment team evaluation is based on the work performed by the individuals during the laboratory analysis (week #1). If the lab group feels all members put in an equal effort, then the % should reflect that, that is, each individual should receive the points the instructor has evaluated the group after their mock trial presentation (see rubric later). If the team feels that a member(s) has not put forth an equal effort, then the team will assess accordingly, for example, if a member has only participated in 80% of the work, then that individual's final point total will reflect that. Let's use the following example; instructor scored your team with an 80/85 pts., and one of the members was assessed at 80% effort; then the instructor will take 80% of 80 resulting in that person receiving a 64/85 while the other two members receive 80/85.

#	**Results Only (Be Brief, No Elaboration)**	**Pts.**	**Scientific Methodology and Explanation of Evidence (*Do Not Fill In; This Space Is for the Instructor Evaluation Only*)**
1			
2			
3			

Signatures of experts validating that the analysis has been performed using sound scientific principles, in an unbiased manner, and that all members agree as to the results.

Team members: A. ______________________________

B. ______________________________

C. ______________________________

__________ pts. for correct analysis of items (15 pts.)

__________ pts. for correct scientific explanation of results (30 pts.)

__________ pts. for research notebook documentation (20 pts.)

__________ pts. for dress, organization, equal participation, and stay w/in time limit (5 pts.)

__________ pts. for quality of visuals/illustrations/PowerPoint (5 pts.)

__________ pts. for returning of state's evidence in its' original condition (5 pts.)

__________ pts. peer evaluation (5 pts.)

__________/ (80 pts.)

STATE OF NEBRASKA § 29-2524.01	**NEBRASKA COUNTY ATTORNEY CRIMINAL HOMICIDE REPORT**	CASE NUMBER

Neb. Rev. Stat. § 29-2524.01 provides that the county attorney must file the following report with the State Court Administrator within thirty days of the ultimate disposition by the court of every criminal homicide case filed by the county attorney.

1. In the District Court of_______________County
2. State of Nebraska vs.______________ DOB:_____
   Address:___________________________
3. Initial charges filed:____
   __________Date:_________, ____
4. Were any of the initial charges reduced? __ Yes __ No. If yes, what were the reduced charges?
   ______________________________________ ______________________________
5. Was the reduction a result from a plea bargain? __ Yes __ No, another reason which was:
   ______________________________________ ______________________________
6. Were there any charges dismissed prior to trial? __ Yes __ No. If yes, they were:______________
   ____
7. On_________, _____, the outcome of the trial was:
   __ Found guilty __ Found not guilty
   __ Charges were dismissed
   __ Found guilty of a lesser included offense:______________________________
   __ Other:____
8. On__________, _____, the following sentence was imposed:______________________________
   ____
9. Was appeal taken? __ Yes __ No Date:_______, _____
10. Sentencing Judge:____
    (Signature)
11. Defense Counsel:____
    (Signature)

DATE:_________, ____

____
County Attorney

____
Print Name

Mail to: State Court Administrator, P.O. Box 98910, Lincoln, NE 68509-8910

Form adopted November 18, 1998.

Appendix 1

Appendix A: Evidence Items in the Erica Holmes Missing Persons Case

Item Number	Description
1	Sample taken of reddish/brown stain (possibly a drop of blood) on the white plastic windshield wiper fluid reservoir under the hood of Erica Holmes' vehicle. Sample taken for DNA analysis.
2	Material (possibly tissue) on the engine block of Erica Holmes' vehicle. Material recovered for histology and DNA analysis.
3	Sample taken of fine specks of reddish stain (possibly blood) around impact hole (possibly a bullet hole) in the firewall (driver's side) under the hood of Erica Holmes' vehicle.
4	Bullet found on driver's side floor under driver's seat in Erica Holmes' vehicle.
5	Sample taken from the braid pattern transfer stain (possibly blood) on the vinyl cargo bay liner of Erica Holmes' vehicle. Sample taken for DNA analysis.
6	Sample taken from the leftmost (driver's side) portion of the large stain (possibly blood) on the vinyl cargo bay liner of Erica Holmes' vehicle. Sample taken for DNA analysis.
7	Sample taken on the right side (passenger's side) of large stain (possibly blood) on the vinyl cargo bay liner of Erica Holmes' vehicle. Sample taken for DNA analysis.
8	Sample taken from the rearmost area of large stain (possibly blood) on the vinyl cargo bay liner of Erica Holmes' vehicle.
9	Fingerprint stain (possibly blood) on rearview mirror of Erica Holmes' vehicle. Sample taken for DNA analysis.
10	Buccal swab from Sarah Holmes.
11	Buccal swab from Dwayne Holmes.
12	Buccal swab from Samdeep O'Neill.
13	Buccal swab from Chuck Beamer.
14	Fiber recovered from braid pattern transfer stain (possibly blood) on the vinyl cargo bay liner of Erica Holmes' vehicle.
15	Fiber (a possible hair) from the large stain (possibly blood) on the vinyl cargo bay liner of Erica Holmes' vehicle.
16	Fiber (a possible hair) adjacent to the braid pattern transfer stain (possibly blood) on the vinyl cargo bay liner. Fiber recovered from within the stain area.
17	Fiber adhering to the bullet (Evidence Item 4) found inside Erica Holmes' vehicle.
18a	Swab of area close to (but not touching) the reddish/brown stain (possibly a drop of blood) on the white plastic windshield wiper fluid reservoir under the hood of Erica Holmes' vehicle. Swab used as a background test for Evidence Item 18b.
18b	Swab taken of reddish/brown stain (possibly a drop of blood) on the white plastic windshield wiper fluid reservoir under the hood of Erica Holmes' vehicle. Swab taken for blood presumptive test. *Note*: Additional swab taken of this same stain and referenced as Evidence Item 1.

Item Number	Description
19a	Swab of area close to (but not touching or within) the reddish/brown speck stains (possibly blood) surrounding an impact hole (possibly a bullet hole) in the firewall (on the driver's side) under the hood of Erica Holmes' vehicle. Swab used as a background test for Evidence Item 19b.
19b	Swab of area within the reddish/brown speck stains (possibly blood) surrounding an impact hole (possibly a bullet hole) in the firewall (on the driver's side) under the hood of Erica Holmes' vehicle. Swab taken for blood presumptive test. *Note*: Another swab (designated Evidence Item 3) was taken of this same area for the purpose of DNA analysis.
20a	Swab of area close to (but not touching or within) the braided pattern transfer stain (possibly blood) on the vinyl cargo bay liner of Erica Holmes' vehicle. Swab used as a background test for Evidence Item 20b.
20b	Swab of area within the braided pattern transfer stain (possibly blood) on the vinyl cargo bay liner of Erica Holmes' vehicle. Swab taken for blood presumptive test. *Note*: Another swab (designated Evidence Item 5) was taken of this same area for the purpose of DNA analysis.
21a	Swab of area close to (but not touching or within) the leftmost (driver's side) portion of the large stain (possibly blood) on the vinyl cargo bay liner of Erica Holmes' vehicle. Swab used as a background test for Evidence Item 21b.
21b	Swab of area within the leftmost (driver's side) portion of the large stain (possibly blood) on the vinyl cargo bay liner of Erica Holmes' vehicle. Swab taken for blood presumptive test. *Note*: A swab (Evidence Item 6) was taken of this same area for DNA analysis.
22a	Swab taken adjacent to (but not within) the right side (passenger's side) of large stain (possibly blood) on the vinyl cargo bay liner of Erica Holmes' vehicle. Swab used as a background test for Evidence Item 22b.
22b	Swab taken from within the right side (passenger's side) of large stain (possibly blood) on the vinyl cargo bay liner of Erica Holmes' vehicle. Swab taken for blood presumptive test. *Note*: A swab (Evidence Item 7) was taken of this same area for DNA analysis.
23a	Swab taken adjacent to (but not within) the rearmost portion of the large stain on the vinyl cargo bay liner in Erica Holmes' vehicle. Swab used as a background test for Evidence Item 23b.
23b	Swab taken adjacent to (but not within) the rearmost portion of the large stain on the vinyl cargo bay liner in Erica Holmes' vehicle. Swab taken for blood presumptive test. *Note*: A swab (Evidence Item 8) was taken of this same area for DNA analysis.
24a	Swab taken adjacent to (but not within) the fingerprint stain (possibly blood) on the rearview mirror in the interior of Erica Holmes' vehicle. Swab used as a background test for Evidence Item 24b.
24b	Swab taken on the edge of the fingerprint stain (possibly blood) on the rearview mirror in the interior of Erica Holmes' vehicle. Swab used for blood presumptive test. *Note*: A swab (Evidence Item 9) was taken of this same area for DNA analysis.
25	Sunglasses recovered from the glove compartment of Erica Holmes' vehicle.
26	Candy wrapper recovered from ashtray (passenger's side) or Erica Holmes' vehicle.
27	Vanity mirror recovered from the glove compartment of Erica Holmes' vehicle.
28	Buccal swab from Alice Beamer.
29	Handgun recovered from Samdeep O'Neill's Ford F150 truck.
30	Buccal swab from Farah Dawood.

Appendix B: Evidence Report

On the following page is an evidence report form you can use to record your analysis of the evidence items recovered in the Erica Holmes missing persons case. If one form is not enough to transcribe all your findings, attach another sheet to the form.

When filling out each report for each evidence item, remember to be as thorough as possible. Any omissions of information gained in your analysis could be seized upon by the defense as evidence of poor record keeping or incompetent analysis.

Evidence Report

Page _____ of _____

Case number: ______________________________ **Victim:** ______________________________

Offense(s): ______________________________

Item number: ______________________________

Description of evidence:

Evidence submitted by: ____________________ **Date submitted:** ____________________

Analysis performed:

Analysis results:

Analysis performed by: ______________________________ ______________

Printed name/signature Date

Witnessed by: ______________________________ ______________

Printed name/signature Date

Appendix C: Glossary of Terms Found in the Text

A

Accuracy: Refers to how close a measurement is to the real, actual value.
Acid phosphatase: Enzyme found in semen.
Acromion: Bony projection of the scapula forming the attachment point of the clavicle.
Adipose: Tissue providing insulation, energy storage, and protective padding for the organs.
AFIS (automated fingerprint identification system): Computer program that identifies the print's minutiae points and compares this information with that of prints in a database.
Agarose: Jell-O-like substance that DNA fragments are forced through when subjected to an electrical field.
Alec Jeffreys: English molecular biologist that discovered the technique of DNA fingerprinting.
Algor mortis: Method of determining time of death by measuring the body's rate of cooling.
Alleles: Alternate forms (polymorphs) of a genetic region.
Alveoli: Site of gas exchange in the lung comprised of thin-walled hollow cavity structures.
Ampere: A unit of electric current.
Annealing: Stage in a PCR cycle where two primers bind to separated DNA template strands.
Anterior: The front of the body.
Antibodies: Molecules that bind antigens as part of their role in providing protection against invading microbes.
Antigens: Molecules that coat the outside of all animal tissues; cause immune system to produce antibodies.
Arch: Fingerprint ridges that show stacks of ridgelines forming a hump shape.
Axon: Part of a nerve cell that contain threadlike fibers that transmit nerve impulses.

B

Base: Component of a nucleotide made up of four different molecules, namely, adenine, cytosine, guanine, and thymine.
Base pair (bp): Complementary pairing of bases, namely, adenine (A) pairs with thymine (T) and guanine (G) pairs with cytosine (C).
Battery: Source of electric power that converts the chemical energy of one or more voltaic cells into electrical energy.
Bifurcation: Fingerprint ridge that splits into two.
Breath analyzer: A device used to measure one's blood alcohol level.
Breech face: Front part of a breechblock; breechblock holds a bullet in the chamber of a firearm.

C

Caliber: Outside diameter of a bullet and/or internal diameter of a shell casing.
Caliper: Measuring instrument that has adjustable arms designed to measure internal and external diameters of an object.
Capacitor: Electrical component that temporarily stores electrical energy.
Cardiac muscle: Elongated, striated, multinucleated cells of the heart.
Carpal bones: Complex of bones forming the wrist.

Cast: The 3D object that results when a liquid material is poured into a cavity, hole, or impression and is allowed to harden.
Castoff: Blood spatter that occurs when blood is flung off an instrument such as a baseball bat or fireplace poker.
Cerebral cortex: Outermost layer of the cerebrum.
Cerebrum: What most people refer to as the *brain*, which controls many of the uniquely human thought processes including speech, language, learning, our social behaviors, and movement.
Cervical vertebrae: Seven vertebrae at the top of spine below the skull; composed of the neck bones.
Chain of custody: Documentation of where, when, and by whom evidence was examined or taken possession of.
Chelex: Resin polymer used to recover DNA.
Chemiluminescence: Chemical reaction that generates light.
Chi-square: A measure of the degree to which the observed values diverge from those expected.
Circumstantial evidence: Type of evidence that is more amenable to scientific examination such as blood, fingerprints, hair, fibers, and DNA.
Clavicle: Collarbone.
Coarse adjustment: Knob on a microscope used for initial focusing.
Coccyx: Tailbone, most distal part of the spinal column formed from fused vertebra.
CODIS (Combined DNA Index System): DNA database maintained by the FBI Laboratory.
Columnar epithelium: Type of skin cells that take on a column-like appearance.
Compact bone: Bone tissue.
Comparison microscope: A microscope that consists of two stages that can be viewed simultaneously through a binocular eyepiece.
Complementary bases: Pairing of adenine (A) with thymine (T) and guanine (G) with cytosine (C).
Composite sketch: A drawing based on an account of an individual's specific features (hairline, eye, nose, and chin shape, etc.).
Contig: Overlapping DNA fragments that represent a contiguous sequence of DNA bases.
Control region: Area of the mtDNA molecular sometimes referred to as the D loop region or the hypervariable region that does not encode for any proteins.
Coracoid process: Hook-like, bony projection on the anterior side of the scapula; attachment points for minor muscles of the chest.
Coronal: Plane that divides the body into front and back halves.
Correlation coefficient: The degree to which data points fall on the regression line.
Cortex: The area that surrounds the medulla.
Cranial sutures: Junction formed between the bones of the cranium.
Cranium: Bony structure that protects the brain.
Crime scene: Encompasses the largest area that might contain physical clues to the circumstances and participants of an unlawful act.
Crossover: Parallel fingerprint ridges joined by an interconnecting ridge (bridge).
Cuticle: The outer surface of a hair shaft.
Cytoplasm: Gel-like fluid of the cell that carries nutrients and acts to support other organelles.

D

ddNTP: Designation used to describe a nucleotide unit where d = dideoxyribose; N = any of the four bases, namely, A,T,G, or C; T = triphosphate; and P = phosphate.
Deciduous teeth: Baby teeth.
Degree of magnification (microscope): Power of the lens within the eyepiece multiplied by the power of the objective lens.
Degrees of freedom: Will be one less than the number of observed data points.

Delta: Triangular-shaped fingerprint ridge buttressed against a loop or whorl.
Delusterant: Material added to a fabric to reduce the sheen in fibers.
Denaturation: Separating the template double helix into single strands.
Dendrites: Cells that have long, branched fibers that transmit electrochemical signals of a nerve impulse.
Deoxynucleoside: DNA molecule made up of a base attached to a sugar.
Deoxynucleotide: DNA molecule consisting of a base, a deoxyribose sugar, and a phosphate group.
Diaphragm: Adjustable opening on a microscope that directs light from the light source onto the object being examined.
Dideoxynucleotide: Nucleotide that has lost its oxygen atoms from both the 2′ and 3′ positions of the ribose sugar.
Differential extraction: Separation of a perpetrator's sperm cells from the victim's epithelial cells.
Direct evidence: Information gathered from statements made by a surviving victim, by suspects, and by eyewitnesses.
Disks: Cartilage found between the vertebra that serve as shock absorbers and prevent the vertebrae from grinding against each other.
Distal: Furthest from the body's trunk.
DNA: Deoxyribonucleic acid; molecule that carries all the information that is needed to make an organism (p. 172).
DNA fingerprinting (typing): Technique used to identify the origin of a DNA sample.
DNA polymerase: Enzyme that attaches nucleotides onto the end of a primer as a new strand of DNA, complementary to the template, is constructed during replication.
DNA replication: Process by which DNA is duplicated.
dNTP: Designation used to characterize a nucleotide unit: d = deoxyribose; N = any of the four bases, namely, A,T,G, or C; T = triphosphate; and P = phosphate.
Dot: Fingerprint ridge of very short length.
Double helix: Describes the overall shape of a DNA molecule comprised of two strands of DNA wound around each other with bonds between complementary bases (A with T and G with C) on opposite strands holding the two strands together.
Drugfire: Database program maintained by the FBI in which digital images of bullets recovered from different crime scenes are archived.
Dye terminator sequencing: Modification of the Sanger method whereby terminated fragments generated in a PCR carry fluorescent dyes on their 3′ ends.

E

Electric circuit: Direction of an electric current from a negative to a positive pole through a defined path.
Electricity: Form of energy that is derived from the opposite charges of protons and electrons—the subatomic particles of the atom.
Electrode: Two fixed points referred to as the anode and cathode through which electricity flows into and out of a battery.
Electrophoresis: Migration of DNA fragments through a gel when subjected to an electrical field.
Epithelial cells: Cells that form the outer layer of skin.
Excluded: Evidence sample that does not match to the suspect or item in question.
Exonuclease: DNA polymerase that displaces and breaks down any strand attached to the template in its path.
Extension: Stage in a PCR cycle whereby DNA polymerase adds nucleotides onto the primers to make new DNA chains.
External acoustic meatus: External opening of the ear canal.
Eyepiece: Viewing component of a microscope used to observe the object under examination.

F

Facets: Provide the means by which adjacent vertebrae move against each other and prevent the grinding of bone against bone.

False positive: A result that indicates, for example, blood is present when in actuality it is not.

Femur: Thighbone; longest bone in the human body.

Fiber: Any threadlike material.

Fibula: Lower leg bone that runs parallel and lateral to the tibia bone.

Fine adjustment: Knob on a microscope that is used to bring the object into its sharpest focus.

Firing pin: Impression or concave indentation made when the firing pin strikes the primer cup.

Follicle: Location where hairs are anchored and formed as pocket of cells.

Forensic anthropology: Study of skeletal remains that are the evidence in a crime or legal dispute.

Forensic botanist: An expert that is trained in identification of plants and associated part of plants to place a person at a unique location or in association with other people or objects.

Forensic entomologist: An insect expert that is trained to identify flies feeding on a corpse to extrapolate time of death.

Forensic odontologist: Specialist dentists called upon to identify a body using dental records, x-rays, dentals casts, and photographs.

Forensic toxicologist: An expert that is trained in the study and detection of drugs and poisons and their effect on the human body resulting in illness and/or death.

Fourth amendment: Right of the people to be secure in their persons, houses, papers, and effects against unreasonable searches and seizures.

Frontal: Skull bone that gives shape to the forehead.

Fuming: Technique used to enhance fingerprints involving chemical vapors adhering to latent prints.

G

Gas chromatography: A chemical technique that vaporizes a sample mixture using heat, which is then sent through a column carried along on a stream of inert gas that results in the sample separating into individual chemical components.

Genotype: Particular genetic makeup or profile for the regions of their chromosomes being examined.

Glenoid cavity: Socket formed in the scapula where the proximal head of the humerus articulates.

Goblet cells: Epithelial cells that secrete a protective mucous layer onto the tissue's surface that lubricates and prevents tissue damage from the enzymes that digest food.

Golgi apparatus: Cell organelle where proteins are processed for secretion.

Granule cells: Small neurons, which, in the granular layer, are very densely packed and account for more than half of all neurons in the entire brain.

Greater sciatic notch: *V*-shaped indentation of the pelvis posterior to the socket joint where the femur articulates. Location of where major nerves and blood vessels pass down to the legs.

Grooves: Markings imparted on the barrel of a firearm during the manufacturing process.

H

Haversian canal: Opening through which nerve cells and blood vessels are channeled through bone.

Hemastix: Strip of plastic carrying a piece of filter paper at one end impregnated with hydrogen peroxide and tetramethylbenzidine, which reacts in the presence of blood (presumptive test).

Hemoglobin: Iron-containing protein in red blood cells responsible for carrying oxygen from the lungs to the rest of the body.

Hepatocytes: Epithelial cells of the liver.

Heterozygous: Different number of DNA repeats from both your parents at a given locus.
High-velocity blood spatter: Fine specks of blood typically less than or equal to 1 mm in diameter.
Histology: The study of cells and tissues by microscopy.
Homicide report: Detailed information from the crime scene that helps investigators file an official report.
Homozygous: Same number of DNA repeats from both your parents at a given locus.
Humerus: Upper arm bone, above the elbow.
Hydrogen bonds: Weak chemical bonds that hold two DNA strands together.
Hydroxyl group: An oxygen atom connected to a hydrogen atom.
Hyoid bone: Bone found below the mandible near the upper part of the neck.

I

Included: Evidence sample that is consistent with the suspect or item in question.
Inferior: Lower than another point.
Intercalated disk: Feature of cardiac muscle that runs perpendicular to the cell's long axis that marks the boundary between two cells touching end to end in cardiac cells.
Involuntary: Muscle tissue that does not contract or relax by conscious thought.
Ion: Positively or negatively charged atoms or molecules.
Ischiopubic ramus: Area of the pelvic bone characterized by a bony ridge of the subpubic region.

K

Kupffer cell: A type of cell whose function in the liver is to break down aged red blood cells and to destroy any invading microbes.

L

Lacrimal bone: Inner wall of the eye socket.
Lamellae: Array of concentric ring structures found in bone.
Lands: Markings imparted on the barrel of a firearm during the manufacturing process creating raised ridges running down the length of a gun barrel.
Laser scanner: Three-dimensional, high-resolution panoramic camera giving a detailed image of a crime scene.
Latent print: Prints invisible to the naked eye.
Lateral: Away from the body's midline.
Light microscope: Microscope that transmits light through a specimen mounted on a stage.
Liver: Organ that produces enzymes and other compounds such as bile needed to break down food, stores glycogen, breaks down red blood cells for recycling, synthesizes plasma proteins, aids in the detoxification of harmful molecules, and manufactures hormones.
Livor mortis: The pooling of blood at the lowest parts of the body due to the pull of gravity; begins within the first hour following death and is complete within approximately 12 h.
Locard's exchange principle: When objects come in contact with each other, a two-way transfer of material takes place.
Loci: Single genetic site on a chromosome.
Loop: Fingerprint ridgelines that fold back on themselves.
Low-velocity blood spatter: Circular blood drops greater than or equal to roughly 4 mm in diameter.
Lumbar vertebrae: Lower five vertebrae comprising the lower portion of the back.
Luminol: Blood presumptive test comprising a yellowish crystal; when dissolved in water and sprayed as a fine mist on a drop of blood, it produces a chemiluminescent bluish-green glow.
Lung: Organ where oxygen is absorbed into the bloodstream and carbon dioxide is released back out.
Lysosomes: Cell organelle that breaks down waste products.

M

Mandible: Chinbone; jaw.
Manufactured fibers: Long chains of single molecules that form a goo-like substance known as polymer.
Mass spectrometry (MS): An instrument that identifies molecules by their mass and charge.
Mastoid process: Bony projection of the skull located behind the external acoustic meatus.
Maxilla: Bone below the eye sockets around and below the nose that gives further shape to the cheeks and to the upper jaw.
Medial: Point lying closest to the body's midline.
Medical examiner: Licensed physician responsible in identifying the individual and certifying their death.
Medium velocity blood spatter: Blood drops from 1 to 4 mm in. in diameter; circular to teardrop shape often formed in a spray pattern.
Medulla: The center portion or core of the hair shaft.
Medullary index: Ratio of the width of the medulla to the width of the hair shaft.
Melanin: Pigments that give hair or skin its color.
Mental eminence: Triangular-shaped protuberance located at the base and midline of the mandible.
Metacarpals: Five long bones in the hand found between the carpals and phalanges.
Metatarsals: Five long bones in the foot between the tarsal and phalanges.
miniSTR: Shorter versions of STR loci, useful when analyzing DNA that has been badly degraded.
Minutiae: Specific patterns formed within the fingerprint ridges.
Mitochondria: Cell organelle that produces an energy-rich molecule called ATP (adenosine triphosphate).
MO (modus operandi or *method of operation*): A pattern of behavior a perpetrator follows when they kill their victims.
Mobile phase: Term associated with chromatography to describe an organic solvent that will carry a sample through a stationary phase.
Mold: Cavity, hole, or impression left by an object.
Monomer: Repeat unit of a DNA base sequence, for example, $[GATC]_{24}$.
mtDNA (mitochondrial DNA): Circular piece of DNA found in the mitochondria made up of 16,570 bp in length encoding 37 genes.
Multinucleated: More than one nucleus per cell.
Multiplex reaction: Amplification of multiple loci simultaneously.

N

Natural fibers: Derived from materials produced by plants or animals.
Nuchal crest: Protuberance at the posterior, midline portion of the occipital bone.
Nucleases: Enzyme capable of degrading and destroying the released DNA.
Nucleotide: Comprises a base such as A, C, G, or T connected to a phosphate group and a ribose sugar.
Nucleus: Spherical body that contains coiled chromosomes of DNA.
Null hypothesis: The idea that there is no difference between the observed and the expected.

O

Objectives: A system of different lenses providing degrees of magnification.
Occipital: Cranial bone that gives shape to the back of the skull.
Ohm: A unit of electrical resistance that a material or conducting substance exerts on an electric current.
Organs: A collection of multiple tissues organized collectively to perform a specific purpose.
Ossification: Hardening of soft tissue into bone-like material.
Osteoarthritic lipping: The formation of a liplike bone mass at the edge of a joint.

Osteocytes: Mature bone cells.
Osteometric board: Tool used to measure the length of bones.
Oxidation: Loss of electrons.

P

P-value: Represents the level of significance under which the test is performed.
Palindrome: Sequence on one strand read in one direction is the same as on the other strand read in the opposite direction.
Palmar: Relating to the palm of the hand.
Parietal: Bone that forms the lower part of the braincase on the left and right side.
Patella: A small, triangular-shaped bone at the knee, where the femur meets the fibula and tibia.
Patent print: Prints formed from a finger that comes in contact with a surface that leaves an impression, indentation, or mold.
Paternity: DNA test to determine who the father is in a dispute of custody, fidelity, alimony, or inheritance.
PCR (polymerase chain reaction): Laboratory method for amplifying a defined segment of DNA.
Pelvis: Lower torso bones (hip) that include part of the body that carries the intestines and reproductive organs.
Perjury: Deliberate testimony that is not truthful.
Peroxidase: Enzyme that reduces hydrogen peroxide (H_2O_2) to water (H_2O).
Phalanges: Bones of the fingers and toes.
Phenol–chloroform extraction: Chemical mixture used to isolate DNA from cells.
Plantar: Relating to the sole of the foot.
Plastic print: Finger in contact with a moldable substance that retains the shape of the ridge pattern.
Point of convergence: Point where lines intersect.
Polyacrylamide gel: Jell-O-like substance that DNA fragments are forced through.
Polygraph: Referred to as a *lie detector*; machine that monitors a body's physiological reaction to stress.
Polymer: Large molecule composed of repeating units.
Polymorphic: Having many different forms.
Posterior: Closest to the back of the body.
Precision: Refers to how reproducible a measurement is when taken with a specific piece of equipment or instrument.
Presumptive blood test: Chemical test to determine if a stain is really blood.
Primer cup: Part of the shell casing that contains the igniting powder.
Primer: Short, single-stranded piece of DNA that binds to the DNA template during a PCR.
Primer: A small shock-sensitive charge that detonates the gunpowder packaged behind the bullet.
Probable cause: A compelling reason to believe that the person or property contains evidence critical to a criminal investigation.
Probe (rtPCR): A short, single-stranded segment of DNA that carries a reporter dye on one end and a quencher molecule on the other.
Probe (sequencing): Short, single-stranded piece of DNA carrying a DNA sequence complementary to a polymorphic region of interest.
Profiling: Evidence that can provide clues about the sex, age, personality quirks, lifestyle, and occupation of the victim and perpetrator.
Prostate-specific antigen (PSA): Protein found in semen.
Proximal: Closest to the body's trunk.
Pubic symphysis: A stretch of cartilage that joins the hipbones at the front of the pelvis.
Punnett square: Mathematical multiplication table that predicts the proportion of offspring displaying a particular trait carried from the parental lines.

Purkinje cells: Cells in the heart that carry electrical signals that coordinate contractions.
Pythagorean theorem: Theorem that states for a right triangle, the square of the hypotenuse is equal in length to the sum of the squares of the lengths of the other two sides.

Q

Quadrupole: A component found in a mass spectrometry instrument consisting of four equally spaced, cylindrical, gold-coated ceramic rods, which detect molecules based on the charge-to-mass ratio.
Qualitative analysis: Nonnumerical analysis or description of an event.
Quantitative analysis: Experiment involving collection of numerical or measureable data.
Quencher: Molecule attached to a DNA probe when in close proximity to a reporter prevents the reporter from glowing.

R

Radius: Forearm bones below the elbow, located on the thumb side of the lower arm.
Real-time PCR (rtPCR): Instrument that quantitates DNA by detecting fluorescent light emitted when a specific segment of DNA is replicated over and over again.
Rectangular coordinates: Using rectangles to map the location and orientation of an item within a crime scene.
Reduction: Gain of electrons.
Reference sample: From a known source.
Regression line: *Line of best fit* through a series of data points.
Reporter dye: Molecular attached to a DNA probe that is the source of light during a real-time PCR reaction.
Resistor: Electrical component that introduces resistance to the flow of current in a circuit.
Restriction endonuclease: An enzyme that recognizes a specific sequence of bases in a DNA molecule and cuts through both strands of the double helix.
Restriction fragment length polymorphism (RFLP): Different size fragments resulting from enzyme digestion at a DNA location.
Retention time: Length of time it takes a molecule to pass through a gas chromatography column.
Reverse dot blot: Lab technique that employs short, single-stranded DNA probes matching different marker alleles, spotted onto strips of nylon paper.
R_f value (retention factor): The distance the chemical component travels divided by the distance traveled by the solvent on a chromatographic surface.
Ribose: Type of sugar molecule that is part of a nucleotide building block of DNA.
Rigor mortis: The stiffening of the body brought on by a rigid interaction between the muscle proteins actin and myosin.

S

Sacrum: Fused vertebra forming a triangle at the base of the vertebral column.
Sagittal: Plane that divides the body into left and right halves.
Sanger method of DNA sequencing (chain termination method): Sequencing technique that utilizes radioisotopes to tag terminated DNA fragments.
Scanning electron microscope (SEM): Microscope that sweeps a finely focused beam of high-energy electrons back and forth across the surface of a specimen.
Scapula: Blade-shaped bone located on the posterior lateral part of the back that forms part of the shoulder.
Search warrant: Law enforcement officer obtaining a judge's permission granting the right to search a person or property.
Sexual dimorphism: Anatomical difference between adult males and females.

Short tandem repeats (STRs): Segments of DNA two to five bases in length that, like VNTRs, are repeated multiple times along a region of a chromosome.
Sine: Ratio of the length of the opposite side to the length of the hypotenuse in a right triangle.
Skeletal muscle: Multinucleated, elongated cells with striations running perpendicular to the long axis.
Smooth muscle: Spindle-shaped cells that are widest in the middle and tapered at each end with elongated nuclei that are centrally located.
Spectrophotometer: Instrument that measures the OD of a DNA sample.
Spinal cord: Nerves that run through an opening within each bone of the vertebrae sending electrochemical signals from the brain to the extremities.
Spinous processes: Hatchet-shaped protrusions along the posterior midline of the vertebra.
Squamous epithelium: Cell layer just below the skin that is comprised of flat and thin layer of cells.
Stage: The platform on a microscope that a slide or specimen is placed for viewing.
Standard deviation: Statistical term to indicate how much a series of measurements varies from the average.
Stationary phase: Term associated with chromatography to describe a solid platform.
Sternum: Breastbone.
Striations: Filaments made of the proteins actin and myosin.
Subpubic region: Area of the pelvis found below the pubic symphysis.
Superior: Higher than another point.
Supraorbital margin: Lateral aspect of the supraorbital ridge.
Supraorbital ridge: Bony ridge above the eye socket.
SWGDAM: Scientific Working Group on DNA Analysis; leading organization involved in establishing best practices for handling DNA evidence.
Synthetic fibers: Derived from cellulose extracted cotton and wood pulp.

T

Tangent: Length of the opposite side divided by the length of the adjacent side of a right triangle.
Taq: Heat-resistant DNA polymerase used to extend the primers in a PCR.
Tarsals: Complex of bones forming the ankle and posterior part of the foot.
Template: The strand of DNA that is copied into a complementary strand during PCR.
Termination: End of a fingerprint ridge.
Thermal cycler: Instrument that carries out the PCR.
Thin-layer chromatography (TLC): Chemical technique that causes a mixture to separate into it individual chemical components.
Thoracic vertebrae: Twelve vertebrae to which the ribs are anchored, upper back region.
Tibia: Shinbone, one of two in the lower leg; larger and more robust than fibula.
Tissue: A group of cells that share a similar structure and a common function.
Trace evidence: Refers to the last detectable remnant of something left behind.
Transfer stain: Formed when a blood-soaked object comes into contact with another surface.
Transistor: Electrical component used to amplify or switch an electronic signal.
Transmission electron microscope (TEM): Microscope that uses electromagnets to focus and transmit electrons through the object being examined.
Transverse: Plane that divides the body at the waist into upper and lower halves.
Triangular coordinates: Technique used to describe the location of an object at a crime scene involving the length of one side and the two angles formed by lines leading from either end of that imaginary line to the object.
Triphosphate: Three-phosphate group carried by nucleotides.
TWGDAM: Technical Working Group on DNA Analysis Methods; leading organizations involved in establishing the best practices for handling DNA evidence.
Twist: Direction a bullet will spin in space when it leaves the barrel of a firearm.

U

Ulna: Forearm bones below the elbow; runs parallel to radius, on the opposite side of the thumb.

V

Ventral arc: Region of the anterior aspect of the pubic symphysis.
Vertebral foramen: Part of the bone that houses the spinal cord of nerve tissue extending from the brain to the rest of the body.
VNTRs (Variable Number of Tandem Repeats): Regions of a chromosome in which a segment of DNA ranging from 5 to 80 bases in length is repeated over and over again, one right next to the other.
Volt: A unit of electric potential difference.
Voluntary: Controlled by conscious thought.

W

Walk-through: A visual observation into a crime scene in which an understanding of the nature and scope of the crime and determine what evidence should be collected and from where.
Weinberg equilibrium: Mathematical description of how the frequency of a trait within a population's gene pool remains constant over time.
Whorl: Fingerprint ridges that look like a *bull's eye*.

Y

Y-STRs: Short tandem repeats profiled on the Y-chromosome used for human identification.

Z

Zygomatic bone: Cheekbone.

Appendix D: Glossary of Words You Might Hear in the Courtroom

Abatement: To reduce in intensity; also, a termination or a temporary suspension of a lawsuit.
Abridge: To shorten; to condense a description into a shorter version without loss of its meaning or major points.
Abrogate: To annul, repeal, or abolish by an official action.
Abscond: To travel secretly out of the jurisdiction of the courts or to hide oneself to avoid arrest or lawsuit.
Accessory: Someone who aids or contributes to the commission of a crime or acts to help a suspect avoid apprehension.
Accessory after the fact: A person who assists or harbors a suspect knowing full well that that suspect has committed a crime.
Accomplice: Someone who assists another in committing a crime.
Accusation: A charge of wrongdoing.
Accuse: To charge someone with a crime.
Accused: The person charged with a criminal act; the defendant.
Acquiescence: Conduct that may imply agreement; implied acceptance such as when an accused person remains silent or passive on a charge leveled against them when they should have raised an objection were they not guilty of that charge.
Acquit: To set free from an accusation by a verdict of not guilty.
Acquittal: A legal finding (jury verdict, court sentence, or other legal process) whereby a suspect charged with a crime is found not guilty and is set free.
Action: A legal proceeding in which a person or business prosecutes another person or business for a wrong done.
Actionable: Grounds for an action or lawsuit. For example, slander, *perjury*, and copyright infringement are actionable.
Adjourn: To briefly delay court proceedings until a later time (as during a court *recess*). When an adjournment extends for a long or indefinite time, it is termed a *continuance*.
Adjudicate: To settle finally; to pass judgment on.
Adjudication: A decision and pronouncement of judgment.
Admissible evidence: Evidence that will aid a judge and jury in a trail and that passes established rules that it was legally obtained and will not bring undue prejudice on the defendant.
Admission: An acknowledgment that an allegation or charge is true.
Admit: To allow into evidence. It can also mean an acknowledgment of guilt or culpability for a wrongdoing.
Adultery: Voluntary sexual intercourse between a married person and someone other than his or her spouse. Adultery is a criminal offense and grounds for divorce.
Adversary: The opponent in a legal dispute.
Affidavit: A sworn statement in writing made under oath before an officer of the court.
Age of consent: The legal age at which a person can marry without parental consent. Also refers to the age below which sexual intercourse is deemed statutory rape.

Aggravating circumstances: Acts to a crime (such as extreme cruelty or depravity) that increase the severity of the charge or the severity of the punishment.
Aid and abet: To knowingly assist someone in the commission of a crime.
Alibi: An argument that a person could not have been at the scene of a crime because they have proof or witnesses that they were elsewhere at the time the crime was committed.
Alienation of affections: A wrongdoing caused by a third party's interference in a married couple's relationship causing a spouse to lose affection for their marital partner.
Allegation: An assertion of fact, often of a wrongdoing, that the person making the charge expects to prove by a legal proceeding.
Amnesty: A pardon to a large group of people who have committed some illegal act against the government.
Annul: To declare a marriage legally invalid and void. An *annulment* completely invalidates a marriage.
Appeal: A request for a higher court to review the decision of a lower court and possibly reverse or issue a different, less damaging verdict. During an appeal, no new evidence is introduced. The higher court only decides if the lower court made an error in legal process or issued a verdict contrary to the evidence.
Appellate court: A court having the power to review, reverse, or modify a decision of a lower court.
A priori: Intuitively true. To accuse someone in a courtroom that they assumed a fact a priori could be to shame them for not arriving at a fact by examining the evidence or careful deductive reasoning.
Arbiter: A person having the court-granted authority to decide a controversy. A court must confirm an arbiter's decision.
Arbitration: The hearing and decision on a case by an impartial person chosen by the two disputing parties.
Arbitrator: An impartial person chosen by two disputing parties to decide a controversy.
Argument: A reason given for or against an opinion or other matter under discussion.
Arraign: To bring a person into the courtroom to answer the charge brought by an indictment.
Arraignment: The process by which a person is formally charged with a criminal offense, served a copy of the indictment against them, and informed of their plea options.
Arrest: To take a person by legal authority into the care of the judicial system to answer criminal charges.
Assault: An attack on another person with the intent of inflicting bodily harm. Physical injury need not be proved to establish assault. When the attacker touches the victim or inflicts bodily injury, the assault is called *battery.*
Attest: Affirm to be genuine or true.
Attorney: A person legally qualified to practice law. Such a person is admitted by the state's highest court or by a federal court to defend a client or prosecute a case in the admitting court's jurisdiction. An attorney is subject to the admitting court's standards of ethical and professional conduct. An attorney not adhering to those standards may be disbarred and forbidden from practicing law.
Authenticate: To certify or to prove genuine. Authentication is often established by expert testimony.
Autopsy: The dissection of a dead person so that the cause of death can be determined.
Bail: Money paid to the judicial system to secure the release of a defendant from jail and that is an offer of good faith that he or she will appear in court as required during a trial.
Bailiff: An officer of the court having responsibility for seating witnesses and spectators, for announcing the judge's entrance to the courtroom, and for keeping order in the court.
Battery: The unlawful contact with another individual, particularly involving the use of force with intent to inflict bodily injury.
Bench: The desk where the judge sits to conduct the trial.

Bench warrant: A court order that directs a person to come into court to answer a contempt of court charge or that compels a witness or defendant to come into court after a subpoena has been served them.

Beneficiary: A person for whom property or finances are led in trust; a person named in a will to receive property from the deceased.

Bias: A preconception or prejudice.

Bind over: A court order that a defendant be placed in legal custody pending the outcome of some court action against him or her.

Blackmail: The extortion of money from a person taken on threat of exposing some illegal wrongdoing or embarrassing act by that person.

Bona fide: Genuine.

Brain death: The cessation of brain function.

Breach: Failure to perform some contracted-for or agreed-upon act.

Breaking and entering: Part of the charge of burglary where physical force is used to remove an obstruction (such as a lock or a closed window or door) designed to obstruct the entrance of unauthorized persons into private or controlled property and entry onto that property.

Bribery: Voluntarily providing something of value to an official of the court or government for the purpose of influencing a legal outcome.

Brief: A written argument stating points of law essential to a client's case.

Burden of proof: The duty of a party to convince the court of the truth of a certain claim.

Burglary: The breaking into a dwelling, building, or vehicle with the intent to commit a theft.

Cadaver: The body of a deceased person.

Capital offense: A criminal offense punishable by death.

Capital punishment: The death penalty.

Carnal knowledge: Sexual intercourse.

Caveat: A warning or statement of caution.

Censure: A reprimand issued by a judge or other official body.

Chain of custody: The documentation that follows a piece of evidence used in a criminal trial from its initial discovery to making note of who has handled it and where it has been stored.

Challenge: An objection that calls into question the validity of something. Also, the objection by a lawyer to the inclusion of a specific person as to their right or fitness to serve as a juror.

Charge: A brief description of an offense.

Circuit court: A part of a system of federal courts extending over a specified geographical area.

Circumstantial evidence: Evidence other than that of an eyewitness account; secondary facts by which a principal fact may be reasonably inferred.

Civil action: An action to compel the hearing of a dispute that provides remedy to a private party who believes they were wronged.

Civil rights: The nonpolitical rights of all citizens, especially those rights relating to personal liberty.

Class action: A suit brought by one or more members of a large group of persons on behalf of all members of that group.

Codefendant: A defendant who is charged with the same crime with one or more other defendants.

Coercion: Any act or form of pressure that compels or induces a person to act against a person's own free will.

Cogent: Compelling and convincing as in a legal argument that appeals forcibly to the mind or reason.

Collusion: Striking a secret agreement with another party to commit fraud or engage in some other illegal activity.

Commutation: Substituting a lesser punishment when a greater one was originally imposed, such as changing a criminal's sentence from death to life imprisonment.

Conclusive evidence: Evidence that is absolute and incontrovertible; evidence that is true beyond question.

Concur: To agree.
Confession: An admission of guilt. A confession is not admissible at trial unless it is made voluntarily.
Confiscate: A government action in which private property is taken without just compensation.
Conjecture: An unsubstantiated inference based upon facts within a person's knowledge. A witness may only testify as to the facts as they know them and may not present their interpretation (a conjecture) of those facts.
Consent: Voluntary agreement.
Conspiracy: An agreement or arrangement between two or more persons to commit an unlawful act.
Conspirator: One involved in a conspiracy.
Contempt of court: An act that interferes with the orderly administration of a trial or that impairs the respect for the court's authority.
Continuance: The postponement of a court proceeding to a later date.
Convict: To determine guilt of a person charged with a crime.
Conviction: The result of finding someone guilty of a crime and upon which sentence or judgment is based.
Coroner: A public official who investigates the causes and circumstances of suspicious deaths occurring within their jurisdiction.
Corporal punishment: Punishment inflicted upon the body that causes pain or direct physical damage to tissue.
Corpus delicti: The objective proof that a crime has been committed. It sometimes refers to the body of the victim of a homicide.
Counsel: Attorney or legal advisor.
Credibility: Truthfulness; whether or not a witness is credible; is capable of being believed.
Criminal: Done with malicious intent, for the purpose of causing injury to person or property.
Cross-examination: The questioning of a witness by a lawyer other than the one who called the witness, concerning testimony given by the witness during direct examination. The purpose is to discredit or clarify that witness' earlier statements so as to neutralize damaging testimony or present facts in a light more favorable to the party damaged by the direct examination.
Cruel and unusual punishment: A penalty tantamount to torture or one that is shocking to people of reasonable sensitivity. A penalty out of proportion to the crime.
Culpa: Fault.
Culpable: Deserving of blame or punishment; at fault.
Custody: The act of holding something within one's personal care and control; having control over a person that ensures his or her presence at a hearing, or the actual incarceration of a person convicted of a criminal offense.
DA: Abbreviation for district attorney.
De facto: In fact; actually. Used to refer to a situation in which an institution is operating as though it were official, but that is not legally authorized.
Defamation: The publication of anything harmful to the reputation of another.
Defendant: The party responding to the complaint; one who is being sued by another; the accused.
Defense: A denial disputing the validity of the plaintiff's case.
Deferment: Postponing until a future time.
Defraud: To deprive a person of property or right by fraud or deceit.
Deliberate: To consider all the evidence and arguments presented in a trial as needed to render a verdict in a criminal case.
Deliberation: The process by which evidence of guilt or innocence of the accused is weighed by jurors so that a verdict can be rendered.

Depose: To give evidence or testimony; the act of interrogating and eliciting testimony during a deposition, usually conducted by a lawyer.

Deposition: A method of pretrial discovery that consists of a transcribed statement of a witness under oath, in response to a lawyer's questions, with opportunity for the opposing party to be present and to cross-examine.

Diminished capacity: The inability to have the state of mind required for the commission of a particular crime. A successful defense of diminished capacity will usually result in conviction of a lesser offense.

Disbar: To take away an attorney's license to practice law because of illegal or unethical conduct.

Discovery: The procedure by which one party gains information and access to evidence held by the adverse party in a criminal case; the disclosure by the opposite party of facts, evidence, and documents held exclusively within their possession or knowledge and that are necessary to support the other party's position.

Dismiss: To terminate a case or some part of it.

Dismissal: A cancellation. Dismissal of a motion is a denial of the motion.

Dissent: To disagree; an opinion that differs from that of the majority of the court.

District attorney: A government official who has the responsibility to prosecute all those accused of crimes. In the United States, district attorneys of the federal government are called United States attorneys.

Docket: A list of cases on a court's calendar.

Double jeopardy: Prosecution or punishment twice for the same offense, which is prohibited by the US Constitution, even if new evidence comes to light.

Due process of law: The principle that the government may not deprive an individual of life, liberty, or property unless certain rules and procedures required by law are adhered to.

Duplicitous: To allege more than one distinct claim in the same indictment.

Duress: Bringing pressure to bear on an individual to compel them to do what they would not otherwise do.

Embezzlement: Fraudulent appropriation of finances from a bank for one's own use.

Eminent domain: The inherent right of the state to take private property for public use, without the property owner's consent.

Entrapment: A defense that excuses a defendant from criminal liability for crimes induced by trickery on the part of the police. To sustain the defense, the defendant must show that if not for the objectionable police conduct, he or she would not have committed the crime or that an ordinary, law-abiding citizen would have been induced, under the same circumstances, to commit the crime.

Escape clause: A provision in a contract permitting a party to renege on its obligation under certain conditions without incurring a penalty or other liability.

Evidence: All the means by which a matter of fact is proved at a trial. Evidence includes the testimony of witnesses, documents, or any physical artifacts recovered from the crime scene or defendant's person that, by their existence, show innocence or guilt.

Exclusionary rule: A constitutional rule of law that provides that otherwise admissible evidence may not be used in a criminal trial if it was obtained as a result of illegal police conduct.

Exculpatory: Evidence or statements that tend to justify or excuse a defendant from alleged fault or guilt.

Executive order: An order issued by the executive head of government that has the force of law.

Exhibit: An item of evidence that has been presented to the court.

Expert witness: A witness having special knowledge, skill, or experience in the subject about which they are to testify.

Extenuating circumstances: Unusual occurrences beyond the control of the accused, which contributed to the commission of a crime.

Extortion: The corrupt collection of money by a public official who uses the weight of their office to bring pressure to bear on a citizen to force them into that payment. The illegal taking of money by anyone who employs threats, or other illegal use of fear or coercion, to obtain money, and whose conduct falls short of the threat to personal safety required for the charge of robbery.

Eyewitness: A person who can testify that they personally saw some part (or all) of a criminal act or who can place another person at the scene of a crime because of their claim that they actually saw them there.

False arrest: Unlawful arrest or restraint of an individual, typically one who is not the perpetrator of the crime being charged.

False imprisonment: The intentional but unjustified detention or confinement of a person.

False verdict: A verdict inconsistent with the evidence and thereby unjust.

Felony: A crime of high seriousness and as distinguishing from a minor offense (a misdemeanor). A felony is typically punishable by imprisonment for more than a year or by death.

Fence: A person who receives stolen property and resells it for a profit.

Fifth Amendment: The amendment to the US Constitution and part of the Bill of Rights that provides citizens with protections that include (1) that a person shall not be charged with a capital or other infamous crime unless an indictment is first issued by a grand jury, (2) that no person shall be placed in double jeopardy such that they are tried twice for the same crime, (3) that no person shall be required to testify against themselves, (4) that neither life, liberty, nor property shall be taken without due process of law, and (5) that private property may not be taken for public use without just compensation.

Filing: Providing documents to the court or with other public officials so that they are preserved as part of the official record.

Finding: A decision of the court that answers questions raised by criminal charges.

First Amendment: The amendment to the US Constitution and part of the Bill of Rights that guarantees freedom of speech, assembly, press, petition, and the free exercise of religion.

Foundation: Preliminary evidence needed to establish the admissibility of other evidence.

Fratricide: The murder of one's brother.

Fraud: An intentional deception, misrepresentation, or nondisclosure of material fact resulting in injury or loss to another.

Frivolous: Unsupported by the facts or incapable of being remedied by law.

Fugitive from justice: One who commits a crime then flees the jurisdiction where the crime was committed with the intent of avoiding the legal consequences of the crime.

Gag order: An order by a court to restrict discussion about a case.

Good faith: An honest attempt to fulfill an obligation.

Gratis: Free.

Guardian: A person who has legal responsibility for the care and management of a minor or person incapable of caring for themselves in full measure.

Guilty: Culpable for having committed a crime as determined by a jury.

Hearing: A judicial proceeding where evidence is examined but in the absence of a jury.

Hearsay: Any statement that a witness may have heard another person say that is offered up as fact.

Homicide: Killing of one person by another.

Hung jury: A jury that cannot reach a verdict because all its members cannot agree unanimously—they are deadlocked in their deliberations.

Hypothetical question: A question that calls for an opinion based on the evidence. Such questions can only be posed to an expert witness who is qualified to give an opinion on the evidence's meaning or weight.

Immaterial: Irrelevant. Having nothing to do with the case.

Immunity: Exemption from penalty.
Impeach: To question the veracity of a witness. To show by the evidence that the witness is not telling the truth or that they should not be believed.
Implied: Not explicitly written or stated. Determined by deduction of the facts.
In absentia: In the absence of.
Incest: Sexual intercourse between members of a family.
Inchoate: Not yet completed.
Incompetent evidence: Evidence that is not admissible.
Inconsistent: Contradictory or not consistent with the facts or evidence.
Incriminate: Show to be guilty of a crime.
Inculpatory: Tending to incriminate.
Indemnity: The obligation to make good on any loss another person has incurred.
Indictment: A formal accusation by the public prosecuting attorney submitted under oath to a grand jury charging a person (or persons) with a crime.
Indispensible evidence: Evidence critical to proving a fact.
Inference: A logical conclusion drawn from given facts.
Injunction: A preventive measure to prevent future injuries.
In perpetuity: Existing forever.
Inquest: An inquiry from a coroner to determine the cause of death of the victim of a crime or of sudden who otherwise died suddenly.
Instruction: A judge's directions to the jury as to how to proceed and participate in the legal proceedings.
Insufficient evidence: A decision by a judge that a prosecutor has failed to provide the minimum amount of evidence required by a jury to decide a question of fact.
Intent: The willful action of performing an act.
Involuntary manslaughter: A homicide resulting from criminal negligence or recklessness such as what might occur when a driver strikes a pedestrian.
Ipso facto: By the fact itself.
Judgment: The determination of the court.
Jurisdiction: The geographic or political entity governed by a particular set of laws.
Jurisprudence: The science of law or the study of legal systems.
Jury: The collection of persons deemed as peers of a person or party charged with a crime tasked with deciding the guilt or innocence of that person or party based on a consideration of the evidence presented in a court of law.
Justifiable homicide: The killing of a person who might have otherwise caused death or serious injury to another.
Kidnapping: The unlawful carrying away of a person against their will.
Larceny: The unlawful taking away of the personal property of another without their consent with the intent of acquiring that property for their own use.
Lay witness: A nonexpert witness who, because of their lack of expertise, is generally precluded from providing testimony in the form of an opinion.
Leading question: A question posed to a witness that is improper because, by its wording, it suggests the answer that the trial lawyer is hoping to obtain.
Liability: An obligation to pay money. Money owed or potentially owed, as opposed to an asset.
Libel: An action that is the consequence of a false or malicious publication aiming to defame a person or to sully the memory of a person deceased.
Liberty: Freedom.
License: A legal permit that allows a certain act to be performed.
Licensee: A person to whom a license has been granted.
Litigants: Those actively involved in a lawsuit, either plaintiffs or defendants.

Litigation: An action by a court to determine a legal outcome.

Litigious: A word used to describe the behavior of being particularly fond or prone to becoming engaged in litigation.

Machination: A hostile scheme artfully plotted out.

Malfeasance: The performance of a wrongful and unlawful act. Any conduct that interferes with the performance of official duty.

Malice: The intent to do a wrongful act without justification and in willful disregard that harm will result.

Malice aforethought: The state of mind that characterizes a homicide as murder as opposed to manslaughter, which does not involve intent and forethought. The state of mind with which a person intentionally commits a wrongful act that results in harm to another person.

Mandate: A judicial command; an official mechanism of communicating the judgment of the appellate court to the lower court.

Manslaughter: The taking of someone's life without malice aforethought.

Material: Pertinent, meaningful, and necessary.

Matricide: The killing of one's mother.

Mediation: A method of settling matters of dispute outside of a courtroom.

Miranda rule: The law requires that a suspect be informed of their right to remain silent so as not to self-incriminate, that they have a right to an attorney, and that any statement they make may be used as evidence against them in a court of law.

Miscarriage of justice: Errors and mistakes made by the court during a trial of such a serious nature that a reversal of the decision is required.

Misdemeanor: A crime less serious than a felony and requiring less severe penalties.

Mistrial: A trial that has been discontinued and declared void prior to rendering of a verdict by the jury because of some extraordinary circumstance such as the death of a juror or attorney involved in the case or because of some fundamental error prejudicial to the defendant that cannot be remedied by any instructions to the jury. A mistrial most often occurs because of a hung jury.

Mitigating circumstances: A set of conditions that might reduce the sentence of the accused. Such circumstances do not exonerate the accused but can make his or her motives more worthy of sympathy.

Modus operandi: The typical or established manner by which a person commits repeated criminal acts.

Moot court: A fictitious court (such as that set up in a classroom) that mimics an actual court of law.

Moral turpitude: Depravity or dishonesty of a high degree.

Motion: A request of the court on the part of its applicant to take an action.

Move: To make a motion.

Murder: The taking of another human being's life with premeditated intent and malice aforethought.

Negligence: Failure to exercise a level of care that a reasonable person would exercise under the same set of circumstances.

Object: To assert that an action in court (presented evidence or line of questioning of a witness) is improper and should not be allowed or continued and that asks the court to make a ruling on its admissibility or legality.

Objection: A challenge to the legality or admissibility of a piece of evidence or line of questioning.

Obstruction of justice: Anything that impedes the proper proceedings of the court.

Opinion: The statement of the reasons for a court's judgment.

Overrule: To overturn or make void a decision of a prior case; to deny a motion, objection, or other point raised to the court. It is the purview of the judge to overrule an objection.

Pardon: To relieve a person of further punishment suffered by a crime for which he or she has been convicted.

Parole: A conditional release from imprisonment such that the convicted party can serve the remainder of their sentence outside of prison.
Party: A plaintiff or defendant; a person directly interested and involved in a case.
Patricide: The killing of one's father.
Pejorative: To make worse. Insulting or derogatory.
Perjury: The criminal offense of making false statements under oath.
Plaintiff: The one who brings the suit; one who seeks justice for an injury or injustice perpetrated upon them.
Plea: A statement of guilty or not guilty in a criminal proceeding.
Polygraph: An electromechanical instrument that measures physiological changes that may accompany the telling of a lie; a lie detector.
Postmortem: After death.
Precedent: A previously decided case that can be sited as the basis for legitimacy of future cases.
Preliminary hearing: A hearing to determine if probable cause for the arrest of a person exists and if an indictment is justified.
Premeditation: Forethought.
Preponderance of the evidence: Evidence strong and convincing enough to lead a jury to make a reasonable and correct determination.
Presumption of innocence: The assumption that the accused is innocent of the crime charged. The burden of proof that they are guilty lies with the prosecution.
Presumptive evidence: Evidence that is indirect or circumstantial.
Probable cause: Knowledge of facts and circumstances that are of sufficient weight that they would cause a reasonable officer of the law to believe that a crime has been committed.
Probate: Actions necessary to establish that a will is valid.
Probation: The procedure under which a defendant who has been found guilty of a crime is released by the court without imprisonment under the supervision of a probation officer.
Probative: Tending to prove that an allegation is true.
Proof: Evidence or argument that establishes fact.
Prosecution: The party initiating a criminal suit.
Prosecutor: The public official who conducts the prosecution against a person accused of a crime.
Putative: Alleged or supposed.
Reasonable doubt: The degree of certainty required of a juror before they can make a determination of the guilt of the accused. In a criminal trial, the evidence against the defendant must be so conclusive that no reasonable doubt of their innocence remains.
Rebuttal: The opportunity for a party in a trial to argue against a claim made by the opposing party. The rebuttal can only address or refute those claims made by the opposing party and cannot raise any new issues.
Recess: A temporary break in a trial.
Reckless: Not heeding of any inherent danger; careless.
Recusal: Disqualification of any participant (judge, juror, or administrative officer) for prejudice or conflict of interest in a proceeding.
Relevancy: The degree to which evidence is admissible. Evidence is relevant if it has bearing on the ability to establish or prove fact.
Remand: To send back (as a judge would remand a jury to go back to further deliberation).
Render: To formally or officially announce a decision.
Repeal: To annul or void a previous law by the enactment of a subsequent statute.
Reprieve: The postponement of a sentence for an interval in which the execution is suspended.
Retraction: The withdrawing of a plea or accusation.
Sanction: To reward or to punish.
Sentence: The punishment ordered by a court for a person convicted of a crime.

Settlement: The resolution of a matter, mutually agreed upon, between parties involved in a civil suit prior to final judgment.

Sixth Amendment: The amendment to the US Constitution that guarantees the accused a speedy trial by an impartial jury, that requires the accused be informed of the charges against them, that guarantees the accused be present when witnesses testify against them, and that the accused has the right to the assistance of counsel.

Slander: Oral defamation of another person's character.

Speculation: To guess at things whose facts are not known.

Statement: A declaration of fact.

Statute: A law.

Statute of limitations: The time after which a crime can no longer be prosecuted.

Stay: A discontinuation of a criminal proceeding whereby the court will not take any further action until the occurrence of some event.

STRs: Short tandem repeats; segments of chromosomes that contain small sequences of DNA (typically 4 to 5 bases as used in forensic science) that are repeated are variable number of times between individuals.

Subpoena: A notice from a court that compels a witness to appear at a judicial proceeding. Failure to abide by a subpoena can place the witness in contempt of court.

Suit: A legal action that requires resolution by the court.

Summation: The last step of a trial whereby the attorneys review the evidence and attempt to persuade the jury as to the strength of their arguments.

Summons: An order by the court requiring the appearance of the defendant and notification that the defendant is being sued.

Suppression of evidence: The disallowing of evidence that was obtained by an unreasonable search or seizure and that violated a defendant's constitutional rights.

Supreme Court: The highest appellate court in the federal court system.

Suspect: One believed to have committed a crime.

SWGDAM: The *Scientific Working Group on DNA Analysis*.

Testimony: A statement made by a witness under oath.

Transcript: An official record, usually prepared by a court reporter, of the proceeding of the court including statements made by the attorneys, witnesses, and defendant.

TWGDAM: The *Technical Working Group on DNA Analysis Methods*; a committee of forensic experts from the United States and Canada who met in the late 1980s to establish guidelines for handling and analyzing DNA evidence to meet standards of admissibility in criminal trials.

Verdict: The opinion rendered by a jury as to the guilt or innocence of the defendant.

Voluntary manslaughter: The intentional taking of a person's life where there is not evil intent such as where the defendant killed the victim in rage, in terror, or out of desperation.

VNTRs: Variable number of tandem repeats; segments of DNA (usually 14 to 80 bases in length) repeated again and again, one next to the other; a variable number of times in different individuals. STRs have supplanted VNTRs as the DNA markers of choice for forensic identification.

Wanton: Grossly negligent or careless.

Warrant: A written order from a court directing the arrest of a person suspected of committing a crime.

Witness: One who swears to facts or gives testimony under oath.

Writ of habeas corpus: A document or filing for obtaining a judicial determination as to the legality of a person's confinement.

Index

A

B

C

D

I

K

L

M

N

O

P

Q

R

S

T

U

V

W

Z